Case
Studies
In
American
Government

The Authors

JOHN H. BUNZEL, co-author of "The California Democratic Delegation," is Assistant Professor of Political Science at Stanford University and a Director of the Northern California Citizenship Clearing House. He has contributed to the *Western Political Quarterly* and the *Political Science Quarterly*.

EUGENE C. LEE, co-author of "The California Democratic Delegation," is Assistant Professor of Political Science at the University of California, Berkeley, and Assistant Director of the Bureau of Public Administration there. He has participated in Democratic political campaigns in California and has also served in a number of administrative posts. He is the author of *The Presiding Officer and Rules Committees in Legislatures of the United States, The Politics of Non-Partisanship,* and other works.

EDITH T. CARPER, author of "The Defense Appropriations Rider," "Illinois Goes to Congress for Army Land," and "Lobbying and the Natural Gas Bill" was formerly a member of the staff of the Inter-University Case Program. She has served as a staff member of several congressional committees and as a member of the staff of the Bureau of Public Administration of the University of California.

SAMUEL A. LAWRENCE, author of "The Battery Additive Controversy," is a member of the staff of the United States Bureau of the Budget. He holds a Masters degree from American University.

THEODORE J. LOWI, author of "U. S. Bases in Spain," is Assistant Professor of Political Science at Cornell University.

CORINNE SILVERMAN, author of "The Little Rock Story," and "The President's Economic Advisers," is a former member of the ICP editorial staff and also wrote *The Office of Education Library*. Her other works include "The Legislative Process in Massachusetts: The Legislators' View," *Public Opinion Quarterly* (Summer, 1954); "A Pressure Group and the Pressured," with Oliver Garceau, *American Political Science Review* (September, 1954); and "Party and the Separation of Power," with V. O. Key, Jr., in *Public Policy,* ed., by Freidrich and Galbraith (Harvard University Press, 1954). Before joining the ICP staff she was chief assistant to Samuel Lubell.

ALAN F. WESTIN is Associate Professor of Public Law and Government at Columbia University. A member of the District of Columbia Bar, he is the author of *The Anatomy of a Constitutional Law Case* and *The Supreme Court: Views from Inside* and has written frequently about the Supreme Court in legal and general periodicals.

Case Studies In American Government

THE INTER-UNIVERSITY CASE PROGRAM

Edited by
Edwin A. Bock and
Alan K. Campbell

PRENTICE-HALL, INC.

ENGLEWOOD CLIFFS, N. J.

JK
21
.I 57

LIBRARY OF CONGRESS CATALOG CARD NO.
62–12624

PRINTED IN THE UNITED STATES OF AMERICA
11943—C

Fourth printing ....October, 1965

PRENTICE-HALL INTERNATIONAL, INC.
London • Tokyo • Sydney
PRENTICE-HALL OF CANADA, LTD.
PRENTICE-HALL DE MEXICO, S.A.

Introduction

This collection of case studies is a product of the Inter-University Case Program, which has sponsored the preparation of case studies in public policy administration since 1948. The cases in this book are intended for undergraduates, especially for those taking the introductory course in political science. They may be used with any text.

The systematic use of case studies in the introductory course in political science or American government is still experimental. For many years the introductory course has been surrounded by controversy about both content and teaching materials. Concerning content, there has been disagreement about whether the course's central focus should be governmental institutions, governmental process, or political theory. Further, there has been a question of whether the course should cover solely American government or whether it should include comparative material as well. Although the pattern which has emerged is by no means uniform, most first-year courses now concentrate on a combination of institutions and processes with emphasis on American government.

There has also emerged general agreement that class assignments should extend beyond the traditional "textbook." This agreement has led to the use of a variety of supplemental materials, including original documents and collections of articles, often combined with field trips and lectures by practitioners of government and politics. Although these aids have undoubtedly added spice to the textbook analysis, they have not proved completely satisfactory. Actual field experience has been difficult to organize on the scale necessary to be meaningful to the student. The readings have been subject to two types of limitation. Some have tended to be as didactic as textbooks, leaving little room for vigorous discussion. Others have succeeded in bringing contemporary political controversies into the classroom but in a highly abstract and therefore somewhat unrealistic context. Yet, despite their shortcomings, field trips and readings have substantially increased the breadth and depth of the first-year course.

In 1957 a five-year grant from the Ford Foundation enabled the Inter-University Case Program to extend its studies into a number of additional areas of political science and public administration. A desire to experiment at improving teaching materials for the initial course in political science moved the Executive Board of the Case Program to appoint a Committee on Cases for the First-Year Course and to provide it with a small budget for case-writing. When the committee first met, at the end of 1957, there were already signs that some teachers of the introductory course in political science were turning to case studies as another useful kind of supplementary material. At first, fictional cases had been included in some textbooks. Carrying titles such as "Getting a Bill Passed" and "John Smith Goes to Washington," these fictional devices did not pretend to present real situations but rather illustrations of generalizations given in the text. More recently there appeared what might be termed "tailored cases," i.e., cases designed to illustrate one single point or process. In order to highlight the central subject, the tailored case is sometimes severely abstracted from its context in reality, and as a further guide the writer may insert his own analysis and some leading questions.

The members of the First-Year Course Committee decided at the start that the case studies in this collection should go further in the direction of reality; that they should seek to show all of the factors that significantly affected the making of a decision or the handling of a problem; and that they should not resist the tendency of governmental situations in real life to be affected by forces and inter-relationships that transcend the chapter titles of textbooks.

The First-Year Course Committee had an ambitious teaching purpose in mind when it decided to produce broad-spectrum cases instead of fictional, tailored, or vignette-size studies. It wanted to introduce into the elementary course case studies which (1) dealt with situations in which important values were at stake in the governmental process, and (2) showed how the fate of these values was affected by key aspects of governmental structure and process. For example, we sought to prepare a case about the Little Rock incident not only to illustrate the conflicting values but to reveal how some of the basic structural and procedural elements of government (federalism, states rights, separation of powers, court system, presidential power) affected the perception, handling, and resolution of the conflicting values. Finally, the committee agreed to search for cases which met its value and process requirements in substantive policy areas that seemed important in modern times: foreign policy, civil rights, science, the military, and government and the economy. In short, the committee's purpose was to develop for the introductory course case studies that presented relatively broad pictures of reality in order to show the interplay of values, substance, process, structure, and, where possible, the individual.

Assigning the Cases

This volume presents the cases under headings commonly used in organizing courses and textbooks. However, because these are broad-spectrum cases, and because they do not ignore the variety of forces and institutions that actually affected a process, they have multiple relevance.

This multiple relevance means first that the cases may be assigned for purposes other than those indicated by the headings under which they appear in this volume—a flexibility also made possible by the exclusion of author's analysis and built-in questions that tie cases to a single subject. For example, *The Little Rock Story,* though listed under Federalism, could also be assigned when dealing with the Supreme Court, the Presidency, Civil Rights, or Interest Groups.

A second advantage of these broad-spectrum cases is that some data in each case will be applicable to later class discussions on different subjects. Thus, while these cases are longer and more complicated than vignettes, the time spent reading each of them will enrich not just one class discussion but several.

Third, experimental teaching indicates that the cases in this collection are mutually reinforcing and that, taken as a whole, they have a cumulative value. Because it shows most of the forces and institutions that significantly affected a particular government matter, each case illuminates not only a single institution at the center of the stage but others on the periphery whose actions condition the principal subject. The reader of the entire collection, therefore, is able to observe a single institution like Congress, for example, in a variety of postures, from a variety of perspectives, exerting a variety of influences. There are cases in this collection that center on the internal workings of Congress and on its relationships with the Executive Branch and with the states. But even cases designed primarily for other purposes, such as *The Battery Additive Controversy* and *The California Democratic Delegation,* show significant aspects of congressional behavior and influence, thereby adding to the student's cumulative appreciation of the role of that institution in American government.

FEDERALISM, INTER-GOVERNMENTAL RELATIONS

The Little Rock Story
Illinois Goes to Congress
The Miracle Case
California Democratic Delegation
(Lobbying and the Natural Gas Bill)
(Defense Appropriations Rider)

INTEREST GROUPS

Lobbying and the Natural Gas Bill
Defense Appropriations Rider
Illinois Goes to Congress
The Little Rock Story
The Miracle Case
Battery Additive Controversy
U.S. Bases in Spain

GOVERNMENT AND THE ECONOMY

President's Economic Advisers
Battery Additive Controversy
Lobbying and the Natural Gas Bill
Defense Appropriations Rider
Illinois Goes to Congress
(The Miracle Case)

POLITICAL PARTIES

California Democratic Delegation
Illinois Goes to Congress
(Lobbying and the Natural Gas Bill)
(Defense Appropriations Rider)

CONGRESS

Defense Appropriations Rider
Illinois Goes to Congress
U.S. Bases in Spain
Lobbying and the Natural Gas Bill
Battery Additive Controversy
President's Economic Advisers
(The Little Rock Story)
(California Democratic Delegation)

PRESIDENCY, EXECUTIVE BRANCH

U.S. Bases in Spain
President's Economic Advisers
The Little Rock Story
California Democratic Delegation
Defense Appropriations Rider
(Lobbying and the Natural Gas Bill)
(Illinois Goes to Congress)

JUDICIARY, CIVIL RIGHTS

The Miracle Case
The Little Rock Story
Lobbying and the Natural Gas Bill
(Battery Additive Controversy)

SEPARATION OF POWERS

The Little Rock Story
Defense Appropriations Rider
U.S. Bases in Spain
President's Economic Advisers
Illinois Goes to Congress
Battery Additive Controversy
(Lobbying and the Natural Gas Bill)

viii   *Introduction*

The Accuracy of Case Studies

Depiction of some aspect of reality is the purpose of a case study, whatever its focus and shape. Yet, although care may be taken to make cases complete and accurate, no case can achieve perfection. No case writer can know everything about any particular process. Memories are faulty, motivations are not entirely conscious, and sometimes the writer must depend on an unrepresentative document that happens to be the only source available to cover a particular point in a case. The reader has the right to expect the Case Program to strive for perfection, and the Case Program has the duty to warn the reader that perfection is impossible. The cases in this collection have been given the same processing for verification and accuracy that the Inter-University Case Program has used for its other studies. A responsible writer is selected and the major participants in a case are invited to review pre-publication drafts. (The footnotes in *The President's Economic Advisers* give an indication of the flavor of the comments sometimes made.) The case is also read critically by members of the ICP First-Year Course Committee and the ICP Executive Board, and their extensive collective background often leads to further checking and rewriting. The case which results is, therefore, the product of many hands, representing painstaking efforts for accuracy and completeness.

Drafts of all the cases in this book were taught experimentally before they were finally revised for publication. Some of the cases have already been published separately in the Inter-University Case Program series (issued by the University of Alabama Press) and have been widely used in first-year courses across the country. On the whole the teaching results have been satisfying. Students have apparently responded well, and instructors have found the cases excellent material around which to center discussions. Teachers have found that the cases, serving a variety of purposes, may be used to raise questions of values, of substance, of theory, of expediency, and of "what is." They indicate the milieu and conflict out of which compromises grow and present policy issues in the context in which they appear to those who have to deal with them.

Improving With Experience

The First-Year Course Committee of the ICP does not intend to cease its experimentation with the publication of this collection. Its future efforts, however, will be materially affected by reactions to this effort. Users of the cases—instructors and students—are invited to address comments and criticisms to the President, Inter-University Case Program, 607 University Avenue, Syracuse 10, New York. The committee hopes that it can profit from the wide teaching experience that will follow the publication of this volume, and from suggestions of useful case studies that might be included in future editions. Teaching experiences, suggestions for cases, and identification of able case writers are all ways by which the quality of the committee's products may be improved.

E.A.B.
A.K.C.

ed, it was decided to experiment with a different kind of material. The
Harvard Business School for many years had been using cases in the teaching
of business administration, providing experience from which the Harvard political
scientists drew inspiration. The use of the case in clinical medicine had also
stimulated their imagination.

Cases written for the Harvard seminar were restricted to use by that institution,
since it was on this understanding that many government officials cooperated in
their preparation. But other graduate schools heard of the experiment and were
favorably impressed by it. Four universities—Cornell, Harvard, Princeton, and
Syracuse—jointly designed a case-writing program supported by the Carnegie
Corporation of New York. Known as the Committee on Public Administration
Cases, this group employed a Staff Director with an office in Washington and
prepared a large number of cases, many of which were later published in a book
called *Public Administration and Policy Development,* edited by the first Staff
Director, Harold Stein.

The purposes of the program were outlined as follows:

1. To provide the basis for realistic concepts, hypotheses, and generalizations
   about administrative organization, behavior, and policy-making by utilizing a
   clinical approach and drawing on case studies of administrators in action.
2. To explore the application and possibility of integration of the various social
   sciences and disciplines in administrative policy-making by collecting and examining a variety of cases which illustrate the complex aspects of decision-
   making in the public policy area.
3. To make generally available a body of case materials which, it is hoped, will
   be particularly useful for teaching purposes, for scholarly inquiry, and to
   practitioners in the field of public administration.

The success of this program was sufficient in the judgment of the participating
universities to justify its continuation after the original funds were exhausted.
It was further decided to broaden the program by including case studies from
other areas of political science and by inviting other universities to participate.
The result of this decision was the establishment of the Inter-University Case
Program, with membership open to all universities and colleges. In 1957 the
Ford Foundation enabled the ICP to expand its coverage to a broader area of
political science and public policy administration. Other ICP committees are

producing cases in the following fields: Foreign and Comparative Government; Overseas Administration; Urban Planning and Development; Regulatory Process; Legislative Policy Making; Executive Leadership; Public Administration and Organizational Behavior. Many of these committees are doing more than preparing cases for teaching purposes. Some are opening up new avenues of insight and knowledge. Some are systematically relating their research to significant hypotheses and curiosities. Throughout its current program the ICP is experimenting in the use of the case study technique for research.

The Inter-University Case Program is directed by an Executive Board elected by the seventy-odd member institutions. The members of the Executive Board during the period of the preparation of this book were:

The following professors served on the First-Year Course Committee from 1957 through 1962 (with the exceptions indicated):

Table of Contents*

* See page vii of Introduction for fuller index.

SIX
GOVERNMENT, SCIENCE, AND THE ECONOMY

ONE

The Constitutional Framework

The Little Rock Story

CORINNE SILVERMAN

It is the inherent paradox of federalism at once to unite and divide. The national government, as part of a larger strategy of building loyalty to the union, tolerates and encourages many diversities in state policy and practice; and the states likewise with their subdivisions. Thereby each leaves some of its citizens, locally in the minority, feeling abandoned to locally dominant elements with contrary views. The minorities appeal for relief to the larger units above them in the name of individual rights. If the more inclusive government moves to protect minority interests by establishing and trying to enforce a uniform national or state policy, it in turn aggrieves powerful local groups who will protest central interference in the name of states' rights or home rule. So diversity may promote unity, and uniformity promote division. The states in their intermediate position face this dilemma both above and below.

—Harvey C. Mansfield
in *The Forty-Eight States,*
American Assembly, 1955.

One: The First Year [1]

In March 1861 an Arkansas convention met to decide whether to join the seven states which already made up the Confederate States of America. The Arkansans voted against secession. It was not until May 6, several weeks after Fort Sumter was fired upon, that Arkansas finally voted to secede from the Union. On Sep-

---

[1] Editor's Note: This case is divided into two sections. The first ends with the arrival of federal troops in Little Rock. The second describes the subsequent court fights to resolve the integration question, including the Supreme Court decision. It also portrays subsequent efforts in the state capital, in the city of Little Rock, and in the Little Rock school district to decide whether Central High School would reopen in the fall of 1959 on an integrated or segregated basis. Each section of the case may be taught separately.

1

tember 10, 1863 the Union forces captured the capital city of Little Rock in the Civil War which Arkansas had not been eager to join.

On the 94th anniversary of the fall of Little Rock—September 10, 1957—Arkansas' Governor Orval Faubus accepted a summons to appear in federal District Court. He was to answer a charge that he was obstructing the plan of the Little Rock School Board to end segregation in Little Rock Central High School. Once again Little Rock citizens were embroiled in an emotional controversy where the first issue was that of constitutional interpretation; where the power of the judiciary was being tested; where the limits of civil obedience were being tried; and where federal troops were to take command of the situation.

This case study of the Little Rock controversy is concerned essentially with the problems of federalism. The Supreme Court decided that segregated schools were unconstitutional, and its ruling was carried out by the federal District Court in Arkansas, by the President, and by federal troops. However, the Governor of Arkansas, the Arkansas Legislature, and the state courts also had jurisdiction over the citizens of Arkansas, and officials in all three branches of the state government acted to carry out their responsibilities as they saw them. Both the federal and state executives backed up their interpretations of the limits of their power with troops at their command. The city officials—the mayor, the city aldermen, and the school board—also had duties and responsibilities as elected representatives of the city of Little Rock. As the events developed, the multiple allegiances, multiple citizenship, and multiple responsibilities which characterize federalism became real, daily questions for the citizens of Little Rock, as local, state, and national elected representatives, the federal and state judiciary, and federal and state armed troops exerted their claims in the question of who should attend Central High School and when.

The Supreme Court Decision

On May 17, 1954 a unanimous Supreme Court delivered its opinion in a set of cases—known as *Brown vs. Board of Education*—dealing with segregated public schools. The opinion overturned the 1896 *Plessy vs. Ferguson* decision which held that segregation did not deprive citizens of equal protection of the laws under the 14th Amendment if the separate facilities were substantially equal. Chief Justice Earl Warren, speaking for the court in the 1954 decision, proclaimed: "Separate educational facilities are inherently unequal."

> To separate [children] from others of similar age and qualifications solely because of their race generates a feeling of inferiority as to their status in the community that may affect their hearts and minds in a way unlikely ever to be undone.

Warren went on to cite the eight psychologists the court had used as authorities, and said:

> Whatever may have been the extent of psychological knowledge at the time of *Plessy vs. Ferguson,* this finding is amply supported by modern authority. Any language in *Plessy vs. Ferguson* contrary to this finding is rejected.

After delivering its opinion on the Brown case, the Supreme Court postponed for one year its decision on another question which had been argued before it: whether the court should decree that segregation end immediately, or whether it should permit desegregation to be instituted gradually. During the next few months the Supreme Court received suggestions from the attorneys general of six southern or border states and from the United States Attorney General. In May 1955 it ruled that desegregation did not have to take place immediately because implementation of its 1954 decision "will involve a variety of local problems." Stating that any proposed solutions could best be evaluated close to the scene, the Supreme Court gave the responsibility for appraising proposed plans to the various federal district courts. However, the chief justice went on, "vitality of these constitutional principles cannot be allowed to yield simply because of disagreement with them."

As a guideline for the district courts, the Supreme Court set as the standard for judgment that

> . . . the defendants make a prompt and reasonable start toward full compliance. . . . Once such a start has been made, the courts may find that additional time is necessary to carry out the ruling in an effective manner. The burden rests upon the defendants to establish that such time is necessary in the public interest and is consistent with good faith compliance at the earliest practicable date.

There were many who hailed the court's 1954 decision as long-overdue. But there were many among those who, while agreeing with the social principle underlying the decision, regretted that the court had rested so heavily upon psychology, since that judicial route led to a variety of criticisms, all of which were soon voiced.

Criticism of the Court

One set of critics pointed out that the justices had been more thoughtful of the psyches of one group than of an-

other. For after all, they argued, if many white Southerners feel it degrading to associate with Negroes, they too are being affected in heart and mind by being forced to give up segregation. Senator Richard Russell of Georgia spoke in a somewhat similar vein on the floor of the Senate the day after the decision was announced, saying that "if the Supreme Court is to abandon law and precedents in favor of psychology in arriving at its opinion, the rights of the States which might remain or the liberties of the American people should not be subjected to the findings of amateur psychologists."

Russell went on to raise still another point of disagreement: that this decision had been a marked departure from what he understood to be general judicial practice. In interpreting sections of the Constitution, he pointed out, the court generally weighed the intention of the framers of the section or amendment in question—in this instance the 14th Amendment—and took note of how contemporaries of the framers construed its meaning. "The very Congress which proposed the 14th Amendment," Russell reminded his senatorial colleagues, "provided for the adoption of a separate school system for the races in the District of Columbia . . . the same legislature which ratified the 14th Amendment proposed by the Congress wrote a constitution for the State of Georgia which contained a provision for separate schools." [2]

Senator Price Daniel of Texas pointed out that at the time of the adoption of the 14th Amendment practically all of the states—both in the

---

[2] The Supreme Court had considered evidence about the intent of the framers of the 14th Amendment and about how their contemporaries construed its words. "At best," the Court's opinion stated, the evidence was "inconclusive."

North and South—had separate schools, and that many states continued this practice after the adoption of the amendment. However, Daniel went on, "No matter how much some of us may disagree with the reasoning and result of the court's decision, we must look to the future with patience, wisdom, and sound judgment to live under the law as it has now been written and at the same time preserve our public school systems and maintain peace, order, and harmony."

Daniel's attitude was echoed by some Southerners, who, while disapproving of the court's decision, nevertheless recognized that the Supreme Court had the power to say, as it did in the 1954 Brown decision, that "All provisions of federal, state or local law requiring or permitting [racial] discrimination must yield. . . ." This power flowed from Article VI, Section 2 of the Constitution:

> This Constitution, and the Laws of the United States which shall be made in Pursuance thereof; and all Treaties made, or which shall be made, under the Authority of the United States, shall be the supreme Law of the Land; and the Judges in every State shall be bound thereby, anything in the Constitution or Laws of any State to the Contrary notwithstanding.

Many Americans drew different conclusions from the history of judicial review and could not agree with Senators Russell and Daniel that the Supreme Court is duty bound to interpret the Constitution in the light of the intentions of the framers. Those who took this view argued that a constitution "that won't bend will break" and maintained that a long line of Supreme Court decisions have served to adapt the Constitution to changing times and attitudes. In this way, they argued, the Constitution, which in a formal sense is difficult to amend, is kept a living instrument, serving the twentieth century as readily as it did the nineteenth.

The position of those who opposed the new interpretation of the 14th Amendment was that the court had usurped the role of the legislature. This view was stated most strongly in a Declaration of Constitutional Principles signed in March 1956 by 77 members of the House and 19 senators, all from the South. Mindful of the fact that for decades anti-segregation measures proposed in Congress had been successfully blocked by Southern senators, they said:

> We regard the decision of the Supreme Court in the school cases as clear abuse of judicial power. It climaxes a trend in the Federal judiciary undertaking to legislate, in derogation of the authority of Congress, and to encroach upon the reserved rights of the states and people.

The court's 1955 implementation decision also became the target of much debate. Some who favored integration were disappointed that the court had not ruled that schools be integrated immediately. Others felt that the court's strategy would allow a more peaceful transition since those areas which wished could desegregate almost immediately without waiting for uniform state action. In the South, many political leaders felt a large measure of relief, some because the decision allowed time for constructive action, some because they saw it as permitting a long period of legal delay.

By its decision the Supreme Court was assigning to the federal district courts a two-fold task: first, approving proposed integration plans, and second, hearing complaints from those who felt that an integration plan should be re-evaluated or was not being carried through properly—in effect, the district courts were to administer their own decisions. The Supreme Court had assigned this role to district courts in some anti-trust cases, but never before in civil liberties cases—or if it had, the cases were so obscure that qualified constitutional lawyers could not bring them readily to mind. In applying its practice in anti-trust cases to the desegregation decision, the court was following the recommendation of the United States Attorney General who had suggested precisely this course in his argument on the *Brown vs. Board of Education* cases.

Reaction in the South

The strongest sentiments against the desegregation decision were expressed in the Southern states which had the largest proportion of Negro residents and the firmest policies against integration. In Mississippi, where Negroes comprise 45 percent of the population, Senator James O. Eastland asserted that the South "will not abide by nor obey this legislative decision by a political court." In border states such as Oklahoma, where only eight percent of the population is Negro, desegregation in the public schools got underway immediately, and by 1957 almost 97 percent of the Oklahoma school districts had begun integration.

In Tennessee, when the board of education in Clinton integrated the high school in 1956, a mob congregated outside the school and did not break up until the local police used tear gas. The next day, the Governor sent 650 National Guardsmen with tanks to enforce the District Court's order to integrate, and the Negro students remained in the school.

Arkansas is neither a border nor a Deep South state. As of 1950 only 23 percent of the state's population was Negro. In only six of its 75 counties did Negroes outnumber the whites, in contrast to Mississippi, for example, where Negroes outnumber whites in 31 of the state's 82 counties. In more than half of Arkansas' counties less than 10 percent of the population was Negro.

In North Arkansas, Fayetteville integrated its public high school in 1955 with almost no protest. Hoxie, Arkansas, on the other hand, was the scene of much public disturbance when the board of education announced it was planning to integrate 25 Negro students with 1,000 white students.

Little Rock, the state capital, lies on the dividing line between the Arkansas hill country of the northwest (home territory of Governor Orval Faubus) where no county is more than 25 percent Negro, and the cotton-raising counties of the southeast where the Negro population is as high as 66 percent. By far the largest city in the state, with over 100,000 people, Little Rock's population is about 22 percent Negro. Its citizens enjoy a considerably higher educational and income level than do those in most parts of the state, which is two-thirds rural. The city relies on diversified light industry for its income and in recent years has joined most Southern cities in an intensive drive to attract more industrial plants.

The Negroes in Little Rock are not completely clustered residentially but live in almost all sections of the city, although fewer of them live in the fourth and fifth wards than in the first three wards. (These first three wards contain Central High School, the Governor's mansion, and the state capitol building.) Although the schools, hotels, restaurants, waiting rooms, and wash rooms were still segregated in 1957, the city buses had been integrated in 1956, and there were several Negro policemen on the Little Rock police force.

The Little Rock Implementation Plan

On May 20, 1954, three days after the Supreme Court's desegregation decision, the six-man School Board of the Little Rock Independent School District issued a statement announcing that it would comply with the decision. A year later the school board approved a plan for integrating the city's public schools. The plan envisioned integration in the high schools in 1957, in the junior high schools within the next two or three years, and complete integration of all grades by 1963.

In February 1956 parents of 33 Negro children, represented by the National Association for the Advancement of Colored People, brought a suit against the members of the school board in the federal District Court in Little Rock, arguing that the planned integration was not rapid enough. The federal district judge upheld the plan of the school board, and the Negro parents appealed the decision to the United States Court of Appeals. In April 1957 the plan was upheld by the Court of Appeals, and the Negro parents decided not to appeal further. This was the first stage of *Aaron vs. Cooper,* which was to be argued and re-argued for months.

During the spring and summer of 1957, Superintendent of Schools Virgil T. Blossom, Little Rock's 1955 Man of the Year, put on a campaign for general acceptance of the plan, making more than 150 talks and speeches in the community. He made it quite clear that he and the school board members felt the law required desegregation, but that, as the school board said, "The plan was developed to provide as little

integration as possible for as long as possible legally. . . ." At this time there was not much evidence that the plan would run into great difficulty. That March, the two members of the six-man Little Rock School Board who were up for re-election under the staggered-term system had been opposed by two announced "segregation" candidates. Both incumbents had been returned to office by an almost two-to-one majority in the light vote customary in school board elections. Thus, the citizens of Little Rock could be said to have given the school board a mandate to proceed with its plan.

But these same citizens were also part of a larger community—they were also citizens of Arkansas—and in the November 1956 election the voters of Arkansas had also given what could be considered a mandate, and one quite different from that implied by the city school board election. In the November election the state voters had been presented with a resolution and an amendment to the state constitution proposed by State Senator James Johnson, Director of the Citizens Councils of Arkansas. (Johnson had run for Governor on a strong segregation platform and had been defeated handily by Faubus in the 1956 spring primary.) The resolution called for an amendment to the United States Constitution which would prohibit the federal government from exercising any control over the operation of public schools. The proposed amendment to the Arkansas Constitution would require the Arkansas Legislature to oppose the Supreme Court's decision in every constitutional manner. This package was approved by 55 percent of the state's voters, sufficient to pass it. Three times as many citizens of Little Rock voted in this election as in the School Board balloting, and they voted almost exactly 50-

50, approving the measure by 50.1 percent.[3]

The State Legislature Acts

In the winter of 1957, the Arkansas Legislature passed four acts under the authority granted by the new amendment. One of the provisions of new Act 84 made it illegal to require any child to enroll in or attend any school in which both white and Negro children were enrolled.

This act, presumably, could be interpreted either as a modification of the compulsory school attendance law, or as an act to prohibit integration. The constitutionality of this provision, or its precise effect, had not been tested by the time the public schools opened in September.

A month before the Little Rock schools were due to start classes, a group called the Mothers' League of Central High School was formed to resist integration.

Governor Marvin Griffin of Georgia was due to arrive in Little Rock on August 22 to address the city's segregationist Capital Citizens Council. Governor Faubus telephoned Griffin for reassurance that his speech would not be inflammatory, and then invited him and Georgia's Citizens Council leader Roy Harris to stay at the Governor's mansion. Little Rock Congressman Brooks Hays later reported Harris' reaction to the invitation:

> We had to accept Faubus' invitation to stay at the Mansion, but we had to apologize to the [Citizens] Council folks for staying there. When we got to

the airport there at Little Rock, Marv went over and greeted the Governor's delegation—the state troopers and all —and that gave me time to get to one side with *our* people. I apologized and told 'em that Marv figured it was just courtesy to accept another governor's invitation, and that being discourteous wouldn't do any good. And then I told 'em, "Why, having us two there at the Mansion's the worse thing could happen to Faubus. It'll ruin him with the integrationists and liberals." And they said, "We never thought of it that way. That's fine." [4]

Griffin and Harris made their speeches, with the Georgia Governor urging Arkansans to join Georgians in an all-out effort to resist integration.

On August 27—registration day at Central High School—a petition signed by 250 members of the Mothers' League called upon Governor Faubus "to prevent forcible integration of the Little Rock schools as now planned by the Little Rock School Board."

None of the Negro students eligible for entrance into Central registered that day, at the suggestion of Superintendent Blossom. Blossom wanted to instruct them first and give them a special tour of the high school before classes began. Of the 900 Negro children of high school age, only thirteen had passed the rigorous screening by the superintendent and the principals of the three senior high schools. Only nine of the thirteen "eligibles" decided to transfer to Central, which had about 1,900 white students. All nine were near the top of their classes at the new, modern, all-Negro high school.

Earlier that month a committee of the Negro PTA Councils had met with Blossom, Pulaski County Sheriff Tom

---

[3] The boundaries of the Little Rock Independent School District do not coincide exactly with the city boundaries. Three or four city precincts are outside the city school district, and a few villages outside the city limits are included in the city school district.

[4] Brooks Hays, *A Southern Moderate Speaks* (The University of North Carolina Press, 1959), pp. 131–132.

Gulley, and Little Rock Chief of Police Marvin H. Potts to discuss plans for police protection of the nine Negro students in case of any disturbance. This committee, together with Mayor Woodrow Wilson Mann, worked out a plan whereby 48 policemen (out of a 175-man total force) would patrol the area surrounding the high school to keep crowds from forming. Two policemen in civilian clothes would patrol the school grounds.

The State Court Rules

On August 29, the Little Rock School Board became the target of a second court suit, this time by white opponents of integration. This suit was brought in the state court (in Arkansas, called Chancery Court) before Chancellor Murray O. Reed by Mrs. Clyde A. Thomason, recording secretary of the Mothers' League. This suit asked that the school board be enjoined [5] from starting integration because such a plan would be contrary to the legislative act passed by the State Legislature. The school board, she said, was requiring that children in the Little Rock School District enroll in a school where both white and Negro students were about to be enrolled. She went on to say that she feared there would be "civil commotion" if the plan were carried out in this period of "uncertainty of the law, conflicting court decisions, and general state of confusion and unrest."

Governor Orval Faubus appeared in Chancery Court that day under subpoena by Mrs. Thomason and strongly supported her allegation that violence was brewing. He said, for example, that he had been given reports—al-

though he did not identify the source of these reports—showing that weapons sales had risen significantly and that revolvers had recently been taken from both white and Negro students.

Chancellor Reed declined to rule on the constitutionality of the various amendments and legislative acts, stating that he felt the Chancery Court was limited to judging whether there was likely to be violence and civil commotion. Reed then granted the injunction against the school board, restraining it from integrating the schools. The testimony of Mrs. Thomason, he said, and especially that of the Governor had considerable value as evidence tending to show that "through certain events over which the school board had no control public sentiment has undergone a swift change and that a probability of violence and civil commotion exists."

The school board now faced a citation for contempt of court from Reed if it proceeded with its integration plan, and from the federal District Court if it did not carry it out. (Since the school board's plan had been approved by the federal courts in *Aaron vs. Cooper,* it would need a federal court order to modify it, and the plan called for integration to begin September 3, 1957.) Attorneys for the school board, although they could have appealed Reed's decision in the State Supreme Court, promptly petitioned the federal District Court, asking for an injunction to prevent anyone from using Reed's orders and from interfering with the board's integration plan. The attorneys also asked for protection against a contempt citation from the Chancery Court if the school board went ahead with its integration program.

Judge Davies Reacts

The board's petition was heard by District Judge Ronald Davies who had

---

[5] To enjoin is to restrain by a court order called an injunction. Disobedience of an injunction may result in a citation for contempt of court.

been brought to Little Rock from Fargo, North Dakota, on August 26. He was filling in until February, since the District Court of the Arkansas Eastern District (containing Little Rock) had two vacancies. Although federal district judges generally sit in their home districts, they may be rotated. Generally they rotate among the districts which comprise the circuit containing their district. Davies was one of the judges of the 8th Circuit Court area which includes the districts in North Dakota, South Dakota, Nebraska, Minnesota, Iowa, Missouri, and Arkansas.

Davies rendered his verdict immediately, and on Friday, August 30, ruled that the State Chancery Court did not have jurisdiction to interfere with the operation of the school board's plan which had been made "in good faith" and which had been approved earlier by the federal District Court. The injunction the state court had directed against the school board was, therefore, invalid. Davies then enjoined all persons from "interfering with and preventing the opening of integrated high schools . . . on September 3, 1957," and enjoined all persons from taking steps to obtain a contempt citation against the school board for disobeying the state court's ruling.

The school board had brought its problem to the federal court because that court was empowered to administer the original decision in *Aaron vs. Cooper*. Davies, by denying legitimacy of the state court's jurisdiction, was relying on the fact that the integration plan involved a federal right, and, he said, the effect of the state court's order would be "to paralyze the decree of this court entered under Federal law which is supreme under the provisions of Article 6 of the Constitution of the United States."

That Sunday, two days before school was to open, Mayor Mann was telephoned by Chief of Police Potts who reported that he had begun to receive a number of anonymous telephone calls warning of "caravans" of automobiles from all parts of the state which were on their way to Little Rock to protest the integration of Central High School. Mann asked Potts to check these reports as quickly as possible and report back to him. Late that same night Potts called again to say that thorough investigation had failed to substantiate the warnings.

Calling in the National Guard

Monday night, September 2, more than 200 armed and helmeted members of the Arkansas National Guard surrounded Central High School. An hour later Governor Faubus broadcast a special address over three television stations, announcing that the troops had been summoned on his orders. Neither the mayor, the chief of police, nor the school board had requested such assistance from the Governor, nor had Faubus consulted them.

In explaining his action, Faubus pointed out that he had been told there were many indications of impending violence, among them that a telephone campaign was under way for white mothers to assemble at Central the next morning, and that automobile caravans were due to arrive at the high school Tuesday morning. Faubus repeated the points he had made in Chancery Court: that weapons sales had increased substantially; that revolvers had been taken from both white and Negro students; and that the legal situation surrounding the new constitutional amendment and the legislative acts was not resolved.

He summed up his message by saying

It is my opinion—yes, even a conviction that it will not be possible to restore or to maintain order and to protect the lives and property of the citizens if forcible integration is carried out tomorrow in the schools of the community. The inevitable conclusion, therefore, must be that the schools in Pulaski County, for the time being, must be operated on the same basis as they have operated in the past.

.   .   .   .

The mission of the State Militia is to maintain or restore order and to protect the lives and property of citizens. They will act not as segregationists or integrationists, but as soldiers called to active duty to carry out their assigned tasks.

The school board met in emergency session that Monday night and then issued a statement that in view of the situation "we ask that no Negro students attempt to attend Central or any white high school until this dilemma is legally resolved."

The jurisdictional struggle over Central High School had become very complex. On the one hand was Judge Davies, representing federal jurisdiction over the constitutional rights of United States citizens. Davies had acted in line with previous decisions by the federal judge for the Eastern District of Arkansas and in line with decisions by the 8th Circuit Court of Appeals and the United States Supreme Court.

On the other hand was Governor Faubus, acting in his capacity as chief executive of the state, responsible under the state constitution for preserving peace and order among its citizens. As commander-in-chief of the state's military forces, Faubus had called out the National Guard, thereby removing the direct responsibility from the city's elected and appointed officials—the mayor, the school board, the superintendent of schools, the city chief of police, and the county sheriff.

Classes Open at Central High School

The next morning, September 3, 1957, a subdued crowd of two or three hundred people watched the white students arrive for opening classes at the guarded high school. No Negro students appeared.

The school board immediately filed a petition with Judge Davies requesting instructions, and after a ten-minute hearing that same day Davies issued an order affirming his August 30 direction to integrate the school on schedule.

That evening Mayor Mann was questioned by Little Rock newspaper reporters who wanted to know if Mann was considering ordering a police escort for the Negro children the next day. Mann answered that in his opinion local police did not have jurisdiction to escort anyone through a guard of state troops and suggested that, again in his opinion, only a federal guard had such jurisdiction. Mann's own preference for such an escort was a contingent of federal marshals—the administrative officials of the federal court districts.

The next day Mann fired off a strongly-worded statement to the press, placing himself in direct opposition to Faubus.

. . . The Governor has called out the National Guard to put down trouble where none existed. He did so without a request from those of us who are directly responsible for preservation of peace and order. The only effect is to create tension where none existed. I call the Governor's attention to the fact that after almost a week of sensational developments brought about by his own actions, the Little Rock police have not had a single case of interracial violence reported to them. This is clear evidence that the Governor's excuse for calling out the Guard is simply a hoax.

Mayor Mann was not speaking from a position of strength, as many were to point out. A local insurance man, Mann had been elected in 1955 in a campaign in which school segregation or desegregation had not been an issue. He had not had a quiet and smoothly-run administration, and in November 1956 the citizens of Little Rock had voted by an almost seventy-percent majority to change from a mayor-plus-ten aldermen system to a city manager-plus-seven city directors plan of government. Mann was, therefore, a "lame duck" mayor, serving only until November 1957, when the new directors were to be elected.

Washington Intervention?

Tuesday afternoon in Washington, President Dwight Eisenhower held his weekly press conference and was questioned on his view of the events in Little Rock. The President informed the reporters that he had already been in contact with United States Attorney General Herbert Brownell's office which was in the process of gathering information for him. One reporter asked the President if he had any plans to take a personal part in the school integration problem, such as speaking on it or getting in touch with Governor Faubus. The President answered, some felt in a rather equivocal way:

My speaking will be always in this subject, as I have always done, urging Americans to recognize what America is, the concepts on which it is based, and to do their part so far as they possibly can to bring out the kind of America that was visualized by our forebears.

. . . .

Now it is for this reason, because I know this is a slow process, the Supreme Court in its decision of 1954 pointed out that emotional difficulties that would be encountered by a Negro, even if given—or by Negroes if given —equal but separate schools, and I think, probably their reasoning was correct, at least I have no quarrel with it.

But there are very strong emotions on the other side, people that see a picture of a mongrelization of the race, they call it. They are very strong emotions, and we are going to whip this thing in the long run by Americans being true to themselves and not merely by law. [*New York Times Transcript*]

The reporter who asked that question, Anthony Lewis of the *New York Times,* filed a more complete story on the position of the United States government as he had gotten it from his various sources. "The legal obstacle to any federal intervention in the Little Rock case at this point," Lewis wrote, "centers on the fact that it [*Aaron vs. Cooper*] is a private lawsuit. It was brought by Negro parents in the Federal District Court in Arkansas with the Little Rock school officials as defendants. . . . Thus the federal government is not a party to the case." Lewis' story was accurate, as far as legal intervention was concerned, but, of course, the President is always in a position to influence opinion by public statements.

The President's failure "to act more positively to support Judge Davies against the Governor of Arkansas and his National Guard troops" drew a response of mingled disappointment and criticism from editorial writers and news commentators outside the South. The Little Rock situation was now front-page news throughout the country and would remain so for weeks. Nor was attention confined to the United States. Descriptions of events at Little Rock began to fill newspapers and radio commentaries in most countries of the world. Critics of the Presi-

dent and supporters of integration began to point out that Radio Moscow
and other propaganda organs of the
Soviet Union and its allies were capi-
talizing on the defeat of integration
plans at Central High School. Many
commentators stressed the unhappy
consequences of the Little Rock controversy on United States relations with
the rising countries of Africa and Asia,
where "American racism" was a favorite theme of anti-United States propa-
gandists.

Wednesday, September 4, the second
day of school, a crowd of about 400
people gathered around Central High
School, but this was not the quiet gathering of the day before. When the nine
Negro students appeared and attempted to enter the school, the crowd
shouted, hissed, and booed. The National Guardsmen barred the doors to
the Negroes, who soon withdrew.

Faubus, at a press conference later
that day, confirmed that the Arkansas
National Guard had blocked the Negroes' entry into the school on his orders issued late the previous evening
to Adjutant General Sherman T.
Clinger, head of the guard. Reporters
pointed out that the Governor had
said in his television address Monday
that the guardsmen were to be neither
segregationists nor integrationists.
Faubus replied that he had changed
his orders because of the change in the
situation—the increased tension in the
community. It was his responsibility
as Arkansas chief executive, he
stressed, to preserve peace and prevent
bloodshed. He expanded his view in a
telegram sent to President Eisenhower
that evening:

. . . The question at issue at Little
Rock this moment is not integration
vs. segregation. . . . The question now
is whether or not the head of a sovereign state can exercise his constitutional powers and discretion in main-

taining peace and good order within
his jurisdiction, being accountable to
his own good conscience and to his
own people.

When Faubus was asked later why
local and state police could not have
dealt with violence if it occurred, he
answered that "it is better to preserve
peace than to quell disorders."

F.B.I. men and other agents of the
Justice Department were already at
work investigating the situation in Little
Rock and had been asked by Davies to
report their findings to him. Faubus referred to these investigations in his telegram to the President, contending
that these activities were aggravating
the "explosive" situation and warning
that "if these actions continue or if
my executive authority as Governor to
maintain the peace is breached, then I
can no longer be responsible for the
results. The injury to persons and property that would be caused—the blood
that may be shed will be on the hands
of the federal government and its
agents."

Eisenhower answered Faubus on
Thursday, also by telegram:

. . . When I became President, I
took an oath to support and defend
the Constitution of the United States.
The only assurance I can give you is
that the federal Constitution will be
upheld by me by every legal means at
my command.

Eisenhower also referred to the Justice Department's investigation:

You and other state officials—as
well as the National Guard which is,
of course, uniformed, armed and partially sustained by the government—
will I am sure, give full cooperation to
the United States District Court.

Faubus replied on Friday, informing
the President that his personal counsel

and the director of the Arkansas State Police were available to the investigators to discuss the evidence upon which he had acted, and ended by affirming that he would "cooperate in upholding the Constitution of Arkansas and the nation."

Implicit in these exchanges were the overlappings of power: both chief executives had sworn to uphold the federal Constitution and to protect the rights of the states under their respective constitutions. In terms of military power the Governor had at his disposal the State Police; the President, the United States armed forces and the United States marshals. Both had authority over the National Guard— Faubus directly and Eisenhower by his power to call the same troops into federal service.

More Court Action

Meanwhile, the School Board had filed a new petition with Judge Davies on Wednesday, the day the Negro students first appeared at the school. The petition asked that the court modify its decision made in *Aaron vs. Cooper* and suspend temporarily the integration order because of the rising tension.

On Friday, Davies received a response to the new petition from the attorneys who had represented the 33 Negro parents in *Aaron vs. Cooper*. Their two-paragraph response quoted the language of *Brown vs. Board of Education* that "the vitality of these constitutional principles cannot be allowed to yield simply because of disagreement with them."

On Saturday, Davies held an open hearing on the School Board's petition. He handed down his decision that day, ruling against the school board petition that the integration plan be delayed. The judge referred to Mayor Mann's newspaper statement that there had been no incidents of interracial violence, and expressed his own view that testimony on the school board's petition had been "anemic." He said, "In an organized society there can be nothing but ultimate confusion and chaos if court decrees are flaunted, whatever the pretext."

That afternoon, Mayor Mann posed a number of questions to Arkansas' Attorney General relating to Mann's possible authority to use the city police force in the Central High School area while the National Guard was still on the grounds. Two hours later he received the Attorney General's written response to the effect that Mann's only course in challenging the National Guard's policing of Central High School was by appeal to the courts.

That weekend, Governor Faubus received a statement of support from eight of the ten Little Rock Aldermen who said that they knew

> . . . that there was, and still exists, racial tension between our people because of the United States Supreme Court's decision concerning our schools. We believe that Governor Faubus took the proper course in calling out the Arkansas National Guard in this crisis to protect the lives and property of all our people.

The Governor's motives were questioned in a number of newspapers inside and outside the state. Some commentators pointed out that Faubus had already been elected Governor twice and suggested he was seeking new support to give him the added strength to buck the state's strong anti-third term tradition. Faubus had run strongly, in his 1956 successful primary fight, in the northwestern section of the state, which had also voted most heavily against the constitutional amendment to nullify the Supreme Court's decision. Some commentators argued that since this was Faubus' home territory, he might feel that he could hold its more integration-minded voters while looking for his new support among the more pro-segregation voters.

The Governor rejected this interpretation of his actions, as well as the accusations that his "true colors" as a segregationist were being shown, pointing out that his son was at that moment attending an integrated college. His only motive, he insisted, was to maintain the peace.

Enter the United States

Monday, September 9, Judge Davies received a 400-page report on the situation in Little Rock from Attorney General Brownell's Department. An hour later Davies issued an order requesting Brownell and Osro Cobb, the United States Attorney for the Eastern District of Arkansas, to enter the case as "friends of the court." [6] He also directed that they file a petition against Faubus, Arkansas National Guard head Clinger, and Lt. Col. Marion Johnson, head of the National Guard unit in Little Rock. The petition, Davies directed, should ask for injunctions to be filed against these three to prevent "the existing interferences with and obstructions to the carrying out of the orders heretofore entered by the court in this case."

The petition by the United States Attorney General was filed the next day, Tuesday, September 10, and Davies made Faubus, Clinger, and

---

[6] The role of a friend of the court, or *amicus curiae,* as it is called in law, is defined by *American Jurisprudence* as being one in which the *"amicus curiae* is heard only by leave and for the assistance of the court upon a case already before it. . . . His principal function is to aid the court on questions of law."

Johnson parties to *Aaron vs. Cooper* and set a hearing for September 20. The Governor was now a co-defendant with the school board, and had to defend himself against the charge that he was delaying the plan authorized by the federal District Court.

Constitutional Issues Raised

Faubus and the National Guard officers immediately filed a motion to dismiss the petition and order. Their motion rested on a number of points. First, they cited *American Jurisprudence* to the effect that an *amicus curiae* is supposed only to aid the court on questions of law and is specifically prevented from becoming a party in the action or instituting any proceedings in a case. Thus, they claimed, the United States, as *amicus curiae,* had no right to petition for additional persons to become parties to the suit against the school board, and the court had no right to hold a hearing on the petition.

The Governor's brief went on to point out that in the recent debates in Congress on the Civil Rights Act of 1957 there had originally been a section proposed which would have permitted such intervention by the United States, but the proposed section had been stricken from the bill by both the Senate and House. Thus, both by legal practice and by specific jurisdiction delineated by the Congress, the Attorney General's petition was illegal, Faubus believed.

The major constitutional question raised by the Governor, though, was that this would be an action between the United States of America and the State of Arkansas, and only the Supreme Court of the United States has jurisdiction in such a case. The difficult question to be determined in these cases, the Supreme Court has ruled, is whether a suit brought against a government officer is directed against his actions in his role as a sovereign, or against his actions as an individual. If the suit is directed against an individual, even though he is also a government officer, for actions *unrelated* to his sovereign power, then lower federal courts have jurisdiction. In this case, Faubus claimed, he was clearly acting as the Governor of Arkansas, who by authority of the state constitution has the power "in case of insurrection, invasion, tumult, riot or breach of the peace, or imminent danger thereof, or to preserve the public health and security and maintain the law and order, to order into the active service of the state any part of the militia that he may deem proper."

The Legal Precedents

In support of this point, Faubus cited the 1909 precedent of *Moyer vs. Peabody,* in which the Supreme Court had decided that the governor is the final judge of the use of the military to suppress violence within his state. In this case, a man had been imprisoned for two-and-a-half months for allegedly inciting violence during a labor dispute which had led to a declaration of martial law by Colorado's Governor. The court had used as its criterion the assumption that a state of insurrection had existed and that the Governor had imprisoned the man while putting down the violence, although he had not had sufficient reasons for his actions. But, the court held, "So long as such arrests are made in good faith and in the honest belief that they are needed in order to head the insurrection off, the Governor is the final judge. . . ."

Faubus' motion was not answered until the September 20 hearing.

Meanwhile, legal experts debated about which constitutional precedents applied. One group of constitutional lawyers debated the relative force of the Supreme Court's interpretation of the 14th Amendment against the weight of the 10th Amendment which Faubus had cited over and over again in his public statements. The 10th Amendment reserves to the states and to the people those powers "not delegated to the United States by the Constitution, nor prohibited by it to the States." Faubus maintained that the states reserved the power to preserve law and order—the police power; and many of his supporters went further, pointing out that, since the Constitution said nothing about education, the power to oversee the education of its citizens was reserved to a state.

Another group of constitutional lawyers was debating the merits of the Moyer case as a precedent, and one which Faubus claimed was ruling, against another decision by the Supreme Court, *Sterling vs. Constantin,* decided in 1932. In the Sterling case, the Governor of Texas, because of a slump in the price of oil, proclaimed that a state of insurrection existed in the oil fields, declared martial law in the area, and directed the National Guard commander to use troops to close the wells. This sequence of events was directed at limiting oil production and, so the Governor hoped, raising the price of oil. Here, the Supreme Court had retreated somewhat from its position in the Moyer case by ruling that the federal courts do have the power of reviewing actions of a governor "where there is a substantial showing that the exertion of state power has overridden private rights secured by [the federal] Constitution. . . ." The Sterling case, though clearly rejecting the earlier view that a governor has unlimited authority not subject to judicial review, still left a broad range of discretion to a governor in determining in an emergency situation what means are necessary to preserve or restore law and order. Thus, even among those who held that the Sterling case was more apt than the Moyer case, there was disagreement on whether the situation in Little Rock had indeed been an emergency situation, and whether the actions taken by Faubus had been justified.

Judge Davies' Final Decision

Little Rock had been in the headlines of newspapers throughout the world for almost two weeks. The White House was under heavy pressure to respond to both domestic and foreign opinion by breaking the deadlock. Faubus was under equal pressure from his supporters in Arkansas to uphold his rights as state chief executive. In this situation of growing tensions, Little Rock's Congressman, Brooks Hays, decided to try to break the stalemate. "I was tormented," Hays was to explain later, "by the realization that my home city was drifting toward a terrible crisis. A head-on clash between state and federal authorities seemed imminent. . . . Nothing was being done to avert it." Hays telephoned Presidential Assistant Sherman Adams—a longtime friend— and proposed a meeting between the Governor and the President. "I explained that in dealing with Governor Faubus he would not be confronting a stubborn, last-ditch segregationist governor, and pointed out that quite aside from the question of the propriety of the Governor's action . . . one would have difficulty in proving insincerity . . . my one great concern was that the Governor not be driven into the arms of the few extremists in the Southern governors' group. . . ."[7]

Adams felt Faubus would have to ask for the meeting himself, and the Governor agreed. Hays and Adams drafted a telegram which Faubus sent on September 11—the day after Faubus had presented his motion to Davies—asking Eisenhower for a conference on the Little Rock situation. Eisenhower answered immediately, inviting Faubus to join him within the next two days at Newport, Rhode Island, where the President was vacationing.

On Saturday, September 14, the two chief executives met for a brief private session at Newport, followed by a two-hour conference together with Hays, Adams, Attorney General Brownell, and Presidential Press Secretary James Hagerty. Faubus explained his position: he felt there should be some way to relieve the federal court pressure until the Supreme Court had ruled on the various state laws which had been passed in 1956 and 1957. The President took the position that he, as the executive, could do little; that the problem was completely within the jurisdiction of the judicial branch. Brownell was apparently opposed to any delays to consider the validity of the state laws.

Eisenhower had sought Brownell's legal advice on his power and duty as President to assist federal courts in enforcing their orders. Brownell had advised that "it is the primary and mandatory duty of the authorities of the state to suppress the violence and to remove any obstruction to the orderly enforcement of the law." The President adopted this as his position, making it clear to Faubus at Newport that he regarded the states as responsible for maintaining law and order. As Hays recalled it, the President told the Governor: "I do not criticize you for calling out the Guard—our only difference is that I would have given them different instructions."[8]

---

[7] *A Southern Moderate Speaks*, p. 137.

[8] *Ibid.*, p. 149.

These interchanges, however, were not made public for many months. The only news released to the press was by prepared statements in which the President and the Governor indicated that each had an understanding of the problems of the other, and that the meeting had been "constructive."

The weekend passed. Central High opened its doors Monday morning still surrounded by National Guardsmen; the school board's request that the Negro students remain home had not been rescinded.

Hays proposed to Faubus that he write to the parents of the Negro children asking them voluntarily to keep their children out of school for a few weeks, and offering to provide tutors for them in the interim. In addition, Hays proposed, Faubus should guarantee to use his office and influence to bring about peaceful conditions. Faubus appeared to be considering this, provided he could be assured that the federal government would not engage in court actions in the interim, and provided that the date for integration were set for the end of September. However, the Justice Department would not make any such commitments.

On Wednesday Hays talked to Adams again, seeking to find a way out of the impasse. They discussed the possibility of removing the National Guard from Faubus' control by transferring it into federal service. This would give Faubus a face-saving "out." However, Adams rejected this plan as a solution at that time.

On Thursday Faubus added another legal move to his pending motion to dismiss the petition of the United States Attorney General. Faubus filed an affidavit requesting that Davies disqualify himself since the Governor believed that the Judge had a "personal prejudice against him, and has a personal bias in favor of the plaintiffs. . . ." Faubus cited in support of this affidavit the various steps Davies had taken to bring the United States Government into the case, concluding that by this activity Davies had "departed from the role of imparitial arbiter of judicial questions presented to him and has, in fact, assumed the role of an advocate. . . ."

Brownell filed a counter motion, citing various precedents in support of the view that Davies' actions were "a proper exercise of a federal court's authority. . . ."

Davies, according to standard legal procedure, decided between the merits of the affidavit and the counter motion. He ruled against the Governor and remained on the bench.

On Friday, September 20, Davies held the hearing on Brownell's petition to enjoin Faubus and his National Guard commanders from interfering with the integration plan. Both General Clinger and Colonel Johnson of the Arkansas National Guard were present in the courtroom, but Faubus was absent, represented by his attorneys. Faubus' attorneys presented the Governor's brief with its arguments challenging the constitutionality of bringing an action against the chief executive of a sovereign state in a court other than the Supreme Court. Davies dismissed the Governor's motion and asked, "Any further preliminary matters?"

One of Faubus' attorneys rose and said: "The position of the respondent, Governor Faubus, and his military officers must be firm, unequivocal, unalterable. The Governor of the State of Arkansas cannot and will not concede that the United States in this court or anywhere else can question his discretion and judgment as chief executive of a sovereign state when he acts in the performance of his constitutional duties under the Constitution and laws of this state.

"Since the respondents do not and cannot concede that the Governor may be so questioned, obviously they can proceed no further in this action. . . . In view of that, if the court please, may counsel for respondents be excused?"

"You may be excused," Judge Davies said, and Faubus' attorneys left the courtroom—before the hearing began.

The attorneys for the school board and the Justice Department had subpoenaed 105 witnesses but called only eight: Superintendent Blossom, Mayor Mann, the Little Rock Police Chief, the Principal of Central High School, the President of the School Board, and three of the nine Negro children.

Davies noted that none of the witnesses gave evidence that they had thought violence imminent. Blossom confirmed this and also testified that he had not asked the Governor to call out the guardsmen.

The Judge granted the petition for a temporary injunction prohibiting Faubus, Clinger, Johnson, or anyone under their orders, from interfering with the integration plan. He recognized the question of state versus federal powers when he stated:

The Governor of Arkansas, as chief executive and commander-in-chief of its military forces, has a vital interest in the maintenance of law and order and broad discretionary powers to suppress insurrection and to preserve the peace.

However, Davies went on:

If it be assumed that the Governor was entitled to bring military force to the aid of civil authority, the proper use of that power in this instance was to maintain the Federal Court in the exercise of its jurisdiction, to aid in making its process effective and not to nullify it, to remove, and not to create, obstructions to the exercise by the Negro children of their rights as judicially declared.[9]

Davies also mentioned Faubus' contention that this was in essence a suit against the State of Arkansas and thus properly belonged only under the jurisdiction of the Supreme Court. In Davies' view, the action did not seek to "invalidate any provision of Arkansas statute or of the Arkansas Constitution. It merely seeks to enjoin the Governor and other officials of the state from committing acts beyond their lawful authority and contrary to the Federal Constitution."

Three hours later, by order of the Governor of Arkansas, the National Guardsmen were withdrawn from Central High School. The arm-chair lawyers were spared the problem of debating whether a federal judge had the power to hold the governor of a state in contempt of court.

Showdown at Central High School

Sunday afternoon there was a meeting between Congressman Hays, Mayor Mann, former Governor Sidney McMath, Harry Ashmore, editor of Little Rock's *Arkansas Gazette,* and two lawyers close to McMath. The group discussed plans for providing protection for the Negro students. The Justice Department had not approved use of deputy marshals. The group considered and rejected using the Marine Corps Reserve component in Little Rock or the Air Force Military Police from the base outside Little Rock. There was consensus that the major obligation rested upon Mayor

---

[9] Judge Davies here was following the argument of the majority decision in the 1932 Sterling case.

Mann's use of local police facilities, with whatever outside help he could muster.

Later that afternoon, Superintendent Blossom telephoned Judge Davies to ask him to authorize the use of United States marshals to accompany the Negro students. The Judge referred Blossom to United States Attorney Cobb. Cobb, in turn, felt he needed authorization from the Justice Department, and contacted it, but to no avail. Hays later conjectured that Brownell had refused because the United States Senate had removed from the 1957 Civil Rights Bill a proposed section authorizing Justice Department participation in civil rights suits. Hays felt that Brownell had interpreted this as a congressional declaration that the Attorney General should refrain from taking the initiative.

The following Monday, September 23, more than 100 city and state police were stationed at the high school to keep order while the Negro students attempted once again to enter classes. The streets and surrounding sidewalks grew increasingly clogged as more and more people joined the crowd. By 8:30 there were nearly 1,000 people milling around the school. Suddenly just as the opening bell rang the crowd exploded. Several members had caught sight of four Negro newsmen and began chasing them away, raining blows on them. While this turmoil was going on at the front of the school, the Negro students were entering at the side. The crowd grew noisier; some of the white students staged a walk-out from classes. By the noon break, both school and city officials agreed the Negroes should leave the school. They were called from classes and sent home.

That afternoon, President Eisenhower issued a statement, calling the morning's events "disgraceful," and sent out a proclamation to the Little

Rock citizens, commanding "all persons engaged in such obstruction of justice to cease and desist therefrom, and to disperse forthwith." (See Appendix One for full text.)

During the course of events that Monday, Congressman Hays intervened again, this time to telephone Sherman Adams to suggest that federal marshals be sent immediately to maintain order. Mann discussed the situation with several of his confidants in Little Rock. That afternoon, Hays telephoned Washington, and Mann was told it would be in order to call directly to the White House to Maxwell Rabb, Eisenhower's special assistant on minority matters. Before Mann had time to place a call, however, he received a call from Rabb who asked for a report. Mann described the situation as he saw it. Since Mann had been told that Hays' suggestion had been rejected, he proposed that federal troops be sent and that the National Guard be called into federal service to remove military command from the Governor. (Only five people in Little Rock knew of Mann's contact with Rabb—Congressman Hays, Blossom, Harry Ashmore, former Governor McMath, and the United States Attorney, Osro Cobb.)

Mann called Rabb at 5:30 Tuesday morning to find out whether any decision had been made for federal intervention. Rabb said Mann's report had been given to Brownell but no decision had yet been made. He asked Mann to keep him informed of developments in Little Rock.

A crowd began forming around Central High although at the request of Mann the *Gazette* had printed an announcement that the Negro students would not attempt to enter the school that day.

At 8 a.m. Mann called Rabb again to tell him the President's proclamation had not done the job—that the crowd was again outside the high school trying to break through the police lines.

At 8:24 a.m. Mann called Rabb again. This time Rabb said Mann should prepare a telegraphed request for federal troops to be sent if the decision were made in Washington to use the troops.

At 9 a.m. Rabb called Mann for the latest news. The crowd was still there, reported Mann, although there had been no rioting. Mann read Rabb the text of his proposed telegram, and Rabb, after making some changes, approved it. At 9:15 a.m. Mann sent off his request to the President.

Mann talked to Rabb again at 9:48 a.m., reporting that no violence had yet occurred, although the crowd had not yet dispersed.

The President had been receiving reports on the developing situation and had been consulting Brownell. Brownell advised him, first, that he had the power to use federal force. However, Brownell continued, the local strength of the United States Marshal in Little Rock was insufficient, it was probably impractical to try to enlist the local citizenry to aid the Marshal, and time was too short to bring in marshals or deputy marshals from other areas. The President himself rejected the notion of using F.B.I. agents.

At 10:22 a.m. Eisenhower issued Executive Order 10730 "Providing Assistance for the Removal of an Obstruction of Justice Within the State of Arkansas." He ordered the Arkansas National Guard into the federal service, thus removing it from Faubus' command, and sent 1,000 soldiers of the 101st Airborne Division of the United States Army to surround Central High School and enforce the order of the District Court. By that evening the first paratroopers had arrived in Little Rock.

Wednesday morning an Army station wagon picked up the Negro students and brought them to the school. The crowd was gathering again, standing silent while the major in charge asked them to disperse. No one moved.

At an order from the major the paratroopers advanced with bayonets drawn. The crowd dispersed.

Faubus, who had been in Georgia attending a meeting of the Southern Governors, returned hastily. He said he had not expected to see federal troops in Little Rock, for as he read the statute books (10 U.S.C. Sec. 331) federal troops could be sent to a sovereign state "whenever there is an insurrection in any state against its government . . ." only at the request of the governor or state legislature. However, Eisenhower was relying on statutes other than the one Faubus had read (10 U.S.C. Secs. 332, 333, 334), one of them based on the statute used by George Washington to suppress the Whiskey Rebellion in 1794. And, in fact, Eisenhower used the wording of the old statute rather than the 1956 revision:

> Whenever, by reasons of unlawful obstruction, combinations, or assemblages of persons, or rebellion against the authority of the Government of the United States, it shall become impracticable in the judgment of the President to enforce, by the ordinary course of judicial proceedings, the laws of the United States within any state or territory, it shall be lawful for the President to call forth the militia of any or all the states and to employ such parts of the land and naval forces of the United States as he may deem necessary to enforce the faithful execution of the laws. . . .

The troops remained stationed at the high school for several months. On November 5 the citizens of Little Rock went to the polls to elect the seven new City Directors. One of the candidates was Mrs. Clyde Thomason, Secretary of the Mothers' League and the woman who had brought the suit in Chancery Court in August.[10] She and five of the other "segregation" candidates were defeated by narrow margins.[11] Only one of the "segregation" candidates was elected. The next day the paratroopers' forces were cut to 250. By November 27 the paratroopers were withdrawn, and the subsequent patrolling was carried on by members of the federalized Arkansas National Guard.

Eight of the nine Negro students finished out the year at Central High. It was not a peaceful period. The Negro students were harassed frequently by some of the white students, and there were bomb threats. One of the Negro students was expelled, and one of the white students was suspended. The federalized guardsmen did not attempt to control the students but patrolled outside the school building.

The day after classes ended in May, President Eisenhower directed the withdrawal and return to state control of the 400 federalized guardsmen. One of the Negro students graduated a few days later in an integrated commencement ceremony unmarred by commotion.

Thus ended the first year of the integration struggle in Little Rock. The Governor's main weapon had been executive power, and his major argument his responsibility to maintain the peace. The weight of the case for federal power had been carried by the federal judiciary relying on the "supreme law of the land" clause of the United States Constitution. At the height of the conflict the ability of the President to neutralize the National Guard and to invoke federal force tipped the balance.

Two: The Second Year

Before the school year had ended, the school board had appealed to the district court to suspend integration at Central High until 1961. This move set off a whole new series of local, state, and federal maneuvers designed to determine whether Central High would open in September integrated or segregated.

The Governor was to turn to the Arkansas Legislature to augment his battery of weapons. The Governor and the Legislature were to act on the

theory that the United States Constitution said nothing about public education, and that this silence plus the refusal by Congress to pass any specific integration law, guaranteed the rights of the states to regulate public education—rights secured, they were to argue, by the 10th Amendment.

The school board was to contend that this position of the state officials, backed up by speeches and state laws, was creating such tension in Little Rock that continued attempts by the board to abide by the court orders would destroy the school system.

The federal government would continue to rely primarily on the judicial process, maintaining, through the President, that the law must be obeyed, and through the Attorney General and Solicitor General that the courts could not bow to violence.

[10] See Appendix Two for analysis of this and all other elections discussed in this case.

[11] In this, as in most elections in Little Rock, *all* candidates proclaimed themselves segregationists. The choice was between candidates who favored defying federal court decisions or orders and those who held they had to accept them. Throughout this case candidates who favored defiance of the courts will be labeled "segregationists" and their opponents "moderates."

Eventually the dispute would return once more to the Supreme Court. After its decision, the Governor would order Little Rock high schools closed and a referendum vote would support him. The schools would reopen August 12, 1959, with four Negroes attending the two former white high schools, and with a procession of extreme segregationists marching on Central High School after attending a mass meeting on the steps of the state capitol.

The Lemley Decision

Public hearings were held in June 1958 on the School Board's petition to suspend integration at Central High until 1961. The hearing was held before District Judge Harry J. Lemley, whose home court was in Texarkana, Arkansas.

On June 21 Judge Lemley granted the School Board's petition. The Judge pointed out that public disapproval of desegregation did not constitute grounds for delaying integration. However, he ruled, the School Board was faced with more than passive community disapproval. The school year had been marked by "repeated incidents of more or less serious violence directed against the Negro students and their property, by numerous bomb threats directed at the school, by a number of nuisance fires started inside the school, by desecration of school property, and by the circulation of cards, leaflets and circulars designed to intensify opposition to integration."

Lemley repeatedly quoted the standard set by the Supreme Court in its 1955 implementation decision: once a start had been made, the courts might find that additional time was necessary, provided the delay was in the public interest and "consistent with good faith compliance at the earliest practicable date. . . ." The Little Rock School Board had made a prompt start, Lemley pointed out, and it had demonstrated to Lemley's satisfaction that the educational program at Central High was being undermined by the "chaos, bedlam, and turmoil" resulting from the presence of the Negro students in the school.

> . . . while the Negro students at Little Rock have a personal interest in being admitted to the public schools on a non-discriminatory basis as soon as practicable, that interest is only one factor of the equation, and must be balanced against the public interest . . . in having a smoothly functioning educational system. . . . There is also another public interest involved, namely that of eliminating, or at least ameliorating, the unfortunate racial strife and tension which has existed in Little Rock during the past year.
> . . . while troops can disperse crowds and keep the Negro students physically within the school . . . the presence of troops cannot reduce or eliminate racial tension, or create a climate that is conducive to education.

Lemley, in granting the two-and-a-half year "tactical delay," also noted, "There may also be some change of the personalities involved in the dispute."

This decision, like all court decisions, did not take effect when the Judge issued a mandate for its implementation. Sometimes this mandate is included in the decision itself. More often there is a delay of a few days in order for the loser to decide whether or not to appeal. If notice of appeal is filed, the mandate is usually stayed until the higher courts have ruled on the appeal. In this case the Negro parents at once announced they would appeal Lemley's decision to the United States Court of Appeals, and they filed the appropriate papers with Lemley. The Judge, however, issued the mandate to make the decision effective on June 23. It might take months to carry the case through the higher courts, he explained, and since he had agreed that the situation at Central High was "intolerable," it would not be in the public interest to leave Judge Davies' integration decision in effect.

In an interview with a *New York Post* correspondent, Superintendent Blossom, despite his victory in Lemley's court, expressed bitterness with all levels of government officialdom. He and the board members, he complained, had received help "from no one."

> Our Governor Faubus and the rest of the state government fight us. The federal courts order us to integrate and then give us no help and no protection. The Justice Department refused to prosecute the trouble-makers, and Attorney General [William] Rogers [12] even inadvertently encourages them to make more trouble when he announced that no prosecutions are planned.
>
> . . . As long as we have a Justice Department and an administration in Washington which does nothing, the answer must come from Congress. It is intolerable to expect a school board, standing alone, to fight the whole community. . . . I am an educator, not a policeman.

The Appeals

Faubus had suffered one setback. On April 28 the United States Court of Appeals had affirmed the decision of Judge Davies that Faubus should withdraw the National Guard. Faubus announced he intended to carry his case to the Supreme Court. In another sense

the Governor's campaign for a third term, in full swing by early summer, was also an appeal—to the voters of Arkansas.

July 29 was primary election day in Arkansas. Faubus, running against two opponents, won the Democratic nomination for an unprecedented third term with a landslide seventy percent. (Both opponents had criticized his action in calling out the National Guard.) But he carried Little Rock by just over fifty percent. (He received 27 percent in the predominantly Negro precincts of the city, and 55 percent in the predominantly white precincts.)

Six days later, on August 4, all seven judges of the 8th Circuit of the United States Court of Appeals convened in St. Louis.[13] They met to hear the Negro students' appeal from Lemley's decision—technically still another phase of *Aaron vs. Cooper*. On August 18 the judges reversed Judge Lemley by a vote of six to one. Although the majority agreed with Lemley's findings of fact, it disagreed with the conclusions he drew from them. The six judges agreed, for example, that opposition to integration had solidified when Central High opened as an integrated school in the fall of 1957; they agreed that there had been considerable disruption of the school routine during the year; and they agreed that the school board met the test of good faith. However, they disagreed with Lemley's legal conclusions. Judge Marion Matthes (of Missouri) wrote for the majority:

> Over and over again, in the testimony, we find the conclusion that the foregoing turmoil, chaos, and bedlam directly resulted from the presence of the nine Negro students in Central High School, and from this conclusion,

---

[12] In October 1957, just about a month after federal troops had been sent to Little Rock, Attorney General Herbert Brownell resigned to return to private practice, and Assistant Attorney General William Rogers was appointed to the post.

[13] Two of the seven judges were from Nebraska. The other five were from North Dakota, Minnesota, Iowa, and Missouri.

it appears that the district court found a legal justification for removing temporarily the disturbing influence, i.e. . . . the Negro students. It is more accurate to state that the acts of violence were the direct result of popular opposition to the presence of the nine Negro students. To our mind, there is a great difference from a legal standpoint when the problem in Little Rock is stated in this manner.

Judge Matthes summed up the heart of the matter, as the majority saw it:

This issue plainly comes down to the question of whether overt public resistance, including mob protest, constitutes sufficient cause to nullify an order of the Federal court directing the board to proceed with its integration plan. *We say the time has not yet come in these United States when an order of a federal court must be whittled away, watered down, or shamefully withdrawn in the face of violent and unlawful acts of individual citizens in opposition thereto.* [Italics in the original.]

The school board immediately notified the Court of Appeals that it intended to appeal to the Supreme Court. At the same time the board petitioned the Appeals Court to stay its mandate until the Supreme Court had ruled. Three days later, on August 21, Chief Judge Archibald Gardner (of South Dakota)—the dissenter in the six to one Appeals Court decision—granted the stay. Thus, with the Appeals Court decision stayed and Lemley's mandate issued, the Lemley decision reinstating segregation continued to be binding on the school board. The Supreme Court was in summer recess until October 1, and Little Rock schools were due to open September 2. Under the existing legal situation Central High School would open as segregated, and the Ne-

gro students who had been attending would have to return to the all-Negro schools.

While the Court Acted

Much activity filled the three days separating the Court of Appeals decision and Gardner's granting of the stay of mandate. In Little Rock, on August 19, Faubus issued a statement castigating the school board:

Does the Board intend to continue to promote the complete integration of the Little Rock schools while muttering insincere, half-hearted protestations, or does it intend to fight in every legal way possible the integration by force, with such dire consequence for education in the affected schools, and the peace of the community?

Faubus urged the school board members to find some way of avoiding integration or to resign.

At his press conference on August 20 President Eisenhower opened by announcing that he did not think it appropriate to express his view on the question of integration in Little Rock because a case was pending in the courts. But, he went on to say, no matter whether one agreed or disagreed with the final outcome, it was the duty of all Americans to obey court orders. "My feelings are exactly as they were a year ago," the President said.

This last remark was widely interpreted to mean that the President was prepared again to use troops to enforce the court orders. A few newspaper commentators pointed out that since the effective court order at this time was Lemley's decision to delay integration, the President might find himself in the ironic position of enforcing the Lemley order to segregate the Little Rock schools.

Others felt that what the President had given with one hand in this prepared statement, he had taken away with the other when later on in the press conference he was asked by the *New York Times* correspondent to express his own personal feeling about whether schools should be integrated:

> I have always declined to do that for the simple reason that here was something that the Supreme Court says . . . is the meaning of the Constitution.
>
> Now I am sworn to one thing, to defend the Constitution of the United States, and execute its laws. Therefore, for me to weaken public opinion by discussion of . . . separate cases, where I might agree or might disagree, seems to me to be completely unwise and not a good thing to do.
>
> I have an oath; I expect to carry it out. And the mere fact that I could disagree very violently with a decision, and would so express myself, then my own duty would be much more difficult to carry out, I think.

Eisenhower seemed determined to keep out of the substantive controversy. To some it appeared he felt it best to refrain from supporting one side or the other in Little Rock in order to hold the prestige of his office "in reserve" for the support of law and order. Critics interpreted his statements as evidence of an unwillingness to lead public opinion.

Later that day Governor Faubus convened a press conference. He had no hesitancy about discussing the pros and cons of integration or the role of the Supreme Court. For the first time he publicly attacked the 1954 integration decision by contending that it was not the law of the land. Free people, he said, think of the law of the land "in terms of laws passed by their own votes at the ballot box, or in terms of laws passed by their elected representatives." The people of Arkansas, he pointed out, had voted overwhelmingly against integration. Secondly, he went on, no law had been passed in Congress to forbid segregation. Many eminent lawyers had expressed the view, said Faubus, that since Congress had not passed any such act, the Supreme Court decision of 1954 was therefore without basis of law.

The next day, August 21, brought Gardner's announcement of the stay of the mandate. Faubus immediately notified the Arkansas Legislature to stand by for a special session the following Tuesday, August 26. It was clear that Faubus was not going to wait quietly for court action. It appeared that he was going to ask the legislature to pass laws paralleling Virginia's "massive resistance" program—laws which would authorize the closing of public schools ordered to integrate by federal courts.

Simultaneously, the Justice Department announced that to avoid the use of federal troops it was now considering deputizing citizens as federal marshals to control mobs and to arrest ringleaders. The department added that it might request the federal District Court to issue injunctions against those inciting violence.

That same day the United States Senate was acting on the last of a series of bills aimed at curbing the United States Supreme Court. None of the bills had been drawn specifically in response to the Supreme Court's integration decision. Rather, they were reactions to recent Supreme Court decisions interpreting the anti-sedition Smith Act of 1940. However, the bills attracted support from many southern congressmen—led by Arkansas Senator John McClellan—who saw them partly as a means of slapping back at the Court for its integration action. Each bill was defeated. On August 21 the last of the bills was rejected by a vote of 41 to 40 with the aid of Texas Democrat Lyndon Johnson, the Senate majority leader. It was considered likely that similar legislation would be introduced in the next session of Congress, and some observers wondered if the possibility of congressional action —strengthened by criticism leveled at the court at the annual Conference of State Chief Justices—would affect the court's subsequent decisions on integration and on other matters.

How Will Central High Open?

Friday, August 22, white students began registering at Central High. The fall term was due to begin in twelve days. Would the school open as segregated or integrated? As matters now stood, the Appeals Court's integration decision would not be implemented unless the Supreme Court upheld it. Until then Judge Lemley's segregation decision governed. The school board members, under strong pressure from Faubus, had asked the Court of Appeals to stay its mandate: they certainly were not going to try to secure Supreme Court review before school opened. On the other hand, since the Negro children had won the Appeals Court decision, it was not up to them to initiate an appeal to the Supreme Court. It appeared that the school board had won the tactical battle and that Central High would open as segregated.

However, the attorneys for the Negro children found a way to break the legal log jam. Thurgood Marshall, chief counsel for the NAACP, who took over the case from the local NAACP attorney, sent a special petition to Su-

preme Court Justice Charles Whittaker asking him to set aside Judge Gardner's stay and thereby make the Court of Appeals decision effective immediately. If this were done Central High would have to open under court orders to integrate and would remain integrated unless the Supreme Court overruled the Court of Appeals. Alternatively, Marshall asked Whittaker to stay the Lemley decision itself.[14] If both the Lemley and the Appeals Court decision were stayed, the only court decision in effect would be Judge Davies' integration decision of the previous year. Either way, Central High would open as integrated. The school board was notified by Whittaker's office that it should reply to the NAACP requests by Thursday, August 28.

Faubus moved immediately. He issued the call for a special legislative session to convene at 11 a.m. Tuesday, August 26. The Governor also released a statement explaining why he was taking this step. First, if Justice Whittaker granted either of the NAACP's requests, the schools would open as integrated, and this, Faubus said, would threaten the peace and tranquility of the state. Second:

> In a republican form of government, the people speak through their elected representatives in Legislature or in Congress.
>
> It is the responsibility of the Chief Executive . . . to preserve the peace and good order of the state.
>
> I, therefore, have no alternative but to convene the General Assembly in extraordinary session, for the purpose

---

14 A single Supreme Court Justice has the power to stay a District Court judgment or to vacate a District Court stay. The precedents are not clear on whether a single Supreme Court Justice can set aside a United States Circuit Court stay or whether full Supreme Court action is necessary.

of considering these matters of such grave concern to the people, and which threaten the peace and tranquility of the state.

The Governor had acted none too soon. On Monday Chief Justice Warren announced that the entire Supreme Court would convene in special session on Thursday, August 28, to consider the NAACP petition on the stays. Warren also invited the United States Government to participate in the case.

The Little Rock School Board met that evening and decided to postpone the opening of school until September 8 in order to "remove the shortage of time for both the Supreme Court of the United States and the Arkansas Legislature."

The Special Legislative Session

The special legislative session opened Tuesday, August 26. The Arkansas legislators received six bills from the Governor and a number of bills from Arkansas Attorney General Bruce Bennett.

The most important of the Governor's proposed new bills was one which granted the Governor the power to close any or all public schools of a district under any one of three conditions:

(a) in order to maintain the peace against actual or impending violence which endangers the citizens, students, teachers, and others or to provide for the safety of buildings and property;
(b) wherever integration in any school or schools in the district has been decreed by any court and federal force is employed on or about the school grounds to enforce the order;
(c) whenever it is determined that a general, suitable and efficient educational system cannot be maintained in

any school district because of the integration of the races.[15]

If the Governor did close any school, the bill provided, an election had to be held in the school district within thirty days. If, at that election, a majority of the *eligible* voters—in contrast to the more usual provision of a majority of those voting—voted to open the schools on an integrated basis, the schools would be opened and integrated.

The Governor's bills received their first two readings that same day. The school closing bill passed the Arkansas House of Representatives the next day by a vote of 94 to 1. The Arkansas Senate passed all the bills unanimously.[16]

Not all the legislators were completely happy with the bills, although they had voted for them. One of the representatives from Pulaski County —the county containing Little Rock— felt that the bill "stacked the school closing election" by requiring a majority of eligible voters. "We don't want

---

[15] There had been speculation whether the legislature could grant such powers in view of the Arkansas constitutional provision that ". . . the State shall ever maintain a general, suitable and efficient system of free schools whereby all persons in the State between the ages of six and twenty-one years of age may receive gratuitous instruction." Apparently Faubus intended to follow the lead of the Virginia Legislature which had adopted an act that an "efficient" school is one in which there is no racial integration.

[16] Some of the other bills provided for additional funds for the Arkansas Attorney General in handling school legal affairs; provided for the withholding of state funds from a school closed by order of the Governor (about forty per cent of local school district funds in 1958 were provided by the state); provided for additional funds for the Governor for school segregation problems (for example, for holding school district elections); provided that students might transfer to schools outside their normal district to avoid having to attend an integrated school.

to go through the farce of a stacked election," the representative said. "We feel that we can win a segregation election without stacking the deck."

In Washington that day—the day before the Supreme Court hearing—President Eisenhower was holding his weekly press conference. A *New York Post* reporter asked the President to verify an item in the current issue of *Newsweek*. The magazine claimed that Eisenhower had told friends in private that he wished the Supreme Court had never handed down its decision, and that integration should proceed much more slowly. The President said the story was not correct. He went on to explain the basis for the item:

> . . . it might have been that I said something about "slower" . . . because I do say, as I did yesterday or last week —we have got to have reason and sense and education, and a lot of other developments that go hand in hand . . . if this process is going to have any real acceptance in the United States.

The same day, however, Eisenhower's new Attorney General, William Rogers, told the American Bar Association convention in Los Angeles: "The decision of the Supreme Court . . . is the law of the land. . . . Compliance with the law of the land is inevitable."

In Virginia, federal District Judge Walter E. Hoffman withheld his opinion on the integration of public schools in Norfolk pending the Supreme Court opinion. If the Supreme Court upheld Lemley, Hoffman told the city officials, "come back to me and I'll end all your troubles." Several other school districts in Virginia, under court orders to integrate, also waited for the Supreme Court's decision. School opening had been postponed in some of these districts, and in others the district judge allowed the schools to re-

main segregated until the Supreme Court decision.

The Supreme Court's Special Session

At 3:30 a.m. Thursday, August 28, a line began to form outside the United States Supreme Court chamber. By the time the session opened at noon there were 500 people waiting, but only thirty members of the public could be seated. The other 140 seats were filled by such interested spectators as Virgil Blossom, three of the school board members, Arkansas' Senator William Fulbright, who had asked permission to file a special *amicus curiae* petition supporting the school board, numerous Washington lawyers, members of Congress, and guests of the court.

The nine justices filed in—three of them appointed since the 1954 integration decision. Technically they were not being asked to consider whether Central High School should be integrated now or in two-and-a-half years. They were being asked to review the stay procedure, and it was to that question that Thurgood Marshall, NAACP chief counsel and the Negro students' representative, addressed himself in his written brief and in the oral argument.

Marshall's written brief had set forth the argument on the technical question: the only decision currently in effect was the Lemley decision; school was now due to open on September 8. "If Judge Lemley's order remains in effect until the opening of school," Marshall's brief pointed out, the Negro students "will be returned to segregated schools for at least one year and [the school board] will have secured the relief [it] sought. The rights of those petitioners who are scheduled to graduate from high school next year will be permanently and effectively nullified."

In his oral argument Marshall went

further to suggest that the Supreme Court might also give a decision on the merits of the case—the question of whether integration should be postponed or not, even though the school board's petition for *certiorari* had not yet been filed with the court and the question, technically, was not properly before it.

The justices turned to the School Board attorney, Richard C. Butler, to question him:

> *Chief Justice Warren:* Mr. Butler . . . has the School Board determined what it will do toward desegregation . . . in the event this court declines to grant the stay?
>
> *Butler:* No, sir, it has not decided, because it is almost compelled to see what statutes are passed by the General Assembly now in session, and various other things which it has no way of determining.
>
> *Chief Justice Warren:* Well, as to these specific children, have they been assigned to any school?
>
> *Butler:* Yes, sir; they have now been assigned . . . to the all-Negro school, the new high school there of Horace Mann.
>
> *Chief Justice Warren:* Isn't that . . . segregating them again?
>
> *Butler:* Oh, yes, sir. It is, it is, and that was done under the order of Judge Lemley's decision.
>
> *Chief Justice Warren:* Yes. Well, then, my point is this: If this court does not stay the order of the Court of Appeals withholding its mandate, then the school board will proceed to segregate these pupils who are plaintiffs in this case?
>
> *Butler:* Yes, sir.

The justices soon turned to questions beyond the technical procedure, and Butler began to explain the school board's position:

> *Butler:* The Little Rock public school board is composed of outstanding citizens of our community. There are two medical doctors on the board. There is a civil engineer. . . . There is a certified public accountant. There is a leading business man of one of the large baking companies there . . . the president of the Little Rock school board is a wise and experienced lawyer who has practiced there many years.
>
> These men are unpaid. They are public servants. They have tried to do the best they could under as trying circumstances as any public servant has ever been faced with.
>
> Now, when other boards of education were refusing to recognize the basic change that the Supreme Court had made in the law in the Brown decision, this board was studying and formulating ways and means of complying. They knew it was not an easy task, but they were willing to do their best.
>
> . . . From bitter experience, however, they have discovered that they could not operate a public school system under the existing climate in Little Rock as of this time. . . .
>
> *Justice Frankfurter:* Would you summarize what Mr. Blossom testified as to why two and a half [year's delay], not one and a half, and not three and a half, was selected?
>
> *Butler:* . . . this school board determined that they were entitled to know what the law was. And so long as editorialists . . . were saying that this was not the law of the land, and that there were ways to get around it, and one court was saying one thing and another court was saying another, and there were laws on the statute books of Arkansas as well as other states throughout the South diametrically opposed—some of them could be reconciled, some of them could not, with the decision in the Brown case— it left the people of our community . . . in actual doubt as to what the law was. . . . It is the opinion of this school board . . . that in that period of time . . . a national policy could definitely be established, that laws could be tested so that the people would know, the people who want to obey the final words. . . .

Justice Frankfurter: Mr. Butler, why aren't the two decisions of this court . . . a national policy? . . . There was a national policy and the federal courts recognized it. It was sustained by the district court over the opposition of the parents or whoever acted in behalf of these children, went before the Court of Appeals and the Court of Appeals said, "Yes, this is a fair carrying out of that which the Supreme Court laid down."

I do not understand what is meant by saying "Let's wait until we get a national policy," if that isn't a national policy.

Butler: Your Honor, in answer to that, I simply say this: That it certainly was not anticipated at the time that plan was formulated that the Governor of the State of Arkansas would call out troops to keep integration from taking place.

. . . .

Chief Justice Warren: Mr. Butler . . . the question crossed my mind, suppose every other school district in the South would do the same thing, say, "We will carry on segregation for a number of years until the law is clarified," how would it ever be clarified?

Butler: Well, your Honor, I think the only answer to that is that many districts do not have that problem . . . in Arkansas there are some districts . . . where . . . it has worked successfully. [But the Little Rock School Board] was faced with actualities which are undermining and which are going to destroy the public school system, and that when it is destroyed, it will be destroyed not just for the white students. It will be destroyed all the way up and down the line unless they are given an opportunity to work this thing out in a climate of calm, rather than in a climate of hysteria.

Chief Justice Warren: My recollection is that in one of those opinions . . . we did say that mere public opposition to the policy and to the program would not be a cause either for denying integration or for extending it.

Butler: We understand that, and of course your Honor is correct . . . and we find no fault with the basic statement . . . but when a school board is confronted with facts which of themselves will force the destruction of the public school system, then this board feels and Judge Lemley decided that time should be given for cooler heads, a calmer atmosphere to come to the front. . . .

A little later Butler pointed out that he was straying from the technical questions of the stay procedure, but he agreed with Marshall that the basic issues were so intertwined that it was impossible to discuss one without the other.

At one point, Butler raised Governor Faubus' point that only the legislative branch could make basic government policy. In asking the court to take notice of the political effects of the Governor's stand, Butler drew a reproof from the Chief Justice:

Butler: Now one other point, and perhaps I did not emphasize this enough. Regardless of whether or not the people of Arkansas should recognize the United States Supreme Court decisions as the law of the land, the plain fact is that they have not, and it is most difficult for them to do so if not impossible, when the Governor of the state says that that is not the law of the land, that only Congress can really say what the law of the land is.

Now as lawyers, we may take the position, well, they are not informed, but that is a fact, and . . . as long as our Governor says that it is not the law of the land, not the settled law of the land, Mr. Chief Justice, you have been the Governor of a great state—

Chief Justice Warren: But I never tried to resolve any legal problems of this kind as Governor of my state. I thought that that was a matter for the courts, and I abided by the decision of the courts. . . .

Butler: . . . The point I am making

is this: that if the Governor of any state says that a United States Supreme Court decision is not the law of the land, the people of that state, until it is really resolved, have a doubt in their mind and a right to have that doubt.

Chief Justice Warren: But I have never heard such an argument made in a court of justice before. I never heard a lawyer say that the statement of a Governor as to what was legal or illegal should control the actions of any court.

Butler's central argument was that when the school board members first formulated the plan, they had assumed it would be backed up by the other state officials in its effort to win public support and obedience. But state officials had attacked it, and the climate of opinion among the people had shifted. Therefore the school board felt justified in asking for a re-assessment of the time table.

The third person heard that day was Lee Rankin, the Solicitor General, who argued for the United States Government. Rankin agreed that the school board probably "could not be blamed for cause of the harassment that they have suffered." However, he continued, the federal government took the position that before the school board asked for a delay, it should have first exhausted all possible steps available to help it carry out the court order. There were at least two things the school board had not done, said Rankin. First, to control the situation inside the school, it could have insisted on having firmer discipline enforced among the students. Second, to try to control the situation outside the school, it could have sought injunctions against the people who were causing the trouble.

To many the kernel of Rankin's argument lay in his concluding words:

. . . when you talk about a deterioration of the educational process in this school, it seems to me that one of the things that all educators . . . would recognize is that . . . part of their responsibility is to get across to these teachers, and for the teachers to get across to the children . . . that we do live in a country where we seek to maintain law and order for the benefit of all the people, and the Constitution and each of the rights that every citizen has under it is precious to every one of us, not just the right that I like and want for me, or that you like and want for you, but all of them, for every man and woman.

And that if you teach these children in Little Rock or any other part of the country that as soon as you get some force and violence, the courts of law in this country are going to bow to it, they have no power to deal with it, they will give way to it, will change everything to accommodate that, I think that you destroy the whole educational process there.

Butler was asked if he wished to respond to Rankin. Butler was in a difficult position, as indeed he had been in the entire hearing. He was the attorney for the school board, not for Faubus or the National Guard or the rioters of Little Rock. The school board had sought to comply with the court orders. Rankin had very eloquently made the case against the disturbers of the peace, and with that Butler undoubtedly had no disagreement. But to him the basic point remained: under the circumstances, the school board felt unable to proceed with the original plan.

Butler countered Rankin's criticism that the board should have sought injunctions:

Butler: Well, of course, it is the school board that takes the brunt of it. . . . Now the fact is . . . that the NAACP, which has rather vast resources and certainly able counsel, had a perfect right to come in and ask for injunctive relief and it did not do so. The Justice Department had every right to put forth any criminal actions that were in order, and it did not do so, and now we have the President of the United States saying that the process should go slower, if we are to read the newspapers accurately and if the newspapers reported it accurately.

Now that is exactly the position that the Little Rock School Board is taking. The School Board has recognized from the beginning, and still does; first that the ultimate decision of any question of this kind is a question of law and that the final decision of the United States Supreme Court must stand.

The court recessed at 3:33 p.m. At 5:10 it reconvened, and the Chief Justice read the decision: the Supreme Court agreed with all three lawyers who had recommended that the court go on to consider the basic question of integration in Little Rock. Therefore, the court deferred until September 11 its decision on the technical question of which mandate should be stayed. On September 11 the justices would hear argument on the basic issue. Warren noted that the decision was based on the assumption that the opening of school would be postponed until September 15.

Opinions in Arkansas

The Arkansas Legislature was still in special session. On Friday, August 29, the State Senate passed Arkansas Attorney General Bennett's bill which provided that an election to recall members of a school board would be held upon petition by fifteen percent of the voters of the school district. All three members of the Pulaski County delegation to the Senate voted against the measure as being aimed solely at the Little Rock School Board. One of them argued on the floor that the school board was "up there now [in Washing-

ton] fighting the battle on the side of the segregationists as earnestly and sincerely as it can." In response one of the supporters of the bill pointed out that he had "no quarrel—and no brief —for the Little Rock School Board," but, he added, the board members were "fighting a battle for which they are largely responsible."

On Sunday, Governor Faubus was the guest on the Columbia Broadcasting System's radio and television program, *Face the Nation*. Interviewing him for the benefit of the national audience were three reporters, including Jack V. Fox of the United Press.

Fox asked whether the Supreme Court laid down the law of the land, and the following exchange took place:

> *Governor Faubus:* There are a great many people in this state and in this nation at this time who firmly believe that the Supreme Court has no authority in law to make the decision which it did. . . . Many, many people . . . believe that the Supreme Court made a law, itself; and it is well known that the Supreme Court has no such authority.
>
> *Fox:* Well, Governor, would you accept a declaration or a law by Congress on this?
>
> *Governor Faubus:* Well, I think if the Congress passed a law, then it would be a law of the land, and there would be no means of questioning it legally. There would still be the question of the difficulty or ease of enforcement, depending on the will of the people in a given area.
>
> You know the amendment setting up Prohibition was adopted by the states themselves, and yet it was found to have so much opposition, that it was so difficult of enforcement, that it was finally repealed.

The Governor then went on to list some of the evidence for his contention that he was not a segregationist but a moderate:

But in this state, we have integrated all the transportation systems, all the institutions of higher learning; I'm the only Southern governor who recommended and put on the State Democratic Central Committee members of the Negro race. . . . I can further point to the fact that my son attended an integrated college, state-supported, last year, and that is more than can be said for the President's grandchildren, who attend private schools, and also for one member of the Supreme Court whose children attend private schools, and that's more than can be said for some ministers in Little Rock who condemn my actions. . . . Why do they want to put all of this burden of this new experiment on the children, like a minister will say that he wants the schools to integrate, but he still refuses to integrate his church?

Arkansas Gazette editor Harry Ashmore was also being interviewed that day on a national network. Appearing on the National Broadcasting Company's television program, *Comment,* Ashmore said he believed the United States Supreme Court should "grant this beleaguered city a stay of execution. . . . The real question is not who will win the struggle between the state and the federal government: it is, can anybody win?"

Other newspaper editors in Arkansas were expressing their opinions too. Just north of Little Rock in Batesville, Paul W. Buchanan, managing editor of the *Batesville Guard* considered, for example, the effect on America's reputation abroad:

Whatever develops, we can't afford to let another howling mob light a fuse at Central High or any other school. In an explosive situation such as this, one spark might touch off a holocaust that could spread across Dixie like a prairie fire. Don't you know the Kremlin would love to see that happen!

On Monday, September 2, the school board voted five to one to postpone the opening of high school until September 15. Dissenting board member Dr. Dale Alford issued a statement that he favored opening Central High on September 8 as planned—as an all-white school, since the Lemley decision was still binding—rather than await the court's ruling.

Faubus lashed out at the board majority, again saying he was "not a bit surprised. . . . They never have displayed any real inclination to listen to the will of the people of the school district, or any reasoning."

The president of the segregationist Mothers' League of Central High School promptly announced that if the Governor signed Arkansas Attorney General Bennett's school board recall bill into law the Mothers' League would start immediately to collect signatures for the petition to recall the school board members—except for Dr. Alford. (Faubus had not signed any of the new bills yet, frankly explaining that he was waiting to see what the Supreme Court would decide.)

Arkansas Senator John L. McClellan announced that he felt the Supreme Court should have the courage to reverse its 1954 decision. The basic issue, continued the senator, was whether the United States was a republic of sovereign states or a collection of provinces under a centralized government.

The Supreme Court hearing was only a few days away. The parties to the suit filed their briefs; their arguments were essentially the same as their earlier ones. The school board, however, included a strong section answering Solicitor General Rankin's suggestion that it should have sought injunctions. In the first place, the brief pointed out, the school board had only a limited amount of money. This money was raised by taxes for the purpose of education—not for litigation. Butler then went on to repeat his contention that it was the function of an agency of the federal government to defend federal law.

> It is not the function of a school district to act as a buffer in a contest between state and federal authority, and certainly not to act as the bulwark of federal authority in such a contest. . . .
> To enforce the law of the land is obviously a duty of a law enforcement agency . . . how can [a school district] possibly enforce the federal law, and where is it to obtain funds to be used for the purpose?

The school board's brief crossed in the mails two letters from Attorney General Rogers. One letter was to School Board President Wayne Upton, telling Upton that the Justice Department would assist the board if it wished to make applications for injunctions in District Court. The second letter was to Little Rock's City Manager informing him that because the Supreme Court might soon order integration in Little Rock, Rogers had made arrangements for the "temporary expansion" of the present staff of the United States Marshal's office. These new deputy marshals would be ready and available to assist the city police in enforcing court orders, Rogers said.

A few days later four Justice Department attorneys arrived in Little Rock to assist United States Attorney Osro Cobb and his staff. Within a few days there were 150 deputy marshals in Little Rock. This increased activity on the part of the Justice Department was interpreted by some commentators as being intended to reassure the Supreme Court justices that the executive branch of the federal government was prepared to support the judgment of the judicial branch if it ordered immediate integration at Central High School.

The Supreme Court Considers the Merits

Thursday, September 11, oral arguments were heard before the Supreme Court on the merits of a delay of integration. Richard Butler, counsel for the school board, spoke first. Butler repeatedly argued that the school board was not denying the legitimacy of the Supreme Court's 1954 ruling, but that it needed a cooling-off period in which the "hysteria" could die down.

For the next hour or so Butler was questioned, first by one of the Supreme Court justices, then another, until almost all had posed in different words the same question: if the school board is granted a two-and-a-half-year delay what will it do, and what will happen at the end of that time? Will the schools then be integrated?

To each, Butler, in essence, gave the same answer: neither he nor the school board could predict what the situation would be in two years, but the school board would seek solutions and attempt to "reconcile the differences that exist in this conflict."

> . . . people are more and more at this point going into the extremes. The moderate people and their thinking have been brushed aside for the moment. The School Board feels that with a reasonable period of time for postponement, that perhaps these extreme views on either side can be overcome by the calmer people. . . .

Butler was asked by Justice Frankfurter to comment on Rogers' letter to Upton offering aid in obtaining injunctions. Butler answered succinctly: the offer came at least a year late.

Butler then offered an alternative course. He pointed out that for integration to work there had to be first an integration plan and secondly a means of enforcing it. The school board had prepared the plans, but there was still no means of enforcement.

> The least relief that the school district should have is a stay of the plan of desegregation until the District Court is satisfied that a plan of enforcement is in operation and is sufficient to insure an adequate educational climate during the operation of the plan of desegregation.

NAACP counsel Marshall spoke next. In response to Butler's continued pleas for maintaining some adequate educational program, Marshall said, "It's according to what type of education you're talking about."

> I worry about the white children in Little Rock who are told, as young people, that the way to get your rights is to violate the law and defy the lawful authorities. . . . I don't worry about the Negro kids' future. They have been struggling with democracy long enough. They know about it.
> This is actually laid bare, the State of Arkansas, with the Governor holding these bills, refusing to sign them, and saying publicly that he holds them to see what this court is going to do. Maybe it has happened before, but I don't know of any other instance where the Governor of a state has tried to hold something over this court.

Marshall attacked Faubus again when he closed by asking the Supreme Court to affirm the Court of Appeals decision to integrate immediately, and to affirm it "in such a fashion as to make clear even to the politicians in Arkansas that Article VI of the Constitution means what it says."

Solicitor General Rankin, repeated the essence of his original argument:

> There can be no equality of justice for our people if the law steps aside, even for a moment, at the command of force and violence.

The Decision

The Supreme Court announced the substance of its decision at noon the next day, Friday, September 12. It affirmed unanimously the Court of Appeals decision and revoked the stay. Integration was to take place immediately. The full written decision of the court would follow.

The members of the school board issued a statement at 3 p.m. that day that Little Rock schools would open on Monday, September 15, and would admit both white and Negro students. One member of the board—Henry Rath—then announced that he was resigning in protest against the Supreme Court's decision.

Within two hours, Governor Faubus signed all the bills passed by the special session of the Arkansas Legislature and then signed a proclamation closing the four Little Rock high schools—Negro as well as white.

Virgil Blossom, flying home from the Supreme Court sessions in Washington, learned of Faubus' actions when he landed at the airport. One reporter asked, "Where do you go from here?"

"To the United Nations," Blossom answered. "Isn't that the only place left?"

In Virginia, the Warren County High School closed and Governor J. Lindsay Almond took over all power and control of it. In a few days four other Virginia schools were to be closed, and by the end of the week more than 10,000 Virginia students were affected.

In Newport, Rhode Island, vacationing President Eisenhower issued a statement urging public support of the Supreme Court's decision, but the plea came after the two Southern governors had already acted.

The School Closing Vote

Governor Faubus set September 27 as the date for the voters of the school district to decide whether or not they wanted to reopen the schools on an integrated basis. As 3,300 senior high school students enjoyed an extended summer vacation, the community organized for the election. Some fifty women formed themselves into a "Women's Emergency Committee To Open Our Schools." The segregationist Mothers' League announced it was circulating petitions for the recall of all the school board members except Alford. A private school corporation was set up in anticipation of a vote to keep the public schools closed.

On September 18 Faubus spoke on a statewide television program explaining his private school plan. He defended its legality, pointing out that the federal government had no authority to require any state to operate public schools. He noted that there was already a law on the Arkansas statute books—it was passed in 1875—providing that whenever a public school building is not in use, the school directors may permit a private school to make use of the school house.

Now it is crystal-clear that if the voters of the Little Rock School District vote against integration on September 27th these facilities will become surplus and not needed for public school purposes. This will leave the School Board free to lease the buildings to a suitable private agency.

A few days later 61 Little Rock attorneys bought space for a quarter-page ad in each of the city's newspapers to advise citizens that, as lawyers, they disagreed with the Governor's legal position.

It is our opinion that existing public school facilities of this district cannot be legally operated with any public funds as segregated private schools and, consequently, that the real issue before the voters . . . will be whether we open our schools under the Court ordered plan of limited integration or close them altogether.

A limited integrated school system . . . is distasteful to many in our group, but the alternative of no public school system is even more distasteful.

A few straw polls were taken—one in Hall High School and one in Central High. (Hall High School was situated in Ward 5, the highest income ward and one with almost no Negro residents.) Hall High students voted 71 percent for open schools, integrated if need be; Central High students voted 71 percent for the schools to remain closed rather than open as integrated.

Two last-minute television speeches were broadcast, one by the Governor who repeated his opinion that schools could legally be made private and segregated, and one by Alford who announced he would vote for segregation.

School integration was rejected 19,-470 to 7,561.

The Opinion of
The Supreme Court

While Little Rock citizens were still pondering the consequences of the school closing vote, the Supreme Court released the text of its opinion in its September 11 decision which had reversed Lemley and affirmed the

Court of Appeals integration decision.

The court decided that the precarious state of education was "directly traceable to the actions of legislators and executive officials of the state of Arkansas." From the point of view of the 14th Amendment, the court said, the school board members and the school superintendent "stand in this litigation as agents of the state." They must, therefore, be held responsible for the actions of the state.

The Supreme Court then went on to make a broad ruling—far broader than the NAACP had asked or expected:

. . . the constitutional rights of children not to be discriminated against in school admission on grounds of race or color declared by this Court in the Brown case can neither be nullified openly and directly by state legislators or state executives or judicial officers, nor nullified indirectly by them through evasive schemes for segregation whether attempted "ingeniously or ingenuously."

The court went on to restate its interpretation of the role of the Supreme Court and the legitimacy of its rulings. Ever since the 1803 *Marbury vs. Madison* decision, the Supreme Court pointed out, it has been accepted and respected principle that the federal judiciary is supreme in the exposition of the law of the Constitution. "It follows that the interpretation of the Fourteenth Amendment enunciated by this Court in the Brown case is the supreme law of the land. . . ." Thus a governor cannot nullify a federal court order, for if he could it would be his order, and not the United States Constitution, which would be the supreme law of the land.

The court then spoke to the contention that supervision of education is not specifically delegated to the federal government, and thus by the 10th Amendment, reserved to the states.

It is, of course, quite true that the responsibility for public education is primarily the concern of the states, but it is equally true that such responsibilities, like all other state activity, must be exercised consistently with federal constitutional requirements as they apply to state action. . . .

State support of segregated schools through any arrangement, management, funds, or property cannot be squared with the [Fourteenth] Amendment's command that no state shall deny to any person within its jurisdiction the equal protection of the laws.

The Voters Speak Again

The Supreme Court ruling did not end the litigation. The school board was under pressure to lease its buildings to the private school corporation, and the NAACP was equally anxious to prevent such a move. Accordingly, the NAACP applied to the District Court, now presided over by John E. Miller, who was ordinarily assigned to Fort Smith, Arkansas. The NAACP asked Miller to forbid the school board to lease any of the school property for the purpose of private, segregated education. Miller ruled that he had no power to make any decision on the question. His ruling was appealed to the Court of Appeals.

While the appeal was pending, the November elections arrived. In the primary election the previous spring, Congressman Brooks Hays had won the nomination to his ninth term in the United States House of Representatives, beating his segregationist opponent by a comfortable 59 percent. Since each Democratic candidate in the primary must sign an oath that he will abide by the results of the primary and will not run as an independent or on any other ticket, Hays had felt his nomination was tantamount to election. However, nine days before the election Dr. Dale Alford—the perennial dissenter on the school board—announced he would run a write-in campaign against Hays.

The day before the election, Arkansas Attorney General Bennett issued an opinion that it would be legal for voters to paste in stickers bearing Alford's name instead of having to write the name themselves. On election day many voters found the stickers waiting for them on the tables of the election inspectors at the polls.

Alford defeated Hays by 24,026 to 18,504—getting some 56 percent of the total vote cast in the five-county Congressional District. Little Rock itself voted for Alford by a margin of 51.1 percent. (The predominantly white precincts in the city gave him 56 percent.)

On November 10 the Court of Appeals ruled on the NAACP petition to forbid school leasing. Not only did the court forbid any leasing program, but it returned the case to federal District Judge Miller with instructions to oversee integration. The court did not specify when integration should take place, nor how it should be enforced. These matters were left to the school board and Judge Miller.

The next day all the school board members resigned except Alford. The next school board election was scheduled for December 6 (according to a new law passed in 1957 by the State Legislature), and the board members felt the people of Little Rock "should have the right in the December 6th election to select a complete new board." The resigning members went on to say: "We recognize the utter hopelessness, helplessness, and frustration of our present position." They re-

minded future candidates that the court orders were directed to the school board, not to any of the members as individuals. The orders, therefore, "will continue in force regardless of the make up of the Board."

In a press interview later, former Board President Wayne Upton said that he and the other four members had resigned because they were "tired of being Governor Orval Faubus' whipping boys. . . . He had used us to win or help win three elections. We were tired of it. All members of this board are segregationists in feeling. But we are confronted with the problem of enforcing the law. Our integration plan would have worked if it hadn't been for political interference."

On December 6 all six positions were to be filled. (Alford, who had not resigned, was up for re-election in any event, and announced he would not run for a new term.) There were two slates. One was filled by a group running at the insistence of a number of local businessmen who felt it was necessary for somebody to run to preserve a position of respect for the courts and the law. A second slate was running with the backing of the segregationist Citizens Council and Governor Faubus. Both slates professed to be segregationist. The difference was in perspective. As one of the Faubus-backed candidates put it, he would go to jail before integrating the schools. The other slate merely claimed it would not "voluntarily" integrate.

If the old school board thought the December 6 election would settle anything, its resignation had been in vain. In a district-wide election the voters split right down the middle, electing by a narrow margin three of the extremists, and three of the moderates. One candidate had had no opponent. None of the other five new board members won by more than one percent of the vote.

The September 27 vote—on the school closing issue—had clearly shown that, given a choice, the great majority of Little Rock voters preferred to have schools segregated. The Hays-Alford and the December 6 school board elections showed another stand just as clearly: the city was being torn apart over the question of whether it wished to obey or to defy an objectionable ruling of the Supreme Court.

August 1959: The Schools Reopen

The situation in Little Rock remained deadlocked for several months. During January United States District Judge Miller held hearings to receive suggestions from "interested parties" on what affirmative steps could be taken. School board member Laster pointed out that under Act 4 (the school-closing act passed at the special session of the legislature) it was a misdemeanor for a board to reopen a school closed because of a desegregation controversy. Laster asked, "Can any court order anyone to commit a crime?"

Judge Miller took the position that the mandate from the Court of Appeals "clearly" did not require him to order the schools opened, but that if they were to be opened they must be desegregated. However, Miller was inclined to agree with Laster. He knew of no way, he said, to open desegregated high schools while the state law remained in effect. There were then two suits pending to test the acts passed in the special session; one in the Arkansas Supreme Court and one in the United States District Court.

Meanwhile, sentiment was growing in Little Rock to resolve the situation. The Chamber of Commerce was disturbed by the impact the school crisis was having on Little Rock's industrial development. In the two years prior to 1957 ten new industries had located in the Little Rock area. Since the fall of 1957 not one new firm had moved in. In March the Chamber of Commerce took a poll of its members: 819 favored opening the schools with minimum integration; 245 favored keeping the schools closed to prevent integration.

On April 27 the Arkansas Supreme Court upheld the school-closing law by a vote of four to three. If the act had empowered the Governor to close all public schools permanently, the state court held, it would have violated the provision of the state constitution calling for a system of free public schools. But the act was clearly designed to be a temporary measure to protect the peace and welfare of the community. It was as legitimate to close the schools temporarily to prevent violence as it would be to close them in an epidemic.

The situation was soon to change. On May 5 the three segregationist members of the school board proposed that some 44 teachers and employees be discharged on the grounds that they favored the minimum integration plan or had cooperated with those who believed in complying with the Supreme Court. The three moderate board members protested that to discharge them without advance notice or hearings of any kind was contrary to regulations and unfair. Vote after vote was taken at the May 5 meeting; each was three to three. Finally the moderates left after reminding the remaining three that the rules of the school board called for a quorum. The three segregationist members then decided that they were not bound by the rules of the previous board and were free to act. They voted to discharge seven principals, 34 teachers, and three secretaries.

There was a violent reaction in the community. The Little Rock PTA Council promptly issued a protest resolution, and every night that week the council held protest rallies in the community, some attended by as many as 800 citizens. A citizens' committee formed within three days, calling itself the committee to Stop This Outrageous Purge (STOP). STOP issued a statement protesting the denial of the teachers' basic rights and the threat to academic freedom. The committee began circulating petitions to recall the three segregationist members of the school board. The segregationist Mothers' League and the Citizens Council immediately began circulating petitions to recall the three moderate school board members. By May 12 STOP had collected 9,603 signatures, the Mothers' League 7,150, enough for a recall election on all six candidates. A few days later a new committee was formed; the Committee to Retain Our Segregated Schools (CROSS). The recall election was scheduled for May 25.

Little Rock newspapers were filled with advertisements placed by STOP, CROSS, and numerous private citizens. The STOP group continued to maintain that the issue was "fair play" for the teachers. The CROSS group proclaimed that the only issue was segregation versus integration. The evening before the election, Faubus in a TV address made a strong appeal for the retention of the three segregationist members and for the recall of the three moderates. The issue, he said, was whether there should be segregation or integration in the schools.

The election was a victory for STOP and the moderates. All three segregationist school board members were recalled; all three moderates were retained in office. Approximately 25,000 people voted, and the results were very close.

On June 18 the United States District Court ruled on Arkansas' school-closing law. The three-judge court held that the law was unconstitutional. The Supreme Court had ruled, the court held, that violence or threat of violence couldn't justify a state using its police power to deprive citizens of their rights under the United States Constitution.

The school board (with the three vacancies filled by appointment by the Pulaski County Board of Education) immediately announced it would open the schools in the fall—under the minimum integration plan. The board also expunged from the record all action taken in the May 5 meeting.

The board called for the schools to be opened early in August. Some 54 Negroes applied to the three formerly all-white high schools. The board utilized the pupil placement law, and by the time school opened on August 12, one Negro was scheduled to attend Central High School and three were assigned to Hall High School.

On August 12 three Negro students entered Hall High School as a few curious spectators watched. Central High School's first day was not so placid. A crowd of more than 1,000 attended a segregation mass meeting on the steps of the State Capitol. Compared to some who addressed the crowd, Governor Faubus was quite moderate. The issue would not be decided in a day, he said, and he cautioned the listeners against violence and against getting injured needlessly. Other speakers urged the crowd to act, with the result that some 200 persons marched in the blistering heat from the capitol toward Central High School. The procession marched up to a line held by Little Rock police and firemen under the direction of the chief of police, who had been appointed about a year earlier by the new city manager. Some of the marchers tried to push past the chief and his aides. Nightsticks and fire hoses were used, 21 demonstrators were promptly arrested, and the demonstration dispersed. The police and firemen continued their heavy guard at both schools during the first week, but there were no further incidents. Compliance with the Supreme Court decision appeared to have resumed at Little Rock, but no one could predict what the next year, or even the next few weeks, would bring.

Chronology

1954

May 17: Supreme Court decision in *Brown v. Board of Education* ends segregation in public schools.

May 20: Little Rock School Board announces it will comply with decision.

1955

May: Supreme Court announces implementation decision.

Little Rock School Board approves integration plan.

Nov.: Woodrow Wilson Mann elected Mayor.

1956

Feb.: Thirty-three Negro parents bring suit against School Board, asking for more rapid integration.

Apr.: Faubus defeats Johnson in gubernatorial primary. Arkansas voters approve resolution to nullify Supreme Court decision.

Aug.: Federal District Court approves Little Rock School Board plan.

Negro parents appeal to U. S. Court of Appeals.

1957

Mar.: Two members of School Board re-elected over segregation candidates.

Apr.: U. S. Court of Appeals approves Little Rock School Board plan.

Aug.: Mothers' League of Central High School formed to resist integration. Governor Marvin Griffin of Georgia urges Arkansans to resist integration. Local officials make plans for police protection of Negro students.

Mrs. Clyde Thomason brings suit in Chancery Court to halt integration.

District Judge Ronald Davies voids Chancery Court injunction.

Sept. 2: Faubus orders Arkansas National Guard to guard Central High School.

School Board meets in emergency session; orders Negro students to stay home.

Sept. 3: First day of school; small, quiet crowd around school.

School Board petitions Davies for instructions; Davies orders integration.

Eisenhower holds press conference.

Sept. 4: Mann issues statement in opposition to Faubus. Negroes attempt to enter school; crowd becomes violent.

Faubus holds press conference; says he ordered National Guard to keep Negroes out.

Faubus sends telegram to Eisenhower protesting interference by federal investigators.

School Board files petition with Davies asking him to suspend integration order.

Sept. 5: Eisenhower answers Faubus, urging co-operation with federal investigators.

Sept 6: Faubus answers Eisenhower, saying he will co-operate with investigators.

Sept. 7: Davies denies School Board petition; orders integration to proceed.

Faubus receives statement of support from eight of the ten Little Rock aldermen.

Sept. 9: Davies receives report from Brownell; directs Brownell and Cobb to enter case as *amicus curiae*.

Sept. 10: Brownell and Cobb file petition to enjoin Faubus and National Guard from interfering with integration.

Sept. 11: Faubus asks Eisenhower for conference.

Sept. 14: Eisenhower and Faubus meet at Newport.

Sept. 19: Faubus files affidavit, asking Davies to disqualify himself as prejudiced; Brownell files countermotion.

Sept. 20: Hearing on Brownell-Cobb petition to enjoin Faubus-National Guard; Davies denies Faubus' motions, enjoins Governor *et al* from interfering with integration.

National Guard withdrawn.

Sept. 23: City-state police guard High School; unable to curb disorder; Negro students withdrawn.

Eisenhower issues proclamation ordering citizens of Little Rock to stop obstructing justice.

Maxwell Rabb calls Mann; Mann suggests federal troops.

Sept. 24: Eisenhower federalizes National Guard; sends paratroopers to enforce integration.

Negro students re-enter Central High.

Nov. 5: Six of seven segregation candidates for city directorships defeated.

Nov. 27: Paratroopers withdrawn; federalized National Guard patrols school.

1958

Feb.: School Board petitions Lemley to delay integration.

Apr.: Court of Appeals upholds Davies.

June 21: Lemley agrees to two-and-a-half year delay in integration.

June 23: Lemley orders decision effective immediately.

July 29: Faubus wins re-nomination.

Aug. 18: Court of Appeals reverses Lemley.

Aug. 21: Gardner stays Appeals Court mandate.

NAACP asks Supreme Court Justice Whittaker to vacate stay; Faubus announces special legislative session; U. S. Senate defeats last of bills to curb Supreme Court.

Aug. 25: Warren announces special Supreme Court session for August 28.

Aug. 26: Arkansas special legislative session opens.

Aug. 27: Arkansas Legislature passes school-closing bill.

Eisenhower indicates integration should go slower.

Aug. 28: Supreme Court hearing on School Board petition to vacate stay; calls for hearing on merits for September 11.

Aug. 29: Arkansas Legislature passes Bennett's school board recall bill.

Sept. 11: Supreme Court hearing on Lemley decision.

Sept. 12: Supreme Court orders immediate integration.

Faubus closes schools.

Sept. 27: School-closing vote. Integration rejected by Little Rock voters.

Sept. 28: Supreme Court releases full text of decision; condemns "evasive schemes."

NAACP petitions District Judge Miller to forbid the leasing of public school property; Miller declines to rule.

Nov. 6: Alford defeats Hays in write-in campaign for Congress.

Nov. 10: Court of Appeals forbids school leasing.

Nov. 11: School Board members resign.

Dec. 6: New School Board elected—three moderates, three segregationists.

1959

Jan.: U. S. District Judge Miller holds hearings in accordance with Court of Appeals ruling to devise "appropriate steps" to implement integration.

Apr. 27: Arkansas State Supreme Court holds school-closing act constitutional.

May 6: Little Rock School Board meets. Moderates walk out. Segregationists vote to remove 44 teachers and school employees.

May 12: Moderates file petition to recall segregationist members of School Board; segregationists file petition to recall moderate School Board members.

May 25: Recall election held. The three moderate School Board members retained; three segregationists recalled.

June 18: U. S. District Court holds school-closing act unconstitutional.

Aug. 12: Little Rock Schools open, four Negroes attending Central and Hall High Schools.

Appendix One

PROCLAMATION 3204
[22 F.R. 7628]

OBSTRUCTION OF JUSTICE IN THE STATE OF ARKANSAS

By the President of The United States of America

A Proclamation

WHEREAS certain persons in the State of Arkansas, individually and in unlawful assemblages, combinations, and conspiracies, have wilfully obstructed the enforcement of orders of the United States District Court for the Eastern District of Arkansas with respect to matters relating to enrollment and attendance at public schools, particularly at Central High School, located in Little Rock School District, Little Rock, Arkansas; and

WHEREAS such wilful obstruction of justice hinders the execution of the laws of that State and of the United States, and makes it impracticable to enforce such laws by the ordinary course of judicial proceedings; and

WHEREAS such obstruction of justice constitutes a denial of the equal protection of the laws secured by the Constitution of the United States and impedes the course of justice under those laws:

NOW, THEREFORE, I, DWIGHT D. EISENHOWER, President of the United States, under and by virtue of the authority vested in me by the Constitution and statutes of the United States, including Chapter 15 of Title 10 of the United States Code, particularly sections 332, 333 and 334 thereof, do command all persons engaged in such obstruction of justice to cease and desist therefrom, and to disperse forthwith.

IN WITNESS WHEREOF, I have hereunto set my hand and caused the Seal of the United States of America to be affixed.

DONE at the City of Newport, Rhode Island this twenty-third day of September in the year of our Lord Nineteen hundred and fifty-seven and of the Independence of the United States of America the one hundred and eighty-second.

DWIGHT D. EISENHOWER

By the President:

JOHN FOSTER DULLES,
Secretary of State

Appendix Two

The Vote in Little Rock

From the time the Little Rock School Board first drew up an integration plan in 1955 until December 1958 there were seven occasions on which Little Rock voters could express their opinions at the polls on segregation issues or candidates. Table I below shows the results of these elections,[17] separating the predominantly white precincts from the predominantly Negro precincts of the entire city.

[17] The December 6, 1958 election returns are official. All others are from the figures printed in the *Arkansas Gazette*.

Table I

ISSUE	WHOLE CITY ACTUAL VOTE **	PERCENT VOTING TO RESIST COURT		
		Whole City	*Predom. White Prec.*	*Predom. Negro Prec.**
NOV. 1956 Nullification amendment to Arkansas Constitution	12,835 — 12,181	50	53	39
MARCH 1957 School Board election; vote against Wayne Upton, president	2,322 — 4,144	35	38	22
NOV. 1957 For Mrs. Thomason for Board of City Directors	9,655 — 10,490	48	51	28
JULY 29, 1958 Democratic primary. Faubus third term bid	14,188 — 7,210 — 6,333 (Faubus, Finkbeiner, Ward)	50	55	27
SEPT. 27, 1958 Against re-opening schools as integrated	17,609 — 7,028	71	77	37
NOV. 1958 For Alford in Hays-Alford congressional election	12,658 — 11,783	51	56	26
DEC. 6, 1958 School Board; vote for Robert ("Jail Before Integration") Laster	6,825 — 6,746	50	53	31

* The Negro precincts cast about fifteen percent of the total city vote. There are minorities of whites in every precinct in this column.
** The segregationist, anti-compliance vote is in the left column.

The economic and racial classification of the precincts is based primarily upon information supplied the author by the city editor of the *Gazette*. From his impressionistic descriptions, the author classified the precincts into the four categories: upper income white; middle income white; lower income white; and Negro. The areas were also checked against the statistics in the 1950 United States Census of Housing, Volume 5 (Block Statistics), part 98 (Little Rock). In the nine years since the census there has been some annexation by the city, and there has also been an outward expansion of the middle and upper income population. The census

As Table I shows, the vote in the predominantly white precincts remained close to a fifty-fifty split in almost every election. The September 27, 1958 election—where the division was approximately seventy to thirty—was the only occasion in which the question was posed: "Do you want integrated schools?" In all the other elec-

data on Wards 4 and 5 were therefore considered by the author to be unreliable. The census data on the central portion of the city matched the city editor's descriptions.

tions the question was whether to support compliance with, or obstruction to, court rulings.

Table II subdivides the city's precincts according to the income level of the residents. (Two precincts—3A and 3G—were omitted because they contain such a racial and economic mixture as to prevent classification.) An "X" in the column indicates that a majority of voters in that precinct voted in the direction of opposing compliance with the Supreme Court decision.

Table II shows both the consistency

Table II

PRECINCTS	Nov. '56 Nullification	Mar. '57 School Board	Nov. '57 Thomason	July '58 Faubus	Sept. '58 To Open Schools	Nov. '58 Hays-Alford	Dec. '58 School Board
ISSUES *							
UPPER INCOME (WHITE)							
4E					X		
4F **			X				
5C					X		
5D	X				X		
5E					X		
5F					X		
5G					X		
MIDDLE INCOME (WHITE)							
1A	X			X	X	X	X
1D			X		X	X	X
3B	X	X	X	X	X	X	X
3D	X	X	X	X	X	X	X
3E	X		X	X	X	X	X
3F	X			X	X	X	X
4A	X	X		X	X	X	X
4B	X		X	X	X	X	X
4C	X	X	X	X	X	X	X
4D	X	X	X	X	X	X	X
5A	X		X	X	X	X	X
5B					X		
LOW INCOME (WHITE)							
2A	X	X	X	X	X	X	X
2B	X	X	X	X	X	X	X
2C	X	X	X	X	X	X	X
1C	X		X	X	X	X	X
NEGRO							
1B							
1E							
2D	X						
2E							
3C							

* The upper income white precincts cast about twenty percent of the vote; the middle income about fifty percent; the lower income about ten; and the Negro precincts about fifteen. The two precincts omitted cast about three per cent of the vote. These proportions did not vary more than a percent or two with each of the seven elections.

** Precinct 4F is not in the Little Rock School District and thus did not participate in the school closing or school board elections.

of the voting and the basic cleavage in the city: the majority of voters in the Negro and upper income white precincts voted consistently against the "segregationist" position, except for the school-closing vote in the case of the upper income white precincts. The majority of voters in the middle and low income white precincts were just as consistently in favor of the segregationist position.

This division is not peculiar to Little Rock. In almost every Southern city where a school integration referendum has been held since the Supreme Court's 1954 decision, the upper income white precincts show up along with the Negro precincts as least segregationist. A number of interlocking factors contribute to this division. One is that Negroes are less likely to live in upper income areas than in other parts of the city. The public schools in these areas would be almost entirely white no matter what the law. Here, too, live the people most likely to be able to afford to send their children to private schools. Another factor is that the Southern business and professional people in the rapidly industrializing cities are more likely to be sensitive to Northern opinion than the lower income groups, which are constantly fed by in-migration from the rural Southern areas. Negroes are in most direct economic competition with the lower income occupational groups. They offer almost no economic threat to the upper income business and professional people.

Table III shows what evidence there is of a shift of opinion over the two-year period ending December 1958.

Table III

INCOME GROUP	PERCENT VOTING FOR SEGREGATION POSITION **						
	Nov. '56 *Nullifi- cation*	*Mar. '57* *School Board*	*Nov. '57* *Thomason*	*July '58* *Faubus*	*Sept. '58* *To Close Schools*	*Nov. '58* *Hays-Alford*	*Dec. '58* *School Board*
Upper Income (White)	46	18	32	39	62	40	29
Middle Income (White)	53	46	59	59	81	61	60
Low Income (White)	54	53	60	60	82	63	66
Negro *	41	22	28	27	37	27	31
Whole City	50	35	48	50	71	51	50

* The precincts classified as predominantly Negro range from a precinct which is split between Negroes and lower income whites—with Negroes predominating—to Precinct 1B which is about seventy percent Negro, according to the census data. The vote in precinct 1B for these elections is as follows: November 1956, 28%; March 1957, 9%; November 1957, 13%; July 1958, 14%; September 1958, 19%; November 1958, 14%; and December 1958, 18%.

** Figures for the May 1959 school board recall election are not given here. The issues in this election involved fair treatment of teachers as well as segregation and compliance with the Supreme Court decision. However, the votes followed fairly closely the pattern of the other elections. Taking the vote to retain segregationist board member Laster as an example, the upper income white precincts voted 21% for Laster; middle income precincts 55%; low white precincts 58%; and Negro precincts 26%. Laster did not carry one upper income white precinct and lost only one precinct in the middle and low income white groups.

The Defense Appropriations Rider

EDITH T. CARPER

Editor's Introduction

In 1955 Congress attached a legislative rider to the annual defense appropriations bill. Its purpose was to give two congressional committees the right to disapprove the shut-down by the Department of Defense of certain of its local installations and activities. The Defense Department had embarked on a "decompetition program"—that is, a program of closing down certain military installations or activities which were producing goods or services that could have been purchased from private business. In carrying out its decompetition program, the Defense Department was acting under administration policies which had originated in at least three quarters: (1) Republican campaign promises to "get the government out of business"; (2) representations from national trade and business associations; and (3) a widely-publicized report by a body formally known as the Commission on Organization of the Executive Branch of the Government but more popularly called the Second Hoover Commission. The Senate Small Business Committee had also urged government departments to curtail activities that competed with, or duplicated services available from, private firms.

One reason for the 1955 defense appropriations rider was strong pressure on congressmen from constituents who felt their localities would suffer if existing installations were closed. Some of these protests came from government workers concerned about their jobs. Others seemed motivated by local pride. But many came from local businessmen who preferred keeping government installations and payrolls in their areas to having them closed out in favor of private firms in other parts of the country. An ironic aspect of these local protests was the fact that many of them were registered by local businessmen—and then amplified by congressmen—who strongly supported the principle of the Hoover Commission recommendations and who believed fervently that as a general rule the government should curtail any activities that could be performed equally well by private enterprise.

The defense appropriations rider was passed only after considerable debate. Some of it concerned the overlapping jurisdictions of the Appropriations committees and the Armed Services committees in the two houses of Congress. And much of it concerned the propriety of writing legislative riders into appropriations bills that Presidents could seldom afford to veto. As Congress expected, President Eisenhower decided he could not veto the large appropriation bill, even though it contained the rider giving congressional committees the right to disapprove the shut-down of individual government installations. But, after signing the bill, the President and other administration officials indicated that they would ignore the rider because they believed it was an unconstitutional usurpation by Congress of powers that belonged to the executive branch. Congressmen who had supported the rider replied that it would be unconstitutional for the President to exercise an informal veto of one provision of the act.

The balance of the case study describes how Congress and the administration fought for their respective points of view. It is told with particular reference to a venerable Navy installation in Boston known as the Boston ropewalk. The story thus has its setting in the controversy about the decompetition program. Its recounting can enlighten the reader about relationships between the executive and legislative branches; about the strength of local influences in national policy making and administration; about the role of interest groups; and about certain aspects of the operations of the Congress and of its committees.

The Hoover
Commission and the Ropewalk

The United States government has engaged in various kinds of business operations from its earliest days. Government-operated powder and ammunition plants date from the Revolution. The Philadelphia Army Quartermaster Clothing Factory antedates the Constitution. In 1837, by direction of an Act of Congress, the government opened a Boston ropemaking plant, in its day the most modern of factories. (The factory was —and is—called a ropewalk because workmen walked along a narrow platform, playing out strands of rope onto a wheel.)

In the twentieth century, government-operated business and commercial enterprises expanded and proliferated, largely because of the impact of two world wars and the great depression. Enterprises operated by the military departments, following the pattern of the past, outnumbered those maintained by other government agencies. Shortly after the end of World War II the Defense Department had a larger payroll, a greater number of employees, a wider scope of operations, and more business/commercial enterprises than any other department. Its activities included the operation of arsenals, shipyards, sawmills, aluminum sweating, scrap metal baling, clothing, paint, orthopedic and ophthalmic manufacturing factories, auto repair shops, laundries and dry-cleaning plants, and many other enterprises. The Defense Department's investment in these operations represented $15 billion at a time when the assets of all industrial corporations in the United States were over $800 billion.

There were many reasons for this extensive involvement, most of them deriving generally from the nature and mission of military establishments: private enterprise could not supply all military demands and services; military units in isolated areas had to be self-sustaining; some service requirements involved classified information and work of a hazardous nature; troop morale had to be maintained through post exchanges, movie theaters, and the like. In addition it was felt that the military had to carry on advanced research and development, and that it needed a standard by which to judge commercial products.

The Decompetition Drive Begins

The degree to which the government was engaging in business or industrial activity began to be seriously questioned after the close of World War II. As the economy shifted to a peacetime basis, demands for an examination arose in Congress. The election of 1946 saw the Republicans gain control of Congress. One of the early acts of the 80th Congress was to create a bi-partisan commission to survey the entire organization of the federal government. Headed by former President Herbert Hoover, and known as the "Hoover Commission," its special function was to promote greater economy and efficiency in the federal government. The commission recommended in March 1949 that some thirty percent of the government's business activities be eliminated. However, there was no effective follow-up to this recommendation, and the outbreak of the Korean War in 1950 further dampened interest in the subject.

The matter continued to be of concern to the legislative and executive branches, though, and during the Korean War a congressional committee investigating the military supply system focused attention on the Defense Department's business operations. Of particular concern to the committee was the finding that each service relied too heavily on its own supply system instead of using centralized depots and facilities. Accordingly, Congress specifically instructed the Defense Department to consolidate supply services.

The Defense Department, in turn, called on the military departments to survey "existing commercial and industrial-type facilities," to end duplicating operations, and to eliminate those supplying services or products that could be filled at equivalent prices by private enterprise.

However, the drive to get government out of business did not take clear shape until after the election of 1952, when the Republicans won the presidency for the first time in twenty years. The question of government-operated business had been injected into the campaign when Republican candidate Dwight Eisenhower specifically promised that "no Federal project will be undertaken which private enterprise can effectively undertake." This, he said, was one way "to bring government closer to the people."

The new Republican Congress set up a second bi-partisan study commission, again headed by Hoover. The Second Hoover Commission was directed to study government services, activities, and functions with a view to abolishing those deemed unnecessary or competitive with private enterprise, and to turning over other appropriate activities to state and local governments.

The issue of government in business seized the imagination and attention of the executive and legislative branches. The new administration began to lay out its program, supported by substantial Republican majorities in both House and Senate. Several congressional committees launched investigations. One of the first to open up the issue was a subcommittee of the House Committee on Government Operations, the Harden subcommittee chaired by Representative Cecil Harden of Indiana. This subcommittee held hearings during 1953, taking testimony from over 100 witnesses representing business firms, trade associations, and government departments. Representatives of the paint and varnish industry, printing and graphic arts, retail food and liquor dealers, barge and tugboat operators, ice cream, wooden box, and rope manufacturers, all contended that the Defense Department's operations in their respective areas menaced the profitability of their enterprises.

The Ropewalk Is Noticed

While this activity was going on in the legislative branch, the Defense Department was carrying on its own drive. Its decompetition program actually had been launched by a directive issued the previous November, just as the Democrats were preparing to leave office. In the early months of 1953, under authority of this directive, the department ordered a survey of business operations to determine which could be abolished. One of the first commercial operations scrutinized was the Boston ropewalk, which manufactured cables and hawsers used for mooring and towing ships.

The ropewalk was also attracting the attention of the Harden subcommittee. The Cordage Institute, the trade association of commercial hard-fiber cord and twine manufacturers, testified that it was able and anxious to take over the ropewalk's production.

Boston interests reacted in strong protest. As early as May 1953, the Boston Chamber of Commerce—breaking away from the United States Chamber's encouragement of the decompetition drive—took a firm stand against shutting down the ropewalk. The local chamber asserted its position was based on economy, on the desirability of retaining the skills of the workers, and on the importance of carrying on research.

The local groups enlisted the aid of Democratic Representative Thomas P. O'Neill whose district encompassed the ropewalk. He, in turn, drew in Representative John McCormack of the adjoining Twelfth district who was the second-ranking Democrat in the House. The combined efforts of the local groups and the congressmen resulted in the shelving of the plans for closing the ropewalk.

The Defense Department's November 1952 directive had not proved generally effective, and the slow pace of divestment was brought to the attention of Defense Secretary Charles E. Wilson, formerly president of General Motors. One of the reasons given for slowness was that the language of the existing directive was too permissive, since it called for "decompetition" but also for maximum utilization of existing facilities. As a result, the department issued a new directive in November 1953 that dealt exclusively with commercial/industrial activities. This directive stated that, consistent with national security, business operations would be terminated to the maximum extent possible. Continued operation could be justified only on the basis of "substantial savings to the government resulting from performance at a government facility." [1] Several months later the department issued detailed follow-up instructions directing the Army, Navy, and Air Force to set up systematic review and evaluation programs. Each service was told to analyze its facilities and to recommend to the Secretary of Defense those which could be shut down.

The report of the Harden subcommittee, issued in February 1954, buttressed the Defense Department's drive. The subcommittee reported that

The federal agencies have entered into so many business-type activities

---

[1] Commissaries, post exchanges, and officers clubs, financed with non-appropriated funds, were excluded.

that they constitute a real threat to private enterprise, imperil the tax structure and are, in many industries, a step toward socialization. . . . It is recommended that a permanent, vigorous, preventative, and corrective program be inaugurated . . . it is essential to develop competitive industries as soon as possible and the government should step out of the picture at the earliest date.

The Harden subcommittee further recommended that the operating agencies, the Bureau of the Budget, and congressional committees make a "thorough annual review" of all existing businesses.

But the eight-man subcommittee was only a part of the thirty-man Committee on Government Operations. The full committee did not endorse unanimously the recommendations of the Harden subcommittee. Eleven of the fourteen Democrats on the committee, including the House Democratic whip, John McCormack of Massachusetts, said they did not feel that "government activity in many fields is, *per se,* a bad thing."

The pressure from the administration increased. In a December speech, Rowland Hughes, Director of the Bureau of the Budget, decried the "alarming" extent of the government's business activities. It was "amazing," Hughes said, that the government of the United States, "the citadel and the world's principal exponent of private enterprise and individual initiative," should operate over 100 different business-type activities.

Within a matter of weeks the Executive Office of the President, through a Budget Bureau directive, ordered a cutback of business operations throughout the federal government. The January 15, 1955 directive provided that

. . . the federal government will not start or carry on any commercial activity to provide a service or product for its own use if such product or service can be procured from private enterprise through ordinary business channels. Exceptions to this policy shall be made . . . only where it is clearly demonstrated in each case that it is not in the public interest to procure such product, or service from private enterprise.

The Defense Department followed through by issuing a new policy directive of its own on Feburary 8. This charged the Assistant Secretary of Defense (Supply and Logistics) with responsibility for carrying out the program; and it directed the secretaries of each of the three military departments to analyze and review commercial/industrial facilities. The directive also provided for continuation of the business activity only if it were "clearly demonstrated" that private enterprise could not supply the service or product. Five criteria were set out to justify continuation:

inaccessibility of commercial facilities;

inability of private enterprise to supply according to fluctuating military demands;

provision of training facilities that might be needed in a combat zone;

necessity of preserving classified information;

other considerations involving the "public interest" as certified by the Secretary of Defense.

Notably absent from the list was the criterion that government enterprises would have to provide their particular goods or services at lower costs than those of private firms. This omission was not due to a lapse of memory on the part of Defense Department officials. Earlier, the department had made attempts to obtain figures on the cost of operating each business. Defense

Department auditors had reported that since the government's accounting system did not provide for such overhead items as interest, personnel, and depreciation, the cost-accounting methods used by the government could not provide an accurate basis for comparing the costs of government-produced items and those of private industry.

Protests rained on the department when the omission of the economy criterion was discovered. First heard from was a private group, organized some years earlier chiefly to get the government out of business. This group, the National Associated Businessmen, Inc., publicized the new criteria in its February Newsletter sent to its 1,000 members. A month later the chairman of the House Committee on Government Operations wrote Secretary Wilson, protesting the omission. A new directive on April 27, 1955 restored the criterion that products of government enterprises should cost less.

The Ropewalk Is Threatened

Meanwhile, the Army, Navy, and Air Force had been carrying out their review programs in accordance with the previous directives. The ropewalk came into prominence again. A sharp difference of opinion developed between the Defense Department and the Navy, the "proprietor" of the ropewalk. The Navy argued that research and development should continue, with production limited to the amount necessary "to provide manufacturing feasibility and to maintain the plant in ready condition." Secretary Wilson did not accept the Navy's position. In December 1954 he issued a memorandum to the three service secretaries:

> The statements of the President, the widespread interest in this program in industry and in the Congress require a far more aggressive approach to our program.

Coffee roasting and the manufacture of rope and paint, he told the secretaries, would have to be halted "unless you see compelling reasons to the contrary. . . ."

The Navy capitulated. In February 1955 its Assistant Secretary announced, "I have now determined that the entire operation should be discontinued . . . the manufacture of rope by the Navy will be phased out completely within six months."

The Massachusetts congressmen responded immediately. McCormack, once again House Majority Leader after the November 1954 elections, wasted no time. He organized a bipartisan group of Massachusetts congressmen to plead to the Pentagon the case for continuing production not only at the ropewalk, but also at the chain forge factory, another activity of the Boston Naval Base. It was to no avail. Five days after the first announcement, the Navy notified McCormack that its final decision had been made. The ropewalk would be closed. McCormack carried his case to local groups in Boston. He informed the newspapers, labor unions, and business groups of his efforts, and he told his constituents:

> If they had left it at the legislative level, I know I could block it. I blocked it in the last Congress, which was Republican controlled, and I know I could block it in this Congress, which is Democratic controlled, but it is going to be action by the executive branch.

The *Boston Globe* devoted its February 11 editorial to the coming fate of the ropewalk, deploring the Navy's action:

Few New Englanders will applaud the decision [to close down] the famous ropewalk at the naval shipyard in Charlestown. A year ago an attempt to end this important adjunct to the fleet drew widespread protests. They would seem to be in order once more.

This ropewalk is the only one the Navy possesses. In addition to being an old institution, it produces cordage for the fleet at about 25 percent less cost than would be the case were its product purchased elsewhere. Also, it employs 100 skilled men. The decision entails needless expense as well as adding to the problem of unemployment in this area.

McCormack also carried his crusade to the floor of the House. On February 28 he announced from the floor that his campaign to dissuade the Navy from closing the historic institution was going to be unsuccessful. He said the decision to close was made "on the highest level, by the President himself, and with the Hoover Commission pressuring for it."

McCormack drew no sympathy from the administration. In April, Budget Director Hughes made a widely publicized speech in which he castigated prior Democratic administrations for "creeping socialism." Speaking to a Texas Chamber of Commerce group Hughes said:

> Over the years . . . the tentacles of government competition embraced more and more areas and the number of business-type activities in which the government was engaged grew steadily. New areas of competition with business were rationalized—rather than justified—and more and more there was a tendency to blur the distinction between what was absolutely necessary . . . and what was merely expedient. . . .

He praised the Defense Department for its "especially active" efforts in the preceding two years and noted that plans for further shut-downs were soon to take effect. He added that the plans called for early termination of all armed forces coffee-roasting activities and for shutting down the Boston ropewalk. Other transfers were to take place in orderly succession.

Sikes Is Aroused

Hughes' words sounded ominous to some members of Congress, particularly those whose districts contained "other transfers." Democratic Representative Robert Sikes of Florida began to receive letters from some of his constituents—employees of the Navy communications system[2] at Pensacola Air Force Base. The Navy had announced a plan to transfer the communications system to private enterprise, and the workers, concerned about their jobs, asked Sikes to block the change.

Sikes, as yet unaware of Representative McCormack's interest in the ropewalk, investigated the Pensacola situation. He concluded that a transfer would be unwise. It would, he felt, bring about greater cost to the government, dislocate the employees and possibly throw some out of work; and, since the aircraft control system involved classified information, the transfer might endanger security arrangements. Sikes approached the Defense Department. Although he was rebuffed initially, he finally succeeded in having the transfer plan dropped.

With his interest aroused, Sikes soon discovered that other members of Congress were similarly concerned. Democratic Representative Porter Hardy of Virginia and Republican Representative John F. Baldwin, Jr., of California,

[2] The installation was a telephone exchange and aircraft control system.

were both worried about plans to shut down Navy-operated paint manufacturing plants in their districts.

Sikes began to feel that Secretary Wilson was pushing the shut-down program with a celerity and enthusiasm not welcomed by congressmen. On March 21, 1955 Sikes introduced a bill, H.R. 5115, to prohibit the Defense Department from disposing of work traditionally performed by civilian components of the department. The bill was referred to the Armed Services Committee.

A month or so later, in May 1955, unions representing employees in the affected installations began to issue public protests. First to act was the Government Employees Council, AFL-CIO, representing 600,000 federal workers. The Council asked Congress to modify the administration's drive. Its statement explained:

> The entire policy is being predicated without regard to increased cost to the taxpayer, national security, and the government's moral obligation to federal employees, who have devoted years of their life in the service of the federal government. . . . The policy has further disregarded the adverse social and economic impact upon communities and states in which these government functions are located. . . . There is also a lack of proper evaluation of the vast sum of taxpayers' monies which have been invested. . . .

Two other employee unions, the AFL American Federation of Government Employees and the International Association of Machinists (AFL-CIO), joined in the campaign to save the jobs of the employees. They pleaded to congressmen the "human side" of the precipitate shut-downs—the dislocation of government employees, the long years of faithful service that would be summarily terminated, and the civil service benefits that would be lost.[3] Representatives of the machinists had private talks with members of the Defense Subcommittee of the House Appropriations Committee.

But there did not seem to be many friendly congressmen. Up to now two congressional committees and one subcommittee had taken some sort of interest in the question of government in business. The Harden subcommittee had reported in favor of the decompetition drive more than a year before; its parent committee, the House Government Operations Committee, had split, with the Democrats skeptical of labeling government activity "bad." At the same time the Senate Appropriations Committee, in its 1954 report, had called for a report by the Defense Department on the extent of competition between government-operated enterprises and private enterprises. Now a third congressional committee weighed in. In a May 30, 1955 report, the Senate Select Committee on Small Business expressed alarm at departmental competition with small business and called for a "straight-forward, aggressive attack upon a steadily growing cancer in our economy." The report referred specifically to government competition in the areas of railroading, coffee roasting, logging and sawmill op-

---

[3] The Defense Department recognized that serious personnel problems would undoubtedly occur when and if the decompetition program started moving rapidly. The workers employed at the plants being closed faced an uncertain future at best. However, it was felt in the Department of Defense that existing reduction-in-force programs of the three service departments were adequate. Under them the government would help to find new jobs for the dismissed employees, an installation would be shut down only after a reasonable notice to the workers, and other government agencies would give priority to "riffed" workers whenever a vacancy occurred. There was no personnel directive at the Defense Department level.

erations, laundries, tire retreading, and paint manufacture.

The Impetus of
The Hoover Commission

Just at this time, the Hoover Commission issued its reports. The May 15, 1955 report recommended that the Defense Department terminate about 1,000 of its 2,500 business-type facilities and transfer their functions to private enterprise. The transfer, the commission claimed, would:

> . . . result in the return of large sums of investment capital to the Treasury, effect economies in government expenditures, increase the tax revenues of the government, and create a more healthy economic system.

But the Hoover Commission felt that the transfers were essential for more than economic reasons:

> Far more important than the dollar savings are the beneficial results to our economy from eliminating Government competition to the greatest practicable extent . . . the private enterprise system is the basis of the military strength of this Nation and of its unparalleled standard of living. Further strengthening of the private enterprise system is the best way to further these objectives.

The commission praised the Defense Department for its "constructive" work aimed at eliminating unnecessary facilities. However, the Hoover Commission's Subcommittee on Business Enterprises felt the department's pace was too slow and called on service chiefs in the field to "implement aggressively the well formulated policy set forth by the Defense Department."

Eleven of the Hoover Commission's twelve members signed the report. Commissioner Chet Holifield, Democratic Congressman from California, also signed, but he issued a general dissent. He did not object to the underlying philosophy but to "the summary, mechanical, and sometimes arbitrary manner in which the commission's report would dispose of many such activities. . . . An effort was made to catalog a multitude of complex government functions and to dispose of them right and left with only the barest consideration." Holifield also criticized the commission's recommendation that government agencies expand contract operations with private companies. Holifield was sensitive to the fact that only recently there had been a furor over the decision of the Eisenhower administration to contract with a private firm—the so-called Dixon-Yates combine—for the construction of a power plant to serve the TVA area.

A steady stream of favorable publicity and editorial comment followed the Hoover Commission reports. The commission's recommendations to the Defense Department were featured on front pages of major newspapers. A *New York Times* headline read: "HOOVER UNIT ASKS GOVERNMENT END 1,000 ENTERPRISES."

Several factors contributed to the favorable climate in which the commission's reports were received. It was able to capitalize on the reservoir of good will and public acceptance of the original commission. No one wanted to quarrel with the commission's goal for government—economy and efficiency. An additional factor was the careful publicity planning on the part of the commission's own staff. The editorial director was an experienced newsman and a former official of *The New York Times* who was able to foster good relations with the press. Reports were released to the press in time to be featured in Monday morning editions or other times when the news supply was low. They were accompanied by well-prepared press releases.

In addition, members of the commission and its task forces, prominent national figures in the business, professional, and political world, were effective advocates. Joseph B. Hall, chairman of the Subcommittee on Business Enterprises in the Defense Department, and Charles R. Hook, chairman of the Commission on Business Organization of the Defense Department, spoke at a New York meeting of the National Industrial Conference Board the same week the commission reported on Defense Department competition with private enterprise. Their appearance before the board, a research and fact-finding organization of business and trade association leaders, government officials, and educators, stimulated discussion of the recommendations to the Defense Department to discontinue many of its business operations.

A private group, the Citizens Committee for the Hoover Report, did a great deal to publicize the recommendations. It stimulated political action through a vigorous grass roots campaign. Originally organized in 1949 to educate, propagandize, and lobby for adoption of the first Hoover Commission's recommendations, it was reactivated in 1955 as the second commission began to issue its reports. It maintained offices in New York and Washington, worked closely with scores of organized national groups, issued news letters, bulletins, and political action directions to state and local organizations in all of the 48 states.

The Sikes Rider

Representative Sikes took careful measure of the heavy build-up of sentiment in favor of decompetition. He

quickly decided that his bill, H.R. 5115, had little chance of getting through Congress or passing the White House without a veto, but he still believed some brakes should be put on the program. He felt that Secretary Wilson was "making the cases fit the policy rather than the reverse," and that unless Congress acted quickly, many installations would be closed, with consequent injury to the public interest, the employees involved, and the communities affected. Sikes had been a member of the House Appropriations Committee since 1949, and it was natural for him to hit on the idea of attaching a rider to the military appropriations bill. He knew that only rarely did a president veto any of the eighteen or so appropriations bills that are passed each year. Accordingly he drafted a new section, subsequently designated Section 638, to be added to the bill, providing annual appropriations for the Defense Department (H.R. 6042). Sikes' rider provided that before the Defense Department could shut down a going installation, the appropriate congressional committee had to be apprised and its agreement secured.[4]

Sikes' rider had first to clear the House Appropriations Committee. Highly influential among the fifty members were Democratic Representative George Mahon of Texas, Chairman of the Defense Appropriations Subcommittee; Democratic Representative Clarence Cannon of Missouri, Chairman of the full committee; and Repub-

---

[4] "No part of the funds appropriated in this Act may be used for the disposal or transfer by contract or otherwise of work traditionally performed by civilian personnel of the Department of Defense unless it has been justified before the appropriate committees of Congress that the disposal is economically sound and that the related services can be performed by a contractor without danger to national services."

lican Representative John Taber of New York, ranking minority member of the full committee.

Sikes was no political neophyte. He had served with the Democratic National Committee from 1936 to 1946 and had been a member of Congress since 1940.

Mahon could see both advantages and disadvantages to Sikes' proposal. First of all, he opposed on principle the idea of introducing controversial legislation as a rider to an appropriations bill. Second, as a personal matter, he himself believed in "keeping the government out of business as much as you reasonably can." Third, he knew the Republican crusade against "big government" and "government-in-business" was receiving both wide public attention and praise. Mahon saw the possibility of a political trap in Sikes' Section 638. He did not want the Democrats to be maneuvered into a position of favoring government-operated business as opposed to "free enterprise."

On the other hand, Mahon was sympathetic to the view that certain business and manufacturing operations were best carried on by the government. (There was an airfield in Mahon's district, but there was no substantial government-run business located there. Nor did the districts of any of the members of the Defense Appropriations Subcommittee house such a business.)

Apparently no other committee member felt more strongly than Mahon. Along with Mahon they accepted Sikes' proposal, and Section 638 became a rider to the appropriations bill.

The Formal Report and the Reaction

On May 5, 1955 the House Appropriations Committee formally reported the defense appropriations bill to the House. Its report [5] voiced the committee's concern over Defense Department plans to transfer many of its businesses to private operation. Such transfers, the report said, were sometimes desirable, but on other occasions they represented "a radical departure from established custom." The report pointed out that "it is conceivable that contract operations could, if carried to extremes, result in a loss of trained personnel and know-how in the departments," and that the shift might cost more money, particularly in case of sudden emergencies. The report concluded:

> The Committee has no desire to hamper legitimate transferral of government activities to private business where it can properly be shown that this is economically sound and that the related services can be performed by contract without danger to national security . . . because of the Committee's responsibility in the matter of appropriations it is felt that a justification of transfers before the appropriate committees of Congress is proper before the transfers take place.

All this was the introduction to Congress and the public of Sikes' Section 638.

Telegrams and letters of protest began to pour in to members of the Defense Appropriations Subcommittee and to the subcommittee offices as well. Chambers of commerce, trade associations, taxpayers' groups, and individual businessmen protested, claiming that Section 638 would slow the Defense

[5] Reports are adopted by majority vote of committees. That there were no minority views or dissents did not mean that all fifty members of the full committee supported every provision. Only on unusual occasions does the committee report include minority or dissenting views.

Department program to get the government out of business. Letters and wires of protest to the subcommittee filled a file drawer. It was believed that the flood of protests had been stimulated by the Citizens Committee for the Hoover Report as well as by trade associations.

The House Acts on 638

The House began debate on the $31 billion defense appropriations bill on May 11. The debate was carried on under a rule from the House Rules Committee waiving points of order.[6]

Debate centered first on the major issue, a proposed cutback of 87,000 in manpower strength of the Army, with token reductions in Navy and Marine Corps strength. Despite Democratic opposition, the troop reductions recommended by President Eisenhower were approved. The House then turned to the Sikes provision, Section 638.

Sikes was a vigorous pleader. When debate began, he spoke earnestly of the importance of giving Congress an opportunity to check the Defense Department's plans to shut down going business operations. Some congressional committee—Armed Services, Government Operations, or Appropriations—should scrutinize the proposals. He said the procedure of "justifying" would not require much time for Congress or great effort by the Defense Department. "I have no desire to hamper the operations of private business or to obstruct improvements in operating procedures in the services. But I do want Congress to know what is going on and for that I have no apologies."

The language of Section 638 was carefully drawn, he said, to allow the Defense Department as much flexibility as possible in reporting to Congress. He intended that the Department should report on and "justify" the winding up of major business enterprises in operation many years. He felt the same information the department used could easily be made available to Congress.

Representative Thomas P. O'Neill of Massachusetts exhibited lively interest and asked if Sikes' provision might mean reprieve for the Boston ropewalk in his district.

The pros or cons of the Sikes provision were not the only points involved in the debate. Also at issue was the recurring problem of the clash between subject-matter committees and fiscal committees dealing with the same area of responsibility. In this instance, the Defense Appropriations Subcommittee was initiating military legislation. Since the Armed Services Committee was formally charged with that responsibility, some of its members exhibited concern. The fact that the provision was protected from a point of order by a special rule granted by the Rules Committee also caused rancor among Armed Services Committee members.

Jurisdictional conflicts between committees have enlivened the legislative

---

[6] One of the standing rules of the House (and of the Senate) is that general legislation should not be written in an appropriation bill. However, the principle is habitually violated, and over the years substantive legislative provisions have crept into appropriation bills. (For example, the Sherman Anti-Trust Act was passed as a rider to a deficiency appropriations bill in 1890.)

Ordinarily any member could prevent a rider from being attached to an appropriation bill by raising a "point of order" from the floor—a parliamentary procedure which takes precedence over any action on the floor and which questions whether proper procedure is being followed. If the presiding officer sustains the point of order, it is carried. However, under the special rule no such points of order could be raised. Rules Committee members explained the rule was needed to guard a complex financing method against technical points of order and to protect legislative items.

process since the birth of the standing committee system. It is difficult if not impossible to mark clearly the boundaries between congressional committees, and it is only by the restraint exercised by committee chairmen and by a mutual respect for jurisdictional territory that frequent open conflicts are avoided. The Appropriations Committee's power over the purse strings gives it a measure of policy control over the military; thus it is in a way a standing threat to the Armed Services Committee.

Vinson Opposes

Tempo of the debate quickened when the Chairman of the Armed Services Committee, Democratic Representative Carl Vinson of Georgia, rose to seek recognition. Vinson, a canny politician, a specialist for 24 years in military and naval affairs, and a veteran of 41 years service in the House, proposed an amendment striking Section 638 in its entirety. He was angered over what he considered the increasing encroachments on his committee's jurisdiction by the Defense Appropriations Subcommittee. On January 11 of that same year he had introduced a bill (H.R. 2034) designed to enact into permanent law some of the military matters that were being included year after year in appropriations bills reported by two Appropriations Committee subcommittees, the Subcommittees on Defense and on Military Construction.

Vinson felt strongly about Section 638. He considered it an unconstitutional trespass on an executive function, and he opposed interfering with the transfer of certain Department of Defense functions to private companies, especially in the area of small business. He called Section 638 a device to retain useless government enterprises

and an unconstitutional incursion into the area of executive authority. He made a biting attack on the substance of Section 638, and he lashed at the Appropriations Committee for giving it a free ride on the appropriations bill.

He said the special rule amounted to a safe-conduct pass; otherwise the provision would certainly be struck out as legislation in an appropriation bill. "Were it in order for me to do so I would make a point of order objection to this section because it is clearly subject to one. But again I am precluded because of the nature of the rule under which we are now proceeding."

Turning to the subject matter of the provision, Vinson said its purpose was:

> . . . to keep the government manufacturing things that the government wants to get out of . . . until some committee back here in the Congress has had a review of it.
>
> Let the House understand this. If you want the government in business, you put Section 638 in the bill. I do not want the government in business. I want private enterprise in this country to operate; I want small business in this country. Private enterprise has to support this country. You have to get taxes out of business to maintain the Defense Department.

He promised that his Armed Services Committee would act soon on the separate Sikes bill, H.R. 5115, which, he observed, was "almost identical" with Section 638. The Armed Services Committee had given it no further consideration after receiving a routine unfavorable recommendation from the Defense Department.

Democratic Representative Overton Brooks of Louisiana, a member of the Armed Services Committee, supported Vinson. "Is this not just another attempt on the part of the Congress to really run the executive branch of the government? Is this not just another effort to prevent the Defense Department from handling its own executive business, not legislative business but executive business, as was intended to be prevented by the Constitution . . . ?"

Democratic Representative Mendel Rivers of South Carolina, also a member of the Armed Services Committee, felt no qualms about requiring the Defense Department to justify its plans and to submit to legislative judgment. Ordinarily he didn't like legislation in an appropriations bill, he said, "but this is a time when it comes in pretty handy." Valuable knowledge and skills would be lost if Navy manufacturing operations were stopped, particularly the paint factory at Norfolk (where the Navy had developed a special paint for ships' bottoms), the parachute plant at Philadelphia, and the ropewalk at Boston. (Charleston, S. C., Rivers' home town, was the headquarters of the Sixth Naval District, and a naval shipyard and several other Navy installations were located there.)

Rivers proposed an amendment giving the Armed Services Committee rather than the Appropriations Committee the authority embodied in Section 638 to pass on Defense Department shut-down proposals. It was a clear-cut issue as he saw it and stated it:

But I want to tell you this now. This amendment puts this control in our committee where it belongs. It does not hurt the bill that has been referred to. The gentleman from Florida is to be commended. They will not veto this appropriation bill but if we get one [meaning Sikes' bill] out of our committee, God knows where it will end up. Since we are going to legislate, since the Committee on Rules has given them authority to legislate in this bill, let us legislate right. Let us send this [veto authority] to our committee

and the gentleman from Georgia and I will take care of this country, as we have been doing.

I know they are quite intrigued about getting the government out of business, but we do not want to destroy Joe Martin's Navy yard, we do not want to destroy Jim Van Zandt's Navy yard, we do not want to destroy Porter Hardy's Navy yard.[7] And we are not going to ask you to do it under the guise of getting the government out of business when you and I know that that condition does not altogether exist.

Vinson responded that the Armed Services Committee did not want such a veto function—that his committee "should not be required to trespass upon an executive function."

Representative Porter Hardy, a durable and persistent debater and also a member of the Armed Services Committee, then asked Vinson if he were not being inconsistent, citing a 1951 law requiring the approval of the Armed Services Committee for any Defense Department real estate transaction over $25,000. Vinson was not impressed with virtues of consistency.[8] He observed merely that government has the duty, "when it buys anything, to say upon what terms and conditions it buys."

In a bit of joshing, Hardy said his

---

[7] He referred casually to the Boston Naval Base as belonging to House Republican Leader Joseph Martin although it was actually located in Representative O'Neill's district. Representative James Van Zandt (R., Pa.) represented the district in which the Philadelphia Naval Base was located and Representative Porter Hardy (D., Va.) the district containing the Norfolk Naval Base.

[8] In the 1951 debate on that bill, Vinson had denied that it trespassed on execution functions. ". . . instead of delegating to a bureau you delegate it to yourselves, delegate it to a committee here in Congress. . . . It is Government property and Congress should have some control over Government property."

"beloved chairman," Mr. Vinson, "was off the beam" on this issue. Vinson retorted tartly, "I would be on the beam if I had a navy yard in my district, as the gentleman has."

Sikes chided Vinson for his stand. By now he had warmed to the attack. As he described it, voracious big business was pushing the administration to shut down commercial installations so it could grab the plums:

> I am greatly surprised that my wise and astute friend from Georgia could be taken in by such maneuvering. Big business does not want any stumbling blocks placed in the way of the giveaway programs. Big business does not want any possible interference from Congress. . . . They have no idea what language it [Section 638] carries. But apparently they have been told by the Defense Department that Section 638 could upset the gravy train; might put a stop in the handing out of nice, fat, juicy plums. So they, or people in the Department, have been pulling strings all over the nation. As a result a mounting flood of telegrams has been piling up, protesting this section.

Democratic Representative Edward P. Boland of Massachusetts, a member of the full Appropriations Committee, endorsed the Sikes proposal. He said evidence from his own district convinced him Congress should check the shift to private enterprise. Contracts for the Garand M-1 rifle, which was designed and produced at the Springfield Arsenal in his district, had been handed over to private industry. Boland said the International Harvester Company, "one of the beneficiaries of the Defense Department's largesse," was producing the rifle at greater cost and lesser quality.

McCormack took no part in the floor debate.

The Vinson amendment to delete Section 638 was rejected May 12 on a roll call vote of 184 to 202,[9] and the appropriations bill then passed unanimously.

Democratic votes swamped Vinson's amendment; 168 Democrats and 34 Republicans voted against it, while 37 Democrats and 147 Republicans supported it. Some of the votes, as usual, were cast with mixed motives. Republican Representative Gerald Ford, Jr., of Michigan, a member of the Defense Appropriations Subcommittee, supported the Sikes proviso not to protect an installation in his district but rather in the hope that Sikes would vote with the administration in favor of Army manpower cuts. He considered that "a far more important Defense matter." Although he had no agreement with Sikes for exchanging support on the two measures, he voted against the Vinson amendment to attract Sikes' vote on manpower ceilings.

The only Massachusetts congressman who voted for the Vinson amendment was Republican Representative Donald Nicholson, whose district contained a privately-owned rope company. Republican Leader Martin, Democratic Leader McCormack, and Republican Richard B. Wigglesworth, ranking minority member of the Defense Appropriations Subcommittee, all fellow Massachusetts representatives, voted against the Vinson amendment. Martin in the past had frequently spoken out against businesses operated by the government. In 1952 he had criticized past Democratic administrations for allowing the government to invade "the field of business to compete with private enterprise, turning

---

9 The Rivers amendment—to give veto authority to the Armed Services Committee—was a perfecting amendment to the Vinson proposal. Consequently, under parliamentary procedure, when the Vinson amendment failed, the Rivers amendment was also lost.

profits into Government deficits." Early in 1955 he had noted that the Eisenhower administration was "selling the competitive federal operations which thrived on tax dollars to the detriment of free enterprise." [10]

Only two members of the Defense Appropriations Subcommittee voted "against" the recommendation of the committee—that is, against Sikes and for the Vinson amendment: Republicans Harold Ostertag of New York and Glenn Davis of Wisconsin.

The Senate Accepts the Principle

During the Senate Appropriations Committee hearings, from April 4 to June 6, 1955, business groups attacked Section 638 as (1) being contrary to sound administrative principles, (2) inviting political manipulations and logrolling among members of Congress, (3) hindering the commendable administration effort to reduce the degree of government competition with private enterprise, and (4) being technically defective in draftsmanship. Witnesses included representatives of the United States Chamber of Commerce, National Association of Manufacturers, box, ice

---

[10] The situation reminded one observer of the following passage in Alexis de Tocqueville's *Democracy in America* (1835):

"It frequently happens that the members of the community promote the influence of the central power without intending to . . . such persons will admit, as a general principle, that the public authority ought not to interfere in private concerns; but, by an exception to that rule, each of them craves its assistance in the particular concern on which he is engaged and seeks to draw upon the influence of the government for his own benefit, although he would restrict it on all other occasions. If a large number of men applies this particular exception to a great variety of different purposes, the sphere of the central power extends itself imperceptibly in all directions, although everyone wishes it to be circumscribed."

cream and paint manufacturers, warehousemen's, movers' and steamship groups, and nurserymen's, and photogrammetrists' associations.

DeWitt Schieck, executive secretary of the Cordage Institute, testified that his trade group had been trying for a number of years to halt the manufacture of commercial-type rope at the Boston ropewalk. He produced a letter from the Chief of the Navy's Bureau of Ships dated February 9 reporting the decision to close the ropewalk. Schieck said he feared that Section 638 might prevent the Navy from carrying out its decision.

The Department of Commerce officially opposed Section 638 on the ground that it would seriously interfere with the decompetition program. The Secretary of Commerce wrote on May 27 and "strongly recommended" deletion of Section 638.

A number of government employee unions sent letters and telegrams approving congressional scrutiny of Defense Department cutbacks.

The Senate Appropriations Committee reported out a revised version of Section 638 that gave the Defense Department more discretion than did the House draft. Under it, the Department could continue to do away with or transfer facilities in operation 25 years or less. A change in the status of older facilities would have to be cleared with the Appropriations committees of the House and Senate. The Senate bill was the first to specify by name the committees which would hold the veto power.

The Senate debated the Defense Department appropriations bill on June 20. As in the House, a Republican, Senator Karl Mundt of South Dakota, offered an amendment to delete the entire section on the ground that it would impede the government's effort to close "socialistic" enterprises. Enumerating areas of competition, he called the attention of Republican Senator Leverett Saltonstall of Massachusetts to the government's fabricated textile mills which he said might threaten private mills in New England. He also reminded senators from furniture manufacturing areas about furniture manufacturing and upholstering enterprises run by the government.

Democratic Senator A. Willis Robertson of Virginia said the rider was inserted to ensure that such "legitimate Government activities" as Navy yards should not be transferred to private enterprise. He criticized the United States Chamber of Commerce for "misrepresenting" the Hoover Commission's recommendations. He said many of the Chamber's publications implied that the commission wanted an end to all the Defense Department's 2,500 business operations.

Robertson declared: ". . . we are just as dedicated to the principle of private enterprise as is any member of the United States Chamber of Commerce, but we think the people are entitled to the deliberate majority judgment of their duly elected Senators and Representatives. . . ."

Saltonstall, who was Senate Republican whip, and Democratic Senator John F. Kennedy of Massachusetts both supported the principle of congressional review. Kennedy, whose father was a member of the Hoover Commission, spoke in debate of the "struggle to preserve the ropewalk at the Boston Navy Yard. . . ."

The motion to delete Section 638 was defeated 48 to 33.

Conference Committee

The House and Senate versions of Section 638 were not identical, and members from both houses were appointed to a conference committee to attempt to harmonize the differences. The conference committee was unsuccessful, and its report was presented to the House on June 30. Representative Mahon then proposed a draft which was passed immediately by the House of Representatives and accepted by the Senate the same day.

With Mahon's draft the proponents of strict congressional control gained greater congressional control than they had originally asked. The Texas Representative's version allowed either the Senate or the House Appropriations Committee to withhold approval of Defense Department plans to close any facility in operation three years or more. The department had to "justify" its plans at least ninety days before the closing date, and the Appropriations Committee of either house could disallow the proposed shut-down within that period. The provision incorporated a device that made it virtually self-enforcing: no funds were to be used to pay for goods or services if contracts were made without approval of the appropriate committee.

No part of the funds appropriated in this Act may be used for the disposal or transfer by contract or otherwise of work that has been for a period of three years or more performed by civilian personnel of the Department of Defense unless justified to the Appropriations Committees of the Senate and House of Representatives, at least ninety days in advance of such disposal or transfer, that its discontinuance is economically sound and the work is capable of performance by a contractor without danger to the national security; provided, that no such disposal or transfer shall be made if disapproved by either committee within the ninety-day period by written notice to the Secretary of Defense.

The Executive Branch Threatens to Ignore the Rider

When the appropriations bill reached the White House, the President and the Defense Department faced a decision. A veto was never seriously considered despite the fact that the bill contained two provisions offensive to the administration: Section 638 and a provision that barred the purchase of foreign-made spun silk yarn for cartridge cloth.

The Defense Department's General Counsel, closely following the language changes of Section 638 as the bill advanced toward passage, found no cause for alarm. The original House version required "justification" for a proposed shut-down but did not require a waiting period. The Senate version also called for "justification" but incorporated a sixty-day waiting period, regardless of whether the designated committee approved or disapproved. However, the final language enlarged considerably the authority of the appropriations committees and the duties of the Defense Department.

A series of conferences was held immediately after the bill passed. Attending were representatives of Defense's General Counsel, its Supply and Logistics Division (which administered the decompetition program), the White House, and the Justice Department's Office of Legal Counsel. The conferees agreed to draft a presidential message that would strongly condemn Section 638.

The Defense Department did not consider oppressive the requirement of "justifying" shut-downs and transfers. However, it regarded as unconstitutional the authority given either committee to forbid a proposed transfer. Consequently, the President's message concentrated criticism on that language,

and the President served notice that he intended to disregard any committee attempt to block the Defense Department.

President Eisenhower said he would have vetoed the bill but for the department's urgent need for the money. In his message to Congress on July 13, 1955, he said the Attorney General had advised him that Section 638 was unconstitutional. ". . . the Congress has no right to confer upon its committees the power to veto Executive action or to prevent Executive action from becoming effective."

The President went on: "Since the organization of our government, the President has felt bound to insist that Executive functions be maintained unimpaired by legislative encroachment, just as the legislative branch has felt bound to resist interference with its power by the Executive." He considered it a "dangerous precedent" to "acquiesce" in a provision that encroached on executive authority:

To the extent that this section seeks to give to the Appropriations Committees of the Senate and House of Representatives authority *to veto or prevent Executive action, such section will be regarded as invalid* by the executive branch of the government in the administration of H. R. 6042, unless otherwise determined by a court of competent jurisdiction. [Emphasis added.]

The Attorney General issued a statement July 14 bolstering the President's legal position. He pointed out that the practical effect of the proviso was to vest the power of administering the program jointly with the Secretary of

Defense and the Appropriations committees

> . . . with the overriding right to forbid action reserved to the two committees. This, I believe, engrafts executive functions upon legislative members and thus overreaches the permitted sweep of legislative authority. At the same time, it serves to usurp power confided to the executive branch. The result, therefore, is violative of the fundamental constitutional principle of separation of powers prescribed in Articles I and II of the Constitution. . . .

The Attorney General also found Section 638 defective because it gave to committees of Congress power that Congress was unable to delegate. Congress, he said, could certainly enact legislation governing contract making, but

> . . . it may not legally delegate to its committees or members the power to make contracts, either directly or by conferring upon them power to disapprove a contract. . . . Apart from the right of the Congress as a whole with respect to contractual authority, it is quite clear that committees of the Congress do not have the legal capacity to enact legislation.

Finally, the Attorney General concluded from the legislative history that Section 638 was "separable" from the rest of the act, that Congress did not intend the act to lapse if it were not observed in its entirety. "Section 638 is in the nature of an addendum and does not bear upon the Act as a whole or any other particular portion of it." He therefore concluded that the President might subject it to an "informal veto" without "prejudice to the rest."

Congress had a different view. The Capitol Hill reaction was an angry one, and some congressmen said the President himself was guilty of breaching the law—that he was utilizing a device long sought by the executive branch, the item veto. Sikes said it was "unbelievable that the Chief Executive . . . would in this way seek to place himself above the law and to set aside a section of law that he does not like. This is veto by paragraph. . . ." McCormack called it nullification. Democratic Senator Dennis Chavez of New Mexico, Chairman of the Defense Appropriations Subcommittee, observed sarcastically that Eisenhower had enunciated a new principle of statutory construction—that a provision of law duly enacted by Congress "may be considered invalid [by the Chief Executive] until proved otherwise by a court of competent jurisdiction."

The *St. Louis Globe-Democrat* called Section 638 a "shotgun rider." "What congressmen did in this matter was arbitrary, a design to prevent the President or Defense Secretary Wilson from abandoning shipyards, arsenals, even government paint plants from bailiwicks of influential congressmen. It is overtly a political shenanigan."

Porter Hardy of Virginia did more than deplore the action of the Chief Executive. Long a member of the House Government Operations Committee, which receives and checks the reports of the General Accounting Office, Hardy wrote the GAO [11] August 3 to inquire how the Comptroller General planned to handle this announced re-

---

[11] The GAO, an arm of the Congress created by the Budget and Accounting Act of 1921, is charged with making an independent audit of the financial transactions of the executive branch. It has power to disallow expenditures made without proper authorization. It reports to Congress in special and annual reports its findings on the government's financial operations. See ICP Case Number 35, *The General Accounting Office: Two Glimpses,* by Gerald G. Schulsinger (University of Alabama Press, 1956).

bellion. "Specifically, I should like to know what the GAO intends to do in the situation at hand," he wrote. He pointed out that previous comptrollers general "took firm steps"—"even to the extent of withholding funds from the agency involved"—when they learned of an "intention not to conform to duly enacted provisions of law."

On receiving a reply, Hardy issued a press release featuring the Comptroller's stand. On August 17 the Comptroller General said:

> On the fundamental basis that it is for the Congress to say how and on what conditions public monies shall be spent, the position of the GAO, as

the agent of Congress, must be, in this case and always, to accord full effect to the clear meaning of an enactment by the Congress so long as it remains unchanged by legislative action and unimpaired by judicial determination.

Accordingly, you are advised that where we ascertain that expenditures of funds are made in contravention of the provisions of Section 638 of the Department of Defense Appropriations Act, 1956, we will take appropriate action to disallow credit for such expenditures in the accounts of accountable officers, and hold such officials, and their sureties, financially liable for such payments. Also, we will furnish a full report thereon to the Congress for its consideration.

Congress Gets Its Way: The Ropewalk Is Reprieved

The first session of the 84th Congress adjourned August 2, and most members left Washington. Some went home to mend fences, to politick, and to rest. Others traveled to inspect overseas bases, attend international conferences, and see how United States funds were being spent abroad. Committee and office staffs remained on the job in Washington to carry on congressional business.

The Defense Department meanwhile prepared to carry on the decompetition program according to Section 638 as it was to be interpreted by responsible officials in the department. The President and the Attorney General had set the course when they announced a policy of disregarding any committee veto.

The Defense Department's General Counsel worked closely with the Supply and Logistics Division in the interpretation and administration of Section 638. On July 1 the General Counsel had notified Supply and Logistics that

Congress had worked out a new, more demanding version. A month later, on August 1, the General Counsel had given Assistant Secretary Thomas P. Pike a full-dress opinion on the duties that Section 638 imposed on the Supply and Logistics Division. The section applied "to those activities of a manufacturing or commercial nature where the contemplated transfer is to private industry" and not to those operations being brought to a halt. Counsel inferred that without a more precise standard than the phrase "work that has been for a period of three years or more performed by civilian personnel," the Defense Department was obliged to furnish information to Congress on establishments of any size, large or small, whose functions were to be transferred informally or contracted out to private enterprise. This involved 1,755 individual commercial/industrial operations which received appropriated money.

The General Counsel's opinion said

further that the vague language of Section 638 meant that difficulties of interpretation would undoubtedly arise. It also noted the President's message and stated that if Congress disapproved a projected action, "this need not be complied with."

Less than a week after Congress adjourned, the Defense Department filed its first notification to the two committees under Section 638. It requested authority to close the Boston ropewalk and thirteen other installations, including four coffee-roasting plants (at Atlanta, Georgia; Auburn, Washington; Oakland, California; and New York City), two paint manufacturing plants (at Norfolk, Virginia and Mare Island, California), five cobbler shops, a bakery, and a dry-cleaning plant. Up to the time Section 638 was enacted, 171 projects had been discontinued.

Secretary of Defense Charles E. Wilson flicked a defiant phrase in the direction of Congress. He said the act of filing notice with the committees did not "meet the challenge of whether the legislation is legal or not." He said the "issue would have to be met" if permission were refused. An indication that the administration's position was already shifting came when Wilson turned down an opportunity to make a categorical statement that the department would adhere to the position previously enunciated by the President and would refuse to recognize either committee's veto. When a reporter asked if the fourteen installations would definitely be closed even if one of the committees withheld permission, Wilson replied that the question was "too iffy" for him to answer.

The Department Does Explain

The Defense Department notice, dated August 8, consisted of the name of each facility, the number of employees at each, and justification for discontinuance. The notice called attention to the department's general policy as set forth in the Defense Department directive and the Bureau of the Budget bulletin. These had provided that the department would discontinue all commercial or industrial facilities except those furnishing necessary military items, products, or services that could not be obtained from private sources at a reasonable price. With these guidelines in mind, the Supply and Logistics Division had decided to close the ropewalk only after "a careful and painstaking study." The following factors, officials said, had led to the decision: (1) the ropewalk's small production, representing only about four percent of the national output; (2) the steady decline in recent years of the price of commercial rope, making it more economical to buy from private industry; and (3) the depressed condition of the rope industry.

The decision to close the two paint plants was based on a determination that Navy manufacture was not a military necessity and that the commercial paint industry, with its wide resources and high degree of competition, could provide satisfactory paint at reasonable prices.

On coffee roasting, the department said there was no question but that private industry could supply military needs at a reasonable price. Statistics submitted included information that the military roasted only 1.8 percent of the total coffee beans roasted in the United States in fiscal 1955.

Justification for closing other facilities included the availability of commercial products at equal or lower prices and such special factors as the dilapidated condition of some of the bakeries. Employment figures were submitted not only for major facilities such as the ropewalk but also for a dry-

68   *The Constitutional Framework*

cleaning plant at Fort Benning, Georgia, employing no personnel (since the plant operators were carried on personnel records as laundry employees and would continue to man the laundry); for a cobbler shop at Chanute Air Force Base, Illinois, with one part-time employee; and for four other cobbler shops employing five persons in all.

The Defense Department notice was addressed to the chairmen of the House and Senate Appropriations committees. The ninety-day waiting period during which the committees were authorized to act would expire long before Congress was to convene in January.

The chairman of the House Appropriations Committee was away from Washington when the notification came. Key members of the Defense Appropriations Subcommittee, including Chairman Mahon, were out of the country. The following day, August 9, Representative Cannon, Chairman of the full committee, issued a sharp rebuke to the Defense Department from his home in Elsberry, Missouri. He said the notice "puts us at a disadvantage because there are fifty members on my committee, scattered over nearly all of the 48 states. It would be a serious inconvenience to get them together during the recess. This was perfectly obvious to the administration and the administration is being quite inconsiderate of us." He considered taking a plebiscite of committee members by mail or wire but deemed it better to have a quorum physically present in Washington to take formal action, since the section's constitutionality had been called into question.

However, the Chairman of the Senate Appropriations Committee, Democratic Senator Carl Hayden of Arizona, was in Washington, and a way was found to postpone action on the ropewalk. Hayden had not previously exhibited any

interest in the Defense Department's program. After a poll of the committee's 23 members, he announced that there was no objection to any of the projected transfers except the ropewalk. He asked that the status quo be continued at the ropewalk "until the committee will have an opportunity to take up these matters in orderly procedure in January."

During the next two months, staff members of the Defense Appropriations Subcommittee of the House carried on active correspondence with the Supply and Logistics Division to try to get accurate cost figures. They wanted dollars and cents comparisons of the cost of a product turned out at a government factory with that produced by private industry. Dissatisfied with the estimates, Chairman Cannon wrote October 19 chiding the Supply and Logistics Division for its failure to cooperate.[12]

At the same time Cannon formally requested the department to waive the ninety-day time limit within which Section 638 empowered the committees to act. On November 3 the Defense Department agreed to suspend action on the fourteen facilities for another ninety days.

The department filed new notices November 3, November 17, and January 4, 1956 listing 56 additional facilities to be phased out or discontinued. The November 3 letter included a re-

[12] One example of the difficulty of determining accurate government costs showed up in a contract made by the New York Naval Shipyard with an armaments firm for an inspection and overhaul job. The firm requisitioned hundreds of items from the shipyard ranging from nuts and bolts to Diesel oil and metal figure and letter stamps—all these items being carried as overhead costs on the shipyard's budget. Thus, the figures presented a lopsided view of the cost to the government of having private industry carry out the job.

quest to close the chain forge factory in the Boston Navy Yard, two cement mixing plants, three cobbler shops, one acetylene manufacturing plant, six tree and garden nurseries, and nineteen office equipment repair shops. Again, the department supplied full information on each installation, including the fact that six persons worked approximately one hour per day per person at the Navy cement mixing plant at San Diego, making three-fourths of a man day. However, it added that there would be no reduction in personnel with discontinuance of the plant, since certain standby facilities for producing small quantities of concrete were being retained. The Navy cement mixing plant at Keyport, Washington, was shown as employing one person in "indeterminate part-time work."

House Committee
Airs Reasons for Closing

The formal action promised earlier by the chairman of the Senate Appropriations Committee took place early in January 1956. Chairman Mahon of the House Defense Appropriations Subcommittee scheduled three days of hearings starting January 9 to explore the decompetition program and to act on specific facilities. The subcommittee heard testimony from Supply and Logistics officers, members of Congress interested in specific installations, and a variety of private groups and associations.

Deputy Assistant Secretary of Defense (Supply and Logistics) R. C. Lanphier, Jr., presented the case for the Pentagon. Committee members questioned him closely on the instances in which there had been disagreement between the Defense Department and the various services. Lanphier conceded that the Navy had opposed abolition of the ropewalk and the paint plants at Norfolk and Mare Island, and that the Army and Marine Corps had also opposed discontinuation of certain enterprises.

Democratic Representative Daniel Flood of Pennsylvania scolded the military departments for being "intimidated" by their overlord, the Defense Department. He admonished the Army, the Navy, and the Air Force each to maintain its own integrity and to speak in its own interest, not that of the Defense Department or private enterprise.

Five members of Congress from Massachusetts, including Majority Leader McCormack, appeared before the subcommittee to plead for continuation of the ropewalk and the chain forge factory. As lead-off witness, Mc-Cormack emphasized the ropewalk's continuous operation since 1837; its service in production, research and development, and testing; and the plight of the highly-skilled workers facing unemployment. The three Massachusetts Republicans in the group, Representatives William H. Bates, Edith N. Rogers, and Laurence Curtis, were equally fervent in their plea that the ropewalk and chain forge continue as government-operated enterprises. All three had supported the Hoover Commission recommendations and had spoken out frequently against "creeping socialism."

Five persons from the Boston area representing government employee organizations, veterans groups, and labor and fraternal organizations asked the subcommittee to intercede on behalf of the ropewalk and the chain forge. Mc-Cormack personally introduced each witness to the subcommittee.

Two other members of Congress appeared before the subcommittee as friends of the paint plants. Hardy, after a brief plea for the Norfolk plant, introduced five representatives of labor unions at the Norfolk Naval Base. Testimony was developed that the plant produced special-purpose, long-lasting paint for ships' bottoms according to a formula not available to commercial manufacturers. A transfer would mean the Navy would have to turn over the formula to private industry.

Republican Representative John Baldwin of California defended the Mare Island plant in his district on similar grounds. He said that a costly inspection system would have to be developed if private industry took over the manufacture; also the special skills of the fifty employees would be lost. The Defense Department, however, felt the commercial paint industry could supply the Navy's needs without additional cost and without impairment of national security.

Chairman Mahon then asked Baldwin: "Do you believe in socialism or government competition with private business, ordinarily, or not?"

Baldwin said ordinarily he did not believe in socialism but "this plant is only producing a particular specialized type of paint only designed for ships' bottoms."

Mahon then asked if "the chamber of commerce and the Rotary Club and the 'big shots' of your district are going to complain about the fact that you want to continue government competition here?" Baldwin said no.

Mahon continued his questioning. ". . . Are you a Democrat or a Republican, Mr. Baldwin?"

Baldwin: "A Republican, Mr. Chairman."

Mahon: "Do you have a record of opposition to Government interference with private business or competition with private business except in cases where such is urgently necessary, or not? What is your attitude there?"

Baldwin: "I have taken positions in some cases against the Government competition with private business. My general view is that if the private business can actually do whatever is required at no risk or expense to the national defense, then I think that the basic thesis that there should not be Government competition with private industry is sound. But in this case I do not think that this transfer can be made without a risk and expense as to national defense."

Mahon: "I should like to say that I am sure that every member of this committee feels that the Government ought to get out of private business wherever it is reasonably possible. We do not believe in Government competition with private business. I do not, and I do not believe any member of the committee does. It is just a question of what should be done about this particular type of case."

Testimony by members of Congress was brief. None submitted memoranda, tabulations, or statistics dealing with the economic or military contributions of the commercial/industrial facilities in question.

Representatives of the National Coffee Association, the Cordage Institute, National Associated Businessmen, Inc., and the National Paint, Varnish and Lacquer Association supported the Defense Department's request to shut down the installations.

Arguing on behalf of commercial rope manufacturers, the secretary of the Cordage Institute asked that the ropewalk be closed down, preserved, and its production turned over to private industry. He said unrestrained imports of rope and twine had brought domestic industry to the edge of a depression. To bolster his request for relief, he cited the report of the Harden subcommittee of the House Government Operations Committee in 1954; that group had said that faced with a choice of closing a government factory or aiding a taxpaying commercial enterprise, especially a depressed one, "it would seem all too evident that private industry should be favored."

The cordage representative explained that private industry supplied the needs of the Coast Guard and Maritime Commission. He said the ropewalk produced only a small part of the Navy's rope, and private industry the rest.

Representatives of the paint trade supplied information on the principal objections to closing the two Navy plants. One witness extended an offer, originally made two years earlier, to absorb the workers displaced if the paint plants were closed. Another argued that industry could match the so-called secret formula paint since it was able to meet the stiff requirements of Army Ordnance and the Air Force for special coatings. Industry favored continuation of research and development in new coatings by the Navy.

The United States Chamber of Commerce praised the Defense Department for efforts to rid itself of business-type activities but noted that Section 638 was slowing down decompetition. "We recognize that the objective of Congress in adopting Section 638 was to prevent hasty or ill-considered action. We respectfully suggest that such purpose would be far better served . . . if Congress would enact legislation prescribing standards and criteria which should be used as a guide by all administrative departments in their 'decompetition' program."

On January 13, 1956 the Mahon subcommittee formally denied permission to close the ropewalk, the chain manufacturing plant, and the paint plants.

Hearings were held April 16 to take testimony on the Navy chronometer repair shops at Norfolk and Puget Sound. Hardy appeared once again to protest. He charged that private indus-try was unable to do the job with the precision the Navy required. A statement expressing similar views was filed by Democratic Representative Don Magnuson of Washington.

Hardy also proposed enactment of Section 638 on a permanent basis. He added that the reviewing authority should be entrusted not to the Appropriations Committee but to the "legislative committee," by which he meant the Armed Services Committee.

On May 3 Mahon's Defense Appropriations Subcommittee allowed the Defense Department to close 51 facilities (motor pools, tree and garden nurseries, office equipment repair shops, and cobbler shops) but forbade the closing of the two chronometer repair shops and three photographic equipment plants (at Mare Island, California; Puget Sound Naval Shipyard, Bremerton, Washington; and Philadelphia Naval Shipyard). The group stated that considerations of economy governed in the case of the photographic shops. With respect to chronometer repairs, the subcommittee did not feel that commercial companies could do as satisfactory and precise a job as the Navy was doing.

The Appropriations Committee Looks Ahead

The House Appropriations Committee, looking back on a year's test of Section 638, was satisfied with the intent of the law but displeased with the Defense Department's interpretation of it. The committee reprimanded the Department after the Mahon hearings on Section 638.

The Committee is dissatisfied with the manner in which this provision of law has been administered and with the poor judgment shown in certain of the proposals for discontinuing activities made to the Congress thus far. Provisions of the section are recommended for inclusion in the Department of Defense Appropriations bill for 1957.

It was a foregone conclusion that the principle would be retained in the current appropriations bill even though the congressional scrutiny had cost much time and immersion in details. When the full committee reported out the Defense Department Appropriations Act for 1957 (on May 3, 1956), it sternly reproved the Defense Department for burdening it with trifles.

Section 633 [the renumbered 638] is continued in its present form, an adequate and convincing justification for its deletion not having been presented. The Committee is not fully satisfied with the interpretation followed by the Defense Department in the administration of this provision of the 1956 Act. The provision was intended to maintain the broad principle of Congressional review of significant actions in the Department involving the expenditure of funds.

Officials of the Defense Department during the current fiscal year have advised the Committee of proposals to discontinue 112 commercial or industrial-type facilities. In nine instances the Committee has expressed disapproval of such proposed action. The Committee strongly favors the basic principle that free competitive enterprise should be fostered by the Government and disapproved the nine proposals only because it felt that for defense and economy reasons such action was warranted. Indications are that Section 638 has affected relatively a very few people and worked no hardship on the Defense Department.

In ten of the cases submitted employment was on a part-time basis and at least nine cases involved the part-

time employment of one person. In one case the request indicated that the item was so inconsequential the Department could not determine the extent of the work. It would appear that this is stretching the intent of the Congress to unreasonable lengths and that in the future similar inconsequential activities need not be submitted. The Committee recalls one of the oldest maxims of the law, that is, "The law takes no account of trifles."

Several of the Appropriations Committee members went farther. Democratic Representative Harry Sheppard of California said the Defense Department had "prostituted the law. I do not know whether you did it for the purpose of embarrassing Congress or not. You have come up with a lot of shoeshine stands or cobbler shops and items like that. . . ." Republican Representative Errett Scrivner of Kansas was even more forthright. He said that "it was taking a lot of the time of the committees of Congress to determine what seemed to be some very picayunish matters, details that were so minor that they did not merit the attention of this committee at all. . . . The matter of a cobbler shop on some base is altogether too minor to take up the time of the Pentagon and this committee and the corresponding committee of the Senate." Republican Representative Gerald Ford of Michigan said the time the fifteen-man subcommittee spent reviewing Defense Department proposals "was the greatest and most complete waste of time I have ever experienced on that subcommittee."

Yet, although the Defense Department had forced the members of the Appropriations committees to pay the price of scrutinizing much trivial detail, the legislators could claim the larger victory. The threat made earlier by the executive branch—that because the rider invaded the jurisdiction of the executive branch it could be subjected to an "informal veto"—had not been carried out. And the ropewalk and a number of other enterprises had not been closed down.

Rep. Vinson Reaches for Jurisdiction: the "Point of Order" Bill

Several factors brought to a head the differences over jurisdiction between the Appropriations and the Armed Services committees of the House.[13] For one thing, the active involvement of the Appropriations Committee in such minutiae as the life or death of a cobbler shop at Eglin Air Force Base, Florida, did little to add to the dignity of Congress. For another, some of the members of the Appropriations Committee were disgusted with the operation of the rider after a year's test. Finally, the congressmen most anxious to protect local installations did not care where the authority was vested so long as Congress was given an opportunity to check the Defense Department. Since the constitutionality of the rider had been questioned and the method of enactment criticized, a more acceptable instrument was felt to be in order.

When Congress convened in January 1956, Representative Vinson, the doughty Chairman of the House Armed Services Committee, introduced a new bill to return to his committee some of the substantive items of legislation that were being regularly enacted as riders on appropriations bills. H.R. 7992, called the "point-of-order" bill, was similar to the bill Vinson had introduced the year before. The principal difference was Section 27, a provision that called for the repeal of Section 638 of the 1956 Defense Appropriations Act.

On May 8, 1956, when the House Rules Committee scheduled a hearing on a rule for the Defense Department appropriations bill, the Armed Services and the Appropriations committees clashed head on. The new appropriations bill included the language of Section 638 [14] again. Mahon and the ranking Republican, Wigglesworth of Massachusetts, asked again for a rule waiving points of order.

Vinson vigorously opposed granting the rule. He said that by Mahon's own account, the defense appropriations bill contained over fifty legislative items. (None was of major importance. A typical one was a provision enabling military lawyers to attend civilian law schools.) Vinson appealed to the Rules Committee "to protect the jurisdiction of the House Committee on Armed Services."

Vinson then described his own bill, H.R. 7992, which he called a tidier, less controversial way of handling not only the principle of congressional scrutiny in Section 638 but the other perennial legislative details in appropriations bills. He said his own com-

---

[13] The jurisdictional problem is not so acute in the Senate, since there is a good deal of cross-membership between the Senate Appropriations and Armed Services committees. Three members of the Armed Services Committee serve also as ex-officio members of the Senate Defense Appropriations Subcommittee. However, in the House the members of the Appropriations Committee do not serve on any other committee.

[14] The section was numbered 633 in the 1957 act but will continue to be referred to herein as 638.

mittee "would soon report a bill which would enact these legislative provisions, making it wholly unnecessary for them to be improperly included in an appropriations bill."

Vinson felt deeply about the growing amount of military legislation that was being passed each year by attaching riders to appropriations bills. He was genuinely concerned that the method was unconstitutional, and he felt equally strongly that the military items should be acted on by his own committee rather than the Defense Appropriations Subcommittee. In that way, controversial items would be accepted or rejected on their merits, not passed on as addenda to appropriations bills. However, Vinson's appearance was to no avail. The Rules Committee granted the rule waiving points of order. A repetition of the previous year's events seemed to be imminent.

The day after the Rules Committee hearing, Vinson convened the Armed Services Committee to act on his "point of order" bill, H.R. 7992. The only witness at the hearing was Thomas P. Pike, Assistant Secretary of Defense (Supply and Logistics). His position was friendly to the bill, and he supported the repeal of Section 638. Members of the Armed Services Committee listened while the Assistant Secretary spoke of the difficulty the Defense Department had encountered in complying with Section 638. Then, as Pike moved away from the witness table to the rear of the hearing room, the committee amended the Vinson bill in such a way as to alter drastically the shape and effect of the simple repealer originally embodied in Section 27. The new language reinstated congressional authority to veto the transfer of specific commercial/industrial enterprises but gave to the entire Congress the authority previously lodged with the Appropriations committees.

Under the terms of this carefully drawn amendment, the Defense Department was required to file with the Speaker of the House and the President of the Senate any proposal to "transfer by contract" any commercial establishment in operation for three years and employing as many as ten people. During the ensuing sixty days of "continuous session" any member could propose a resolution disapproving the action. The resolution would be referred to the "appropriate committee" which was to be the same committee in every instance: the subject matter being the Defense Department, the review committee would be the Armed Services Committee and not the Defense Appropriations Subcommittee. If the committee failed to act within ten days, the resolution could be brought to the floor as privileged matter and debated. As one of the Armed Services Committee attorneys explained, if either body disapproved, "that's the end of it."

The term "transfer by contract" was used, Armed Services Committee counsel explained, with the ruling of the Comptroller General in mind. The Defense Department was presumed to have ample executive authority to curtail any operation by reducing or abolishing it. However, under Section 27 the Defense Department would be required to get permission from Congress to abolish an activity and then contract with private industry for performing the same function. Without such permission, the Comptroller General would disallow funds to pay the bills for the work done by private industry. Counsel explained that the department could halt any commercial/industrial operation with or without Section 638 on the statute books "but if it stops it and is required to go into the private industry market to get that product, the present language prevents the expenditure of appropriated funds to get the product from private industry."

The language of Section 27 was based on established precedents. The Rubber Disposal Act of 1948 and the Reorganization Act of 1949 gave Congress authority to act as final arbiter of proposed executive action. Vinson explained that the Speaker of the House himself was responsible for the draftsmanship of the Rubber Act. The Speaker had proposed an amendment transferring authority to act from the Public Works Committee to the entire House.

Vinson's view of the irresponsibility and unconstitutionality of giving Congress the last word on administrative matters was unchanged. However, he was willing to go along with the sentiment of members of the Armed Services Committee, and, as he gauged it, there was strong feeling that Congress should have authority to block the closing of certain facilities. Committee members Hardy, Rivers, Philip J. Philbin (D., Mass.), and Bates pressed hard for retaining congressional authority in some form.

The language of Section 27 was the work of the committee, and Vinson supported the committee position.[15]

---

[15] Close associates say that once the Armed Services Committee takes a position, Vinson will support it whole-heartedly and fight for it regardless of his own convictions on the matter. "If the Committee's position is 180 degrees away from the Chairman, he will go to the floor and fight as though he were the author of the provision in dispute."

Section 27 was intricately drawn to (1) meet some of the constitutional objections to Section 638 raised by President Eisenhower in 1955, (2) give every member of Congress an equal chance to block a shut-down in his own district, and (3) defend the jurisdiction of the Armed Services Committee.

Assistant Secretary Pike, present all the while, was asked his opinion of the change. Answering cautiously, he said he judged that "it would lessen the administrative burden both on the members of Congress and this committee as well as upon my staff." He agreed with the principle of transferring authority from one committee to the entire Congress.

Vinson told the committee that the subject of Section 27 had been broached with Majority Leader McCormack, who "manifested a great deal of interest in it." He said there had been some diplomatic exchanges with Sikes of House Appropriations and that Section 27 was all right with Sikes. Vinson then gave his blessing to the appropriations bill, as it would be altered by the deletion of Section 638; he said he thought that with this correction, the Armed Services Committee could support it. He said it was certainly "improved by putting in what we have done here today . . . because then the President won't have any ground to talk about vetoing."

The committee, with twenty members present, reported H.R. 7992 unanimously.

The House Removes the Rider

Congress often dawdles over appropriations bills, sometimes not completing them until after the beginning of the new fiscal year. However, that spring the appropriations bills were moving rapidly through the House. On May 8, 1956 the Defense Department appropriations bill got a rule. On May 10 the bill came to a vote. (The action of the

Armed Services Committee did not affect the appropriations bill that faced the House. Section 638 was in the bill, and its repeal or retention was up to the members of the House.) At least one hour of the six hours of debate on the $33.7 billion defense appropriations bill was devoted to Section 638.

This time House Republicans were organized to cut Section 638 out of the bill. The Republican leadership acted through Leo Allen of Illinois, ranking minority member of the Rules Committee, who moved to strike out Section 638. He was strongly supported by Les Arends of Illinois, GOP whip; Mrs. Marguerite Church of Illinois; Davis of Wisconsin; Dixon of Utah; Richard H. Poff of Virginia; Thomas M. Hand of New Jersey; Charles B. Brownson of Indiana; and George Meader of Michigan, all Republicans. When T. B. Curtis of Missouri observed with regret that only Republicans were opposing Section 638, Vinson rose to his feet and observed with dignity: "I have a very bad throat. I am for the Allen amendment. I only wish I could speak on it."

The Republicans offered five arguments against Section 638:

1. *The Hoover Commission argument that government-in-business was an anomaly in a capitalistic, free-enterprise system.* The point was made by Mrs. Church and Brownson. Mrs. Church called Section 638 a "roadblock . . . against the progress of the Defense Department in eliminating and turning over to private enterprise its unnecessary business and industrial-type activities." She said she herself had introduced 77 bills during the 84th Congress to carry out Hoover Commission recommendations. Brownson said Section 638 was "socialistic." He indicated that the Hoover Commission recommendations had had a powerful effect in his district. "My constituents

are writing me daily in increasing numbers. They are clamoring and demanding economy and efficiency in government to pave the way for tax reductions."

2. *Straightforward support of the administration.* This was represented by the Allen-Arends axis. Allen said that by retaining Section 638 ". . . we force the Department of Defense to operate and supervise governmental enterprises despite the fact that that department says they do not need them, they do not want them, and that certain of those enterprises are inefficient and unprofitable." Arends said Section 638 "retards, delays, and obstructs the splendid job our Secretary of Defense has been doing in taking the government out of business in competition with private enterprise. And, in my judgment, taking the federal government out of those enterprises and activities that rightfully belong to private enterprise is one of the major undertakings of the present administration."

3. *The view that the Armed Services Committee should have the job.* Arends, a member of the committee, also spoke to this point.

4. *The general inappropriateness of giving such authority to a congressional committee.* Davis of Wisconsin said the rider was "harmful" because "it is an open invitation to backscratching among members of the Appropriations Committee." He also said it was "incongruous" that the committee appropriated $33.7 billion "under terms of great latitude and discretion and yet we will not permit the Secretary of Defense to exercise his judgment on the question of a ropewalk or a telephone exchange."

5. *The loss of congressional dignity, prestige, and power involved in performing such tedious, administrative jobs.* Meader said Congress should not try "to engage in ministerial and ex-

ecutive activities, including day-to-day decisions of the character here involved. In fact, our attempt to invade executive functions and to assume them makes it less likely that we can recapture the policy-making authority which we have lost, because our time is limited and there is just so much we can do."

Mahon announced that he favored the amendment, after originally opposing it in committee the year before. Congress appropriated the money for establishment of the Defense Department's business operations, he reasoned, and "Congress should have some say-so in what is done with these activities. Expensive government machinery should not be abandoned and heavy losses to the taxpayers incurred without Congress having an opportunity to take action." However, he stated that the government, with or without the amendment, regrettably, was not making great headway in divesting itself of its business ventures. "If you knock the action out of the bill . . . please do not think that free enterprise, which we all represent, has won a signal victory."

The only Democrat active in debate was Sikes. Vinson pleaded his bad throat; McCormack abstained; Hardy said he was indifferent to whether the authority were exercised by the Appropriations or the Armed Services Committee.

Sikes contented himself with saying that the past year's results had demonstrated the value of congressional scrutiny. He said he opposed the Allen amendment but told colleagues that the Armed Services Committee had taken action to claim the authority in the name of jurisdictional propriety. "If you want the final measure on this, the House Committee on Armed Services has prepared a bill, and will present it shortly, which carries on this same

operation. It is in different language, yes, but it will carry on the same activity. . . ."

The House dropped Section 638 on a roll call vote of 222 to 156. Only 23 Republicans left the fold to join 133 Democrats in voting to retain Section 638 and thus to keep the authority with the Appropriations Committee. There were 158 Republicans and 64 Democrats who voted in favor of the Allen amendment which would eliminate Section 638.

Only two members of the Massachusetts delegation, Joseph Martin and Donald Nicholson (both Republicans), voted to strike Section 638.

All the Democrats on the Defense Appropriations Subcommittee voted to retain the section. They were joined by two Republicans, Wigglesworth of Massachusetts and Scrivner of Kansas. The subcommittee's other four Republicans (Ostertag, Davis, Ford, and Miller) voted to scrap Section 638.

Chairman Cannon of the full Appropriations Committee voted to retain Section 638 while John Taber, ranking minority member, voted to strike.

Thirteen of the seventeen Republican members of the Armed Services Committee voted for the Allen amendment. Two members (Bates of Massachusetts and William Bray of Indiana) voted against it. The three others did not vote.

Democrats on the Armed Services Committee split, with nine members for and nine against. However, the ranking Democrats (Vinson, Brooks of Louisiana, Paul Kilday of Texas, and Carl Durham of North Carolina) supported the Allen amendment. Rivers and Hardy voted against it.

The House vote to delete Section 638 from the appropriations bill relieved the Defense Department of specified legal duties. However, the Senate

Appropriations Committee noted its continuing interest in the decompetition program by including an obiter dictum paragraph in its report on defense appropriations for 1957. In a report of June 16, 1956 the committee directed the department to continue to report plans for closing commercial facilities. The committee noted that the House had deleted the veto authority, and so it directed the department to continue to maintain commercial/industrial operations "unless such disposal or transfer is economically justified, and unless no increased costs result. The Defense Department is directed to report periodically to this committee on actions taken regarding such disposal or transfer."

The Vinson Bill

The May 10 House vote to shear the supervisory authority away from the Appropriations Committee left the Congress without authority to oversee the Defense Department's decompetition drive. Four days later, the Vinson bill was reported to the House and referred to Committee of the Whole. Finally on July 21 it came up for consideration. Vinson rose to explain it.

There was nothing new or controversial in 29 of the bill's 33 sections, he said, as these were taken directly from appropriations bills of recent years. He admitted Section 27 was "controversial," but he said he hoped it would not "obscure the more important objective of this legislation.[16] The House Armed Services Committee is trying to protect its jurisdiction."

Vinson referred only once to the fact that the previous year he had proposed striking Section 638 from the appro-

priations bill. "While I am sure it was not intended . . . ," he said, "a strict legal interpretation of the language [of Section 638] required the Defense Department to report commercial activities which were being performed by only one civilian employee of the Defense Department. So it was quite onerous to both the Defense Department and the Appropriations Committees."

Vinson stressed that Section 27 gave every member of Congress an equal chance to be heard on a scheduled shut-down. ". . . we are on sound ground on the procedure, and the proper way to run the Department is to give the Congress in the well of the House an opportunity to say whether or not this or that installation should be closed."

Rather than accuse the Appropriations Committee of jurisdictional raiding, he laid the blame on the Defense Department. Section 27 was necessary, he said, to keep the Defense Department from legislating in appropriations bills "when it suits their convenience and meets with the approval of the Appropriations Committees."

Sheppard of California, chairman of the Navy panel of the Appropriations Committee, also spoke on this point. Sheppard said he had recently had to rebuke the Navy for interlarding its budget requests with legislative details. He said he had warned the Secretary of the Navy "that if all his presentations coming up in the next fiscal year budget are not cleared of legislative requirements, they would not get a quarter for it."

When Curtis of Missouri asked how the executive department felt about congressional authority to supervise, Vinson responded that ". . . the department was never consulted about it. . . ." Curtis persisted. He said he understood the administration strongly opposed the proviso. "The gentleman's

---

[16] Section 27 gave to the entire Congress the authority which, in the days of Section 638, had been lodged in the appropriations committees.

statement as to the attitude of the administration," Vinson said, "is the first information I have that they have expressed any opinion pro or con." Curtis retorted that the President's message of last year "opposed this very principle."

McCormack praised Section 27 as "a sound protection. It preserves the dignity of Congress and enables us to have a voice in the determination of these activities which go back through the years." He said many members shared his view. Several, he said, reported to him that they had voted to strike Section 638 only because they knew the principle was incorporated in the Armed Services bill.

Tempers became frayed in the course of the afternoon as the debate wore on. O'Neill of Massachusetts said Leo Allen certainly couldn't have any "federal installations in his district because, surely, if he has or if he had had, he would not be in opposition to this section." Taber, member of Congress since 1923 and an unswerving supporter of economy, declared that in spite of "a great big setup in my district," he had never opposed the transfer of any facility to private enterprise. Bates, too, declared his objectivity. "May I advise the committee that I have no installation in my district, but as a member of the House Committee on Armed Services I believe it is my responsibility to see what the military do with such projects as these."

Mrs. Church said she felt that she must have been "magically asleep for about two months and have just awakened and am still listening to a debate on the floor of the House on the 10th of May. . . ." She said she preferred an outright grant of authority to the Armed Services Committee to approve or disapprove. "Not that I do not trust the membership but . . . I can imagine no Member of the House who could very easily refuse to introduce a resolution . . . against the closing down of an activity within his own area."

The debate took place on Saturday afternoon, but the actual vote was postponed. When it came on the following Tuesday, the House approved Section 27 on a record vote of 201 to 185. Party lines held firmly: 179 Democrats and 22 Republicans joined to pass the measure; 16 Democrats and 169 Republicans voted against it. Representative Vinson's bill itself was passed on a voice vote.

Democratic members of the Armed Services Committee approved Section 27 unanimously. They were joined by four Republicans: Leroy Johnson of California, Bates of Massachusetts, Bray of Indiana, and Wilson of California.

The Defense Appropriations Subcommittee members scattered their votes. Wigglesworth and six Democrats voted to retain Section 27; Mahon and four Republicans voted to strike it.

Vinson's Bill Dies in the Senate

There was no companion "point of order" bill in the Senate. The House bill was referred to the Senate on July 25. Even though adjournment was looming, a sudden storm of messages urging Senate rejection of Section 27 deluged the Senate Armed Services Committee. Most of them appeared to have been instigated by the Citizens Committee for the Hoover Report, which considered Section 27 as baleful as Section 638. Senator Saltonstall of Massachusetts, ranking Republican on the committee, was the target of a number of the protest messages. He replied to their authors that he did not believe the Senate Armed Services Committee would report out the bill. He was right. Congress adjourned two days later on January 27, and the "point of order" bill died in committee.

Epilogue

With Section 638 stricken and the "point of order" bill a lost cause, Congress no longer possessed statutory authority to prevent the Defense Department from closing industrial/commercial installations. However, even without such formal authority, Congress continued to exercise influence against shut-downs of installations with strong local support. One means was an instruction issued by the Senate Appropriations Committee in its June 1956 report on appropriations for the Defense Department for fiscal 1957. The committee called on the department to maintain all facilities except those whose transfer to private enterprise could be justified on economic grounds. This instruction was, technically, without legal force, but the department could not ignore such an instruction from Congress—particularly from a committee that processed its appropriation requests. Yet, not long after the Senate committee insisted on clear economic justification, the Defense Department received from the Bureau of the Budget a directive announcing that it was now the position of the administration that the criterion of lower costs was no longer to be used as a fundamental reason for continuing or discontinuing a government enterprise. The Budget Bureau gave several reasons for withdrawing the economy criterion: (1) Since government enterprises paid no taxes, their costs were not comparable with corresponding business costs. (2) Government accounts were kept in a different manner from business accounts, and comparisons were difficult and often misleading. (3) "Above all, the decision whether to continue or discontinue a government activity solely on an ap-

parent cost basis runs counter to our concept that the government has ordinarily no right to compete in a private enterprise economy."

Even though Section 638 and the "point of order" bill were not in effect, Defense Department officials could not forget the possibility that congressmen, if aroused over the shut-down of local installations, might vote to insert similar provisions as riders to future appropriation bills. In fact, renewal of congressional veto power appeared as a threat again in 1957. The military public works authorization bill reported by the House Armed Services Committee in June of that year contained a section almost identical to Section 27 of Vinson's 1956 "point of order" bill. It would have compelled the Defense Department to report to Congress on plans to close commercial establishments, and gave either House power to veto such plans. A motion to strike the section was defeated on the floor of the House, but the Senate bill failed to include similar language, and the section was dropped in conference.

Defense Department officials thus faced conflicting pressures. The Defense Department was bound by administration policy, by Hoover Commission recommendations, and by its own previous directives to reduce drastically the number of its commercial/industrial enterprises. These formal mandates were continually reinforced by policing and pressure from the Citizens Committee for the Hoover Report and various business groups. Also the Senate's Small Business Committee and the House Government Operations Committee had gone on record some years earlier in favor of eliminating without delay operations that competed with private enterprise. On the other hand, Defense Department officials had learned that some congressmen and local business groups who vigorously supported "decompetition" programs, would strongly resist the closing down of installations that threatened to deprive their localities of government installations and payrolls. And Defense Department officials had learned that, if it chose, Congress could make its will felt in preventing the shut-down of local installations.

In the events of 1955–1956 described above, it seemed clear to many observers that the Defense Department had backed away from the policy of defiance enunciated by the President in his July 1955 message. The President had indicated that the administration would comply with the notification requirement but would disregard any committee attempt to block a proposal to shut down an installation. But when powerful congressional interests had supported continued operation of the ropewalk, the chain forge factory, and the paint plants at Norfolk and at Mare Island, and when these congressional interests had strengthened their position by securing support from the Comptroller General, the administration appeared to have given in. By the end of the year the ropewalk and the Boston chain forge factory as well as the paint plants at Norfolk and Mare Island were still in operation.

On the other hand, the Department of Defense took the position that it had not departed from the standard set down in the President's message. After Congress had refused permission to close the ropewalk and the other installations, the department, a spokesman maintained, had not given in. It had "reconsidered" its plans and had concluded that wisdom dictated continued operation of the controversial installa-

tions. In a letter to the author, dated September 31, 1959, the Acting Assistant Secretary of Defense, Supply and Logistics, explained the Defense Department's position in the following manner:

There was no decision made subsequent to the President's signing the Appropriations Bill which was contrary to the position stated by him at that time. There was no reason during the period that Section 638 was applicable of not advising the committee of plans to discontinue or curtail commercial-industrial type activities. Following advice from the [House Appropriations] Committee, we did on occasion, where the facts presented by the Committee warranted, give additional consideration to certain proposed discontinuancies. In the case of the Ropewalk and the chain manufacturing plants, further study resulted in their being continued as government-owned and operated activities, but on a substantially curtailed basis. In the case of the paint factories it was found that private suppliers could meet the needs of the national defense, and these activities were discontinued with the exception of a small activity retained for purposes of research and development.

The Department of Defense officials did what they could to steer a course between the conflicting pressures. Although they sometimes deferred to the wishes of members of Congress on specific installations, by December 31, 1957, the Department reported that 585 installations had been, or were scheduled to be, closed. By June 1958 it succeeded in closing the paint plants at Norfolk and Mare Island. The ropewalk proved more resistant. The department could only curtail its operations. The ropewalk was continued as a research and development facility, with its production limited to the amount necessary to carry on experimental and testing functions.

TWO

The Courts and Civil Rights

CASE **3**

The Miracle Case: The Supreme Court and the Movies

ALAN F. WESTIN

Introduction

This is an account of a United States Supreme Court case—called *Burstyn v. Wilson*—about state censorship of the motion picture, *The Miracle*. The narrative traces the litigation from the start of the dispute (between the Paris Theater in New York City and the City Commissioner of Licenses), through city and state agencies and courts, to the Supreme Court decision in 1952. Then the story describes the effects of the court's decision on movie houses, local censorship boards, and courts throughout the nation. Although the account ends early in 1961, the issues raised are likely to be controversial for a good many years to come.

This study raises questions about censorship of motion pictures by government agencies and about the way in which private groups associate themselves with constitutional cases as they progress upward through the courts. It depicts the way in which judges balance values in deciding cases—precedent versus social change, freedom of expression versus community morals, religious freedom versus state enforcement of religious doctrines, and "subjective" judicial rules versus "objective" standards.

The Making of a Constitutional Law Case

In 1950 over 80,000,000 admissions per week were recorded in American motion picture houses. The 16,000 "permanent four wall" theaters and several thousand drive-in establishments which attracted these crowds did a gross annual business of $1,247,000,000. As a whole, the movie industry employed over 200,000 persons and had a capital investment of over $2,500,000,000. Over 420 new feature films were placed on the market

83

in 1950, about sixty of which were foreign made.

In 1947 and 1948 the movie industry had been shaken by the widely-publicized hearings on "Communist influence" in Hollywood held by the House Committee on Un-American Activities. The year 1950, however, was more calm, despite a proposal by Senator Edwin Johnson of Colorado that a system of federal licensing and censorship be instituted to keep film-making "moral"—a proposal which stirred no action in Congress. But regardless of the fact that its political difficulties had subsided, the industry found 1950 no better than an average year as far as protests, bannings, and picketings of "controversial" movies were concerned. The censorship boards of six states— Kansas, Maryland, New York, Ohio, Pennsylvania, and Virginia—continued busily about their work of screening and licensing films; some 150 to 200 cities also maintained review boards operated by special commissions, mayors, police chiefs, or individual censors. Altogether the movie industry paid about $1,800,000 annually in fees and expenses to comply with state and local censorship boards.

In 1950 the New York Board of Regents refused exhibition licenses to *Birth of a Baby, A Bullet for Stefano, Flesh Will Surrender, The Paris Waltz, A Royal Affair, Scandals of Clochemerle,* and *The Sinners.* A host of Southern cities from Tennessee to Texas banned *Pinky* and *Lost Boundaries,* two films dealing sympathetically with the Negro's problems under segregation. In Chicago another film involving race relations, *No Way Out,* was shelved temporarily on orders of the police chief because it showed violence between Negroes and whites. The protests of several Jewish groups against the "anti-Semitic overtones" of the British film *Oliver Twist* caused its

producer to withdraw that film for a year. The American Humane Association called for suppression of scenes involving cruelty to animals in the movie *The Brave Bulls. I Was a Shoplifter* was banned in Atlanta because the censors thought "it gave too much information to amateur shoplifters." Two widely acclaimed Italian imports, *Bicycle Thief* and *Bitter Rice,* were denied exhibition in many cities, with Catholic War Veteran and National [Catholic] Legion of Decency protests leading the attack. In New Jersey, American Legion pickets were successful in persuading a number of movie exhibitors not to show any films of Charlie Chaplin because of his "left-wing affiliations."

Nor were these all the disputes that year. Newsreels shown in Ohio were censored by the Division of Film Censorship. The National Association for the Advancement of Colored People protested against the showing of *Birth of A Nation* in several communities on the ground that the film's portrayal of Reconstruction was "anti-Negro." Ingrid Bergman's affair with Italian movie producer Roberto Rosselini, her divorce from her American husband, and the early birth of Rosselini's child stirred much national comment and placed a number of both Bergman's and Rosselini's films in difficulty. *Stromboli,* produced by Rosselini and starring Bergman, had been approved by censorship boards before the disclosure of their personal affairs, but it was re-examined and banned in several cities after local church groups attacked the "lax morals" of the film's principals.

Despite these and other incidents indicating that the risks in "controversial" movie-making were by no means gone, most observers of the motion picture industry remarked that films from 1945 to 1950 had been exploring important social issues more frequently than they had in the 1930s. *Lost Weekend* in 1945 had dealt with alcoholism. *The Best Years of Our Lives* in 1946 had probed the conflicts facing returning war veterans. *Gentleman's Agreement* in 1947 was an outspoken criticism of anti-Semitism. *All the King's Men* in 1949 was an acid portrait of the Huey Long type of political machine. Each of these motion pictures had won an Academy Award as best picture of the year and had made profits for its producers. Encouraged by public response to frank movies dealing with formerly "untouchable" problems, the movie industry was reported in October 1950 to be readying a test case to raise before the United States Supreme Court the question of the constitutionality of state and city censorship of movies.

The Legal
Status of Movies, 1915–1950

The position of motion pictures in American law was governed by a 1915 decision of the United States Supreme Court, *Mutual Film Corporation v. Industrial Commission of Ohio*.[1] A description of the state of movie-making and exhibition in that era will help the reader to understand the court's ruling.

The first "moving picture" was seen in 1896. The next decade saw the rise of arcades where customers looked into individual viewers. The modern industry began in 1905 with the success of the "nickelodeon" projection theater. By 1908, 10,000 nickelodeons were showing one-reel films of various kinds to an audience of millions. Subjects ranged from literary films such as *Uncle Tom's Cabin* and travel sagas such as *Wonders of Canada* to such spicy items as *A Hot Time in Atlantic City, The Bride and Groom's Visit to the New*

York Zoological Park and *Beware: My Husband Comes.*

About 1910 multi-reel films were introduced by the major producers, and the day of the "feature film" began. Social and political topics were explored in *Capital vs. Labor, The Factory Girl,* and *Russia, Land of Oppression.* Patriotic films such as *The Hand of Uncle Sam* occupied the bill along with moral and family-theme features such as *The Drunkard's Reformation, Gold is Not All,* and *The Life of Moses.* Comedies ranged from Mack Sennett's Keystone cops to the early works of Charlie Chaplin. Many feature films continued the tradition of risqué comedy and spicy drama.

By 1907–1910 some civic and religious groups had launched a drive for protective censorship of both nickelodeons and features. In 1907 Chicago set up the first official censorship board, under the Chief of Police, and banned *The James Boys.* In 1911 Pennsylvania became the first state to require licensing of films. By 1915 two other states had followed suit—Ohio and Kansas— and several dozen municipalities joined the march, including Kansas City, Mo.; Houston, Tex.; Pasadena, Calif.; and Seattle, Wash. Producers with substantial investments in the films which had encountered censorship bans were not long in challenging such government licensing in the courts.

The *Mutual Film* case in 1915 involved Ohio's statute requiring all films to be submitted for approval to a Board of Censors under the State Industrial Commission. The board passed only films found to have "a moral, educational, or amusing and harmless character." Mutual Film Company sought an injunction in the federal district court for northern Ohio to prevent the state from enforcing this law. The company argued that the Ohio statute interfered with interstate commerce and

---

[1] 236 U. S. 230 (1915).

that pre-exhibition censorship was a denial of freedom of speech and press protected by the Ohio Constitution. (No question of *federal* free speech rights could be raised since it was only after a 1925 case, *Gitlow v. United States* (268 U. S. 652), that the speech and press guarantees of the First Amendment were held to apply to state action, through the due process clause of the Fourteenth Amendment.)

In a unanimous decision the United States Supreme Court denied the exhibitor's contentions. The opinion stressed that films were capable of being "used for evil," and it was "against that possibility" that "the statute was enacted." As for freedom of speech, the court said:

Are moving pictures within the principle [of free speech], as it is contended they are? They, indeed, may be mediums of thought, but so are many things. So is the theater, the circus, and all other shows and spectacles, and their performances may be thus brought by the like reasoning under the same immunity from repression or supervision as the public press. . . . [But] it cannot be put out of view that *the exhibition of moving pictures is a business, pure and simple, originated and conducted for profit, like other spectacles, not to be regarded, nor intended to be regarded by the Ohio Constitution, we think, as part of the press of the country, or as organs of public opinion.* They are mere representations of events, of ideas and sentiments published and known; vivid, useful, and entertaining, no doubt, but as we have said, capable of evil, having power for it, the greater because of their attractiveness and manner of exhibition. It was this capability and power, and it may be in experience of them, that induced the state of Ohio, in addition to prescribing penalties for immoral exhibitions . . . to require censorship before exhibition. . . . We cannot regard this as

beyond the power of government. [Emphasis added.]

The same day, the court upheld a Kansas movie censorship statute. Although the decision simply approved the state's general police power, one of the grounds for denial of a license in this Kansas statute was that a film was "sacrilegious."

Between 1915 and 1950 the motion picture industry underwent great changes, from the introduction of sound in 1926 (and the censorship problems that it raised) to the introduction of a self-regulation system for Hollywood by its own detailed Production Code Administration. By 1950, six out of 48 states had enacted movie censorship laws, and between 150 and 200 municipalities had municipal censorship programs.

In the years after 1915 the United States Supreme Court had adhered steadily to the Mutual Film rule, usually by refusing to hear cases attacking the status of state or local movie censorship boards. However, in a 1947 decision, *United States v. Paramount Pictures,*[2] involving an anti-trust action for monopolistic practices in producer-distributor relations, Justice William O. Douglas had commented in the course of his opinion for the court, "We have no doubt that moving pictures, like newspapers and radio, are included in the press whose freedom is guaranteed by the First Amendment." This was a casual remark not essential to the decision of the case—what lawyers call a "dictum." But it seemed to encourage the view that, if a movie censorship case could be brought before the Supreme Court of the 1950s, the basis of the *Mutual Film* case might be overturned, and, with movies regarded as more than "a business, pure and simple," the court might consider what, if any, prior

----

2 334 U. S. 131.

state restraints on movie exhibition were constitutional.

Enter The Miracle

This was the setting when, on December 12, 1950, a movie called *Ways of Love* opened at the Paris Theater, a small foreign film house on West 58th Street in New York City. *Ways of Love* was a grouping of three short films into one feature. Two of these were French-made: *A Day in the Country,* based upon a story by Guy de Maupassant and directed by Jean Renoir; and *Jofroi,* directed by Marcel Pagnol. The third was an Italian picture written and directed by Roberto Rosselini from a story by Federico Fellini and featuring the volatile and celebrated Italian actress, Anna Magnani. Each film was presented as illustrating a different aspect of love and was introduced by a frame showing alternative definitions of the word "love" from the dictionary. All three films had English subtitles. *A Day in the Country* and *Jofroi* were received warmly by the critics and by the public, and at no time did they create a controversy. It was only *The Miracle* that caused explosions.

The Miracle was in four scenes and ran for forty minutes. A demented peasant woman living in a primitive Italian village is tending her goats when a bearded stranger strolls by. She thinks he is St. Joseph, returning to earth to bring her "grace." She gives him food and wine, drinks wine herself, and the scene closes with the clear implication that he seduces her. Toward the end of this episode, a deep voice on the soundtrack recites from the Bible (Matthew 1:20): "Behold, the angel of the Lord appeared unto him in a dream, saying, Joseph, thou son of David, fear not to take unto thee Mary thy wife: for that which is conceived in her is of the Holy Ghost." In the second scene,

months later, she talks with two priests about the "miracle" which has happened to her. Later, while dancing after a church service, she faints, and the village women learn she is pregnant. In scene three, she refuses to work because she must "honor" the coming child. She is taunted by the young people of the village, who put a basin on her head, sing a religious hymn to "Mary," and throw her out of town with a mocking religious procession. In the final scene, after living alone for months in a grotto, the demented woman goes to an outbuilding of an abandoned but locked church on a mountainside, and in a moment of combined pain and religious ecstasy, delivers her own child.

The Miracle played to mixed notices. Howard Barnes of the *New York Herald Tribune* wrote: "The less said about *The Miracle* the better, except that it would be wise to time a visit to the Paris in order to skip it. Rosselini has imagined that an idiot shepherdess meets a handsome stranger whom she mistakes for St. Joseph and bears him a child. The Italian director has dragged out the theme with a great deal of revolting attitudinizing. Anna Magnani has the bad luck to play the subject of the supposed miracle and Federico Fellini is guilty of having written the tasteless script as well as having acted in it. Altogether it leaves a very bad taste in one's mouth." Rose Pelswick in the *Journal-American* echoed the view that the film was "in questionable taste" but added that it offered "a striking performance by Rosselini's pre-Bergman star, the fiery Anna Magnani." Alton Cook in the *World-Telegram and Sun* considered *The Miracle* as "charged with the same overwrought hysteria that ran through [Rosselini's] *Stromboli. . . .* In addition to the unrelieved tone of hysteria, the picture has an unpleasant preoccupation with filth and squalor. The verdict in this corner on *Ways of Love* is two excellent films and one exceedingly trying experience." Archer Winsten in the *New York Post* found Miss Magnani's performance "profoundly impressive" but remarked that "the parallels with Christ's conception, birth in a manger and hard times give this picture implications and overtones that could well prove offensive to the religious. . . ."

Praise came from Bosley Crowther in the *New York Times*. Calling *The Miracle* the "most overpowering and provocative" of the three films and "probably the most intense dramatic piece that we have had from the sensational Italian director," Crowther predicted this would "certainly cause a lot of stir."

Played by Anna Magnani with a passion and fluid forcefulness as could only come from a Latin who is inspired yet fully disciplined, this bold and extravagant character is a creature of such tragedy—and it is so subtly framed by Rosselini—that she may be interpreted in two ways. She may be logically accepted as a symbol of deep and simple faith, horribly abused and tormented by a cold and insensitive world; or she may be entirely regarded as an open mockery of faith and religious fervor—depending upon your point of view. However, it must be acknowledged—Rosselini's caustic picture is the topper to a brilliant lot of film.

Enter Commissioner McCaffrey

What audiences' reactions to *Ways of Love* would have been if it had continued its run at the Paris Theater unmolested will never be known. On December 24, 1950, twelve days after the first performance, the New York press reported that showings of *The Miracle* had been stopped the previous afternoon on orders of the New York City Commissioner of Licenses, Edward T. McCaffrey.[3] McCaffrey had a letter delivered to the manager of the Paris, Mrs. Lillian Gerard, on Friday, December 22, declaring that he found the film "officially and personally blasphemous." In a telephone call earlier the same day, a representative of the Commissioner's office warned Mrs. Gerard that the theater's license would be suspended if *The Miracle* were shown at that day's 1:00 p.m. opening performance or thereafter. Mrs. Gerard contacted the distributor of the film, Joseph Burstyn, for advice. She asked the Commissioner's representative for a short period of grace to consult her attorneys. This was not granted, and Commissioner McCaffrey could not be reached to discuss the legal implications of withdrawal. For the two afternoon showings that Friday *The Miracle* was withdrawn and another film screened in its place.

At the same time that he notified the theater, Commissioner McCaffrey had a letter delivered to Burstyn. This stated that "all theaters under the jurisdiction of this department" were being advised by the commissioner that he intended "to take immediate steps against their licenses in the event they are found showing such a film, which I find to be a blasphemous affront to a great many of our fellow citizens." McCaffrey called on Burstyn to "cooperate" by eliminating all bookings of *The Miracle* in New York City.

---

[3] The License Commissioner of New York City is appointed by the Mayor and serves at the Mayor's pleasure. The appointment is made after consultation with party leaders and does not involve negotiations with professional or other interest groups, as would, for example, the appointment of a Health Commissioner. The License Commissioner has authority over 77 different occupations or activities and is empowered to license and supervise these to protect the public from unfair practices or improper conditions.

McCaffrey's suggestion was a potential economic disaster for Burstyn. His company was not an importer of large numbers of foreign films but rather of a few which Burstyn took on because he thought they had unusual artistic merit. He had brought *Paisan, Open City,* and *Bicycle Thief* to American audiences, and it was his practice to work with "100 percent effort" on one film at a time. He had a heavy financial investment in *Ways of Love* already, in preparation and advertising costs, and it was his major film of the winter season, 1950–1951. The New York City market was the most important in the nation for foreign films, and a ban in New York based on Catholic protests threatened to set off censors in other key cities such as Chicago or to frighten away theater owners even in cities without government censorship. Burstyn decided that he had to fight for his film, for economic reasons as well as for civil liberty.

The first thing Burstyn did after receiving McCaffrey's letter was to phone Mrs. Gerard and to agree that they should keep the ban out of the news, in an attempt to straighten it out with the License Commissioner. However, a *New York Times* editor attending the theater became curious about the substitution and broke the story in his paper. When Burstyn learned that the theater had withdrawn *The Miracle,* he informed Mrs. Gerard that failure to show the film was a violation of the theater's contract with him, and he persuaded her to stand up to the commissioner. At the two evening performances on Friday, *The Miracle* was restored to the trilogy.

Commissioner McCaffrey was apparently keeping close tabs on the Paris. A letter delivered by messenger the next morning (Saturday, December 23) notified Mrs. Gerard that the theater's license was under suspension because of the Friday evening showings. While not required to do so, the commissioner said he would give the theater a hearing before any further step of revocation was taken. At a press conference Commissioner McCaffrey told reporters that he had acted after having seen the film personally, not because he had received any outside complaints. "Officially, as a representative of the city government," McCaffrey explained, "I felt there were hundreds of thousands of citizens whose religious beliefs were assaulted by the picture."

During the next few days developments came rapidly. The National Legion of Decency, the agency which reviews films on behalf of the Catholic Church in the United States and publishes its findings to guide its communicants, placed *Ways of Love* in its "C" or "Condemned" classification.[4] The film was described as "a sacrilegious and blasphemous mockery of Christian-religious truth." The Catholic War Veterans announced its full support for Commissioner McCaffrey's position. On the other hand, the New York Film Critics voted thirteen to three to register a vigorous protest against the commissioner's action as "dangerous censorship"; leading theater figures such as Howard Lindsay protested against making eight million residents of New York City depend upon Commissioner McCaffrey's personal judgment on movies; and the American Civil Liberties Union telegraphed a notice to Mayor Vincent Impellitteri that the action of his commissioner violated the First Amendment's protection of freedom of speech and of the press. The ACLU offered help to any theater

---

[4] The Legion's classifications are: "A-1," Unobjectionable for general patronage; "A-2," Adults and adolescents; "A-3," Adults only; "B," Objectionable; and "C," Condemned.

that decided to test the commissioner's ban.

Joseph Burstyn took action by engaging the law firm of Basil O'Connor and John Farber, a firm with prominent Catholic members, to sue the City of New York. A motion for the issuance of a temporary injunction against Mc-Caffrey was filed and scheduled for hearing for Friday, December 29. Reporters at City Hall could get no direct comment from Mayor Impellitteri, who was said to feel that the issue should be left to the courts.

The management of the Paris Theater convened its Board of Directors—it was owned by French interests—and decided to seek legal guidance before taking further action. Meanwhile, it showed a substitute film for *The Miracle*.

Restraining Commissioner McCaffrey

In New York the state court of general jurisdiction for cases in law and equity is called the Supreme Court, and it is here that legal disputes are first tried before a single justice and, if the case is one involving jury trial, before a jury as well. For purposes of Supreme Court operations New York is divided into ten judicial districts, each with its own set of Supreme Court justices. After cases are heard in the Supreme Court, certain constitutional and statutory classes of cases may be carried to the Appellate Division of the Supreme Court. For Appellate Division review, the state is divided into four judicial departments. The Governor designates who will sit on the Appellate Division from among the roster of the Supreme Court justices; his appointments are for five-year terms. At the top of New York's judicial system is the New York Court of Appeals sitting in Albany, composed of a chief judge and six associate judges. The Court of Ap-

peals hears cases appealed from the Appellate Division and passes almost exclusively on questions of law and practice, not on factual issues. The judges of the Supreme Court and Court of Appeals are popularly elected for fourteen-year terms.

On Friday, December 29, 1950, Earle Koons of O'Connor and Farber, representing Joseph Burstyn, appeared before Justice Henry Clay Greenberg of the Supreme Court for New York County to argue for the issuance of a temporary injunction restraining Commissioner McCaffrey from banning showings of *The Miracle*. The commissioner was represented by Saul Moskoff, Assistant Corporation Counsel for the City of New York.

Koons explained to the court that *The Miracle* had been approved by United States Customs authorities when it was first brought into the country; that a license to exhibit the film had been issued to Lopert Films, Inc., on March 2, 1949 by the Motion Picture Division of the Department of Education of New York, which was authorized to pass upon movies for censorship purposes; and that another license to exhibit the trilogy, *Ways of Love,* including *The Miracle,* had been issued to Joseph Burstyn, Inc., by the Motion Picture Division on November 30, 1950.[5]

---

[5] Motion picture censorship in New York State was established in 1921 and was administered by a three-man commission. In 1926 New York transferred this function to a Motion Picture Division lodged in the Department of Education. The Director of the Motion Picture Division and his staff were charged with the duty of examining all motion pictures which were to be publicly exhibited. These were to be licensed "unless such film or a part thereof is obscene, indecent, immoral, inhuman, sacrilegious, or is of such character that its exhibition would tend to corrupt morals or incite to crime." Newsreels were exempt from licensing. Scientific and educational films not for exhibi-

After describing *The Miracle* and noting that it had been shown at the Venice Film Festival in 1948 "without objection from Vatican representatives present at the Festival," Koons charged that Commissioner McCaffrey's action in banning the film was illegal and should be enjoined. Moskoff replied that McCaffrey had acted within his powers, but he had not proceeded very far in this argument when Justice Greenberg said that he had "great doubts" about that. Reading from the complaint the sections concerning the clearance by customs and by the Motion Picture Division and on the lack of Vatican objection, Greenberg asked Moskoff: "You mean to say, in the face of all that, aside from the Commissioner's power, his action should not . . . be deemed to be arbitrary?" Moskoff insisted McCaffrey had not "overstepped his powers." This drew from Justice Greenberg the observation that administrative officials could "arrogate" powers which were not theirs. "Now here is a case," the judge continued, "where a License Commissioner has seen a film; he finds that it is 'personally and officially' obnoxious to him, and he closes the picture down and after he closes it down, in effect, offers [the theater owner and film owner] a hearing to determine whether or not what he has done was right or wrong. That is the same as convicting a man and then asking him what he has to say. . . ."

Justice Greenberg, warming to his theme, added:

I don't think, really, Mr. Corporation Counsel, that it was the intent of the statute to which you have called my attention to vest such drastic powers in the License Commissioner, conceding the honesty of his purpose and intention. . . . The court is required to stand between, at least, semi-tyranny and the rights of individuals, whether they be personal or property—I just can't subscribe to this kind of action. . . .

With this, the judge announced that he would sign a restraining order forbidding Commissioner McCaffrey to interfere with *The Miracle* until a final determination of the film's status was made. However, Justice Greenberg said he would declare a five-minute recess to let Moskoff ask Commissioner McCaffrey if he desired to "compromise." Following the recess, during which he spoke to McCaffrey by telephone, Moskoff informed the court that the commissioner "does not want to give the impression of being tyrannical" and was willing to permit showing of the film "until the matter was adjudged in Special Term" of the Supreme Court. With the ban lifted, Justice Greenberg signed an order setting a hearing for January 3 before the Supreme Court for New York County on the question of the License Commissioner's authority to censor films by revoking theater licenses. At the Paris Theater, the projectionist put the print of *The Miracle* back into the projector, and *Ways of Love* ran again in its original form.

Conversation in Venice

Meanwhile, public discussion of *The Miracle* continued. The Right Reverend Monsignor Walter P. Kellenberg, Chancellor of the Catholic Archdiocese of New York, issued a statement on December 30 calling *The Miracle* "an

---

tion were automatically given licenses. Films shown solely for education, charitable, or religious purposes (non-commercial showings) were licensed without examination of their contents. Failure to obtain a license before publicly exhibiting a film was made unlawful. The Motion Picture Division and its parent body, the Department of Education, were under the authority of the New York State Board of Regents.

open insult to the faith of millions of people in this city and hundreds of millions throughout the world." It was disclosed also that *The Miracle* had been seen by a representative of the Legion of Decency at the 1948 Venice Film Festival and that "a vigorous protest" had been made against its further distribution. The facts of this protest—not elaborated in Monsignor Kellenberg's statement—were as follows: Mrs. Walter Looram, representing the National Legion of Decency of the United States at the 1948 Venice Festival, had watched the film and found it thoroughly "sacrilegious." When she saw Joseph Burstyn talking to Rosselini's lawyer, Mrs. Looram asked Burstyn, "You aren't going to buy *that* film, are you?" Burstyn laughed and told Mrs. Looram, "Lots of things are all right for the Legion after cuts, aren't they? You approved *Forever Amber* and we'll see what can be done with *The Miracle.*" Mrs. Looram expressed doubts that "cuts" would cure the problems here. When she returned to the United States, Mrs. Looram reported the "sacrilegious" character of *The Miracle* to the directors of the Legion, but since *The Miracle* was not presented that year or the next, the matter rested with her report. When *The Miracle* opened in 1950, the Legion immediately entered the fray. It drew up a memorandum on the film's content, explaining why it was sacrilegious, and contacted all the dioceses in New York City.[6] The Legion's alert had preceded Commissioner McCaffrey's action.

---

[6] This was the first film that the Legion had condemned as "sacrilegious" since its formation in 1934. In 1936 it had condemned Russian director Serge Eisenstein's film about Mexico, *Time in the Sun,* as "anti-religious"; but Legion spokesmen said they had "generally ignored" Soviet imports and the foreign "art film" market in order to concentrate on the "mass-audience" American-made movies.

While Catholic denunciation of *The Miracle* increased, a number of Protestant ministers in New York announced that they did not find the movie sacrilegious but rather a powerful attack upon the cruel disregard of religious beliefs. In the midst of the ministerial "reviews," the New York Film Critics announced that *Ways of Love* had been selected as the "best foreign film of 1950."

In Supreme Court, Special Term

On January 3, 1951 in Special Term, Supreme Court for New York County, the question of Commissioner McCaffrey's power to censor movies was presented in a suit for a temporary injunction by Joseph Burstyn, Inc., before Justice Aron Steuer. Earle Koons argued on behalf of Burstyn that there was no right remaining with the City of New York to censor films after the Motion Picture Division of the State Board of Education had passed a film and licensed it for exhibition in the state. New York City Corporation Counsel John P. McGrath replied that there was a gap in the censorship law in that no provision was made for appeal from an "approval" by the Board of Education. (There was provision for appeal from a denial.) Because of this gap, he argued, the city was permitted to act through its License Commissioner. McGrath notified the court that a letter had been written (but not yet mailed) summoning the management of the Paris Theater to an administrative hearing to show cause why its license should not be suspended. "You'd be in a better position here today," Justice Steuer interjected, "if that proceeding had been followed originally." "No comment," was McGrath's reply.

Justice Steuer advised that it might be better for the License Commissioner to wait until after a definition of his powers before he held a hearing. When Koons offered to show *The Miracle* to the court, Justice Steuer flatly refused to view it, saying that this would make him a "censor." He promised to rule on the request for an injunction within 48 hours.

The ruling came down on January 5. Explaining that he would not discuss whether the Municipal Charter gave the License Commissioner power to act as he had done or whether "blasphemy per se" could be grounds for suppressing a movie, Justice Steuer said that he found the key question to be whether a municipal officer could interfere with a motion picture "duly licensed" by the official state censoring board. This question he answered in the negative. The ruling went on to note:

> It may not be amiss to state that the Commissioner of Licenses is not the protector from affronts of a large portion of our citizens or even all of them. . . . They can protect themselves, first by ignoring the exhibition and secondly any individual can seek to have the Board of Regents revoke its permit or if he can show that the license was granted through an abuse of power he will find the courts as ready to give relief against such an abuse as it is to restrain this one.

At about this time, *Life* published an article reviewing the controversy. It called McCaffrey's ban "a striking example of how minor bureaucrats can find ways to establish their personal prejudices as law." On the merits of the film, the *Life* report appraised the story as truly religious and ennobling in concept.

Enter Francis Cardinal Spellman

With *The Miracle* now playing to packed audiences, the head of the Ca-

tholic Archdiocese of New York, Francis Cardinal Spellman, took a personal hand in the affair. He issued a statement that was read at all Masses at St. Patrick's Cathedral on Sunday, January 7, and made the headlines on Monday. The Cardinal's statement began by reminding Catholics that they had recently taken the annual "pledge of the Legion of Decency," promising to "remain away from indecent and immoral films, to unite with those who protest against them, and to stay away altogether from places of amusement which show them as a matter of policy":

> Today, we call upon you to make that pledge effective against a motion picture entitled *The Miracle,* and against any theater that is showing it now or may show it henceforth. Not only do we address this admonition to the one and a quarter million of our fellow Catholics of the Archdiocese of New York but also to the 26 millions of our fellow Catholics in these United States of America.

Cardinal Spellman summarized the condemnation of the film by the National Legion of Decency and mentioned its condemnation in Rome by the Pontifical Film Commission. Noting the report in Saturday's press of Justice Steuer's ruling, the Cardinal said:

> It is indeed a blot upon the escutcheon of the Empire State that no means of redress is available to the people to correct a mistake made by the State Board of Censorship. And in licensing *The Miracle* our State Board certainly made a mistake offending and insulting millions of people for which it will be censured by every decent man and woman. . . . Since the civil law sustains the showing of such a vile and harmful picture, we, as the guardians of the moral law, must summon

you and all people with a sense of decency to refrain from seeing it and supporting the venal purveyors of such pictures which are so harmful to morality and the public welfare. Moreover if the present law is so weak and inadequate to cope with this desperate situation then all right-thinking citizens should unite to change and strengthen the federal and state statutes to curb those who would profit financially by blasphemy, immorality and sacrilege.

The Cardinal then explained to his audiences why *The Miracle* was offensive:

The theme of *The Miracle* is the seduction of an idiotic Italian woman. What is there in this theme to be approved or licensed? The seduction of any idiot-woman, regardless of race, is revolting to any decent man or woman. It is art at its lowest. And to give to this story of the seduction of an idiot-woman the title, *The Miracle,* is diabolical deception at its depths. The picture should very properly be entitled, *Woman Further Defamed,* by Roberto Rosselini. . . .
The Miracle is a despicable affront to every Christian. It is a mockery of our Faith. We believe in Miracles. This picture ridicules that belief. . . .
In a secondary way, *The Miracle* is a vicious insult to Italian womanhood. It presents the Italian woman as moronic and neurotic and, in matters of religion, fanatical. Only a perverted mind could so represent so noble a race of women. . . .
We are a religious nation. The perpetrators of *The Miracle* unjustly cast their blasphemous darts of ridicule at Christian Faith and at Italian womanhood, thereby dividing Religion against Religion and race against race. . . .
Divide and conquer is the technique of the greatest enemy of civilization, atheistic Communism. God forbid that these producers of racial and religious mockeries should divide and demoralize Americans so that the minions of Moscow might enslave this land of liberty.

Reminding Catholics of their pledge, Cardinal Spellman closed by expressing confidence that "all good Americans will unite with us in this battle for decency and Americanism."

In the wake of the Cardinal's message, the Catholic War Veterans set up a picket line outside the Paris Theater from opening to closing time. The pickets carried signs reading, "This Picture is an Insult to Every Decent Woman and Her Mother," "This Picture is Blasphemous," "Please Stay Out of This Theater." Some placards read, "Write to the Board of Regents in Albany to Remove the License of this Picture." The Ancient Order of Hibernians and New York Assemblyman Samuel Roman of the Fifteenth District telegraphed Governor Thomas E. Dewey to stop the exhibition of the picture, and the New York Chapter of the Knights of Columbus called on the Governor to "correct this error." A protest demonstration by 3,000 men of the New York Archdiocesan Union of the Holy Name Society was set for the following Sunday to picket in the plaza across from the Paris Theater.

Circulars were handed out by the pickets with questions and answers for passers-by and potential customers. For example:

Question: Can you give me one good reason why I shouldn't go in and see the picture?
Answer: What now happens to us may some day happen to your Belief. If you give your O.K. to anti-religious pictures by patronizing them, then don't be surprised if a picture is made attacking your own religion. . . .
Question: I saw the picture and I didn't see anything wrong with it.
Answer: Nobody knows the Catholic Religion better than the Catholics themselves and they are therefore better able to know what is attacking their Belief.

Question: I am a Catholic and I liked the picture.

Answer: You are evidently either ignorant of the teachings of our Church or you are actually defying our Church and are then not a real Catholic. Since the Church has condemned the picture, you are therefore disqualifying yourself as a Catholic by acting contrary to what the Church has told you.

Interviewed at his office the following day, Joseph Burstyn told reporters that he had no quarrel with Cardinal Spellman for objecting to the picture and calling upon Catholics to boycott it. "But they have no right to impose their opinion on anyone else," he said, referring to the proposal for state censorship. "I am pretty certain citizens of the state will resist censorship by one group." The accounts of Burstyn's reaction also disclosed that since its opening *The Miracle* had been seen by approximately 100,000 persons and that no objection had been made to the theater management by any member of the audience. (Catholic groups said that such objections had been made.)

At this point in the affair two issues arose which were to continue throughout the long controversy—apart from differing interpretations of the film's meaning. The first related to whether the Vatican had ever "approved" the showing of *The Miracle*. Burstyn released to the press on January 8 documents showing that the film had been licensed by the Italian government for exhibition in Italy; he noted that under the Lateran Accord, publications which "may offend the Catholic religion" are not permitted. He also noted that after *The Miracle* opened in Italy Roberto Rosselini had received Vatican approval to make a film on the life of St. Francis of Assisi, with members of the Franciscan Order participating as

actors.[7] This, Burstyn said, must have meant that the Vatican did not regard Rosselini as a blasphemer. And he noted that *The Miracle* had been shown at Venice, where films objected to by the Vatican as "blasphemous" would not be included, according to the Director of the Venice Film Festival.

The Legion of Decency and Cardinal Spellman, on the other hand, disclosed that the Catholic Cinematographic Center (CCC), the Italian counterpart of the Legion, had condemned *The Miracle* as an "abominable profanation," and Catholic Action in Italy had warned Catholics to shun it. The CCC on October 19, 1948, a month after the Rome premiere of *The Miracle,* had published the following judgment:

The Miracle constitutes in effect an abominable profanation from religious and moral viewpoints and we must earnestly deplore both its production and exhibition. It seems incredible that anyone dared to conceive and present to the public a parody of a sacred mystery, a parody of that sublime evangelical narrative which forms the basis of every Christian belief. We advise everybody, nobody excepted, not to see the film.

The critic of *L'Osservatore Romano,* the semi-official Vatican newspaper, remarked that "objections from a religious viewpoint are very grave and they were not lessened by the madness of the protagonist, inasmuch as the [film's] author was not mad." The account praised the "scenes of undoubted screen value" and closed by saying, "notwithstanding all this we still believe in Rosselini's art and are waiting for his next work." [8]

---

[7] Later, ironically, it was Burstyn's firm which distributed *The Flowers of St. Francis* in the United States.

[8] AMTORG, the firm which buys western movies for exhibition in the Soviet Union

Commercially, the film was a failure in Italy, grossing only $30,000, or less than half its cost. It is not clear whether this was because of CCC condemnation or because, as Italian film exhibitors reported, the audience "found it boring." There were some favorable reviews in the secular Roman press. *Il Populo,* the official newspaper of the pro-Catholic Christian Democratic Party, for example, judged the movie "a beautiful thing, humanly felt, alive, true and without religious profanation as someone has said, because in our opinion the meaning of the characters is clear and there is no possibility of misunderstanding."

Both the supporters and the opponents of *The Miracle* in the United States, then, could argue their side by citing "the Vatican." The film had not been banned in Italy, as it could have been by formal Vatican objection, but it had been branded a "profanation" by Vatican spokesmen. According to the Rome correspondent of the *New York Times,* Vatican officials fully supported the position of United States Catholics in seeking to have the film banned in the United States. Monsignor Albino Galleto, head of the CCC, stated in February 1951 that a film profaning a dogma of the Catholic Church and belittling its religious tenets was more dangerous in a nation with a non-Catholic majority than in a country like Italy, where the population was overwhelmingly Catholic and would not easily be misled.

The second disagreement between critics and supporters which prevailed throughout the controversy was somewhat less important. This involved the issue of whether the stranger and the demented woman were dressed to suggest Biblical figures or were in modern

clothing. The speeches made by Catholic spokesmen, their literature, and eventually the descriptions used by several of the boards and courts of New York spoke of the stranger in the film as a man "dressed in a manner similar to the traditional images of the Saint. He is bearded and wears flowing garments reminiscent of the clothing used in the Holy Land at the time of Christ." Actually the stranger's dress consisted of a United States Army green field jacket, United States Army olive-drab trousers, a United States Army fatigue cap, and "G.I." shoes. In later arguments of the case before the United States Supreme Court, one of Burstyn's attorneys had "still" photographs made from the film and showed that the stranger wore army garb.

Picketing and Counter-Picketing

After Judge Steuer's ruling on January 5, lawyers for the Regents of the New York State Board of Education were said to be studying the power of the board to reopen consideration of *The Miracle,* and the City of New York prepared its appeal from Judge Steuer's ruling as to the License Commissioner's powers.

On January 8, following Cardinal Spellman's denunciation, a picket line manned by members of the Catholic War Veterans marched in front of the Paris Theater. On January 9, two counter-pickets from a Protestant "interdenominational" group appeared at the Paris with signs protesting censorship.

On January 12 a cablegram was made public from Roberto Rosselini to Cardinal Spellman. In a previous film, Rosselini said, he had tried to show how the absence of charity made for "immense sorrow."

In *The Miracle* men are still without pity because they have not gone

---

and satellite countries, viewed *The Miracle* but refused to distribute it on the grounds that it was "pro-Catholic propaganda."

back to God. But God is already present in the faith, however confused, of the poor, persecuted woman and since God is forever, a human being suffers and is misunderstood. *The Miracle* occurs when, with the birth of the child, the poor demented woman regains sanity in her maternal love. They were my intentions and I hope that Your Eminence will deign himself to consider them with paternal benevolence.

Public discussion continued. Bosley Crowther, film critic of the *New York Times,* discussing *The Miracle* and *Oliver Twist,* called for a "free screen" in both cases and an end to pressure group controls. Reaching a different conclusion, the *Independent Film Journal* criticized release of *The Miracle* and *Oliver Twist* and said they had "set the industry's public relations effort back at least ten years." The Authors League of America, many Protestant clergymen, and the American Book Publishers Council joined the anticensorship ranks to add new voices to the dispute.

On Sunday, January 14, over 1,000 pickets took turns marching in front of the Paris, with the largest group at one time consisting of a 200-man double line from Fifth Avenue west to a point midway in the block, past the theater. Among the signs carried were: "This is the Kind of Picture the Communists Want," and "Don't be a Communist—all the Communists are Inside." In the next two weeks the picket lines became increasingly noisy, with a good deal of shouting at patrons entering the theater. Ephraim London, Burstyn's lawyer, had drawn up papers asking for a court injunction against the mass picketing, which he felt to be "clearly illegal." But the Paris management at first held back from this step. Despite the picket lines the theater was packed at every performance, producing the highest grosses that had

ever been taken in. However, the pickets began to get noisier in the days following January 14, and the Paris told London to go ahead with the injunction motion.

To get solid proof of the "massed" and "obstreperous" character of the picketing, London arranged by telephone to take movies and sound recordings in front of the theater. But when the movie company and London arrived at the theater there was no noise, and only a few pickets were walking. The next day, the pickets increased and the noise resumed. London, after checking to make sure that Burstyn, the Paris management, and the film company had not disclosed the plans, concluded that a "leak" had taken place and decided to try a decoy operation. A telephone call to Burstyn from London's office made arrangements to place a microphone in the marquee to record the noise. Secretly, London arranged to have a second microphone placed in another location outside the theater. When London arrived at the Paris on the scheduled night the cord to the microphone on the marquee was cut, but the microphone not discussed on the telephone was unharmed. "I don't know just who it was," London later reminisced, "but there was somebody tapping our telephone wire."

On another front, the New York film critics announced that they were shifting the ceremony of their best-film awards from Radio City Music Hall to the Rainbow Room of the RCA Building. The manager of Radio City had received a telephone call from Martin Quigley, publisher of the *Motion Picture Herald,* co-author of the Hollywood Production Code, and one of the original sponsors of the Legion of Decency. Quigley warned the manager that Catholic Church leaders would be gravely offended if an award to *The Miracle* were presented there, that they might urge a boycott of the theater, and pickets might take up positions. When informed of this, Howard Barnes of the *New York Herald-Tribune,* president of the New York film critics, made inquiries of Catholic spokesmen. He concluded that Quigley's impressions of sentiment at the Archdiocesan office were not correct, and he advised the manager of Radio City to ignore the message.

Barnes and the manager were soon corrected. Monsignor Walter Kellenberg, Chancellor of the Archdiocese, informed the manager by letter "unequivocally" that the assumption that holding the ceremony "would not incur the disfavor of the Catholic church and that you would not offend his Eminence [Cardinal Spellman] is absolutely false." To avoid embarrassing the management of Radio City, the critics moved their ceremonies but issued a protest against the "insidious pressure" exerted by the Church.

Agitation grew at the Paris during the last two weeks in January. On January 20 the police emptied the theater for 45 minutes after the manager received a call saying that a bomb would be thrown inside. A capacity audience, 25 pickets, one counter-picket, and 200 persons waiting to buy tickets stood patiently outside while 25 policemen searched the theater. No bomb was found. However, a fire inspector present issued a summons to the Paris management for allowing standees in violation of the fire code. The management considered this a clear instance of harassment, since it was the first summons it had received since the theater opened in September 1948, and it had understood that a small number of standees was permitted in practice. Ephraim London urged the management to fight the summons. But on the theory of "Pay the two dollars," the Paris pleaded guilty and paid a $100 fine.

A series of similar bomb threats took place during the next few weeks. Each time the police emptied the theater, and each time they found no bomb. As if to even the score, someone wrote Cardinal Spellman threatening to bomb St. Patrick's Cathedral. Special police details were posted around the building and inside the Cathedral at all Masses, but no explosions went off there either.

Reviewed by the State Board of Regents

                    With   Commissioner McCaffrey enjoined, *The Miracle* showing to packed audiences, and Catholic protests mounting, the New York State Board of Regents stepped onto the scene.[9] (The reader will re-

---

[9] The regents, thirteen in number, were elected one each year for thirteen-year terms by the State Legislature in joint session. Regents served without pay and were usually citizens with substantial civic and educational qualities. Party affiliation was usually made the basis for election, reflecting the majority in any given year in the joint legislative body. In 1952, two of the thirteen regents were Catholics.

call that the Board of Regents headed the Department of Education. The Motion Picture Division in that department had issued the license to exhibit *The Miracle.*) On January 15 a three-man committee of the Board viewed the movie, and its members declared it to be their unanimous opinion that *The Miracle* was "sacrilegious." Dubbed "the All-American committee," its members were William J. Wallin of Yonkers, a Protestant (and Chancellor-Emeritus of the Regents); John F. Brosnan of Manhattan, a Catholic; and Jacob Holtzmann of Brooklyn, a Jew. On January 19 the licensees of *The Miracle* were directed to appear before this committee in New York City to show cause why the film's license should not be withdrawn. With this, the City of New York ceased to be an actor in the drama; the city's appeal from Judge Steuer's ruling was never heard.

In an attempt to prevent the Regents Committee from acting, Burstyn's lawyers filed a motion in Albany on January 29 before Supreme Court Justice Roscoe V. Ellsworth to enjoin the hearing, alleging that the board had no authority under the movie censorship statute to revoke a license once granted. Justice Ellsworth ruled that whether or not there was revocation power in the censorship statute, the Regents might decide not to revoke the license, so that the danger from which Burstyn was seeking protection might never occur. On this basis he denied the motion for an injunction.

At 3:00 a.m., January 19, in the building of the Association of the Bar of the City of New York, the Regents Committee opened its hearings. Present were the three Regents and Charles A. Brind, Jr., Counsel for the State Education Department. Chairman Wallin rapped a gavel and announced:

> The hearing is called to order. . . . I would announce to you that we are a committee appointed to hear and report back to the Board of Regents. We have no other or further power. As we see it, there are two questions to be discussed. One is the power of the Board of Regents to revoke and the second is the factual question, is this picture, *The Miracle*, sacrilegious?
> There will be nobody heard except the licensees. Other people may file briefs. So far as the licensees and their counsel are concerned, we say that you may appear here specially, if you care to, for the purpose of challenging jurisdiction or otherwise, or inasmuch

as we are seeking light on the matter, you may appear generally, and we will stipulate on the record that all your legal rights are reserved, with the same force and effect as if you had not appeared. . . .

John C. Farber was the first speaker. He was present, he said, "on behalf of Joseph Burstyn, Inc.," appearing "specially" to "challenge the jurisdiction" of the committee and the Regents to conduct any revocation proceedings. Farber said that the statute gave no such power and that the precedents in New York courts had already determined that such power did not exist. Farber asked for a ruling on a motion that the committee take no further action. "We are not prepared to rule on such [a] motion," Wallin said. "We are still studying the matter."

Farber then proceeded to the second part of his prepared statement, which noted that the committee had seen the film and called it "sacrilegious." "It is submitted," Farber said, "that this committee has made a prejudgment of the issue with respect to which it was to receive evidence. . . . I move that this committee disqualify itself. . . ."

"Denied," the chairman ruled, "on the ground that there has been no predetermination and cannot be. The committee is not clothed with power. It is a committee to hear and report back only."

"In the circumstances," said Farber, "Joseph Burstyn, Inc. shall respectfully refuse to participate in the hearing . . . and we are now withdrawing Joseph Burstyn, Inc. from the hearing."

After some spirited debate with counsel for private groups who sought the opportunity to testify, the hearing was declared closed. Briefs and statements were filed with the committee by 24 individuals and eight organizations, the latter including the Coordinating Committee of Catholic Lay Organizations; the New York State Catholic Welfare Committee; Catholic War Veterans; the Ladies Auxiliary, Division 11, Ancient Order of Hibernians; the American Civil Liberties Union; and the National Council for Freedom From Censorship. Besides discussing the nature of the film, many of the briefs reviewed the question of statutory authority of the Board of Regents to revoke an earlier grant of a license. The Catholic briefs maintained that review of its own decisions was recognized as the common law right of an administrative agency under New York law. The pro-Burstyn briefs argued that while review authority had been granted for scientific and educational films, licenses for commercial films could be reviewed only for the grounds given in the statute, which were "misrepresentation" or alteration of the film after issuance of the license. Several briefs argued that the censorship statute was itself unconstitutional because, they declared, it constituted a prior restraint on freedom of expression.

Claims of Harassment

While the Regents Committee was deliberating, the management of the Paris told reporters that it was being singled out systematically for violations of the fire laws in a manner calculated to harass the theater. The manager explained that a summons had been written by a fire inspector after one person strayed from a group of standees awaiting seats in the rear of the theater and stood for a moment in the aisle. He was seated, the manager noted, even before the summons could be completely written out. Fire Commissioner George P. Monoghan denied that his officers were singling out the Paris, but the theater's owners said that they could not recall that the Fire Depart-

ment had ever exercised so close a watch before. On February 10 the Fire Department opened an investigation of "bribe-giving" to fire inspectors by the Paris Theater. According to the Paris management (and theater owners generally), it was "accepted practice" in New York City to give the fire inspectors a few dollars now and then. This was done also by many store and building owners. The Paris regarded the practice as so routine that it even entered the payments in the account books. When the management denied giving gratuities, Commissioner Monoghan had the books subpoenaed and issued the summons. Several hearings were held before the Fire Marshall at which the Paris admitted paying $20 a month since its opening and defended this as the "universal practice." The accusation of "harassment" was withdrawn by the management.

The Regents Hear and Decide

On February 15 the Regents Committee submitted its report to the full board. After reciting the history of the dispute and the facts of the hearing, as well as the terms of the censorship statute, the committee declared:

> The Board of Regents is the constitutional head of the Department [of Education] and as such it is its duty to administer and enforce the law as it is enacted. By Chapter 153 of the Laws of 1927, the Legislature saw fit to place the responsibility for the administration of [the censorship] law in the Education Department and thus it has become the duty of the Regents to administer it as it is written. It must be emphasized that it is not within our jurisdiction to pass upon the wisdom of that law or upon its constitutionality, or the validity or desirability of the standards of exclusion set forth therein.

As to the authority of the Board of Regents, the committee stated:

> We cannot sustain the challenge to the jurisdiction of the Board of Regents to act in this matter. As head of the Department of Education, it not only has the power, but the duty to inquire into the actions of one of its subordinates [the Motion Picture Division] and to determine whether this act in issuing the license did or did not contravene the Law. . . . The Legislature said in so many words: "The Board of Regents shall have authority to enforce the provisos and purposes of Part II of this Article" (Section 132) [and the Regents have this constitutional power under Article V, Section 4 of the State Constitution].

On the power to revoke a license once awarded, the committee's report stated:

> The statute prohibits the issuing of a license for the exhibition of a film, any part of which is obscene, indecent, immoral, inhuman or *sacrilegious*. The granting of a license to a film that comes within this condemnation would be an illegal act. It is inconceivable that it was ever intended that the head of a Department could not have the power to vitiate an illegal act performed by any "sub-department, division or bureau" under its supervision and for the acts of which it is by law specifically made responsible. . . .

The report concluded that there was "no legal obstacle" to the regents passing upon the propriety of the film, and it recommended that the board "view such motion picture."

The board saw *The Miracle* at a private showing on February 15. On February 16 ten members of the board, sitting as a committee of the whole, issued a unanimous report. Accepting the judgment of its committee that it had power to revoke, and reciting the ban on "sacrilegious" films, the report maintained:

> In this country where we enjoy the priceless heritage of religious freedom, the law recognizes that men and women of all faiths respect the religious beliefs held by others. The mockery or profaning of these beliefs that are sacred to any portion of our citizenship is abhorrent to the laws of this great State. To millions of our people the Bible has been held sacred and by them taught, read, studied and held in reverence and respect. Generation after generation have been influenced by its teachings. This picture takes the concept so sacred to them set forth in both the Protestant and Catholic versions of the Bible (St. Matthew, King James and Douay Versions, Chapter I, verses 18-25) and associates it with drunkenness, seduction and lewdness.

A motion to rescind the license issued to Lopert Films, Inc. for *Il Miracolo* and to Joseph Burstyn, Inc., for *Ways of Love* was unanimously passed. Burstyn was given permission to file for a license for the two French portions of *Ways of Love*.

As soon as the regents' decision was announced, John Farber filed a motion on behalf of Burstyn before Justice Kenneth MacAffer of the Supreme Court for Albany County, asking for a review of the regents' decision by the Appellate Division. The case was set down for hearing at the March term of the Appellate Division, but Justice MacAffer refused to issue an order staying the cancellation of the license while the court considered the case. *The Miracle* was again taken out of the projection machine at the Paris.

Though *The Miracle* had stopped playing in New York, it was scheduled to open in Los Angeles on March 7. California had no state censorship of films. Archbishop Francis McIntyre of

Los Angeles was reported as saying that to denounce the movie would only publicize it more, and that he would let it run its course without public comment. The *New York Times* remarked that Catholics were less numerous and less politically powerful in California than in New York, and that this might account for the difference in tactics. All was not smooth for the California showing, however. At the behest of Archbishop McIntyre, a Jewish attorney (who normally represented the major movie studios) persuaded the movie distributors in Los Angeles not to book the film. Burstyn wound up renting a private theater in order to show his movie. The film was exhibited in Washington, D. C. without legal or picketing difficulties.

The Shape of Public Opinion

By early March quite definite lines of group opinion had formed over *The Miracle*. There was clearly no common "Christian" position. Ministers drawn from all of the major Protestant denominations—Unitarian and Congregationalist to Methodist, Baptist, and fundamentalist—issued public statements that they did not regard the movie as sacrilegious. (Statements from almost a hundred Protestant clergymen to this effect were collected by counsel for Burstyn after special showings of the film in New Jersey and Boston, Mass., and were later presented to the courts.)

Jewish religious leaders were also opposed to the censorship measures. They said little about the "sacrilege" aspect during the public discussions, perhaps because they felt this was a matter to be fought out within the Christian camp. (Ephraim London, Burstyn's personal attorney, was unable at that time to get more than two or three statements by rabbis supporting the film, although he had no trouble ob-

taining dozens of statements from Protestant ministers.) Several Jewish religious leaders commented, however, that if the law were made to reflect "offensiveness" felt by particular religious denominations, then Orthodox Jews could object to many passion-play movies, crucifixion treatments, and other portrayals, because of the classic relationship between crucifixion emphasis and anti-Semitism. This, said these Jewish commentators, would be unfortunate, but it would follow from acceptance of the "offensiveness" rule in *The Miracle* episode.

Some individual Protestant and Jewish religious leaders disagreed and stated that *The Miracle* should not be shown. Typical of this response was a sermon delivered by Rabbi Max Felshin at the Radio City Synagogue. In the key part of his address, Rabbi Felshin stated:

The very fact that the leadership of the Catholic Church, which has millions of devout adherents in this city alone, considers the film offensive and sacrilegious should be sufficient grounds for the immediate withdrawal of the picture from further showing in our midst. True Americanism requires a sympathetic regard and due deference for the feelings of all fellow Americans. We must not willingly outrage the sanctities of any loyal, law-abiding group of any faith, especially when the insistence upon this public exhibition of a controversial film by the flagrantly-immoral Rosselini is particularly obnoxious to the Catholic section of our population.

Some time ago, when the producer J. Arthur Rank, not an American, was requested by the Jewish section of our American population to withdraw his objectionable English film, *Oliver Twist,* he hastened to do so as a real gentleman of high character. Why cannot similar kindness, courtesy and consideration be shown by an American exhibitor. . . . The offensive film . . .

should be withdrawn at once in the interest of public peace and true Americanism.

Within the Catholic community, the hierarchy in New York and other communities, most of the diocesan press, and virtually all organizations such as the Knights of Columbus, Holy Name Societies, and Catholic War Veterans demanded suppression of the film. As the controversy lengthened, however, some minority voices began to be heard in the Catholic camp.

The film critic of the *Catholic Messenger,* a diocesan paper in Iowa, deplored "the violence of New York Catholic reaction," especially since Burstyn in the past had brought into the United States "much of what film art is entering the country." The critic placed much of the explanation for the ruckus on a desire to "get" Rosselini for his affair with Ingrid Bergman:

> The thing that made Rosselini's fall uniquely unforgivable was that his partner was an American star whom American Catholics, or rather those of them who are movie fans, had just finished canonizing as a popular saint. She had played a nun a couple of times, and she had played a saint. She had become, for the American Catholic fan, the symbol of feminine sincerity.

The "ambiguous sounding" story of *The Miracle,* the critic concluded, "provided a splendid opportunity to strike back at the man who had debauched a saint."

A number of leading Catholic laymen in the field of arts and letters made statements protesting the Catholic campaign against *The Miracle.* Allen Tate, poet and critic, said in the course of a letter to the *New York Times:*

> Is there any institution in the United States, civil or religious, which has

the legitimate authority to suppress books and motion pictures, however disagreeable they may be to certain persons on theological grounds? In my opinion there is no such institution under a system that separates church and state. . . . Has any secular body [like the Regents] the legitimate authority to decide a theological question? As a Catholic, I cannot see that it has. . . .

> It should be borne in mind that Cardinal Spellman has full authority to denounce this picture as sacrilegious, but that his opinion of its effect upon Italian or any other womanhood is not authoritative and is no better than yours or mine. In the long run what Cardinal Spellman will have succeeded in doing is insulting the intelligence and faith of American Catholics with the assumption that a second-rate motion picture could in any way undermine their morals or shake their faith.

Otto Spaeth, past president of the Liturgical Arts Society and an American delegate to the First International Congress of Catholic Artists at Rome in 1950, published a discussion of the case in the *Magazine of Art.* "At the outbreak of the controversy," Spaeth wrote, "I immediately arranged for a private showing of the film. I invited a group of Catholics, competent and respected for their writings on both religious and cultural subjects. The essential approval of the film was unanimous."

> There was indeed "blasphemy" in the picture—but it was the blasphemy of the villagers, who stopped at nothing, not even the mock singing of a hymn to the Virgin, in their brutal badgering of the tragic woman. The scathing indictment of their evil behavior, implicit in the film, was seemingly overlooked by the critics.

In an article in *The Commonweal,* a nationally-known liberal magazine edited by Catholic laymen, William Clancy of Notre Dame University's English Department wrote a long article, "The Catholic as Philistine," denouncing the suppression efforts.[10] As did Spaeth, Clancy linked *The Miracle* with Catholic pressures against Charlie Chaplin movies and other instances of group intervention which "involve the attempt to limit [the choice of the artist] by appeals to mass emotion and by subsequent mass pressure."

> The end result . . . has been a semi-ecclesiastical McCarthyism, accompanied by some of the odious methods which this now implies: its "guilt by association," its appeal to prejudice and non-intelligence, its hysteria. This has made the matter of art and prudence a question for debate in the marketplace, and it has called into the debate thousands of well-meaning but misguided voices

[10] The movie reviewer of *The Commonweal* had originally condemned the film. Noting that Rosselini "may have had the most sincere intentions," Philip Hartung called the "finished result" so "dangerously close to being sacrilegious that it would have been better to leave this material alone." However, *The Commonweal* later denounced the censorship action in its editorials.

that appear to know very little of the profound meaning of that which they so noisily argue about. It is a spectacle which many of us, as Catholics, can view only with shame and repulsion, for we know that neither art nor prudence, religion nor country, intelligence nor morality can be served by such means.

The minority protests of the Catholic laymen were answered by articles in the Catholic press, usually with the statement that Cardinal Spellman and the Legion of Decency were better able to judge what was "sacrilegious" than were "amateur theologians."

These positions—heavily Protestant, Jewish, and secular opposition to banning *The Miracle* and predominantly Catholic support for its suppression—continued for the eighteen months that the issue was in the courts. Many articles were written on the film and on the issue of censorship generally, with the arguments repeating the basic stands taken above rather than introducing any new issues. After March 1951, however, the dispute shifted to the courts, and the cadences of legal debate began to permeate the discussion.

The Miracle in the New York Appellate Courts

On March 12, the Appellate Division of the New York Supreme Court heard three hours of argument in what had come to be known as *Burstyn v. Wilson,* or, as the full heading of the case read: *In the Matter of the Application of Joseph Burstyn, Inc., Petitioner, For an Order Pursuant to Article 78 of the Civil Practice Act, against Lewis A. Wilson, Commissioner of Education of the State of New York, and John P. Myers, William J. Wallin, William Leland Thompson, George Hopkins Bond, W. Kingsland Macy,*

Edward R. Eastman, Welles V. Moot, Caroline Werner Gannett, Roger W. Straus, Dominick F. Maurillo, John F. Brosnan and Jacob L. Holtzmann, as Regents of the University of the State of New York, Respondents. John C. Farber argued the case for Burstyn, with Earle R. Koons, Ephraim S. London, and Clendon H. Lee as participating counsel on the brief. Charles A. Brind, Jr., counsel for the Regents, argued in behalf of the Department of Education.

Speaking first, as counsel for the

party which brought the appeal, Farber presented three points: that the Board of Regents had no power to revoke a license issued by the Motion Picture Division; that the censorship statute and the action of the regents under it violated the United States Constitution's guarantees of religious liberty and of separation of church and state; and that censorship of motion pictures was a previous restraint of speech and press in violation of the federal and state constitutional guarantees of free expression. Brind, in his presentation, asserted the opposite side of each of these issues and stressed the harmful consequences of abolishing censorship or of allowing *The Miracle* to be shown.

The two lawyers clashed frequently. Farber declared that only Catholics had protested against the film and that Protestant clergymen and other religious leaders approved it. Brind told the court that letters had been received from non-Catholics "in a stack this high" (indicating a space about a foot off the counsel table), "which I have in my office." [11]

Counsel debated whether motion picture censorship was "still constitutional" in the eyes of the Supreme Court of the United States. Brind, joined by Patrick C. Dugan, counsel as "friend of the court" for the New York Catholic Welfare Committee, argued that it was constitutional and cited the case of *RD-DR Corporation v. Smith,* 340 U. S. 853 (1950). In that case, a federal Court of Appeals had upheld an Atlanta movie censorship statute, citing the *Mutual Film* case of 1915 as "on the books for

---

[11] Brind never produced these letters in court. Burstyn's lawyers felt that most of the letters written to the Regents were by Catholics who had never seen the film but were protesting out of their agreement with the position taken by the Legion of Decency and church authorities.

years, not only unchanged but uncriticized [in the Supreme Court]. . . ." The United States Supreme Court had denied certiorari in the *RD-DR* case, which meant that the court would not consider the case. This left in force the Court of Appeals decision.

Farber, joined by counsel from the Civil Liberties Union and the National Council of Freedom from Censorship, argued that the Supreme Court was moving in a different direction. They cited Justice Douglas' dictum in the *Paramount Pictures* case and relied upon statements in a number of recent "free speech" cases involving sound trucks, speeches in public parks, and magazine censorship to indicate Supreme Court disapproval of restraints such as that imposed against *The Miracle.*

After hearing the arguments and receiving the briefs of interested parties, the court announced that it was taking the case under advisement. The court then proceeded to view *The Miracle* itself.

On May 9 the ruling of the Appellate Division was issued—a unanimous decision upholding the regents' action in revoking the license of *The Miracle.* After describing the movie (including a reference to the stranger being "garbed in a dress reminiscent of Biblical times"), Presiding Justice Sidney F. Foster's opinion stated that the constitutionality of censorship of motion pictures was not "an open issue" before the court. Citing the *Mutual Film* case, the *RD-DR Corporation* ruling of the federal Court of Appeals, and a New York case upholding state censorship (*Pathe Exchange, Inc. v. Cobb,* 202 App. Div. 450, 236 N. Y. 539), the opinion held that "In view of this situation it is not appropriate for us, as an intermediate court, to re-examine the issue."

As to the argument that the standard,

"sacrilegious," was an unconstitutional one, the opinion maintained:

Petitioner cited the fact that what may be sacrilegious to one group of citizens may not be so to other groups; and hence it reasons that no enforcible meaning can be given to the term for the purpose of censorship. The Board of Regents based its revocation solely on the ground that the picture is sacrilegious; that it parodies in effect the Immaculate Conception and the Divine Birth of Christ as set forth in the New Testament. By millions of Christians these doctrines are held sacred, and any profanation thereof regarded as sacrilege. Concededly there are other groups who do not accept these beliefs. May the state bar on the ground of sacrilege a motion picture that profanes the religious beliefs of one group, however large, when the profanation is not common and universal to all groups?

Answering its own question "in the affirmative," the opinion proceeded to a discussion of the meaning of "sacrilege" as a standard for judgment.

The term "sacrilege," according to modern semantics, means the violation or profanation of sacred things. It is derived from the Latin word, "sacrilegium," which originally meant merely the theft of sacred things, but its meaning has since been widely extended. Even as far back as Cicero's time it had grown in popular speech to include any insult or injury to things deemed sacred. (Encyclopedia Britannica, Vol. 19, p. 803.) Obviously the legislature used the term in its widest sense, and we think it was intended to apply to all recognized religions, not merely to one sect alone.

Turning to the issue of religious liberty, the opinion said:

We fail to see how such restraint can be construed as denying freedom of religion to anyone, or how it raises the dogma of any one group to a legal imperative above other groups. As we construe the statute all faiths are entitled to the same protection against sacrilege. This is not to say that full inquiry and free discussion, even to the point of attack, may not be had with regard to the doctrines of any religion, including Christianity, by those who are free-thinkers and otherwise (*Commonwealth v. Kneeland,* 20 Pick. 206; *Cantwell v. Connecticut,* 310 U. S. 296). However, motion pictures, staged for entertainment purposes alone, are not within the category of inquiry and discussion. A view of the picture in question would convince any reasonable mind that it was conceived and produced purely as an entertainment spectacle, and not as a vehicle for inquiry or discussion as to the merits of any religious dogma. The statute . . . [bars] a visual caricature of religious beliefs held sacred by one sect or another, and such a bar, in our opinion, is not a denial of religious freedom.

In its closing sections the opinion held that the Motion Picture Division had not been created as an independent agency by the legislature but as a subordinate agency of the Board of Regents, and as such it was subject to review by the regents. Since it was "against common sense" for the legislature to have intended the continued showing of indecent or immoral films once mistakenly licensed by the division—and free from penal proceedings because of the 1950 law making a license a bar to prosecution—the court held a review power to be inherent in the regents' general authority.

Finally, as to the question whether the regents were "arbitrary and capricious" in their finding, the court said that whether or not the film was "sacrilegious" to a large body of Christians was a question of fact. Courts could interfere with an administrative agency's findings of fact only when the determination was one "that no reasonable mind could reach. While some of us feel that the importance of the picture has been exaggerated," the court said, "we cannot justly say that the determination complained of was one that no reasonable mind would countenance."

Opponents of *The Miracle* reacted to the ruling with satisfaction. At the same time, the critics of censorship noted that at the vital points of the case, it was the unwillingness of the Appellate Division to re-examine the status of movies as more-than-spectacle that had deprived Burstyn's argument of much of its force as to prior restraint on speech and press. Burstyn's lawyers immediately took an appeal and the case was set down for argument before the highest court in New York, the Court of Appeals. Everyone settled down for the next round.

Religious Issues on The National Scene

The Court of Appeals heard the arguments on *Burstyn v. Wilson* in June. Charles A. Brind, Jr., represented the Regents, and Ephraim London took over the appeal for Burstyn. (He was to be Burstyn's courtroom advocate at all stages of the case from then on.) On July 12 the Court of Appeals announced that it was deferring decision of *The Miracle* case until the fall.

At the same time the Court of Appeals, in a six-to-one decision, upheld the New York State system of released time religious education under which public school children whose parents made written request were dismissed from school earlier than their classmates in order to attend religious schools. The court rejected the argument that this violated constitutional mandates of separation of church and state. In the released time case, known

as *Zorach v. Clauson,* the Catholic community was deeply committed in favor of released time and considered this a crucial matter of national legal policy. In contrast to *The Miracle* issue, however, the Protestant and Jewish communities were not overwhelmingly united on the opposite side. Most Protestant denominations and a segment of ultra-Orthodox Jewish opinion supported released time. Several Protestant groups and all the major Jewish civic groups opposed it. Still, the debate had strong pro-Catholic and anti-Catholic overtones—opponents of the plan pointing with alarm to the Catholics' "growing drive for power," Catholic spokesmen denouncing the "Godlessness" and "atheistic materialism" supported by their antagonists. To the list of religious issues of 1951–1952 can be added the question of compulsory Bible-reading in the public schools, federal aid for education, and the controversial nomination by President Harry Truman, in October of 1951, of General Mark Clark as United States Ambassador to the Vatican. Most Protestant and some Jewish groups opposed the Clark nomination as an improper governmental recognition of the Catholic Church. The period was one in which religious controversies received much national attention. Since many of these issues were expected to wind up in the Supreme Court of the United States, there was a feeling in the air that powerful changes in the American law of church-state relations might be in the offing.

On the motion picture front, the theme of interference by religious leaders was sounded in a steady series of articles by the influential movie critic of the *New York Times,* Bosley Crowther. Crowther, a staunch foe of censorship and a close personal friend of Joseph Burstyn, carried on his campaign not only in the *Times* but also through outside speeches and writings, including a widely-quoted article in the *Atlantic Monthly* specifically on *The Miracle* case. Crowther maintained that *The Miracle* was not an isolated issue but had been chosen by the Catholic Church "for a calculated showdown test of strength." The Church was aiming, he felt, to extend to the foreign film market the hold which it already had over Hollywood. Since "the producers of these films, particularly the French and the Italians, are not conditioned to our rigidly charted morals," Crowther wrote, the Church had decided it should intervene.

On the other hand, spokesmen for the Legion of Decency, looking back later on *The Miracle* dispute, felt that those who wished to wipe out state and local censorship of movies had seized on the row over *The Miracle* and used it cleverly for their own purposes. It was easier to make a case on an inter-religious question involving sacrilege, Legion spokesmen felt, than on the issue of whether immoral, obscene, or indecent films should be censored. As for the condemnation of *The Miracle* being part of an effort to extend "control" to the foreign film market, Legion officials stated that they judged films by their content, not their origin.

In retrospect, it might be correct to say that both camps rallied to basic positions once the dispute moved from the local level, involving one theater and a License Commissioner, toward the United States Supreme Court level, where it became a question affecting movie censorship, religious group pressures and counter-pressures, and church-state relations for the entire nation.

In the New York
State Court of Appeals

On October 18, the Court of Appeals of New York State ruled five to two that the regents had been legally justified in revoking the license of *The Miracle*. There was an opinion for a four-man majority, a concurring opinion for one judge, Justice Charles S. Desmond, and a dissent for Judges Stanley H. Fuld and Marvin R. Dye. The opinions took up about thirty closely printed pages.

The opinion of the court, by Justice Charles W. Froessel, discussed five contentions made by counsel for Burstyn. First, that the regents were powerless to review the action of the Motion Picture Division; as to this, the court brushed aside the argument that Burstyn, acting on the basis of the license, had spent a great deal of money advertising and promoting the film. As a matter of statutory construction, the court held that the legislature had not intended to make the Motion Picture Division an autonomous body and that review by the regents was perfectly valid.

Second, that in using the term "sacrilegious," the statute delegated legislative power without adequate standards; as to this, the court held that the "dictionary . . . furnishes a clear definition thereof, were it necessary to seek one, e.g., 'the act of violating or profaning anything sacred' (Funk & Wagnalls' New Standard Dictionary, 1937). There is no difficulty in recognizing the limits of the criterion thus established, and the courts have had no problem either with the word 'sacrilegious' or with its synonym, 'profane.' " In support of this contention, the court cited three Supreme Court cases in which statutes using the terms "sacrilegious" or "profane" had not been challenged for those terms.

Third, that the regents, even if empowered to act, had acted unreasonably in finding *The Miracle* "sacrilegious"; to this the court replied:

> We have all viewed the film in question. The so-called exhibits [pre-

sented by counsel for Burstyn], which are simply unsworn communications expressing personal opinions, are of little help to us. The principal basis for the charge of sacrilege is found in the picture itself, the personalities involved, the use of scriptural passages as a background for the portrayal of the characters, and their actions, together with other portions of the script and the title of the film itself.

The opinion reviewed each of these aspects of the film, interpreted them as supporting a finding of "sacrilegious," and held that the regents' judgment could not be overturned as unreasonable.

Fourth, that denial of a license on the ground of sacrilege entailed a religious judgment by the censoring authority and constituted an interference in religious matters by the state as well as a denial of religious freedom, since "one man's sacrilege is another man's dogma." The court rejected the first part of this argument by saying that there was "nothing mysterious" about the standard and no religious judgment by the state. "[The] fact that some benefit may incidentally accrue to religion is immaterial from the constitutional point of view if the statute has for its purpose a legitimate objective within the scope of the police power of the State. . . ."

> We are essentially a religious nation (*Church of the Holy Trinity v. United States,* 153 U. S. 457, 465), of which it is well to be reminded now and then, and in the *McCollum* case [333 U. S. 203] the Supreme Court paused to note that a manifestation of governmental hostility to religion or religious teachings "would be at war with our national tradition" (at p. 211). The preamble to our State Constitution expresses our gratitude as a people to Almighty God for our freedom. To say that government may not intervene to protect religious beliefs from purely private or commercial attacks or persecutions, whatever the underlying motive, and however skillfully accomplished, as distinguished from the assertion of conflicting beliefs, is to deny not only its power to keep the peace, but also the very right to "the free exercise" of religion, guaranteed by the First Amendment.

Mockery and ridicule "can be a deadly form of persecution" the opinion noted, and prohibiting it was within the legitimate sphere of state power.

Fifth, that the statute was unconstitutional *in toto* because motion pictures were to be treated as the press and were not subject to prior restraint. On this issue, the court affirmed its belief that the *Mutual Film* case had been rightly decided by the United States Supreme Court in 1915 and should be adhered to still.

Justice Desmond, in a concurring opinion, based his position concerning the status of motion pictures on the assumption that movies were included within the protection of the First Amendment (citing Justice Douglas' dictum in the *Paramount Pictures* case), even though certain well-defined and narrowly-limited classes of expression could be censored. This included matters that were lewd, obscene, libelous, and profane or "fighting words." *The Miracle* could be banned as coming within one of these censorable categories. To hold that "any prior censorship at all of any motion picture is unconstitutional" Desmond concluded, would mean "that the floodgates are open."

The dissenting opinion by Justice Fuld, for himself and Justice Dye, was as long as the majority opinion and made two points. On the first, the dissent argued that the legislature had never intended the regents to have power to revoke a license once issued.

The second point of the dissent focused on the freedom of expression issue. Arguing that the "consistent course of decision by the Supreme Court of the United States in recent years . . . persuades me that [the *Mutual Film* case] no longer has the force or authority here claimed for it," Justice Fuld proceeded to re-examine the entire setting of the New York censorship law. This law, the opinion stated, was a prior restraint on the right to disseminate ideas via motion picture—the "baldest form" of censorship. While it was true that the freedoms of the First Amendment were not absolute, the dissent noted, "they are as near to absolute as our judicial and political system recognizes." Some restraint might be accepted in cases where there was "pressing public need," but such, it was argued, was not present in the case being decided. There was no "captive audience" on the public streets to protect. Moreover the reliance upon "sacrilege" was itself constitutionally infirm. "Over a century ago, the Supreme Court declared that 'the law knows no heresy and is committed to the support of no dogma. . . .' (*Watson v. Jones,* 80 U. S. 679, 728). Just as clearly it is beyond the competency of government to prescribe norms of religious conduct and belief."

As for the use of "sacrilege" as a standard, the "inherent indefinability" of this term "is apparent upon the merest inquiry." There are more than 250 religious sects in the United States, the dissenting opinion noted, and it asked: At what point does the search for truth by one overlap into a challenge to the dogmas of another? Probing the definitions adopted by the regents, the Appellate Division, and the majority consensus, the dissent charged that "the adherents of a particular dogma become the only judges as to whether that dogma has been offended! And if that is so, it is impossible to fathom how any governmental agency such as the board of regents, composed as it is of laymen of different faiths, could possibly discharge the function of determining whether a particular film is 'sacrilegious.' " As to the United States Supreme Court cases where the terms "sacrilegious" and "profane" had been cited by the majority, the dissent said that none of them had involved direct considerations of those words by the court and that the word "profane" had been used not in the sense of religion but as a synonym for "swearing and epithets."

The dissenting opinion concluded with a plea that the First Amendment be meaningfully interpreted for the contemporary scene.

A belief does not lose its character as a belief, an idea does not become less of an idea, because, instead of being expressed by the "air-borne voice," the printed word, or the "still" picture, it is put forward by a "moving" picture. The First Amendment does not ask whether the medium is visual, acoustic, electronic or some yet-unheard-of device. . . . The *Mutual Film* case should be relegated to its place on the history shelf. . . .

The Miracle in the United States Supreme Court

The highest court in New York having upheld the ban, Burstyn and his supporters now turned their hopes to Washington. Getting a case into the Supreme Court is far from automatic. For example, during the 1951 term (October 1951 to June 1952) lawyers filed 1,107 cases in the Supreme Court. The justices accepted and decided only 200 of these, 101 being cases brought on "appeal" and 99 on "certiorari." Burstyn's petition was an appeal from the decision of the state's highest court based on the claim that Burstyn's federal constitutional rights had been infringed by the state. A request for review was filed by Ephraim London on December 4, 1951 and a "Statement As To Jurisdiction" on January 12, 1952. It remained to be seen whether the Supreme Court would take this case, since the *RD-DR Corporation* case and others on lower court decisions of state movie censorship laws had been denied review in the court. There was not long to wait, for the Supreme Court announced on February 4 that there was "probable jurisdiction." With this, *The Miracle* case moved into the nation's high court for determination.

Group Developments

Supreme Court rules permit the filing of *amicus curiae* (friend of the court) briefs by persons or groups not directly involved in the case as litigants. In theory the amicus briefs present to the justices arguments which have not been fully treated or even raised by counsel for the parties. Sometimes, amicus briefs are filed on behalf of the government. Sometimes private associations of an economic, civic, religious, or racial character intervene in order to express their constitutional position or because it is assumed that an expression of concern by the organization might have an effect on the justices beyond that of reason alone. To prevent too many amicus briefs from clogging its rationed time, the Supreme Court's rules require that counsel for each side of the case agree to the filing of each amicus brief. Even if one attorney refuses to permit filing, the court retains power to accept the brief if the court feels that it would be useful to have it.

In *The Miracle* case, several aspects of the amicus situation deserve mention—the Catholic briefs, the civil liberty and non-Catholic religious group briefs, and the position of the Hollywood film industry.

The New York Catholic Welfare Committee had filed an amicus brief supporting the Regents' ruling in the New York appellate courts, and it was prepared to present a brief to the Supreme Court. Drafting the brief was Porter Chandler, a partner in the Wall Street firm of Davis, Polk, Wardwell, Sunderland & Kiendl. Chandler was legal adviser to Cardinal Spellman, particularly on property matters relating to the Archdiocese of New York.

A Liberal Catholic Committee

However, as noted, not all New York Catholics shared the position taken by Cardinal Spellman and by the State Catholic Welfare Committee. During 1951 a group of Catholic writers, teachers, editors, and lawyers in the New York City area, some of whom had voiced individual disagreement publicly over *The Miracle* ban, decided that more than individual statements would be necessary if the American public were to understand the division of Catholic opinion. The fact that the only Catholic briefs in the New York courts had been those supporting censorship convinced these persons that it was essential for them to file a brief in the Supreme Court, as Catholics, taking the opposite side.

By January 1952 a Committee of Catholics for Cultural Action had been formed. Its organizing board was made up of Joseph Bennett, William P. Clancy, Robert Fitzgerald, Robert Giroux, Frederick Morgan, James Johnson Sweeney, and David DuVivier, legal counsel for the committee. A draft of a brief was prepared and circulated to like-minded Catholic laymen throughout the country. They were invited to join the committee and participate in the presentation of the brief as the first step in a course of actions designed to demonstrate Catholic support for intellectual and cultural freedom in the United States. The invitation stressed that "enemies of the Church in the United States" had made much of "what they call the 'monolithic' character of American Catholic cultural and political life," and of the consistent appearance of this attitude "on the side of censorship and suppression, a narrowly short-sighted sectarianism, and an anti-Communism which is too frequently uncritical, sterile, and negative." To show that there is a "wide area for a healthy and constructive disagreement among Catholics," the letter of invitation continued, the committee would take public stands in controversies involving "politics, art or education," expounding "the Catholic tradition of essential freedom in civil and cultural matters."

News of the committee's formation appeared in the press. Later in January the executive officers of the committee were invited to a conference at the Chancery Office of the Archdiocese of New York. The Chancellor of the Archdiocese, Monsignor Walter Kellenberg, indicated strongly to the group that theirs would be an unwise action. It would undermine the authority of the Cardinal, give comfort to the enemies of the Church, and support the cause of licentiousness and sacrilege in films. Spokesmen for the committee received the advice respectfully but informed the Monsignor that, while they did not question the Cardinal's powers to warn Catholics against immoral films, they felt it their right as Catholics and as American citizens to oppose both state censorship of films and lay Catholic vigilantism.

Previously Porter Chandler had in-

vited members of the committee to a luncheon at the Harvard Club and had urged them not to file a brief. Given the legal issues before the Supreme Court, he warned, the committee would be forced to support the propositions that the state could not censor movies or that sacrilege could not be a ground for denial of a license. Chandler did not think the committee would want to support such far-reaching and dangerous propositions. Actually, the committee had included exactly those two points in its brief, and it went ahead with its plans to file.

During February and early March, however, a dispute broke out between Solicitor General Wendell Brown of New York and Ephraim London concerning who, if anyone, would be allowed to file an amicus brief. In December 1951 Brown had agreed to the filing of a brief by the American Civil Liberties Union (ACLU), supporting Burstyn. By February, additional requests had been made to Brown by the American Jewish Congress, the Metropolitan Committee for Religious Liberty, and the Catholic Committee for Cultural Action. Brown advised these groups that to keep the number of briefs "within reasonable bounds" New York would consent to the filing of only one amicus brief on each side of the case. He suggested that the three other groups and others desiring to file might join in the ACLU brief.

The ACLU Board refused to let other groups join its brief, however, on the ground that "a brief on pure civil liberties grounds filed by an organization interested solely therein should not be joined by groups of a specific sectarian nature or those which naturally have a special interest in the outcome." (Artists Equity had by then asked permission to file a brief of its own.) The ACLU counsel proposed to Brown that New York allow additional briefs to be filed if counsel writing them looked at the ACLU brief and avoided duplication.

Meanwhile, London had his own tactical situation to protect.[12]

He was naturally anxious to get the Catholic Committee for Cultural Action brief before the justices in order to show the diversity among Catholics. Having read the ACLU brief, which focused on freedom of expression, and the brief written for the American Jewish Congress by Leo Pfeffer, which dealt with state intrusion on religious grounds, London was especially concerned to have the Pfeffer brief reach the Supreme Court. To advance these goals, London wrote Patrick Dugan, official counsel to the State Catholic Welfare Committee, indicating refusal to permit Dugan to file his amicus brief because New York would not let Protestant, Jewish, and Catholic groups submit briefs on Burstyn's side. To have the State Committee's brief as the only religious group presentation, London said, would create "an erroneous impression with respect to the attitude of religious groups toward the issue."

Faced by this situation, New York offered to admit two briefs for the anticensorship cause, the ACLU brief and one joined in by "all the other organizations." However, the other groups would not agree to a collaboration. Then New York stated that it was with-

drawing consent to any amicus briefs, since London would not let the State Catholic Committee enter. On receipt of that news, the ACLU Board reconsidered and voted to allow other groups to "join or endorse" its brief. Brown told Herbert Monte Levy of the ACLU that he would accept this joint brief if London would let the State Catholic Committee file. Levy replied that London would be "better disposed" to consent if the Catholic Committee for Cultural Action could also file. Brown agreed, and in late March the way was finally clear for two amicus briefs supporting Burstyn and one defending New York's position. The joint brief, in which the ACLU argument on freedom of expression was joined with the American Jewish Congress exposition about religious freedom, was presented on behalf of those two groups plus the International Motion Picture Organization (a group of foreign film importers founded in 1950, with Joseph Burstyn and Mrs. Gerard of the Paris Theater among its directors) and the Metropolitan Committee for Religious Liberty. The American Book Publishers Council and the National Lawyers Guild were refused permission by New York to file but sought permission from the Supreme Court and were allowed to submit their briefs.

Talks at the Chancery Office

Legally, the Catholic Committee for Cultural Action could now present its brief. Beginning March 31, though, spokesmen for the committee had attended a series of informal meetings at the Chancery office with Monsignor John S. Middleton, representing the Archdiocese's interests. (At no time did Cardinal Spellman meet with the committee, but committee members "understood" that His Eminence was aware of the negotiations and guided their

---

[12] In the spring of 1951, London had corresponded with the leaders of several Protestant groups—the Committee on Religious Freedom of the Baptist World Congress, the Episcopal League for Social Action, and the American Protestant Defense League—in an effort to present amicus briefs to the courts on behalf of organized Protestantism. But no briefs were ever filed by these groups, largely, it seems, because Protestant denominations singly and the National Council of Churches as their confederate spokesman moved very slowly in such matters and rarely filed briefs in constitutional cases.

general course.) Monsignor Middleton heard the committee directors present their concern over such actions by Catholic lay groups as the picketing of the Metropolitan Opera House for the portrayal of the Church in Verdi's *Don Carlo,* Catholic War Veteran threats to a New York television station which planned to show some old Chaplin films, and similar examples of "cultural intolerance." Monsignor Middleton expressed a deep interest in helping to prevent extremist actions by lay groups and to foster a climate of cultural freedom. He indicated that some lay activities had been a source of growing concern at the Chancery.

He went on to suggest that a better result might be achieved for both the Church and cultural freedom if the committee did not file a brief in the Supreme Court. He said that there were serious problems involved in the arguments the committee was making, problems of Catholic and secular character. If the committee withdrew, Monsignor Middleton suggested, the views of the committee would be solicited by the Chancery in future censorship issues and the Chancery would use its offices to prevent extremist action by the laity.

The directors of the committee met to consider this proposal and debated it at length, weighing the importance of speaking out in a leading controversy and keeping up their organizational momentum against the advantages of having the Chancery support cultural freedom within the Catholic community. A decision was made to withdraw the brief. Several of the members felt that if the Chancery performed as desired, a larger battle would be won; if the Chancery did not, the committee could always speak out in the next controversy.

The committee put its decision in a letter to Monsignor Middleton on April 9. It indicated that it still adhered to the correctness of its constitutional positions. But, the letter continued, the committee would not file "chiefly out of consideration for the larger ambiguities in the situation and out of filial deference and respect for the position of his Eminence the Cardinal Archbishop."

Following its withdrawal, the committee was invited to read Chandler's brief for the State Catholic Committee. Several objections were made to statements therein, and some of these were modified to meet the criticisms. However, the basic constitutional position of the Chandler brief remained diametrically opposed to the position of the Committee of Catholics for Cultural Action.

DuVivier wrote London that the committee had decided not to file a brief. London, who had a draft of the brief in his files and had been maneuvering vigorously to see that it got to the justices, was terribly disappointed and attributed the withdrawal to Chancery pressures. DuVivier told him that the reason for the committee's decision could be found in the Gospel according to St. Matthew, Chapter 18, Verse 15. There, London found the lines:

> . . . If thy brother shall trespass against thee, go and tell him his fault between thee and him alone; if he shall hear thee, thou has gained thy brother.

London also could quote Scripture. He answered DuVivier that the next verse, 16, was equally relevant:

> But if he will not hear thee, then take with thee one or two more. . . .

The Industry Supports Another Case

The final group activity to be related here concerned the position of Hollywood and the major producers, who furnished more than ninety percent of the films shown in the United States. Throughout the dispute, Burstyn had been ignored and even criticized by leading figures of the movie industry. Several times Burstyn had thought seriously of dropping the fight, telling his friends that he felt "isolated" and that the issue was taking up all his waking hours. Bosley Crowther had been asking repeatedly why the industry did not strike out at state and local censorship and support *The Miracle*. On February 27 in *Variety,* the show business paper, an article appeared giving the industry's story. The Motion Picture Association of America had decided to support an appeal to the Supreme Court in another case known as the *Gelling* case. William Gelling, manager of a theater in Marshall, Texas, had been convicted and fined $200 for showing *Pinky* in violation of a ban by local censors. The industry considered this "a clear-cut, uncluttered test of the constitutionality of film censorship," and the major studios were prepared to carry the case from the Texas Supreme Court to the United States Supreme Court if the latter would take it. "In contrast," the article went on, *"The Miracle* case is mixed with a religious issue, since the principal protest against it came from Cardinal Spellman of New York." In addition, while movie attorneys "think Burstyn may well win," this would be "merely by a decision that 'sacrilegious' is too loose a criterion as used in the statute. Thus, there'd be nothing gained from an industry standpoint other than that *The Miracle* would be permitted to play in New York. . . . [The] lawyers would rather save their ammunition for the Gelling case."

In the Supreme Court of the United States

By April 18, Burstyn's brief and the brief for the State of New York (with the Attorney General of the state, Nathaniel Goldstein, joining Charles A. Brind, Jr. for the regents) had been filed with the Clerk of the Supreme Court. These were lengthy and comprehensive statements of the facts and the law in the case as each side saw it, and they included as their main themes the arguments already described above in the various proceedings.

Oral argument before the Supreme Court was held on April 24, and observers watched closely for any signs as to which way the justices were leaning. London argued for Burstyn; Brind and Wendell Brown, Solicitor General of New York, argued on behalf of the State of New York. The presentation lasted from 12:10 until 1:55. As is customary in arguments before the Supreme Court, the justices interrupted frequently to probe arguments being presented by counsel. The court was composed of Chief Justice Fred Vinson and Associate Justices Hugo Black, William O. Douglas, Stanley Reed, Robert Jackson, Felix Frankfurter, Harold Burton, Tom Clark, and Sherman Minton.

The question of the regents' power to review the action of the Motion Picture Division and to revoke the license was a matter of interpretation of New York law. On such issues the United States Supreme Court accepts the construction of the state supreme court. Therefore only "federal questions" could be raised by Burstyn. London summarized these in his opening remarks:

> The questions raised are these: One, is the film censorship statute void as an unconstitutional abridgment of the right of free communication? Second,

is the standard that was applied in this particular case unconstitutional? May a film be suppressed if found sacrilegious?

The Supreme Court had attended a private showing of *The Miracle*. Counsel for both sides, in reviewing the film's content, referred the justices to the specifics of the film.

An account of the argument and the questions of the justices was presented by *United States Law Week* at the time. Selections from this account are included below:

Continuing his history of the film's appearances in the United States, Mr. London stated that the film was not found sacrilegious by ministers and theologians of many Protestant sects who saw the film in the Community Church in Boston and in the Union and Princeton Theological Seminaries.

"What is the direction of this argument?" Mr. Justice Frankfurter wanted to know. "What is the purpose of all this?"

Mr. London: "To show that there is a religious controversy involved."

Taking the position that the Mutual Film case "has been all but explicitly overruled, and may no longer be considered controlling authority," Mr. London insisted that motion pictures are a medium of expression and communication and therefore are entitled to the "privileges, immunities and freedom guaranteed the press by the Constitution." The New York statute provides for censoring and licensing of communications prior to their distribution or publication. The main purpose of the First Amendment's prohibition of interference with the press is to prevent the imposing of restraints before publication.

Mr. Justice Frankfurter: "You do not urge that an exhibitor of an obscene or sacrilegious film could not be prosecuted after the showing, but that such a system of prior licensing must fall."

Mr. London: "Yes, your Honor, such a system must fall."

Mr. Justice Frankfurter: "Under your view, if no license is required and the exhibitor is prosecuted, that wouldn't affect the continued showing of the picture."

"Well, then you have the same situation as in the case of books and magazines. A person in his right mind wouldn't continue showing a film if he had been criminally prosecuted for showing it."

"Well, as a matter of law, it wouldn't stop him."

Mr. London agreed, stating that all he was contending for is that the same standards be applied to motion pictures as are applied to books and magazines.

"What about theatrical plays?" Mr. Justice Reed queried.

"I would say that the same thing applies to theatrical plays. But, as a matter of fact, I don't think New York has ever censored theatrical plays."

Mr. Justice Minton: "What about television?"

"Well, we have a strange situation with regard to television. Persons who can't see a film in a theater because it has been censored can see the same film on television."

"Would you argue," Mr. Justice Minton asked, "that even if the film is sacrilegious it cannot be censored?"

"That is my next argument. My position is that a movie cannot ever be censored in advance."

"Not even for obscenity?"

"That's right."

.   .   .   .

His final argument was that the statute violates the First Amendment's guarantee of freedom of religion, which protects "statements of religious disbelief as well as statements of religious beliefs." On this point, Mr. London claimed that his position could be sustained without overruling the Mutual Film cases, which, he said, involved the inclusion of motion pictures within the constitutional guarantee of a free press.

Mr. Justice Frankfurter: "Has Ohio a provision regulating religious movies?"

"Yes, it did."

"Then that same issue was involved there."

"Yes, I believe it was."

New York's Argument

Charles A. Brind, Jr., counsel to the Board of Regents of the University of the State of New York and the State Education Department, began the State's argument by pointing out to the Court that the licensing statute in question is a very narrow one—in fact, much narrower than the Ohio censorship statute upheld in the Mutual Film cases. First of all, the Education Department must license all films "unless" it finds that a particular film is obscene, indecent, immoral, or sacrilegious. Second, "current event" films may be exhibited without inspection and without permits or fees. And finally, permits for scientific, educational, and religious films are issued without examination upon the filing by the owner of a description of the film and a statement that it is not to be exhibited at a place of amusement.

In outlawing the showing of "sacrilegious" films, Mr. Brind continued, the New York statute prevents the vilifying and reviling of the religious beliefs of any segment of the population, whatever segment and whatever religious persuasion may be involved. It is not applicable to any one religion and therefore does not involve the religious opinions of the censors.

Mr. Justice Frankfurter: "Do you mean that whether or not a film is sacrilegious can be mechanically determined?"

Mr. Brind insisted that it could.

"How do you find out that it profanes a religious doctrine? To what authority do you refer?"

In reply Mr. Brind stated that in this case the Regents reached the conclusion that "The Miracle" was of such a nature as to be offensive to the American public.

Mr. Justice Frankfurter: "The Regents didn't profess to say that there is an established Catholic doctrine and that the picture ridiculed it?"

Mr. Brind: "That's right."

"What I want to know is how they reached that conclusion without considering religious beliefs. . . . The criterion is in their minds. Is that it?"

"That's right."

Mr. Justice Black: "Is there any term other than 'sacrilegious' involved here?"

"No, your honor."

Mr. Justice Frankfurter: "The Regents didn't profess to go on any proclaimed doctrine of any religion?"

"That's right."

"They proceeded on their own judgment of the religious doctrine?"

"That's right."

Later, in connection with Mr. Brind's statement that religious pictures could be shown without prior examination by the censors, the Chief Justice asked: "What do you call a religious picture?"

"If a church wishes to show a picture they term religious, all they have to do is file a statement with the Board and the picture is licensed. However, if they wish to show it in a motion picture house where admission is to be charged, then it must be inspected by the censors."

Mr. Justice Frankfurter: "Do I understand you to say that if they consider this as a religious film and wish to show it in their community houses, you could be . . . compelled to issue a license?"

"That's right."

"If a foundation uses this picture as a religious picture and subsidizes a picture house so that it can show the picture without charging, you would have to issue a license?"

"That's right." However, Mr. Brind suggested that if the Education Department issued a permit for such a religious film and later received complaints that it was sacrilegious, it might have to inform the police authorities of this fact.

Mr. Justice Black: "Do I understand that the Board of Regents has power in New York to stop a church from showing a sacrilegious film?"

Mr. Brind admitted that he thought the Board should revoke the church's permit to show the film if it found out that the film violated the statute's standards. However, he also stated that the standards would differ where a church was showing the film for its own purposes, since in such a case the general public would not be witnessing the film.

Mr. Justice Jackson: "Suppose a church group that doesn't accept Divine Birth takes this particular film and says that we are going to show this film to show you that the doctrine is wrong. Could they show it?"

"I think they could. It would not be sacrilegious then."

"Well, is it or isn't it? If they used it to show how ridiculous they thought the belief is, wouldn't that be sacrilegious?"

"I don't think it would be if used in a church."

"But this picture was being used for entertainment rather than religious purposes, while a church would be using it directly for the purpose of 'lampooning' the doctrine."

"I think that if the picture is used by a church and not in a public theater, we would have no jurisdiction."

"Is this a correct statement of your view of New York law: New York law prohibits sacrilege for pay but not sacrilege for its own sake?"

"Well, I didn't want to get into that part of the argument. Mr. Brown was going to present those arguments. The only thing we are dealing with here is whether the Board has power to censor pictures which are sacrilegious and are being shown in a theater."

"And a distinction is made on the basis of charging a fee?"

"That's right."

At this point, Wendell P. Brown,

Solicitor General of New York took over the State's argument. He began by opposing the appellant's claim that the Mutual Film cases may no longer be considered controlling authority.

The Chief Justice: "You recognize that this Court has made certain statements that run counter to your argument?"

Mr. Brown: "Yes, there are such statements, but—"

The Chief Justice: "The Mutual Film cases were decided in 1915. Justice Douglas' dictum in the Paramount Pictures case [334 U.S. 131] indicated that moving pictures are covered by the First Amendment."

"But that statement was purely dictum."

"But the statement was made. . . . That was an indication—well, it shows what it shows."

"But it does not show as much as this Court's affirmance of this very statute in the Eureka case."

Mr. Justice Jackson: "Do you read Mutual Films as meaning that movies are not entitled to any protection under the First Amendment?"

"No, of course not."

"If that were true the Court would not have had to discuss the problem at such length."

"That's right, and we make no such contention."

Resuming his argument, Mr. Brown challenged his opponent's statement suggesting or implying that television films are not subjected to any censorship. He pointed out that the Communications Act specifically provides for the revocation of the broadcasting license of any station which does not reserve some control over the subject matter of its programs.

Mr. Justice Burton: "Is that to be exercised before showing or after showing the film?"

Mr. Brown: "I believe that any film distributor is obligated to submit the script before showing the film and that the station is under an obligation not to permit the showing if it is obscene, immoral, or sacrilegious. And the Federal Communications Commission may revoke its license if it does not do so."

Mr. Brown then asserted that the motion picture industry itself is not opposed to censorship, and, in fact, refused to participate as amicus curiae in this case.

Mr. Justice Jackson: "Well aren't foreign films the only ones to which this case is important, as a practical matter."

"That's right."

"Doesn't the domestic motion picture industry voluntarily submit its films to the Church for censorship?"

"It has its own censorship committee."

"Then the only application this case has is to foreign films?"

"Yes, except that there are a few independent producers who will be affected."

That the portrayal of the sacrilegious in a motion picture is an expression of the exhibitor's constitutional freedom of religion was denied by Mr. Brown. "On the contrary it is a violation of the public's freedom of religion." The right guaranteed by the First Amendment is the "right to follow one's own religious faith in an atmosphere of tolerance, respect and understanding." None of the Court's decisions protecting the expression of religious views involved a "burlesque of a religious belief for the sheer purpose of producing a motion picture that would make money at the box office. . . . It is wholly within the guarantee of religious freedom that the State prohibits that which seeks to destroy religion."

To support his contention that the word "sacrilegious" should be held sufficiently definite to satisfy the requirements of due process of law, Mr. Brown cited decisions by the Supreme Court sustaining the use of words such as "loud and raucous" and "public interest, convenience and necessity." "Sacrilegious" is a word of "common speech," which popularly conveys the meaning of irreverence of religious beliefs and precepts. Although it was

his position that the Supreme Court was required to accept the definition of "sacrilegious" adopted by the New York Court of Appeals, Mr. Brown said he had no "personal objection" to the Court's adoption of its own definition.

On the church-state separation point, Mr. Brown denied that a restraint on the ridiculing of a religious belief is an aid, adoption, or enforcement of any religious belief. The revocation of the license for the motion picture "The Miracle" did not enforce upon any one the Christian concept of Christ as "established" religion. "Indeed, to prevent the sacrilegious in a film is the very 'neutrality' for which appellant argues."

Mr. London limited his rebuttal to a denial of Mr. Brown's statement that motion picture producers do not object to censorship. He called the Court's attention to the fact that an appeal had recently been filed with it [Gelling v. Texas, No. 707] by a motion picture producer objecting to censorship.

Mr. Justice Jackson: "Don't they submit to voluntary censorship?"

"Yes, they say 'this is the democratic way of doing it.' "

"But if they submit to censorship, they don't object to it."

"But they don't submit the film to an outside censor; they submit it to themselves. They have their own censorship committee."

The Supreme Court Decision

On May 26, 1952 the Supreme Court handed down a unanimous decision reversing the New York Court of Appeals and striking down the ban on *The Miracle*. The opinion for the court was written by Justice Tom Clark. Justice Reed wrote a short concurring opinion, and Justice Frankfurter contributed an extended concurring opinion which was joined in by Justices Jackson and Burton.

Justice Clark's opinion for the court,

after reciting the facts and earlier proceedings, examined first the question of whether motion pictures were entitled to the protection of the First Amendment. Reviewing the *Mutual Film* case, Clark noted that it had been decided eleven years before the advent of talking pictures and prior to the rulings of the Supreme Court holding that liberty of speech and press in the First Amendment were guaranteed against state invasion by the due process clause of the Fourteenth Amendment. Clark concluded that the *Mutual Film* rationale was simply "out of harmony" with the court's present views. Films were "a significant medium for the communication of ideas," and their importance was "not lessened by the fact that they are designed to entertain as well as inform." That motion pictures were made for profit was declared irrelevant, since books, newspapers, and magazines were also made for profit and had traditionally been protected as forms of expression. And even if it were accepted that movies had a "greater capacity for evil, particularly among the youth of a community" than written works, "it does not follow that motion pictures should be disqualified from First Amendment protection. If there be capacity for evil it may be relevant in determining the permissible scope of community control, but it does not authorize substantially unbridled censorship such as we have here."

To hold movies protected by the First Amendment did not mean that there was "absolute freedom to exhibit every motion picture of every kind at all times and all places," Clark noted, any more than the court gave absolute protection to other media of communication. Applying the court's rules as to freedom of expression to the New York statute invoked in *The Miracle* Clark began by noting that the state law did not punish subsequently but

required "that permission to communicate ideas be obtained in advance from state officials who judge the content of the words and pictures sought to be communicated. This Court recognized many years ago that such a previous restraint is a form of infringement upon freedom of expression to be especially condemned," citing *Near v. Minnesota,* 283 U.S. 697 (1931), a case involving prior censorship of newspapers.

Therefore, Clark stated, the state had "a heavy burden" to demonstrate that the situation was one justifying prior restriction. The New York Court of Appeals formula, "that no religion, as that word is understood by the ordinary, reasonable person, shall be treated with contempt, mockery, scorn and ridicule . . ." is, Clark found, "far from the kind of narrow exception to freedom of expression which a state may carve out to satisfy the adverse demands of other interests of society. . . . [The] censor is set adrift upon a boundless sea amid a myriad of conflicting currents of religious views, with no charts but those provided by the most vocal and powerful orthodoxies." Censors would find it virtually impossible to avoid favoring one religion or banning unpopular minority sentiments, and such applications of the "sacrilegious" test would raise questions as to the First Amendment's guarantee of separation of church and state. On a free speech basis alone, however, the Court noted "it was enough to point out that the state has no legitimate interest in protecting any or all religions from views distasteful to them. . . . It is not the business of government in our nation to suppress real or imagined attacks upon a particular religious doctrine, whether they appear in publications, speeches, or motion pictures."

In conclusion, Clark stated that the court was not considering the power of a state to censor movies under "a clearly drawn statute designed and applied to prevent the showing of obscene films. . . . We hold only that under the First and Fourteenth Amendments a state may not ban a film on the basis of a censor's conclusion that it is 'sacrilegious.' "

Justice Reed wrote a one-paragraph concurring opinion:

> Assuming that a state may establish a system for the licensing of motion pictures, an issue not foreclosed by the Court's opinion, our duty requires us to examine the facts of the refusal of a license in each case to determine whether the principles of the First Amendment have been honored. This film does not seem to me to be of a character that the First Amendment permits a state to exclude from public view.

Justice Felix Frankfurter's concurring opinion (joined in by Justices Jackson and Burton) opened by quoting an account of *The Miracle's* content and meaning by Bosley Crowther, who was described by Frankfurter as "a practiced hand." Frankfurter then summarized fully the history of the film's reception in Italy and New York. Moving into the constitutional issues, Frankfurter commented:

> Arguments by the parties and in briefs amici invite us to pursue to their farthest reach the problems in which this case is involved. . . . We are asked to decide this case by choosing between two mutually exclusive alternatives: that motion pictures may be subjected to unrestricted censorship, or that they must be allowed to be shown under any circumstances. But only the tyranny of absolutes would rely on such alternatives to meet the problems generated by the need to accommodate the diverse interests affected by motion pictures in compact modern communities.

These broader problems the court would have had to meet, Frankfurter noted, had the New York Court of Appeals given "sacrilegious" the "meaning it has had in Catholic thought since St. Thomas Aquinas formulated its scope. . . ." But the New York court, said Frankfurter, did not so limit its use of the word but viewed it as "a self-defining term," based upon quotation from Funk and Wagnalls' Dictionary: "The act of violating or profaning anything sacred." This did not define at all, but introduced two new words which leave "wide open the question as to what persons, doctrines or things are 'sacred' . . . [and] what representations on the screen will constitute 'profaning'. . . ."

Frankfurter's opinion then presented a painstaking survey of the meaning of the word "sacrilegious" as drawn from a look at legal dictionaries and indices, world history from early religious eras to the present, church law, English law, leading dictionaries through the ages, and contemporary sources. The clear import of this survey was that "sacrilege" was a concept limited to the physical abuse or misuse of property dedicated to religious uses, such as church vestments, ornaments, or monies. As used by the New York courts, the term had been expanded to mean something closer to the offense of "blasphemy," which was clearly distinguished from "sacrilege" by all the authorities canvassed by Justice Frankfurter.

With the meaning of "sacrilege" so expanded, said Frankfurter, grave problems presented themselves. "Blasphemy was the chameleon phrase which meant the criticism of whatever the ruling authority of the moment established as orthodox religious doctrine." In the United States, decisions of the Supreme Court had been clear in rejecting the idea that an official orthodoxy could be imposed by government, and New York's use of "sacrilegious" opened the way for intrusions into beliefs.

To allow "such vague, undefinable powers of censorship," Frankfurter stated, would have a stultifying effect upon art and literature, and history "does not encourage reliance on the wisdom and moderation of the censor as a safeguard in the exercise of such drastic power over the minds of men." Thus, Frankfurter concluded, the New York statute offended due process in two ways. It did not forewarn persons of what might be predictably found to be "illicit" by the state authority. And where the initial judgment was made by an administrative agency, "judicial review is in effect made inoperative."

> On the basis of such a portmanteau word as "sacrilegious," the judiciary has no standards with which to judge the validity of administrative action which necessarily involves, at least in large measure, subjective determinations. Thus, the administrative first step becomes the last step.

Related Decisions

During the spring of 1952, the United States Supreme Court handed down two other related decisions, one involving church and state and the other an application of First Amendment guarantees resembling that in *Burstyn v. Wilson*. On April 28 in *Zorach v. Clauson,* a six-man majority upheld New York's system of released time for religious instruction. Justice Douglas' majority opinion stressed that there was no evidence that students were coerced into joining the released time program or that public school funds, teachers, or property were used in the religious instruction. The dissents by Justices Black, Jackson, and Frankfurter argued that the state's machinery

was still being used to aid religion in a way which offended the "wall of separation" of the First Amendment, and that coercion was involved.

On April 28 the second ruling was issued, in the case of *Beauharnais v. Illinois*. Beauharnais, a leader of the White Circle League, had distributed leaflets attacking the "mongrelization" of the white race by Negroes and protesting the need to take measures against the "rapes, robberies, knives, guns and marijuana of the negro. . . ." Beauharnais was convicted under a 1917 law which forbade publications which portray "depravity, criminality, unchastity, or lack of virtue of a class of citizens, of any race, color, creed or religion" in a way which "exposes the citizens . . . to contempt, derision, or obloquy or which is productive of breach of the peace or riots. . . ." Five justices upheld the conviction and the statute in an opinion by Justice Frankfurter, concluding that Beauharnais' right to free speech did not prevent the state from punishing a criminal libel directed at certain defined groups and thereby preventing racial and religious violence such as the Chicago race riot in 1919 which had led to the Illinois Act. Justices Jackson, Reed, Douglas, and Black, in their various dissents, argued that freedom of speech was infringed, that terms such as "virtue," "derision," and "obloquy" were too ambiguous to be constitutional, that no "clear and present danger" of violence was shown, and that traditional defenses to libel actions such as "fair comment," "truth," and "privilege" had been denied to Beauharnais.

Reaction to the Supreme Court's Ruling

On May 27, the day after the Supreme Court's ruling in *Burstyn v. Wilson* was handed down, the Board of

Regents restored the license of *The Miracle.*

Burstyn was elated. He told the press that "this marks the beginning of adult days for the film industry." Bosley Crowther in the *New York Times* said:

> The highest tribunal in the land cut through what has been an inhibition for thirty-seven years—to wit, the reactionary notion that movies are but childish "spectacles" and may therefore be legally restricted by pre-release censorship.

Eric Johnston, head of the Motion Picture Association, applauded the ruling as a "giant step forward toward removing all the shackles of censorship from the screen." New York newspapers had high praise for the decision, as did some 37 newspapers across the country sampled by the Motion Picture Association. Writing in the trade paper, *Boxoffice,* Ivan Spear discussed what remained to be done by the industry:

> Still to be captured and permanently razed are the censorship hurdles constantly being erected by pressure groups, large and small. They regularly spring into existence under the tattered banners of religious, moral, or patriotic interest in motion pictures, but all too often and all too transparently they stem from selfish machinations and desires of individuals or organizations for headlines, self-aggrandizement or personal financial gain.

On Wednesday, June 25, a luncheon honoring Joseph Burstyn for his fight in *The Miracle* case was tendered by the International Motion Picture Organization. Three hundred and ten members of the industry attended. One of the speakers, Arthur Garfield Hays, praised Burstyn and London for accomplishing what the big film companies "with all their money," had been unable to achieve.[13]

Criticism of the Supreme Court's ruling came as fast as the praise. Frederic L. Vorbeck, executive chairman of United Catholic Organizations for the Freeing of Cardinal Mindszenty, called the decision "intolerant and insulting," one which "has torn to shreds the sensibilities of 28,000,000 American Catholics by blessing the showing of the scurrilous film." Vorbeck stated that his group, and others, would resume picketing of theaters which showed *The Miracle.*

Reaction in leading Catholic periodicals ran a wide gamut. Writing in the Jesuit magazine *America,* its editor, Father Robert C. Hartnett, acknowledged that the standard of "sacrilege" as applied by the New York authorities

> . . . might well be . . . too jejune to serve as a statutory guide. Mr. Justice Frankfurter called "sacrilegious" a "chameleon phrase."
>
> One gets the feeling, nevertheless, that the same colorful expression might equally well be applied to dozens of terms the Supreme Court habitually interprets and enforces: "liberty," "unfair," "reasonable," "clear and present danger," "interstate commerce," "political" and so on endlessly. What are courts for, if not to build up, case by case, working definitions of "indefi-

[13] The cost to Burstyn of fighting the ban from the first action by Commissioner Mc-Caffrey to the United States Supreme Court was between $55,000 and $60,000. Of this, about $40,000 was legal expense, including lawyers' fees, printing of briefs and record, and court fees. The remaining $20,000 was spent for such activities as showing the film at Protestant theological seminaries and elsewhere to obtain endorsements, wiring cultural leaders for statements, taking films of picketing, and other related matters. Since all of this was in defense of his property rights in the film, Burstyn was able to deduct the entire cost on his income tax as an expense against the profits earned by the film.

nite" terms? Incidentally, if a Catholic had been on the Supreme Court, he might have helped to keep the discussion closer to the real meaning of "sacrilege." As it was the Justices strayed far afield.

Warning that government and the legal system must not be a force for "further secularizing American culture" Father Hartnett ended his article:

> The Supreme Court, one must conclude, has just about emptied our law of respect for Almighty God. It upholds laws against "group libel," but not laws prohibiting "sacrilegious" films. Are "groups" more sacred to us than the things of God? On this score, the court is eroding the very cornerstone of respect for both individuals and groups. It had better modify its rather one-sided Burstyn verdict.

Writing in the influential archdiocesan paper of Boston, *The Pilot,* its editor, Monsignor Francis Lally, remarked:

> For some strange reason the impression has got about that Catholics are uniformly unhappy about the recent ruling of the Supreme Court on the occasion of *The Miracle* case. This simply is not so. The unanimous decision of the Court had nothing to say about the grossly insulting nature of the film or its sacrilegious character, and those who found it offensive artistically and religiously can continue to hold their views. Similarly, those who wish to boycott it and persuade others to do the same have no reason to desist. . . .
> We are faced with the question of the function of the state in a society where various religions are conscientiously held by their adherents. The civil power must protect the consciences of its citizens in those matters which do not damage the general welfare; it will scarcely do for the civil authorities however to determine what

is sacred, or what is sacrilegious. When they speak in these accents they assume a competence which is not theirs.

The Pilot editorial concluded by counseling Catholics to stay away from the film, to write or phone theaters which showed a picture insulting to many of its clients, and thus to touch the movie industry in its "box office receipts."

The National Council of Catholic Men made up a special one-page sheet of questions and answers about "The Miracle Case," prepared by the Legal Department of the National Catholic Welfare Conference. Among the fourteen questions and answers was the following:

> What can be done about it? The whole controversy must be fought in the forum of public opinion; for in the last analysis the only effective bulwark against pictures which are immoral, short of being obscene, is public opinion manifested through such an organization as the Legion of Decency. The alternative is the motion picture industry's self-regulation, and undoubtedly this will fluctuate in accordance with public opinion.

Two Catholic publications came out in firm support of the Supreme Court's decision. The *Indiana Catholic and Record,* official paper of the Archdiocese of Indianapolis, declared that it viewed the film itself as "utterly blasphemous and offensive to all Christians," but found it "hard to dispute" the logic of the Supreme Court's holding. Prior censorship by the state of all films "could become a dangerous weapon."

And an editorial in *The Commonweal* stated:

> What was really at stake in *The Miracle* controversy was this uniquely

lay character of the American State. The civil power was in danger of playing the role of theologian by attempting to determine a properly religious concept. . . . Far from this being an "anti-religious," or "secularist-motivated" decision, it is one which rests on [an] . . . enlightened, rational, and truly liberal philosophy of civil and religious freedom. . . . Catholics might well make it clear that they accept the modern "lay" state . . . and resist any such attempts to vitiate or alter the character of this state as were present in the New York [episode]. . . .

Once the first flurry of newspaper and periodical commentary had subsided, lawyers and group spokesmen began to consider carefully just what the decision meant and how far its impact swept. Industry lawyers were quoted as saying that the ruling did not challenge the basic power of state censor boards as such and that it would take the outcome of many more cases, such as the pending *Gelling* case on *Pinky,* before the reach of the decision became clear. By itself, though, *The Miracle* ruling seemed to open the possibility of a general attack on local and state bans by industry lawyers armed with the implications of the ruling for movies as instruments of expression under the First Amendment. Specifically, it was said, the decision was narrow; it prevented only "sacrilege" from being a ground for prior restraint, and no other film was currently in trouble on that charge.

The immediate situation of *The Miracle* itself helped to clarify just what the decision would mean to censorship practices. *The Miracle* reopened in New York City, not at the Paris but at ten theaters in Manhattan, the Bronx, and Brooklyn. The advertisements in the press announced:

The World's Most Talked About Movie—See for Yourself—The Original Uncut Version . . . Exactly as it Was Approved by the UNITED STATES SUPREME COURT.

In New York State, the film had a good run; in Buffalo, for example, it broke box office records. However, in Nassau County (Long Island) and in Philadelphia, performances were canceled because of threatened boycotts by Catholic lay organizations. Pickets marched at several New York City theaters. In Maryland, the state censor board reiterated that the movie was "an obvious indignity to religious personages and beliefs" but issued a license to it with the statement that there was "no legal alternative."

In other areas, the film ran into a brick wall despite the Supreme Court's ruling. The Ohio censors banned the film because its seduction scene was "disgusting," because it "exploits immoral conduct, if not directly, certainly indirectly," and because there was "grave danger that in an unrestricted audience the immature adolescents may accept as reasonable the behavior and distorted values of the unfortunate girl. . . ." Pasadena, Calif. also kept its ban on the movie. In Chicago, the board which had banned it earlier for mocking religion now continued its ban on the ground that the film was "obscene."

Burstyn announced that he would fight the new bans, but some of them proved difficult to dislodge. In Chicago, for example, after much maneuvering to create a test case, the American Civil Liberties Union had the ban reversed by a trial court. The Illinois Supreme Court overturned this action in 1955, construing the censorship ordinance as permitting bans for obscenity and sending the case back to the trial court. At this proceeding, a new trial judge found the movie obscene. In 1957 the Illinois Appellate Court reversed this second ruling and found the picture *not* to be obscene. By now the city decided to submit, and in 1957 a license was issued to *The Miracle*. However, Burstyn had died in 1953; his company no longer owned the rights to the film, and thus *The Miracle* was never shown in Chicago.

Meanwhile, on June 3, 1952, the

United States Supreme Court unanimously struck down the ban on *Pinky*.[14] A short opinion cited *Burstyn v. Wilson* but did not discuss the basis for judgment or the issue of censorship on grounds other than sacrilege.

---

[14] *Gelling v. Texas,* 343 U. S. 960 (1952).

From Rule to Reality: Applying the Miracle Case

To leave a discussion of *The Miracle* case in June of 1952 would be to assume that constitutional decisions are thunderbolts in a void or that a judicial ruling is entirely self-executing. The truth is that a new rule such as *Burstyn v. Wilson* opened up a host of questions.

When the Supreme Court overturned the *Mutual Film* case, it chose not to announce a comprehensive guide as to proper or improper censorship. Often, the court follows such a course, deciding large issues on small grounds in order to feel its way cautiously and build up case-by-case experience. However, the Supreme Court must also concern itself with establishing standards for administrators and guides for private action. The tension between those two values soon became evident in the court's use of the *Burstyn* precedent.

Between 1952 and 1958, the court decided four additional movie censorship cases, in each instance after the justices watched a private screening of the films.

1. In the *Superior Pictures* case (1954),[15] the court overturned two bans imposed by Ohio censors. *Native Son* had been banned as contributing to "racial friction." *M* had been ruled to be "harmful" because of its theme of crime with an underlying motif of homosexuality.

2. In the *Commercial Pictures Corp.* case, decided in conjunction with *Superior Pictures*,[16] the court overturned a New York ban on a French film, *La Ronde*. The regents had considered the film "immoral" and tending to "corrupt morals."

A seven-man majority disposed of these two cases with a short memorandum opinion which simply cited *Burstyn v. Wilson* as the controlling precedent. Since none of the three movies involved sacrilege, observers were somewhat at a loss to know how *Burstyn* covered the new situations. In both cases, Justices Douglas and Black declared in a separate statement that they believed movies to be fully protected by the First Amendment and wanted the court to hold them free from prior censorship.

3. In 1955 a unanimous court overturned a Kansas ban upon *The Moon is Blue*.[17] The censors had condemned its "sex theme" and had found it "obscene, indecent and immoral." Again, a brief per curiam opinion simply announced the result, this time citing *Burstyn* and *Superior Pictures*. Justices Douglas and Black did not register individual views.

4. In 1957 a Chicago ban upon the movie, *Game of Love* (for being "im-

---

[15] *Superior Pictures, Inc. v. Department of Education of Ohio,* 346 U. S. 587 (1954).

[16] *Id.*

[17] *Holmby v. Vaughn,* 350 U. S. 870 (1955).

moral and obscene") was reversed.[18] A memorandum opinion for seven justices cited none of the previous movie cases; instead, a 1957 decision involving books was cited.[19] That decision had held that while "obscenity is not within the area of constitutionally protected speech or press," the standards applied by government must not bar material "which does not treat sex in a manner appealing to prurient interest."

Between 1952 and 1958, then, the court had, without saying that it was doing so, stretched the *Burstyn* doctrine to cover racial themes, crime, and sexual frankness. Yet the majority had drawn back from the suggestion by Justices Douglas and Black that all prior censorship of movies was forbidden.

Lady Chatterley's Lover

In 1959, a unanimous Supreme Court struck down New York's refusal to license *Lady Chatterley's Lover*.[20] A 1954 amendment to New York's movie regulations had provided:

> . . . the term "immoral" and the phrase "of such a character that its exhibition would tend to corrupt morals" shall denote a motion picture film or part thereof, the dominant purpose of which is erotic or pornographic; or which portrays acts of sexual immorality, perversion, or lewdness, or which expressly or impliedly presents such acts as desirable, acceptable, or proper patterns of behavior.

Lady Chatterley's Lover had been banned because the film's subject matter was held to be "adultery presented as right and desirable for certain people in certain circumstances."

For six members of the court, Justice Potter Stewart held that the New York Court of Appeals had construed the statute to forbid advocacy of "an idea —that adultery under certain circumstances may be proper behavior." Even though the state said this ran counter to moral standards and even to law (adultery is a crime in New York), Justice Stewart held the "idea of adultery" to be one which could still be advocated. Citing the *Burstyn* case for the protected status of movies under the First and Fourteenth Amendments, Stewart held that the New York law cut too "close to the core of constitutional freedom" to be sustained. However, state censorship was still not completely outlawed, and no further boundary lines were drawn.

Five other opinions were written. Justice Clark elaborated and defended the majority position. Justice Black— noting that he would no longer look at films—deplored the fact that the Supreme Court was becoming a national censorship board and stated that he considered all prior censorship unconstitutional. Justice Douglas echoed this view.

An opinion by Justice Frankfurter and one by Justices John M. Harlan and Charles E. Whittaker adopted different approaches to the same result. These justices questioned the broadness of the majority opinion and its blow at the whole statute. Noting that the court did not make all previous restraint invalid, they argued that the proper procedure was a case-by-case weighing of specific films and standards. On such an examination, they thought *Lady Chatterley's Lover* was not properly classifiable as obscene.

[18] *Times Film Corp. v. City of Chicago,* 355 U. S. 35 (1957).

[19] *Albert v. California,* 354 U. S. 476 (1957).

[20] *Kingsley International Pictures Corp. v. Regents,* 360 U. S. 684 (1959).

The Supreme Court's Impact on
The Movie Industry, 1952–1960

During the eight years which followed the ruling in *Burstyn,* movies became "bolder," "franker," and "more daring" than they had been for decades. The Legion of Decency viewed this trend with alarm. In 1960 the Legion found over 24 percent of Hollywood's output objectionable, compared to 14 percent in 1959. This represented an "alarming departure from previously accepted and respected standards," the Legion's 1960 report concluded. The Roman Catholic Episcopal Committee for Motion Pictures, Radio and Television accused Hollywood of a "new-found predilection for pornographic and perverted subject matter." Protestant groups also displayed increased concern over the content of films, but did not abandon their general position against government censorship. An editorial in *Life* commented that the "bluer movies" today were not, as formerly, low-budget, "B-films" or foreign imports but major productions from Hollywood, such as *Psycho; Suddenly, Last Summer; Desire in the Dust;* and *Butterfield 8.* There is "little doubt" what caused this trend, *Life* noted. "The Supreme Court, the Hollywood Production Code, and general public sentiment (including that of the Legion itself) have combined to relax the old Hays Office taboos in favor of more 'mature' and lifelike screen standards. In law and in fact we are a less puritanical country than we were five or 10 years ago." This has produced "generally better movies," said *Life,* but "also a wave of smut."

Hollywood reaction to these criticisms in 1960 was unusually firm, although by no means defiant. Hollywood spokesmen noted that many criticized films were foreign-made, that the industry itself deplored the few ex-

amples of "sordidness" by domestic producers, that the public's standard of taste was changing (Radio City Music Hall, the nation's "family theater," was showing in 1960 *The World of Suzie Wong,* concerning a Hong Kong prostitute), and that movies had to meet competition from television by providing adult fare. Furthermore, most of the challenged American movies were renditions of books or of plays that had been shown and widely acclaimed for their value as serious drama.

How concretely the Supreme Court's rulings had been felt in this period can be learned from a look at the state censorship scene. State courts in Massachusetts, Pennsylvania, and Ohio ruled that their state censorship statutes were unconstitutional under the *Burstyn* doctrine. Several boards, as in Maryland, passed "questionable" films with public statements that they had no other choice under "Supreme Court rules." By 1961, only four states were left with state boards. Municipal censorship agencies had declined from about 175 in 1950 to fourteen in 1961. In addition, state courts, as in Illinois, steadily reversed the findings of unsuitability as to specific films banned by the state or municipal boards, in contrast to wholesale state court acceptance of censor board findings before 1952. Even those states which kept censorship, such as New York, and many of the remaining municipalities, revised their laws to attempt compliance with Supreme Court standards suggested in *Burstyn, Gelling,* and *Superior Pictures.*

However, censorship was not gone— or even inactive during these eight years. Dozens of films were banned for a wide variety of reasons. Some of the bans appeared to be clearly improper under Supreme Court decisions; others, such as those based on nudity, obscenity, and pornography, did not seem to be covered precisely by the precedents. With a record of unbroken victories in the Supreme Court since 1952, the movie makers and distributors entered the 1960s ready to test these bans— and the very process of pre-exhibition censorship itself.

The Decision in the
1961 Times Film Case

One of the most active censorship boards during 1952–1961 was in the city of Chicago, where examination of films rested with the police. After the Chicago police had ordered cuts in a number of his films which had shown across the nation without incident, the president of the Times Film Corporation told the firm's lawyer to prepare a total challenge to the city's authority. A harmless movie named *Don Juan,* a film rendition of Mozart's opera, *Don Giovanni,* was chosen for the new test. Times Film paid the license fee, refused to submit a print of the film, and demanded a permit. When this was refused, Times Film sued in federal district court to compel issuance of a permit. The suit was dismissed, and the federal court of appeals affirmed the dismissal saying that there was no issue presented because the film had not been proffered and denied a permit.

When the case was argued before the United States Supreme Court, questions put to counsel for Times Film indicated that some of the justices were disturbed by the claim that films could be shown at the will of exhibitors and that no governmental licensing requirement was permissible whatever its form and whatever the standards used. Industry lawyers and Supreme Court specialists noted this reaction and speculated that perhaps the court had been presented with the one situation most likely to reverse the trend of

anti-censorship victories—a "hypothetical" case denying all state power to censor.

On January 23, 1961, by a five to four vote, the Court rejected Times Film's position.[21] Justice Clark's opinion for the Court reviewed the holding in the *Burstyn* case that motion pictures were entitled to free speech guarantees but noted that the case had also said that "it does not follow that the Constitution requires absolute freedom to exhibit every motion picture of every kind at all times and all places." Cases after *Burstyn* had turned on specific standards, he said. The *Burstyn* decision had also noted that each method of expression presented "its own peculiar problems," so that the comparisons made to books, newspapers, and the like were not valid. The court would not hold that there was an absolute privilege against all forms of state licensing. Clark's opinion closed by noting carefully that the court was not passing on the validity of any of the standards set forth in the Chicago ordinance. Such issues would have to await a "concrete case involving a specific standard. . . ."

There were two dissenting opinions. One was written by Chief Justice Earl Warren for himself and Justices Black, Douglas, and William J. Brennan, Jr. (the latter being the only Catholic on the court). While the majority said it was leaving the question of unlimited movie censorship "for another day," Warren warned, it was really allowing a violation of freedom of expression, abandoning the court's precedents forbidding prior restraint in speech and press cases, and endangering the freedom from licensing of all forms of communication. The dissent recited several pages of examples of movie

---

21 *Times Film Corp. v. City of Chicago,* 365 U. S. 43.

bans, showing censors imposing the vaguest and most imprecise standards and putting into law a variety of prejudices about politics, morals, labor and race relations, religion, and the like. The court's opinion, he said, "officially unleashes the censor and permits him to roam at will, limited only by an ordinance [in Chicago] which contains some standards that, although concededly not before us in this case, are patently imprecise." Warren stressed the lack of due process involved in administrative licensing and concluded that the court was crippling a basic principle of the Constitution by its doctrine. A separate dissent by Justice Douglas, joined by Chief Justice Warren and Justice Black, discussed the principles of government censorship and took the position that its evils were so apparent that no censor could operate constitutionally "as long as the First Amendment survives."

Prospects for the Future

Some saw the *Times Film* case as a self-inflicted wound. A number of Hollywood lawyers had maintained all along that careful reading of the 1952–1959 decisions made it apparent that a majority of the justices was not willing to outlaw all censorship of movies. However, just as Joseph Burstyn won a constitutional victory for motion pictures on his own, unaided by the "majors," so Times Film, on its own, lost some battleground for the motion picture industry. The "majors" had played no part in the framing of the *Times Film* suit. It was only when the case reached the Supreme Court and the possible dangers to the industry were seen that the Motion Picture Association filed an amicus brief in the case. Times Film argued that there was a constitutional right to show a movie at least once, without prior examina-

tion by public officials, and this would apply no matter how obscene or pornographic the film might be. Put thus baldly, as the majority saw it to be put, *Times Film* was an extreme case. Indeed, in his dissent, the Chief Justice, in trying to shift the focus to the censorship dangers, took pains to say that "the Court is not bound by the petitioner's conception of the issue or by the more extreme positions" that the petitioner had argued.

The immediate result of the *Times Film* ruling of 1961 was to set off a wave of campaigns for municipal and state censorship laws. It also produced an unprecedented solidifying of the ranks of communication media. Times Film asked for a re-hearing of its case and was joined by amicus briefs for the American Society of Newspaper Editors, the National Association of Broadcasters, the American Book Publishers Council, the Motion Picture Association, the Independent Theater Owners Association, *Playboy* Magazine, and many other groups. Newspaper editorials throughout the nation were overwhelmingly in disagreement with the majority ruling.

What the future would produce remained in doubt. Would specific bans on films as "obscene" or "immoral" now be upheld, from time to time, by the Supreme Court? Would censorship systems be allowed to operate if they did not provide for full hearings, submission of briefs and evidence, and other aspects of due process? Did the *Times Film* case mean, as Ephraim London argued, only that the government could require presentation of films for licensing but that no approval of censorship had been given by the majority?

As of July 1961 the community groups assembled in *The Miracle* case —supporters of an uncensored screen and of movie-goer sovereignty on the one side versus supporters of government-imposed minimums as to taste and propriety on the other—continued to confront one another in passionate disagreement. The Legion of Decency, the American Jewish Congress, local Councils for Decent Literature, Protestant associations, parent-teacher organizations, license commissioners, state legislatures, movie makers, and state courts continued to grapple over the censorship issue directly as well as over its related manifestations—police pressure upon theater owners, economic boycotts, picketing, and production codes. The contest promised to be a lively—and permanent—feature of American constitutional law in the coming decades.

THREE

Politics

CASE 4

The California Democratic Delegation of 1960

JOHN H. BUNZEL

and

EUGENE C. LEE

Introduction

Had a Martian arrived at Hollywood's Hotel Knickerbocker, headquarters of the California delegation during the 1960 Democratic National Convention, and said "Take me to your leader," he would have been pushed and pulled in 162 different directions. There would have been still more guides had not the delegation been limited to 162 members. The Governor of California was the "favorite son" and head of the delegation, but he was to learn the hard way that never had so few been led by so many.

The politics of a state are writ large in the deliberations and calculations by which any of its political parties select delegates to a national convention. They also affect the way in which the delegates vote when the convention selects a presidential candidate. These generalizations are true in spite of the fact that politics differ from one state to another. What is possible in one state (or in one party) may be politically out of the question in another. To this extent no state can be considered typical, particularly not one with the size and variety of California. Theodore White has put it this way:

Note: The many quotations of conversations contained in this study are based primarily on off-the-record conversations and correspondence the authors have conducted with delegates and other political figures in California and elsewhere. Quotations from newspaper accounts have also been used but have not been footnoted. Other than these, the only source from which verbal quotations have been taken is Edwin Self's two-part article, "An Unrequited Love Affair With Adlai Stevenson," in the magazine *San Diego* (August and September 1960).

There are fifty states in this union, each of them endowed with a separate sovereignty by the Constitution. These sovereignties are genuine; they create in each state two major parties; and within each party from two to four separate political groups contend for capture, first of the state party's leadership, then of the state's sovereignty. Where true power lies in these hundreds of revolving, dissolving, nascent and fading political groups is known only by local folklore, below the threshold of public report. Such information is the trade gossip of politicians, the treasures of wisdom that political reporters exchange among one another from state to state, a baffling perplexity for academic political scientists who seek permanent truths, the aspect of mystery that the average voter confronts as he seeks to understand who controls his government.[1]

In 1960 California's 81 convention votes were a big prize, or at least they were thought to be by all of the men who were seeking the Democratic presidential nomination—Senators John Kennedy, Stuart Symington, Lyndon Johnson, and Hubert Humphrey—and by Adlai Stevenson, who entertained the hope to the very end that the convention would seek him. Governor Edmund G. (Pat) Brown and other leaders of the Democratic Party in California were aware of the national significance of California's votes. They were also aware of local considerations which could be dismissed only at great risk to continuation of their party's political power in the state. These local considerations they accorded as high a priority as the national business of the convention itself.

---

[1] From *The Making of the President 1960* by Theodore H. White, pp. 135–136. Copyright © 1961 by Atheneum House Inc. Reprinted by permission of Atheneum Publishers.

The California Democratic Party

In 1959 the leaders of the California Democratic Party hoped that they could send to the national convention in Los Angeles the following year a united delegation formally committed to Governor Brown. They hoped to avoid a heated primary contest that would cause party leaders to take sides against one another in support of opposing candidates for the presidential nomination.

The leaders were conscious that the party had much to lose in such a fight among competing delegations pledged to different candidates. For years California voters had elected Republicans at the state level despite a preponderance of registered Democrats over registered Republicans.

The Democrats had won the governorship and control of both houses of the legislature in 1958 for the first time in the twentieth century. Although there had been a fairly steady rise in Democratic state voting since 1952, the leaders were aware of the uphill road they had traveled to achieve the 1958 victory, and they were equally conscious of the fact that party dissension might send them rolling back into the political wilderness.

Political parties in California faced obstacles not present in most states. Cross-filing in primary elections—a system which had allowed candidates to run in the primaries of both parties—prevailed until 1959. It was also possible to change one's party registration before each primary election. Further, the "good government" spirit had long been at work in the state. Party labels were not used in municipal elections. Civil service systems at all levels made party patronage relatively scarce. The party organizations in California also had the task of cooperating with, and making maximum use of, sizeable volunteer groups. For the Democrats these groups took the form of local Democratic clubs, separate from the official Democratic Party organization, composed of volunteers of liberal persuasion. These clubs had been largely organized after 1952, usually around a nucleus of Stevenson supporters in each locality. They came together, in a manner of speaking, in the California Democratic Council (CDC). It would have been difficult in any circumstances to hold together a political party in such a large and dynamic state. The many criss-crossing sectional, economic, and social forces in California were comparable to those in the entire eastern and southern United States seaboard with a desert state thrown in. The state's population had doubled between 1940 and 1957, when it was estimated at about 14 million. In 1960 it was still growing at a rate of a half-a-million persons each year. The Census Bureau predicted a population of 18 million by 1965. Much of California's growth was the result of migration from other states. Its population was seen by some as tiers of immigration waves, the "old timers" being those who had migrated before the 1940s. Expanding to accommodate the new residents from all over the country, searching for more room, jobs, and water for its growing population, the state struck some observers as unlikely ever to settle down. Northern and southern Californians had long been battling for scarce water supplies—to the point where northern secession had been publicly advocated. The cultures of the two major metropolitan areas, Los Angeles and San Francisco, were notably different. In addition to capital-labor opposition, differences between old and young about pensions, and sectional differences about irrigation, the state included a host of varied industrial and agricultural interests.

In such a climate, party unity was a cherished commodity. As Democratic leaders saw it, with Stevenson, Kennedy, Humphrey and other factions competing in the June 1960 primary, the tenuous cohesiveness on which their party depended to retain state power could be shattered for years. The leaders, including Governor Brown, therefore determined to support a slate pledged to Brown as a favorite-son candidate. This meant they would have to convince the presidential contenders to accept the favorite-son slate and to stay out of the California primary. Since all of the hopefuls felt that they needed the Golden State's 81 votes to win the nomination, each insisted that he receive full and equal consideration from California and that its delegation stay pledged to Governor Brown throughout the pre-convention period. In 1959, however, it appeared that it would take a lot of political ingenuity to still the anxiety of one presidential hopeful in particular—the ambitious and resourceful junior senator from Massachusetts, John F. Kennedy.

The Early Stages

In the spring of 1959, Kennedy made his first visit to California as a very probable presidential candidate. He arrived at the Governor's office in Sacramento for a press conference, which was conducted in an easy and relaxed fashion. The Governor paid no intense attention to what was said until the senator was asked if he had made any plans regarding the California primary. Kennedy paused for a moment, stared at the desk in front of him, and then went on to praise the leadership of Governor Brown and the splendid record of his new administration. He said he understood the Governor was thinking about leading a favorite-son delegation to the Democratic convention, but as for his own plans, they were not yet firm. The Governor took note of these remarks. No one in California had given much thought either to the state primary or to the presidential convention, which were still over a year away. From that moment the situation began to change rapidly.

Governor Brown, The Favorite Son

Edmund G. (Pat) Brown, the first Democratic Governor of California since 1942, had grown up as a Catholic in an Irish-American atmosphere in San Francisco. He graduated from San Francisco Law School, was admitted to the bar in 1927, and (as a Republican) ran unsuccessfully that year for the state Assembly. In 1943 he was elected District Attorney of San Francisco and went on as a Democrat to win the office of state Attorney General in 1950. In 1954 he was the only state officer to capture the nominations of both political parties and was reelected with the highest total primary vote ever received for a contested office. As the only Democrat in a Republican administration—he served with Governors Earl Warren and Goodwin Knight—Brown had managed to build up considerable support from independents and Republicans alike and at the same time had avoided any clearcut alignment with either the conservative or liberal groups in his own party.

In 1958 Brown was elected Governor, defeating Senator William Knowland by more than one million votes. His impressive victory, and Democratic control of the legislature, led to a strong legislative program in which California Democrats took immense pride. One of the major Democratic legislative efforts was approval of a statewide water plan, a long-standing, thorny issue that had traditionally divided northern and southern Californians. Brown's record and his sponsorship of fair employment practices that were more advanced than in most states brought him national prominence. He was sometimes mentioned by Democrats as a possible presidential or vice-presidential candidate.

Brown's position in the 1959–1960 period was a difficult one, if, at times, of his own making. For one thing, following his highly successful record in the 1959 legislature, visions of the White House were observed floating above the State Capitol in Sacramento. In part these were the creatures of the Governor's staff, in part an attempt to establish California's bargaining position in the convention, still almost a year away. But in part, too, these dreams of a dark horse coming out of the West were those of one Edmund Brown. One month before, Brown had turned the Western Governors' Conference at Sun Valley into what one reporter termed a "one-man show . . . a stepping-stone on the way to the Democratic presidential nomination. . . . The governors headed for home after being more thoroughly dominated by one man than at any other time in this history of their annual conference." The party's state chairman stated that the Democrats were prepared to go "all the way" for Brown, and an even more enthusiastic supporter announced the formation of "Brown for President" clubs.

But as winter approached, even in sunny California a chill of realism overtook the Governor and his aides. To begin with, in his campaign for Governor in 1958, Brown had repeatedly charged his opponent, Senator William F. Knowland, with attempting to use the Governor's office merely as a way-station to the presidency. For Brown to turn around now and do the same thing was to lay himself open to serious attack. More importantly, perhaps, Brown had watched New York Governor Nelson Rockefeller try to launch himself as a presidential candidate in the Republican Party. Brown believed that if he wanted the nomination he would have to do the things Rockefeller had done, only better. "I would need a tremendous research staff," he told a press conference in December 1959. "I would have to go on tour nationally. I would have to put aside my duties as Governor to campaign. I have started no research program," he said. "I have made only three speeches out of the state. I do not expect to change my course in the next six months."

"Then you will take no active part in seeking the nomination?" he was asked.

"That is right," the Governor replied. But his remarks were still not unequivocal. "Of course, if someone comes in to seek delegates in California, I might seek delegates in other Western states," he added in another of his warnings to Democratic presidential hopefuls to stay put. The Governor made it clear he wanted to lead the state's large delegation to the Democratic convention as California's favorite son. "I want to do this in a way that will help insure the best possible choice by the convention of a presidential nominee. I hope for a delegation with open minds which during the next six months will seek the man who will best serve the interests of the party." These sentiments, however, appeared as nothing more than platitudes to Senator Kennedy and the men around him.

In January 1960 Governor Brown announced officially: "I have decided to allow a delegation to be formed pledged to me as head of the Democratic Party in California for the state's presidential primary next June."

The Governor's announcement followed by only a few days a statement from Senator Kennedy that he had been "entertaining" the idea of entering the California primary. The fact that Kennedy was considering it at all was enough to make party leaders shudder. Brown had been a favorite-son nominee in 1952. He had campaigned as head of an uncommitted slate and had been soundly defeated by Senator Estes Kefauver in the primary. The experience led him and other party leaders to conclude that when faced with a choice between an active presidential candidate and a favorite son who was not a *bona fide* national candidate, the Democrats of California would vote for the former.

The Kennedy Threat

Private soundings taken by California Democratic leaders throughout the state in the early months of 1960 indicated that Kennedy could defeat Brown in a primary contest. The Governor believed it, and so did the senator. As far as the Democrats in California were concerned, the problem was to keep Kennedy out of the state, for his candidacy in California might well lead other contenders to join the fray.

The Californians were not primarily motivated by a protective feeling for Brown's favorite-son candidacy. Their concern was for what Kennedy's entry would do to the party, to the Governor's legislative program, to the state's other political races, to the November election, and even to Senator Kennedy himself. They were convinced the immediate result of a bitterly contested primary would be a deeply divided party, tearing many of the local campaigns to shreds and leaving the Republicans the sole beneficiary. A primary struggle would also come at an awkward time for the Governor. A special session of the State Legislature was to convene in the spring, and the $1,750,000,000 water bond issue, the heart of the Governor's program, was to go to the people for a vote in November. Brown faced a hard political fight to get it approved, and a divisive primary battle at the same time could endanger his entire program.

Therefore, when talk swung to the possibility of Senator Kennedy's entering the June primary, California Democrats winced. As one party leader said, "If Kennedy wins it will seriously endanger the chances of our capturing the state legislature again in 1960." Whoever controlled that body in 1961 would draw the new boundaries of the state legislative and congressional districts. This was a fact of more importance to many legislators than the question of who would be nominated for president, particularly since, as a result of the census, California was gaining eight new congressional seats. They felt certain that a Kennedy primary victory would put an entirely new faction in control of the party organization, since almost everybody who was anybody in the party was now behind Governor Brown. There was no doubt in their minds that the foremost concern of the Kennedy group would be the nomination of Senator Kennedy and little else.

What if Senator Kennedy ran in California and lost? It was generally agreed his candidacy would suffer a serious blow. Beyond this feeling was the conviction shared by most California Democrats that in a primary battle Kennedy would lose even if he won. "If he came in, he would reap the undying rancor of Democrats on all levels," one party leader affirmed. "The fight would destroy so much of what we have worked so hard to build up over the years. If he then won the nomination and lost the presidency he would get little support in California if he wanted to try again in 1964 or 1968."

In early February some of Kennedy's political lieutenants attended the Western Democratic Conference at Albuquerque, New Mexico, and told Democratic leaders that if Kennedy announced he would not run against Brown, the Governor in turn should issue a reassuring statement that he would release the California delegation after the first ballot. One of the persistent fears of the Kennedy team seemed to be that some secret commitment might be made by Brown's delegates to another candidate. The Governor was asked if he intended to make the statement requested by the Kennedy people.

"I do not," he replied. He went on to say that Senator Kennedy had not asked him for any deal of any kind. "He [Kennedy] said he felt his success in other primaries would determine what he would do in California."

Yet everyone knew that Kennedy could wait only so long. He was entered in the nation's first primary, in New Hampshire, on March 8, and if he decided to invade California the names of his nominating committee would have to be filed with its Secretary of State by March 9. Then he would have until April 8 to decide whether to file a slate of candidates pledged to his candidacy. Moreover, his second primary, in Wisconsin, was on April 5, only three days before he would have to fish or cut bait in California. The probability was that if Kennedy failed to score a big victory over Humphrey in Wisconsin, he would enter the California primary—and that Humphrey would undoubtedly follow.

"If this happens," a leading Democrat in the state remarked, "it will be a real mess. The Governor would have no choice but to stand and fight. But what Kennedy doesn't know—no one knows at this point—is whether Brown would do this by going it alone against all comers or entering an alliance of some sort with Senator Humphrey." The next move was up to Senator Kennedy.

The CDC Convention

In mid-February 1960 the California Democratic Council gathered for a weekend meeting in Fresno. More than 3,000 members, representing local clubs of California liberals from all parts of the state, assembled for their annual issues convention. Born in the 1952 presidential campaign of its patron saint Adlai Stevenson, the CDC was the most dynamic political organization of grassroots volunteers in the state. It had played an instrumental role in the Democratic Party's rapid rise to power in California during the 1950s. No one claimed that the beliefs of these issue-oriented partisans were the beliefs of all California Democrats or that their preference for a presidential candidate would determine the Democratic Party's selection of a standard-bearer. But it was generally believed that the CDC was influential and that its viewpoint would be reflected in the make-up of the delegation.

While the council would endorse no candidate and its leaders would support the favorite-son candidacy of Governor Brown, the feelings of the CDC members themselves about the various presidential candidates were important to observers. The most illuminating moment of the entire weekend, the *Christian Science Monitor* reported, came when Brown in his keynote address mentioned all the possible Democratic candidates.

First, he named Senator John F. Kennedy, who won warm applause; then Senator Hubert H. Humphrey, who won even warmer applause; then Senator Stuart Symington, who got less than either; then Senator Lyndon B. Johnson, who got virtually none.

When the Governor named Chester Bowles, there was overwhelming applause. Governors G. Mennen Williams, of Michigan, and Robert Meyner, of New Jersey, won a token response. And when Governor Brown ticked off the name of Adlai E. Stevenson, the convention rose to its feet in a prolonged ovation.

The Kennedy people assessed the situation quickly and accurately. Stevenson was the obvious sentimental favorite, but since neither he nor Chester Bowles was actively seeking the nomination, Humphrey seemed to be the choice of the California liberals. This did not mean, however, that Humphrey was the favorite of California Democrats generally. Most recent rank-and-file polls showed that, next to Stevenson, Kennedy was the popular choice.

Where did this leave the other two candidates, Symington and Johnson? The Johnson boosters at the Fresno CDC convention could have met in a telephone booth. But evidence of considerable Symington strength in other quarters was reflected in a poll of the state's Democratic legislators, many of whom would sit on the 81-vote delegation. When asked who they thought would win the Democratic presidential nomination, 25 said Symington, 19 said Kennedy, and 17 forecast Stevenson. But, when asked whom they liked best, it was the same old story: Adlai E. Stevenson of Illinois. It was clear that in selecting a strong favorite-son delegation, one which would probably include at least some support for each of these nationally boosted Democratic candidates, Governor Brown had his political work cut out for him.

The Election Code and the Executive Committee

The legal requirements for the selection of delegates are set down in California's *Election Code*. They distinguish California from other large presidential primary states. It requires that a small executive committee be organized to select delegates and alternates from each of the congressional districts in the state and to secure enough petition signatures (about 15,-000 in 1960) to qualify these persons as the delegation to appear on the primary ballot. The delegation is organized and voted upon as a single statewide slate on an all-or-none basis. There are no separate district or convention elections as in other large states. Only South Dakota has a similar provision.

The Code also requires that the executive committee obtain the endorsement of the candidate for the presidential nomination to whom the delegation is to be pledged. In reality, the candidate almost always selects the executive committee in the first place. Once chosen, the delegation must meet before going to the convention and must elect a chairman. The final stipulation is that each delegate, "to the best of his judgment and ability," must support the candidate to whom the delegation is pledged. The delegation must be pledged to someone. In 1960 there was no provision—as in New York, Illinois, and Pennsylvania, for example—for an unpledged, no-preference delegation.[2]

The deadlines imposed by the Code had the effect of forcing California Democratic leaders to commit themselves to a strategy of delegation-selection before it could be known how Kennedy would do in the spring primaries. Similarly, the several candidates had to make judgments concerning California which—in their opinion—were premature and which, conceivably, would have been quite different if they could have been postponed for a few weeks.

In view of the unanimous support of the party leaders for a united front, the formation of the executive committee was almost a pro forma matter. It was, in effect, an ex officio body composed of the leaders of the several official elements of the party: besides the state chairman, the executive committee included the northern California chairman, the state women's vice-chairman, the national committeeman and committeewoman, the president of the California Democratic Council, the president pro tempore of the state Senate, the speaker of the state Assembly, the chairman of the Democratic congressional delegation, and one other congressman to be recommended by the congressmen and United States Senator Clair Engle. It was the job of these executive committee members to choose 162 delegates and 80 alternates from 1,000 or more "dedicated," "deserving," and especially demanding party faithful. (Each of the thirty districts—under state law—was assigned five delegates, leaving ten to be filled at-large.) [3]

To make matters even more difficult, the number who clamored to be chosen in 1960 was inordinately high, since

---

[2] In 1961 the California Legislature amended the law to make possible the elec-

tion of an "unpledged" delegation in future years.

[3] Within multi-district counties (e.g., Los Angeles) the assignment of delegates could be made without regard to district lines.

the convention was being held in Los Angeles. Each delegate and alternate had to contribute to the delegation treasury ($100 in 1960) as a condition of his selection, no matter where the convention was held. The additional expenses for traveling to a convention out of the state had usually served as a convenient screening factor. But this year California was the host state, and as one of the leaders from the San Francisco Bay Area pointed out, "There are always all sorts of problems for the host state. For example, everybody in Los Angeles County wants to get into the act this year, and there are more screwballs per square mile down there than any place in the country."

To "assist the committee to form a fair, representative and united delegation," the Governor designated a 29-member advisory group, again a largely ex officio body representing the official party leaders not on the executive committee. The advisory group never met and was not expected to. However, several of its members did submit lists of names to the executive committee for its consideration.

In accordance with 1956 practice, congressional district caucuses composed of local party leaders were invited to submit nominations to the committee for consideration. (The district caucuses were instructed not to nominate partisan office-holders from their district, since these would be considered separately by the committee.) The weight accorded these recommendations depended on the status of the local leaders involved. In some cases, the executive committee merely ratified the caucus recommendations, which had themselves been unofficially "ratified" by other local leaders and key legislators from the district. In other cases, local caucus recommendations were generally disregarded and the opinions of other persons in the district were given greater weight. And in yet other circumstances, the executive committee threw up its hands at the local recommendations and substituted its own judgment. There were 162 delegates to be named. As it turned out, of the 289 district caucus nominees, 47 were selected as delegates, 39 as alternates. Whether this number was sufficient recognition of "grassroots sentiment" remained a minor bone of contention throughout the life of the delegation.

The Smoke-Filled Sanctuary

The selection of the delegation took place at a private meeting of the executive committee late in February. The setting was the wedding chapel of the Carmel Highlands Inn, a beautiful resort on the California coast. Chosen because of its remoteness from the "outside world," especially the press, the chapel soon became known as the "smoke-filled sanctuary." In addition to the executive committee, three important political figures attended: the Governor's executive secretary, the party secretary for northern California, and a leading assemblyman and supporter of the Governor from southern California. Participation by the Governor's secretary was intended to guarantee final ratification of the delegation by the chief executive, and, in fact, Brown subsequently made only two or three minor adjustments in the list.

Although the meetings of the committee were closed, and tight security was maintained, there was one important exception. Unknown to the rest of the committee during its deliberations, one of the group would slip out of the chapel from time to time to confer with an aide of the Kennedy organization who had managed to plant himself close to the proceedings. These periodic rendezvous, held on the back steps of various motels, were kept out of sight to conceal manifestations of pressure by the Kennedy people. The senator was acutely interested in what was taking place during this forty-eight-hour period, and, in truth, it was important to the California Democratic Party leaders that he be given all possible assurance that his political interests were receiving serious consideration. Kennedy had been advised, even by his most ardent backers in California, that in the long run he would profit by staying out of the primary. "Why come into California, spend hundreds of thousands of dollars and maybe wreck a state party," he was told by one of his earliest supporters, "when if you win the other state primaries you can probably have a majority of our delegates on your side?" But would "probably" be good enough for Kennedy? The primaries were still ahead of him, which meant he had to take another close, perhaps last, look at California now—this weekend. Eighty-one convention votes were at stake, and Kennedy knew he was almost assured of capturing them all if he decided to make the effort. However, there were risks, too, and for this reason he wanted to see what the Brown delegation would be like before finally making up his mind.

The party strategists were already thankful for one mercy: the tremendous Stevenson strength throughout the state lay dormant, not yet aroused by the "potential candidate" himself or any of his devoted local followers. Had there been any Stevenson agitation at this time, the California leaders had no doubt that Kennedy would enter the primary on that ground alone.

The people on the executive committee who wielded influence in the selection of the delegation were important elected office holders and other top party leaders who were equally responsible for the party's organizational and political activities. Their guiding principle in the entire process of selecting the California delegation was to put together as much political muscle as could possibly be assembled. "It was our hope," one of the members of the executive committee said later, "that Senator Kennedy would be so impressed with the delegation's broad-based representation of the party leadership and its solid support of the Governor that he would decide he would not care to come in and take on everybody running for partisan office in California."

The delegation, as it finally emerged, included supporters of each of the presidential candidates as a further inducement to have them all keep out of the primary. But there was an even more urgent consideration in taking this course of action. Not only was the delegation broadly representative as a result of Kennedy's continued threat to fight it out with Brown in the primary; it included every conceivable group, to insure that no faction of any political importance remained around which the Kennedy forces could organize a rival slate.

"The idea of 'political muscle' never meant putting a large number of Kennedy supporters on the delegation," the committee member explained.

As a matter of fact, there were very few known Kennedy people at this time, and those who *were* personally sympathetic to the Senator—people like Congressman Jack Shelley, Ed Heller, Joe Houghteling, Bill Malone and one or two others—never favored his contesting the Governor in the June primary. We were all united in wanting to go to Los Angeles pledged to Brown, and we would wait to see what developed when we got there.

Another member of the committee pointed out one of the little ironies in the politics of assembling this particular delegation:

. . . the constant and mounting pressure from the Kennedy organization to enter the primary—and hell, let's face it, they were threatening us very effectively right down to the wire —forced us to create a broadly representative delegation that would not be easily subject to anyone's control and would certainly not be pro-Kennedy. And the end result was that at the convention Kennedy probably wound up getting fewer votes from California than he might otherwise have had if he hadn't kept the pressure on so tight back there in January and February.

We were looking out for the interests of the Democratic Party in California [the first committee member continued]. Kennedy certainly wasn't going to. We started with the assumption that most of the Democratic congressmen, state senators, assemblymen, and other constitutional officers in the state would at least be invited to be on the delegation. If one of them didn't want to be a delegate we asked *him* to nominate somebody in his district to be his replacement. We were trying to get the idea across to Senator Kennedy that if he came into California and tried to put together his own delegation, our people—the ones going on the Governor's delegation—would be on the defeated slate if Kennedy won the primary. They would not be overly enthusiastic then about supporting Kennedy for President in their local campaigns. And any presidential candidate hoping to take a state like California in November wants to be assisted by the local candidates running for office all the way down to the sheriff, if they're partisan, or as far down the partisan line as you can get.

Thus the leaders in the Carmel Chapel picked a 162-man convention delegation that included 15 congressmen, 24 assemblymen, 17 state senators, and one United States senator, a total representation of 57 legislators that constituted more than one-third of the whole slate and was four times the legislative membership of previous years. In addition, eleven assemblymen and four state senators were appointed as alternates.

There were other considerations which had to be kept in mind in picking a delegation. All of the various groups in the state which the Democrats normally called upon in an election year to raise money and help get out the vote had to be given representation. These included the heavy financial contributors who were expected to make generous donations before the primary and in the presidential campaign to follow; the hundreds of campaign workers who constituted the core of the party's organization in the precincts and counties; men and women from the ranks of organized labor whose work in registering their own union members was indispensable to a Democratic victory; and representatives of religious and ethnic minority groups whose allegiance to the Democrats could no longer be taken for granted. Agriculture, which could not be overlooked, was automatically included when people from the Central Valley were put on the delegation. The north and south also had to be equally represented, but since the thirty congressional districts were evenly divided in California, this balance was easy to attain. By the time the delegation was finally assembled it was apparent that there was no single center of power. More than half-a-dozen factions and sub-factions within each of these were represented in the delegation. The California delegation was put together with the short-run purpose of bringing in all the diverse elements of the party to avoid a primary fight; the long-run goal was the hope that this diversity could somehow be unified later in the common cause of nominating a President.

There was almost no historical precedent for such a delegation. Ever since the presidential primary had first been adopted in California in 1912, California Democrats had gone to conventions committed to an active contender for the presidential nomination. (The one exception had been in 1920 when the voters had selected an unpledged delegation then permitted by the prevailing law.) The delegates had always made a presidential choice in advance of the primary; that decision had been ratified by the voters at the primary; and the delegates had gone to the conventions united in support of a single candidate. The job of leadership had been not to persuade the delegates whom to support, but how best to conduct their business to maximize the chances of their candidate. Moreover, Californians had generally stuck with their candidate to the bitter end, as with Kefauver in 1952, or with McAdoo for 100 ballots in 1924, or with Garner—until the famous switch to F.D.R.—in 1932. California Democratic delegates, in sum, had rarely had to make up their minds at a convention.

In 1960 everything was to be different. The delegation had been picked entirely on bases *other* than preference for a single candidate. The voters in the June primary would be asked to ratify not a prospective presidential nominee but the state party organization itself.

What mandate would the voters be conferring upon the delegates? For some, their selection as delegates and their election in the June primary on a Pat Brown slate would mean "follow the Governor." Others, it was understood, were on the delegation on what might be termed an "ex officio" basis because of their leadership of some particular constituency. These persons would feel that their mandate was from the constituency in question: labor organization, Democratic club, minority group, etc. For yet a third category of delegates, selection was made in recognition of their place in the party hierarchy—as financial contributor, as an important legislator or state officer. Although selected to run on a slate pledged to the favorite son, they were not chosen because they were beholden to Brown but because they would add their independent political weights to the formation of a slate of delegates so powerful that no outsider, particularly Kennedy, would lightheartedly assail it. In other words, they did not conceive their selection as involving an obligation to follow the Governor.

The decision not to have a "controllable" delegation was deliberate. There was no thought or proposal that the Governor, for example, should submit his own list of people who would be pledged to him. Brown looked upon this procedure as dictatorial. Moreover, California society is so big and so multifarious that any attempt to assert control in this manner could not have been made without —to quote a key supporter of Governor Brown—"causing great controversy and lasting division throughout the state among active Democrats. Recognition of the limitations of the Governor's power, I think, is probably the most important thing needed before he can move to actual effectiveness."

The Role of the Legislature

The Governor had another reason for wanting a balanced delegation and, in particular, the inclusion of so many legislators. At hand was the 1960 spring legislative session with a setting charged by the politically explosive Caryl Chessman case.[4] One week before the Carmel meeting of the executive committee, the celebrated "red light bandit" had been saved from the gas chamber by a 60-day reprieve from Governor Brown. The matter had caused intense controversy abroad as well as in the state and nation. The Governor had aroused a storm of crit-

[4] Caryl Chessman was arrested on an eight-count combination sex offense-kidnapping-robbery charge in 1948. Under California law he was sentenced to death but then proceeded to embark on legal appeals which were to keep him in court for the ensuing twelve years. His crimes, trial, and sentence and his published writings during his long confinement on Death Row gave him world-wide notoriety. At one time in the weeks preceding his execution as many as a thousand letters a day flooded the governor's office, mostly requesting clemency. However, under California law the governor is powerless to act in a case such as this without the affirmative recommendation of a majority of the state supreme court, which was denied on two occasions by a 4–3 vote. Chessman's plight became a matter of controversy in many foreign countries, and the controversy increased at home and abroad as the day of his execution (February 20, 1960) drew near. On February 18, the Vatican newspaper, *Osservatore Romano*, urged a pardon. On the eve of Chessman's scheduled execution, February 19, 1960, Brown received advice that United States State Department officials were concerned over the damaging impact the execution would have on President Eisenhower's pending Latin American trip. Brown then granted a 60-day reprieve and placed the entire question of capital punishment before the legislature. Bills supported by Brown to abolish capital punishment or to provide for a moratorium on a trial basis failed to clear the judiciary committee of the state senate. Chessman was executed on May 2, 1960.

icism by reprieving Chessman and tossing the whole affair into the laps of the legislators with a personal recommendation that capital punishment in California be abolished. The legislators' response to Brown's actions was swift and bitter. The major business before the legislature was to work out a budget for the coming fiscal year, and few legislators were anxious in an election year to engage in a prolonged debate on what to do about the death penalty. Some Democrats said privately they wished Brown would abandon the whole thing, fearing it would cost them control of the legislature. Others reacted more bitterly. But the Governor, who had long been a conscientious foe of capital punishment, went ahead with his plans. In a very short time he was caught up in the most tumultuous fight of his career. His political stock dropped so quickly that Senator Kennedy, the *San Francisco Examiner* reported, "may decide within 48 hours to enter California's Democratic primary against Governor Edmund G. Brown, largely because of Brown's reprieve of Caryl Chessman." Larry O'Brien, a top Kennedy advisor who had been present, "on the fringes," when the Democratic brass met at Carmel to pick the delegation, told a high-ranking California Democrat and a Brown supporter, "It looks as if you may be having company."

The Carmel meeting was held in the emotional climate of the Governor's action in throwing this hottest of "hot potatoes" to his Democratic brethren. At the very least, the committee's previous decision to give substantial recognition to the legislature was strengthened and reinforced by the need now to close ranks.

The death-penalty issue aside, the executive committee fully understood that recognition needed to be given the legislators in order to stabilize the Governor's influence in Sacramento. Close cooperation with the legislature was one of the first undertakings of the Brown administration from the time it took office. "During the first two years of the Governor's term," one of his top aides remarked, "we tended to go all out for the legislators largely on the theory that this was the way to get a really impressive legislative program. I think we got the program, but it may be we used a disproportionate amount of our political bank account in doing so." This consideration argued for bringing the legislators into the delegation "as a means of giving recognition and reciprocating for votes past and prospective."

In 1956 only 51 Democratic state legislators had had to be considered in constructing a delegation—which had been pledged to Stevenson—and only 13 were selected. (Another three had appeared on the "rebel" Kefauver slate.) Following the 1958 landslide, there were 73 Democratic state legislators, of whom 56 were chosen for the 1960 convention delegation. In 1960, considerations of executive-legislative relationships in furthering the party's local fortunes were paramount along with the quest for a delegation slate with "political muscle."

There was still another reason for having a large number of legislators on the delegation. One of the most influential and knowledgeable Democrats in California spoke on this point with rare candor:

If the legislators were not used, then we could have turned more heavily to contributors, who have a somewhat tarnishing effect, if used in too large numbers; or we could have turned to the CDC [the California Democratic Council, the official designation of the clubs]. . . . The CDC certainly was never close to the Governor person-

ally; beyond that, I think that most of the people who were in on the discussion as to how to construct the delegation have never had great confidence in the CDC, although the rest would probably deny that for purposes of public consumption. I think they [CDC leaders] are a very useful political development, but they still do not have the requisite stability either over the long haul or at the moment of major decision. They do not relate to the California community at large, but to a particular ideological base. Stated another way, they relate to their own ideas rather than human beings, and to their own emotions rather than the general public feel. In any event, once the conclusion is reached that the CDC is not to have practically free rein (at least in southern California), it is only natural to fill the vacuum with the legislators, who have proved themselves electable and oriented towards other Californians.

Thus it was that the California Democratic delegation came into being. Its composition was the result of careful consideration of a multitude of problems ranging all the way from a prudent regard for political matters within the state and the party to a calculated effort to show Senator Kennedy (or any other contender) that if he came into the primary and defeated this delegation he would inherit the ill will of practically everyone concerned. Kennedy, however, was still tempted to flout the wishes of all factions in the party and go after the whole eighty-one vote delegation.

A Deal is Made

At this point the Brown forces played their last card. Edward Heller, San Francisco financier and a long-time member of the inner circle of the California Democratic Party, intervened to secure a pacifying compromise.

"Heller was in a position to do so," wrote columnist Joseph Alsop some months later,[5] "since he and his wife are among the most generous supporters and the most respected behind-the-scenes figures of the California Democratic Party." Moreover, they had been early Kennedy supporters. The compromise Heller proposed to Governor Brown was simple enough in principle. The Governor would withdraw his favorite-son candidacy in favor of Kennedy before the first ballot, if Kennedy won the Wisconsin primary and all the others he had entered. In return for this assurance, Kennedy would stay out of California. If the senator failed in any of his primary contests, Brown would then have complete freedom to move in any direction he wished.

According to Alsop, the Governor accepted, and the news was passed on to Senator Kennedy. He agreed, with

one important exception. The Oregon primary was viewed by Kennedy with something less than confidence, for it was generally believed that Senator Wayne Morse would be unbeatable in his home state. As a matter of fact, Kennedy looked to the California primary, coming immediately after Oregon, to cancel the damage done by a Morse victory. To meet this problem it was specified that Brown would back Kennedy if he won all the other primaries and ran *second* in Oregon. In a final direct conversation between Kennedy and Brown, Alsop reported, the understanding was, in effect, signed and sealed. Although the agreement was never publicly admitted, it was clear that Brown would be in Kennedy's debt if the latter did not enter the primary.[6]

---

[5] *New York Herald Tribune*, July 12, 1960.

[6] The extent to which a formal "deal" was actually consummated is challenged by some observers, although none deny that the Alsop story had some basis in fact.

A Delegation Is Elected

On March 9, the first primary filing deadline, it was still not absolutely certain that Kennedy would stay out of California. Backers of Senator Kennedy and Senator Humphrey filed petitions that day technically entering their names in the primary in opposition to Governor Brown. Within minutes, however, both senators sent telegrams repudiating the filings.

But before the last-minute Kennedy-Humphrey flurry, the name of pension promotor George McLain was placed in nomination on the Democratic ballot. The secretary of his endorsing committee said thousands of older voters were unhappy with Brown's record on welfare benefits for the senior citizen and wanted McLain

as their own favorite-son candidate. In order to qualify for the ballot, McLain's sponsors had to file 15,701 signatures of registered voters by April 8 to validate the slate of 162 convention delegates yet to be picked. But this requirement was looked upon as a technicality. "One hundred seventy-five meetings a week; everything we need we've got," McLain's associate said. California, he pointed out, had 1,650,-000 voters of aged 60 or older, and those on old age pension rolls had 640,-000 close relatives. The Governor's supporters, including virtually all the Democratic Party's leadership, looked upon McLain's entry into the primary as a political nuisance, perhaps inspired by aides of Vice President Richard Nixon. They were much more concerned with mustering a large enough Brown-delegation vote to out-total the vote for the unopposed Republican delegation pledged to the nomination of Nixon.

The Primary Campaign

The key to this popularity contest between Democratic favorite-son Brown and Republican leading-candidate Nixon was two-fold: Could the GOP by superior turnout offset the 3-2 registration advantage possessed by the Democrats? How many Democrats would vote for McLain or simply fail to vote as a protest against the Governor, whose controversial role in the Chessman affair was still alive in the public mind? Predictability was hindered by the fact that the 1960 primary election was held under new rules; cross-filing had been abolished by the 1959 legislature. The great bulk of the races went uncontested, with virtually all of the incumbent officeholders facing little or no intra-party opposition.

Thus, the primary was destined to be a low-pressure election, with relatively little at stake. Nixon chose to remain at his post in Washington, while Brown would not dignify the McLain candidacy by serious opposition. Instead, the Governor attempted to portray his favorite-son delegation as a group of high-minded Democratic leaders energetically and objectively looking for the best presidential candidate. This search was dramatized by the Governor in a personally conducted "man-in-the-street" poll in several of the state's metropolitan areas. The "survey," which was carried out in full view of newspaper reporters, revealed a surprising Stevenson strength in California to a degree which threw Brown and his allies off balance. Their freedom of action was in danger of being circumscribed by a poll of their own creation.

Almost as if in response to this rumbling, each of the announced candidates for the nomination (but not Stevenson, of course) entered the state to make a formal appearance at one or more of the Democratic fund-raising dinners held during the primary campaign. The avowed purpose of these dinners was to give the national leaders a chance to express their affection for "my old friend Pat Brown" and to urge the election of Brown's delegation. The real purpose was to capture delegates behind the banner of Kennedy, Symington, or Johnson, as the case might be. Practically, the dinners provided funds (about $50,000) to finance the primary campaign and the earlier costs of qualifying the delegation.

The outcome of the June primary was never in doubt, although the interpretation of the results was anything but clear. Only 63 percent of California's registered voters cast a ballot, and of these some 200,000 Democrats and an equal number of Republicans actually went to the polls but failed to vote for *any* of the presidential delegations! Nixon's slate received 1,517,652 votes and Brown's 1,354,031, but Democrats replied that the combined Brown-McLain vote of just over 2,-000,000 demonstrated the superiority of their party's strength. (McLain had received almost one-third of the Democratic total.) In any event, the Brown delegation was now official.

The Ziffren Affair

A state delegation to a national convention is formed quadrennially for one main purpose, and, with its mission accomplished, passes out of existence. But two officers chosen by the delegation do continue, the national committeeman and the national committeewoman.[7] Controversy over the choice of the first of these dominated the early days of the California delegation, persisted throughout its entire life, and, in fact, was to endure long after the delegation had held its last meeting.

Paul Ziffren had been in the political spotlight ever since he had become California's national committeeman in 1953, and his supporters were as enthusiastic about him as his enemies were hostile. He was lauded by many for becoming a close political ally of Paul Butler, then national chairman of the Democratic Party, and was credited with being responsible for bringing the convention to Los Angeles. He was a staunch figure among California liberals and received overwhelming support for re-election from the great majority of the directors of the California Democratic Council. So well known was his name in Democratic circles outside the state that to many people Paul Ziffren was "Mr. Democrat" of California.

Nevertheless, during the early spring of 1960 four or five party leaders were publicly touted as rival contenders for Ziffren's post, and several more were talked about privately as possible compromise choices to avert a party split. Since it was expected that Mrs. Elizabeth Smith of northern California would remain as national committeewoman, the national committeeman, by tradition, would have to be from southern California. Prominently mentioned for Ziffren's post was Dan A. Kimball, president of the Aerojet-General Corporation and former Secretary of the

Navy under President Truman. Hugo Fisher, second-year state senator from San Diego, was favored by some of the legislators on the delegation, and a number of Democratic congressmen gave strong support to Assemblyman William A. Munnell of Los Angeles County, chairman of the Democratic State Central Committee. Lionel Steinberg of Palm Springs, southern regional Democratic vice-chairman, was an avowed candidate. The intra-party squabble shaping up was in many respects the outgrowth of Democratic confidence of victory in November. The national committeeman from California would then be in a position to play a key role in the future plans of the party. It was no secret that Ziffren's job was regarded as a prize.

Ziffren himself had been variously reported as ready to fight to keep his post and as willing to retire, but finally he announced he was a candidate for another term. Governor Brown had never been close to Ziffren and shared the belief of some other top Democrats that as national committeeman he had not concerned himself enough with California affairs. The feeling was widespread that he was much less interested in helping to solidify the position of the Democratic Party in California than he was in striking sharp ideological notes and becoming the leading voice of California liberals in the nation's capital. One leading California Democrat spoke of him in this fashion:

> His relations with our contingent in Congress were anything but warm and friendly. Without consulting anyone he supported Paul Butler in his clash with the Democratic leadership in Congress and kept challenging every move of the majority leader in the Senate to the point where Lyndon Johnson was no longer helping California achieve its legislative program in Washington.

---

[7] Not all states follow the same procedure in the selection of the national committeeman and committeewoman. See V. O. Key, Jr., *Politics, Parties, and Pressure Groups* (New York: Thomas Y. Crowell Company, 4th ed., rev. 1958), p. 348.

Many of our people in the House of Representatives complained that they would pick up a Washington paper in the morning and find that Ziffren had made another public pronouncement on something as if he were declaring what Democratic policy was on every issue. It got so they continually had to apologize for Ziffren's behavior. It wasn't at all surprising that, when it came time for the delegation to decide what to do about Paul, the congressmen played a much stronger role than they usually do.

The congressional delegation resented Ziffren's elevating himself to a policy-making role when, it believed, he was supposed to be a party functionary who, along with the national committeewoman and state chairman, served as a link between the Governor and the national committee. The elected officials, they felt, were intended to be the policy-making leaders of the party. Thus, the northern and southern chairmen of the party, the national committeewoman, every state senator but two, every assemblyman but four, and every congressman but one subsequently voted against Ziffren's retention in his post.

There was still another reason why the Governor wanted to replace Ziffren. Brown felt strongly that a party attempting to maintain unity in the face of a primary election and in anticipation of the presidential convention could not afford to have as its national committeeman someone who was in opposition to the Governor. A high-ranking Democrat close to Brown tells the following story:

The Governor was convinced that Ziffren had urged Kennedy to come into the primary on a number of occasions. I remember a small luncheon given in Kennedy's honor in 1959 in San Francisco. About sixty people were invited on the very practical assumption that in this sixty Kennedy would perhaps have thirty or forty delegates. These people were pretty much "naturals" to be on the delegation. No commitment was asked—it was just an exposure to Kennedy. During the meeting an influential Democrat from the San Francisco Bay Area and a strong supporter of the Senator said to me, "Did you know that our national committeeman has urged Kennedy to come into the state primary?" I was astonished. I didn't know exactly what to do with this information, and finally decided I would ask Kennedy himself if this were true. He looked a little startled, and said, "Yes, it is." I said to him, "Well, I don't think he was doing you a favor." Ziffren was apparently willing to see Kennedy come into the primary because he believed that if he did he would win, and that then Kennedy would appoint him to head the delegation to the convention. As a matter of fact, the Kennedy people outside California kept using Ziffren as a threat, saying if they set up a delegation it would most likely be headed by him.

It made little difference that Ziffren vigorously denied he had ever urged Senator Kennedy to come into California. Governor Brown, convinced that he could not trust Ziffren, assumed the leadership in securing a replacement. For his part, Ziffren indicated he would fight any attempt to remove him from office and commenced a campaign among the delegates to gain support. Thus, almost before it could draw its first breath, the California delegation found itself torn by dispute. It was clear that this was not only a struggle over the national committee post per se but a contest for power and influence among the sharply competing factions of the Democratic Party in southern California. Ziffren represented one group and made no bones about it.

The selection of the national committeeman and woman was scheduled for the first official caucus of the delegation, to be held in Sacramento on June 18, just eleven days after the primary election and three weeks prior to the convention itself. If the Governor was going to find a replacement for Ziffren, a quick decision had to be made, one which would command the support of a majority of the delegates. Although it seemed clear that Ziffren could be defeated if the right person were chosen, none of the reported candidates seemed suitable or was willing to face a contest. The choice was made one week before the caucus when the Governor persuaded Attorney General Stanley Mosk to seek the post. A liberal, a southern Californian, and (like Ziffren) a member of the Jewish faith, Mosk could not easily be attacked. The Ziffren supporters claimed that Mosk lacked time for the job, pointing out that only three weeks earlier the Governor had indicated his preference that the post should not go to anyone in public office. However, the Governor's office virtually ignored the previous statements of the chief executive, which had been made to stifle the ambitions of Assemblyman and State Chairman William Munnell. An intensive telephone campaign to the delegates on behalf of Mosk was initiated by party leaders from the Governor on down.

The Sacramento caucus was a crowded and exciting affair. All but 26 of the 162 delegates were there along with a host of alternates. The Governor and his aides had done their work well, and the decision was quickly reached. Mosk's popularity, antagonism toward Ziffren, and a desire to support the Governor combined to result in an overwhelming victory for the Attorney General. The vote was 115 for Mosk, 37 for Ziffren. Even among southern California delegates Mosk gained more than twice as many votes as Ziffren.

The Formal Organization Of the Delegation

With its first difficult decision completed, the delegation was ready to adjourn—shortly to meet again in Los Angeles. The only remaining formality was the selection of delegation officers. This meant giving the delegates the opportunity to ratify the decisions of the Governor and those around him who had assumed the lead in selecting the delegation, in operating the primary campaign, in making arrangements with convention authorities concerning hotel space, and in a score of other problem areas. This group was small and informal, but its authority was never questioned. Included at its heart were the Governor's executive secretary, the Democratic Party executive secretary for northern California, and the Governor's leading supporter in the state Assembly, a southern Californian. To this group were added the party chairman, the national committeeman and committeewoman, and others as the occasion demanded.

Earlier, the Governor had announced that United States Senator Clair Engle would be the chairman of the delegation. It was customary for the chairmanship to go to a ranking elected officer, and Engle was the natural selection. From the start he participated in the decisions of the working committee described above, and constant contact was maintained between Democratic headquarters in San Francisco or the State Capitol and Senator Engle's Washington office.

The officers suggested by the inner group and ratified by Engle and the Governor were predestined, given the broadly-based character of the delegation. The party chairmen, north and south, were proposed as vice-chairmen of the delegation, the secretary was president of the California Democratic Council, the parliamentarian a senior member of Congress, and the treasurer held the same office in the Democratic Party for northern California. Only the sergeant-at-arms, the personal choice of the chairman, was relatively unknown.

These officers were presented to the delegates and unanimously approved without discussion or division. The officers were regarded as representing various segments of the party. None were selected as "Governor's men," nor were they expected—as officers— necessarily to support Brown in his actions or decisions. Moreover, none were selected because of their position for or against any of the presidential candidates. As officials of the delegation they were expected to perform as neutrals in the various contests that might ensue. As delegates, on the other hand, they were free to go their own way.

As if in recognition of the essential neutrality of the formal organization of the delegation, the delegates gave the chairman power to appoint a steering committee and representatives to the various committees of the convention, the most important being the Platform Committee. The twenty-man steering committee, as with the previous executive committee which had selected the delegation, was again representative of the various factions within the delegation and included most of the leaders of these groups. If California had been pledged to a bona fide candidate, this steering committee would undoubtedly have been the chief instrument in developing political strategy. In view of the division among the delegates and the committee itself, however, it assumed only

administrative and housekeeping responsibilities at the convention.

Behind the activities of the California delegation were a score or more of workers who devoted long hours to its administration. Some of these were paid personnel, some were loaned by other party organizations and officials, some were volunteers. As previously noted, each of the delegates and alternates was required to provide $100 for the delegation treasury as a condition of his selection. This sum of approximately $24,000 was administered by the delegation treasurer under the supervision of a special three-man budget committee appointed by the chairman. The funds were used to cover hotel charges for the headquarters, press, and caucus rooms; telephone installation and service; the rental of duplicating equipment and paper; and payments to a small number of staff carried on the delegation budget. Approximately one-third of the total was used to meet a portion of the expenses of the primary campaign.

The delegation had the benefit of being an "official" group, supported by party leadership and staff that had been through the mill at previous conventions—both state and national. In 1952 the Democrats had sent a "rebel" delegation to the convention, and the lack of experience of this group had been a serious handicap. In 1960, in contrast, the delegation was strongly organized and effectively staffed. But as the delegates now turned their attention to the convention, many expressed the hope that the unity of the 1952 delegation could somehow be captured.

Pre-Convention Politics

In January 1960 Governor Brown had hoped that the delegation would be "representative of all the several shades of party loyalty among party workers in the state, so the delegation will go to the Los Angeles convention uncommitted to anybody but the governor." In March he had stated the hope that the delegation would vote as a bloc, but admitted he had "no way of knowing what the delegates will do." In support of this position, State Controller Alan Cranston, a top Democrat, had expressed his view in April that ". . . the delegation will stay with Brown as long as Brown wants it to stay. And, if and when it leaves Governor Brown, I hope it all goes some place together." The experienced political editor of the *Sacramento Bee* had declared in May that the favorite-son candidacy "might be termed a holding operation until California's Democratic *leaders* can decide which one of their party's nationally touted nomination seekers *they* want to support."

Almost until the opening of the convention, the delegation was frequently portrayed in this light: a group of rational, unified Democrats who would come to Los Angeles and, in the quiet of the caucus, listen to their leaders and decide which presidential candidate best suited the needs of the nation. To a certain extent the description was accurate. With only a few exceptions, the delegates responded to the request of the Governor that they not publicly declare their preference for a nominee, and many, perhaps most, *were* undecided, awaiting the latest primary results, survey findings, candidate statements, and the like.

On the other hand, there was growing evidence that this description was not completely apt. As far back as March 1960, a poll conducted by secret ballot had suggested the division among California Democrats. Thirty-five of the 162 delegates had indicated a preference for Kennedy, 35 for Stevenson, 15 for Humphrey, 12 for Symington, 4 for Johnson, and 3 for Bowles. Twenty had stated no preference other than favorite-son Brown, and 38 had failed to reply. Shortly thereafter, a subsequent poll assuming "release by the Governor" indicated a somewhat different pattern among the 98 delegates replying: Symington, 24; Stevenson, 21; Kennedy, 20; Humphrey, 8; Bowles, 5; Johnson, 5; no preference, 15. Furthermore, as the convention approached it was evident that the leaders of the delegation were no nearer a consensus than the delegates as a whole.

The Candidates Woo The Delegates

Ever since the delegates had been selected, each had been sent correspondence and literature from the announced candidates and their supporters. Many of the delegates had met the three senators at the $100-a-plate dinners attended by the candidates during the primary campaign.

Senator Kennedy's operation in the Fairmont Hotel in San Francisco had been the best organized. During the afternoon preceding the dinner, each of the northern California delegates had been invited to visit the senator in his room overlooking the bay. As the delegate entered the two-room suite at the time suggested in the invitation, he was met by an attractive secretary (a long-time Democratic politico in the area) who checked off his name and introduced him—if an introduction was necessary—to one of the ten or so persons in the crowded room: other delegates and Kennedy staff and supporters. After a short wait, the delegate was invited out on the balcony which joined the two rooms, and there was taken in tow by Representative Jack Shelley of San Francisco, one of the few delegates who had announced his choice for the nominee early in the year. Shelley and the delegate quickly disappeared into the second bedroom where the delegate was introduced to the senator. Shelley returned to the balcony, leaving the two alone for a few moments or minutes, depending on the delegate's importance. The pattern was repeated, with little variation, until all the delegates had been met.

Later in the afternoon, the delegates attended a cocktail party given by the supporters of Stuart Symington, meeting the Senator from Missouri as he circulated throughout the room. In the lobby and at the dinner a comely group of Johnson supporters appeared, garbed in red, white, and blue cowboy dress, and wearing large buttons reading "All the Way With LBJ."

These outward events were but a surface indication of the mounting pressures that were being brought to bear upon the delegates as the convention approached. In Washington, for example, the Democratic congressmen from California felt the hand of Speaker Sam Rayburn as he led the drive for his fellow-Texan Lyndon Johnson. Passage of legislation favorable to a congressman's district was, at times, contingent upon his support of the Johnson cause. Many trade-union delegates had long and friendly ties with Stuart Symington, arising out of the senator's favorable voting rec-

ord and the excellent labor-management relationships which he had encouraged as an industrial executive. Other Californians from areas with large defense contracts had also worked closely with Symington when he had been Secretary of the Air Force in the Truman administration.

Stevenson's California Strength

Looming over all the California campaigning of the three candidates—Kennedy, Johnson, and Symington—was the spectre of a fourth. Undeclared, yet refusing to rule himself out of the race, Adlai Stevenson was the imponderable element whose behavior would profoundly shape the character and life of the California delegation. The strength of this influence was not fully appreciated by politicians from outside the state. Nor did the state's own Democratic leaders entirely recognize the extent of the former Illinois Governor's appeal.

Stevenson was, in fact, the prime reason why many of the California delegates had entered politics in the first place. His 1952 campaign had provided much of the manpower and leadership from which had sprung the California Democratic club movement. Stevenson had appeared on the platform with many of the legislators in every campaign from 1952 through 1958 and was associated by many with the California Democratic victories of recent years. In 1956 he had fought and won a bitter primary battle against Estes Kefauver in California, and in November of that year California had been one of the few states to give Stevenson a larger share of its vote than it had in 1952. Stevenson had been the house guest of a number of Democratic leaders throughout the state. With all of his infuriating indecision, the two-time presidential candidate was *the* leader as far as many party officials were concerned, and most had come to power during the Stevenson era. These were some of the factors propelling the continuing undercurrent to "Draft Adlai."

Backers of Governor Stevenson realized that California was the key to the convention. Only if California went strongly for him could he develop the second, third, and fourth ballot support from other states that might lead to victory. But just as many Californians underestimated Stevenson's strength, so did his supporters overestimate the ability of the California delegates to remain uncommitted (or committed to an undeclared candidate) in the face of pressure from the forces of Kennedy, Symington, and Johnson. California leaders flew to the Stevenson farm in Libertyville to divine what their preferred candidate planned to do. Would he declare? Would he fight for the nomination? Whom would he support if it became clear that he could not gain the nomination? To all such questions Stevenson remained noncommittal, but he continually stressed his desire that California delegates should remain "loyal" to him. For several key California Democrats, such a position was unrealistic. They returned home to declare, "Governor Stevenson simply can't win on this basis; I'm not going to support someone on the faint hope that there will be a deadlock after two or three ballots." For these persons, having made the difficult and soul-searching decision no longer to support Stevenson, the choice was clear: Kennedy. But for many others, the cord could not be cut so easily. For reasons of loyalty, ideological commitment, friendship, personal advantage—and a host of other factors—the Stevenson movement gained strength.

Brown's Dilemma

And what of the favorite son? After a show of leadership in the national committeeman dispute, and with the convention now three weeks away, would Governor Brown move to mobilize the delegates into a cohesive body? *Could* a delegation with so many diverse allegiances be brought to support one candidate? Should the Governor declare his preference for his candidate early and vigorously attempt to lead the delegation to support his choice? Or would it be better to wait as long as possible in the hope that the situation would itself shape the delegation's decision? The latter course would avoid a public split among the California party leaders and would preserve, before this national gathering of Democratic leaders, the appearance of unity and possibly even of gubernatorial leadership.

In a sense, some of these questions had been answered the moment it was decided to form a delegation broadly representative of the party as a whole. While this was a delegation of party leaders headed by the Governor, it was not the "Governor's delegation," and he knew it. Nevertheless, the question remained, would the Governor attempt to minimize the inherent division within the delegation, or would he let it go its own way? With only three weeks left, the decision could not long be put off.

But put off it was. As the days sped by and the convention neared, no decision was made, and the forces of division within the delegation increased.

Brown had probably been a Kennedy supporter since mid-1959, although it is certain he had not extended a clear commitment of support at that time. But with the 1959 decision to mount a favorite-son candidacy, the Governor was early put in a position of public neutrality. He could not openly declare for a candidate prior to the June primary election without stretching the theory of the presidential primary law beyond recognition. He knew, too, that an early declaration of preference would lead immediately to a formal repudiation of his leadership by leaders of other candidate factions within the delegation. Relations with the State Legislature also dictated a decision not to announce for any candidate. And, with respect to the national political scene, an open position appeared to be the only realistic course of action to take throughout most of the spring of 1960. Presidential primaries were yet to be held, state conventions were in the offing, and no advantage was seen for a large state in reducing its freedom of action. In fact, Brown's agreement with Kennedy—under which the Senator agreed not to enter a slate in the California primary—was predicated upon Brown holding up any public announcement until after the Oregon primary.

Yet another set of factors had kept the Governor silent during the spring. His closest political advisers, both in and out of the executive office, were not sold on the Senator from Massachusetts. Others in key positions were equally uncertain about Kennedy and urged the Governor to keep an open posture, while supporters of Johnson and Symington were insistent that the favorite son remain just that.

To all these forces was added the unanticipated fervor for Stevenson that the Governor had uncovered in his widely-publicized sidewalk polls. "When Pat went out to sample public opinion on the streets," said a close observer, "he became aware for the first time of the depth of the Stevenson sentiment in California." What had

been conceived as merely a public-relations gimmick to build up support for the Brown delegation in the presidential primary became a factor influencing the Governor's own attitudes and actions. He could not test public opinion—even as just a campaign device—and immediately turn around and repudiate that opinion, which had turned out so overwhelmingly for Stevenson.

All these influences of the spring months converged on the Governor as the convention neared. In a sense, the publicly neutral position which he had been forced to employ during the spring made a clear expression of leadership more difficult, now that it was appropriate. The Governor had been captured by the favorite son! And, as a friend observed of Brown's habits of action: "The Governor was never willing to burn all the bridges but one. He just couldn't bring himself to it." [8]

_____

[8] Brown's dilemma has been well-described by Theodore White in his discussion of a June meeting held with Stevenson managers Mike Monroney (United States Senator from Oklahoma) and John Sharon (Washington attorney): "In California they dined with Governor Brown at his Sacramento mansion; they shook him as they described the glowering clouds of war and disaster in the outside world. Yes, Brown admitted, Stevenson was far and away the best-qualified man to be President. On into the night the conversation went, Brown wavering in indecision. As they left, the perplexed and troubled Governor of California pleaded with them to remember what he owed Jack Kennedy—if Kennedy had come into the California primary, he would have clobbered the California Governor." From *The Making of the President 1960* by Theodore H. White, p. 124. Copyright © 1961 by Atheneum House Inc. Reprinted by permission of Atheneum Publishers.

In a slightly different vein, Joseph Alsop reported on July 12, 1960: "The existence of this problem of Brown's [his obligation to Kennedy] was not publicly admitted. Yet Brown's curious way of dealing with his problem has been the key to the whole Cali-

In these final days the Governor could fully mobilize the influence of his office behind his chosen candidate (whether or not he declared for the candidate publicly); or, he could declare the delegation to be free and remove himself from any special claim or obligation to exercise leadership. He chose neither course. With two weeks to go the *Sacramento Bee* reported that the Governor, "insistent that he is personally uncommitted, has voiced hope that his delegates may be persuaded to vote as a unit in the convention for a single candidate, admitting doubt in the same breath, however, that they will agree to do so."

However, as this statement was is-

fornia political drama, as well as an important element in the national Democratic drama, during all of these last months. Brown's way of dealing with the problem was, in effect, to listen to the anti-Kennedy side for a long while. The Stevenson backers at first did not want Brown to withdraw. The Johnson backers, headed by the powerful oil man, Ed Pauley, to whom Brown is obligated, were even more insistent that Brown ought to maintain the empty parade of his favorite-son candidacy."

sued, the Governor's *office* had joined the Kennedy campaign. A few days previously, the decision had finally been reached to talk with each of the delegates and to indicate that the Governor was going to come out for Kennedy and hoped that the delegation would vote as a bloc. Key leaders in the party who were known to be members of the Brown administration team, if not devoted Kennedy followers, were given lists of delegates to call. But such an effort depended for its success upon the full—and increasingly open—support of the Governor himself, and this support was not forthcoming. "We'd convince people to vote for Kennedy," said one of the senator's top campaigners, "and then the Governor would unconvince them by telling them 'to vote their conscience'; and off they'd go to Stevenson!" Brown continued to portray himself as the leader of the delegation but refused to undertake the steps which alone might make this leadership a reality. A close associate summed up the entire pre-convention campaign: "Pat's just not a whip-cracker at heart."

Los Angeles: The First Three Days

Writing after the convention, Theodore White observed:

A national convention, always a universe in itself, is usually bound together in a compact huddle of down-town hotels in some compact, clotted city so that geographical nearness throws delegates together until they can simmer into a common boil. But this convention was a diffuse one with only two focal points, the Biltmore Hotel and the Sports Arena. . . . The universe of this convention was atomized and dispersed—as was the greater universe of reality outside and beyond it.[9]

[9] "The Changing of the Guard," *Saturday Review,* August 6, 1960.

For the Californians, the universe was the Hollywood Knickerbocker Hotel, the delegation headquarters. Fifteen miles from the Biltmore and an equal distance from the Sports Arena, the California delegates met and talked largely with each other.

If the convention itself was dispersed and decentralized, so was the California delegation. Although many delegates lived at home, the hotel was not large enough to house those who needed space. Surrounding motels were employed, and a station-wagon bus system to and from the hotel was initiated. Problems of communications mounted as the nearly 250 delegates and alternates arrived. Incoming letters and wires ran into the thousands, and volunteers worked full-time sorting and distributing mail. A telephone center in the lobby of the hotel, manned around the clock, took messages for hundreds of calls. A daily mimeographed newsletter was prepared and distributed to each delegate's hotel room (and to the surrounding motels) advising him about the delegation meetings, social events, and steering-committee decisions concerning the conduct of delegation business.

The entire life of the delegation was influenced by the fact that the convention was held in Los Angeles. This fact made possible the attendance of a full roster of delegates and alternates. It also made possible the attendance of a full roster of wives, friends, hangers-on, party camp-followers, and a rich variety of southern California exotica. The Californians were forced to do business under conditions of public scrutiny and pressure far beyond those facing the typical delegation. While other delegates were receiving letters and wires, the Californians were receiving midnight phone calls and personal visits.

The Governor, more than any other, felt the impact of a convention in California. Public attention across the nation was focussed on him as chief executive of the host state, and he was subject to special demands and pressures. Much more than would have been the case if the convention had been in Philadelphia or Chicago, the delegation was pictured as a battle-ground in which his local leadership and prestige were at stake. And, of course, the government of the state had to be carried on. For almost a week, the Knickerbocker became the State Capitol for the conduct of important state business. As one of the leading

state senators pointed out, in addition to the delegates, their alternates, and state and federal office-holders, the convention had attracted almost everyone having a connection with government and politics. "Everyone's here," he said, "so we can get a lot of work done in addition to the business of nominating candidates and adopting a platform. We can mend fences, listen to complaints, and do business informally and quickly."

For the California delegation the first official business was to be a caucus held on Sunday afternoon, July 10, immediately preceding the opening of the convention on the following day. (The convention's first ballot for the presidential nomination was scheduled for Wednesday evening.) During the previous weeks it had been widely reported that, at this meeting, the Governor would release the delegation from its pledge to support him and would announce his own personal choice for the nomination. There was now no question in anyone's mind that Brown would support Kennedy. As the delegates began to arrive at the Hollywood Knickerbocker, the strategy of the competing groups became clear.

The Candidates Look to California

In this 24-hour period before the convening of the convention, the position of the state and of its Governor was highly important to the Kennedy cause. One of the state's leading political figures put it this way:

Beginning at the National Governors' Conference in late June, where Governor Brown talked to leaders of other uncommitted states, and continuing right up to the eve of balloting itself, the Governor's position was important to a great many people—in Pennsylvania and Illinois to a certain extent, and in Iowa, Kansas and New Jersey to a greater extent. The fact that Brown was coming out for Kennedy and that this fact was known for a week to ten days before the convention had great impact. The Kennedy bandwagon had to appear to keep moving and to have a strong possibility of getting over on the first ballot. For that purpose California was absolutely essential.

The other three candidate factions, divided in their choice of a nominee, were unanimous on one point: the California delegation should be required to cast its first-ballot vote for the favorite son under whose banner its members had been elected. In this way the Kennedy blitz would be slowed, and the nomination would be forced into a second or third ballot. Equally important was the question of when the delegation would be polled about its preference for the party's nominee and thus definitely reveal for the first time the actual strength of the several candidates. At the start, the Governor and the Kennedy leadership favored an early California vote in order to swell the senator's unofficial total. But one of the closest observers of the scene reported:

> Countervailing pressures built up quickly. The delegation showed it was sharply divided not only among the candidates, but even within each candidate's group of followers. Some wanted to announce their preference so as to add to their candidate's total strength. Some wanted to duck for personal reasons until the convention consensus was clear; some were just confused, without any cause to advocate.

As the Stevenson movement gained strength, many of its supporters in the California delegation—while continuing to press for a first-ballot vote for

Brown—clamored for an early "advisory preference poll" of the delegates. Such a showing would, they hoped, dramatically indicate the division within the delegation and advance the "stop-Kennedy" cause. Symington and Johnson leaders in the delegation also supported this strategy. In reaction, the Kennedy forces decided to delay polling. By so doing they would have more time to persuade wavering delegates and would lighten the impact of the split California delegation upon the other states.

Furthermore, several key legislators appealed to the Governor on Sunday morning to "keep them off the pan" as long as possible by postponing a vote. This, the legislators hoped, would reduce the pressure on them from their districts for another day or two. By then, perhaps, the outcome of the race would be a foregone conclusion and they could take their stand with the winner without losing support at home.

This approach would also preserve the unity of the delegation. If everything went right, the Californians could climb aboard the band-wagon without ever revealing the deep division that had actually existed. Just as the organization had attempted to present a united front to the voters at the primary, now it might be able to survive the convention itself without internal conflict. True, California might not get credit for being in the vanguard of the winning candidate's convention drive, but this might be a small price to pay to avoid the bitter strife that would result from an open split. State Senator Hugo Fisher from San Diego, one of the delegation leaders, put it this way:

> Down to the wire there will be only two candidates—Johnson and Kennedy. Right now we're all under tre-

mendous pressure from the clubs and
our mail for Stevenson. But as we get
closer to the balloting it will become
clearer to everyone that Stevenson is
not a candidate. He can't be, and he
won't be. If we poll the delegation
now, he'll display substantial strength,
Brown will take an unnecessary licking,
and the issue will be even more confused.

The Sunday Caucus

The caucus convened in the
crowded Knickerbocker conference
room on Sunday afternoon, July 10.
Immediately, the Governor rose to
make his long-awaited statement:

We are here to make up our minds
on the man who will most surely be
both electable and clearly competent
to lead this Nation at a time of the
greatest promise and peril this country
has ever faced. I want to make it absolutely clear that every delegate has
to exercise his own independent judgment as this critical decision is made.
I am sure that in this delegation there
are supporters of all of the four major
presidential possibilities. I hope and
am confident, however, that there will
be a consensus by a clear majority of
us. . . . For my own part—and I
know I speak the minds of a great
many other members of this delegation, I am for Senator John F. Kennedy for president. . . . As for my
favorite-son role, I do not want it to
be a barrier to full consideration of
the men who are genuine presidential
candidates. I have repeatedly made
clear throughout the primary as I did
in my campaign in 1958, that I would
not be a serious candidate for anything
except to be the best possible Governor for the full term to which I was
elected. . . . In the primary I said I
would bring to the convention a free
delegation so that each delegate could
exercise his own judgment on the best
candidate to be nominated here. I have
done my part. You are now in a position to exercise that independent judgment. I want to consult closely with
you on the procedure the delegation
and I, as Governor, follow between
now and Wednesday.

To several of the reporters facing
immediate deadlines, the meaning of
the statement was clear. While the
meeting was still going on, the headlines began to roll off the presses:
"BROWN RELEASES DELEGA-
TION." Not until the close of the caucus did the reporters find out that this
was not the case. The Governor explained, "No, I haven't released the
delegation. I only meant that they are
now free to come out and say whom
they're for." Asked when had he decided not to free the delegates, Brown
replied, "This morning." He added,
"I won't release the delegation prior
to Tuesday and will make a judgment
then as to whether to do so or let my
name be put in nomination." The plot
was further thickened by the discovery
and publication of an earlier draft of
the Governor's speech, which fell into
the hands of a reporter. The draft
stated: "I have decided finally and
firmly not to allow my name to be
placed in nomination and to release the
delegation," but this phrase had been
struck from the final statement used
by the Governor and released to the
press.

Within the caucus itself, a strange
parliamentary struggle developed involving two long-time legislative associates. Assemblyman William Munnell, majority floor leader for the
Democrats in the lower house and the
state chairman of the party's central
committee, had been regarded for
some time as a supporter of Lyndon
Johnson. The previous day, however,
Munnell had announced that he was
for Stevenson, a pattern of behavior
followed by several other erstwhile
Johnson supporters, who decided the

stop-Kennedy cause in California could best be advanced by supporting Stevenson. Munnell's seat-mate in the Assembly was Jesse Unruh, chairman of the powerful Ways and Means Committee and a spokesman in the Assembly for the Brown administration. Unruh had assumed leadership of the Kennedy delegates in southern California. Unruh started the parliamentary fight by moving that the delegation be polled in the next day or two at the discretion of the chairman of the delegation. Munnell countered with a substitute motion that the delegation be polled at once, but he withdrew the proposal when it became clear that this course would not be approved by the delegates. In a vote based on uncertainty and confusion the delegation proceeded to defeat the Unruh motion which, at the time, probably expressed the sentiments of the majority. Unruh then abruptly called for adjournment. As much in resentment against the author's tactics as against the motion, the delegation strongly expressed its disapproval.

As tension mounted, Representative Chet Holifield rose to accuse the Governor of "bad faith." The Governor had told the congressmen, Holifield stated, that the delegation would vote its first ballot for the favorite son if the congressmen would refrain from pre-convention commitments to the several candidates. This the congressmen had done, and now the Governor was letting them down. Brown denied such a commitment, regretting that this interpretation had been placed on his conversations with the congressmen. (Subsequently, Senator Clair Engle stated that he did not believe the Governor had broken faith.) Holifield, a close associate of Munnell's, moved again that the delegation be polled at once, "so that we may know what the situation is and decide whom each one

of us will support." Again, the motion was tabled. The Kennedy supporters, those still undecided, and those wishing to postpone a public announcement of their position were still in the majority.

Munnell then moved that the delegation nominate Brown as the Democratic candidate for President and cast its vote for him on the first ballot, whether or not the Governor released the delegation and regardless of his wishes to be put in nomination. "The people who voted for the Brown delegation in June have a right to expect that we shall cast a first ballot for the Governor," asserted Representative Harry Sheppard, dean of the California legislators in Washington and a Johnson supporter. Munnell argued that California and the Democratic state administration "could use the publicity" that national coverage of the nomination would bring. This brought State Senator George Miller, Jr., to his feet. Miller, a leader of the Stevenson forces and a powerful member of the upper house, said Munnell's motion would make California a "laughing-stock." To have to vote for the Governor against his will would make the delegation look "ridiculous." To this most delegates agreed, and a motion to table was easily passed.

Finally, with a sense of relief, the delegation adjourned to reconvene on Tuesday at 1:30 p.m. For two hours the delegation had debated motions and amendments; none had passed except adjournment.

Forty-eight Hours to Go

In most other states, the decision about whom to support had been reached long ago. Presidential primaries or conventions had expressed a clear preference for one or another bona fide candidate to whom the particular delegation was pledged. Party leaders in solid control of their delegations had come out for Kennedy or Johnson or Symington. In other states, the candidates' organizations, particularly Kennedy's, had been effective in obtaining commitments from most delegates. For all these delegates, speculation centered around what would happen if they had to go to a second, third, or fourth ballot. But with national attention focussed on the first ballot, the pressure was decidedly off most of the delegations for the moment. Delegate attendance at Disneyland soared.

Not so for the Californians! Neither primary nor convention had suggested a real choice to the delegates. Nor were party leaders in agreement, much less in "control" of the delegation. Also, the organization of Senator Kennedy had not been particularly effective in influencing California delegates, partly because of the failure of the Governor to play a decisive role in the days preceding the convention. Part of this ineffectiveness related also to the choice of the key Kennedy spokesman in southern California. In the jungle of Los Angeles politics, Assemblyman Jesse Unruh represented one of the chief combatants in the factional disputes which had so long divided Democrats in that area. His assumption of leadership meant the almost automatic opposition of other delegates in the area to the Kennedy movement. The same would have been true for almost anyone selected to head the Kennedy forces in the Los Angeles region.

State Candidate Factions

As the indecisive Sunday caucus adjourned, the members of the California delegation found themselves confronted with the need for decision. The organization forces seeking to crystallize decisions were primarily those factions supporting particular candidates. Each group had its leaders and meetings and made its decisions. The Kennedy and the Stevenson advocates in the California delegation were quite formally organized; the Johnson and Symington forces, being smaller, were less formal and met less frequently. Not all delegates associated themselves with a faction; some who did not had made up their minds but, for a variety of reasons, did not wish to participate in any organized effort or campaign for their favorites. Other delegates belonged to *more* than one faction.

The Stevenson caucuses were typical. One observer described the scene as follows:

> On arriving in Room 601 we were admitted by friends to the crowded room. There was an atmosphere of expectation and pressure. Carefully, painstakingly, Toby Osos, a prominent Democratic woman leader, and Don Rose, chairman of the Los Angeles County central committee, went over the list of delegates to determine whom they should count on, who they should firm up, who was hopeless, who might be switched over. "Now just remember," someone was saying, "don't panic. We've got more votes than Kennedy. We can win if we work." The delegates rushed out of the room almost as if they had just been given a half-time pep talk in the dressing room by the coach.

From such meetings as these, intelligence about the direction in which California was moving was transmitted to the respective headquarters of the candidates. Arthur Hoppe of the *San Francisco Chronicle* painted a picture of the Kennedy headquarters:

> The lobby of the Biltmore Hotel was, as usual, a swirling mass of hoopla.

Bands played feverishly. Pretty girls begged each passerby to accept a button. Delegates yelled and marched and cheered, each as though the future of the Nation hung on his fervor for his candidate.

By contrast, the small corner room high up on the eighth floor seemed as quiet and as remote from convention realities as an ivory tower. Three men in shirtsleeves sat around a coffee table. One was reading a newspaper. Another was checking over a list and a third was muttering into a telephone. . . . The room, which had been functioning for the past three weeks, was one of the many scattered outposts of Senator John F. Kennedy's smoothly functioning organization. The three men were responsible for the Kennedy vote in the key California delegation. Each of the three was an able, professional politician.

The man with the telephone was California Assemblyman Jesse (Big Daddy) Unruh, a great bear of a man and a rising power in Democratic politics. The tall, lean young man checking the list of delegates was Assemblyman Tom Rees, a very likable guy hatched from the same political mold as Unruh. The man behind the newspaper was Larry O'Brien, a longtime Kennedy staff aide and a man whose coolness and political savvy both Unruh and Rees have come to admire.

A short, white-haired labor official wandered in. Rees gave him a list of members of the California delegation to contact. Unruh continued talking into the phone, discussing the number of votes he is counting on. "It's good," he said, hanging up.

From one viewpoint the Kennedy organization appeared superbly organized. Lists had been prepared months before, persons had been assigned to contact delegates, reports were received and analyzed. But between the quiet room on the eighth floor of the Bilt-

more and the hectic lobby of the Knickerbocker much could and did happen. Within the California delegation were a variety of factions, leaders, and loyalties. An assessment of an individual delegate's leanings, much less the temper of the delegation as a whole, was a risky undertaking and subject to frequent change. There were so many places where things could go wrong and statements could be misunderstood. Wishful thinking was an occupational hazard.

And there were the "grassroots"! While Stevenson headquarters were in downtown Los Angeles, the heart of his movement was in the Hollywood Knickerbocker with the California delegation. Here was the redoubt from which the supporters of the two-time candidate would sally forth to capture the nomination, if only they could hold the fort for a second or third ballot. "I'm getting afraid to walk through the lobby," said one of Brown's key lieutenants in the legislature. "It's alive with club members from my district. I counted thirty or forty of them in here this morning. These damn California Democrats won't give up!" Meanwhile, the letters, wires, and calls mounted, both in number and intensity of feeling. "IF YOU DON'T VOTE FOR ADLAI, DON'T COME HOME," delegates were warned. "AM CHANGING REGISTRATION UNLESS STEVENSON GETS THE NOMINATION. DON'T COUNT ON ME FOR HELP IN YOUR CAMPAIGN UNLESS HE DOES," ran a similar theme, addressed to the many legislators up for re-election. Delegates from the great Central Valley of the state felt the editorial weight of the three *Bee* papers, the McClatchy chain, which daily championed the Stevenson cause. The extent of the split in the California delegation resulting from pro-Stevenson feelings was publicly displayed with the announcement by Lieutenant Governor Glenn Anderson that he was supporting Stevenson. Anderson's open break with Brown was seen as an important gain by Stevenson supporters and as an act of disloyalty to Brown or of opportunism by pro-Kennedy delegates.

Added to this pro-Stevenson activity was the full brunt of the stop-Kennedy drive, for it was clear that—almost alone among the big states—California was still in the balance, still wavering, still to be had. "The eyes of Texas" were upon more than a few California delegates. "Don't be steam-rollered," they were told. "Let's have a free and open convention," which meant, in effect, "Don't vote for any candidate who's gained enough strength to win on the first ballot."

The Deeper Pulls

While the life of the delegation seemed outwardly to revolve around the several candidate factions, inwardly there were other associations which had great impact. Delegates in each of the three legislative groups—congressional, state senatorial, and Assembly— had long worked with one another. Channels of communication and leadership, which cut across candidate preferences, had existed before the convention had begun and were expected to last long after it had adjourned. Delegates from the same district were bound by ties of acquaintance, if not friendship, while officers and active members of the Democratic club movement had a history of personal contacts and shared activities. Trade union members had yet different traditional associations and loyalties, and Negro delegates and alternates had their own informal meetings and leadership. None of these groups was mutually exclusive. In the short and hectic existence of the delegation these pre-existing informal associations became an influential force.

In his suite at the Knickerbocker, Governor Brown was beginning what he would later describe as "the roughest week of my political career." Now publicly off-the-fence, Brown was probably in as unenviable a position as any one of the 1,500 delegates in Los Angeles. Once a "dark horse" and then a "favorite son," the Governor now found himself merely a leader of one faction within the delegation. To be sure, he had still to render the all-important decision about when to release the delegation, but beyond that his power fell off sharply.[10]

Even as "BROWN CLAIMS MAJORITY OF CAL DELEGATES" headlines were appearing the Governor knew he was in deep trouble. He was, in fact, confronted with two opposing objectives. On the one hand, he was committed to Senator Kennedy, resulting from Kennedy's agreement not to enter the California primary and from Brown's personal decision that the young senator was the strongest Democratic candidate who could be put forward. On the other hand, Governor Brown found himself the leader of a political party whose unquestioned emotional favorite was Adlai Stevenson, a candidate who refused to declare himself either in or out and for whom the Governor could find no real support outside the state. Brown had hoped that when the delegates reached Los Angeles Stevenson's lack of national support would become obvious to

---

[10] The power to release the delegation was based on tradition, not law. If Brown had tried to hold the delegation through the first ballot, the tradition would have been sorely tested; many Kennedy delegates would have been under pressure to vote for their candidate, and there was no legal provision which would have prevented them from doing so.

them. After attending a Governors' Conference in Glacier National Park a few days previously, Brown tried to alert the delegates to the fact that "there is no Stevenson movement outside California." But the concentration of the delegates in Los Angeles prevented them from detecting any lack of a strong national Stevenson drive. Rather than communicating with the outside world, the Californians saw only each other. Moreover, the Stevensons began to talk only to Stevensons.

> If we can do this well in California, certainly the other states will see the light.
> Those Kennedy statements are just band-wagon stuff.
> There are 50, 100, 250 delegates waiting to switch to Stevenson on the second ballot, and then we'll be on the way!
> How many telegrams have you received from *your* district? I've never seen anything like it.
> My assemblyman says *he* doesn't feel committed to Brown, and I certainly don't see why I should.

Almost in frustration, a Governor's aide ordered a large sign prepared for the hotel lobby on which could be posted the state-by-state wire service predictions of delegate strength. Meanwhile, the Governor talked to individual delegates in his suite, urging their support of the Kennedy cause. But the hour was too late, the external pressures too great, and the Governor too much of a "good guy" to use coercive tactics. The division within the delegation mounted.

Delegates' Opinions

And what of the individual delegates themselves?

Delegate A, a California Democratic club president, truly and objectively felt Stevenson to be the best man for the job, and as a delegate he wanted to do the best for his party and for his country. *Delegate B,* an attorney, felt the same way about Kennedy, and this was his primary motive for standing up to the pressures of his local suburban Democratic club to shift to Stevenson.

Delegate C, also an attorney, was tired of being on the losing team and of seeing California fail to pull its weight in national Democratic politics. Besides, he and his wife had long talked about the excitement of a Washington assignment. His choice—Kennedy.

Delegate D was a trade union official, and the state and national leadership of his union was strongly in the Symington camp. As a team player, *D* would go along with the labor leadership. He always had. *Delegate E* was also an organization man, in this case a woman, but her primary loyalty was to the official party machinery and to the Governor. "I'll go down the line with Pat," she said, "and if he's for Kennedy, that's the way it's going to be."

Delegate F was also for the Governor, but for a somewhat different reason. As a Brown appointee to an important state office, *F* felt he had no choice but to repay a political debt by supporting the Governor's position.

Delegate G, a congressman, was also in political debt, but his obligation extended back to the Capitol. There, it had been made very clear, successful passage of a bill crucial to the congressman's district, carried with it a price. Besides, *G* rationalized, "Johnson has the greatest experience and would make a fine president."

Delegate H, a young state senator, was not in debt to anyone, but he wanted to build his ties with several of the leaders of the upper chamber, and they were for Stevenson.

Delegate I, also a state legislator, was facing a hot race in November.

He would need every bit of club support he could get, and the wires and letters he was receiving made their preference clear—Stevenson.

Delegate J had long had business connections with associates in Texas. Not only did Senator Johnson most closely represent his political views, but it would be a "neighborly" thing to do to support his candidacy. *Delegate K* was also in the Johnson camp, but when the word came that the cause could best be supported by a Stevenson vote, *K* switched at the last minute.

Delegate L, housewife, was a longtime supporter of national committeeman Ziffren; in fact he was the most inspirational Democratic leader she had ever known. She had never forgiven Pat Brown for failing to support Ziffren's re-election bid, and here was a way to get back at the Governor, particularly when all her friends were supporting Stevenson. (She was able conveniently to side-step the fact that Ziffren was himself backing Kennedy.)

Delegate M of Los Angeles aspired to be a party leader. He was tired of the incessant wrangling of the clubs in the area and of their "ultra-liberal" stands on certain issues. He saw advantage to his faction of the party in southern California by a vote for Kennedy.

Perhaps no single delegate made his choice solely on the basis of any one of the types of influences suggested above. Almost all the delegates were subject to a multiplicity of demands and desires, many unexpressed. For every delegate the pressures were conflicting, and the attempt to resolve them to the point of a decision was difficult for more than a few. How and when the decision was reached was unknown to the delegates themselves. For some it had been months ago, for others almost literally the moment before having to announce their votes.

From the Knickerbocker to NBC

The closed Sunday caucus resulted in one firm decision, other than adjournment: namely, the next caucus would not be closed. Press, radio, and television were united on one point: the decisions of the California delegation were public business and should be covered just as the convention itself. They pointed to the misconstruction of the Governor's statements concerning his release of the delegation as evidence of the evils of piecemeal and handout information. Delegation officials were also moved by the persistence of the reporters. At the Sunday session an aide to the Governor had found a tape recorder secreted behind the curtains of the caucus meeting room, while a news photographer dressed as a janitor had been flushed out of an airvent in the ceiling. These incidents suggested that no further advantage could result from off-the-record sessions of a group numbering almost 250, each of whom would talk to the press at the slightest pretext.

The hotel had no space large enough to hold the delegates and alternates, plus the press, plus the large television floodlights and cameras. Thus, the most important meeting of the California Democrats took place in a Hollywood NBC television studio a few blocks from the hotel, under bright stage lights and in full view of more than one hundred representatives of the news media. It seemed a long way from the "smoke-filled sanctuary" in Carmel.

The appearance of two of the candidates and a representative of a third suggested the importance of the meeting. It is doubtful that any California votes were influenced, but the groundrules of the 1960 Democratic Convention seemed to require that each candidate make a brief speech to as many delegations as possible. Symington, the first to appear, pointed to his varied experience in executive and legislative fields as qualifying him for "the biggest management job in the world."

As Symington departed, Kennedy entered. In an attempt to capture the support of the liberal club delegates, the senator was accompanied by Chester Bowles, a popular figure among many California Democrats and a strong Kennedy supporter. Kennedy stressed the fact that while he had triumphed in seven presidential primaries during the spring, he had refrained from entering California upon the urging of Democratic leaders of all factions. As the tension and excitement mounted, the candidate left the television studio. His principal California contender, Adlai Stevenson, was not to appear. In response to the invitation of the delegation, he had wired that he did not care to address them in the role of a candidate, but, in a phrase not calculated to dissuade delegates, he thanked the Californians for their support both in the past and the present.

Nor did the last of the four major contenders, Senator Lyndon Johnson, address the delegates. There were other states where his presence would be more decisive, and Oscar Chapman, former Secretary of the Interior, spoke in his behalf. Chapman urged the delegates to look at Johnson's voting record which was, he asserted, far more liberal than the senator had ever been given credit for.

Brown Releases the Delegation

Finally, with the preliminaries over, the chairman recognized Governor Brown. "Each of you signed a pledge to support my candidacy 'to the best of your judgment and ability,'" the Governor stated, quoting from the language of the *Elections Code*. "Each of you has faithfully complied. You've worked hard, and I appreciate it from the bottom of my heart. But it's time we get along with the nomination of the next President of the United States. For that reason, I ask my name not be placed in nomination, and I hereby release you from your pledge."

The decision to release had been made by the Governor only a few hours before. The longer he held onto the delegation, the more he was pressured not to release at all. On the other hand, if the delegation were to be released, the Governor was urged to do it sooner rather than later. Caught in the middle, his staff felt the time had arrived to get their boss off the hot seat and shift some of the burden of decision to the delegates themselves. The boss agreed.

Despite the release, the strategy of the Kennedy leaders remained one of delaying the actual polling of the delegates. As of mid-Tuesday it was clear that Stevenson was running strongly in California. The best that could be done was to contain the tide and keep the other delegations in doubt. For their part, the Stevenson leaders were also willing not to press for an immediate poll unless the Johnson or Symington forces moved first. State Senator George Miller, Jr., perhaps the key man in the California Stevenson camp, had spoken earlier with his caucus against appearing to force a ballot. Arguing with those who wanted to push for an immediate vote, Miller urged, "Let the others take the lead; let's not embarrass the Governor unnecessarily." As for the other candidates, Miller advised the Stevenson group to be friendly with them all. "Cheer their guys, too," he said. "Cheer like hell."

For Lyndon Johnson, however, Wednesday was too late. If Kennedy was to be stopped, then he had to be stopped in the next 24 hours. Evidence of the California split had to be dramatized and made concrete, and time had passed for considerations of the Governor's reputation. Johnson owed nothing to Brown, to say the least, nor to California for that matter. If the Stevenson delegates wouldn't move themselves, they could still be used. As Roger Kent, a Kennedy supporter and delegation vice-chairman, moved that the delegation be polled on Wednesday morning, Representative Cecil King, long-time follower of the Texas senator, jumped to his feet to offer an amendment: "I move that we be polled immediately!"

The Delegation is Polled

The Stevenson delegates believed that to support delay, now that a motion to poll had been made, could only be interpreted as weakness. Amid the confusion, the various delegates tried to get their signals straight. Kennedy spokesman Jesse Unruh once more tried the action that he had unsuccessfully employed at the Sunday caucus. He moved adjournment, a motion which took precedence over all other business. The response was immediate and loud. "Railroad," went the cry. "That'll cost us five votes," muttered one Kennedy worker. Tempers grew short as the chairman called for a standing vote. It was against adjournment.

The vote to poll the delegation "immediately" was the first roll call since the national committeeman dispute four weeks earlier. For the first time in Los Angeles, the delegates would have to declare themselves publicly.

The vote on the procedural motion became a test of sentiment on the substantive issue, in this case the choice of a presidential candidate.

All but one of the 61 delegates who a few minutes later would vote for Kennedy supported the Kent motion to delay balloting for another 18 hours. In contrast, nearly nine out of ten Stevenson-Symington-Johnson supporters favored an immediate polling, and these votes were sufficient to decide the issue. Eighty-one delegates chose to vote on the presidential candidate immediately; 76 preferred to delay. The moment of truth had finally arrived.

From Allamprese to Ziffren, the delegates were called by name and announced their choice. As the balloting commenced, Stevenson ran to an early lead, but midway through the voting Kennedy forged narrowly ahead. There were exclamations of surprise when Senator Engle announced that his vote was going to Stuart Symington. Many had assumed that, as delegation chairman, Engle would go along with the Governor. The roll call continued with three out of each four votes going to either Stevenson or Kennedy. Finally, the secretary announced the results:

Stevenson	63
Kennedy	61
Symington	18
Johnson	13
Brown	5
Bowles	1
Not voting	1
	—
	162[11]

As though a balloon had been punctured, the tension went out of the delegation. It was not that an end had come to political maneuver. In fact,

---

[11] Each of the 162 delegates had half a vote.

with everyone on record, the points at which pressure could be applied during the next 24 hours to change a vote were more evident than ever. But the act of going on record had liberated more than a few delegates. They had finally reached a point of decision and, for better or worse, that was that.

The Final Vote

Times Square on New Year's Eve, the circus, a championship basketball tournament, the subway at rush hour, Cape Canaveral at the countdown—all these and more describe a national political convention. Imagine a crowded gymnasium with several thousand spectators in banked seats around the sides and with the floor itself packed with some two thousand additional chairs. Between the sections of seats range scores of TV, radio, and news reporters, crowding the aisles until movement is almost impossible. Over all an amplifier is blaring a piece of political gospel, the speaker ever louder as he tries to make an impression on 10,000 persons, all of whom are talking themselves. In the midst of this, place 162 delegates, constantly moving, leaving their chairs to speak with one another, to find a much-needed sandwich, to converse with a politician from some neighboring state.

This was the environment in which the California delegation now found itself. Consideration had already been given to how the delegation could transact its business away from its center of operation, the Knickerbocker. Arrangements were established to poll the delegates on the floor of the Sports Arena, if the occasion arose. A list of delegates in each row was prepared, and at each convention session delegates were required to "sign in" by initialing the roster opposite their names. A similar listing was prepared in ballot form, with space for the delegate to indicate his vote for a contested office or issue.

The system was perfect with one exception. The signup sheets were useful only for the fleeting moment the delegate remained in his chair. The moment he left, it was immediately occupied by a reporter, a friend from out of town, weary strangers needing a rest, or movie starlets. The empty seats of the delegation were available to anyone persistent and lucky enough to gain entrance to the floor of the arena, and these numbered in the hundreds.

And there were the alternates, 80 party leaders who, either by their own self-sacrificing decision or by choice of the selection committee, had been assigned to second-class status. Although they had paid the same $100 required of all the California delegates, their seats were in the farthest reaches of the Sports Arena, at such a distance from the California delegates that field glasses were necessary to determine what was taking place on the auditorium floor. The goal of each and every alternate was to spend as much time in the delegates' section as possible. To accomplish this end, a delegate had to give up his badge, this to be carried by a runner to the alternates' section, several hundred yards, one escalator, and two long stairs away. By use of a walkie-talkie between the floor and the balcony, it became possible to seat an alternate within ten minutes.

In the final hours preceding the Wednesday balloting, the most serious reading was the California roll call of the preceding day. Delegation leaders pored over the lists attempting to locate persons they thought could be persuaded to switch their votes, if not on the first ballot, then on the second. Additional reading for the Californians was provided by the headlines: "BROWN TAKES DUMPING"; "BROWN GETS BLACK EYE"; "BROWN MISSES KENNEDY BOAT." For the first time, delegates began to sense the price of "independence." Their Governor, their favorite son, the head of their party, was taking a public shellacking, and many of them had contributed to it. More to the point was the realization that the party's reputation and the reputation of the Governor could not easily be separated.

For the Governor himself there was little more to be done except to put the best possible face on the situation. "I'm not disappointed. In California we haven't any bosses and that's the way our free and independent delegation wanted it. The votes Kennedy gets from California will put him over the top on the first ballot." But no one doubted that Pat Brown was angry and hurt and sad. In the special house trailer located for his use a few hundred feet from the arena, the Governor and a few friends sat in silence awaiting the start of the evening session and the first ballot.

The Governor knew that his lieutenants were at work. In the roll call of the states, California was fifth, the first of the large states to announce its vote. It would be highly advantageous to the Kennedy cause if he could show more California votes than Stevenson. But as the Kennedy leaders within the delegation pushed to find an extra eight or ten delegates, the Stevenson-Johnson-Symington workers strove equally hard to hold their position. Especially vulnerable were the five delegates who had voted for Brown and the one man who had voted for Bowles. "Don't waste your vote," they were

urged. Thirteen additional delegates had not voted at all on Tuesday but had been replaced by alternates. Significantly, these included eleven legislators (four senators, four assemblymen, and three congressmen), at least some of whom were anxious to keep out of the limelight as long as possible. They were particularly fair game in the last-minute hunt for additional votes.

The procedure for changing one's vote (or changing an alternate's vote) had been thoroughly discussed by the steering committee. A prepared mimeographed form had to be signed and placed by the delegate in the hands of the delegation secretary on the floor of the convention before the beginning of the call of the states. No oral switches were to be recognized; no one other than the delegate himself could deliver the form. Unless a form was delivered, the delegate would be reported as voting for the candidate indicated at the Tuesday caucus. No full roll call would be taken. Insofar as an accurate count could be brought out of the chaos of the convention floor, the Californians would do it. Alternates were told that they would have to be content with their remote vantage point, and all but one of the 162 delegates were in their seats as the session began. The absent delegate was from Los Angeles County, and, in accordance with established procedure, the first alternate on the alphabetical list from that county—Allen—was called down from the balcony. The day before, Allen had been absent himself and alternate James Brown had cast the ballot for the missing delegate. Brown was a Stevenson sympathizer; Allen was for Kennedy. A vote hung on the question of the first letter of a last name.

The Stevenson Demonstration

The nominating speeches were made and the endless "spontaneous demonstrations" enacted. The professional bands and the paid marchers (so many per candidate) earned their fee as weary delegates followed a shuffling parade around the crowded floor and then, after convention chairman Le-Roy Collins pounded his gavel, returned gratefully to their seats.

For all the candidates but one, the demonstration was a formality, required by ancient and wornout writ. For the leaders of the Stevenson movement, however, this was their last chance. If only they could show that the "people" still wanted Adlai, the delegates might respond. "Willkie did it in 1940," the Stevenson lieutenants insisted, overlooking the fact that the "popular" demonstration from the balcony in that Republican convention culminated a rigorous and well-organized campaign and that there had been important sources of strength on the floor.

The Stevenson demonstration in which so many of the Californians were deeply involved seemed, to some, a sad ending to the presidential campaign of the former Illinois Governor. He had begun on a high note in Chicago in 1952 with an intellectual appeal to the American people. His campaign ended in 1960 with an emotional appeal by his followers to a stacked gallery.[12]

"I was sitting in a section on a complimentary ticket which Paul Ziffren had given me," a well-known political scientist later observed.

"For about a half-hour prior to the Stevenson demonstration the rows in front of me would be filled up. Then the crowd would go out in the lobby. A few minutes later a completely new group of people would come in. This was repeated about three or four times, and I suspect the same thing was taking place all around the hall. When the Stevenson demonstration erupted, all these people moved in to the hall, chanting, shouting, waving signs."

On the floor, only a few score delegates left their chairs to join the march. For the other demonstrations, those in the balcony had watched the delegates on the floor, but now the delegates watched the audience.

As the allotted time for the demonstration ran out, Governor Collins began to call for order, but the crowd persisted. Again and again he insisted that the demonstrators take their seats, but in defiance they yelled even louder. "Nobody can be nominated if we conduct ourselves like hoodlums," shouted Collins. The delegates, still only observing, began to move uneasily as they sensed a crowd on the verge of

---

[12] It would take little short of a formal investigation to unearth fully the true story of the gallery-packing episode. Theodore White states that the demonstration was the result of a "sharp, well-planned organization" and goes on to detail how the Stevenson group came into possession of almost 4,000 tickets. From *The Making of the President 1960* by Theodore H. White. Copyright © 1961 by Atheneum House Inc. Reprinted by permission of Atheneum Publishers.

Others credit Paul Ziffren, publicly a Kennedy supporter, as being the key to the successful effort to obtain tickets for the demonstrators, utilizing his prestige and position as host national committeeman. Those capable of comprehending the complexities of

southern California politics conclude that Ziffren felt it necessary to assert leadership among his host of followers, almost all of whom were solidly for Stevenson. Ziffren disavows playing any role in the packing but offers a different explanation than White's as to how it was done. He suggests that the Stevenson organization was able to obtain extra tickets if it would agree to have its people "demonstrate" for the lesser favorite-son candidates.

In any event, it is clear that the demonstration was made possible by the fact that the convention was held in Los Angeles, the heartland of the Stevenson movement, and that local Stevenson supporters were active in convention arrangements.

becoming a mob. "I doubt if he had anything to do with it, but Stevenson's losing a good deal of his halo in this affair," said a friend of the former Illinois Governor.

Finally, the demonstration died, and with it the 1960 "Stevenson for President" campaign.

The Roll Call of the States

Within the California delegation there was continued excitement: the secretary had begun to accept and record vote changes. Television cameras and reporters moved in to capture the tally, for this appeared to be the only state where last-minute shifts were taking place. If the outcome of the convention itself seemed increasingly assured, here at least was minor drama within a delegation. Delegates came to the front to obtain vote-change forms, just in case. Floor leaders looked anxiously to see whether any of "their" delegates had taken such a precipitous step and moved quickly to confer with them if they had.

The secretary held up a large pad of paper with the latest California tally: Kennedy, 61; Stevenson, 61. The word swept through the delegation. Then a flurry of change sheets with Kennedy votes and a new total: Kennedy, 66; Stevenson, 59. In a last-minute attempt to reverse the tide, Johnson votes began switching to Stevenson. One delegate who had switched from Johnson to Stevenson, switched back to Johnson; another switched, inexplicably, from Symington to Johnson and from Johnson to Stevenson; a third changed from Stevenson to Symington and then went back again. Another delegate started to switch from Stevenson to Kennedy, but ended up in frustration, tearing her ballot into little pieces.

Finally, Governor Collins announced, "The roll call of the states will now commence," and as the convention clerk called out, "Alabama," the California delegation secretary made a final double-check of the tally and turned to Brown. "Governor, we've still got a half-vote for you which has to be reported. Shall we announce your name first or last?" Brown replied, "If you've got to announce it at all, make it at the end." As the television cameras of the nation zoomed in on him, Senator Engle announced California's vote: "Johnson, 7½; Symington, 8; Stevenson, 31½; Kennedy, 33½; and our great Governor Pat Brown, for whom we would all have liked to vote as a favorite son, ½." The pro-Stevenson gallery gave vent to their anger by prolonged booing of Brown's name, and the Governor's humiliation was made complete with this final public evidence of challenge to his state leadership—made at his party's national convention and before a coast-to-coast audience. Around the delegation the question was asked, "Who cast their vote for Brown?" The reply: "Assemblyman Hawkins of Los Angeles." "That's the first vote Hawkins has given the Governor in two years," said another assemblyman bitterly. He looked over at the Governor. "You know what's wrong with that man? He's got too big a heart." A fervent Stevenson delegate from San Francisco had tears in her eyes. "Most of us are for Pat, too. We love him. We really do."

The Morning After

Although the convention still had two more days to run, it was over for most of the delegates. Rarely does a presidential nominee throw the vice-presidency up for grabs as had Adlai Stevenson in 1956. This would not be Kennedy's strategy in 1960, and the individual delegates did not see much more to do.

For the presidential nominee and his staff, however, there was great utility in continuing a convention past its climax. The congregation of so many state and national political leaders would not occur for four more years. State chairmen had to be selected as soon as possible, staff had to be appointed, major strategy outlined. Also, there were innumerable fences to be mended. Bitter rivals of the day before now had to appear as comrades-in-arms against the foe; delegates who had only hours before denounced the nominee had to be persuaded that his election was essential to the nation. The concluding hours of the convention constituted a critical beginning period in the presidential campaign.

It was in this atmosphere that the 1960 California Democratic delegation closed its existence in the final hours of the convention. For the Californians there was, as usual, something extra. Just as the last days of the convention provided an occasion for the national party to patch up its wounds, so for this deeply-divided delegation was there now a need to close ranks, for if it could not unite in a common fight against the Republicans in November, the California Democratic Party could be doomed to another term of minority status.

Thursday morning, only a few hours after California had announced its vote for the presidential nominee, Brown called key members of the delegation to meet in his hotel suite at the Knickerbocker. Here he extended the olive branch to those who had been working so hard to oppose him during the previous week. There would be no recrimi-

nation, no head-chopping.[13] In return, the fifteen party leaders present "pledged united support to Governor Brown and his administration, commending his record of achievement."

That same day, the Governor paid homage to the presidential nominee, meeting briefly with the senator to discuss campaign plans for the coming months. Kennedy had reportedly had some hard words to say about California during the past weeks, but his meeting with Brown was free from criticism or rancor. The emphasis was on the future, not the past. The senator knew that Brown had been through the wringer in recent days, some of it of his own making, but much of it on behalf of the Kennedy candidacy. It appeared, too, that the national election might be won or lost in California, and Brown's reputation could well be a factor in this contest, even though he would not be running on the ticket. Just as Kennedy expected support from the Democratic Governor, so was it essential that the nominee now do whatever he could to strengthen Brown's standing with his fellow partisans and with the general public. The mere act of receiving the Governor was a gesture in this direction, but Kennedy went beyond this in making clear that he regarded Brown as the head of the California party and, as such, the leader of the Kennedy campaign in the state.

Although the convention was bound by tradition to endorse any vice-presi-

---

[13] Fifty-six of the 73 Democratic state legislators had been appointed to the delegation. Only one-third had supported Brown in his advocacy of Senator Kennedy as compared with almost one-half of the remaining delegates. It appeared that the legislators had been more vulnerable to local pressures and less sensitive to pleas to support the Governor's party leadership.

dential candidate put forth by Senator Kennedy, the announcement that this would be Senator Lyndon B. Johnson put a strain on the custom. Within the California delegation, reactions ran the gamut from enthusiasm to bitterness. "This is great statesmanship," said George Killion, San Francisco shipping executive and one of the few delegates who had voted for Johnson. But a labor delegate growled: "Kennedy's pulled a fast one. It looks like a winning ticket —in New England and the South." And Assemblyman Byron Rumford, one of the state's two Negro legislators declared, "I didn't come here to vote for Lyndon Johnson. The people of my district aren't for him."

When the delegation reached the arena, this dissatisfaction was quickly demonstrated as petitions were circulated to hold a caucus. Chairman Engle was informed that thirty-six signatures had been obtained, a few more than the necessary 20 percent that the steering committee had established as sufficient to require a call for a meeting. Rumors swept the convention floor naming persons who would be put in nomination in opposition to Johnson. But there was no willing sacrificial political lamb for the liberals. Since the vice-presidential nomination would be decided by acclamation, not by roll call, there would be no need for a caucus or for polling the delegation.

When the voice vote actually did take place those in favor rose to their feet. Those opposed sat glumly on their hands. "Thus," one reporter put it, "the California delegation kept its perfect record of being split on everything that came up in the convention."

An Act of Unity

But unity prevailed again in the final act. Just before adjourning to the Los

Angeles Coliseum to hear the acceptance speeches, a final "kiss and make up" caucus was held at the hotel. It seemed an eternity since the delegates had last met in this room to hear Brown declare his support of the now successful Kennedy. On that occasion, only five days earlier, the Governor's appearance had been the kick-off to acrimony and dispute. Now, the entire delegation rose and applauded Brown for a solid five minutes.

Thus did the California Democratic delegation of 1960 pass into history. Born out of a desire to avoid splitting the party and its leadership in a contested presidential primary, the delegation had split wide open at the convention itself. No one believed that the display of unity in this final meeting meant that true harmony had come to the party organization. The factions within the party had not suddenly ceased to exist, nor had the competing ambitions of various politicians been satisfied. These had been on the scene long before the delegation had been formed and, in fact, had formed the basis for its organization. They would endure after the convention had adjourned. But there was an election to be won. For the moment, the party's fortune was inseparable from the fortunes of the individuals and factions which comprised it. As it does at each election, the stake in unity had become personalized. But the scars were deep and the feelings intense. The events of the 1960 convention would affect the party for some time to come.

FOUR

The Legislative Process

CASE **5**

Lobbying and the Natural Gas Bill

EDITH T. CARPER

Introduction

Congress was the focus of unusually strong pressures from conflicting interest groups as it considered the Harris-Fulbright bill during 1955 and 1956. This case is the story of how some of those pressures were mobilized and applied.

The Harris-Fulbright bill sought to clear up an ambiguity in the Natural Gas Act of 1938, an ambiguity which —along with the growth of natural gas consumption since 1945—had led to years of conflict between producers and consumers. The overall conflict centered on two questions which could mean billions in profit or cost to either side: (1) Did the Federal Power Commission have authority to regulate the price of natural gas sold to interstate pipeline companies by "independent producers" (i.e., producers not affiliated with interstate pipeline companies)? (2) If so, should prices be determined by the FPC as if gas were a utility or as if its production was inherently more risky and therefore de-

serving of a higher rate of return, such as one based on market value.

The fight over the Harris-Fulbright bill in 1955–1956 was the latest battle in a war over these two questions that had begun around 1940. This war between consumers and producers had increased in intensity in the postwar period as pipelines began carrying natural gas from producing states—such as Texas, Louisiana, Oklahoma, Kansas, Mississippi, Arkansas, and New Mexico—to almost every other state in the union.

The fact that this story deals with lobbying in Congress should not cause the reader to conclude that this was the only branch of government that the consumers and producers sought to influence. Past battles in this struggle had also been fought before the Supreme Court and in the executive branch, and, especially, in the Federal Power Commission, an independent regulatory agency created by Congress. Its five commissioners

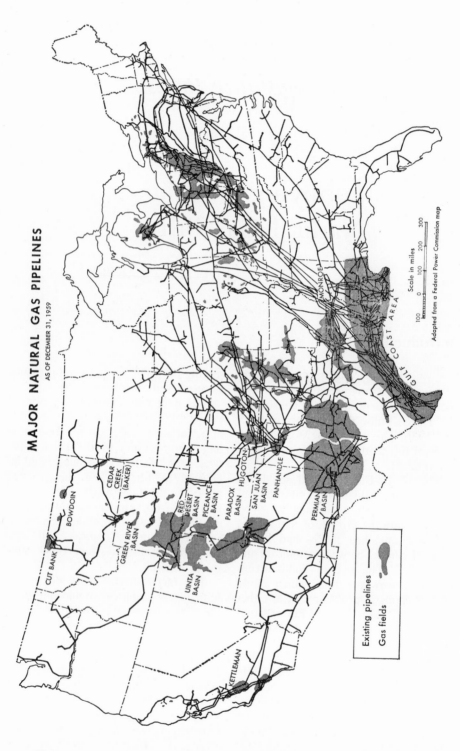

MAJOR NATURAL GAS PIPELINES
AS OF DECEMBER 31, 1959

Scale in miles

100   0   100   200   300

Adapted from a Federal Power Commission map

Existing pipelines ——
Gas fields

CUT BANK
BOWDOIN
CEDAR CREEK (BAKER)
GREEN RIVER BASIN
RED DESERT BASIN
PICEANCE BASIN
PARADOX BASIN
UINTA BASIN
HUGOTON
SAN JUAN BASIN
PANHANDLE
PERMIAN BASIN
KETTLEMAN
MONROE
GULF COAST AREA

were appointed by the President and approved by the Senate. The commissioners and their staff carried out regulatory duties in accordance with powers granted by Congress in legislation such as the Natural Gas Act of 1938.

With so much at stake in the struggle between natural gas consumers and producers, a victory in one branch of government was regarded by the other side as only temporary, as one that it would seek to undo the following year, possibly by an offensive in another branch of government. While either of the two powerful groups had strength left, no settlement would ever be regarded as final. The issue is still being fought as this is written, at the beginning of 1962.

This battle over the Harris-Fulbright bill in 1955–1956 has been selected as a case study subject because lobbying by both sides became a collateral public issue of such intensity that it precipitated two congressional investigations. These inquiries spread on the public record an unusual amount of detail about the activities and techniques of the opposing forces. The material in this story comes from those public hearings and documents, from newspapers and periodicals, and from house organs and publications of the oil industry, the utility industry, and the public relations field. Documentary sources have been supplemented by interviews with some of the participants.

Lobbying and Its Regulation

Lobbying has often been regarded as a bad word connoting the effort to win from legislators some special privilege as a result of special access and special pleading if not actual bribery. It was this repugnant connotation that made charges of extensive lobbying useful weapons to incite public opinion during the debates over the Harris-

Fulbright bill. In its neutral and nonpejorative sense, lobbying is understood as any effort to influence or persuade a congressman about a particular piece of legislation. It includes efforts at persuasion by the provision of facts and specialized data. Lobbying is a common means used by groups of all kinds in attempting to advance their fortunes in the governmental process. Legislators and civil servants sometimes rely heavily on lobbyists for expert counsel, specialized knowledge, and help in rallying public opinion.

With the passage of the Federal Regulation of Lobbying Act of 1946, Congress signified its belief that lobbying was a natural concomitant of the legislative process and that the issue was not how to eliminate lobbying but rather how to curb its excesses. The act required individuals and organizations seeking to influence legislation to register with the House and Senate and to file quarterly reports listing contributors, expenses, publications issued, and statements of legislative objectives. Subsequently, the Supreme Court upheld the right of Congress to regulate lobbying, but it narrowed the definition of this activity to "representations made directly to the Congress, its members, or its committees" for purposes of influencing any legislation. The court's reason for using strict construction was to avoid abridging constitutional rights of free speech and freedom to petition.[1]

The definition of lobbying in the act does not extend to many other activities by which pressure groups seek to advance their interests through governmental action. It applies only to efforts to influence specific legislation and not to public relations campaigns aimed at winning public support for institutions or causes. As interpreted in court de-

---

[1] *U. S. v. Rumely,* 345 U. S. 41, 1953; *U. S. v. Harriss,* 347 U. S. 612, 1954.

cisions, it refers only to direct influencing of congressmen by lobbyists and not to "indirect lobbying," such as campaigns designed to cause citizens to appeal to their representatives. It does not apply to persuasion directed at those officials of regulatory agencies or of the executive branch who decide how programs authorized by Congress are to be carried out.

The Natural Gas Industry

To understand what was at stake in the fight over the Harris-Fulbright bill and in the larger struggle of which that fight was a part, the reader will need to know something about the natural gas industry.

Furnishing gas to consumers involves three stages: producing and gathering, transporting, and distributing.

Producers and gatherers (approximately 8,100) explore for natural gas, which is of two kinds: that found in connection with crude oil (casinghead gas) and that found in distinct wells (well-gas). About two-thirds of the gas in interstate commerce is of the latter type, and both kinds require varying degrees of processing to remove by-products and impurities. The price charged at the wellhead is called the field price.

Interstate pipeline companies (approximately 100 in number) buy gas from the producers and gatherers and transport it through high-pressure pipelines to consuming states, where they sell it at the city gate to utility companies for distribution. Another type of consumer is the large industrial concern which buys directly from the pipeline company. Some pipeline companies also produce natural gas which they "sell" to themselves or to other pipelines, but nine-tenths of United States gas reserves are owned by independent producers.

Ambiguity In the Natural Gas Act of 1938

The postwar struggle between producer and consumer interests over federal regulation of prices of gas sold by independent producers to interstate pipeline companies has stemmed from two sources. One was the ambiguous wording of the Natural Gas Act of 1938; the other was an almost sevenfold increase in United States consumption of natural gas between 1938 and 1956.

In the early days of the oil industry, natural gas was treated as a waste product arising incidentally from oil drilling. The gas was flared off, or burned, at the well site. In Louisiana, Texas, and Oklahoma, oil fields at night were bright with flared gas even in the late 1930s. Although seamless tubing had made possible the construction of long high-pressure pipelines, the supply of natural gas before 1940 was still vastly greater than the demand. Consequently, pipeline companies were able to purchase gas at a low figure.

At the consumer end, in bargaining with utilities, the pipeline companies were also in a strong position. Natural gas was a cheap fuel. Once a local utility hooked its lines to an interstate pipeline, it could not shop around for other suppliers. The cost of laying pipelines was extremely high, and competition of lines was as unthinkable as having competing water pipe systems. The maximum prices that local utilities could charge ultimate consumers were usually set by state regulatory commissions. The standard used in utility regulation was cost of service and a fair return (five or six percent) on capital investment. The pipelines, being interstate carriers, were beyond effective state regulation and could charge the utility companies what the market would bear. The utilities could pass these costs on to the consumers as part of their cost of service.

The interstate pipeline companies were thus in a strong position in relation to both consumers and producers. To bring them under regulation, Congress passed the Natural Gas Act of 1938. Section 1(b) of the act provided that the jurisdiction of the Federal Power Commission should apply:

> . . . to the transportation of natural gas in interstate commerce, to the sale in interstate commerce of natural gas for resale for ultimate public consumption . . . and to natural gas companies engaged in such transportation or sale . . .

But its very next words qualified this grant of jurisdiction:

> . . . but [FPC jurisdiction] shall not apply to any other transportation or sale of natural gas or to the local distribution of natural gas or to the facilities used for such distribution *or to the production or gathering of natural gas*. [Emphasis added.]

With the expansion of natural gas consumption after World War II, the question of whether the FPC had power to regulate prices of gas sold by independents to interstate pipelines became a critical dispute for the national economy. Were such prices exempt from federal regulation because of the act's qualification about "production or gathering"? ("Gathering" refers to the independent producer bringing gas from his wells in several areas into a common pipeline prior to sale.) Or were they under the FPC's regulatory authority by virtue of the first part of Section 1(b)?

Although consumption of natural gas had increased greatly during World War II, at the end of the war there began an even more dramatic expansion of interstate pipelines and a staggering increase in the consumption of gas. Pipelines were now carrying natural gas to almost every state. Demand more than doubled between 1947 and 1956. Not only was current demand increasing rapidly, but pipeline companies were becoming concerned about future supplies.

The producers of natural gas now found themselves in a sellers' market and in a favorable bargaining position in dealing with pipeline companies. The weighted average wellhead price for Texas-Oklahoma-Louisiana which had stood at 2.94 cents per thousand cubic feet in 1945 increased to 9.31 cents per thousand cubic feet in 1956. No longer would independent producers sign long-term contracts at low rates because no one else wanted their product. Postwar contracts called not only for higher prices but provided escalator and "most favored nation" clauses that would enable prices to be adjusted upwards in accordance with anticipated rises in future market prices.

As pipelines proliferated to many states, as the number of consumers increased by the millions, and as field prices rose in reflection of greater demand, so did the political force of consumer pressure increase for vigorous federal regulation of the field prices of the producers. The producers in vain sought to assuage the growth of this consumer concern by noting that only a small fraction of the increased price paid by the consumer was the result of the rise in field prices. They pointed the accusing finger at the pipeline companies, at the local utility companies, and at the general increase in the cost of living. But their arguments could not divert consumer attention from Washington and from a demand for federal regulation to halt the rise in field prices.

Just who or what was the "independent producer" who was now in such a strong bargaining position? In the literature of spokesmen for the natural gas industry, the independent producer was the wildcatting explorer for oil and natural gas who operated on a narrow margin and who had the luck to strike oil and/or gas deposits. In the literature of the consumer interests, the independent producer was the big oil company, like Humble Oil, chief subsidiary of Standard Oil of New Jersey. Actually the spectrum of the 6,000 or so independent producers extended from the wildcatter and the small family well owner on one extreme to the giant oil company on the other.

According to *Fortune* (September 1959) the 200 largest independent companies produced more than 90 percent of the natural gas. Of firms reporting reserve ownership in 1953, the ten largest owned 40.2 percent of proven reserves. In 1954, 70 percent of the gas sold in interstate commerce came from 35 producers. Twenty-two of these were major oil companies, and they owned most of the nation's proven reserves.

What Type of Price Regulation?

In addition to the fight between producers and consumers over the interpretation of the Natural Gas Act of 1938, there was the question of what pattern of price regulation should be used by the Federal Power Commission if it did have jurisdiction. The Federal Power Commission, which also regulated interstate electric and water power utilities, had been following a practice of setting prices on the basis of "actual legitimate cost" of the natural gas producer. This pattern, which was constructed to fit "regular" utilities, was unintelligible and unacceptable to the speculatively-minded oil and gas producer.

The oil and gas man was likely to point out that drilling for oil and gas was a risky business, in the style of gold prospecting. In a typical year, an industry source reported, 10,550 exploratory wells had been drilled. One thousand had struck oil, 350 gas, and 9,200 were dry holes. The sale by the independent producer of his gas to a pipeline company that, in turn, transported it and sold it to a local utility across the country did not, in the judgment of the independent, justify the application of normal utility regulation (cost plus moderate rate of return on investment) to his highly speculative and risk-oriented ventures. The ordinary utility did not have to search. Its plants could continue to produce electricity, but once gas was used it was lost to the owner forever. If the oil and gas producer had wanted the regular, government-guaranteed five or six percent return that utilities received, he would not have gone into the speculative oil and gas industry in the first place.

Thus the independent producer— large or small—wanted more than a "fair return" on cost and investment from any government agency regulating his prices. He wanted some kind of market price that took account of the value and scarcity of what he had dug for and discovered. Moreover, a theory of utility regulation on a cost basis seemed to him absurd because it would result in different prices for different wells in the same field, due to differences in their costs of drilling.

Consumers of gas, on the other hand, wanted as low a price as possible, and their spokesmen favored the traditional utility regulation methods. Also, consumers tended to regard producers as pirates seeking inordinate profits. The

Large Nontransporting Natural Gas Companies, 1953

Rank	Company	Annual Sales To Interstate Pipelines In Billion Cubic Feet	Reserve Holdings Reported, Trillion Cubic Feet
1	Phillips Petroleum Co.	457.4	13.2
2	Stanolind Oil & Gas Co.	202.6	9.9
3	Humble Oil & Refining Co.	196.6	16.0
4	Magnolia Petroleum Co.	157.5	7.5
5	Shell Oil Co.	156.3	(?)
6	Chicago Corp.	155.6	(?)
7	Gulf Oil Corp. & Gulf Refining Co.	138.4	4.0
8	Atlantic Refining Co.	95.2	2.2
9	Shamrock Oil & Gas Corp.	81.4	1.7
10	Skelly Oil Co.	74.6	2.3
11	Sun Oil Co.	69.0	(?)
12	The Texas Co.	67.4	10.5
13	Carthage Corp. plant	66.6	(?)
14	Republic Natural Gas Co.	63.2	(?)
15	Superior Oil Co.	62.5	(?)
16	Sunray Oil Corp.	53.7	1.5
17	Union Oil Co. of California	53.0	1.6
18	Continental Oil Co.	52.9	2.2
19	Southwest Gas Producing Co. Inc.	50.8	(?)
20	Panoma Corp.	48.6	(?)
21	La Gloria Corp.	48.0	(?)
22	Pure Oil Co.	48.0	3.7
23	Ohio Oil Co.	47.8	2.1
24	Abercrombie, J. S., Co.	46.9	(?)
25	Tide Water Associated Oil Co.	45.4	1.8
26	Sinclair Oil & Gas Co.	43.4	1.7
27	American Gas Producing Co.	43.3	(?)
28	Southern Production Co.	42.1	1.3
29	Western Natural Gas Co.	39.2	1.4
30	Taylor Oil & Gas Co.	32.9	1.1
31	Union Sulphur & Oil Corp.	28.2	.5
32	United Carbon Co.	28.1	(?)
33	California Co. (subsidiary of Standard Oil of California)	26.4	4.5
34	Columbian Fuel Corp. (subsidiary of Columbian Carbon Co.)	26.3	1.6
35	Sohio Petroleum Co.	25.8	.7
36	Cullen, H. R.	25.6	(?)
37	Hugoton Plains Gas & Oil Co.	25.5	.5
	Other producers with interstate sales of less than 25 billion cf (about 250 firms)		6.9
	Total reported		100.4

Source: E. J. Neuner, "The Natural Gas Industry," University of Oklahoma Press, 1960. Reprinted with permission.

fact that the oil and gas industry was already being treated with what critics called extraordinary favoritism by a 27½ percent tax depletion allowance exacerbated this feeling.[2]

Producers of natural gas, on the other hand, tended to be outraged by critics of the depletion allowance who did not understand the need to encourage discovery of new reserves. They regarded natural gas consumers who pressed for utility price regulation as foolish persons who demanded the golden nugget without paying the prospector the market rate for his product.

This, then, was what the war was all about. As one informed observer has written:

> The ultimate question Congress had to decide was who was to be the principal beneficiary of the marvelous cheapness and desirability of natural gas. The producers—and the states that taxed them—had a good claim. They had found and developed the great fields. Their price to the interstate pipe line was a small part of what the ultimate consumers paid, and they could multiply it several times before the final cost of natural gas approached that of oil or coal. The consumers had a case, too. It was not the discovery or development of natural gas that made it valuable, but the millions of dependable consumers on the other end of the pipe line. If it were not for them the East Texas night still would be bright with the flames of flared gas. And it was they, with their rapidly increasing number, who would make natural gas a public utility—all the

way back to the well head—if they could. . .[3]

Prelude to the Harris-Fulbright Bill

The efforts of the producers, and later the consumers, to press for a resolution of the two basic issues (ambiguity of the act and market vs. utility standard in price regulation) began shortly after the passage of the 1938 act. The industry and its spokesmen in Congress paid particular attention to who was appointed to the five commissionerships of the FPC. In 1940 the FPC itself determined that it lacked authority under the Natural Gas Act to regulate the field prices of independents. In 1943 the commission reversed this position. In 1947 the Supreme Court upheld the commission's position and actually expanded the FPC's powers with a judgment that all natural gas sales in interstate commerce were subject to regulation under the act and that "producing or gathering" exceptions were to be "strictly construed." (*Interstate Natural Gas Company v. Federal Power Commission,* 331 US 682.)

Because the Interstate case dealt with a pipeline company that also produced natural gas, its relevance to the independent producer was not clear; but as a portent of the court's position, it upset the producers. The industry's response was to stir up congressmen from producing states to introduce legislation to amend the 1938 act in order to remove producer prices from FPC control. The five FPC commissioners were themselves divided. In 1947 a majority of the commissioners

---

[2] The tax depletion allowance was enacted and retained by Congress with strong support from representatives from oil states. Owners of natural resources (oil, gas, uranium, etc.) were allowed to deduct a percentage of the income derived from these properties to represent the value used by extraction. The oil depletion allowance permitted a flat deduction of 27½ percent from gross income.

[3] Ralph Huitt: "National Regulation of the Natural Gas Industry" in E. Redford, ed.: *Public Administration and Policy Formation* (Austin, Texas, 1956).

approved an order *denying* that the 1938 act gave the FPC power over independents' field prices. In 1948, with one vacancy, the commissioners divided 2–2 on this question. In 1949 President Truman appointed a commissioner who sided with the two favoring control over field prices.

Also in 1949, Senator Kerr of Oklahoma introduced a bill to exempt sales by independent producers. The same year, led by Lyndon Johnson, senators from producing states sought to block confirmation of President Truman's reappointment of Commissioner Leland Olds, who had served on the FPC since 1945 and had been a vigorous proponent of regulating independents' field prices. Olds had also incurred the wrath of the producers and their friends in Congress by mobilizing newspaper opposition to the Kerr bill when it was being quietly considered by a Senate committee. Although President Truman sought to make the Olds case a matter of Democratic Party loyalty, the Democratic senators from producing states joined with Republicans and decisively turned down the nomination of Olds. President Truman was forced to make another nomination.

Later, in 1950, Congress passed the Kerr bill. President Truman, on the advice of three of the five commissioners, vetoed the bill on the grounds that regulation of producers was in the public interest "because of the inherent characteristics of the process of moving gas from the field to the consumer." Unlike producers of coal and oil, "purchasers of natural gas cannot easily move from one producer to another in search of lower prices."

The President also cited the limited amount of competition among producers, the phenomenal growth of the natural gas industry, and the advantages of natural gas as a fuel. These factors, he said, made for the "clear possibility that competition will not be effective . . . in holding prices to reasonable levels."

After the President vetoed the Kerr bill, the FPC withdrew its 1947 ruling which had denied its power to regulate field prices.

In 1948 the Federal Power Commission tried once again to clarify the limits of its jurisdiction in a case involving the Phillips Petroleum Company, the biggest independent producer and one of the giants of United States industry. In 1951, in a 4 to 1 decision, the FPC held that Phillips' sales to interstate pipelines were an integral part of its extensive gathering process, and were thus exempted by the Natural Gas Act. Several petitions for review were filed in the United States Court of Appeals for the District of Columbia. Arguing for reversal of the FPC decision were the State and Public Service Commissions of Wisconsin; the County of Wayne, Michigan; and the Cities of Detroit, Kansas City (Missouri), and Milwaukee. Arguing to uphold the FPC decision were the State and Oil Conservation Commission of New Mexico, the Corporation Counsel of Oklahoma, and the Railroad Commission of Texas, as well as the Phillips Company. The division was between consuming and producing interests.

On May 22, 1953 the Circuit Court of Appeals reversed the FPC, ruling that the Phillips Company *was* subject to FPC regulation. The decision was appealed to the United States Supreme Court which, after first refusing to hear the case, upheld the Circuit Court in a 5 to 3 decision on June 7, 1954. The court was in the unusual position of interpreting the FPC's jurisdiction more broadly than the agency's commissioners wanted. The Phillips decision established definitively that the Natural Gas Act gave the FPC the authority to regulate the field prices of independent producers.

The Harris-Fulbright Bill

With this decision, producers felt that only a change in the Natural Gas Act could preserve them from utility-type price regulation, and the Harris-Fulbright bill was designed for this purpose. The measure limited the FPC's power over field prices. It did empower the government to see that the producer was paid no more than a "reasonable *market* price" [emphasis added] for his product, but opponents felt that this phrasing was a sham— and was worse than an actual decontrol bill. They charged that the Harris-Fulbright bill promised regulation but, because the standard was too vague to be enforced, could not deliver it.

The oil and gas interests were able to mobilize great resources to throw into the campaign to enact the Harris-Fulbright bill. The stakes were high: an increase or decrease of only 5 cents per 1,000 cubic feet in the field price would amount to $116 million a year earned or lost by the companies operating in seven states (Texas, Louisiana, Oklahoma, Kansas, Mississippi, New Mexico, and Arkansas), and would mean a difference of $3.5 billion in the value of their existing reserves. These states contained about 84 percent of the gas reserves of the United States.

Oil and gas interests made up the backbone of the forces promoting the Harris-Fulbright legislation. The many thousands of gas producers—big and small—placed the weight of their numbers behind it; they were supported by the giants of the petroleum industry—

the major oil companies that produced both gas and oil—as well as the small companies and lone prospectors, or "wild-catters."

Virtually all of the oil-producing industry was in the fight because most producers, through sales of casinghead gas or ownership of gas wells discovered while drilling for oil, had major interests in gas. Business and industrial concerns that serviced the oil and gas industry also supported the bill. Pipeline companies joined on the side of the producers and the producing states. A third force that helped promote the bill was a segment of business not directly affected, but which nevertheless feared that any extension of federal regulation would strengthen the network of controls already imposed on business activity.

Three groups predominated in the fight against the bill. They were labor unions, municipal organizations, and gas utility companies. All represented themselves as spokesmen for the consumer. There was no organization of actual gas consumers to oppose the bill.

Broadly speaking, Congress reflected three viewpoints on natural gas: producer state representatives favored exemption; consumer states favored regulation; and states whose economy was based largely on the coal industry wanted direct sales of natural gas to large industrial users brought under federal regulation.

The oil-gas lobby knew it could count on effective and articulate representation from congressmen from producing states—and not only because of the substantial campaign contributions that industry men regularly made. The economies and tax systems of most producer states were heavily dependent on oil and natural gas. An Oklahoma representative once said, "We oil congressmen represent our people. It is my duty to represent their views. I would be replaced otherwise, and I would deserve it." Senators and representatives from producing states were often influentially situated in their legislative bodies.

The opponents of the Harris-Fulbright bill could not count on a comparable loyalty among consumer state representatives. The "consumer" is a stock character with diffuse interests, and the legislator cannot rely on his support at the polls or his largesse with contributions. The consumer in this case was represented by a utility company coalition, a group as powerful and experienced as the gas-oil lobby but one that entered the campaign late and operated on a lower budget. Indeed, private utility companies had not traditionally counted themselves on the side of advocates of regulation. As they explained it, their ideological shift on this issue resulted from the view that continually-rising prices, which they were able only with difficulty to pass along to the consumer, made it imperative that producers be brought under regulation.

The oil-natural gas industry had many seeming advantages in the coming struggle over the Harris-Fulbright bill. But one of these—the large number and great variety of industry interests and spokesmen—meant that one problem would be getting everyone to act in accordance with a wise overall strategy. Oil and gas men, reflecting the speculative atmosphere that hung over their industry, were not susceptible to central regulation or coordination from any source. There would be considerable "wildcatting" in the industry's efforts to support the Harris-Fulbright bill despite efforts by the larger firms and by industry associations to mobilize support in terms of a coordinated strategy.

The American Petroleum Institute

Even before the Supreme Court decision in the Phillips case, natural gas producers had begun to plan for new legislation should the decision be adverse.

Backstopping any specific effort was the continuing work of the American Petroleum Institute (API), the industry's major trade association. Organized in 1919 to promote the industry and "to afford a means of cooperation with the Government in all matters of national concern," it had grown by the 1950s to include over 10,000 members and a staff of 360, with headquarters in New York City. The API brought together producers, refiners, marketing firms, and oil, gas, and natural gas pipeline companies. It had 200 committees that dealt with all phases of the petroleum industry, and it was thought to be influenced largely by the interests of large integrated oil corporations.

The institute was able to congratulate itself in 1947 for having achieved a high degree of industry-government cooperation:

As a result of such Government-industry cooperation, industry standards find wide Government acceptance and proposed Government regulations and procedures receive careful industry study as to their necessity, practicality and effectiveness.

As far back as 1946 the API had organized a continuing nationwide campaign to win friends and create a praiseworthy impression of the industry in the public mind. It was designed to increase public understanding of the oil industry "through a carefully planned series of specific steps that will create a constructive, favorable impression of the oil industry in the public mind. We want the public to like the oil industry."

As a result of various soundings conducted by opinion survey forces, the term "progressive" had been selected as characteristic of the industry, and a slogan was devised describing the campaign as "progressive public relations for the progressive petroleum industry." [4]

In 1947 the institute established an Oil Industries Information Committee to handle public relations. This committee set up fourteen district offices throughout the country to distribute literature and films, to furnish speakers, and to promote special events. The outstanding feature of the special events program was Oil Progress Week, when a network of 25,000 oil company employees—gas station operators, jobbers, and employees—acted as volunteer public relations men in 5,000 cities and towns. They visited clubs, churches, schools, newspapers, and radio and TV stations to draw attention to oil in every possible way. The promotion squads concentrated particularly on the schools, where volunteers distributed material featuring the petroleum industry's importance in science, social studies, economics, and conservation.

Although the API had always carried the burden of representing petroleum to the government and interpreting the industry to the public, industry leaders agreed to set up special instruments to press for legislation nullifying the regulatory power of the FPC as interpreted by the Supreme Court in the Natural Gas Act. Two ad hoc groups were organized, the General Gas Committee to lobby for legislation, and the Natural Gas and Oil Resources Committee to inform the public of the problems facing the oil industry if the Supreme Court's mandate were enforced. The two bodies tackled their problems of organization immediately, and by the end of 1954 both were ready to carry out their missions.

The General Gas Committee

On May 22, 1953, after the Circuit Court of Appeals for the District of Columbia had held that Phillips Petroleum Company was subject to federal regulation, "consternation reigned throughout the entire gas-producing industry." In November, when the American Petroleum Institute staged its convention in Chicago, no subject was more widely discussed than the Phillips decision.

In this atmosphere, 25 persons met for breakfast to launch a plan of industry action. Maston Nixon, president of Southern Minerals Corporation of Corpus Christi, an independent oil and gas producer, was chairman of the informal group. Nixon's company was not involved in interstate sale of natural gas. The group, calling itself the Gas Study Committee, met again in New York on January 24, 1954 and agreed not to press for legislation until after the Supreme Court acted. Meeting again in Dallas on June 24—following the court's decision on June 7—it decided that the congressional session was too near its end for effective intervention at that time; the committee would wait until the following year to press

---

[4] Thirteen years later the same word was still considered effective. Posters, booklets, and handouts in the 1959 centennial celebration of the oil industry featured the slogan, "Born in Freedom, Working for Progress."

for a law exempting gas producers from federal regulation. The steering committee also agreed to make "every effort to secure the widest possible support throughout the industry." Acting on this decision, 77 persons met in New York on July 13, 1954.

After two more meetings of the steering committee, at which ambitious plans were made and the form of a larger organization was drafted, the group, in San Antonio on October 4, 1954, agreed on an organization called the General Gas Committee (GGC). Nixon continued as chairman; he was assisted by Charles E. Simons—executive vice president of Mid-Continent Gas and Oil Association—as secretary of the GGC. The General Gas Committee began work October 25, 1954 at an office in Fort Worth, but on January 1, 1955 the main operation was transferred to Washington.

Organization of the GGC

The GGC worked through five committees: steering, cooperation with other groups, legal, legislative, and evidence.

The committee on cooperation was directed to line up support from such diverse groups as farmers, ranchers, and cattlemen, gas distributors and marketers, railroads and railroad brotherhoods, the coal industry and coal unions, oil and gas unions, the sulphur industry, chambers of commerce, the Attorneys General Association, the Interstate Oil Compact Commission,[5] state governments, the League of Municipalities, and the National Association of Railroads and Utility Commissions.

------

[5] A compact among producing states for the promotion of oil conservation.

The legal committee's function was to identify oil industry personnel and others who would make presentable, qualified witnesses before congressional committees.

The legislative committee's assignment was to see that the desired legislation was introduced and acted upon in Congress, and to work with the Federal Power Commission to ensure its support of legislation acceptable to the industry.

The evidence committee's task was to put together data and testimony for the industry witnesses before congressional committees.

Membership and Financing

By April 1955 the GGC had 667 members, including individual producers, oil company executives and employees, pipeline company men, representatives of various oil and gas associations, and attorneys. Other business and industrial groups joined: banks with large loans to the gas industry; steel mills (Bethlehem Steel, Jones and Laughlin) that had supply companies dealing in tubular goods for the pipeline industry; and auxiliary and service enterprises, such as drilling companies. The membership list contained the names of recognized leaders and notables in the oil industry including such well-known oil magnates as H. Lester Hunt, Sid Richardson, and Clint Murchison.

GGC's total accountable funds, $118,625, represented contributions by corporate members. The largest contribution was $3,855, the smallest $25.

The Work of the GGC

When the GGC registered under the lobbying act, Nixon stated its objective as seeking "to secure corrective legisla-

tion that we consider necessary to restore to the producers of natural gas
the exemption that we thought we had
in the Natural Gas Act of 1939."

The GGC, its officers said, did not
lobby as a group. Only the member
companies actually lobbied—that is,
discussed legislation with members of
Congress. Many of the members were
officials of major oil companies or of
independent firms with valuable political connections in their home states and
in Washington. They worked through
their contacts—state governors, members of the state regulatory or railroad
commissions, municipal officials, and
others—to push the notion of producer
exemption. They talked informally,
both before and after bills were introduced, to senators and representatives
with whom they were friendly. When
bills were before Congress, GGC members saw to it that expert witnesses were
on hand to present the best case for
exemption to congressional committees.
As an organization, GGC's purpose
was to develop, collect, and distribute
information and statistics favorable to
producer exemption.

The work of the GGC was divided
into three phases. Initially it concerned
itself with organizing, planning, assigning industry personnel to committees,
financing, and "stabilizing" industry
views on acceptable legislation, that is,
ironing out conflicting viewpoints that
might jeopardize a united front.

The next step, of course, was a bill,
but GGC officers felt that any decision
they made on specific details of legislation would be wasted motion until they
knew what the President's Advisory
Committee on Energy Supplies and Resources Policy—appointed the previous
year—would recommend. They reasoned that the committee's position
might well be the best the industry
could expect in the way of legislation.

Report of the President's Advisory Committee

The GGC was reasonably satisfied
with the broad recommendations of the
report when it appeared. It recommended that gas prices be controlled
by having the FPC forbid the pipeline-
purchaser to pay more than a "reasonable market price" for gas. The report
set standards for the commission to
consider in determining the "reasonable
market price": whether or not the price
was arrived at competitively, what
effect the contract would have on future
gas supplies, and what effect the contract would have on existing or future
market field prices.

In summary, the report asserted that
for reasons of national defense, assurance of reasonable prices and supplies
to consumers, and the development of
adequate reserves,

> . . . we believe the Federal Govern-
> ment should not control the produc-
> tion, gathering, processing or sales of
> natural gas prior to its entry into an
> interstate transmission line.

Shortly after the report was issued,
Democratic Senator Paul Douglas of
Illinois charged that the gas and oil industry had "infiltrated" the Advisory
Committee and successfully slanted its
report. Some of the task force members
and many of the technical consultants,
he pointed out, were persons from the
oil and gas industry. The task force
member responsible for the oil and
gas studies, the senator said, was a
banker, a former oil company president, and trade association leader.[6]

---

[6] Douglas was referring here to J. E. Warren, New York banker and prominent businessman. Warren, a petroleum engineer with
25 years experience in the field, was a former

Senator Douglas' charges did not slow up the pace of the work being done at GGC headquarters. GGC's Washington members met daily for a time after the release of the President's Advisory Committee report. The basic question to be settled was whether to "accept" its recommendations for regulation in terms of the "reasonable market price" standard or to go beyond them to try, with another "Kerr bill," for exemption from regulation. Sometimes as many as fifty people attended these strategy sessions: lobbyists for the major oil companies, highly-placed public relations men from the home offices of the major companies, and several company counsel. The producer interests were in the majority, but pipelines also were represented.

GGC and the Harris Bill

GGC people did not have a formal draft of legislation, but they were soon given one that came from Representative Oren Harris of Arkansas. Harris, the group was told, was going to introduce the bill shortly.

---

president of the Independent Petroleum Association of America, a former president of API, and a member of the National Petroleum Council. He had been deputy administrator of the Petroleum Administration for Defense in 1952–1953. The other task force members were the president of a coal company, a former federal judge, and an investment banker.

The President's Advisory Committee had also used four technical consultants on gas, and six on oil. They included an officer and director of the Humble Oil Company, the chief foreign economist for The Texas Company, the assistant to the board chairman of Continental Oil Company, the president of Southern Natural Gas Company of Birmingham, a director and vice-president of the Independent Petroleum Association of America, and an executive of the United Pipeline Company.

The Harris [7] draft embodied the Advisory Committee's recommendations (1) that the FPC allow the pipeline-purchaser to pass along only a "reasonable market price"; and (2) that the commission should determine "reasonable market price" by considering the same three factors listed in the advisory report. The Harris bill, however, carried one additional proviso: with respect to price, the pipeline company was to be allowed to pass on to the utility companies the "reasonable market price" *plus* a "fair gathering charge."

Not all the members of the GGC were happy about the Harris bill. But the hope of the GGC, as one official, Hines H. Baker, president of Humble Oil, said, was that "the oil and gas industry in all of its branches and aspects might have a common viewpoint" and stand together on a law to "remedy" the Phillips decision.

> We felt that this decision was a threat to our whole free enterprise system, that if regulation of the price of gas in the hands of a producer by the Federal Government should be established, it is only another step to oil, and to coal, and to wheat and to other products. . . .

And, as chairman Nixon explained:

> There [was] great conflict within the industry, that is, between pipeline companies which also produce gas and independent producers that want to get themselves clear but leave the pipeline companies' production subject to the FPC. My principal job, the job of my committee, was to bring about a meeting of minds to where the industry

---

[7] Harris had not been approached by anyone from the working level of the GGC. Probably he had heard from oil company executives who were among his constituents.

could present to this Congress an intelligent, solid front for all producers of natural gas. . . .

Nixon's harmony campaign was more successful with producing groups than with pipeline companies. He was unable to get the pipelines to agree to bring direct sales to industrial consumers under FPC regulation, and GGC feared that a bill without such a provision would offend coal state representatives. The coal industry, prominent in West Virginia, Pennsylvania, Ohio, and Kentucky, had lost ground—according to its spokesmen—because gas pipelines sold gas at "dump" prices which undercut coal.

The industry finally decided to support the Harris draft, despite some disappointment. On March 2 Nixon wrote a GGC colleague in Texas, "Congressman Oren Harris will introduce in the House today a bill that represents the views of the General Gas Committee." Harris announced on the House floor that the bill (H.R. 4560) had been prepared after he had conferred with "our beloved Speaker," Sam Rayburn of Texas, "who has announced his wholehearted support for this corrective legislation." Harris went on to say that the bill had been drafted in the light of the President's Fuels Advisory Committee report.

The GGC's immediate concern was to find an effective sponsor of a comparable bill in the Senate. Much to the surprise of GGC leaders, on March 18 Republican Senator J. Glenn Beall of Maryland introduced a producer-exemption bill (S. 1498). Soon afterwards, one of the GGC's legislative experts went to see the Maryland senator to explain the views of the GGC, to clarify any questions Beall might have, and to provide whatever technical data he needed. At the same time other GGC men tried to find other Senate sponsors already familiar with the general problems of the industry. Oren Harris conferred several times with his Arkansas colleague, Senator William Fulbright, and on April 18 Fulbright introduced S. 1853—a bill identical to the Harris House bill.

Supporting the Harris Bill

With legislation before both the Senate and House, the GGC turned to the task of preserving the Harris bill during hearings of the House Interstate and Foreign Commerce Committee and assuring its safe journey, without major amendments, through the House.

Two GGC subcommittees, the legislative and the evidence subcommittees, worked actively in the early months of 1955. The legislative committee was composed of five registered lobbyists: Fayette B. Dow of the National Petroleum Association of America, John A. Ferguson of the Independent Natural Gas Association of America, Ray C. Hinman of Socony-Vacuum Oil Company, Harold L. Kennedy of Ohio Oil Company, and Frank W. Rogers of Western Oil and Gas Association.

The evidence subcommittee prepared other material: a speech for the Governor of Illinois to deliver to the Interstate Oil Compact Commission, and a memorandum for the Governor of Louisiana on the effect of the Phillips decision on gas producers in Louisiana. Frank Rogers of the Western Oil and Gas Association worked actively as a member of the evidence subcommittee. When Oren Harris sought assistance from GGC to publicize his bill, Rogers, a former newsman, was assigned to draft a press release.

GGC leaders realized that the major task confronting them was accumulating authoritative data to support the industry's position. The Humble Oil Company's general counsel had recommended to Humble's chief economist, Dr. R. J. Gonzalez, that GGC should have a qualified industry economist to direct research. Writing Gonzalez in December 1954, the general counsel had said:

> In connection with the work of the Evidence Committee it is most important that we have a top-flight economist who could devote for several months his full time to the work of the Committee. Although the Committee felt you were the most qualified of any economist available, they agreed with my suggestion that (1) it may be embarrassing for you to work with the Evidence Committee after having served on the task force of the Energy Supplies and Resources Policy Committee and (2) in view of the time you had given to the work of the task force, it would be unfair to ask Humble to release you for another several months.

For these reasons GGC chose Dr. John Boatwright, chief economist for Standard of Indiana, to direct research —which occupied him from January 1955 until Congress adjourned in early August. He returned to Washington late in 1955 to prepare material for Senate consideration in 1956. According to Nixon, Boatwright's documents and pamphlets were used only "to inform and educate" GGC members and others who requested that kind of information. Some $39,000 was spent for printing, mailing, and distributing literature.

Boatwright testified in favor of the exemption bills before both the House and Senate committees. He identified himself as an economist for Standard of Indiana, but he said he was testifying "on behalf of all producers of petroleum and natural gas." He said his company had loaned him to the American Petroleum Institute for that purpose.

Throughout the time that GGC was an operating body, individual members, as part of the GGC plan, called on their political friends to warn of the consequences to the consumer and the country if gas producers were regulated. Whenever a state regulatory commission, a governor, or a municipal league issued a statement calling for regulation, one of GGC's members went into action to counteract or neutralize it. Members called on senators and representatives to urge a favorable vote. If, for instance, a senator from a "doubtful" or uncommitted state were not readily accessible to some GGC member, GGC staff persons dug into the senator's background and more often than not found some mutual friend through whom to channel the message. In a number of cases congressmen themselves sought out GGC for technical information, data, and statistics.

As Nixon explained it, however, GGC's only activity was amassing data —it did not lobby as a group. When GGC members telegraphed or spoke to congressmen, they did so as individuals and not as representatives of GGC. "Everybody in the oil and gas industry," Nixon said, "discussed it with their congressmen and the senators, and discussed the merits of the legislation like it is proper. The only thing we did was to provide factual data that they could use in any way they wanted to. But we did not direct them to contact their congressmen or their senators."

GGC Takes Alarm

Late in April 1955 Mayor Joseph Clark of Philadelphia and mayors from other large gas-consuming cities appeared before the House Commerce Committee and presented a strong case for federal regulation. The GGC took alarm. News accounts that had featured industry testimony now began to give space to consumer arguments favoring regulation. Nixon called for redoubled efforts on the part of GGC members.

On April 25 Nixon wrote on GGC letterhead to Hines Baker of Humble, a member of the GGC steering committee. He called Baker's attention to the "steadily increasing opposition" from several groups, including the gas utilities, and urged Baker to "continue your efforts to arouse your employees and others to the dangers of federal control." He asked Baker to see that Humble's future mailing pieces include a "direct request" to recipients to write Congress. He also proposed a special mail campaign with Humble's oil and gas royalty owners, especially those in non-producing states where "we need the greatest effort." He dispatched similar letters to other oil company executives.

Tests of the oil industry's efforts came soon. On June 7 the House Commerce Committee met to decide whether to report out the Harris bill, which by this time had been modified—after lengthy hearings spread out between March 22 and May 2—to meet some of the objections raised by mayors and utility companies. The revised bill (H.R. 6645) gave the FPC jurisdiction over certain price increases that formerly went into play automatically under long-term contracts.[8]

---

[8] These were price increases in the "favored nation" category. This term referred to a contract, say with producer X, which provided that if at some time in the future the pipeline company bought gas from some other supplier at a higher rate than it was paying X, it would modify its contract with X to pay him the same higher rate. The revised bill provided that if a pipeline company based its request for a higher rate on an increase in field prices under a "favored nations" provision in the contract, the FPC should determine in a hearing whether the increase represented the reasonable market price of the gas.

The committee vote was a tie, but the next day, with the committee's entire membership of 31 mobilized, the bill was reported out by a 16 to 15 vote.

The one-vote margin shocked Nixon, and on June 20 he issued a call to arms to GGC members:

A series of conferences have been held in connection with HR 6645, better known as the Harris bill, as reported out of the House committee. I think the industry was thoroughly shocked at the close vote in the committee. It may prove beneficial in that it clearly showed to the oil and gas industry the real fight [needed] to secure its passage.

The opposition is terrific, well organized, and using every political trick. If we are to pass this bill, it's going to be necessary for every member of the GGC, as well as others in the industry, to go out right now in their own way to get congressional votes. We can win or lose by a very narrow margin. The success will depend on the work out in the country in an intelligent way by the right people in contacting the Members of Congress.

It is useless to restate the real need for passage of this legislation. I assume that every member of the GGC realizes its importance. I plead with you to put your best effort in this fight for Congressional votes during the next two weeks, when the battle will either be won or lost. The oil industry has never failed, and surely it cannot in this, its most crucial fight.

The next step was clearance by the House Rules Committee. The vote on July 26 was 6 to 5 to clear the bill, with one member not voting.

The bill came to the House floor July 28 and passed that day by a margin of six votes. Congress adjourned on August 2.

Nixon was jubilant. On August 1 he

wrote R. F. Windfohr of the Fort Worth oil producing firm of Nash, Windfohr and Brown, congratulating him on the job he had done as chairman of the GGC steering committee.

> Friday morning I sent Sam [House Speaker Sam Rayburn of Texas] the enclosed wire. I think the industry owes a debt of gratitude to the Speaker. Without his solid support, the Harris bill could have been killed on the rules vote, and certainly I feel sure that he was good for more than the six-vote majority. Quite frankly I am terrifically pleased that the Harris bill has passed the House. With Lyndon's [Senate Majority Leader Lyndon Johnson of Texas] improvement in health and with only 96 Senators to hold the pulse and discuss the logic of the Fulbright bill, I feel our task in the Senate is not so tough. This work in the Senate can be done bodily, without a lot of fanfare and notoriety and with Lyndon's leadership, we should be able to send the gas legislation to the White House in the first month of the next session.

A bill of such scope and controversy could not be expected to pass the Senate in the few remaining days of the session. It was important to the gas and oil forces backing the bill to launch its Senate counterpart early the following year.

Preparing for the Senate Vote

The third phase of GGC strategy was preparation for Senate consideration and passage. The battlefront in the fall of 1955 shifted to the states. Intensive campaigns were planned in the hope of getting favorable votes from the senators from certain states, particularly Connecticut and Alabama. The states singled out were those where GGC strategists saw hope of winning over an opposition senator.

GGC asigned key men to consumer states in which municipal leagues were working actively for federal regulation. The general counsel of Gulf Oil Company, Archie D. Gray of Pittsburgh, was instructed to head off any resolution that mayors' groups in Pennsylvania might make opposing the Harris-Fulbright bills. Gray worked through Gulf's district sales managers to intercede with the mayors. Sidney Swensrud, chairman of the board of Gulf Oil and a GGC officer, talked informally with Republican Senator James Duff of Pennsylvania.

Howard Guleickson, head of the Denver legal department of Shell Oil and a former Democratic attorney general in Montana, was asked to intercede with Montana Democratic Senator Mike Mansfield.

Frank Rogers contacted about three-quarters of the members of the California delegation in the House and supplied written material to the two California senators. He also presented additional technical and legal material to three senators—Kuchel of California, Monroney of Oklahoma, and Beall of Maryland—at their request.

F. B. Dow, accompanied by an executive of Phillips Petroleum, discussed technical aspects of the pending legislation with Vermont Republican Senator Ralph Flanders. Dow also discussed the merits of the bill with Wyoming Democratic Senator Joseph O'Mahoney.

GGC furnished last-minute, up-to-date briefings to industry members before they went to Capitol Hill to speak to their senators. In January and February of 1956 anywhere from one to ten persons a day—most of them independent producers, but also company general counsel and other highly-placed executives—dropped by GGC headquarters to get the latest statistics and data on natural gas in order to present the most effective possible case.

The Natural Gas and Oil Resources Committee

During the year GGC had been working as a lobbying organization, a second industry group worked just as actively to rally popular sentiment in favor of the bill. As conceived by gas and oil company leaders, it would not be a lobby group. Its function was to educate and inform the public not only about the merits of producer exemption but the problems of the entire gas industry as well.

Entitled the Natural Gas and Oil Resources Committee (NGO), it actually had been planned for several years, but was organized October 20, 1954, after the June Supreme Court decision in the Phillips case. It was designed to foster a favorable "image" of the natural gas industry and in so doing to create a climate of opinion in which the desired legislation could be passed.

The NGO was formally launched in New York at a meeting attended by 24 gas and oil producers. The president of Continental Oil Company of Houston, L. F. McCollum, called the meeting. (The GGC had been set up eleven months earlier, and was by this time a going organization.) McCollum represented the formation as the culmination of years of discussion in the industry on how to "carry our story to the public. . . . Public misunderstanding, compounded by widespread misrepresentation, has been so great that a substantial information program will be required over an extended period of time if we are to set the record straight in the public mind." Other NGO officials, however, were clear that creation of the NGO had been triggered by the Phillips decision and the favorable press comment on that decision.

There was some feeling that the public relations facilities of the American Petroleum Institute could have been used for this program, but the view prevailed that a new organization devoted exclusively to natural gas matters would be a better vehicle.

McCollum was named chairman; Paul Kayser, president of El Paso Natural Gas [pipeline] Company, vice-chairman; and J. C. Donnell, II, president of Ohio Oil Company, treasurer. Within a week NGO had engaged the New York public relations firm of Hill and Knowlton and had retained legal counsel.

Baird H. Markham became executive director. Markham had begun in the auto industry, had switched to oil, and in 1934 had started working for the API. He organized and directed the API Industries Committee and was registered as a lobbyist for it. A former Adjutant General of the Oklahoma National Guard, he was addressed as General Markham. His duties with NGO were full-time, and he drew a salary of $67,000 between October 1954 and June 1956. He was assisted by economists and other technical experts detailed by their oil and gas employers to perform specific assignments. However, the bulk of the staff work at the New York City headquarters office was performed by Hill and Knowlton personnel. At its peak the headquarters staff numbered 17 full-time Hill and Knowlton employees and 15 to 20 persons who worked part-time on the NGO account.

NGO operations were financed by contributions from oil companies based on a formula keyed to production. A fund of $1,972,545.58 was received from over 1,000 contributors. About

80 percent of the contributions came from 26 gas and oil firms.

The NGO did not register under the Federal Regulation of Lobbying Act, since it considered its function that of conducting an information and education program without any direct legislative contact work. The NGO's counsel, the eminent downtown New York law firm of Davis, Polk, Wardwell, Sunderland and Kiendl, agreed.

The Davis-Polk opinion, dated November 4, 1954, said that the NGO was different from the GGC, which had been formed "for the express purpose of carrying on such [direct legislative] discussions."

> This second group consists of officers and employees of the same petroleum and gas companies whose personnel serve on the Committee. While the members of both groups will presumably express the views of the petroleum and gas companies with which they are associated, and while the second group may distribute to Congressmen literature written or developed by the Committee, no person will be a member of both groups and neither group will direct the activities of the other.

The Hill and Knowlton Plan

Hill and Knowlton had had earlier experience with the petroleum industry. Past clients had included The Texas Company and Caltex Petroleum Company. Executive vice-president Bert C. Goss was in charge of the NGO.[9]

---

[9] Goss, who later became president of the firm, had headed the Washington office before being transferred to New York. Holder of a Ph.D. degree in economics from New York University, Goss had taught at NYU for a few years. He had then become business editor of *Newsweek,* and in 1945 he had joined Hill and Knowlton.

Hill and Knowlton presented a work plan on November 4, 1954, calling for:

1. a public relations and advertising program originating from and directed at the headquarters level;

2. a simultaneous appeal to public opinion at the grassroots level to be achieved through a network of oil and gas company volunteers or persons selected by their employers to make speeches and to seize or create opportunities for making favorable news about the industry;

3. an appeal for the support of other business, and trade and professional associations, to be carried out by oil and gas company executives;

4. and a series of campaigns within each oil and gas company directed to employees, stockholders, credit-card customers, and royalty owners.

Specifically, the plan recommended the immediate establishment of field offices to be supplied with "how to do it" manuals on soliciting the support of other industries, meeting the press and arranging press tours, utilizing publicity opportunities, and working with local civic, service, educational, and business groups. The field offices were to be activated with the support of the oil and gas industry.

The Hill and Knowlton plan for field offices was put into effect immediately. The country was divided into fifteen districts with a regional chairman for each. Operations in each state were headed by a state chairman, and local forces were activated—down to the county and municipal level in some areas. About 2,100 people, devoting varying proportions of their time, kept the field operations going. There was no expenditure of NGO funds for these people; the oil and gas industry continued to pay their regular salaries.

Timing and Strategy

Publicity was timed carefully to accompany spot news developments, such as the request from a local community for gas service, the location of a major industrial plant within an area, or the discovery of a new gas field. The advertising campaign was to follow after the area had been awakened to the issues by "natural publicity." Industry ads were to appear, the Hill and Knowlton people advised, only "when the publicity program is well underway and the control controversy has begun to become a public issue. Timing is of fundamental importance, for studies indicate that institutional advertising seldom arouses public interest unless it deals with a live issue."

State and regional chairmen attended a briefing and indoctrination session in New York on December 13-14, 1954. McCollum and Kayser headed the list of industry speakers. The field men returned home with tools for organizing local campaigns: organization manuals, speakers' kits, background material, press releases, feature stories, fillers, and prepared scripts for local radio and TV stations.

On December 29 Hill and Knowlton recommended that the advertising follow these basic principles:

1. The program should reflect the fact that it was being waged on behalf of thousands of producers, small and large, and not just by a few "big companies." Practically speaking this meant a conspicuous effort to subordinate New York headquarters and magnify grassroots support.

2. The program should be impressive enough to gain wide-spread attention, but not so flamboyant as to make it appear to be backed by limitless resources.

3. To combat charges of "sneak" and "giveaway" the program should stress that the public was being invited to examine the issues fully. Repeated use of such phrases as "The American public is entitled to know the facts" was suggested.

4. Care should be taken to avoid the appearance of challenging the entire Supreme Court. In fact, Hill and Knowlton counseled against mentioning the court in ads whenever possible. When referring to the court, the use of such phrases as "a 5 to 3 majority of the Court" or "the existing law as interpreted by a 5 to 3 majority of the Court" was suggested.

5. Diversified arguments stressing regional characteristics should be employed. For example, Wisconsin and Minnesota, considered to be regulation-minded areas, might be moved by the argument that federal control of a competitive commodity like gas opens the door to control of oil, grain, and other commodities. For heavy consuming areas, the argument that freedom from regulation means more gas at less cost to consumers might be meaningful. In states-rights areas a popular argument might be that federal regulation of production infringes on certain state conservation powers.

The Hill and Knowlton advice was buttressed by a public opinion survey made in early 1955 by Opinion Research Corporation of Princeton, New Jersey. The $10,000 survey was conducted to weigh the public's opinion of the natural gas industry and to test the value of certain arguments for and against regulation of producers. Based on interviews with so-called "thought leaders"—editors, high school and college teachers, clergymen, doctors, lawyers, and businessmen—the survey indicated that NGO faced a "formidable" task in building support for producer exemption. Fifty-six percent of those interviewed thought producers should be regulated; 36 percent thought not. Even among the group categorized as "free enterprisers," the results were not much more favorable. Forty-three percent of these favored regulation. Those favoring regulation preferred federal to state regulation by a two-to-one margin.

The survey adjudged lack of knowledge of the oil and gas industry to be influential in producing the high percentages favoring regulation:

> Further evidence that people do not distinguish between the producing and distributing sides of the natural gas industry comes from the reasons given for favoring regulation of producers' prices. Among the frequently mentioned reasons are the two ideas that producers are not competitive and that they are public utilities. It is also evident that many people feel that the price paid to producers is a considerable factor in retail prices, for the chief reason volunteered in favor of regulation is that it will protect the consumer by keeping prices down.

Those interviewed, when asked to evaluate some arguments against regulation, reacted most favorably to the discussions built around a competition theme. Of eleven reasons advanced for not regulating producers' prices, the three most attractive were:

> 1. Producers, in contrast to pipelines and distributors, are keenly competitive and should not be regulated.
> 2. Competing fuels such as coal and oil are not regulated; therefore, natural gas should not be.
> 3. Because there are thousands of natural gas producers, competition suffices to keep prices reasonable.

The survey concluded with this recommendation:

> If majority support from thought leader groups is to be obtained, it will first be necessary to get them to differentiate producers from the rest of the industry. In doing this, emphasis on the competitive characteristics of natural gas production is likely to be persuasive to thought leaders.

The Advertising Campaign Opens

A page-one story in the *Wall Street Journal,* January 12, 1955, carried details of industry strategy. The story, under a Houston dateline, said the industry had put up $1.5 million to institute a "king-sized publicity campaign" to persuade the consumers "that their best interest lies in removing the federal control decreed by the Supreme Court. . . ." The *Journal* reported that a gigantic newspaper campaign would begin the following Monday, January 17, with the heaviest concentration of publicity to fall in "key" eastern consuming areas. The headlines read: "GAS PRODUCERS ENLIST CONSUMERS IN BATTLE AGAINST FPC CONTROL" and "INDUSTRY MOBILIZES GIANT LOBBY TO BACK LEGISLATION TO UPSET PHILLIPS PETROLEUM DECISION."

The campaign unfolded as the *Journal* story predicted. On January 17 a full-page ad—entitled "What the Regulation of Gas Supply Means to 25 Million American Families"—appeared in 1,273 daily newspapers with a total circulation of 50 million. In March a second ad, entitled "Why Scrap Free Competition," ran in 1,754 dailies with a combined circulation of 55 million. This ad bore the trademark developed for NGO's material, a tiny gas flame with the slogan "Protect the Public Interest Through Free Competition." No ad was attributed to the national organization, but each listed as sponsors the NGO chairmen of the state organizations. Sixteen basic ads were used, many including local data based on such factors as newly-discovered oil and gas fields or extension of gas service to the area.

Throughout the spring of 1955 NGO ran other ads in farm and ranch publications, in the oil and gas industry press, and in business magazines (*Time, Newsweek, U.S. News and World Report, Business Week, Barrons,* and the monthly magazines of the Rotarians, Lions, and Kiwanians). A two-page "advertorial" or "quality" ad appeared in *Harpers* and the *Atlantic Monthly* in May 1955. Labeled a "public interest" advertisement, it warned that producer regulation threatened free competition. The ad (called by a college English professor "the finest example of formal argumentation to be found in current periodicals") closed with this statement: "The public interest lies in this freedom to compete. The issue goes far beyond natural gas. It goes to the very roots of America's greatness."

According to Markham, the advertising campaign was designed to reach the general public through newspapers, intellectuals through *Harpers* and the *Atlantic,* and opinion leaders through business magazines.

Two double-page ads were run in the editorial trade press—*Editor and Publisher, American Press, National Publisher,* and *Publisher's Auxiliary.* One was a reproduction of the first newspaper advertisement, with a note that NGO was using newspapers to tell its story.

Monitoring teams were set up in key cities to read newspapers and check radio and TV for adverse publicity. An attempt was made immediately following to "correct" whatever was deemed a misrepresentation.

A number of special advertisements appeared later in selected areas. Based on the survey findings, they were de-

signed to "overcome misunderstanding." One of the most common "misunderstandings" was that the producer received the largest share of the cost of gas to the consumer. An ad designed to correct this impression ran in May, June, and July 1955; it was headlined "It Isn't the Two Cents a Day Paid the Producers that Determines the Size of Your Gas Bill." [10]

NGO paid almost $1.5 million for its advertising and printed material. Expenses, according to records, were as follows (from NGO's inception to March 31, 1956):

Advertising	$798,304.59
National publicity	87,032.89
Field program, booklets and printed material	499,181.77
Film and TV aids	27,079.36
	$1,411,598.61

Editorial Contacts and Briefing Sessions

The campaign to get gas into the news and editorial columns began on January 26, 1955, when NGO put on a briefing session in New York for 31 representatives of trade publications, financial journals, and the wire services. Soon after that, one industry member of the NGO staff and a Hill and Knowlton representative began making calls on editors of popular maga-

---

[10] The average price producers received for gas varied widely and was a product of many factors. In 1952, when the household consumer paid about 83¢ per 1,000 cubic feet, wholesale rates were about 30¢, and Texas field prices averaged 7¢. Fainsod, Gordon, and Palamountain, *Government and the American Economy* (New York, 1959), p. 675.

zines—*Saturday Evening Post, Time, Newsweek, Business Week,* and *Colliers.* This task took several weeks. McCollum reported to the NGO directorate that, as a result of these editorial contacts and the distribution of new authoritative data and information, two newspapers, the *Washington Post and Times-Herald* and the *Chicago Sun-Times,* reversed earlier unfavorable editorial expressions.

NGO was sometimes able to get access to the news columns. McCollum wrote signed news stories for the *New York Herald-Tribune* and the *New York Journal of Commerce* warning of the dangers of federal control. Both his business and NGO affiliation were carried along with his byline.

The industry story reached other publications. The bi-monthly magazine *Steelways,* trade publication of the American Iron and Steel Institute, carried a three-page article in June 1955 on the "miracle" of the natural gas industry. It concluded with quotes from industry officials that federal control of producers represented a cloud on the horizon. It noted that uncertainty about the status of producers had forced postponement of three pipeline projects and the resulting shutdown of a major pipemill. The April 1955 issue of *Nation's Business,* published by the United States Chamber of Commerce, featured a story on the natural gas issue which NGO characterized as "excellent."

Regional rallies were given for field personnel in March. At a series of one-day meetings held in Atlanta, Boston, Chicago, Denver, and Philadelphia, NGO's top staff members distributed new material and encouraged the volunteers to trade experiences in various promotional efforts. To counter any possibility of a "let-down" resulting from the favorable editorial support, Markham staged a conference telephone hook-up with regional and state chairmen from March 29 through April 1. In his talks he issued instructions on what should be done in the next sixty days, urged renewed contact with newspapers, suggested intensive cooperative effort with local chambers of commerce, and offered a preview of speech and publicity materials that were planned for early distribution. This material included news stories localized for each state and prepared editorials to be distributed through commercial syndicates.

Materials for the Education Campaign

The campaign to mold public opinion involved all media of communication—newspaper and magazine advertisements, radio and TV programs, films, news releases, interviews, speeches, and numerous miscellaneous items. During the first eight months of 1955, NGO distributed over five million pieces of literature. In at least one state—Minnesota—stationery on which to write to congressmen was included in the distributed material. Republican Senator Edward J. Thye reported that much of his mail from different areas of Minnesota was written on identical stationery.

The field force distributed three types of materials. The first type, consisting of materials for speakers, included speeches tailored to the interests of specific audiences and press releases for advance and follow-up publicity. It also included radio and TV scripts; general background material on natural gas, including attractive pamphlets for general distribution; a reprint of the McCollum article in the *New York Herald-Tribune*; and a history of the natural gas industry. The second type of material was an Editor's Information File containing glossy prints, background, suggested editorials, and filler material. The third was a press kit to accompany a 16-minute film entitled "You the People." Each volunteer worker was equipped with instructions on ways to make effective use of the materials. NGO headquarters kept the field forces abreast of developments in a bulletin published every two weeks.

The film, which was financed primarily by the Ethyl Corporation at a cost of around $25,000, was shown approximately 500 times. As Markham explained its selling points, "We picked out a man that was a natural gas man in the State of New Mexico, and he came in and made a talk about how the whole situation affected him about gas, and the amount of reports that he had to make out." The others in the film were a producer, a farmer, a lawyer, and an oil jobber, none of them professional actors.

One of the radio scripts in the speakers' file was a 15-minute interview to be set up with a prominent woman in the community, an oil company manager (the NGO spokesman), and the radio announcer.

The interview opened when the woman, responding to a question, said she really knew nothing of where the gas came from that she used for cooking and heating her home.

> *NGO representative:* "Do you remember the stories of the prospectors for gold of the old days—the men who spent years panning streams for nuggets?—your particular fuel is the result of some 'prospectors' digging—looking—hoping—losing—finally hitting 'pay dirt'—natural gas. When you turn on this flame in your kitchen range or your furnace, the gas comes direct by pipeline from the source itself, an actual well, perhaps in Texas, which was discovered some years ago by a dogged prospector."

> *Woman:* "That does sound romantic. . . ."

> *Announcer:* "These 'prospectors' as you call them, how do they go about locating a natural gas well? Don't they know pretty well where to look for it?"

> *NGO:* "A good question. I'll bet many of them wish they did. The fact is, when a gas producer drills exploratory wells, past experience in the industry tells him that, on the average, he will drill eight DRY holes before he hits one that produces. Dry or not, these wells will cost him an average of around $100,000 each and some range up to more than $1 million. So you see, when he does finally run into some luck, he's got an awful lot of bills to pay from what he earns."

> *Woman:* "But my goodness. With all the initial expense of discovering the well, and then the gas having to go from there to a pipeline and then to a gas company, why does it cost so little?"

> *NGO:* . . . "Abundance of gas, resulting from competitive prospecting, has made it inexpensive. Most of what you pay for is the cost of getting that gas to your home. Out of every dollar you pay for gas service, the producer receives only about a dime for the actual gas."

The discussion turned to finding means of assuring adequate supplies to customers and extending service to those who wanted it:

> *NGO:* "I told you earlier that the pipelines and your local gas utility company are regulated. Usually there's only one gas company in a town and one pipeline serving that company. So their rates are fixed by local or federal agencies—because they have no competition. But, the government is now trying to regulate producers too, even though they are entirely different. They don't have any exclusive market. They have to compete for their busi-

ness—just like people who produce cotton or corn or automobiles or anything else. I hope we're soon going to have an end to government interference."

Ads for Harris Bill

Although the NGO's stated aim, repeated many times by officials and by the literature, was to inform the public and not to influence legislation directly, some of its paid advertisements urged support for the Harris bill. After the House passed H.R. 6645, ads referring to the Harris bill appeared in newspapers in Washington, D.C. and in Alabama. The Washington ad, headed "The Facts on Natural Gas Controls," stated that "A handful of utilities, led by big Eastern interests" were advocating utility-type controls for natural gas producers. A box in the ad read: "The Harris bill protects consumers." It added that the Harris bill, as amended in committee, supplemented the protection already given consumers through competition by requiring the FPC to allow producers "a reasonable market price."

The ad that ran in Alabama newspapers contained, in addition to the same box on the Harris bill, textual material geared to the exploration then under way for gas and oil in Alabama.

Alabama stands today as America's new oil frontier. The recent activities in the Pollard and Citronelle fields open vast new horizons. Qualified geologists have stated that at least 60% of the state is potential gas and oil land. . . . The prospects are that the $1 million which the state already is receiving in gas and oil revenues is only a beginning. . . . Yet, all of this potential prosperity is risked by the zeal of those advocating controls. . . . Obviously the best interests of Alabama, whether in natural gas use or

production, lie in a continuation of this historic competition which has resulted in the bold and risky exploration that underlies the vigorous development of an area's resources with benefit to producers and consumers alike.

General Markham justified the reference to pending legislation. He said the usage had been approved by NGO's attorneys because, as he explained it, the Harris bill had then passed the House and the attorneys did not consider it "pending." Markham said that following legal advice NGO had scrupulously refrained from referring directly to the Harris bill during the time it was under consideration in the House. As Markham understood it, NGO—as an educational and not a lobbying group—was barred by the Lobbying Act from referring directly to pending legislation. However, as he interpreted the attorneys' opinion, it was all right to make such a reference once the bill was no longer "pending." Bert Goss, Hill and Knowlton president, was also satisfied with the attorneys' opinion of the legality and propriety of referring to the Harris bill. He said that he, "as an average ignorant layman," thought that the Harris legislation was no longer before the Congress if it had been passed by the House.

Support from Other Groups

Markham reported to the NGO on September 1, 1955 that the effort to win support from other groups was highly successful. He said that 120 organizations in 34 states had passed resolutions supporting the producer position and that the groups had acted voluntarily in doing so.

Statements from three organizations were incorporated in booklets distributed by NGO, which included a quotation from the Farm Bureau: "Since the field price of natural gas is adequately regulated by competition, we favor legislation providing that field prices of natural gas shall not be regulated by the FPC." Another quotation, from the American Cattlemen's Association, read: "Gas is an important product of ranch and farm land.

This decision . . . [in the Phillips case] may well be the beginning of laws to regulate all industries in this country, including the livestock industry." And from the National Wool Growers Association: " We believe [the Phillips] decision is fundamentally and dangerously wrong."

Lobbying by Individual Companies

Before, during, and after the NGO campaign, oil and gas companies carried on their own efforts with their employees, stockholders, customers, and the public. Some examples are given here.

Standard of Indiana

Standard-Indiana operated in fifteen middle western states in the manufacture and sale of petroleum products. The chief subsidiary on the East Coast was American Oil Company; its Rocky Mountain subsidiary, Utah Oil Refining Company. The company employed about 50,000 persons and had approximately 140,000 stockholders. Company policy, according to the president, was to persuade all department heads and plant managers "to take a real interest in what is going on and the issue behind any type of legislation that might indirectly or directly affect our business."

Early in January 1956, when it was clear that the Senate was nearing a vote on the Fulbright bill, an official from Standard's home office in Chicago traveled to Minnesota to discuss plans for securing Senator Thye's vote. While Democratic Senator Hubert Humphrey's public statements opposing the bill indicated to company strategists that it was a waste of time to try to sway him, they felt that Thye had not yet made up his mind. (He had voted against the Kerr bill in 1950.)

On January 10, shortly after arriving in Minneapolis, Joseph Markusich, who was assistant supervisor of the production department, met with several of the company's representatives to discuss the Harris-Fulbright bill. According to William C. Kniefel, regional manager, the talk "centered on ways in which we might make it clear to Senator Thye that there was widespread support for the Harris-Fulbright bill in Minnesota. Someone suggested the possibility of having a large number of telegrams sent to Senator Thye. Time was short." They agreed to go ahead with a telegram campaign, and Markusich assured them that Standard would pay for the wires.

The plan was set in motion by a series of telephone calls. It involved the cooperation of 402 agents who operated bulk plants, 41 bulk-station salesmen who supervised the agents, and a number of other company employees.

Keith Thomson of Duluth was one of the participating salesmen. He had worked on the NGO "education" campaign in 1955 when Standard-Indiana had made his services available. Before that he had gained public relations and contact experience on special assignments with the American Petroleum Institute during "Oil Progress Week."

On January 11, 1956 Thomson got a phone call from Standard's assistant sales manager in Duluth, who "instructed me to drop whatever I was doing" and contact ten bulk stations and "secure three telegrams from each bulk station town to be sent to Hon. Edward Thye, with relation to support of the Fulbright bill." The wires, to be sent that week, were modeled on a form telegram furnished by the company.

Thomson immediately set forth on the 500-mile trip around his territory. Just before he got to each of his stations, he telephoned the bulk agent, explained the company plan, and said, "We have to have three people not connected with the oil business to send a telegram in favor of the Fulbright bill." Thomson, new to the territory, had met some of the agents before but was not personally acquainted with the townspeople. He had covered the territory only once prior to undertaking the special assignment. In some cases the local agent had no trouble finding three people willing to lend their names to wires urging support of the gas bill. Thomson or the agent then dispatched the message. In other cases, according to Thomson, he was so pressed for time that he had to rely on the agent's word that the dispatch of a telegram was accomplished. Thomson himself secured the consent of ten persons whose names were signed.

On arriving at Grand Rapids, Minnesota, after driving part of the night, Thomson said that he received three names from the local agent—all persons connected with the First National Bank. However, he did not send the wires until he got to the crossroads village of Remer, some twenty miles distant, the next day. There he got names of three Remer residents from the local agent and sent from Remer six wires signed by the three Grand Rapids names and the three Remer names. He said he thought permission had been granted in each case.

On Friday, January 13, J. E. Swear-

ingen, Jr., vice-president of Standard's production department, called on Senator Thye in Washington to present the company's views on the merits of the Fulbright bill. The Senator spoke of the flood of telegrams from Minnesota.

Although there was no definite link to Standard-Indiana, Swearingen, on his return to Chicago on Monday, called in Markusich to find out what sort of efforts the field people in Minnesota were making in behalf of the gas bill. When he was told about the telegram campaign, Swearingen—according to the president of Standard-Indiana—ordered that it be stopped at once. Swearingen told Markusich that it was an "ill-conceived activity, that it was extremely embarrassing to the company." Standard did not report to Senator Thye that it had initiated the campaign.

As a result of Standard's grassroots effort, some 900 telegrams were sent to Senator Thye from Minnesota on January 12 and 13. Standard-Indiana paid the $1500 charges, listing the item as a marketing expense.

Standard's other agents in Minnesota worked in a variety of ways to fill their quotas. In Nashwauk one confined his efforts to his family, sending wires signed by his wife, his brother, and his father-in-law. In Coleraine two wires bore names, similar to those of local residents, that were actually contrived —though typical—Minnesota names. One bulk agent, who regularly purchased two trucks a year, had no trouble convincing the truck salesman to authorize his signature on a wire. In other instances, the salesman stopped in a cafe or restaurant and secured the permission of friends or acquaintances to send telegrams in their names.

Senator Thye's office replied to the wires. Two of the alleged senders denied sending the messages. Others said they had sent, or had authorized sending, a message, but that they then disassociated themselves from the request that the senator support the Fulbright bill. Thye's office concluded that the wires were in no way representative of the sentiment of his constituents. Other factors earmarked the effort as contrived. Many of the wires were identical; none came from Minneapolis or St. Paul, largest cities in the state; and often as many as six wires were sent from the same Western Union office at the same minute.

The Work of Paxton Howard

The oil industry exerted special efforts to persuade Alabama and Connecticut congressmen and senators to vote for exemption bills. Alabama was generally thought of as a "consumer" state, but recent exploration had uncovered oil deposits in the southern region. Industry therefore couched its arguments in terms of the possibility of Alabama becoming a big producing area.

Connecticut was without question a consumer state, but industry strategists felt that Republican Senator Prescott Bush, a former investment banker, might be persuaded to vote for exemption. His colleague, Republican Senator William Purtell, an active advocate of regulation, was considered already irrevocably committed.

The principal instrument for carrying out the industry missionary task in both states was Paxton Howard, Shell Oil Company attorney of Midland, Texas. A recognized expert in natural gas matters, Howard had been with Shell for twenty years. Other oil company executives helped on the Alabama assignment—Herman Pressler, a director of Humble Oil and a member of both GGC and NGO, and Harold Skinner, associate general counsel of Continental Oil Company and an NGO

official. These two made special trips to Alabama during 1955 to speak to business groups and other organizations. They hoped to neutralize the campaign being waged against the gas bill by the Alabama League of Municipalities.

In addition to meeting with local gas and oil people, Skinner of Continental conferred several times in October 1955 with persons active in Alabama politics and with close friends and supporters of the two Alabama senators. They included George Lemaistre, a Tuscaloosa attorney, who had campaigned actively for both Senators Sparkman and Hill; Gessner T. McCorvey, an attorney of Mobile; and J. Finley McRae, president of a Mobile bank. Howard said that these men were brought in to give advice on Alabama politics. Later, one oil company employed Lemaistre as attorney, and he made several trips to Washington for conferences with Senators Hill and Sparkman. He did not register as a lobbyist.

Howard was instructed by his company—specifically by W. F. Kenney, vice-president and general counsel—to go to Alabama to try to overcome opposition among municipal officials. (Kenney was a member of the GGC steering committee.) Many Alabama towns and cities had municipally-owned gas systems, and the mayor was in effect the president of the local gas company.

Howard first came to Alabama in the late fall of 1954, and also made one or two trips in 1955. On instructions from Shell, he started his campaign by getting in touch with James J. Britton, executive secretary of the Alabama Petroleum Industries Committee, an arm of the API that monitored state legislation affecting the oil industry. (APIC in Alabama, like its counterparts in other states, had an executive committee of eight to ten persons and was headed by a full-time executive secretary who directed the operations of a grassroots organization extending to the county level.) Britton knew the Alabama scene and was on friendly terms with many business people. Howard said he "didn't know a soul in Alabama."

On one occasion Howard spoke at a meeting of Alabama wholesale oil dealers and their business friends. He concentrated on explaining the provisions of the revised Harris bill then before the House. He said the House Committee had tightened up the original bill, and that it was now one that municipal officials could wholeheartedly support. He urged the oil men to persuade their local mayors to communicate their views to Congress.

Telegrams from Alabama

About 100 telegrams urging an exemption vote were sent from Alabama municipalities to Washington. Britton guessed that most came from mayors who had not previously expressed opposition.

Howard was credited with bringing about a complete reversal of the position of the Alabama Public Service Commission.[11] The commission, as of April 12, 1955, had opposed the Harris bill. That day a telegram signed by the three members had asked the Alabama delegation in the House to vote against the proposed bill. "Urge your opposition to passage of the Harris bill," the message read. "By removing

regulation of the wellhead price of natural gas this bill would place in the hands of natural gas producers the privilege of controlling a major element in the cost of natural gas service to Alabama consumers." The commission's opposition was predicated on the relative nearness of Alabama to supplies of natural gas. Members felt that without federal regulation, pipelines serving Alabama would have to bid for supplies against pipelines serving more distant areas, with ensuing higher prices to Alabama.

Three months later the commission recommended a vote in favor of the bill. The new position was based on the commissioners' understanding that the bill, "as amended, will give the FPC the authority to grant the pipeline companies only that amount of their cost of gas at the wellhead that the FPC thinks is reasonable and just as far as rate-making purposes are concerned. This being the case it seems to me that the ultimate consumer would have adequate protection which would remove my objection to the bill; in fact, I recommend its passage under these conditions." The letter, dated July 13, 1955, was signed by the president of the commission, with the notation that the other two members agreed with the position.

According to W. F. Kenney, Paxton Howard "personally went over and talked to them [the members of the commission], and after he had talked to them or explained to them what the facts of life were on the Harris-Fulbright bill, although they had previously issued or come out with a resolution against the bill, they completely reversed their position."

Howard and the Senators

Howard's next assignment took him to Washington in early January 1956,

---

11 Howard himself would not comment on the victory he allegedly had brought about. Nor did the three commissioners recall any occasion on which Howard talked to them about the bills. The secretary of the commission said in a letter to the author on October 21, 1959 that "the Commissioners have no recollection of such a person having visited the Commission."

just prior to serious Senate consideration of the Fulbright bill. Again Kenney instructed him to make the trip. His mission was "to talk to industry people, and I would be available to talk to anybody that would listen to me on the gas bill." He was able to speak to Senators Williams of Delaware and Hickenlooper of Iowa, appointments having been made through the state secretaries of the Petroleum Industries Committee.

Howard did not register as a lobbyist. He said he did not regard any of these activities as lobbying. He carried out the special assignments on instructions from Shell, his salary and expenses were paid by Shell, and for his work he received a $5,000 bonus from Shell. He expressed only the cloudiest knowledge and scantiest information about the organization, personnel, and purpose of either the GGC or the NGO. He conceded that when he was in Washington he often dropped by the GGC headquarters.

Britton, too, on a trip to Washington in January 1956 talked with Alabama's congressional delegation about the gas bill. He came to Washington on other business, but he spoke to Democratic Senators Lister Hill and John Sparkman and to six or seven representatives. "I invariably go by and visit with them when I am in Washington and discuss anything that is of interest to Alabama and to our business," he said.

Alabama congressmen had voted 8 to 1 in favor of the Kerr exemption bill in 1950. In 1955 sentiment had changed. Their vote was 7 to 2 against the Harris bill.

The good offices of Paxton Howard were also employed in Connecticut on Senator Bush. One of Howard's neighbors back in Midland, Texas, was Senator Bush's son, George Bush, president of a drilling company and partner in

a newly-organized oil company, Zapata Petroleum Corporation. Howard said George Bush "was very much for the gas bill" and "wanted his father to get the facts on this bill; George was particularly anxious that I contact the Senator and lay the case before him." Therefore Howard discussed the legislation twice with Senator Bush, once in Florida, another time in Washington. However, the senator let it be known publicly that he intended to vote against the bill.

The public statements of Senator Bush involved his son George in another episode growing out of the gas bill controversy. One night in January 1956 George Bush received a midnight telephone call from a Fort Worth oil man who identified himself as Ed Hill of the well-known producing firm of Richardson and Bass. Hill told Bush that the position of his father and others like him was ruining the oil business. Hill threatened to use his own influence to see that local companies boycotted young Bush's newly-established oil business.

Promptly the following day George Bush reported the telephone call to one of the firm's senior partners, a personal friend. The partner assured Bush that the firm had no knowledge of such a telephone call and apologized for the incident. Hill himself telephoned later and apologized to Bush; he requested Bush to overlook anything he might have said, particularly the boycott threat. Bush thereafter regarded the matter as closed and was reluctant to discuss it publicly lest he be branded an "informer."

Connecticut's delegation in both the House and Senate opposed the Kerr and the Harris-Fulbright bills. Only one favorable vote was cast from the entire delegation on both bills when Representative Morano, a Republican, voted for the Harris bill.

El Paso Natural Gas Company

NGO's vice-chairman, Paul Kayser, felt strongly the responsibility of the pipeline industry to press for legislation negating the Phillips decision, and he was clear about the interests of his company, El Paso Natural Gas Company:

> We were very much interested in any framing of a statute to repeal the Phillips decision. We were interested two ways. We are in the pipeline business, and the language of that statute could be so framed that it would materially and seriously hurt our business. We had our counsel follow all of the discussions as best we could, the language that we figured would be put on it. That was just as much a part of the business of El Paso Natural Gas Company as any other administrative or executive part of its business, to my notion.

El Paso assigned its executive vice-president, Howard Boyd, to Washington as a member of the GGC steering committee to follow the progress of the Harris bill and "to be helpful in language" of the bill "so that we would not have another Phillips decision."

The best time for engaging in either an education or a lobbying campaign, Kayser felt, was before legislation was drafted. "It may be too late when the bill is dropped in the hopper to do anything effectively about its language. If you have any common sense, in following this matter, you would like to know what is going on from the beginning."

Kayser had realized as early as 1952 the desirability of informing the public about the problems of the pipeline in-

dustry. As president of the Independent Natural Gas Association that year, he had launched an industry advertising effort costing about $100,000 a year; its purpose, he said, was to give the public the facts behind the effort to bring gas from the sands to the burner.

His interest grew out of a panel discussion at the Omaha convention of the pipeline industry in 1952. Panel members, representing producers, pipelines, distributors, and one state regulatory commission—California's—had had a lively discussion about natural gas.

The producer argument had so impressed Kayser that he organized a group within the pipeline industry to carry the message to the world. "I ran into a brand new idea . . . in respect to the business that I had been in practically all of my business life, and that was . . . that both our supplies of oil and gas and natural gas service is wholly dependent for its continuity on exploration, the findings of additional supplies." He said that this realization jarred him. If he, whose business it was, didn't realize the importance of unfettered exploration, how could he expect "a man who simply turned a little valve and burned the gas to understand it."

El Paso, with 6,700 miles of pipeline, was the nation's second largest pipeline company. It had some production facilities "primarily to protect the investment that we have and to undertake to insure the supply," Kayser said. In 1956 total assets amounted to $909.5 million, and operating revenues were $221.5 million.

Kayser's pipeline group emphasized these ideas: (1) that more than two-thirds of the energy that fed the United States economy was supplied by oil and natural gas; (2) that natural gas exploration should be carried on independently of the search for oil, without government controls on gas prices so that gas could pay its own way; (3) that consumers, to get gas, should be willing to pay for it.

Humble Oil and Refining Company, Houston, Texas

Humble, a major subsidiary of Standard Oil of New Jersey and organized as a Texas corporation to produce, refine, and market natural gas, crude oil, and by-products, was the largest contributor to the NGO. It donated $175,000, which it charged off as an operating expense for income tax purposes; a $3,855 donation to GGC, however, was treated as a lobbying expense.

Humble actively assisted GGC in other ways: Hines Baker, president of Humble, was a member of the steering committee and the committee on co-operation with other groups; Herman P. Pressler, a director, served on the legal committee. As contact man for GGC, Baker was in communication with several groups before the Harris-Fulbright bills were introduced. He contacted landowner groups, ranchers, farmers, cotton growers, and coal people to determine their reaction to general exemption legislation.

Humble stepped up the pace of its activities after the Phillips decision. It engaged a lobbyist, it issued publications alerting employees and outside groups to the danger of treating natural gas as a public utility, and its executives made speeches to warn the public of impending danger. Because the Phillips decision, in Baker's words, "tended to make the gas-producing business, which is a very risk-taking enterprise, a public utility, and to get away from the private enterprise system—we took an active interest in all education processes

and an active interest in the enactment of legislation to overcome it."

Baker "had contact," he said, with "a number of members of Congress, with our two Senators from Texas" with Representative Harris and Senator Fulbright, and with Senator George (Democrat of Georgia). He said the conversations were more or less casual discussions with persons who already favored the legislation. (Senator George had voted for the Kerr bill.)

Humble chose for the lobbying assignment a former lieutenant governor of Texas, Walter F. Woodul. Woodul, a Houston lawyer, had served in Washington for ten years as a lobbyist for Texas railroads.

The purpose of the discussions with those who were generally committed, Woodul said, was to secure agreement on amendments. He refused to try to change the viewpoint of opposition legislators, even though he "knew a lot of them personally. . . . I didn't think my argument would appeal to them. There are plenty of other people in their own bailiwicks."

The JCCP

Late in 1955, after the Harris bill had passed the House, the gas and oil forces were joined by a hybrid group of mayors and two small producers who organized to promote the Fulbright bill. The Joint Committee of Consumers and Small Producers of Natural Gas (called JCCP) was to serve as a counterweight to the well-publicized group of mayors who opposed the bill. Alex Clark, former mayor of Indianapolis, headed this organization, whose activities consisted generally of following developments on the legislation, issuing press releases, and distributing literature to members of Congress. The group employed a public relations firm at a cost of $12,000.

In April 1955 Clark declined an invitation to join the "eastern" Mayors' Committee, which opposed the legislation. Several mayors from producing areas urged Clark to make clear to Congress that the eastern group was not speaking for the United States Conference of Mayors. Accordingly, he presented his views supporting the Fulbright bill to the American Municipal Association meeting in Miami. Mayor Hayden Burns of Jacksonville, Florida, a member of the JCCP, complained of outrageous lobbying by utility companies at the convention. He said (in a letter of January 18, 1956 to Senator Holland of Florida) that "lobbyists and various representatives of certain big Eastern gas utilities" besieged the members in a vain attempt to block resolutions favoring the Harris-Fulbright bills.

On December 28, 1955, a few weeks after the utility group opened a Washington office, the JCCP group announced its own formal campaign to promote the Fulbright bill. Its press release stated that "certain big Eastern utilities . . . enjoying monopolistic franchises, have joined in a movement to perpetuate direct Government price-fixing of natural gas at the producer level."

JCCP was financed by contributions from gas producers and others aggregating $37,000. Clark was paid $5,500, plus expenses.

The JCCP was made up of mayors of Indianapolis, Indiana; Kansas City, Missouri; Cumberland, Maryland; Jacksonville, Florida; Ann Arbor, Michigan; Wilmington, Delaware; LaCrosse, Wisconsin; Elkins, West Virginia; Atlantic City, New Jersey; Moorehead, Minnesota; Bradford, Pennsylvania; and Los Angeles, California. The two producers were from Kimball, Nebraska and Granville, Ohio.

Opponents of the Bill

As early as 1947 municipal officials and some utility companies in non-producing states had begun to oppose—before the FPC, in the courts, and in Congress—efforts by the producers to secure exemption from regulation or substitution of market standards of price regulation for utility standards. The success of the industry in spreading pipelines to almost every state and in vastly increasing the number of consumers burning natural gas had the political effect of increasing the size of its potential opposition. This opposition sought to bolster its ranks by enlisting groups in states that had only recently begun to use natural gas. It drew strength from articles and speeches of liberals complaining about favored tax treatment accorded to the oil-gas industry by Congress. It had frequent opportunities to exercise its ability to influence government and to oppose industry influence in hearings on exemption bills, in controversies over appointments of FPC commissioners, and in hearings before the FPC. As noted above, some state and municipal bodies had participated as parties to natural gas cases in the federal courts.

The legislative offensive on behalf of the industry that followed the Phillips decision and that led to the introduction of the Harris-Fulbright bill, did not, therefore, find the anti-industry forces unprepared. In 1955 mayors, city attorneys, labor unions, and utility spokesmen were ready, as before, to argue before congressional committees that producer exemption would mean, to consumers, uncontrolled gas prices.

Like the oil-gas industry, they had been spreading their side of the story among the public for many years. Unlike that industry, however, they did not seek overall coordination of their efforts, which remained separate and, in some cases, sporadic.

The anti-industry forces were apparently taken by surprise by the unprecedented scale of the industry's campaign before the public and before Congress on behalf of the Harris-Fulbright bill. As the extent of the oil-gas campaign began to be clear, and as a parade of blue-ribbon witnesses for industry (state governors, lawyers, economists, etc.) took the stand to make effective presentations for the Harris-Fulbright bill, the opposition blocs became alarmed. One of their first reactions was to turn the size and scope of the industry's campaign against the industry by portraying it as a multi-million dollar lobbying effort.

A coalition of mayors from big "consumer" cities in the East was the first new group to organize a campaign against the bill. During the congressional recess a second pro-regulation organization entered the field to fight the exemption bill in the Senate. This group, the Council of Local Gas Companies, was made up of eastern utility companies long resentful over contract provisions for automatic price increases regardless of market conditions.

All told, four groups actively opposed the gas bill. Two, the United Auto Workers (UAW) and the National Institute of Municipal Law Officers (NIMLO), were mature organizations whose principal activity was in other fields; the others, the mayors' committee and the utility group, were ad hoc organizations thrown into the controversy at the eleventh hour. The bloc operated on total expenditures amounting to about $96,329. (NIMLO

had no funds; expenses of members to testify came from city treasuries.)

The only group to register as a lobby organization was the Council of Local Gas Companies.

NIMLO

The oldest organized opponent of exemption legislation—and the one with the widest technical knowledge—was the National Institute of Municipal Law Officers, a non-profit organization made up of 985 municipalities in the United States and its territories. Steadfastly supporting the position that the Natural Gas Act of 1938 did, in fact, provide for federal regulation, it had opposed a producer exemption bill in the 80th Congress in 1947. Its mandate of authority to oppose such legislation was regularly and without incident renewed at annual conventions.

In 1954, however, members attending the San Francisco convention found themselves the target of pressures they later described as terrific, unprecedented, and unremitting. James H. Lee, chairman of the Committee on Electric, Gas, and Telephone Rates, said that oil industry representatives or prominent lawyers "contacted" everybody at the convention to plead for a resolution repudiating the Phillips decision. The effort failed. NIMLO's resolution opposed any federal legislation "which would weaken or impair the jurisdiction and functioning of the FPC under the Natural Gas Act as now written. . . ."

NIMLO did not lobby as a group. Individual attorneys, representing their cities, did lobby actively against the Harris-Fulbright bills. Lee, as assistant corporation counsel of Detroit, talked with Michigan's two senators and with several representatives. Lee testified before the House and Senate committees, presenting Detroit's formal opposition to the legislation. He also presented to the committees all the resolutions passed by cities throughout the country. The city of Detroit paid his expenses.

NIMLO was used as a resource organization by members of Congress and some mayors. Lee said the chairman of the House committee "told us that he appreciated very much the . . . manner in which we expedited the presentation of our side of the story to his committee." Two days after Lee's appearance before the Senate committee, on May 20, 1955, Democratic Senator Pat McNamara of Michigan related to the Senate what had happened during Lee's appearance. Just as Lee was beginning his testimony, McNamara said, "a slanderous mimeographed sheet" issued by Mid-Continent Oil and Gas Association was circulated in the committee room. According to McNamara, the statement charged Lee with being "an unwitting victim of Fabian Socialist tactics" in his opposition to the gas bill. It said further that "Mr. Lee, in his testimony . . . apparently swallows whole the salami tactics by which socialism has been sold to many European countries —slice by slice."

McNamara said the statement was made by R. F. Windfohr—chairman of the GGC steering committee—and he charged that the "scandal sheet" was financed by the $1.5 million "slush fund the oil and gas people have thrown into this fight as a preliminary installment on the tens of millions of dollars they are prepared to spend to gain their immoral ends." McNamara considered publicity the best antidote for such tactics. In publicizing the matter on the Senate floor, he left "it to my colleagues and to the American people."

NIMLO helped to organize a consumer group, headed by Wisconsin Republican Senator Wiley, that called on President Eisenhower on March 18, 1955. The delegation included NIMLO's general counsel, city attorneys, mayors, and Governor Kohler of Wisconsin. The President, they reported, listened attentively to their appeals to oppose the Harris bill but would not go beyond stating that he was keeping an open mind on it.

Mayor's Committee

Hearings on the Harris bill began in the House committee on March 22, 1955. The first testimony was taken from proponent groups and individuals, and newspapers carried front-page stories of the strong case made by the industry. Sentiment began to grow among the floating islands of opposition for a unified counter effort.

The Democratic Mayor of Philadelphia, Joseph Clark, after advice from two of his assistants, decided to try to organize a committee of mayors, as representatives of the gas-consuming public, to oppose the bill. The Philadelphia City Council on March 17 urged the President and Congress to prevent enactment of exemption legislation. (The gas utility system of Philadelphia was municipally owned.)

Clark telephoned the mayors of New York City and Pittsburgh and found them receptive to the idea. On April 6 he and his assistants began a formal recruitment campaign. GGC had been in existence over a year and NGO some six months by this time. Clark's telegram, sent to mayors of over 90 cities of 100,000 or more inhabitants, read:

Regarding proposed legislation to exempt natural gas producers from Federal price regulation, greatly concerned that urban consumer interests are not being sufficiently weighed and represented.

We therefore ask your support in forming mayors' committee to oppose passage by Congress of HR 4560 and similar exemption bills. Time being short, would appreciate early reply to following questions: (1) Will you participate? (2) Would you join in testifying against HR 4560 or authorize the undersigned, as steering committee, to arrange testimony and appropriate public release? (3) Would you attend informal meeting of interested mayors in Washington 2 p.m., April 16, to plan further action?

Please reply to Mayor Clark, Philadelphia.

The response from "consuming" states was good, but Sacramento, California was the only city from a producing state to join. Mayors representing some of the large cities in Pennsylvania, New York, Maryland, Alabama, Massachusetts, Connecticut, New Jersey, Illinois (Chicago), Ohio, Colorado, Michigan, Minnesota, Indiana (Gary), Tennessee, Kentucky, Oregon, Rhode Island, and Virginia participated.

Many refused, including mayors from Albany, New York; San Jose, San Francisco, Berkeley, Oakland, and Los Angeles, California; Des Moines; Evansville, Fort Wayne, and Indianapolis, Indiana; Fort Worth; New Orleans; Tulsa and Oklahoma City; Phoenix; Salt Lake City; Savannah; Shreveport; Tampa; Washington, D.C.; and Wilmington, Delaware. Clark said the mayor of New Orleans, a personal friend, originally joined but "changed his mind because of the representations made to him by the oil interests in Louisiana, and by the Chamber of Commerce in New Orleans." Clark said also, without amplification, that in one or two other cases mayors agreed to join the committee but changed their

minds after being influenced by proponents of the legislation.

Clark and several other mayors appeared before the House committee during a week of "consumer" testimony in late April 1955. Clark paid tribute to the work accomplished by the group and its NIMLO allies for making possible an "effective presentation" before the committee. One of the accomplishments of the effort, he felt, was the fact that many newspapers, particularly those in cities where the mayor or city attorney testified, carried more accurate accounts of the legislation after consumer testimony before the House committee.

The oil and gas lobby, which has been operating a gargantuan propaganda mill in Washington on behalf of the Harris bill, went to such extreme lengths in trying to counteract the testimony of the city spokesmen that their material and tactics actually boomeranged. Newspapers discovered that they were receiving distorted statistics on gas prices, and also slanted accounts of our testimony which were at complete variance with the stories filed by the papers' own Washington correspondents.

On May 11 Clark sent to members a strategy bulletin summing up the effect of testimony before the House committee and issuing suggestions for future efforts. He called for political action and painstaking homework, predicting that the House committee vote on the Harris bill, expected soon, would be "extremely close" and urging any mayor who "can muster any influence with committee members" to act "without delay."

He also asked each mayor to help in compiling a tally sheet on the Congress by telephoning congressmen from his area and trying to get a commitment against the exemption principle. At the same time he suggested ways in which the mayors might prepare for their appearance before the Senate committee: (1) each mayor should concentrate on telling the story of gas prices in his city only; (2) he should avoid getting entrapped in the general field of gas regulation; (3) he should contact the local gas utility—"who in nearly every case you will find cooperative"—or the state utility commissions for facts and statistics, prices and trends. He warned that preparation was necessary. "There are members on both the House and Senate committees who know the issues thoroughly and will fight hard to promote the producer viewpoint."

The committee's total budget, about $20,000, consisted of contributions from city councils and utility companies.

United Auto Workers

Often active in an area of legislation with a "consumer" interest, the CIO United Auto Workers Union resolved at its Cleveland convention on April 1, 1955 to defeat the bill that would "strip the FPC of authority to regulate the field price of gas."

The Washington office began work immediately to prepare testimony for presentation to the congressional committees and to issue information bulletins and a call to action on the part of union members and others. Washington Director Donald Montgomery appeared before the House committee on April 25 and before the Senate committee on May 31. The office worked closely with some of the congressmen opposing the bill. Representative Wolverton of New Jersey enlisted Montgomery's help in drafting the minority report on the Harris bill signed by himself.

Beginning May 14 the Washington office sent out periodic reports to local groups concerning the status of the Harris bill. Eight bulletins, including a twelve-page report on House action, the House vote, statements by Senators Wiley and Douglas, and two pamphlets issued by the Council of Local Gas Companies, were distributed between May and January 16, 1956. The union's monthly newspaper also carried information on the character of the legislation and its progress in Congress. Coverage to the union and the public was augmented by union radio and TV programs.

The UAW campaign was carried on through interaction with other similarly minded groups. The Washington representatives conferred with other CIO unions and with representatives of local gas utility companies to try to coordinate the opposition. After House passage, a report went out to a list of sixty leaders in consumer, women's, welfare, religious and other organizations.

The mandate to continue efforts to block the bill was renewed and reinforced by a resolution passed December 5, 1955 by the merged AFL-CIO unions.

As debate reached a climax in the Senate in late January 1956, the UAW ran a full-page ad in 27 daily newspapers in 25 cities in eight states and the District of Columbia urging public opposition. The ad featured a gunman accosting a customer, with the bold legend: "YOU HAVE JUST THIS WEEK TO STOP THE GREAT GAS ROBBERY!" The ad carried in the *Des Moines Register* told readers "Iowa gas consumers alone will pay $17,981,-400 more a year" and urged letters to the Iowa senators. The ads, costing $32,858.35, ran between January 30 and February 2.

On February 4 and 5 the UAW ran 30-second spot radio announcements urging listeners to write their senators to vote against the Fulbright bill. These spots, carried on 26 stations in 27 cities in three states and the District of Columbia, cost $5,302.02.

An additional $584 was spent in 1956 to encourage wide dissemination of a fifteen-minute broadcast by Senators Pastore, Douglas, Potter, and Purtell. The senators were able to obtain free radio time as a public service on some fifty stations. The union had extra recordings made to be mailed to additional stations.

The union's representatives called personally on a number of senators to ask for a "no" vote. One dropped by the office of Democratic Senator Anderson of New Mexico, who was already on record as favoring the bill. Asked how he would vote, Anderson said, "I think I have pretty well made up my mind what I am going to do. I live in a gas-producing state. The money goes to our public schools." The visit lasted about five minutes.

Walter Reuther, UAW president, characterized the UAW activities as lobbying. "I wish to state clearly and emphatically that we were trying to influence votes. . . . We were lobbying against it, and the purpose of the education work we did was to persuade others to lobby against it."

Montgomery and two other UAW Washington staff members registered regularly as lobbyists. UAW itself had not registered since it felt that lobbying was not a major part of its work. The registration statement carried the lobbyists' salaries and expense accounts but not the money spent for the newspaper ads and miscellaneous expenses of the campaign on the gas bill. The total UAW cash outlay was $38,762.-43. Some fifty union employees devoted a part of their time to the lobbying campaign.

Council of Local Gas Companies

A few months after the House passed the Harris bill and a year after forma-tion of the NGO, a group of utility companies determined to pool their efforts to battle the Fulbright bill in the Senate. Gas distributors for the first time were advocating federal regulation of producers. One distributor, explaining the modification of the utilities' traditional opposition to regulation, complained that field prices of gas had risen 30 percent from 1950 to 1955.

After informal talks in September and October 1955, eastern utility executives invited that part of the industry outside the producing states to join in opposing the bill. Accordingly, the Council of Local Gas Companies was set up at a breakfast meeting on October 18, 1955, during the convention of the American Gas Association in Los Angeles. (Utilities were the backbone of the AGA. However, its membership included producers, pipeline companies, and equipment and appliance manufacturers.) Leading figure in the formation and work of the Council was chairman John E. Heyke, president of the Brooklyn Union Gas Company of Brooklyn, New York. Some sixty companies in twenty states were represented on the council.

At the AGA convention the year before, the principal speaker, pleading for a united front, had spoken of the identity of interests of utilities and producers. K. S. Adams, chairman of Phillips Petroleum, had said that the regulation decreed by the Supreme Court would mean less gas in the interstate market and less business for the utilities. "It means the death blow to your future gas supply," he had warned.

The Phillips executive had also called on distributors to tell customers the facts about their gas bills. He had proposed an information campaign to tell the public that the bulk of the charges levied by the gas company went to pay investment costs in construction and operation of the pipelines and the utilities, both of which were heavily regulated.

> You have everything to gain by informing your customers of the facts; you stand to lose everything if they are not sufficiently informed to demand Congressional action which will remove this threat to their gas supply and their pocketbooks.

However, utility companies, aroused by rising gas prices, concluded that they should try to block passage of the Fulbright bill in the Senate. Sentiment at the Los Angeles meeting favored a coordinated utility effort. The companies felt they had accomplished very little in their testimony before the House and Senate Commerce Committees in 1955. The utility view, as advanced by Consolidated Edison (New York), was that the basic problem was the escalation clause whose "operation is a one-way street on which a producer can receive more and more revenue, but never less, and the ultimate users must pay more and more, but never less." As the Consolidated Edison spokesman saw it, the increases rarely resulted from any change in the producers' expenses or in the value of the gas, but rather from "artificial extraneous circumstances." The Harris-Fulbright bills, the Consolidated Edison spokesman claimed, would write the escalation clauses into the Natural Gas Act. This would mean that in some areas higher-priced gas would no longer be able to compete with coal or other fuels. Utilities, though their earnings were closely regulated, were not guaranteed those earnings.

Late in November 1955 the group set up operating headquarters in Washington manned by W. E. Himsworth, assistant vice president of Brooklyn Union, and Charles H. Frazier, executive engineer of the Philadelphia Gas Works. Frazier was in general charge of the operation, working under the direction of Heyke and a steering committee of officers of East Coast companies. He spent about a third of December in Washington, almost all of January, and about half of February. Himsworth concentrated on "public information" and on liaison with other opponent groups. Other utility company employees—engineers, economists, lawyers, and rate specialists—donated time to the council. The council paid no salary to its staff; all were continued on their company payrolls.

Operations were financed through contributions solicited on the basis of $50 for each $1 million of revenue in 1954. Receipts amounted to $37,567.43. Principal expenses included $6,688 paid to public relations counsel, $6,085 for living expenses of the Washington staff, $4,469 for professional services, and $5,457 for printed matter.

Members of the council included a few of the giants of the utility world such as the Consolidated Edison Company,[12] but most were gas companies from medium-sized cities such as the Council Bluffs Gas Company, the Lynchburg Gas Company, the New Bedford Gas and Edison Light Company, and the Worcester Gas Light Company. The largest contributor was the Consolidated Natural Gas Company combine (which operates through subsidiaries in Ohio, Pennsylvania, West Virginia, and New York), whose five members gave a total of $10,650. Consolidated Edison contributed $3,700, as did the Public Service Electric

---

[12] One of the largest operating utilities in the world, it served a highly-concentrated population of over eight million in New York City and vicinity. It received 80 percent of its revenue from electric energy, 15 percent from gas and 5 percent from steam. In 1955 its total assets were $1,919,828,280; total revenues were $493,684,370.

and Gas Company of New Jersey. Some of the donors were municipally-owned gas companies.

The council, engaged in lobbying and "education" activities, sent out strategy suggestions to members, distributed forms or leaflets to be enclosed in monthly gas bills, forwarded to members and others form letters for writing senators, and distributed large quantities of literature and data. The literature consisted of a technical evaluation of the Harris-Fulbright legislation, a popularly-written pamphlet on natural gas ("The Natural Gas Issue Before Congress"), and a technical study—the Smith Report—prepared by the former head of FPC's Bureau of Accounts, Finances and Rates ("Prices and Pricing Practices of Producers of Natural Gas, with particular reference to their effect on Consumers and Distributors").

The original plan to limit legislative contacts to individual companies dealing with their own senators was soon modified. Since only twenty states were represented on the council, some way had to be found to reach other members of the Senate. Consequently the council assumed the task of making direct representations to senators. In December the council, Frazier, Himsworth, and David K. Kadane, general counsel of the Long Island Lighting Company, registered as lobbyists.

The council's staff worked closely with Senators Pastore, Douglas, and Potter, the leaders of the opposition to the Fulbright bill, and helped develop technical material to assist them in debate on the Senate floor. One of the difficulties the council found was that no one senator acted as opposition leader, so that the work of imparting technical data and coaching had to be repeated on a senator-by-senator basis. Frazier and Himsworth were able to talk to about half the senators or their principal assistants.

In lining up their own contacts, Frazier and Himsworth put together a checklist on which they ticked off the names of the senators and estimates of their stand on the bill. The chart had three columns: one listed senators known to oppose the bill because of strong public statements; the second, those who might reasonably favor it ("they come from producing States and I thought it would be a waste of time"); and the third, possible favorable votes ("ones I felt should have an interest in our side because they consumed more gas in those States than they produced").

As part of the legislative activity, two member companies provided two engineers, who followed the Senate proceedings carefully, noted points requiring rebuttal, and helped develop pertinent answers.

As part of its generalized campaign, the council kept various state public service commissions advised about its activities, either directly or through member companies, and distributed the Smith Report to various state governors. In each state represented on the council, one company was designated to coordinate all the efforts within that state.

As Senate debate reached a climax, the council concluded that the odds favored the Fulbright bill and that there was not a chance of defeating it. The staff then modified its strategy and tried to improve the bill through amendment. A lawyers' committee, headed by the chief counsel for the Commonwealth Natural Gas Corporation, helped to draft amendments. Senator Bush had come forward with a suggestion for a "fair and equitable" standard as a substitute for the "reasonable market price," which the bill had originally made the measure of the price pipelines were to pay producers. The council, in late January, helped Bush and other Republican senators to draft and simplify a definition of the "fair and equitable" standard so that it would be more easily understood in debate. None of the amendments passed.

White House Visit

While the Senate was considering the bill, the council members felt they needed to pin down a "rumor" that the administration "was supporting" the Fulbright bill. Heyke said, "Circulation of a story that the administration was behind this bill was harmful to us, and we attempted to clear that one up." To do so, Heyke, who was a bank director, a director of the Brooklyn Institute of Arts and Sciences, and prominent in business circles, sought and was given an appointment with the President's principal assistant, Governor Sherman Adams. He told Adams, during the brief visit, that "it was necessary, if this was not an administration measure, for the word to get out," but he was unable to get a yes or no from Adams. Adams, he said, "gave me the impression" that the bill was not backed by the administration, "but that was only an impression. . . ." The two did not discuss the report of President Eisenhower's Advisory Fuels Committee.

Assessment

Weighing results, the council took little or no pride in its campaign to win votes. When the campaign was initiated, Frazier and his associates tallied some thirty "no" votes. They felt they could take "some credit" for the additional eight votes against the bill, but concluded that the final decision was "almost as decisive a defeat as might have resulted had no efforts been made."

One of the council's difficulties was attributed to lack of time to mount an effective campaign. The Himsworth effort to win support from consumer, civic, and service organizations was handicapped by the complexity of the issue. "It was impossible in the time at our disposal to get any of the better known organizations—such as the General Federation of Women's Clubs or the League of Women Voters—to pick up an issue as complex as ours." The council ascribed part of its failure to the FPC. Because of its "inaction, we could not point to a positive, business-like plan of regulation which would establish a reasonable climate for continued exploration."

On the other hand, it was felt that the campaign proved valuable in relations with consumers. The distributors had hoisted their colors on behalf of consumers, and Heyke had repeatedly stated that utility companies "have an inherent obligation to millions of gas customers to provide them with the best possible gas service at the lowest possible cost."

The Fate of the Gas Bill

The debate in the Senate had been going on for almost three weeks, with little prospect of success for the opponents of the bill, when Republican Francis Case of South Dakota rose in his seat on February 3, 1956 to make what he called a difficult speech. Senator Case said he could not vote for the Fulbright bill because certain forces who stood to win "inordinate profits" if it passed had tendered him a $2500 campaign contribution. The senator said he would return the money.

> Had this incident not happened, I suppose that I would have followed the course recommended by the overwhelming majority of telegrams and letters from my State and voted for

the bill . . . but, Mr. President, I cannot vote to place upon the freedom of political thought chains that would be bought and paid for by the very people placed under bondage. . . .

I cannot vote for the bill as it stands. In the light of evidence personal to me that the bill has prospects of unusual monetary profit to some, and that with that profit would go the means for a continuing effort to influence the course of government for private gain, I must vote to maintain in people's Government the opportunity to control the profits from a monopoly product.

Senator Case's statement caused a national sensation. What lay behind it was some lobbying by a relatively small member of the oil-gas industry, the Superior Oil Company of California. Superior, an oil-producing company that did business in six western and southern states, had some international holdings and owned an interest in a pipeline company. Superior took part in the GGC campaign, but it also acted on its own and in other ways to advance the cause of producers.

Around 1947 Howard B. Keck, president of Superior, had established a special account from his personal funds for campaign contributions. He entrusted the funds in this account to one of Superior's attorneys, Elmer Patman. Patman, a Superior employee since 1943 and a former enforcement officer of the Texas Railroad Commission,[13] decided whom to support and distributed the money as he saw fit. Keck, who trusted Patman completely, required only a casual verbal accounting of how the money was disbursed. Usually Keck turned over about $5,000

or $6,000 a year to the fund, but in both 1954 and 1955 he raised the amount to $8,000 or $9,000 a year.

On October 1955 Patman engaged a legal assistant, a Nebraska lawyer and an old friend, John Neff of Lexington, Nebraska. Neff was hired on a long-term basis at a retainer of $1,000 a month. Although Neff was engaged to do general legal work, he devoted himself entirely to other matters for the next four months.

His first assignment from Patman was to find out how the two Nebraska senators planned to vote on the Fulbright bill. Patman also told him that there was $5,000 available as a campaign contribution to the Republican Party of Nebraska. (Neither of the Nebraska senators was up for re-election in 1956.) Within two weeks Neff had completed his inquiries. He reported to Patman in Washington, D. C., in late October and at that time turned over $2,500 of the Keck money to the Nebraska Republican Committee.

In November Neff went to Sioux Falls, South Dakota, to find out how Senator Francis Case stood on the bill. (Case had voted against the Kerr bill in 1950 in the House.) He determined that Case was favorably inclined toward the bill and so informed Patman on a trip to Washington in January. Patman turned over $2,500 to Neff for delivery to Case, and on a subsequent trip to South Dakota Neff delivered the money. This was the contribution that impelled Senator Case to vote against the bill.

Neff traveled to three other states— Iowa, Montana, and Wyoming—to determine the attitude of their senators. For the four months from October 1955 to February 1956 Neff's duties consisted entirely of efforts to influence the outcome of the Fulbright bill. Pat-

---

[13] The Texas Railroad Commission is that state's regulatory agency for its oil and gas industry.

man approved Neff's expense accounts for the period and wrote "Natural Gas Bill" across the face of three of them when he sent them on to Superior for payment. Neff had not registered as a lobbyist.

Senator Case's dramatic announcement that the attempted bribe had swung him away from support of the Fulbright bill came when most senators were already drawn from the tension. Party loyalties had been strained; state delegations were split. Senator Mike Mansfield had lost ten pounds in two weeks. Ugly charges and countercharges had been made about lobbying.

In the turmoil caused on the floor by the Case statement, Senator Fulbright pressed Case for the name and association of the man who had offered the bribe. Case only indicated that the donor represented interests that stood to make enormous profits if the Fulbright bill passed. Fulbright suggested angrily that Case might have been duped—that utility companies might have set up the bribe attempt to "throw" the Senate vote.

"May I respectfully suggest that Senators may not want to press the point too far," Case said. Democratic Senator Mike Monroney, Fulbright's principal ally, quickly retorted: "I should like to press it as far as it can be pressed, . . . I resent the implication of the Senator's statement."

During the weekend, the Senate's majority and minority leaders and their assistants announced plans to investigate the incident. Fulbright continued to denounce Case, accusing him of bad faith, of timing his statement with deliberate attempt to influence the upcoming vote, and with evasiveness. Fulbright warned that Case should make a full disclosure if he expected to stay in public life. The Federal Bureau of Investigation interviewed Case to see whether federal law had been violated. It was also disclosed that the "bribe offerer" was a lobbyist for Superior Oil Company.

On Monday, February 6, resolutions calling for investigations were introduced. The vote on the Fulbright bill followed, and it passed by the comfortable margin of 53 to 38.

On February 17 President Eisenhower vetoed the Harris-Fulbright bill because of "arrogant lobbying." The President said that he supported its principles, but felt that faith in democratic processes would be undermined unless he vetoed the bill. Congress made no attempt to override the veto.

Was Lobbying Effective?

The oil-gas forces had been proud of their lobbying campaign and were particularly bitter that the zeal of wildcat lobbyists had resulted in a presidential veto. Together, groups on both sides had spent substantially more than $2 million in seeking to affect the outcome of this legislation. The $2,500 contribution proffered by Superior to Case had doomed the bill. But what had the rest of the money, and the thousands of hours of lobbying and writing and persuading, accomplished?

Lobbyists, being human, tend to over-emphasize their role in the legislative process and to attribute any shift in voting behavior to their own efforts. But neither political scientist nor lobbyist can say with certainty what impels a congressman to vote as he does. The final vote on the Harris-Fulbright bill reflected factors too numerous to assess. Nevertheless, some possibilities are suggested in comparing the final vote on the bill with the voting on the Kerr producer-exemption bill in 1950, for which there had been no extraordinary lobbying operation:

KERR BILL (1950)				HARRIS-FULBRIGHT BILL (1955–56)		
Rep.	Dem.	Total		Rep.	Dem.	Total
			House of Representatives			
79	197	176	For	123	86	209
57	116	174 [a]	Against	67	136	203
			Senate			
16	28	44	For	31	22	53
22	16	38	Against	14	24	38

[a] Includes one independent

The leading states in gas production and proved reserves included Texas, Louisiana, Oklahoma, Kansas, Mississippi, and California. The congressional delegations from the first five of these states voted almost unanimously for both the Harris-Fulbright and the Kerr bills. (California's variegated economy, less dependent than the others on gas and oil, makes it difficult to assess the factors behind the votes of its congressional delegation. Its senators and representatives divided on the Kerr bill, but both senators and a majority of representatives supported the Harris-Fulbright bill.)

The House delegations from the producing states of New Mexico, Utah, and Wyoming voted as a unit for the Harris-Fulbright bill, although they had split on the Kerr bill. Florida, which does not rank high in actual production, but which has vast untapped offshore oil deposits, supported both measures unanimously. Three other southern states—Georgia, and North and South Carolina—supported both, overwhelmingly.

The states consistently opposing both bills were the "consuming" eastern states of Connecticut, New Jersey, New York, and Rhode Island. States in which coal mining was an important industry also opposed the bills. These included West Virginia, Missouri, and Pennsylvania. (The Pennsylvania House delegation divided on both bills but voted against both by a slight margin.) The northern tier states of Michigan, Minnesota, and Wisconsin also opposed both bills.

On the other hand there were some significant changes:

SENATE

Both Senators Supported Kerr Bill But Opposed Harris-Fulbright	*Both Senators Opposed Kerr Bill But Supported Harris-Fulbright*
Georgia [a]	Delaware
Kentucky	Idaho
Ohio [b]	Iowa
Tennessee	Maine [c]
Virginia	Maryland
Washington	Massachusetts [c]
	Montana
	New Hampshire
	Vermont [c]
	Wyoming

[a] Both supported Kerr bill; one opposed Harris-Fulbright, other did not vote

[b] Both supported Kerr bill, split on Harris-Fulbright

[c] Both opposed Kerr, split on Harris-Fulbright

HOUSE

Majority of Delegation Supported Kerr, Opposed Harris	*Majority of Delegation Opposed Kerr, Supported Harris*
Alabama	Illinois
New Hampshire	Indiana
Tennessee	N. Dakota
Virginia	S. Dakota

[The oil-gas lobby sought to emphasize in 1955–1956 the recent discovery of oil and natural gas in Alabama, North and South Dakota, and Montana. Other states with gas reserves, in addition to those mentioned in this section, included Michigan, Ohio, Indiana, and Illinois.]

Postscript

Subsequently, two Senate select committees conducted investigations growing out of the Case incident. The George committee, which dealt exclusively with the offer made to Case, concluded that the contribution was clearly an attempt to "influence" the Senate, that it was "manifestly improper," but not "illegal." A federal grand jury disagreed and returned indictments in July 1956 against Superior Oil, Neff, and Patman. The defendants pleaded guilty to violating the Lobby Act. The court fined Superior $10,000 and the two agents $2,500 each.

The second committee, chaired by Democratic Senator John L. McClellan of Arkansas, conducted a fourteen-month investigation into "political activities, lobbying, and campaign contributions." It heard testimony from groups and individuals that lobbied on both sides of the gas legislation and it sought advice from scholars and experts on a model lobby law.

The McClellan committee recommended a general overhaul of both lobbying and election laws. It proposed broadening the coverage of the 1946 Lobby Act to "indirect lobbying," defined as a written communication in which as many as 1,000 persons are asked to get in touch with congressmen concerning legislation. It proposed criminal penalties for some cases of filing false information with Congress or influencing the dispatch of spurious messages to Congress. The election law changes proposed abolishing ceilings on spending in presidential campaigns and increasing the spending limits in congressional elections.

Complaints were also voiced against the pressure tactics of opponents of the bill. Senator Holland of Florida was critical of the utility lobbyists who tried to influence the American Municipal Association to oppose it. Senator Monroney accused opponents of gutter politics. He was angry at the UAW for the full-page newspaper ad depicting the gas producer as a holdup man with a gun leveled at the consumer.

The same complaints had been made by congressmen when the Harris bill was being considered by the House. Representative Hayworth of Michigan told colleagues of a great flood of telegrams from constituents who supported the Harris bill on grounds that regulation of producers jeopardized free enterprise. He explained that in his district "we are all enthusiastically for free enterprise. But I could not understand why this passion for the American economic system was suddenly inspiring so many householders to invite an increase of several dollars a month to their gas bills." He said his Flint office, after making a check, discovered that the senders were all oil company employees or persons whose support had been "solicited" by an oil company employee. Hayworth, a member of the House Interstate and Foreign Commerce Committee, signed one of the minority reports on the Harris bill and voted against it.

Representative Hale of Maine spoke of being pressured by opponents.

> Not a day goes by but that a lot of propaganda is laid on my desk about this bill. I do not think I ever got a single piece of propaganda in favor of this bill, but I have had and continue to get an enormous amount of propaganda against this bill, all of it coming from consumer groups who are either misleading themselves or very much want to mislead other people. . . .

Despite these complaints, the McClellan committee, in 14 months of investigation, was unable to uncover any instances of illegal lobbying. In May 1956 the McClellan committee "urgently requested" fellow senators to come forward with any knowledge or information, hearsay or otherwise, of wrongdoing in connection with the gas bill or other legislation. No information worth inquiry was produced. In June 1956, on the Senate floor, the invitation was extended to the press and public, but yielded no significant information.

Later Efforts to Settle the Issue

The lobbies that organized around the Harris-Fulbright bills in the 84th

Congress have not been reconstituted as formal entities since. The presidential veto and disclosures of the two investigating committees foreclosed any possibility for exemption that session. However, new bills were introduced in 1957 in the 85th Congress. Again the legislation lost any chance of passage through the over-zealous activity of outside interests. In January 1958 a Texas Republican national committeeman requested contributions from a group of Texas oilmen for a fund-raising dinner honoring House Republican Leader Joe Martin. The Texan, H. J. (Jack) Porter, said a large war chest was necessary to ensure passage of the pending gas bills.

> Joe Martin . . . has always been a friend of Texas, especially of the oil and gas producing industries. He mustered two-thirds of the Republican votes in the House each time the gas bill passed . . . As Speaker of the 83rd Congress he led the fight for adoption of the tidelands ownership bill.

The *Washington Post* broke the story on the Porter letter. Headlines blazed: TEXANS RAISE FUND: FETE MARTIN IN HOPE OF EASING GAS CURBS . . . ; STATE GOP DINNER NETTING $100,000 MAY EARN BILLIONS.

The gas bill died quietly in Congress. Although the House Commerce Committee approved it, no bill reached the floor of either house. The furor over the fund was too great.

After 1958 the conflict shifted from Congress back to the regulatory arena. The basic position of the FPC, which favored exempting producers, remained unchanged. However, since Congress had failed to amend the Natural Gas Act, the commission turned to the problem of finding a formula for producer regulation as decreed by the Supreme Court in the Phillips decision in 1954.

Illinois Goes to Congress For Army Land

EDITH T. CARPER

Cast of Characters

Wilber Brucker	Secretary of the Army, Washington, D. C.
George W. Cox	Vice President of Santa Fe Railroad
Everett M. Dirksen	U. S. Senator from Illinois, Republican
Paul H. Douglas	U. S. Senator from Illinois, Democrat
George Eve	President of Cook County Council of Illinois Federation of Sportsmen's Clubs
Franklin Floete	Administrator of General Services Administration, Washington, D. C.
C. R. Gutermuth	Vice President of Wildlife Management Institute, Washington, D. C.
Wayne Morse	U. S. Senator from Oregon, Democrat
Edmund Muskie	U. S. Senator from Maine, Democrat
Glen Palmer	Director of Illinois Conservation Department
Melvin Price	U. S. Representative from Illinois, Democrat
Dewey Short	Assistant Secretary of the Army, Washington, D. C.
William Stratton	Governor of Illinois, Republican
Carl Vinson	Chairman of House Armed Services Committee, Democrat
Floyd Zebell	Secretary of Will County (Illinois) Sportsmen's Club

Chronology

1958

March	Illinois Conservation Department applies to General Services Administration for a grant of Tracts 1, 2, and 3 of Des Plaines property. Industrial groups open negotiations with GSA for same land.
June-July	Business and conservation groups ask Senator Dirksen for help.
July	Illinois Conservation Department amends request to GSA to allow 200 acres to go to industry.
September	GSA Administrator Floete tours Des Plaines land.
October	Floete instructs GSA Chicago office to proceed with disposition of Des Plaines. Sante Fe Railroad makes offer to GSA for Des Plaines.
December	Floete instructs GSA Chicago office to survey Des Plaines and offer it for sale. Illinois conservationists ask Senator Douglas for help.

1959

January	Conservationists ask both Illinois senators for legislation to prevent sale of Des Plaines land. Douglas introduces bill in Senate (S. 747) to convey Tracts 1, 2, and 3 to Illinois without cost. Representative Price of Illinois introduces identical bill (H.R. 3984) in House.

February   GSA advertises for bids on Des Plaines tracts, then suspends efforts to dispose of land. Dirksen asks Department of Army for additional land for conservationists so GSA can sell Tracts 1 and 2 to industry.

March   Senate Government Operations Committee appoints Muskie subcommittee to consider Des Plaines bill. GSA receives bids on Des Plaines, announces opposition to S. 747.

April   Muskie subcommittee holds hearings on Des Plaines bill.

May   Illinois and GSA officials confer in Washington on Des Plaines settlement. Dirksen confers with Army, proposes amendment to S. 747 to have Army give Tract 4 to Illinois, with understanding that state will buy Tract 3. Dirksen announces proposal publicly, and Army assigns matter to Assistant Secretary of the Army Short. Muskie subcommittee processes Dirksen amendment.

             Price bill (to grant Tracts 1–3 to Illinois) is assigned to real estate subcommittee of House Armed Services Committee. Price bill is amended to conform to Dirksen amendment, and House subcommittee holds hearings.

June   Conservationists accept Dirksen amendment. Short reports to Muskie subcommittee Army opposition to ceding Tract 4, offers to give up Tract 5 instead. Conservationists reject Tract 5.

July   Muskie subcommittee reports out S. 747 rewritten to have Army give Tract 4 to Illinois and GSA sell Tract 3 to state. Senate Government Operations Committee accepts, reports out subcommittee bill.

             Short obtains support of House Armed Services Committee Chairman for Army compromise (to cede Tract 5 instead of Tract 4).

August   Committee version of S. 747 goes to Senate floor, passes Senate.

             Army makes formal offer of its compromise to House Armed Services Committee. Action on Price bill delayed in House.

September   Conservationists urge House passage of Des Plaines bill in spite of possibility of presidential veto.

December   Illinois Conservation Director and Representative Price throw support to Army compromise.

1960

January   Dirksen tries for administrative settlement of Des Plaines controversy. Conservationists accept Army compromise.

February   Army rejects proposal for administrative settlement. Dirksen announces agreement on legislative settlement allowing Illinois to buy Tract 3, receive Tract 5 without cost, use Tract 4 part-time.

April   Conservationists mount fresh campaign for settlement on basis of Army compromise.

May   House Armed Services subcommittee holds hearings on Price bill. Subcommittee amends bill to conform to Army compromise. Full committee accepts bill and reports it out.

June   Amended committee bill passes House and Senate.

July   Des Plaines bill becomes law.

Introduction

Every member of Congress spends much of his time doing chores in Washington for his constituents. He may be called upon to secure a government publication, to sponsor a job applicant, to collect information, to sponsor legislation on his constituents' behalf, or to intercede for them with federal agencies in an effort to obtain a special service or to insure prompt action. Carrying out assignments from home is a time-consuming part of a congressman's job.

This study describes how two senators and a number of other congressmen were occupied for two years with conflicting requests from Illinois sportsmen's groups and industrialists, each seeking the same piece of federal land. The land—or at least some of it—was regarded as surplus. Located about 45 miles from Chicago, it was known as the Des Plaines property. Each group competing for it—a business syndicate and a combined force of sportsmen's clubs and conservationists—pressed its case first with Illinois state officials and then with the General Services Administration, the federal agency responsible for disposing of surplus federal property. The opposing groups then turned to the two Illinois senators for intercession with the GSA. Their conflicting requests posed the two senators with a nice political problem.

Later, both groups appealed to their senators to introduce legislation effecting the land transfer. The sale of federal land is usually routinely accomplished by administrative action of the GSA under general laws that prescribe standards and procedures. In this case, however, the senators and other Illinois congressmen—in fact, the entire Congress—became involved in special legislation concerning the Des Plaines property that was in effect a substitute for administrative action by the GSA. Although the Des Plaines land transfer took up a great deal of time in Congress, in the GSA, and in the Illinois state capital, it was, from beginning to end, never considered to be a matter of significant national interest. Yet it featured a characteristic array of postures often adopted by congressmen in dealing with, and acting on behalf of, the interests of their constituents.

Des Plaines: the Background

The Des Plaines Public Hunting and Wildlife Refuge Area was in northern Illinois (Will County), 42 miles southwest of downtown Chicago and close to Joliet (population 62,000). It was part of 32,000 acres that the Army Ordnance Department had acquired during World War II for its Joliet Arsenal. (See map, page 226.) When the war ended and arsenal operations began to slacken, the Army allowed portions of the territory to be used by the public, leasing some land to stockmen for grazing, some to farmers for crops. From 1948 to 1958 the Illinois Department of Conservation leased from the Army several thousand acres in the western end for development as a conservation area, wildlife refuge, and public hunting grounds. This land, the Des Plaines property, was made up of three distinct parcels. (See map, page 227.) Tract Number 1, the northernmost section, contained 620 acres; Tract 2, 848 acres; and Tract 3, 946 acres.

The Des Plaines property contained woods, low shrubs, and many small lakes. The rocky soil was unsuited for agriculture. The northwest corner was at the conjunction of two rivers, the Kankakee and the Des Plaines, the latter a navigable waterway that constituted part of the Inland Waterway System linking the St. Lawrence Seaway and the Great Lakes with the Mississippi River. The property had three miles of frontage on the Des Plaines River and was strategically placed with respect to land transportation. The Santa Fe Railroad ran to within an eighth of a mile of the southeast corner of Tract 3, and other rail lines were close by. The property also had three

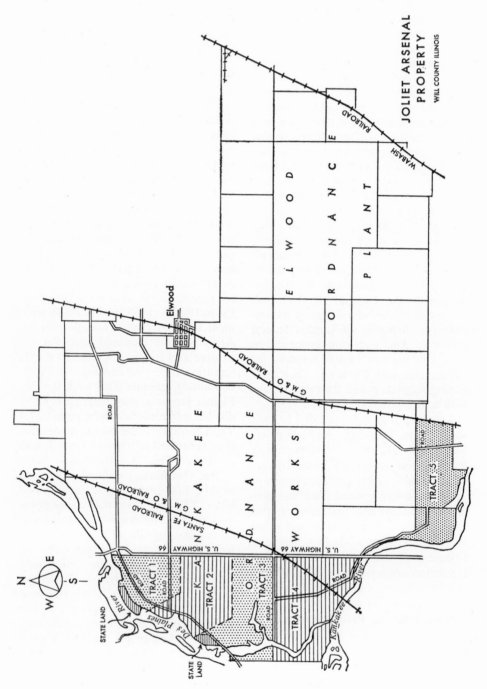

JOLIET ARSENAL
PROPERTY
WILL COUNTY ILLINOIS

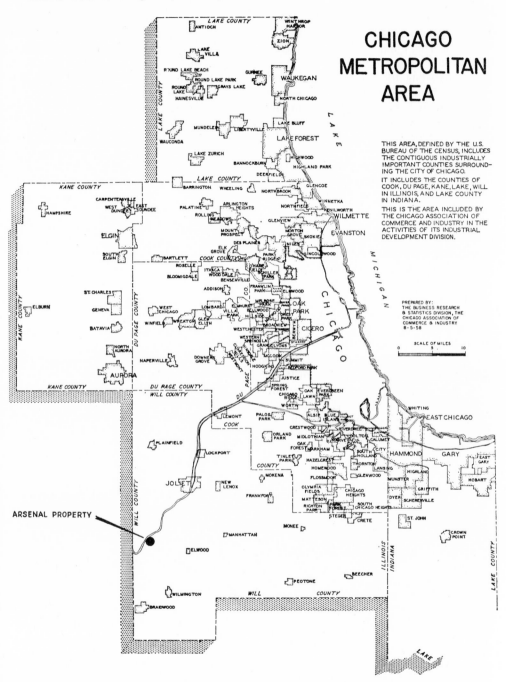

CHICAGO
METROPOLITAN
AREA

THIS AREA, DEFINED BY THE U.S.
BUREAU OF THE CENSUS, INCLUDES
THE CONTIGUOUS INDUSTRIALLY
IMPORTANT COUNTIES SURROUND-
ING THE CITY OF CHICAGO.

IT INCLUDES THE COUNTIES OF
COOK, DU PAGE, KANE, LAKE, WILL
IN ILLINOIS, AND LAKE COUNTY
IN INDIANA.

THIS IS THE AREA INCLUDED BY
THE CHICAGO ASSOCIATION OF
COMMERCE AND INDUSTRY IN THE
ACTIVITIES OF ITS INDUSTRIAL
DEVELOPMENT DIVISION.

PREPARED BY:
THE BUSINESS RESEARCH
& STATISTICS DIVISION, THE
CHICAGO ASSOCIATION OF
COMMERCE & INDUSTRY
8-5-58

SCALE OF MILES
0   5   10

ARSENAL PROPERTY

miles of frontage on U. S. 66, a four-lane highway.

The Des Plaines tracts abounded in pheasants and rabbits, providing a rewarding bag for sportsmen. Mallards, wood ducks, pintails, and black ducks were reared there for release throughout the state. As the only major waterfowl refuge in northern Illinois, Des Plaines provided a rest area for ducks and geese on their migratory flights between Canada and the South.

During the ten-year lease from the Army the state of Illinois made major improvements and constructed facilities for the use of sportsmen. The state's investment amounted to about $500,000.

In 1956 the Army, always under public pressure to reduce its land holdings, decided that the Des Plaines area (Tracts 1–3), along with a contiguous 1500-acre plot (Tract 4), was surplus to its needs. The property thereupon came under the jurisdiction of the General Services Administration (GSA). As required by law, GSA first offered the land to other federal agencies, and another Army unit—this time the Fifth Army in Chicago—took possession of the southernmost part, Tract 4, as a site for reserve training exercises.

The state of Illinois wished to take permanent title to Des Plaines so it could continue to maintain the hunting and conservation area. The state conservation director had filed requests for it with GSA as early as 1956. When the three Des Plaines tracts became available in 1958—no other federal agency having asked for them—the state Conservation Department again petitioned GSA for the land on behalf of Illinois.

Political Figures

Illinois in 1958 was represented in the Senate by two towering political figures: the senior, Paul H. Douglas, a Democrat; the junior, Everett M. Dirksen, a Republican. In many respects, they were opposites. Douglas was a liberal, Dirksen a conservative; Douglas an intellectual, Dirksen a shirt-sleeved politician and proud of it; Douglas an internationalist, Dirksen, at least at times, an isolationist; Douglas an advocate of welfare measures, Dirksen a believer in reliance on individual initiative.

Douglas was a successful "amateur politician," that is, one who had achieved national office after a successful professional career. Elected to the Senate in 1948, he had been a professor of economics at the University of Chicago, had written books on wages, social security, and unemployment problems, was a Phi Beta Kappa, and had been president of the American Economic Association in 1947. Before running for the Senate, the only elective office Douglas had held was as Chicago alderman from 1939 to 1942. He had volunteered for service in World War II, had served in the Marine Corps, and had received the Bronze Star for heroic achievement.

During Douglas' two terms in the Senate, his name had been associated with measures to aid depressed areas, alleviate unemployment, assist underdeveloped countries, and develop park and recreation areas. He was regarded as a conservationist. As a senator he had displayed devotion to ideas and ideals and had showed little fondness for compromise. He had never been regarded as a strong team player or as a member of the Senate's inner club.

Dirksen, on the other hand, was a politician by instinct and practice. He had gained an appreciation of the uses of compromise from much experience in the practice of accommodation, particularly on behalf of his state. Elected to the House of Representatives in 1932, he had served eight terms before being elected to the Senate in 1950. He had been a member of the Republican congressional campaign committee and vice-chairman in charge of the midwestern area for many years. In 1952 he had been appointed to the Eisenhower strategy board for the presidential election and had been named chairman of the Republican senatorial campaign committee. Early in 1959 Dirksen was elected Senate Republican leader. He was a colorful figure, an impassioned speaker with many of the qualities of the old-fashioned "silver-tongued" orator. Considered an old-guard Republican, he opposed such measures as public housing and aid to education.

The son of a German-born painter and decorator, Dirksen had served overseas in World War I, had studied law at the University of Minnesota, and finally had earned his law degree at night school in Washington after being elected to Congress. He was a member of a number of veterans' and fraternal organizations and of the alliance of fishermen called the Izaak Walton League.

With both the Illinois statehouse and the national administration in Republican hands, Dirksen was an important link between his state's executives and Republican leaders in Washington. The Illinois Governor, William Stratton, in 1958–1960 was nearing the end of his second term. The son of a prominent Illinois Republican, Stratton had been state treasurer for two terms and had also served in Congress for two terms as Illinois Congressman-at-Large.

The member of Stratton's official family directly concerned with the Des Plaines property was the Director of Conservation, Glen Palmer, an authority in the field of game breeding and rearing. Palmer, whose earlier career had been in farming and the insurance business, had served since 1953. He had a reputation as an able administrator and a dedicated conservationist.

The chief of the General Services Administration, the federal agency responsible for disposing of Des Plaines, was Franklin Floete, a septuagenarian Republican from Iowa, who had been GSA Administrator since 1956. From 1953 to 1956 he had served the Eisenhower administration as Assistant Secretary of Defense for Properties and Installations. He had been in the construction, land, and lumber businesses before entering government service.

Many Illinois residents, members of conservationist organizations, sportsmen's clubs, and the like, played active parts in the Des Plaines story. The principal actors among them were Floyd Zebell of Wilmington, Illinois and George Eve of Chicago. Eve was president of the Northern Zone Association of Sportsmen's Clubs and a Republican precinct committeeman in Cook County. Zebell, a Democrat, was secretary of the Will County Sportsmen's Club and editor of its monthly newsletter. He had been law enforcement officer in the Illinois Department of Conservation under the Democratic administration of Governor Adlai Stevenson, but had left the department shortly after Stratton became Governor, and was serving as security policeman for the Army at the Joliet Arsenal.

Illinois Applies for Des Plaines

On March 18, 1958 the Illinois Conservation Department applied to GSA for a grant of Des Plaines Tracts 1, 2, and 3 (a total of 2,414 acres) for continued use as a conservation and wildlife area. The state based its request on a 1948 United States statute providing that when real property under the control of a federal agency was no longer required, such land could be turned over, without cost, to a state agency for use as a conservation and wildlife area. To do this the law required, among other things, a formal judgment by the GSA Administrator that the land was "chiefly valuable" for such purposes. Two other choices were open to GSA in disposing of the Des Plaines property. Another law provided that the administrator could sell surplus land to public agencies at 50 percent of the going market value. In all other cases GSA's basic legislative charter required it to sell the land at whatever price it could recover for the federal treasury.

A number of active conservationist and sports clubs in Illinois had sought the transfer of Des Plaines for several years. The area was popular with hunters and fishermen from Chicago and Joliet who, along with conservationists, wanted the state to keep the area as it was. The clubs had carried on a vigorous campaign among their members who, in turn, petitioned members of Congress and the GSA for favorable action. Senator Dirksen, who had been helpful in bringing the land under GSA jurisdiction and thus subject to transfer, had carried on an extensive correspondence with the Illinois sportsmen and conservationists, and in 1958 hoped soon to bring the transfer to a successful conclusion. The Fish and Wildlife Service of the federal Department of the Interior favored the transfer.

Industrial Groups Become Interested

In the spring of 1958, at the same time that conservationists were moving to gain use of the land, various Chicago business and industrial groups also began negotiations to acquire the Des Plaines property. The fact that it was located near a navigable river, railroad sidings, spur lines, and a transcontinental highway increased its industrial potential.

Several groups or individuals were interested in the property, including the Santa Fe Railroad (which acted through its industrial development subsidiary), a Chicago real estate company, two chemical companies, and the Star Peerless Trust of Chicago. They directed their immediate efforts at Joliet business associations and unions, and during the summer of 1958 representatives of Joliet's Association of Commerce and the city's central trade council came to Washington to persuade Dirksen to plead their case with GSA. They told him that industrialization of northern Illinois was important because of the St. Lawrence Seaway, scheduled to open in 1959. Also mentioned was the value of new industry as a source of jobs for those laid off by the gradual contraction of the Joliet Arsenal's activities. (1958 was a year of nation-wide economic recession.)

The Joliet Association also fostered a brisk letter-writing campaign to members of Congress, GSA, and to Illinois state officials. The letters all pleaded the area's need for industrial development and new tax sources. By the fall of 1958 the Santa Fe emerged as the principal bidder for the property.

State Officials

Governor Stratton did not take an active part in the unfolding Des Plaines struggle. Initially he supported the plan of his Conservation Director for obtaining the entire Des Plaines area for continued use as a state game preserve. If Des Plaines could be secured without cost, it would be a nice coup; the constituents of the Conservation Department would be pleased, and the state's treasury would be intact. However, after the Santa Fe and other commercial concerns began to evidence hard interest in the property and to advance arguments about the state's need for industrial development and additional sources of revenue, Stratton saw the value of trying to please both the business community and the conservationists.

Palmer's official responsibilities as Conservation Director did not extend to the state's fiscal condition, and he wanted the entire Des Plaines territory for conservation use. He considered the request reasonable, since the state had invested a half million dollars in building or improving two dams, gravel roads, pheasant pens, and residences for custodial personnel. However, Palmer was willing, if economic necessity dictated, to let a portion of the property be detached and sold to industry. In July 1958 he dispatched an amended request to GSA, asking the agency to turn over approximately 2,200 acres to Illinois for conservation. He enclosed a map showing the 200-acre plot reserved for industry. A copy of the same map was also sent to Dirksen.

State Pressures Trained on Dirksen

In mid-1958 the interested parties—Palmer, the Sante Fe, and the conservationists—asked Dirksen to use his influence to advance the respective courses each was advocating for the Des Plaines property.

Dirksen's original task, which Palmer had asked him to perform, was to persuade GSA to turn over all of Tracts 1, 2, and 3 to the state. Then in July 1958 he was told that the state had decided not to ask for the whole property, as Stratton and Palmer wanted GSA to reserve 200 acres for industrial development. Dirksen was asked (in a letter from Palmer of July 10, 1958) to try to get GSA approval of such an arrangement and to urge Floete to make a speedy settlement.

Dirksen knew it would be a problem to dispose of Des Plaines in a manner that would keep everybody happy. But, as the Republicans' most experienced adjuster and mediator, he was willing to try. He had nursed the transfer of the property from the Army to the GSA for several years, and he wanted to satisfy the Illinois sportsmen. Parks, recreation areas, and wildlife matters were not his legislative specialty, but he rated the sportsmen-conservationist combine as a significant political bloc, one it would be unwise to offend. He also wanted industry to get a portion of the Des Plaines property. Industrial development of the area satisfied his own economic philosophy: let private enterprise pull the area out of the slump. The Joliet and Chicago business groups that were pushing for industrial development also were numbered among his supporters, and he wanted to do them a favor if he could. Finally, Dirksen saw it as his duty to bring about a settlement satisfactory to the Republican national administration—to GSA in this instance.

Dirksen discussed the Des Plaines controversy with Floete. Floete, who often involved himself personally in GSA's real-estate transactions, went to Illinois in September and toured the property, escorted by Glen Palmer. Returning to Washington, he notified Dirksen (in a letter of October 2) that GSA was willing to transfer a "substantial portion" to Illinois without cost and that "a portion of the surplus property adjoining the Des Plaines River" would be offered for public sale. "When such areas are determined, we will advertise for competitive bids thereon and depending upon the amount of the offers received, if any, we will determine whether offers should be accepted or whether the entire property should be transferred to the state of Illinois." Floete instructed the GSA regional office in Chicago to decide which portion should be offered for public sale and which reserved for Illinois.

The Santa Fe, meanwhile, evinced strong interest in the entire Des Plaines plot, or in more than 200 acres of it, and railroad officials conferred several times with the regional officers of GSA in Chicago. Not satisfied with the pace of negotiations there, the Santa Fe sent to Washington George W. Cox, a vice-president and head of the industrial development subsidiary. Cox conferred with Floete on October 22 and offered $500 an acre for 2,200 acres.

Floete and Dirksen, who worked closely on Des Plaines, agreed that GSA should proceed carefully. Certain amenities had to be observed before the agency took final action. It was important, they felt, to establish the market price of the three Des Plaines parcels, which were reasonably well-marked geographic entities, each possessing special features and characteristics. Dirksen agreed that GSA should have the property appraised, both as a whole and by tract. Once a value was established, GSA would decide whether the Santa Fe, or anybody else, would buy one or more of the parcels and what approximate price the land should bring.

On December 1 Floete instructed the GSA office in Chicago to survey the property and to offer it for sale in three tracts. Dirksen and Floete reasoned that the transfer could be handled in this manner without inviting criticism. At bottom was their understanding that the Santa Fe would be allowed to buy Tracts 1 and 2 and that GSA would give Illinois Tract 3, the least desirable as an industrial site. Another reason

for determining the value, in their view, was the possibility that Illinois could enter the competition and bid for other parts of the area.[1] Dirksen summarized the plan in a letter dated December 12, 1958, to one of the conservationists.

> . . . GSA is in a rather awkward position on this particular piece of property because it has a highly marketable value and there are cash bidders for the acreage involved.
>
> GSA deems it a duty to retrieve wherever possible compensation for any kind of surplus property for restitution to a somewhat depleted Federal Treasury and to that end expects to offer this property for sale in three separate and distinct parcels in the hope that this might satisfy not only the industrial but conservationist interests as well.
>
> The State could bid for such portion as it might like to retain for conservation purposes although I do not know whether it has constitutional authority or funds for this purpose.

The news that GSA's Chicago office was surveying the land preparatory to seeking bids stirred up a wave of criticism in Illinois. The conservation organizations asked their members to dispatch letters to Springfield (the capital of Illinois), to GSA, and to Senators Dirksen and Douglas. One peti-

---

[1] Illinois had acquired most of its park, conservation, and wildlife refuge sites by purchase from private individuals or federal housekeeping bureaus. Much of the property the Conservation Department had acquired was swamp land or marginal land unable to command a high price. The Department had paid as low as $20 per acre for marginal land or as high as $200 per acre for farm belt land. The interest of the Santa Fe, or any major industry, in the Des Plaines property could be expected to raise the price for public bodies as well as for any other purchasers.

tioner asked Governor Stratton to request Floete to reverse the GSA stand on Des Plaines and turn over "this vital area" to the Department of Conservation. Glen Palmer explained the state's stand. On December 8 he wrote various sportsmen that the Conservation Department's position had received the general support of the Illinois congressional delegation but that the transfer was being delayed because "certain cash offers by industry have been made for sale of a portion of the area to private enterprise." As consolation he offered the possibility that the Army would soon relinquish some land south of Des Plaines that could be made available to the Conservation Department.

Chicago newspapers sided unanimously with the sports groups, criticizing GSA for acquiescing in a deal to sell off conservation land for "factory sites." The *Chicago Daily News* (December 22) blamed business for interfering with the orderly transfer to Illinois. "SPORTSMEN BATTLE BUSINESS TO KEEP JOLIET-AREA TRACT," a headline said, and noted, "Bid to Buy Land for Railroad Runs into Stiff Opposition." The *Chicago Tribune,* the *Sun-Times,* and the *Chicago-American* carried similar stories.

The Sportsmen Ask for Legislation

When the first session of the 86th Congress assembled in Washington in 1959, the Illinois conservationists and sportsmen stepped up their campaign with Senators Dirksen and Douglas. There was a voluminous correspondence between Illinois and Washington. (The congressional elections of 1958 had returned heavy Democratic majorities with what observers termed a strong liberal flavor. Democrats, of course, organized Congress and headed all committees.) The sportsmen's mo-

rale had been raised by assurances of support from two business concerns, Olin Mathieson Chemical Corporation of East Alton, Illinois and the Outboard Boating Club of Chicago. (One of Olin's divisions produces Winchester rifles and ammunition for sportsmen.) An Olin Mathieson officer told the Will County Sportsmen's Club that while the company could not involve itself in partisan politics a company executive had done "everything possible on a personal basis" to bring about a transfer of Des Plaines to Illinois. Also, some support from organized labor appeared: the Chicago office of the United Auto Workers contributed $100 to the Will County Club.

Now the conservationists not only wanted support; they wanted their senators to sponsor legislation to forestall the GSA sale. The secretary of the Will County Sportsmen's Club, Floyd Zebell, asked both Dirksen and Douglas (in letters dated January 2) to introduce a bill to keep GSA from disposing of the property. Such legislation would give the conservationists time to muster their strength. He suggested that if the senators were unwilling to sponsor a bill, they might turn to a conservation-minded colleague. Some 200 letters from the Harvester Sportsmen's Club of Chicago reached the two senators in January. One was a hectographed form letter warning that although hunters and fishermen do not write many letters, they "DO vote and they will remember the outcome when they go to the polls."

Another request for legislation was directed to Senator Dirksen only, but copies of the letter were sent to President Eisenhower, Senator Douglas, the full Illinois congressional delegation, Governor Stratton, and the Chicago newspapers. The writer was George Eve, an active Republican and an officer of a sportsmen's club in the Chicago vicinity. Eve asked Dirksen to introduce a bill transferring Des Plaines to Illinois, to push it through both houses, and to try to come to terms with Floete. His letter concluded: "We have complete faith in our Senators insofar as getting the job done. However, if you believe it beyond your ability, advise us as to whom we should direct our attack."

When the sportsmen agreed that their best hope lay in legislation, they concentrated their campaign on Douglas. Douglas was well known to his constituents and to the country as a dedicated fighter for park sites and conservation and wildlife refuges. He had gained the gratitude of outdoorsmen and scientists and the antagonism of business groups by his fight in 1957–1958 to save the Indiana dunes area as a national park.

The campaign to enlist Douglas was advanced by the personal pleas of officers of national conservation organizations with headquarters in Washington. Representatives of the Wildlife Management Institute, the Izaak Walton League, and the Audubon Society called on him. The leading figure in the effort at personal persuasion was the vice-president of the Wildlife Management Institute in Washington, C. R. Gutermuth, who talked several times with Douglas and members of his staff.

The interests of the Illinois sportsmen and the national conservation organizations here were identical. The two groups were veterans of many a battle against the bulldozers. Their common purposes were often fostered through the Natural Resources Council of America, a clearing house for conservation organizations, scientific societies, sportsmen, and nature lovers. The 35 constituent units of the council included the American Alpine Club, the American Fisheries Society, the American Museum of Natural History,

the Appalachian Mountain Club, the Izaak Walton League, the National Audubon Society, the National Fisheries Institute, the National Rifle Association of America, the Sport Fishing Institute, and the Wildlife Management Institute.

The Natural Resources Council and its member units were tax-exempt, nonprofit organizations, barred from devoting substantial efforts to lobbying. To get support for legislation, the various member units turned to individual members of local hunting and fishing clubs, many of which were organized to promote the aims of both conservationists and sportsmen. One of these was the Northern Zone (Illinois) Association of Sportsmen's and Conservation Clubs, claiming 20,000 members in the 33 northern counties of Illinois. Its purpose was to encourage protection and restoration of waters and wildlife and to improve hunting and fishing.

Illinois sportsmen and conservationists were well organized in local, state, and regional clubs. The largest was the Illinois Federation of Sportsmen's Clubs, a state association of 367 conservation clubs which claimed a membership of 47,000 persons. One of its units was the 5,000-member Will County Club.

Another national organization, the United Auto Workers, supported the Illinois conservationists. One of UAW's Washington lobbyists called on Senator Douglas, and the Chicago office sent him a telegram asking for help.

Dirksen and Douglas Respond

Toward the end of January both Dirksen and Douglas, without any consultation with each other or any liaison between their staffs, decided that the uproar from home, the wide newspaper coverage of GSA plans, and the intense personal solicitation called for action on the congressional stage. Both senators decided to sponsor legislation affecting Des Plaines.

Their plans were dissimilar. Dirksen, the new Senate Republican leader, was under an obligation to disturb as little as possible the national Republican administration and the state Republican administration in Illinois. He understood and sympathized with Floete's dilemma. He wanted to satisfy the conservationists, who did vote, as they had forcefully reminded him, and the businessmen of Chicago and Joliet, who not only voted but contributed to campaign coffers. Dirksen did not have to face re-election until 1962, but the gubernatorial election in Illinois was barely a year off—in 1960—with primaries to occur in the spring.

Douglas, on the other hand, *was* up for re-election in 1960. Not only did his natural sympathies lie with the conservationists, but a successful battle for preservation of a wildlife area would help him politically. Aware of fiscal and economic problems in his home state, he knew that the Joliet Association of Commerce and others were arguing that industrial development of the Des Plaines section was vital to alleviate Joliet's economic plight. He considered this a proper argument for alert business groups to be advancing, but he felt that the Illinois economy would benefit just as much if the industrial plants were located on some other site. In the course of Senate committee hearings in February 1958 on economic conditions, Douglas had learned that eight percent of the Joliet work force was unemployed and that the rate might rise as high as 11 percent. (The state's unemployment had stood at 350,000 in July 1958, but the rate had been dropping steadily.) However, as a professional economist, he believed that Joliet's economic dislocation was temporary.

Douglas felt that preservation of the area as a hunting and wildlife preserve outweighed the claim of industrial development. He was also anxious to extend the use of Des Plaines by creating trails, camp sites, picnic grounds, and strolling areas. He wanted it to be open for the broadest possible use of an estimated eight million people in Chicago and surrounding areas.

The Illinois conservationists were jubilant when they learned that both senators planned to sponsor legislation. Gutermuth told Floyd Zebell that Douglas was preparing a bill and would fight valiantly for its enactment and that Dirksen was also willing to introduce a bill. "We really do not care who sponsors the proposal. . . . Evidently both of the Senators from Illinois are now eager to become the saviors." Gutermuth said he would see that legislation was also introduced in the House.

The Douglas Bill

On January 28, 1959 Douglas introduced a bill (S. 747) that called for GSA to convey the entire 2,414-acre Des Plaines area (Tracts 1–3) to Illinois without cost for continued use for wildlife conservation or recreational purposes. It also contained the usual clauses providing for title to revert to the United States in the event the property was not used for the stated purposes. The bill was referred to the Government Operations Committee, which had jurisdiction over disposal of real and personal surplus government property.

The Douglas bill caught Dirksen by surprise. He had been planning for some time to introduce legislation transferring Tract 3 to Illinois. His proposed bill was one part of a long-range plan by which Dirksen hoped to satisfy all the competing interests. According to his understanding with Floete, GSA would sell Tracts 1 and 2 to the Santa Fe. To recompense the conservationists for the loss of these tracts, Dirksen would negotiate with the Army for release of additional land, which could then be transferred to the Illinois Department of Conservation, along with Tract 3. He had explained his plans to state officials, and on January 21, 1959 had told Palmer that he was waiting word from GSA before drafting a bill. Floete had asked Dirksen not to introduce a bill until GSA received a better idea of the value of the land.

The Douglas bill caught Floete off guard also, but GSA went ahead with plans to advertise for bids. Its ads in Chicago newspapers on February 3 notified prospective buyers of the location of the property—"THE IDEAL LOCATION FOR INDUSTRIAL SITES NEAR JOLIET, ILLINOIS" —and the sales conditions: "APPROXIMATELY 2325 ACRES— OFFERED AS ONE UNIT, OR AS THREE SEPARATE PARCELS OF APPROXIMATELY EQUAL SIZE."

(Bills similar to Douglas' S. 747, transferring the entire Des Plaines area to Illinois, were introduced in the House within a few days by Illinois congressmen. The House bills contained a sentence referring to the property, incorrectly, as Army land. They were therefore assigned to the House Armed Services Committee.)

The conservationists continued to promote their cause, with strategy being called by C. R. Gutermuth of the Wildlife Management Institute in Washington. When bills had been introduced in both houses, Gutermuth advised Zebell to keep up the flow of correspondence from Illinois. He suggested that Will County Club members continue to ask Douglas and Dirksen to persuade GSA to delay disposing of Des Plaines pending congressional action. (Following a request from the chairman of the Government Operations Committee, Floete agreed to discontinue efforts to dispose of the property until Congress acted.) Gutermuth also suggested letters asking the chairmen of the Senate Government Operations Committee and the House Armed Services Committee to schedule early hearings.

Gutermuth then coached the sportsmen on points to emphasize in committee hearings. He suggested that witnesses stress the need for more recreation facilities near a large urban center, the state's expenditure of $500,-000, and the number of signatures (20,000) gathered on petitions to the Illinois senators.

An official of the National Wildlife Federation also offered counsel. One way to combat the lure of the large Santa Fe bid, he suggested, was to compare the value of Des Plaines to Central Park. The per-acre value of Central Park land might be six figures, but no New York politician would dream of selling it to bring in more money for the city treasury.

Dirksen Plans

The Douglas bill came as a surprise to Dirksen's staff members, who had hoped to have their own bill before the Senate by early March. With S. 747 in the hopper, Dirksen's strategy had to be modified.

Dirksen's belief that the Des Plaines site was well-suited for industrial development was strengthened when he met a delegation of industrial and union leaders in Chicago in mid-February. The Des Plaines tracts, he was told, were the only part of the government's holdings in that area suitable for industrial use.

In reply to the continuous stream of letters and petitions from Illinois, Dirksen then offered the conservationists and sportsmen the hope that they might obtain other suitable land from the Army in the near future. He told one correspondent that he would try to work out something soon with the Secretary of the Army. On February 26 he wrote to the Secretary, Wilber Brucker, describing the situation as follows:

> Sen. Douglas has introduced a bill to turn this tract [the Des Plaines area] over to the State of Illinois, without compensation and without any incumbrance. The General Services Administrator, the better to determine the value of this tract, has submitted it for bid in three separate parcels. . . .
>
> I can appreciate the dilemma of Mr. Floete, the Administrator of GSA, who seems under something of a duty to retrieve for the Federal Treasury whatever cash he can as a result of the sale. At the same time he recognizes the need for outdoor areas for recreational, wildlife and conservation purposes. Accordingly he has been very patient in the matter and we have discussed the equities on a number of occasions.

Dirksen suggested that the Army could easily give up some of its "tremendous amount of acreage," particularly the tract along the Kankakee River, which, being hilly and slightly timbered, was well adapted for conservation and wildlife purposes.

> This is an urgent matter and I am wondering whether you could assign it for immediate exploration in the hope that before 60 days elapse [the GSA deadline for disposing of the property by bid] it might be possible to consummate an arrangement where both industry and conservation could be served and probably as much as $1½ million in cash might be retrieved for the Federal Treasury. I earnestly hope this can have immediate attention.

The Senate
Government Operations Committee

In early February the Senate committee began the routine work of soliciting opinions of S. 747 from the executive agencies that might be affected —the Bureau of the Budget, GSA, and the Interior, Justice, and Agriculture Departments. On March 20 the chairman appointed a special three-man subcommittee to act in the committee's name. He selected the freshman Democrat on the committee, Senator Edmund Muskie of Maine, as chairman and Senators Gruening (D) of Alaska and Capehart (R) of Indiana. The Government Operations Committee rarely had held hearings on transfers of federal land. In 80 percent of similar cases the committee had approved the transfers on the basis of staff recommendations.

The executive agencies began to forward to the committee their reactions to the bill. GSA's answer was delayed until the Des Plaines bids were opened. The high bid—from the Santa Fe Railroad—was $1,351,000 for the entire property (an average price of $560 per acre). On the individual tracts the high bid was $499,100 for parcel 1 (an average of $805 per acre); $559,680 for parcel 2 ($660 per acre); and $286,638 for parcel 3 ($303 per acre). On March 24 GSA notified the committee of its opposition to S. 747 based on two factors: (1) the bill was "special legislation," whereas there was existing law of general application; and (2) the bill involved a financial loss to the federal government. The Bureau of the Budget supported GSA on the same grounds. There was no notice to the Department of the Army or the Defense Department because the formalities concerning the Army's release of the Des Plaines land had been completed. The decision on disposition of the property was up to GSA.

Senator Muskie's Subcommittee Holds Hearings

The subcommittee held hearings on S. 747 for two days, April 9 and 10, 1959. Only two of the three members attended—Chairman Muskie and Senator Gruening. Capehart never participated. Senator Douglas, the first witness, emphasized the importance of preserving open areas for conservation and wildlife and as a retreat for Chicago's teeming population. He spoke of his future hopes for the Des Plaines land:

> This has been used as a wildlife area for hunting and for breeding pheasants, which are then transferred to other wildlife refuges. It can be used, however, and I believe should be used, to a much greater degree for recreational purposes. The shore of the Des Plaines River could easily be developed as a park with picnic grounds, and if we make progress in cleaning up the pollution of the Des Plaines River, . . . the river itself could be used by people who come there for recreational purposes.
>
> So this is not merely to be a public shooting ground, so to speak. It can also be fishing grounds and picnic grounds and a general recreational area.

He did not deal with the ability of Illinois to buy the land or to bid for it in the open market. He was critical of GSA for interpreting the 1948 law (on which Illinois had based its request) so narrowly in terms of "chiefly valuable," saying it was not possible to measure the value of recreation and outdoor life.

Floete, the second major witness, told the subcommittee that, according to GSA construction of the 1948 law, the only land that could be turned over to the state without cost was marginal land unsuitable for other purposes. However, he named other relevant laws under which Illinois might bid for the land, including one which allowed GSA to sell surplus land to public agencies at half the going price. Indicating a willingness to negotiate with state representatives, he held out the possibility of an arrangement concerning Tract 3. He felt that the per-acre price for land in Tract 3, on the basis of the bids GSA had received ($303 per acre), was a price Illinois could afford to pay. Floete firmly opposed the Douglas bill. He felt that GSA could not justly allow parcels 1 and 2 to go free to the state, since the Santa Fe bid was so high.

Governor Stratton of Illinois did not attend the hearing, nor did he respond to committee invitations that he testify. The state's views were given by Glen Palmer, who was in a spot in having to make public and official comments on the Douglas bill. As Director of Conservation, he was committed to his original aim—to get the entire Des Plaines area, or as large a part of it as possible. However, as a member of the Stratton Republican administration, he was duty-bound to advance a compromise that allowed the property to be divided. His hope, like Dirksen's, was for an award of additional land from the Army. Palmer made these points: (1) it was uneconomical to maintain an area less than 2,000 acres for hunting and public shooting; (2) industry would be wise to locate near a city rather than in the comparatively rural

Des Plaines area; (3) the 2,400-acre Des Plaines area, plus Tract 4 (a 1,500-acre parcel held by the Fifth Army and used by the Conservation Department on a permit basis), was an ideal area for the Conservation Department's various activities.

Palmer, when asked whether the state might bid for the land, said Illinois was trying to balance its budget—which was then being considered at the biennial session of the State Legislature—but was anxious to work out an agreement with GSA. Illinois, without jeopardizing its budget, could buy the Des Plaines land, he said, "if it is based on a fair value as far as recreation or out-of-doors usage is concerned." He added that he had just discussed the matter with Stratton, "and I am sure we have the backing of our Governor who, I might say, is very conservation minded." He sidestepped a direct question about the Governor's attitude, saying Stratton believed that "the majority" of the property should be developed as a wildlife area rather than as an industrial area. Palmer never spoke directly about S. 747, the Douglas bill, saying he based his hopes on making an arrangement with Floete.

Dirksen's Testimony

Dirksen strongly opposed the Douglas bill. He told the subcommittee that allowing Governor Stratton to negotiate with GSA was preferable to settling the question by an act of Congress. He nodded toward the platform on which the two members of the subcommittee were seated. "Senator Gruening, you were a Governor, and Senator Muskie, you were a Governor. I think if the committee took action on this bill, it would be something of an affront to our Governor, when he is doing his best to work out a difficult problem." He said he had just talked to Stratton by telephone and had learned that the Governor had enough money to bid for at least some of the land, letting the rest go for industry. He asked the subcommittee to set aside S. 747 and allow Illinois officials and GSA to arrange their own terms.

Chairman Muskie explained to Dirksen the subcommittee's desire to act in the best interests of Illinois. He said he had gained the impression from Palmer's testimony that the Governor supported S. 747. Since it was poor politics for Governor Stratton to be represented as opposed to the Douglas bill, even though it had been introduced by the state's Democratic senator, Dirksen's answer hinted that Palmer, as an ardent conservationist, was unable to visualize the wider responsibilities faced by the Governor. He asked the subcommittee "to make allowances for Mr. Palmer's testimony on this bill" and to consider the position of the Governor, who had many interests to balance—including those of the conservationists and of the industrialists—as well as being obligated to maintain the fiscal stability of his state.

Dirksen indicated a possible solution. The Army could give 5,000 or 10,000 acres (of the approximately 32,000 it still held in the Joliet area) to Illinois for conservation purposes. He threatened a showdown with the Army, "because if they cannot show a real need, they ought to surrender the land." He said he had already suggested to the Army that it could well afford to hand over some of its holdings. Dirksen told the subcommittee the matter could be handled administratively and asked the members to let the Douglas bill languish.

Asked whether he favored giving Des Plaines to the state, Dirksen replied that he favored giving Illinois some of the acreage, but "I think those that have an interest in part of it, at least, for industrial purposes should be heard and should be given consideration." He did not expand his answer or mention possible benefits that industrial possession of the land would bring. (Chicago newspapers reported Dirksen's opposition. "DIRKSEN OPPOSES JOLIET AREA PARK" read a headline in the *Chicago Sun-Times* the next day.)

Army representatives from the Pentagon, present at the hearing, followed proceedings closely but did not testify.

The following day Palmer, recalled to testify, said that Governor Stratton firmly supported continued use of most of the area for conservation, with the detachment of 200 acres fronting on the Des Plaines River for industrial development. (It was this decision, in which the Conservation Department acquiesced, that had led Palmer to amend Illinois' request to GSA in July 1958.)

The Illinois conservationists and sportsmen were represented before the subcommittee by Burton K. Atwood of Winnetka, secretary of the Izaak Walton League; W. E. Hewitt, of the Illinois Federation of Sportsmen's Clubs; Stanley Ekedahl, president of the Will County Sportsmen's Club; and Floyd Zebell. They made short statements at the conclusion of the hearing, emphasizing the points suggested in Gutermuth's briefing.

Gutermuth and other representatives of national conservation groups then testified in favor of S. 747. They stressed the importance to public health and welfare of adequate recreational facilities, and emphasized the proximity of the Des Plaines area to Chicago. In a region containing an extremely heavy concentration of population, they argued, the Des Plaines land was the only site suitable for a recreational area.

Opposing the bill, in addition to GSA and Senator Dirksen, were two representatives of the Joliet Association of Commerce and one each of the Will County Board of Supervisors, the Santa Fe Railroad, and the Chicago Association of Commerce and Industry. They argued that the Joliet area needed industry more than it needed a conservation and recreation area; that the closeness of site transportation made it ideally suited for industrial development; that the cutback in the Joliet Arsenal payroll from a peak of 24,000 to less than 1,500 meant a serious unemployment problem (this cutback had taken place gradually over a ten-year period); and that other land still under Army jurisdiction could be better utilized for conservation and recreation than Des Plaines.

George W. Cox, head of the Santa Fe industrial development subsidiary, testified that his company had long considered the area prime industrial property and had made an effort to get it as early as 1952. Claiming that the Santa Fe favored unified development of the entire area, he predicted that within ten years industrialization would produce annual taxes amounting to over $3 million for Will County and Illinois. It was not worthwhile for the Santa Fe to extend tracks, said Cox, if only 200 or so acres were detached for industry, as Palmer had originally visualized.

There was no unified "labor" position. A UAW representative from Chicago supported S. 747 on grounds that the swelling Chicago population, particularly labor people with shorter working hours, needed recreation. On the other hand, a Joliet steelworkers union official supported industry use of the area to relieve unemployment.

At the conclusion of the hearings, Senator Gruening summed up the subcommittee's dilemma. Its sole concern, he said, was to arrive at a solution that satisfied the people of Illinois. He continued:

It is a little difficult to find out how the people of Illinois feel, because we apparently have a division. The senior Senator from Illinois is in favor of turning this over for recreational and wildlife purposes, and the junior Senator apparently wants to turn it over for business purposes. We have conflicting testimony as to the attitude of the Governor, whose views we would naturally respect and would like to have. The director of the Illinois Department of Conservation testifies that he is in favor of the conservation aspects. And the junior Senator testified that he talked to the Governor not later than yesterday, and he finds him on his side for industrial use of the area.

We find one group of labor people who are in favor of the industrial development, and another group that are in favor of the recreational development.

The Subcommittee Acts after Hearings

The public hearings had developed several alternatives to S. 747. One was the original Palmer plan to snip off 200 acres for industry and transfer the rest of the Des Plaines tracts to Illinois. The Santa Fe, however, wanted all the property, although it was willing to limit its request to Tracts 1 and 2. The second possibility, therefore, was to allow the Santa Fe to buy the entire area for $1,351,000, or Tracts 1 and 2 for $1,058,780. Dirksen suggested a third possibility: satisfy industry and negotiate with the Army for release of additional land for sportsmen and conservation interests.

Since the hearings had not resolved the dispute, the subcommittee chairman wrote Governor Stratton to suggest that he and GSA confer in an effort to come to terms.

A brisk interchange of letters and advice between Washington and Illinois followed as the several groups made preparations for the conference between Illinois officials and the GSA. Zebell offered Senator Muskie his critical interpretation of the plan—which he noted was originally suggested by Dirksen—to let Illinois and GSA work things out. He charged that the move was "designed to take control of the situation away from the Senate and give it to the Administration so they will be free to work out the best deal for industrial interests. . . . We are hopeful the Committee will see to it the Senate does not lose control of the issue even though it may recommend that GSA and Illinois officials sit down together and negotiate."

C. R. Gutermuth offered advice several times during the interim period. He told Palmer he could rely on the unyielding support of Senator Douglas and the national conservation organizations. He hoped Palmer would take a strong stand in his talks with Floete for retaining all three Des Plaines tracts for conservation use. The only acceptable compromise, Gutermuth said, was the detachment of the original 200-acre parcel. He suggested that Palmer take reinforcements to the GSA meeting—somebody from the Wildlife Management Institute (Gutermuth's organization) or from Senator Douglas' office.

GSA and Illinois Negotiate

The conference took place on May 5 in Floete's Washington office. Present were two men from the Illinois administration (Glen Palmer and Morton H. Hollingsworth, the Director of Finance, who acted as the Governor's representative), Floete and an assistant, and representatives from the offices of Senators Douglas and Dirksen.

The conferees agreed that the various points of view could be harmonized if the Army gave up some land. Palmer stated that if Illinois could get suitable land for conservation purposes the state would be willing to pay Floete's price for Tract 3 ($303 per acre, the amount of the Sante Fe bid). Hollingsworth gave assurance that the State Legislature would appropriate the necessary $286,000.

Hollingsworth explained that Illinois could not afford to offer 50 percent of the market value for all three tracts if the Morse formula[2] should be invoked. The conferees did not touch on the fact that Douglas' bill provided for transfer without any cost to Illinois. (If GSA had been able to determine under the 1948 law that the property was "chiefly valuable" for conservation and wildlife, the Morse formula would not have applied.)

---

[2] A formula devised by Senator Wayne Morse to cover disposal of federally-owned land. It required the federal government to charge 50 percent of the appraised value when selling property to other public agencies for public use. It will be more fully explained later.

Floete held to the original GSA plan of selling Tracts 1 and 2. Palmer said he would offer no opposition if the state were given some conservation land in addition to Tract 3. His suggestion tallied with Dirksen's plan to get the Army to give up some of the land it still held near Tracts 1, 2, and 3.

At this point Floete said he would call his friend, the Secretary of the Army, and ask the Army to relinquish Tract 4, the 1,500-acre parcel just south of and contiguous to Tract 3. Floete then tried, unsuccessfully, to get through to Secretary Brucker on the telephone. Since such a transfer would not be a major land transaction for GSA or for the Army, Floete assumed that there would be no difficulty in obtaining the Army's agreement, especially since Brucker would understand that GSA was in a dilemma and needed the parcel. The two men had worked harmoniously when Floete had handled real estate for the Defense Department, and Floete did not anticipate any difficulties.

This substitution proved agreeable to Douglas. His office staff turned its attention to other matters while awaiting word of the GSA negotiations with the Army.

The Bill Is Revised

During the following week Dirksen talked to Pentagon officials by telephone. It was the senator's understanding that the Department of the Army consented to the Floete suggestion to give up Tract 4. On May 13 Dirksen acted to translate the understanding into action. He introduced an amendment to the Douglas bill, providing for the Army to convey Tract 4 to Illinois, without cost, to be used for wildlife conservation and recreational purposes. Dirksen's amendment struck out everything in the Douglas bill after the enacting clause.

Dirksen said the solution was agreeable to Illinois, to the conservation interests, and to industry. He explained on the Senate floor that the amendment was "part of a program which has been achieved after long negotiations with all parties in interest, including the State of Illinois, the conservation interests, and the industrial interests." His program included two other items:

(1) GSA would sell Tract 3 to Illinois for conservation use, and (2) GSA would sell Tracts 1 and 2 to industry. He said the conservationists would gain by the transaction, "which would provide 2,448 acres to be used exclusively and in perpetuity for recreation, wildlife, and conservation purposes."

Dirksen called a press conference the following day (Thursday, May 14) to announce the settlement. Playing down his own part, he said that Governor Stratton, Conservation Director Palmer, and Floete had worked out an arrangement to transfer Tract 4 to Illinois free of charge. A simultaneous announcement at the capital in Springfield stated that Governor Stratton was setting aside a sum of money from the state budget to buy Tract 3. Chicago newspapers were enthusiastic about the terms of settlement, as was the outdoor reporter for the *Joliet Herald-News*. In a column on May 24 the reporter praised Senator Douglas and the sports groups for effective work. He also commended the Santa Fe Railroad and the Joliet Association of Commerce. Without their opposition and strong fight to reserve the two northern tracts for industrial sites, he said, "the Federal government would never have released the backwaters to take off the political heat." The newsman assumed that the statements from Washington and Springfield indicated that the responsible agencies had in fact released Tract 4.

Fifth Army officers in Chicago were jolted at the announcement. They had not been consulted about any agreement to release Tract 4, and their plans for conducting weekend reserve exercises on that Tract were still in effect.

Des Plaines
Legislation in the House

During this time—January to May 1959—while Senator Dirksen and, to a lesser extent, Senator Douglas were involved in negotiations with Illinois officials and federal agencies over the Des Plaines area, a holding action was taking place in the House. Four bills transferring Des Plaines to Illinois had been introduced by four Illinois congressmen—Representatives O'Hara, Price, and Boyle, Democrats; and Representative Church, Republican. The bill acted upon was H.R. 3984, sponsored by Representative Melvin Price.

The bills were assigned to the House Armed Services Committee, since it authorized the acquisition and disposition of military property. They referred to the identical property (Tracts 1, 2, and 3) dealt with in the original Douglas bill. However, the House bills claimed that the real estate was owned by the United States Army whereas the property actually was "owned" at that time by GSA. The Armed Services Committee had itself approved the transfer to GSA in January 1958. Tract 4 was transferred at the same time—by an actual book entry—from Army Ordnance to Army Reserves for use as a reserve training area by the Fifth Army in Chicago. The bills got no attention in the House until May, after the meeting between Floete and the Illinois officials.

The course of events in the House during May remains jumbled. Beginning on May 11 Price tried to get the Armed Services Committee Chairman, Carl Vinson (D) of Georgia, to designate a subcommittee to handle H.R. 3984. Within a short time the bill was assigned to a real estate subcommittee on which Price was the second ranking Democrat. The subcommittee received a formal statement of the Army's view of H.R. 3984 on May 18: the Army had no further need for Tracts 1–3 and was not concerned with their disposition.

However, events in the Senate caused the Army to re-examine its position. Since January 1958 Tract 4 had been under the jurisdiction of Army Reserves and under the immediate jurisdiction of the Commanding General of the Fifth Army in Chicago, General William Arnold.

When Dirksen announced that all parties were satisfied with the plan to transfer Tract 4, the Pentagon saw storm signals and decided that the arsenal property was going to take more than routine handling. Tract 4 was the responsibility of the Army unit devoted to manpower, personnel, and reserve forces, headed by Assistant Secretary Dewey Short. The Army considered the matter important enough to throw the Assistant Secretary himself into the fight. Short was a stalwart fighter and an anchor Republican; in representing the Army "on the Hill" he benefitted from having served as a member of the House for over two decades. For most of that time he had been a member of the House Armed Services Committee (formerly the Military Affairs Committee). After losing his House seat in 1956 he had been appointed to a high post in the Defense Department. Short was in a favorable position to promote the Army viewpoint with his former colleagues on the Armed Services Committee.

Even without such an influential emissary, however, the Army was favored in its dealings with the Armed Services Committee by certain institutional relationships. One was the committee's long-standing and intense interest in military real estate transactions. Another was the fact that the members of the Armed Services Committee held no other major committee posts. Thus they were able to devote a great deal of their congressional time to becoming "specialists" in military problems, and to developing an understanding of military needs.

The committee's interest in military

real estate had begun in the thirties. At that time the Military Affairs Committee, its progenitor and the principal congressional instrument for processing military legislation, had not seriously concerned itself with overall military policy. The committee's attention had focused on matters of concern to the members and their districts: the location of Army posts and Navy yards, construction, and procurement. The committee's special jurisdiction over military real estate transactions dated from 1944.

There were other reasons for the close cooperation between the military chiefs and the Armed Services Committee. The growing importance of military affairs after 1941 resulted in increased congressional involvement in military policy and administration. Congress interpreted its responsibility to mean that it must have access to the views of individual military chiefs rather than just a prepared endorsement of the official Pentagon position approved by top civilian officials. Thus, the House Armed Services Committee became a forum for hearing both sides of military disputes, both majority and minority views.[3]

Dirksen was encouraged when he learned that he would be dealing with Dewey Short on the Des Plaines matter. The two had served together in the House and shared similar views on many economic matters. During a telephone conversation with Dirksen, Short tried to make clear that the Fifth Army was not willing to give up Tract

---

[3] The relationship between members of the Senate Armed Services Committee and the Pentagon was not the same. Senators served on other committees as well. They had neither the time nor the expertise to pay close attention to details of military policy and administration. Also, the Senate committee customarily began consideration of military legislation later in the congressional year than did the House committee.

4. One can only guess that there was a misunderstanding between the two concerning the location or designation of the various parcels, for Dirksen believed that the Assistant Secretary had agreed to release the property. The senator's understanding had several repercussions. Among them was a request from some Illinois conservationists to Representative Price to amend his bill by designating Tract 4 as the area to be ceded to Illinois.

Price agreed to amend his bill and turned the matter over to the staff of the Armed Services Committee toward the end of May, the same time the date for a hearing on H.R. 3984 was set. Price, confident that the session on May 29 would be routine, skipped it to keep a series of speaking engagements in his Illinois district.

The information that the Price bill was to be altered to conform to the Dirksen amendment resulted in a last-minute attempt by the Pentagon to get a clear understanding of the Fifth Army's position. On the night before the House hearings, Short telephoned General Arnold in Chicago. Told by General Arnold that the Fifth Army really needed Tract 4, Short promised he would do his best to keep it.

The House Armed Services Subcommittee hearings opened May 29 in an atmosphere of some confusion. The chairman (Representative Carl Durham) and the witnesses learned that the bill they were to consider had been modified fifteen minutes before the hearing began. The new version, identical with Dirksen's amendment, required the Army to give up Tract 4. The chairman lectured the committee counsel for failing to notify the interested parties of the drastic change in the bill. The counsel protested that he himself had learned of the change only a few minutes earlier.

The Army representative (a civilian from the office of the Chief of Engineers) firmly opposed the revision. He said the Army, upon hearing of the proposal that it give up Tract 4, had rechecked its position the night before and had determined that Tract 4 was definitely *not* excess to Army needs.

The state of Illinois did not have an official representative at the hearing. However, Palmer had designated Charles H. Callison, an officer of the National Wildlife Federation in Washington, to represent him. Callison endorsed the "settlement" involving Tracts 3 and 4. He said that Illinois sports groups were satisfied and that Illinois officials (he had talked to Palmer on the phone just that morning) regarded the Army's agreement as secure.

A representative of the Will County Board of Supervisors came to testify in opposition to the Price bill, as he had to the original Douglas bill. He found out only when he reached the hearing room that the Price bill had been amended.

The hearing was recessed after an abbreviated session, and the revised Price bill was sent to the agencies for comment. The Army's formal reply was not to come for over two months.

The Senate Committee
Processes the Dirksen Amendment

In May 1959 Senator Muskie's subcommittee went to work once again to process the Dirksen amendment, which it referred to the affected agencies for comment. Senator Douglas thought the Dirksen plan was a satisfactory arrangement, but he would not act formally before conferring with state wildlife and conservation groups.

On June 10 Douglas notified the Muskie subcommittee that the state conservationists accepted the "partial substitution" of Tract 4 for Tracts 1 and 2 of the Des Plaines area, but with two qualifications: "First, that the Army agrees to turn [Tract 4] over to the State of Illinois, and, second, that the State will purchase from the GSA 946 acres of Tract 3. . . ." These were the essential terms of the Dirksen amendment.

The Army, now a formal party at interest, received a copy of the Dirksen amendment and a request for its views. As a former congressman, Dewey Short appreciated the importance of maintaining good public relations for the Army. He also wanted to assure himself that the Fifth Army's stated requirement for Tract 4 was based on a genuine military need. He therefore dispatched an aide to Chicago to check on General Arnold's plans for using Tract 4 and to determine whether the Army had another area equally well suited for holding reserve training exercises. On his return to Washington, the aide prepared a memorandum (dated June 16) reporting that General Arnold considered Tract 4 the only area in the Joliet complex suitable for the Fifth Army's needs. The terrain was particularly well adapted to the performance of training maneuvers such as scouting and patrolling, map-reading, command post exercises, river crossing, and tank driving. According to the Fifth Army, no other Army holdings near Chicago offered comparable features. Moreover, the accessibility of Tract 4 to Chicago reservists enhanced its value. The Fifth Army said it had "a vital and continuing need for the 1500-acre tract for use as an outdoor Reserve training area."

The Department of the Army then offered to yield another part of its Joliet holdings to satisfy the needs expressed by the conservationists. After clearing with Secretary of the Army Brucker, Short wrote to the Muskie subcommittee on June 17 to outline the Army proposal. His letter registered formal objection to releasing Tract 4 but offered to give Illinois a 1,375-acre tract (Tract 5), as well as limited use of Tract 4 when it was not employed for military training. This arrangement had the virtue of being satisfactory to Short personally. He opposed the original Douglas plan to transfer Tracts 1, 2, and 3 to Illinois without cost, because such a transaction represented a net financial loss to the federal treasury. He felt that the interests of United States taxpayers, who had financed the original Army purchase of the Joliet Arsenal property, should be considered in working out new arrangements. Thus, the compromise he offered seemed an ideal solution: it added to the treasury, it did not offend the Army, and it was—as Short saw it—a satisfactory arrangement for the conservationists.

A short time later (July 8) the Budget Bureau announced its support of the Army compromise. GSA offered no objection.

The Army move required Douglas to query the conservation people once again. On June 18 he notified them that the Army was willing to continue limited use of Tract 4 and to give up another parcel measuring 1,375 acres. This latter parcel, separated from Tract 3, was across the super-highway, United States Route 66, and was east and south of Tract 4. "BELIEVE ARMY HAS PULLED A FAST ONE," Douglas telegraphed in one message to the conservationists, "BUT WOULD LIKE ADVICE AS TO WHAT TO DO." He said further that he had not received any written assurance from Governor Stratton that Illinois would appropriate the money to pay for Tract 3. "I DO NOT LIKE THE TURN OF EVENTS BUT NEED HELP."

Douglas asked some of the conservationists to inspect Tract 5 to see if it was suitable for their purposes. He was told that not only was the location poor but that the area lacked vegetation, streams, or other natural resources for recreational development.[4] Douglas then notified Muskie that the conservationists and sports people rejected the Army compromise.

Although the Muskie subcommittee had devoted an unprecedented amount of time to solving the Des Plaines dispute, in July it was even farther from a solution than when it had started. The Army plan (to convey Tract 5) was not acceptable to Douglas or to Illinois conservationists and sports groups; the Douglas plan (for GSA to cede Tracts 1, 2, and 3 to Illinois) was not acceptable to Dirksen and GSA; and the Floete-Dirksen plan (for the Army to convey Tract 4) was not acceptable to the Army. Moreover, the Army allowed information to get around that it would ask President Eisenhower to veto the Dirksen bill if it were passed.

Douglas continued to urge his own bill on the subcommittee. On June 18 he wrote Muskie:

> Since you are now confronted with two bills, my bill and Dirksen's bill, may I respectfully urge that my bill be reported. This will put the heat on the Governor and the Army to come up with better and more definite offers. If we take Dirksen's bill we know the Army will oppose it and unless you have received a definite promise from the State Administration, this may fall through. I believe it is desirable to keep pressure on to force a better compromise.[5]

---

[4] Glen Palmer was not aware that any inspection of Tract 5 was being made for Senator Douglas. Palmer had inspected the tract in the spring of 1959 and judged it well-suited for recreational use.

[5] Douglas was not convinced that Stratton

The Army Position

In early July, while Douglas was urging Muskie to report out the original version of S. 747, Short began a round of visits to key members of Congress to drum up support for the Army compromise. He called first on the senators from Illinois. Dirksen, who indicated something of an open mind, believed the Pentagon had welched on what he thought was an agreement to give up Tract 4, but he thought it fruitless to blame Short. He was already looking to the future when, as he saw it, the Army would release more of its Joliet holdings. The meeting between the Senate Republican and the administration Republican was cordial, although Dirksen indicated that he would stand by the proposal he had sponsored (involving Tract 4). No such cordiality prevailed at Short's meeting with Douglas, who was not receptive to compromise.

Short concluded that he had better write off the Senate. He turned to the House, and on July 16 visited Chairman Vinson of the Armed Services Committee. After hearing Short's explanation of the Army position and his assessment of the Senate situation, Vinson indicated understanding of the Army's requirement and sympathy with its position. He advised Short to present the compromise immediately as a formal offer to the Armed Services Committee, along with a legal description of Tract 5 and area maps to show its relationship to the other properties involved.

Scrupulously following this advice, the Department of the Army formally presented the compromise offer in-

---

was sincerely interested in producing a solution adequate for the sportsmen. He thought it advisable to prod the Governor occasionally to ensure that funds were made available to buy Tract 3.

volving Tract 5 to the House Armed Services Committee on August 6, 1959. Secretary of the Army Brucker signed the letter.

In the negotiations at this stage, as earlier, there was no coordination between the two Illinois senators. Dirksen conducted his conferences with the Army without advising the Douglas staff, and Douglas conferred with Illinois sportsmen without reporting to Dirksen. Dirksen's assistants said that Douglas, as always, preferred to work alone, while Douglas' staff said that coordination with Dirksen was useless because they believed Dirksen was interested only in satisfying the Santa Fe.

The Muskie Subcommittee Acts

It is necessary to step back one month in time to pick up the story of Senator Muskie's subcommittee. The group met in executive session on July 10. Army and GSA representatives were invited to participate if either was ready to announce a change of position. Neither was. (Although the Muskie subcommittee knew of the Army compromise involving Tract 5, the formal offer by the Department of the Army was presented—later, in August—only to the House Armed Services Subcommittee.) Army representatives stated only that they would have to recommend a presidential veto of any bill giving away Tract 4.

One of Douglas' aides suggested another compromise. He proposed that the role of "lender" be reversed, with the Army ceding Tract 4 to Illinois. Illinois would then guarantee the Department of the Army the right to hold weekend reserve training exercises there at any time. The Army found this proposal unacceptable.

The subcommittee's two Democrats, Muskie and Gruening, sympathized with the conservationists and wanted—

within political limits—to satisfy them. They were also disposed to aid Senator Douglas if possible, particularly since he faced re-election the following year. Following the July 10 meeting the subcommittee reported out its own version of S. 747 and the full Senate Government Operations Committee agreed on July 23. The committee, while retaining the S. 747 designation, patched together the original bill and the Dirksen amendment. The final version provided (as the Dirksen amendment had) for the Army to turn over Tract 4, but included a proviso (not in the Dirksen amendment) that contingent on that transaction, Illinois would purchase Tract 3 from GSA for $286,000. The committee, mindful of Douglas' objection, decided against constructing a compromise on the Army's offer of Tract 5.

Committee Democrats, who kept Douglas advised of deliberations, learned that the compromise bill was satisfactory to him. Douglas had decided to risk a presidential veto rather than accept Tract 5, which he rated as a shabby substitute. He was convinced, moreover, that the Fifth Army used Tract 4 as a private shooting preserve for its high brass and not as a site for reserve training.

Senate Debate

In August, while the House Armed Services Committee was still receiving reports from interested agencies, the final version of S. 747 reached the Senate floor. Douglas, hoping to have strong assistance from Dirksen in floor debate, telephoned several Illinois conservationists, inviting them to shower Dirksen with letters and telegrams endorsing the bill and asking him to support it. The conservationists obliged by dispatching numerous messages to both Dirksen and Douglas in early August.

Both senators were thus able to state in floor debate that the Illinois interests most directly affected were behind the bill.

Cooperation between the Illinois senators and support from within the state did not ensure smooth passage for the Des Plaines legislation. Senator Wayne Morse, Oregon Democrat and individualist, fearing that S. 747 violated the "Morse formula," announced on the floor that he intended to speak at length in opposition to the bill. Morse's stand thus put him in conflict with his staunch friend and ally, Senator Douglas. The two had stood together for years on many "liberal" measures—often in lonely isolation from the mainstream of the Senate.

This so-called Morse formula, which was to plague the Senate for the ensuing several days, was not a law but an arrangement or understanding that originated in 1946 when the Senate Armed Services Committee, of which Morse was a member, was overseeing the disposal of excess federal real and personal property. The formula provided that public bodies should pay 50 percent of the fair appraised market value for federal land being conveyed for public use purposes, while private individuals, groups, and corporations paid the full market price. Its purpose was to keep states from obtaining excess federal land at giveaway prices.

Senator Morse, arguing energetically, announced that he would offer an amendment to S. 747 forcing Illinois to abide by the Morse formula. He wanted the state to pay half the appraised value of the whole 2,446 acres covered by the bill. His position was based on a literal reading—that Illinois would buy Tract 3 for $286,000, the going market price, but would get Tract 4 without cost. Morse warned that if the parties at interest did not agree to handle the transaction according to the formula, he would move to recommit the bill.

This new complication prompted a quick reaction on the Senate floor. Douglas and the Illinois conservationists were anxious to close the transaction, and Senators Muskie and Gruening did not relish further sessions with the bill in their subcommittee. Since the matter was one of narrow interest, both men, as fledgling senators, preferred to devote their legislative time to issues that would gain them national reputations or enhance their stature with their constituents. Muskie defended the subcommittee's work on Des Plaines:

> . . . the committee devoted long hours—indeed, I would say, in terms of the importance of this issue on the national scene, we have devoted a disproportionate amount of time, to the consideration of the issue before the Senate.

Douglas, defending the bill, denounced the Army as the villain and called its land policy "selfish." He expressed a willingness to negotiate but warned Morse that the land might be lost altogether for recreational purposes by Morse's insistence on applying his formula.

> It is simply one of the facts of life . . . that if we put this land up to the highest bidder and say the locality must meet the bids of factories and large industrial concerns, then we are going to price the recreational values of this land right out of the market, and the local authorities will be unable to meet the price even at one-half the rate.

After the opening round of debate, Douglas and Morse met in an unsuccessful attempt to iron out their differences. Several meetings between their staff aides were no more fruitful.

Debate Resumes

On August 11 Douglas and Morse again faced one another over the Des Plaines bill in the sparsely-attended Senate chamber. Douglas reported GSA's official approval (dated August 3) of the amended bill. The Bureau of the Budget, he announced, favored the Army compromise (using Tract 5). He praised Dirksen for persuading Illinois authorities to accept the compromise by which Tracts 1 and 2 were set aside for industry while Tract 3 was reserved for Illinois. Douglas reiterated his opposition to the Army offer and noted that S. 747 was not a party measure, that it was supported by both Illinois senators, by the Government Operations Committee, and by GSA, and that only Senator Morse and the Army objected to it.

He again deprecated the military opposition by hinting that the Army wanted to keep Tract 4 only because it was adjacent to the Illinois game preserve in Tract 3, thus affording rich shooting for Army officers. He had been told by committee aides that the Army had been notified of the hearing and invited to testify, but had not appeared officially. Douglas believed that the Army had refused to testify openly before the Senate Government Operations Committee, not only because its case for retaining Tract 4 was flimsy, but also because the Army was waiting for the more compatible atmosphere of the House Armed Services Committee before stating its argument.

Morse now took the floor. He again criticized the Muskie subcommittee for requiring the Army to give up land which was not clearly surplus to its needs. He pointed out the firmness of the Army's refusal to relinquish the property and reproved the subcommittee for not bringing the Senate "an adequate and thorough analysis of the is-

sue of whether the property is, in fact, needed by the Army." (He delivered this criticism at a time when both Senators Muskie and Gruening were on the floor.) It was Morse's idea that after recommittal of S. 747 the Muskie subcommittee would decide whether the Army's objection was legitimate. Also, he thought the subcommittee ought to decide how much Tract 4 was worth. Morse brought the Army's position to the notice of the Senate by inserting in the *Congressional Record* Secretary Brucker's letter of August 6 to the House Armed Services Committee.

Tempers flared as debate droned on. Finally, Douglas berated Morse for taking up so much of the Senate's time, especially in the closing days of the session when major legislation was at stake. (A number of major bills awaited congressional disposition, among them the omnibus housing bill which had been vetoed by the President in July. The Senate was scheduled to vote the following day to try to override the veto. Other legislation pending included a major labor reform bill [the Landrum-Griffin bill], aid to education, proposals for increasing the minimum wage, a highway financing bill requested by the President, and depressed area legislation.) Douglas noted that he had used only twenty minutes while Morse had spent two hours and was still talking. Morse, on the other hand, criticized Douglas for offering an inconsequential argument.

The debate finally produced an agreement to schedule a record vote the following day on Morse's proposal to recommit the bill. The motion for recommittal would be the life-or-death test for S. 747. If it carried, the bill was, for all practical purposes, doomed.

Following this agreement, Senator Muskie, who had been presiding during the first part of the debate, took the floor to try to answer Morse's questions. (It was Muskie's first appearance in the Senate as pilot of a bill.) He and Morse debated for another half hour without result.

Dirksen Endorses the Committee Bill

On August 12 the Democratic whips summoned the senators to vote to override the President's veto of the housing bill. (They failed to do so.) Immediately after, pursuant to the leadership agreement, twenty minutes was devoted to debate on the Des Plaines transfer.

Dirksen, appearing for the first time on the floor, took six minutes to explain some of his work behind the scenes and to argue in favor of the committee bill. After noting the original hope of all parties that the entire area could be transferred to the state for conservation, he explained that industrial interests had bid for the land to extend the use of the St. Lawrence Seaway.

Interested persons came here to discuss the matter with me. I had hoped that some of the land could be set aside. Out of all the conferences, out of all the meetings, the GSA which had charge and jurisdiction of the surplus land, finally decided to ascertain what it was worth. They divided the land into three parcels and took bids. On the industrial tract, they figured they could get $1,000 an acre. I thought that was a good deal, because the money goes into the Treasury. On still another tract, of a little less than 1,000 acres, they got a bid of $303 an acre.

So the Governor called me and said, "We will take that 1,000 acres and will pay $303, but I think in all fairness, since we have done a lot of developing out there, you can give us 1,500 acres, or thereabouts."

So when we got it all spelled out, what we had was a package which received the approval of the GSA. It has the approval of the Director of Conservation. It has the approval of the Committee. It has the approval of the Governor. It has my approval.

Dirksen, like Douglas, asked the Senate not to take the Army's disapproval seriously.

. . . Well, the Army will still have 32,000 acres of our land which has been removed from the tax base of the State and counties of Illinois. Considering that the Army has had 36,000 acres for 18 years, and measuring the taxes the State and counties have lost, I wonder whether anyone can ever say that there has been a giveaway.

Both Illinois senators were activated by constituent demands, as the clamor from home was insistent. The Santa Fe and its allies, chambers of commerce, business groups, fiscal men in the Illinois statehouse—all demanded industrial development. Sportsmen and conservationists—both individuals and organized bodies—demanding recognition of their claims, wrote to every senator urging support of the Douglas bill. The Army had no compelling political power in Illinois, and neither senator had anything to lose by calling the Army names. Douglas led the attack; Dirksen, merely reminding the Senate that the Army still retained large holdings, purposely limited his statement to avoid annoying Short and to keep channels open for getting additional Army land for the state.

Of the 96 senators who voted on Morse's motion, only thirteen, including Morse, voted to recommit the bill —ten Democrats and three Republicans.[6] Dirksen and Douglas, of course,

---

[6] Those supporting Morse were Democratic Senators Bartlett, Chavez, Fulbright,

along with all the members of the Government Operations Committee, voted against recommittal.

In spite of this defeat, Morse plunged ahead with his drive to trim S. 747 according to the Morse formula. This time he singled out a new "defect" in the bill—the clause which relinquished the reversionary interest of the United States. The usual clause for such transactions provided that if the state ceased to use the land for wildlife conservation (or for whatever purpose it was conveyed), title would revert to the United States. According to Muskie, Illinois had every intention of using Tract 3 for all time as a wildlife conservation area. However, since Illinois was paying the market price for it, state officers felt that they should be able to reconsider and use it for some other "more valuable" purpose if the occasion should arise. Muskie said GSA had suggested the phraseology of the reversionary clause.

In a subsequent agreement reached on the floor the language was altered, withdrawing Illinois' power to have the reversionary interest relinquished on request. A second amendment was passed restoring to the United States the oil, gas, and mineral rights in the transferred land.

S. 747 was passed by the Senate on August 12. The long debate and the arguments raised by Senator Morse resulted in minor modifications, but the heart of the bill was the same: it provided for Illinois to acquire Tracts 3 and 4. The bill contained a cut-off date of one year.

The debate—in which Douglas and Morse had been the principal combatants most of the time—had occupied the Senate for portions of three days.

Green, Proxmire, Russell, Stennis, Symington, and Young of Ohio; and Republican Senators Cooper, Prouty, and Scott.

Douglas argued for passage, saying the compromise was a happy one. Morse said he spoke for a constituency larger than Illinois—the taxpayers of the United States, the national interest. Dirksen played only a slight part in the debate as he was anxious to avoid becoming entangled in Senator Morse's arguments and being forced into upbraiding the Army. He felt that sooner or later the Army would have to relinquish most of its holdings around Joliet, and Dirksen wanted relations to be amicable so that he could ask for, and hope to get, the additional land. Muskie received praise for his first effort at piloting a bill through the Senate. Leaders of both parties complimented the freshman senator.

Reaction to the Veto Possibility

Even though the House had taken no further action on the Des Plaines land, a presidential veto already loomed as a real possibility to advocates of the Senate bill—which was not general legislation, had limited appeal, and was opposed by both the Army and the Budget Bureau.

Dirksen, as Senate Republican leader, continued to figure in the negotiations even after the Senate had passed the bill, and his office was the target of many requests to help avert a presidential veto. One letter came from the persistent Zebell, the Democratic conservationist.

Zebell wrote on August 20, saying that conservationists and club members were "highly appreciative" of Dirksen's efforts on Des Plaines, including his floor appearance. Apropos of the veto threat, he suggested that Dirksen get in touch with President Eisenhower and pass along this message: "The President should be made aware of the fact that we are not just a bunch of bird watchers, and enough public interest has been generated by this issue that a veto would be writing Illinois off to the Democrats in the 1960 election." Zebell promised that the Will County Newsletter would convey to the club members the full story of Dirksen's efforts if the senator were able to "bring this controversy to a successful conclusion."

Zebell's August Newsletter carried a 400-word story on Senate passage under the head "WAR ON THE PRAIRIE." The story referred twice to the efforts of "faithful Senator Douglas," but did not mention Dirksen. A forthright letter from Dirksen's special assistant was sent on August 27 calling the omission to Zebell's attention.

> I know the Senator is pleased to have your letter about his assistance in the Des Plaines Wildlife Area but I personally am somewhat confused.
>
> I enclose a copy of your latest publication and I note that you apparently overlooked that assistance in reporting to your full membership. . . . Senator Dirksen who while he may not be so faithful at reporting his actions for publicity, does have quite a record for getting things done.

Early House Action Urged

Douglas now tried to stir the House to act on the Des Plaines bill before Congress adjourned. He wrote to Representative Price on August 14 that the bill had passed the Senate with bipartisan support, and asked for Price's continued help. Douglas also called on the Illinois sportsmen to request House action. He wired constituents: "YOUR HELP WILL BE REQUIRED TO ASSURE HOUSE PASSAGE." A few days later (August 17) he wrote Floyd Zebell: "I hope you will let the House know of your interest and urge support for House passage."

Zebell, on his own initiative, suggested in his August Newsletter that club members could facilitate House passage by a series of letters.

> Just write a letter to one of your relatives in another state, explain the problem to them, and ask them to write to their U.S. Congressman and ask them to vote for this bill when it is voted on in the House. Then write the President and ask that he sign the bill. Of course, you also write to our Congressman (Noah Mason), and the President.

There was ample time for the House Armed Services Committee to schedule hearings during that session. However, Douglas' requests to the committee chairman, channeled through Representative Price (a member of the committee) and Representative Charles Boyle of Chicago, brought no satisfaction. Chairman Vinson explained that the Army's unequivocal objection precluded action during 1959. The Army's position "is sufficiently firm to indicate to me that the bill would be faced with a recommended veto by the Army if it should be passed," he told Boyle in a letter of August 19. Vinson, considering the Army objection to be serious, postponed action to give the parties time to negotiate.

The chairman's view indicated that Army disapproval would be more influential with the Armed Services Committee than with the Senate Government Operations Committee. Price found himself in a dilemma. As a long-time member of the House committee, he shared its traditional support for the Army. But he was also a staunch friend of the Illinois conservationists and was anxious to help them. Moreover, he felt that since the Conservation Department had maintained the Des Plaines land for ten years and proposed to preserve it as a hunting and wildlife area, its disposition was a matter of interest to the entire state. Price's first reaction was to blame the Army for obstruction. He said as much in an interview with the *Chicago Tribune* on August 20, explaining that the Army threat to recommend a veto caused the committee delay.

Price planned to deal personally with the Secretary of the Army and with Short. He would point out to them that they could counteract the Army's bad publicity in Chicago by giving in gracefully on Tract 4. Unaware at this time of Short's earlier visit to Chairman Vinson, Price did not realize that Vinson had agreed to support the Army. When Price recognized the futility of trying to alter the Army's position and Vinson's, he began to modify his own views about Tract 4.

The Recess:
Illinois Pressure Builds Up

After Congress recessed on September 15, Douglas and his allies in Illinois worked to fan grassroots sentiment in favor of the Senate bill. The conservationists had reported their dissatisfaction with Tract 5 in June. Douglas now feared, however, that the veto threat and (in his view) the absence of strong leadership from Governor Stratton would induce the conservationists and sportsmen to give up the fight and accept the Army's compromise. He therefore tried to keep their enthusiasm high, and urged them to pelt Army officials and House members with letters.

The Illinois conservationists and sportsmen were disposed to take Douglas' advice. The Des Plaines fight, assuming a symbolic importance in their minds, was seen as a battle that had to be won lest greedy industrial interests seize other lands then reserved for conservation and recreation. Two Chicago newspapers, the *Daily News* and the *Sun-Times,* reflected this sentiment and urged the conservationists to stand fast.

This effort to rally Illinois interests achieved a measure of success in the autumn of 1959. According to orientation, inclination, or instruction, various individuals wrote letters to the Army, to House members, and to the Illinois Conservation Department. The department's mail was of two sorts: a majority of the letters supported the Senate bill; some few favored the Army compromise as a realistic solution. Many correspondents praised Senator Douglas for his unyielding support of the conservationists' position.

In their first reaction to the Senate victory, the various Illinois interests—the sports groups, industry, and the statehouse—found the Senate solution thoroughly satisfactory. By this time the Illinois Legislature had appropriated the funds to pay for Tract 3. The Conservation Department was willing to risk a veto over Tract 4, and Palmer wired the Illinois delegation in the House to support the Senate bill.

The Palmer Plan

Through the autumn of 1959 Palmer became increasingly upset at the shape the Des Plaines controversy was taking. The Senate bill was entirely satisfactory to him as a settlement of the conservation problem, but he found it politically unsatisfactory. In the first place, the Army's opposition represented a veto threat, and he could get no assurance from Dirksen that the Army would alter its position. Second, S. 747 was considered a Douglas bill, a Democratic Party measure. The Price bill would clearly be the House vehicle and it, too, would wear the Democratic label. Since Governor Stratton might seek a third term, party labels on Illinois legislation in Congress began to assume greater importance.

With these considerations in mind, Palmer decided in early December to throw his support to the Army compromise (the gift of Tract 5 and limited use of Tract 4).

Specifically, Palmer was concerned over the deluge of mail coming into his office and the amount of political glory Senator Douglas was harvesting by maintaining his solicitous attitude over conservation lands. He revealed his worries in a letter (of December 31, 1959) to Dirksen:

I am attaching hereto copies of various letters, petitions, and news clippings which are representative of the thousands we have received in this office.

The Illinois Federation of Sportsmen's Clubs, the Illinois Izaak Walton League and many, many other organizations are supporting our request for this land.

It appears that Senator Paul Douglas is receiving much glorification in news articles, etc., and I believe we should take every step to overcome this.

The possibilities for political gain were not lost on Senator Dirksen. Not only were he and Governor Stratton fellow Republicans, but Dirksen's own term of office was due to expire in 1963, and re-election, if he were to seek it, would be considerably easier with a Republican administration in Illinois. He began to cast about for ways "to overcome" the Democratic advantage.

Dirksen saw a chance to siphon off

some of the Democratic credit by disposing of Des Plaines by administrative action. His idea was to trade the Senate bill for the Army's compromise and then arrange for GSA to transfer Tract 5 to Illinois. He notified Palmer of his plan in a letter of January 8, 1960. After reviewing the law and the facts, Dirksen stated his conclusion that administrative settlement was best. Believing the Army would soon declare Tract 5 surplus, he advised Palmer to prepare a formal request to GSA for the land. Dirksen sent a similar letter to Floete, and, at the same time, wrote Assistant Secretary Short to ask that the Army transfer Tract 5 administratively rather than by the protracted congressional process. He argued that congressional handling might take many more months, crowding his own tight schedule and occupying the scarce time of other members.

Meanwhile, Palmer moved to reduce the feverish pitch the Illinois sportsmen were maintaining. He worked through George Eve, Republican committeeman of Cook County, who was president of the Cook County Council of the Illinois Federation of Sportsmen's Clubs in Chicago. Palmer disclosed his strategy to Eve in a letter of February 2, 1960.

. . . I know that Senator Dirksen is very interested in the transfer of the area to our Department for the benefit of the sportsmen, and believe he is going to try and come through. I feel he should be given opportunity of accomplishing this transfer, and added letters to our Congressional delegation could possibly hinder his efforts rather than being helpful. I would suggest we sit tight until April 1 and if it appears that he cannot get the transfer made, I will call on you fellows for all of the help possible.

Eve readily agreed to call a halt to the letter-writing campaign.

However, the administrative details of Army transfer of Tract 5 to GSA were not completed immediately. The political situation, as Palmer saw it, caused him increasing anxiety. Writing to Dirksen on February 4, 1960, he ascribed the bulk of the trouble to Floyd Zebell, whom he called a Democratic agitator. He said he had "fired" Zebell as department law enforcement officer of the Department of Conservation,[7] and also confided to Dirksen that the Des Plaines transfer was laced with politics.

> This matter [the political issue] the average sportsman does not know about, therefore, when he sends such letters statewide as he has been doing, the members of the various clubs do not realize it is done strictly for political purposes but believe that he [Zebell] is a crusader with the interest of the sportsmen at heart. This is one of the reasons, Senator, that I am so anxious to have this transaction completed as quickly as possible, and the purchase of Parcel 3 that we are to buy in order to get the additional acreage.

Palmer asked Dirksen to hurry the transfer so that he, Palmer, could make a dramatic announcement when he addressed a convention of the sports groups on March 27. "There is nothing that I can conceive of that would do more for the Republican Party in Illinois as the completion of this transaction."

Palmer began to see villains everywhere. A week later (February 11) he wrote Dirksen that the Army was postponing declaring Tract 5 officially surplus in order to give Representative Price a chance to amend S. 747 to conform to Army wishes. He again told Dirksen the matter was urgent.

> Naturally, Senator, we want this area and will accept it regardless of how we get it, but if humanly possible, I hope you can have the transfer completed for us without any amendment from Mel Price and, God knows, any assistance from Douglas. We want Senator Dirksen and the Republican Party of Illinois to receive full credit for the transfer of this property.

The Illinois
Sportsmen Accept a Compromise

Palmer and Dirksen received an unexpected stroke of luck. During January and February of 1960, while they were trying to bring about administrative transfer of Tract 5 and at the same time keep the Illinois sportsmen quiet, Representative Price was also working toward the same general goal. When Price had assured himself that the Army would not give up Tract 4, that it based its stand on military requirements, and that it had the firm support of Armed Services Committee Chairman Carl Vinson, his enthusiasm had begun to ebb. Since the Des Plaines area was hundreds of miles from his own district in the southwestern part of the state, its disposition was not a matter of close concern to his constituents. Furthermore, he knew all too well that it was useless to buck the Army and the chairman of the Armed Services Committee; when they were united, they represented an almost invincible combination. Price, therefore, aiming for congressional—not administrative—settlement, began to work out plans to amend his bill.

Price's letters to Illinois conservationists and sportsmen began to take

---

[7] Both Zebell and the Director of Conservation, Glen Palmer, agreed that the termination of Zebell's job was political. Zebell said he was "forced to resign" because his job headquarters was transferred away from the Joliet area. Since he didn't want to move, Zebell said, he obtained other employment.

on a different tone around December 1959. He told correspondents he was convinced of the Army's genuine need for Tract 4 and suggested that the sportsmen would be wise to accept the compromise offer of Tract 5—the compromise was a sure thing, but a bill conveying Tract 4 ran a considerable risk of a presidential veto. He expressed this opinion to Floyd Zebell in a letter of January 6, 1960:

> Under the Army's proposal, only tracts No. 4 and No. 5 are involved. . . . The position which the Army takes is that tract No. 5 would be conveyed in fee to the State while tract No. 4 would be used by the State under a permit in the following fashion: full utilization of the tract all through the year with the exception of weekends (when Reserve training is being carried on) and during the pheasant season.

> I will express it as my personal idea in view of the strong position taken by the Army that it will be extremely difficult to report out and pass S. 747 in its present form. In view of this, it would be my recommendation that your organization give serious consideration to the acceptance of the Army proposal which, so far as I can determine, represents a reasonable compromise and one which would in great part satisfy the needs and interests of the two interested parties.

At the same time Glen Palmer was repeating the same advice to the sportsmen and conservationists. He pictured Tract 5 as more attractive than they had originally rated it. He also counselled them on the virtue of getting and holding a bird in the hand—Tract 5—and continuing the effort to get the more desirable tract later.

The conservationists and sportsmen, after reflecting on this advice—but without checking their decision with either Senator Douglas or the national conservation organizations in Washing-

ton—concluded that they should accept the Army substitute and try for Tract 4 in the future. Among those who agreed were two of the staunchest supporters of the Senate bill, Floyd Zebell and Bob Cary, columnist for the *Chicago Daily News* and vigorous spokesman for conservation. In mid-January they communicated their decision to Price, putting three conditions on their acceptance: (1) the bill was to specify that Illinois would buy Tract 3 (they were worried by its omission from the language of the Army offer); (2) the Army was to convey Tract 5 without charge; and (3) the Army was to go on record that the sportsmen could use Tract 4 on a limited basis. Zebell said that officials of local, state, and zone conservation organizations all accepted the Army offer.

Price, reassuring the sportsmen, wrote to Cary on January 20 that ". . . there is no reason why Tract No. 3 could not and should not be included in the overall plan for this conveyance." He then offered some advice on how to conduct an effective grassroots campaign, suggesting

> . . . that all interested parties get together and make a formal proposal along this line to me and to the GSA [with respect to Tract No. 3]. Naturally, any such proposal must have the official sanction of the State, and I would expect that "all interested persons" actually include everybody who has a personal or official interest in this matter.

Dirksen Reaches for Credit

In the middle of February, Dirksen, annoyed that the Des Plaines settlement continued to drag on, telephoned Dewey Short. He had begun to suspect that the Army was not enthusiastic about transferring Tract 5 by administrative act, and he asked Short how the settlement was proceeding.

The Army's legal staff had advised Short that Tracts 3 and 5 could be conveyed by administrative action but warned that such action might constitute a precedent for disposing of Tract 4. If Tracts 3 and 5 were transferred administratively, Short, who wanted to protect Tract 4 at all costs, feared the Army would be under continuous pressure from the Douglas forces to relinquish it in the same manner. Two other considerations led the Army to take a firm stand against administrative handling: the attitude of the Illinois sportsmen, who preferred a legislative transfer; and the idea that an act of Congress would look open and aboveboard, whereas administrative handling might be criticized as underhanded.

Trying to keep peace with Dirksen, Short brought his aide and a representative of the Army's General Counsel to the Senator's office on February 17 to present the Army's side of the story. Short explained once more the importance to the Fifth Army of keeping Tract 4 and his own unwillingness to override General Arnold. He repeated to Dirksen his regret at being unable to help.

As soon as he got back to his office, Short drafted a letter to Dirksen again setting forth the Army position. The Army was willing to cede Tract 5 to Illinois, he said, but preferred to have the matter handled by statute rather than by administrative action. He asked that the bill omit any reference to Tract 4 but "assured" Dirksen that the Army would make the tract available for recreation and wildlife purposes year-round, with the exception of weekends and a two-week summer training period.

Dirksen was annoyed at what he construed as Short's recalcitrance. Not only did the Army embarrass him by

clinging to Track 4; it even refused to handle the compromise by administrative action. Forced to accept this state of affairs, Dirksen acted immediately to salvage what credit he could for the compromise and for the Republican part in working it out. He released information on the "final settlement" in a letter of February 18 to Stratton, authorizing the Governor to publicize the contents. Dirksen summarized the past negotiations in such a way as to give himself the principal credit for achieving the settlement. He attempted to link his name to the substitute proposal then being developed.

> I am now assured that the Army will assent to legislation along the line which I proposed in my testimony before the Senate Committee on Government Operations . . .[8]

The previous year, he continued, he had made a formal proposal, the Dirksen amendment, which he described as follows: that GSA would sell the two northern parcels to industry and that thereafter Illinois would buy Lot 3 and receive "without compensation an additional tract for conservation purposes, which is customarily referred to as Tract 5."[9] He continued:

> In addition, the Army has assured me that it would permit the State to use the adjacent 1500 acre tract at all times when it is not necessary for training exercises. . . .
>
> I know how deeply you and the Director of Conservation are interested in this matter and likewise the various

---

[8] In his appearance before the Senate committee in 1959, Dirksen had said that the Army could well afford to give up a plot of land to compensate the conservationists for loss of Tracts 1 and 2. He had not presented any formal proposal then.

[9] Dirksen's amendment actually had referred to an entirely different tract.

sportsmen's groups in the state. I have, therefore, undertaken to pursue a course that would achieve maximum conservation and recreation benefits for the sportsmen of the state and at the same time do nothing that would invite a veto . . . because a veto could terminate all our hopes for this Session after so much work has been done on this project. We have nursed it along for more than three years, and I want to see this consummated as soon as possible.

Dirksen also told Stratton that the chairman of the House Armed Services Committee, as well as the ranking Republican (Illinois Representative Leslie Arends), approved the compromise.

Privately, Dirksen was disappointed at the Army's refusal to sanction administrative settlement. "As you well know," he wrote Palmer on February 19, "politics gets into wildlife." He explained that S. 747 was totally unacceptable to the Army and that the Army could make a veto stick. "You know very well that if the Army asks the President to veto a bill because its terms interfere with the Army's training program, the President will accede."

The announcement of the outcome was made in Illinois. Stratton announced "final settlement" of the Des Plaines dispute at a press conference on February 24 in Springfield. Palmer at once formally petitioned GSA to sell Tract 3.

Senator Douglas learned of the "settlement" from the newspapers. He immediately issued a statement, carried by the *Chicago Sun-Times,* condemning it as a "surrender." He described Tract 5 as totally unacceptable for hunting, recreation, or use as a wildlife refuge. He said he was asking Price to support the Senate's bill, and also called on the Illinois sportsmen "to take appropriate action."

In Washington, however, Congress and the Pentagon failed to act promptly on Des Plaines, dashing Palmer's hope of claiming credit for his party. When he addressed the Illinois sportsmen's annual convention on March 27, he played Des Plaines in a low key, only reporting the facts of the situation— the bill the Senate had passed, the impossibility of getting the same bill through the House because of Army opposition, and the attempt then under way to substitute Tract 5 for Tract 4.

Des Plaines Still Stalled

March passed, then April, without any final disposition of the Des Plaines land. The Illinois sportsmen grew increasingly restive, especially those who had heeded the suggestion of George Eve that they remain quiet while Dirksen tried to work out a settlement. They mounted a fresh letter-writing campaign to members of Congress. Many of the sports publications and newsletters, including that of George Eve's group, the Cook County Council, took on a militant tone. The Council's May issue noted that after the two-month silence the time had arrived for club members "to pull out all stops and get as many letter-wires or calls to our Senators asking—nay DEMANDING them to move this bill to the Senate floor at once . . . remember NOVEMBER is X time."

Similar letters and messages pressing for fast action on the Army compromise were sent to Representative Price. Rumors were hatched during the long delay, including one reaching Floyd Zebell that the Army planned to doublecross the sportsmen by allowing use of Tract 5 on a permit basis only. Price promptly assured Zebell that the Army offer was genuine and watertight.

House Hearings

The House Armed Services Committee scheduled hearings on the Des Plaines bill for May. The proponents of the various points of view had largely become reconciled by this time—with the exception of Douglas, who alone opposed the swap of Tract 5 for Tract 4.

The Armed Services hearings began May 11 and continued for two days. The bill being considered was S. 747, as modified by the Senate. Price, who presided as acting chairman of the real estate subcommittee, noted that the "single most important consideration" was the Army's objection.

One of the principal witnesses was Senator Douglas, who urged the subcommittee to enact the Senate version. He pointed out the desirability of having the two contiguous parcels (Tracts 3 and 4) and the importance of setting aside a recreation area. He again suggested that the Army objected to yielding Tract 4 because the generals used it as their private pheasant preserve. He was supported by three Illinois congressmen, Representatives Church of Evanston (Republican), O'Hara of Chicago (Democrat), and Derwinski of Chicago (Republican), all of whom advocated enactment of the Senate version. Representative Noah Mason, Republican of Oglesby, who represented the 15th District (Joliet and environs), took no public position on any of the Des Plaines bills but opposed any solution that resulted in a financial loss to the United States.

Senator Douglas considered his reception by the subcommittee to be courteous and correct but not cordial. He felt he was speaking for the record —nothing more.

The Army Testifies

Assistant Secretary Short entered into the record the Army's objection to S. 747. In a review of his department's position, he noted that the Army had advised the Senate Government Operations Committee on June 18, 1959 of its military requirement for Tract 4—for training reserve units —and hence could not sanction the transfer. The Army had consistently opposed such a transfer from the time the matter was first broached, Short stated. Furthermore, plans had been made and announced publicly for the release of Tract 4 without notice to the Army.

> I want to make it clear for the record now once and for all . . . that at the time this so-called compromise involving Tract No. 4 was first revealed to Congress, the Army had not been approached concerning it; and further that the Department of the Army and the Department of Defense at no time agreed that Tract No. 4 could be made available for transfer to the State.

The Army had not been invited to appear at the Senate hearings, he said, "though the interested Senators knew our opposition to S. 747." (The plan to substitute Tract 4 had not taken shape at the time of the original Senate hearings.) Finally, Short reported, the Army would not object if the bill were amended to substitute Tract 5 for Tract 4, and the Budget Bureau would support such an amendment.

The conservation voice was represented by the executive secretary of the Illinois Federation of Sportsmen's Clubs, Royal McClelland. The clubs preferred the Senate bill, he said, but would accept the compromise "because we are somewhat reluctant to go to war with the United States Army." Three national conservationist organizations, the Izaak Walton League of America, the Wildlife Management Institute, and the National Wildlife Federation, took the same position.

C. R. Gutermuth, however, went farther than any other witness in attempting to assess the political realities of the situation. He expressed the belief that if Senator Dirksen and Governor Stratton, important figures in the Republican Party, had "made a strong enough case that this legislation would be enacted and the bill would not be vetoed."

Gutermuth introduced two additional points into the testimony: (1) the Army should be persuaded to promise formally to give Tract 4 to Illinois for conservationist use once the Army's need ceased; and (2) the original Douglas bill (ceding Tracts 1, 2, and 3) was the ideal solution and could have been enacted if industry had tried to find alternate sites. "You have miles of private land up and down both sides of that river that are just as suitable for industrial purposes as that particular tract."

Representative Price's statements in the course of the hearing indicated that he—and perhaps the entire subcommittee—favored the final Senate version of S. 747. He felt, however, that the Army's need for Tract 4 was genuine and that the only practical solution was acceptance of the Army compromise. The committee's position was this, he said: "If the Army feels strongly about it,—if they were requested [to make] a recommendation after the legislation passed the House and when it went to the President's desk for approval or disapproval, it would appear to me that their recommendation might be adverse and then we would lose everything."

The representative of the Joliet Association of Commerce, hoping for fast action, said the Army proposal was the safest and least controversial. "We would like to see this matter resolved as quickly as possible for two reasons . . . we have lost two industries and will continue perhaps to lose more industries unless the controversy is settled."

Within two weeks the Armed Services Committee endorsed the subcommittee and reported out S. 747, amended to substitute Tract 5 for Tract 4. The committee exacted a price in the form of a loose commitment that the Army would eventually turn over Tract 4 to Illinois. The committee report, issued May 18, documented the "understanding."

> It is the Committee's further understanding that should the Army's need for Tract No. 4 cease at any time in the future, strong and sympathetic consideration will be given to the conveyance of this tract also to the State for wildlife conservation and recreational purposes.

Price told the sportsmen that a "legislative statement" carried a great deal of weight, since the Army must come to the Armed Services Committee every year for its legislative program.

Several members of the full committee, aware of Senator Douglas' low opinion of the compromise, stated firmly that House conferees should oppose any Senate attempt to get Tract 4 back into the bill. Chairman Vinson expressed the committee's position: ". . . we will not consider any amendment with reference to the 1500 acres, No. 4, without further hearing."

With Price in charge, the amended committee bill passed the House June 6 on a voice vote. There was no discussion.

On June 17 Dirksen notified the sportsmen that he was trying to get the Senate to adopt the House amendment, thus avoiding a conference, and by the end of June he informed them that the Senate had agreed. Dirksen took the occasion to claim once again that the bill (ceding Tract 5) was "substantially the same" as the substitute he had introduced the previous spring.

Douglas wired Illinois supporters that he agreed reluctantly to accept the compromise. It was useless to struggle further, he said. He cited these factors: the Army's objection, the "opposition" of the state administration, and lack of support from all quarters. "Had I received more thoroughgoing support we might have been able to win but in view of the actual situation there was nothing to do but acquiesce. At least we have saved something."

The bill became law on July 12, 1960, and within a week GSA announced plans to dispose of Tracts 1 and 2 on a publicly advertised, competitive bid basis. With the legal difficulties settled, Floete contended, the two parcels should command a higher price than in 1959.

Reaction among Illinois sportsmen and conservation people was mixed. Some considered any settlement a victory and a triumph over bureaucratic inertia. Others adjudged the outcome a partial victory only, made palatable by the hope that Illinois would eventually get Tract 4 if ever the Army should release it. Still others viewed the transaction as a political shakedown of the conservationists by a flaccid state administration and an inflexible Army.

One of those most disappointed was the outdoor reporter for the Chicago *Sun-Times,* Jack Griffin, who wrote on July 7, 1960 that the compromise was "reached with a club." He noted that the two tracts were one and one-half miles apart, separated by U.S. 66, often a "hazardous" road.

Some sportsmen's clubs, either through misinformation or in an attempt to impress members with their power, have called this a victory. This is not a victory. It is a defeat, an outrageous disregard for thousands of Chicagoans who found pleasure in the big area. . . . The victory went to the Army and private industry, which started all the fuss in the first place.

Griffin was critical of the state administration's lack of effort:

But despite constant assurances from Palmer that the state desired the area, his boss, Governor Stratton, made no attempt to help in the Washington hearings and Senator Everett Dirksen (R-Illinois) actively opposed all proposals to keep the two tracts together. . . .

Aftermath: 1961

Within a few months Illinois took title to the two properties. The Army carried out its part of the bargain when it signed a quitclaim to Tract 5 on August 17, 1960. Shortly afterward (September 6) GSA turned over Tract 3 for the agreed purchased price of $286,000.

Final disposition of Tracts 1 and 2 required a longer time. When GSA asked for a new round of bids, the Santa Fe emerged as the principal bidder but this time made an offer considerably lower than its previous one of $1,058,780 for the two parcels. In addition, it tied the bid to a request for a right-of-way easement across Tract 3. Although GSA attributed the drop in the bid price to a nationwide slump in real estate values, it was reluctant to accept the offer. Consequently in December it asked once more for bids. When they were opened in March 1961, the Santa Fe offer of

$1,096,960 was accepted by GSA.

Assessing the settlement, the two Illinois senators continued to hold differing views. Dirksen called the settlement acceptable and said he was proud of his part in bringing all parties to agreement. He felt the conservationists were wise to accept half a loaf, as he had counselled them, rather than none.

Douglas, considerably chagrined over the outcome, indicated that he planned to continue his effort in 1961 to get additional land from the Army for park and recreational purposes and wildlife conservation use.

Postscript: 1962

Actually, efforts by both Douglas and Dirksen to obtain more conservation land for Illinois continued through early 1962, when this study was completed. This time there were Democratic administrations in both Washington and Springfield. Each senator's object was now the same—to get Tract 4—but they virtually exchanged strategies.

In 1961 Douglas began negotiations with the Department of the Army to obtain Tract 4 for Illinois. On October 31 the Department reported to the Senate and House Armed Services Committees that it no longer needed the land. A 4,000-acre tract in the Joliet Arsenal had become available to the Fifth Army, which preferred to use the larger area for reserve training exercises.

Douglas had kept the Illinois sportsmen and conservationists informed of his efforts. Telling them that Tract 4 was now surplus, he urged them to ask the new Democratic Governor to apply to GSA for the land. The state filed a formal request with GSA, and Douglas expected the transfer to be effected early in 1962.

On January 18, 1962, however, Dirksen announced on the Senate floor that he was introducing a bill, S. 2704, directing GSA to convey Tract 4 to Illinois for wildlife, conservation, and recreation purposes. Dirksen said he believed that the state stood a better chance of getting the land by an act of Congress than by administrative action. (Both Dirksen's bill and the GSA application would grant the land to Illinois without cost.)

Douglas disagreed, fearing that the Morse Formula might again be invoked, since the bill called for recreational development of the tract. "We have every reason to believe the Defense Department and GSA will approve [an administrative] transfer," he said.

> Introduction by Senator Dirksen of this bill may delay the GSA from effecting the transfer. . . . Under the present financial condition of the State, this [payment of one-half the market value of the land] will be impossible for the State to meet. Now that we have a State administration which, unlike the preceding administration, is anxious to acquire the land, the best way to handle this matter is to let the transfer take place by administrative order, without cost to the State.

Douglas also thought that Dirksen's bill was motivated by purely political considerations. (Dirksen was expected to run for re-election in the fall.)

Dirksen, unperturbed by the criticism, claimed that Douglas was piqued because the initiative had been taken away from him.

FIVE

The Presidency

U. S. Bases in Spain

THEODORE J. LOWI

Editor's Note: This case was prepared as part of a research project on civil-military relations in the United States, sponsored by The Twentieth Century Fund and directed by Professor Harold Stein of Princeton University. It will appear in the forthcoming book, American Civil-Military Decisions: A Book of Case Studies, published in 1962 by the University of Alabama Press for The Twentieth Century Fund and The Inter-University Case Program, and edited by Harold Stein. It is reproduced here, with slight modifications, by permission of the copyright owner, The Twentieth Century Fund.

Introduction

On August 25, 1953 Senator Pat McCarran was presented with the Grand Cross of the Order of Isabella La Católica by the Spanish Ambassador, José Felix de Lequerica, "for his efforts to improve Spanish-American relations." One month later the first military-economic agreement between Spain and the United States was signed in Madrid.

McCarran's decoration symbolized a critical feature of five years (1948 to 1953) of Spanish-American relations: the role played by Congress in bringing about an important shift in foreign and military policy. In 1948 the United States had no ambassador in Madrid, and there were no plans to include Spain in American aid programs. Two years later action was underway—and

was completed in 1953—to include Spain among the recipients of United States economic aid and to make her an important link in Western defense policy.

Led by Senator McCarran, Congress brought an entire spectrum of political techniques successfully to bear on a reluctant Truman administration. Large sums of money were voted gratuitously to Spain; strong public pronouncements were registered in favor of Generalissimo Franco and his country; spokesmen of the administration were badgered in public hearings; officers and civilian officials of all branches of the armed services were encouraged in hearings and meetings to publicize the tactical and strategic importance of Spain; and the issue was

265

surcharged with growing fears of the Communist threat. With the support of key members of the two houses of Congress, the issue of United States military bases for Spain was placed upon the policy agenda of the Truman administration and kept there until action was taken.

In resisting the shift, the administration bargained with the arguments which, until 1948, had proved effective in justifying the policy of avoiding close or friendly relations with Spain. President Truman and Secretary Acheson emphasized the Fascist origin and nature of the Spanish government. They pointed to the delicate balance of the Western Alliance which might be upset by the slightest hint that the United States was inclined toward European defense behind the Pyrenees.

However, during the period from 1948 to 1953 the entire fabric of international relations changed. Anti-communism replaced anti-fascism as the most popular, as well as the most realistic, issue of the day. And economic reinforcement—the Marshall plan—was replaced or augmented by military containment, the consequences of which were fully realized in Korea. Within the new context emerged a substantial, then irresistible, Spanish bloc made up of elements hitherto small and fragmented. (Much information about the internal politicis of the moves to secure the Spanish bases remains unknown, because much of the vital discussion took place in the privacy of the National Security Council and the Joint Chiefs of Staff and within the military services. Thomas K. Finletter, who served during this period as Secretary of the Air Force, characterized the Spanish problem as "something special, like a separate stairway.")

Acheson aligned himself with the proposal for bases in Spain late in 1950. To him the Spanish question had been "magnified by controversy to a position among our present-day foreign problems which is disproportionate to its intrinsic importance." Without Acheson, President Truman remained for many months practically alone against his entire administration. Long after the new Spanish policy had been established with presidential approval, the President continued to express his distaste for it. Nevertheless, the President, albeit reluctantly, had acquiesced in a series of actions which, taken cumulatively, amounted to a national decision.

Background and Setting

At the close of World War II the victorious allies cast uncharitable eyes toward Spain and its military dictator, General Franco. Franco's equivocal neutrality had kept his country out of the war, but his opportunistic flirtations with the Axis had wounded the allies far too deeply for the salve of his latter-day cooperative overtures, and the bitter memories of the tragic Spanish civil war were still vivid.

President Roosevelt expressed the feelings of all the allies on March 10, 1945 in a letter to Norman Armour, the United States Ambassador to Spain. (The style of the letter suggests that it was drafted in the State Department, but there is no reason to doubt that the President knew what he was signing.)

> . . . Having been helped to power by Fascist Italy and Nazi Germany, having patterned itself along totalitarian lines the present regime in Spain is naturally the subject of distrust. . . . Most certainly we do not forget

Spain's official position with and assistance to our Axis enemies at a time when the fortunes of war were less favorable to us, nor can we disregard the activities, aims, organizations, and public utterances of the Falange, both past and present. These memories cannot be wiped out by actions more favorable to us now that we are about to achieve our goal of complete victory. . . .

The fact that our Government maintains formal diplomatic relations with the present Spanish regime should not be interpreted by anyone to imply approval of that regime.

As you know, it is not our practice in normal circumstances to interfere in the internal affairs of other countries unless there exists a threat to international peace. The form of government in Spain and the policies pursued by that Government are quite properly the concern of the Spanish people. I should be lacking in candor, however, if I did not tell you that I can see no place in the community of nations for governments founded on fascist principles.

A year later, on March 4, 1946, the governments of France, the United Kingdom, and the United States, after a series of discussions on relations with Spain, issued a joint statement. In language almost identical with that of Roosevelt's letter, the three governments expressed hope for a peaceful change of regime in Spain and an opportunity for the Spanish people to choose their own government and leaders.

The new United Nations followed suit. At the San Francisco Conference, ending in June 1945, a resolution was adopted barring from membership those "States whose regimes have been installed with the help of military forces which have waged war against the United Nations, so long as those regimes are in power." At the Potsdam Conference of July 17, 1945, President Truman joined with Churchill and Stalin to state that they would not support a request by Spain for admission to the United Nations.

There was some question, however, just how far beyond a United Nations blackball the United States was willing to go in order to encourage reform in Spain. In 1946 Poland presented a resolution calling for UN members to sever all relations with that country. The United States position was presented by its delegate, Senator Tom Connally, before the Political and Security Committee of the General Assembly. The United States, said Connally, believed that the Spanish people should determine their own destiny and would "welcome any democratic change in Spain which protects basic human rights and freedoms." The United States would continue to oppose UN membership for Spain. However, it would also oppose any "coercive measures [against the Franco regime] by the United Nations, such as severance of diplomatic relations or the imposition of economic sanctions," because it was thought that such measures would either unite the Spanish people behind Franco or precipitate disorder within Spain.

On December 12, 1946 the General Assembly adopted a resolution—a compromise between the Polish and American positions—recommending that (1) Spain be debarred from membership in the United Nations and all its agencies, (2) all members immediately recall their ambassadors and ministers plenipotentiary, and (3) the Security Council consider further measures to remedy the situation if a more liberal government were not established in "a reasonable time."

The United States had had no ambassador in Spain since the withdrawal of Norman Armour in December 1945.

To implement the new resolution, the United States simply left the American Embassy in Madrid in the hands of the Chargé d'Affaires, Paul Culbertson.

The United States resisted later attempts to strengthen the original resolution. A November 1947 resolution calling for a reaffirmation of the original ambassadorial ban—to stop the gradual flow of ambassadors back to Spain—was not passed, primarily because of the abstention of the United States. The United States backed a second resolution which expressed the confidence of the General Assembly in the Security Council's judgment to take measures against Spain when such action was required.

Bases In Spain: The Campaign Begins

The story of the Spanish bases began the next year, 1948, in spite of a climate that made even the notion seem preposterous. Both the country and the administration were in a period of transition from the let-down and adjustment of the immediate postwar years to the growing realization of a new phenomenon, the "cold war." The Washington merry-go-round was spinning busily to a dozen different tunes, among them atomic energy, unification of the armed services, and the second session of the 80th Congress. Much of the administration's energies centered around new involvements in foreign relations. Serious congressional debate of the new European Recovery Program (ERP), often called the Marshall Plan, began in January, and the program ran into heavy weather right away. In February eleven European nations signed the Brussels Pact, forming the Western European Union. Shortly thereafter, the United States began conversations with these European countries and Canada about regional security and self-defense arrangements that were soon to lead to the formation of the North Atlantic Treaty Organization (NATO). Of immediate attention at home were the well-publicized hearings of the House Un-American Activities Committee which reached a climax when Whittaker Chambers accused Alger Hiss of previous Communist Party membership and activities. Finally, a presidential election was imminent—the first in years that was not dominated either by the shadow of war or depression or by the commanding figure of Franklin D. Roosevelt.

To understand how and where Spain fitted into this crowded agenda, it is necessary to review the problems of some of those agencies which participate in the making of foreign policy in all its aspects—political, economic, and military.

Postwar Business at the Pentagon

In 1948 the head of the Department of Defense, James V. Forrestal, was beset with overwhelming burdens. Mediating the demands of the three armed services, unreconciled to unification, was proving to be more than a man-sized task, and Forrestal was torn by his desire to pacify factions and still develop a new, balanced defense force. Concerning military policy, as reflected in budgetary terms, Forrestal was also torn between the threat of a possible third World War, the demands of preventing it, and the characteristic postwar budgetary cuts demanded by the President and Congress.

The basic issue was often expressed in terms of the peacetime "defense force in being." In the past it had been national policy to slant the peacetime defense budget in favor of the Navy while depending on emergency measures to rebuild a deteriorated Army and Air Force in the event of war. However, the once natural geographic reasons for this pattern of allocation were hotly questioned after World War II.

Spain held a low priority—if any at all—on the Air Force agenda, for the Air Force at this time was cool to the idea of a string of foreign bases. A minimum of 70 combat groups was being urged (rather than the 55 the Air Force already had), including an enlarged strategic air arm with 100 B-36 "intercontinental" bombers. Intercontinental striking power, especially intercontinental delivery of the atomic bomb, would obviate further dependence upon foreign bases. Also, it would be politically unwise to press simultaneously for funds for bases and for B-36s. Air Force leaders certainly wanted the B-36s first.

The Department of the Army, on the other hand, was preoccupied primarily with the *ignis fatuus* of universal military training and the achievement of a total force of 822,000 men instead of the 782,000 provided for in the Forrestal plans for the coming fiscal year. To add to the confusion, the Joint Chiefs of Staff (JCS) unanimously reported on April 14, 1948 that an 837,-000-man Army would be required—under the new concept of a *balanced* military establishment—to make the Army commensurate with a 70 air-group program.

Additional complications piled up at this time when JCS began to consider what United States relations should be with the Western European Union, recently established by the Brussels Pact. The Army, particularly, was reluctant to assume any responsibility for the defense of Europe unless any agreements with the European powers at least left open the possibility of using the military potentialities of both Germany and Spain. Later, after the creation of NATO, the Army lost its interest in Spain (though not in Germany). NATO's military aspects became primarily an Army project involving decisions on the number and placement of military personnel in Western Europe. In brief, the Army's task in Europe was to build a defense of the entire continent from Western Germany to the sea, not even to consider defense behind the Pyrenees; the possibility of using Spanish troops was either forgotten or shoved aside.

The Navy Department was cool toward universal military training, and it feared the "empire-building" tendencies of the Air Force and the Air Force's lack of emphasis on foreign bases. During 1948 there was a running quarrel between the Air Force and the Navy over "operational control" of atomic bombs. For the Navy to "perform some of its primary missions," some provisions were required for the delivery of atomic bombs, thus pointing to the need for the proposed giant carrier capable of launching atomic bombers.

Naval personnel were particularly aware of weaknesses in the Mediterranean and its Atlantic entrances. Great Britain held the most important bases in the area, those in Gibraltar, Malta, and Egypt. To have a predominant position in the inland sea and the approaches to it, the United States Navy had to have bases of its own. With the build-up of the Sixth Fleet, the Navy greatly feared being bottled-up in or sealed out of the Mediterranean. Moreover, the Navy could hardly bargain with Great Britain over control of the Mediterranean fleet under the North Atlantic Treaty if it had no bases of its own in either the nearby

Atlantic or the Mediterranean. Consequently, the Navy looked warmly upon the Spanish ports of Cadiz and El Ferrol and the North African coastline.

Secretary Forrestal's own leanings were strongly toward the admirals. Because of his previous service as Secretary of the Navy, Forrestal had taken office as Secretary of Defense holding many of Navy's fears of unification, which were reflected in the National Security Act of 1947 (though the responsibilities of office soon changed his mind, as the amendments of 1949 demonstrated). He counted as absurd an imbalance in favor of the Air Force. This, he contended, would mean a plan based on a massive air offensive from Great Britain, a position that might lead to war rather than prevent it.

Furthermore, Forrestal was very much concerned about Middle East oil supplies. Although his appraisal of the importance of this oil was to change drastically later, in 1948 he felt that no precaution should be overlooked in "securing the Mediterranean line of communications."

The State Department, the Election

At the State Department, the problems were just as large and complex. In a letter to Secretary of State George C. Marshall dated October 31, 1948, Forrestal addressed a number of questions in hopes of getting Marshall's guidance in accommodating the Defense Department's allocations to President Truman's $15 billion defense ceiling. Specifically, the questions were: "(a) Has there been an improvement in the international picture which would warrant a substantial reduction in the military forces we had planned? (b) Has the situation worsened since last spring and should we, therefore, be consider-

ing an augmentation? (c) Is the situation about the same?"

Marshall's answer came a week later from Paris. It evaded the real issue of defense requirements—or, at least, gave Forrestal no help—by stating simply that the international situation had not changed in the past eight months. Marshall insisted that the important task was to re-arm Western Europe; consequently, the energies of the State Department would be devoted to the Marshall Plan, just then reaching fruition, and NATO, just then being born.

Marshall had often urged rescission of the UN ban on ambassadorial exchange with Spain. While in Europe, he had actively sought a change of heart in the British and French governments through their foreign ministers. However, bases and ambassadors were entirely separate in the mind of General Marshall. In view of the hostility of the NATO nations toward Spain, and in view of their fear of a policy of defense behind the Pyrenees, it would have been folly to press for Spanish participation in the Marshall Plan even though the plan itself did not include military aid.

In Washington preparations were being made for a presidential election. Prospects were not good for the Democrats, and many members of the Truman administration had practically conceded defeat. President Truman was an implacable foe of Franco Spain, but for the moment he held his peace. He also secured—and quite possibly sought—some domestic political advantage from a bit of diplomatic maneuvering with Spain that could cause no harm and might even be useful. On March 30, 1948 Myron C. Taylor, President Truman's representative to the Vatican, stopped in Madrid en route to Rome. Taylor had instructions to inform General Franco by what means he could gain the acceptance of the Western governments, but it was asserted by some that the visit was intended to demonstrate to American Catholics that the Truman administration was in a conciliatory mood toward Spain.

The Spanish Lobby

In 1948 the Spanish Foreign Ministry began a campaign to change the administration's policies. Overwhelming economic problems were forcing drastic revisions in the Spanish view of the outside world. Since the loss of its once vast overseas empire, Spain had not known decent living standards. Almost ten years after the end of the devastating civil war, the Spanish worker was twice as poor as he had been before, if figured by any accurate statistical standard. The country was plagued by three severe afflictions: inflation, increasing population, and decreasing productivity.

In 1948 it was painfully obvious that Spain was to be the only country in Western Europe without some form of aid from the United States. Further, it would be damaged, in relative terms, by the projected European Recovery Program. The vicissitudes of an American election year encouraged Franco to try to improve Spain's position. The result was "the Spanish Lobby."

Responsibility was given to Senor Don José Felix de Lequerica, an able, experienced diplomat. During the early months of 1948, Lequerica (with the title Inspector of Ministries) became in effect chief of the Spanish delegation in Washington. Through him the Spanish Foreign Ministry sought the aid of interested congressmen in getting the right person to represent its interests. It retained the services of Charles Patrick Clark, a man under 40 who was already regarded as an old-timer in Washington circles. An honor graduate of Georgetown, Clark had served on the staffs of several congressional committees and government agencies. His major distinction, as he took pains to point out, was his war service with the Truman Committee to Investigate the National Defense Program.

It is impossible to measure exactly the influence of interest groups and skilled public relations men in such a complicated milieu, but the Spanish cause began to improve almost immediately after Clark became a part of it. He mobilized effectively the groups that coalesced to form the Spanish Lobby.

Pro-Spanish support came primarily from five separable but overlapping groups. The first might be called the Catholic group. It was made up of some of the most ardent Spanish supporters, such as Senator Pat McCarran (D) of Nevada, Senator Joseph McCarthy (R) of Wisconsin, Representative Eugene J. Keogh (D) of New York, Representative Alvin E. O'Konski (R) of Wisconsin, and others. Very close and partially identical to this group was the extreme anti-Communist group, which viewed Spain as the most zealous anti-Communist nation in Europe and probably the only "reliable" ally in the cause. The third cluster, pro-Spanish bases, was composed in part of Admirals Richard L. Conolly, John H. Cassady, and Matthias B. Gardner, and Secretary of the Navy John L. Sullivan and his successor, Francis P. Matthews. Although most of these men were Catholics, they would no doubt have sought Iberian bases regardless of religion. As the months passed, they were joined by hosts of senators, congressmen, and bureaucrats. The fourth group could be called simply the anti-Trumanists, led by Senator Robert A. Taft (R) of Ohio, a Republican policy leader.

Growing anti-administration feeling brought to the support of bases in Spain Senators Kenneth McKellar (D) of Tennessee, Owen Brewster (R) of Maine, Styles Bridges (R) of New Hampshire, and others. The fifth group was economic, and was led by southern cotton interests. Taken together, these elements gave the Spanish Lobby a surprisingly bi-partisan, supra-sectional, supra-religious, and supra-economic appearance.

Moreover, the identity of some of its congressional members gave the Spanish Lobby, from the beginning, unusual status. For instance, four members, Senators McCarran, McKellar, Bridges, and Brewster, were well-known to the general public, outspoken in defending their conservative views, and members of important Senate committees. All came from one-party states and had seniority in the Senate.

The two Democrats, McCarran and McKellar, were especially influential. In their long tenures in the Senate they had often opposed liberal policies recommended by Presidents Roosevelt and Truman. Pat McCarran, born in 1876, had served as associate justice and chief justice of the Nevada Supreme Court. Elected to the Senate in 1932, he had become a member of the Judiciary Committee and since 1943 had been its chairman when Democrats had a majority in the Senate. McCarran was also a member of the Appropriations Committee; in fact he was chairman of the appropriations subcommittee that reviewed State Department budget requests. Kenneth McKellar's re-election in 1946 made him the only senator from Tennessee ever to serve six terms. He was the senior Democrat on the Senate Appropriations Committee and a member of its subcommittee that reviewed State Department requests.

In March 1948 the Spanish Lobby's first big opportunity arose. The first Economic Cooperation Act implementing the Marshall Plan was on the floor of the House of Representatives, and Representative O'Konski introduced an amendment making Spain one of the participating nations. In a surprising show of support, the House adopted the amendment 149 to 52, but later it was killed in House-Senate conference. Undoubtedly, the sudden burst of support for Spain was due in part to the pressures of an election year. But the surprisingly large vote gave warning in all circles that a basic reappraisal might be necessary.

The Spanish Lobby missed its opportunity in the 80th Congress, but the fight had just begun. On September 30, 1948 Senator Chan Gurney (R) of South Dakota held an hour's interview in Madrid with General Franco. Gurney, Chairman of the Senate Committee on Armed Services, was one of the powerful members of Congress on military legislation. He was accompanied by the United States Chargé d'Affaires in Spain, Paul Culbertson, and several United States military officers. However, when the time came for the interview, Culbertson was left in the waiting room while private discussions were held between Gurney and Franco. When he emerged from the interview, the senator said that he favored "complete re-establishment of all relations between Spain and the United States."

On October 5 Senator Gurney, back in Washington, held conferences with Secretary Forrestal and the three service secretaries: Kenneth Royal, Army; John Sullivan, Navy; and Stuart Symington, Air Force.

Although the opposition to the administration's Spanish policy had now formed, its activities were muffled for the rest of 1948 by the presidential election. The operations of the Spanish

Lobby did not go into high gear until the 81st Congress and the administration of President Truman—now elected in his own right—took office in 1949. The results of the 1948 congressional elections had implications for the cause of closer relations with Spain. The Democrats took control of both the House and the Senate, making Senators McCarran and McKellar the chairmen of, respectively, their chamber's Judiciary and Appropriations Committees. Also, a Joint Committee on Foreign Economic Cooperation was formed in the 81st Congress. Its membership included McCarran and Bridges.

With the advent of a new administration the story of United States bases in Spain splits into three concurrent strands of events, separate but interrelated. These three phases, treated separately in the remainder of the narrative, reflect different though overlapping types of activity on the part of the Spanish Lobby: (1) a congressional drive to vote United States aid funds for Spain; (2) activities by some congressmen and military officials to prod the executive branch into recognizing Spain and including it in Western defense plans; (3) developments within the executive branch which, encouraged by supporters of Spanish bases within the executive, weakened the opposition of the Secretary of State and then the President to closer relations with the Franco government.

Phase One: Congress Votes Money for Spain

The sudden burst of Spanish support in 1948 could be attributed in part to election-year fever, the lenient attitude of Secretaries Marshall and Forrestal toward Spain, and the formation of the Spanish Lobby. After the 1948 election the anti-Spanish bloc, though weakened, was still a majority. With respect to the Spanish cause the most important post-election change was the replacement of Marshall as Secretary of State by Dean Acheson. Acheson, while serving as Under Secretary of State, had been instrumental in formulating the Truman Doctrine and the Marshall Plan, and, as secretary, promptly worked for the establishment of NATO. Particularly sensitive to the problems of European economic and military cooperation, he was in sympathy with the Spanish policy expressed in 1945 and 1946. In 1949, as the new Secretary of State, Acheson helped revivify the established Spanish policy in the executive branch because, or primarily because, a change might adversely affect NATO and ERP.

Acheson's earliest expression on Spain came on May 5, 1949 before the subcommittee of the Senate Committee on Appropriations, meeting for hearings on State Department requests for the next fiscal year. First, with respect to ambassadors, Acheson said, the United States was bound to honor the United Nations ban as long as it stood. Second, since the United States never had severed diplomatic relations with Spain, the lack of an ambassador was a trivial point. Third, concerning money, Spain was welcome to apply to the Export-Import Bank like any other nation. Fourth, Acheson concluded, the rest was up to Spain and the Western allies; Spain would have to liberalize its government and be accepted unanimously by the allies before we could enter into closer relations. On May 11, one week later, Secretary Acheson strengthened his position by stating that the UN ban on ambassadors, though not in itself so important, had "become a symbol" to all the Western democracies.

Although Acheson had President Truman's full backing, the primary reason for the President's opposition was simpler and more direct: Franco had come to power on the coat tails of the Axis and was continuing to follow Fascist patterns of religious and political persecution. Consequently, in response to a July 1949 attempt in Congress to include Spain under the Marshall Plan, Truman went beyond his Secretary of State. The President said simply that the United States opposed the step because relations between the two countries were "not friendly." The situation had not been stated so bluntly since the immediate postwar period. Senator Taft, in exasperation, called on the administration to "shake loose from its Communist-front philosophy" and grant full recognition to Spain.

The Line Officers

Meanwhile, outside of Congress, another source of support for Spain was building up, the significance of which was not appreciated at the time. As was said above, the Navy had been in stiff competition with the British for predominance in the Mediterranean and the nearby Atlantic, and the fight for control increased in 1949 as a consequence of the organization of the fleets under a single NATO command. To prevail, the American Navy needed bases independent of the British and strategically located with respect to both oceans. A glance at the map was enough to appreciate Spain's strategic allure. Floating facilities or mooring rights in Spain bespoke of few political difficulties as far as the Navy was concerned. No construction would be necessary and no United States military personnel would have to be stationed on the Spanish mainland.

Admiral Richard L. Conolly, Commander of the United States Naval Forces in the Eastern Atlantic and Mediterranean, took the first forthright step toward breaking the Spanish ice. Between 1947 and 1949 Admiral Conolly had made repeated requests for permission to take units of the fleet to pay courtesy calls on Spanish ports. These requests were blocked by the State Department until September 1949, when the President (presumably on Acheson's recommendation) authorized an informal visit, which Conolly described as "informal but official." American warships entered a Spanish port for the first time since the civil war on September 3, 1949. There they remained, at El Ferrol, for five days. When Admiral Conolly called on General Franco, who was at his summer headquarters nearby, he was accompanied by four admirals, an Air Force general, an Army general, and the United States Naval Attaché in Madrid, Captain Preston V. Mercer. Captain Mercer, who served under Culbertson, the Chargé d' Affaires, had often openly criticized the policy of the United States government toward Spain.[1]

Conolly's visit was authorized as a test of Franco's intentions and as a feeler of American and European public opinion. No specifics were discussed, and no commitments were made. Conolly and Franco exchanged civilities and discussed problems of mutual interest.

---

[1] In April 1949 Mercer had decided at the last minute to accompany Culbertson on a trip to the United States. This had given rise to widespread speculation that the State Department was making a full-scale review of its policy toward Spain. Acheson, preoccupied with NATO, had not moved to scotch this rumor until his May statements discussed above.

When Admiral Conolly returned to United States in October, he conferred with the White House and with interested members of Congress. The President was not displeased with Conolly's report, which included the fact that Spain was eager to cooperate with the Western powers. However, the core of the President's opposition to Spain still remained. Before the House Armed Services Committee Conolly made a strong plea for naval bases in Spain. "The strategic importance of the Iberian Peninsula is uniquely evident," he reported. Furthermore, "The more friends you have on your flank the better."

The State Department's leaders stood firm. They feared that any friendship with Spain would imperil the Western alliance, soon to be NATO. They had predicted that Conolly's visit was going to cause great furor at home and abroad, but the expected tempest turned out to be a spring squall. Although much of the Western press reaction was unfavorable, it had little of the expected invective and denunciation.

The Conolly visit was not the only evidence of revolt by the line officers against the President's Spanish policy. Other naval units were soon to follow, the first one shortly after the Conolly visit when a task force of the Sixth Fleet paid a call at Barcelona. Another potential dissent was registered when Admiral Forrest P. Sherman requested permission to include Spain in a tour of Europe shortly after his appointment as Chief of Naval Operations in November 1949. The request was not approved. In these activities, Conolly and Sherman had the open support of Admirals Cassady, Gardner, and Robert B. Carney. The Sixth Fleet had turned its big guns on Washington.

Rumblings were also heard from the Air Force. Nine months before Conolly's well-publicized visit, Major General William H. Tunner, chief of the Berlin airlift, had paid an inconspicuous visit to Madrid. Following his visit, General Tunner had been host in Wiesbaden to a party of Spanish officials, including Lieutenant General Apolinar Saenza de Burnaga, Spanish Under Secretary for Aviation.

The exchange of visits between General Tunner and the Spanish officers was part of a more general movement in the Air Force to revise strategies. Like the Navy, the Air Force had developed a pattern of collaboration with the British in the use of RAF bases, primarily on the British Isles. In 1948 arrangements were made for still greater direct use of the British bases. At the same time, there were misgivings that such arrangements would not entirely fulfill the fundamental means of defense against aggression: (1) the general policy of containment; (2) the military axiom of having as many friends on the flank as possible; (3) dispersion of the acutely concentrated base locations of all United States services; and (4) closer proximity all the time to the Soviet Union. Secretary Forrestal encouraged the reappraisal in his fear that over-concentration courted hot war and that lack of suitable bases could mean loss of access to the Middle East.

Two countries were considered well suited for air bases: Spain and French Morocco. Both would require economic and military bolstering, plus the outright construction of military installations. But, whereas the Navy considered mooring rights in Spain a simple matter, the Air Force could foresee insuperable problems of politics and utilization. Morocco, on the other hand, while in essentially the same radius as Spain, was both outside the realm of attention of American political liberals and (at that time) inside the legal shadow of the French Union. For the time being, the Air Force passed over Spain and landed in North Africa, although the makings of Spanish support did not disappear.

The Junketeers

By the fall of 1949, Spain had indeed achieved a new status in governmental circles. This was indicated by the sheer number of congressional junketeers whose itineraries included Madrid.

Charles Patrick Clark led the way. Both his and the congressional visits were a direct result of Admiral Conolly's trip, showing how closely all parties were attuned to possible changes in the official stand. Clark spent several weeks in Spain during September and October, traveling extensively and talking with influential and usually inaccessible Spaniards. On his return, Clark wrote a lengthy report "as requested" to his former superior, the President. This report, dated November 10, 1949, concerned freedom of worship in Spain, specifically as applied to Protestants.

Of the several authorities Clark cited, the most interesting was Max H. Klein. On the basis of his twenty-seven years as president of the American Chamber of Commerce in Spain, Klein attempted to answer the many adverse reports which had been appearing in American newspapers and journals. In part, Klein said, "Protestantism is not a problem in Spain."

> Confining myself to Barcelona, where I usually live, I can be quite definite in saying that the Protestant community is not persecuted and they are free to worship according to their beliefs. In the past years I have several times attended services at the Protestant Chapel and have many friends who attend them regularly without the slightest difficulty.
>
> Spaniards are great individualists and are apt to be very undisciplined. There is just one issue on which they are practically all agreed and that is their religion. Why should we attempt to destroy that unity?

One fact omitted in this report was that Klein himself was a Catholic.

Ending his report to the President, Clark said:

> The writer, in discussing the question of religious freedom, with General Franco, stated that he might have the pleasure of visiting with the President on his return, and, if he should, he would like to take back an expression of General Franco's feeling regarding the religious situation, as well as other matters. The writer would prefer to discuss the Chief of State's message orally. The writer arrived at certain conclusions which he would also prefer to give orally.

The meeting with the President never occurred. But Clark's report and conclusions gained currency in many other circles, predominantly congressional.

At the time Clark was making his survey, many prominent senators and congressmen were visiting Spain. On September 14 Senator McCarran departed for Madrid, announcing to the press that it was his intention to discuss the loan question with Franco. On September 15 President Truman issued a sharp statement that McCarran went as a private citizen and did not represent anyone in the administration.

Following closely on McCarran's heels were Representative James J. Murphy, a New York Democrat, and seven associates. After an interview with the Spanish leader, Murphy said that General Franco impressed him as a "very, very lovely and lovable character." At about the same time, another batch of legislators arrived in Spain including Senator Brewster, and Representatives James P. Richards (D) of South Carolina, Eugene J. Keogh (D) of New York, Noble J. Gregory (D) of Kentucky, and W. R. Poage (D) of Texas.

On November 27, 1949 members of an important subcommittee of the Senate Appropriations Committee arrived in Europe for a five-week tour: Senators Dennis Chavez (D) of New Mexico, John Stennis (D) of Mississippi, Edward Thye (R) of Minnesota, John McClellan (D) of Arkansas, Willis Robertson (D) of Virginia, and Elmer Thomas (D) of Oklahoma. They agreed unanimously on return from Spain that full diplomatic relations should be restored as soon as possible and that some form of economic aid should be granted. Chavez went on to insist that this should also include military aid to Spain to "bulwark Western Europe's security." The flow of important visitors to Madrid continued.

From the standpoint of the administration, however, matters were getting out of hand. This public courtship of Spain was tending to give the wrong impression. Thus, on December 3, several administration supporters on the House Foreign Affairs Committee departed for Spain. On December 11 Representative Joseph L. Pfeifer (D) of New York told the press that where Spanish-American relations were concerned, ". . . it is a matter not simply for the United States to settle. It is in the last analysis a question for Spain and the Spanish people to settle." (Pfeifer was echoing Secretary Acheson's words.) He also warned that Spaniards had given undue weight to the pronouncements of certain individual members of Congress and that

no individual could speak for the entire body. Concurring in this report were Thomas Gordon (D) of Illinois and Clement Zablocki (D) of Wisconsin.

The Spanish press denounced the Pfeifer statement as "offensive and impertinent." And for good reason, in the context of 1949. The major effect of congressional activity of 1948 and 1949 had been to obstruct and frustrate the President's personal animus and the administration's general coolness toward an unreconstructed Spanish regime. Why should Franco yield to the remonstrances of Myron Taylor, Paul Culbertson, Dean Acheson, *et al.,* if he had the encouragement of growing numbers in Congress, from Senators Gurney and McCarran on down?

Congress Takes the Lead

The congressional stage was set. On January 18, 1950, shortly after the opening of the second session of the 81st Congress, Senator Tom Connally of Texas (Chairman of the Senate Foreign Relations Committee), at his request, received clarification of the Spanish policy from Acheson. The contents of this letter will be considered in some detail in a later section, but, for its importance to the legislative process, certain points must be mentioned here.

Acheson explained that the United States policy of withdrawal of ambassadors from Spain "as a means of political pressure was a mistaken departure from established practice." Entirely aside from the present view of the Spanish regime, the United States, said Acheson, was in favor of rescinding the UN ban on ambassadors, but as long as the resolution stood, the United States was obliged to comply with it. However, he reaffirmed the administration's opposition to providing money to Spain to use as it saw fit. Spain would not be discriminated against at the Export-Import Bank, which loaned solely on the basis of need, the merit of the purpose, and the prospect of repayment.

In a sense the Spanish cause had taken the legendary one step forward and two steps backward. While the administration was willing to restore Spain to full diplomatic status, it had reaffirmed its opposition to extending the generosity of the United States to Franco. To give access to American money only through the Export-Import Bank meant in effect no access at all. Spain was unable to offer guarantees of any kind in return for loans. Even its supporter Argentina had curtailed economic assistance in the face of Spanish insolvency.

In the spring of 1950 a series of public attacks on the administration's Spanish policy began, made by congressmen of both parties. (Congressional criticism of the foreign policies of the Truman and Roosevelt administrations was generally intense during this period. Accusations of softness to communism and of responsibility for the loss of China to the Communists were not uncommon.) Owen Brewster delivered the first lengthy attack of the session on March 10, 1950. It was clear by now that the emotional or ideological factor—most notably in the President himself—was the chief barrier to be overcome, and Brewster concentrated his fire in that direction. He stressed, first of all, Spain's important role in World War II, especially in keeping open the western end of the Mediterranean. On the religious problem he quoted Max Klein at length. (By this time, Mr. Klein's name, as an authority on Protestantism in Spain, had become almost a household word.)

The lengthiest exposition in Spain's favor came in June from South Carolinian James Richards, Chairman of the House Foreign Affairs Committee. Richards reaffirmed his faith in Acheson and the administration in general, and Yalta and China in particular:

> At no time in the history of any other government has greater vision or initiative been shown.
>
> There is, however, to my mind, at least one glaring weakness and inconsistency in the foreign policy of the United States. I refer to our attitude toward Spain.

Richards made an earnest attack upon the basic premises of the administration's policy. For each of the President's points concerning Spain's degraded economic and political practices, Richards offered counterpoints, citing countries where the United States did not bother to inquire into such matters before entering into full relations. On the general problem of religious freedom, Richards drew upon the researches of Brewster and Representative Abraham Multer (D) of New York —a close friend of Charles Patrick Clark—who had earlier delivered a speech on the Jewish problem in Spain. All three presentations bore similarities to points in Clark's report.

Senator McCarran Takes Charge

Speeches notwithstanding, it was Senator McCarran who led the way by positive action for Spain in this session. On April 27, 1950 he secured the support of 35 of his colleagues for his unsuccessful amendment to the Economic Cooperation Act authorizing a loan to Spain of $50 million. There was less support for this amendment; unlike previous attempts, it mentioned a specific amount of money. Although this second attempt to put Spain into the Marshall Plan was defeated, there was every reason for optimism. Support for Spain was growing. Moreover, the State Department had weakened on an important point—the UN ban on ambassadors. Diplomatic representation was viewed as the preliminary but inseparable stage to full economic, political, and military rapprochement with Spain.

At the very moment when the pro-Spanish forces were being organized for still another attempt, the Korean War broke out. After the initial surprise passed, the Spanish bloc made preparations. In July, less than a month after the North Korean invasion, McCarran called an unpublicized meeting in his office. It was attended by a few senators and a small group of military representatives from the Pentagon. No names were disclosed "for obvious reasons," the senator reported later.[2]

McCarran announced to the slightly uneasy guests that he planned to introduce another bill in Congress for a Spanish loan, this time for $100 million. The senator then turned the meeting over to the military officers, who repeated generously the strategic arguments that had already been furnished to congressmen for the ever-growing number of floor speeches. The meeting and other individual contacts between members of Congress and the Pentagon occurred without either the express sanction or disapproval of the Defense Department secretaries.

Whatever solid opposition remained in Congress after the Korean outbreak was dispersed during the following few weeks. For, immediately after Korea, there came an urgent demand from the administration for aid to Marshal Tito and the passage of the Yugoslav Emergency Relief Assistance Act. In spite of important distinctions between the Yugoslav and Spanish situations, which the State Department took special pains to point out, the simplest and most immediate impression was that of inconsistency. If the United States could aid one dictator without approving of his political methods, it could aid another on the same basis.

On August 1, 1950 the first Spanish loan was pushed through the Senate. It was a painful defeat for the administration. The vote was overwhelmingly favorable, 65 to 15. Even the Senate Democratic leadership defected to the majority. In a meeting of the Democratic Policy Committee just prior to the vote, Senator Connally and his pro-administration colleagues had decided to capitulate. Scott Lucas (D) of Illinois, Senate Majority Leader, attempted to explain this move to the press on August 4. "We had to make a deal. I don't care what any Senator or anyone else says. I'm a realist, and when I'm licked, I don't hesitate to admit it."

Passage of the $100 million Spanish loan was regarded as the result of shrewd maneuvering. First of all, the bill had been attached as an amendment to the first General (Omnibus) Appropriations bill, which would have to be accepted or rejected *in toto* by the President. Second, none of the proposed ECA funds would be used. The loans were to be made by the Export-Import Bank and administered by ECA, but the money was completely above and beyond the ECA appropriations. Thus the amendment was designed to remove all cause for alarm by the allies, who had expressed fears that Spanish aid could come only at their sacrifice.

On August 3 a motion was entertained to reconsider the Spanish loan amendment. By the same vote, 65 to 15, the motion was tabled—a scant few hours after Truman had publicly

---

[2] Pat McCarran, "Why Shouldn't The Spanish Fight For Us?" *Saturday Evening Post,* April 22, 1951, p. 25.

denounced the loan. His denunciation, obviously, had had no effect.

Throughout August the fate of the Spanish loan lay in the hands of the House-Senate conference, where this minor item was only one of many differences between the House and Senate versions of the Omnibus Appropriations bill. On August 24 the conference report was presented to the House. The House conferees accepted the principle of the Spanish loan at a reduced sum of $62.5 million. In return, the Senate accepted the House demand for a cut in the Point Four (technical assistance) appropriations from President Truman's request of $26.9 million to $15 million and the complete elimination of money for the United Nations Children's Fund.

In response, the President sent a strong appeal for restoration of the full amount for Point Four. House floor leader John McCormack did not read the President's message; he inserted it in the record without comment.

On August 25, with unusual dispatch, the House approved a $34.1 billion omnibus appropriation by a vote of 165 to 90. The bill included the Spanish loan and the full $26.9 million Point Four appropriation. No administration leader spoke against the "mandatory" loan to Spain; no Republican leader spoke against full restoration of the Point Four program. The Senate approved the conference report on August 28 with a minor amendment, and later that day both houses approved the final version by voice vote. The Spanish loan had ridden in on the coat tails of Point Four.

On September 6, 1950 President Truman signed H.R. 7786, the General Appropriations bill. But he gave warning in his accompanying statement that he would withhold the Spanish funds indefinitely. He refused to consider the loan "mandatory"; it was no more than an "authorization."

> Money will be loaned to Spain whenever mutually advantageous arrangements can be made with respect to security, terms of repayment, purposes for which the money is to be spent, and other appropriate factors, and *whenever such loans will serve the interest of the United States in the conduct of foreign relations.* [Emphasis added.]

With this statement, the President set the stage for the later phases of the fight for bases in Spain. Before the United States government would relinquish money liberally to Spain, it would have to have a plan by which the United States would gain something substantial in return.

Phase Two: Congress Urges Executive Action

Until the official policy of the United States administration changed, congressional measures would be of relatively small importance. Truman's statement that the loan was considered an "authorization" and not a "mandate" confirmed earlier fears of the Spanish Lobby that after all was said and done in Congress, the route to Spain had to pass through the doors of the executive branch. Consequently, the congressional fight for financial aid to Spain was only one phase of the battle with the administration.

Money in Search of Policy

Secretary Acheson was the focal point of the barrage. In fact pressure on Acheson for a change of policy began over a year before the monetary victory. Spain was one of the several reasons for the growing unpopularity of Acheson with Congress.

The attack on Acheson was led by his constant assailants, Senators Mc-Carran and McKellar. On May 5, 1949 the subcommittee of the Senate Committee on Appropriations met for hearings on State Department requests for the next fiscal year. The matter of ambassadors arose first, and the cross-examination showed how neatly appropriations hearings could be turned to substantive questions of policy:

Senator McCarran: Mr. Secretary, during the course of these hearings there will come up in this bill the matter of diplomatic items. I should like to ask you why it is that this country refuses to recognize Spain.

. . . .

Senator McKellar: Mr. Chairman, I may say that I feel exactly as you do about our nonrecognition of Spain . . . Spain is a Christian nation and we have had friendly relations with her. She has been a good customer of ours. She has usually paid her debts. I see no reason why we should not have friendly relations with Spain. . . .

. . . .

Secretary Acheson: Senator, I tried to state a moment ago that, acting under this recommendation of the General Assembly, we have not appointed an ambassador.

. . . .

Senator McCarran: Are we to be enslaved to the UN? I never voted with that in mind.

. . . .

Senator McKellar: Neither did I.

. . . .

Senator McCarran: Let me say to you, Mr. Secretary, that so far as I am personally concerned as chairman of this subcommittee I am not in favor of your policy with reference to Spain and until that policy is changed I am

going to examine your appropriations with a fine tooth comb. . . .

The senators' cross-examination then went on to the question of Spain's place in United States security.

Senator Saltonstall: . . . If nonrecognition of Spain is the policy of the Department of State now, I assume it is based on our security because of the attitude of other nations in Europe toward Spain and our wanting to work along with them. Is that a fair statement?

Secretary Acheson: Senator, I think we ought to be very clear that there is no policy of nonrecognition of Spain.

Secretary Saltonstall: I emphasized the word "security."

Secretary Acheson: . . . So far as security is concerned, you are entirely right. Spain is a very important element in the security of the United States, and that is why it is so important and why we have been doing our best to bring about what I call a reintegration of Spain in the west.

In order to bring Spain into a system of collective security in the west, it must be by common agreement. You cannot get Spain into a thing such as the North Atlantic Treaty without some resolution of these difficulties with the other countries. There has to be common desire and common understanding.

. . . .

Senator McKellar: I am in hopes that you will be diplomatically friendly to Spain hereafter. I think it ought to be done. Spain is a great country as far as we are concerned, and just as important as any other western European country so far as our defense is concerned, and so far as our protection is concerned, and I hope you will look into it and change it. I am sure you will.

Senator McCarran: He did not answer you in the affirmative, Senator.

. . . .

Senator McCarran: [A few minutes later after several other topics had been covered.] . . . Is not the Iberian Peninsula on which Spain exists essential to the full success of the North Atlantic Pact?

Secretary Acheson: It is very important. The pact can be successful without it; it can be stronger with it. . . . I do not think we ought to pretend there is any mystery about this. As I said at the outset, this is the result of history. Now it is no secret that the Spanish regime was a fascist regime. . . . At the end of the war . . . it was the idea that this type of authoritarian government was out. However, it has gone on in Spain.

What the western Europeans want is some movement toward the relaxation of those oppressive measures, which is not an unreasonable thing to want and which could be accomplished very easily. If you could bring together the western Europeans and Spain on some basis of mutual adjustment, the problem would very largely be solved.

The highest military authorities were coming in for their share of congressional inquiry also. The substantive congressional committees—particularly the Armed Services and Foreign Relations Committees of the Senate— were attempting to marshal a large body of professional opinion in support of closer relations with Spain. Although the military chiefs were by no means willing to make a public commitment to that effect, it was hoped that the hearings would provide some of the military supporters of Spain with a politically important channel to present views which, until the very last, were unpopular among the chief formulators of foreign policy—the State Department, the National Security Council (with the exception of the Secretary of Defense), and the White House.

Secretary Louis Johnson, who headed the Department of Defense from March 1949 to September 1950, was the chief force behind military planning on Spain. But in 1950 it was still a behind-the-scenes job, and in answering a congressional query on Spain's role in case of war, Johnson replied, "I know that everyone does not agree with my ideas about Spain. I still have the same ideas. I would like to discuss them with you in executive session."

George C. Marshall, who succeeded Johnson as Secretary of Defense, was in a particularly difficult position in view of his support before the 1948 presidential election for improved relations with Spain.

Senator Russell: . . . What are your views on agreement with Turkey or with Spain, or other nations that might be in a position to contribute to the defense of Western Europe?

Secretary Marshall: As to Spain, that is quite a delicate international diplomatic question today. For the Defense Department I would not care to make any comment at this time.

Senator Russell: I thought perhaps since you have served as Secretary of State you would be able to comment from that standpoint. We have had the Secretary of State before us and he has replied that there are a good many military questions involved, and you say it is a question of diplomacy. I had thought, perhaps since you had served in both capacities you might give us the answer.

Secretary Marshall: When I walked out of the door of the State Department I ceased to be Secretary of State very definitely, and a great deal of water has gone over the dam since then.

As a consequence of these probings, the sides of the growing controversy emerged all the more clearly. How long were the "delicate international diplomatic questions" referred to by

Secretary of Defense Marshall to take precedence over singularly pressing desires to push the boundaries of United States defense farther away from its shores? On the one side were those who feared that, although Spain would undoubtedly add to Western military strength, this strength might be more than neutralized by an eventual loss of morale and unity among the allies. There were also some who feared that bases in Spain might prove no more solid than castles in Spain.

On the other side was what was becoming a congressional majority, arguing that Spanish bases would be firm bastions and that any losses of morale among the European allies would be more than compensated for by the collaboration of the most reliable of anti-Communist powers. In the uncomfortable middle remained Marshall, Navy Secretary Matthews, Generals Omar Bradley (Chairman of the Joint Chiefs of Staff) and J. Lawton Collins (Army Chief of Staff), Admiral Sherman, and many other top officials in the Pentagon. The President's obduracy had bound them—some of them were probably also uncertain about the net advantages of a new Spanish policy—and they had, at least, to refuse to be open parties to congressional polemics. Instead, they spoke of the desirability of Spanish affiliation only in terms of a "military point of view," and they shunned the larger question of evaluating the overall effect of Spain's inclusion in the Western alliance.

President Truman's answer to the "mandatory loan" had, however, left the door to policy change ever so slightly ajar. It must be shown that aid to Spain would indeed be beneficial to the United States, and already a majority in Congress believed that such was the case.

Even before the first Spanish loan had been put through the Senate in August 1950, and before President Truman had stated that a *quid pro quo* was essential, Senator Harry Cain (R) of Washington had declared:

> To my mind, it is impossible to separate Spain from a study of the North Atlantic Pact. Those responsible for strategic planning do not hide the fact that they believe that Spain is essential to the reliability and effectiveness of the North Atlantic Pact.
>
> To all intents and purposes Spain is a huge airfield of 195,000 square miles surrounded by water. Its sea coast has many ports and natural first class naval bases. . . .

After the loan was put through, the Spanish bloc did not sit back to enjoy victory. On the day of Senate passage two senior senators, one from each side of the aisle, advocated a military arrangement on just such a "mutually beneficial" basis as Truman spoke of a month later when he declared the loan not "mandatory." Senator Styles Bridges declared, "If Spain wants to be included in arms aid, there is no reason why we shouldn't negotiate for some bases which we could use if there is a Russian attack in Europe." Senator Millard Tydings (D) of Maryland warned, ". . . to go through with this plan [Mutual Security] without putting Spain in the picture, with her great national army, and with her great antipathy to communism, is to lose one of the great assets of national defense without which the picture is not complete."

In 1951 members of the Joint Chiefs of Staff were still elusive about advocating closer ties with Spain. An illustration was provided by the Army Chief of Staff before joint hearings of the Senate Foreign Relations and Armed Services Committees:

> *Senator Wherry:* . . . Do you feel you can have a proper defense of

western Europe without having Spain brought into the family of nations?

General Collins: I think it would materially aid, and again I am speaking from a military point of view.

Senator Wherry: . . . Military experts have also stated it was very necessary to have Spain friendly to the North Atlantic Treaty community. And I was asking your opinion, if you felt that an adequate defense could be built without Spain.

General Collins: Yes, sir; I believe it could be. The alternative would be if Spain were an enemy. If Spain were an enemy the lines of communication through the Mediterranean would be dreadfully threatened but we did operate through the Mediterranean with Spain neutral, during the last war.

A few days later the Chief of Naval Operations was on the stand.

Senator Connally: Of course, Admiral, we want all the help, all the assistance, and all the cooperation we can get, don't we?

Admiral Sherman: Yes. But we do not want to make commitments on which the disadvantages may outweigh the advantages.

Senator Wherry: If those questions could be settled, whatever they are, political, military, or otherwise, do you feel if they would be invited into the North Atlantic community of nations, they would be of tremendous assistance? I say, if the questions could be settled, whatever they are.

Admiral Sherman: In certain cases there are other problems so I cannot answer to that without reservations which require elaboration in executive session.

In March 1951 the Senate Committees on Foreign Relations and Armed Services completed their hearings and, in a joint report on Assignment of Ground Forces to Europe, the committees supported the pro-Spanish bloc:

. . . Spain has 350,000 men under arms; Yugoslavia, 330,000; and Greece, 150,000. . . .

It is fair . . . to say that the addition of over a million armed men, who would fight for their freedom, would contribute immeasurably to the security of Western Europe and be an additional deterrent to Soviet Aggression.

(The joint report arrived at its total of "over a million armed men" by adding, say, 200,000 Turkish soldiers, sailors, and airmen to the assorted 830,000 men in the Greek, Yugoslav, and Spanish armed forces.)

On April 4, 1951, following the recommendation of the Foreign Relations and Armed Services Committees, the Senate, in its resolution authorizing dispatch of troops to Europe in support of NATO, asked that consideration be given to revision of European defense plans to provide for the utilization of Spanish military and other resources.

McCarran Renews His Attack

Senator McCarran was not content to depend upon debate and hearings and resolutions. If the administration was stalling for time, more direct measures were called for. At McCarran's meeting with the senators and military officers in July 1950, alluded to briefly above, he had outlined his program for the future. The $100 million loan was to be only a starter. Later, McCarran had promised, he was going to begin a drive to bring Spain into NATO. The ultimate intent was to send, not merely $100 million, but as many millions as necessary to make Spain's army one of the strongest in Europe. And if bringing Spain into the Atlantic alliance "involves too much international malarky," McCarran hoped to lift the quarantine by sending the economic and military aid and letting "the NATO nations catch up and approve later. . . ."

The meeting had served a twofold purpose. McCarran had turned the gathering over to the military in order to persuade the senators. At the same time the meeting had encouraged supporters in the Pentagon to come out in the open. McCarran did not identify the officers except to say that they were of the "lower echelons."

As McCarran himself reported, he realized that

> . . . political decisions belong to the State Department and the White House, and the President had made it clear he wanted no relations with Spain. This left the technical men in a spot. They could not openly advocate a policy which frightened their superiors, let alone contradict the President, yet their blueprints did just that. Unofficially, the lower echelon made known its views. The meeting in my office was just one of many in Washington.[3]

(McCarran's magazine article describing the meeting was not published until April 1951, when Spain was once again in the limelight.)

The Defense Department was not the only agency singled out for pressure. In May 1951 McCarran held another meeting. The senator was very much concerned that after almost a year only a very small amount of the 1950 mandatory $62.5 million loan had gotten into Spanish hands. If the State Department was delaying action until a de-

cision could be made about what the United States could get in return for the money, McCarran wanted that decision immediately. To this meeting came Carlisle Humelsine, Deputy Under Secretary of State; William B. Dunham, Spanish Desk, State Department; Herbert E. Gaston, Chairman of the Board, Export-Import Bank; Paul R. Porter of the ECA; and, demonstrating that the senator's private State Department was in operation, Ambassador Lequerica.

In the presence of Lequerica, McCarran questioned the officials about the Spanish situation and demanded action. The fiery senator was later roundly denounced in the press and in government circles for his breach of protocol. McCarran conceded that he had "gone a little out of line," but he felt that it had been necessary to get to the truth. It was not as chairman of the Judiciary Committee but as sponsor of the loan that he had called the meeting, he explained.

Wherever there was support for Spanish bases or for more general aid to Spain, McCarran and his colleagues sought to encourage it. While the highest Pentagon personnel were still forced to hedge on the subject, there was no such reticence on the part of their underlings, who shared the knowledge but not the responsibility. And if the officials under State Department control could not be goaded into action, they could at least be embarrassed. Word of these and other meetings drifted down the corridors of Washington, and many began to get the cue.

Phase Three: The Executive Branch Reconsiders

In the preceding section of this study, the congressional battle has been carried forward to the

spring and summer of 1951. It is now necessary to return to executive branch developments from 1950 through the same period.

---

[3] McCarran, *Ibid.*

Acheson and the State Department

The Secretary of State had had an uncomfortable time in 1949 which was due to continue in 1950 and 1951. Congressional criticism on a number of subjects—the administration's China policy, foreign aid, and allegations of Communists in the State Department, among others—was frequent, severe, and often personal. Many observers believed that the criticism in fact constituted harassment.

Acheson's position on Spain was one of the reasons for his growing unpopularity with Congress. Also, many of his peers and close advisers differed with him privately and publicly on this subject. Secretary of Defense Louis Johnson did not hesitate to forward the pro-Spanish point of view on Capitol Hill and in NSC meetings. Even as early as October 31, 1947, George Kennan, by 1950 Chief of the State Department's Policy Planning Staff, had expressed his opposition to unfriendly relations with Spain. The Mediterranean, he had said to Forrestal, could not be considered without considering Spain and the question of transit through the straits of Gibraltar.

Acheson's letter to Senator Connally on January 18, 1950 touched off the beginning of a shift in the State Department's Spanish policy. Included in this letter, along with his admission that the UN ban had been an unsuccessful departure from accepted diplomatic practice, was a lengthy discussion of the general position of the United States toward Spain. In speaking of the UN ban he volunteered some further information:

> Experience since that time has served to confirm our doubts about these recommendations. They were intended as a gesture of disapproval and as an attempt to bring about a change in the Spanish Government. In retro-

spect it is now clear, however, that this action has not only failed in its intended purpose but has served to strengthen the position of the present regime. . . . The Spanish reaction has been no different from that to be expected from any proud people.

Of even greater significance were his comments on the existing outlook of the State Department.

> The policy of the United States toward Spain is based on the recognition of certain essential facts. First, there is no sign of an alternative to the present Government. Second, the internal position of the present regime is strong, and enjoys the support of many who, although they might prefer another form of government or chief of state, fear that chaos and civil strife would follow a move to overthrow the Government. Third, Spain is a part of Western Europe which should not be permanently isolated from normal relations with that area.

Acheson then went on to specify the conditions which he felt must be fulfilled before normal relations could be achieved. "Spain . . . is still unacceptable to many of the Western European nations. . . . We believe that this is a matter in which the Western European nations must have a leading voice." The cooperative projects such as the European Recovery Plan and the Council of Europe, Acheson emphasized, were not a negative reaction to communism. They were part of a "positive program to support and strengthen democratic freedoms, politically, economically and militarily. In that context, the participation of the present Spanish Government, unless and until there has been some indication of evolution toward more democratic government in Spain, would weaken rather than strengthen the collective effort to safeguard and strengthen democracy."

Acheson's attitude emerged from this

communication in two separate points. First, we could not hope for any changes of government. Rather, we should deplore the prospect, for it might reduce Spain again to the shambles of civil war from which it had not recovered after more than a decade. Second, we should not enter into closer economic and military relations with Spain until certain political conditions were fulfilled: until the Spanish government had introduced some liberal economic and political features into Spanish life, and until the Western allies could set aside their fears of defense behind the Pyrenees.

In the months following the Acheson letter, little or no action was taken by the State Department. Congress took the initiative on Spain; debate, hearings, and oratory filled the air, and there were good prospects of a loan. More important, however, the attention of the department was overwhelmingly in other directions, pending participation in and completion of what was to be known as "NSC 68." This document was a monumental attempt to re-evaluate the principles and objectives of American and Western security and to provide a general plan for attaining such objectives or a context within which policy decisions could be more realistically made. The trigger that set off work on NSC 68 was the first Soviet atomic test explosion in September 1949.

What was the nature of world tensions and conflicts: simply a struggle to fill the so-called power vacuums created by World War II, or the prelude to World War III? How capable were we to prevent war? How well-fitted were we to fight in case of war? NSC 68 concluded that, if our basic aims were to develop a world system of politically independent, militarily and economically secure, cooperating states, we were not in good shape at all.

NATO was not an encouraging prospect in the summer of 1950: The member governments were reluctant to provide the shares agreed upon, and the representatives in the NATO councils were jealous of rights and prerogatives. NSC 68 had set 1952 as the "period of maximum danger," when the Soviet Union and its satellites would be most capable of defeating United States purposes.

The Korean war, coming only a few weeks after the circulation of NSC 68, did not change the appraisal of the document. It intensified the efforts of the executive branch to fulfill the aims of NSC 68, provided a practical reason for requesting more defense expenditure, and put Congress into a more propitious mood.

Thus, world events favored the Spanish cause. For it was under these circumstances that the $62.5 million "mandatory" loan for Spain was attached to the Omnibus Appropriations bill in August.

The Problems of Ambassadors and Aid

By the fall of 1950 Secretary Acheson was juxtaposed precariously between Congress and its military sympathizers—with the unanswerable argument that money was available as a *quid pro quo*—and the President, who still bore the grudges coming out of the past fifteen years and the weatherbeaten but hardy conviction that the wishes of the Western allies must be honored.

The skirmishes earlier in the year left President Truman and Secretary Acheson with two immediate adjustments to make. First, the 1946 United Nations ban on exchange of ambassadors with Spain was to be lifted. The administration was committed to some form of action on this situation because of Acheson's letter to Senator Connally in January. Lifting the UN ban was of great importance in the fight for bases. As a practical matter, full and equal diplomatic status must exist before an important treaty could be given serious consideration. The official UN position was an important part of Acheson's argument against changing the situation at all. The second adjustment concerned the unwanted authorization for loans to Spain, enacted in September.

Both were sensitive matters. Up until this point official policy had been one of inaction: watchful waiting for the time when Spain's internal politics would take a turn for the better, or for the time when the Western allies cast toward Spain a more favorable eye. In this context, any positive move would surely have repercussions in Washington and among the allies.

The UN Removes the Ban on Ambassadors

As November 1950 arrived there was no doubt that the General Assembly would lift its ban on ambassadors. The delegates no longer felt any obligation to uphold the ban, which was freely admitted to have been a failure. Most of the states which had espoused the original 1946 resolution had long since disregarded it and had sent ambassadors back to Madrid. When Acheson had recommended rescission of the ban in January, it only remained for the General Assembly to convene in the fall.

The concerted four-year effort of Spain for restoration of full international status reached its climax on October 31, 1950. On that day the Special Political Committee of the General Assembly passed a resolution repealing those portions of the original resolution relating to the exchange of ambassadors with Spain. The vote was 37 to 10 with 12 abstaining, well over the required two-thirds majority of those voting yes or no.

The General Assembly approved the action of the Special Political Committee on November 4 by 38 to 10 with 12 abstentions. On both occasions the United States voted with the majority.[4]

The action was not an unqualified success for Spain. While the ambassadorial ban was erased from the record, some important parts of the original resolution remained. The preamble, which linked Franco to nazism and fascism, was not affected. And the third recommendation, calling upon the Security Council to consider measures "to remedy the situation" if another government had not been established "within a reasonable time," still stood. Furthermore, the Assembly's action was not a request that members send ambassadors to Madrid. It simply stated that those nations wishing to do so could in good grace resume full diplomatic relations.

No one was sure what the United States would do. And, because fighting was still going on inside the administration, no one, including the Secretary of State, could be sure just when the United States would respond to the UN action. On October 7, 1950 the State Department had officially released a volume of German documents disclosing the relations of the Axis with Spain during the late 1930s. Among other things, these documents showed that some $200 million of Nazi money had been invested in the Franco regime. (A similar set of documents on Franco's World War II role had been released in 1946 on the day the original UN Spanish resolution had been approved.)

---

[4] The United States played no formal part in initiating the change. On both occasions the resolutions were sponsored by seven Latin American countries, plus the Philippines.

Ineffective though this October 7 attempt seems to have been, it did indicate that under no circumstances would the administration adopt an all-is-forgiven position. The department was out to prove what it had often emphasized about Spain: exchanging ambassadors with a country did not imply approval of its form of government. Also indicated was the continued existence of a strong determination to maintain a climate of opinion unfavorable to a full political or military embrace.

Griffis to Madrid

Two days before the General Assembly vote, November 2, President Truman told those assembled at his press conference that it would be a "long, long time" before the United States would send an ambassador to Spain and that reporters would have a "long time to think about it."

Two weeks later, on November 16, the President was again confronted by the question of ambassadorial exchange with Spain. When reminded by one reporter that he had said it would be a long, long time, the President replied, "That's right." This time, however, he made a qualification. Although he was reluctant about any appointment, he could be convinced that it was necessary, but he "was not in that frame of mind right now."

The "long, long time" turned out to be slightly more than a month. On December 27 the President announced the nomination of Stanton Griffis as Ambassador to Spain. Griffis, born in Boston in 1887, brought a wide and varied experience to the post. A New York financier, he had served as Ambassador to Egypt, Poland, and Argentina, and in 1948 had headed the United Nations Relief for Palestine Refugees. Griffis also brought a strongly pro-Spanish attitude to his new post.

Almost three years before this appointment, upon transfer from Poland to Egypt, he had confided to Forrestal that he would have preferred Spain. He said that he found it "difficult to understand how we can talk about the control of the Mediterranean at one end and ignore the other points, now that we have no Ambassador in Spain."

To avoid any false impressions about the surprise action, the President issued a statement on the day following Griffis' nomination. Truman insisted that the nomination of Griffis did not represent a change of policy toward Spain. The administration had been deliberating the move since the Acheson-Connally letter of January 1950, the President reported. The exchange of ambassadors was simply a more orderly way of doing business.

Aid to Spain
Prompts a Policy Study

The administration's attitude toward the Spanish loan, set forth in the previous section, was that the money would be delayed until it could be used for the benefit of the United States. Money, ambassadors, and bases were all tied inextricably together. The forthcoming exchange of ambassadors with Spain was an important preliminary for any desirable future action. What might this action be? What would be the actual costs and gains of closer ties with Spain?

To help decide these and other questions, a joint policy committee was formed of staff members of the Departments of State and Defense. Working closely together on the Spanish "policy paper" were William Dunham of the State Department's Spanish desk and James Wilson from the office of the Assistant Secretary of Defense for International Security Affairs. (Working relations between the State Department and the Pentagon had taken a turn for the better as a consequence of Louis Johnson's replacement as Secretary of Defense by General Marshall in September 1950. There had been much enmity between Johnson and Acheson, whereas relations between Acheson and Marshall were cordial.)

Although the details of this paper have never been revealed, its balance of favor was admittedly strongly in the direction of military arrangements in some form with Spain, preferably outside NATO. Work continued on the paper through the fall of 1950, and it was later turned over to another interdepartmental group, the Senior Staff of the National Security Council (NSC), in the persons of Frank Nash and Paul Nitze.

The Korean crisis and the events which followed closely after it had served to increase the desire for a change in our relations with Spain within the administration. The middle echelons in both the Department of State and the Department of Defense, represented by Dunham and Wilson, Nash and Nitze, had begun to shift. In the higher ranks such men as John Floberg, Assistant Secretary of the Navy for Air, and Secretary of the Navy Matthews were now arguing for a change in policy. Although Air Force Secretary Thomas Finletter remained adamantly opposed (because he had no confidence that Spanish bases would remain available after war began), his Chief of Staff, General Hoyt Vandenberg, favored Spanish bases, and Vandenberg became one of the first official United States visitors to Spain after negotiations began. Another key figure in the final shift was the Chief of Naval Operations, Admiral Sherman.

In November 1950—the same month the UN lifted the ban on ambassadors to Spain—the Spanish policy paper awaited Secretary Acheson's approval, which had to be given prior to formal presentation to the NSC. For Secretary Acheson it was a problem of his own values, those of the President, and those of the Western allies.

In November even the exchange of ambassadors was not to come "for a long, long time" as far as President Truman was concerned. For the NSC to discuss anything beyond that would have been unseasonable and impertinent. Consequently, the policy paper did not come before the NSC until January 1951, shortly after Griffis' nomination. In presenting the paper, Acheson accepted the full import of its conclusions. A major purpose of the exchange of ambassadors would be to investigate the situation for a possible military arrangement. The Spanish government had expressed a strong desire for such an arrangement, but what concessions it would be willing to make was not known.

However, there was one last question the policy paper could not answer: to what extent would France and England now react against an agreement with Spain, preferably outside NATO? For, although more and more members of the executive were moving toward a pro-Spanish bases view, the Korean situation might actually have increased the fears of the allies that if war did come the United States would defend Europe from behind the Pyrenees. Finding the answer to this question was the task of Ambassador Griffis and his colleagues in Paris and London.

Griffis departed for Spain in early February 1951. On February 7 Secretary Acheson appeared before the Senate Foreign Relations Committee. When asked directly just what United States policy was with respect to Spain, Acheson replied that the United States had sent "a most able ambassador to Spain" with the hope that "the relations of this country, and I hope of the other countries, with Spain, are now entering a new phase."

Beyond this, the department and Acheson remained close-mouthed. The secretary made no comments after Griffis' first conversations with General Franco. Fairly detailed reports of the Griffis-Franco talks reached the press, but the State Department remained silent. Among the topics covered were the rights of Protestants and military collaboration. On the former, Franco promised to issue a manifesto to the civil governors of every province, instructing them to see that there was no infringement of Protestant rights. On the latter, Franco said that Spain did not desire to become a member of NATO but that he would be delighted to make a bilateral agreement with the United States that would bind Spain to all the obligations of NATO membership—if it received proper military aid.

Shortly after these events, instructions were given to the ambassadors in Paris and London to discuss with those governments the possible role of Spain in general European defense.

What remained? The President must yield, and the pressure for doing so was well-nigh overwhelming.

Truman Stands Alone

One factor which colored the entire Spanish story was the President's strong opposition to negotiations with Spain. Changing his position was painful for him. It required him to take a stand counter to his emotions, and his action would in effect contradict a host of his own strong public statements.

Apparently, when President Truman had said in November 1950 that exchange of ambassadors would not come for a long, long time, he had meant it. On their first encounter, prior to the December 27 announcement, Griffis told the President that he would be

happy to accept the appointment if he were allowed a few weeks' vacation. To this the President said, "That's great and exactly what I want. I don't want you to go for the present—so soon after what I said a few weeks ago. I have been a little overruled and worn down by the [State] Department."

The President went on to say:

. . . I don't know what your religion is, I do not even know if you have any, but I am a Baptist and I believe that in any country man should be permitted to worship his God in his own way. The situation in Spain is intolerable. Do you know that a Baptist who dies in Spain must even be buried in the middle of the night?

Obviously, President Truman had not relied upon the findings of Charles Patrick Clark and the travelling congressmen of the year before. Also, it appears that political and religious factors—and, to a lesser extent, NATO morale—were the central considerations in the President's mind. As far as the President was concerned, the improvement of civil liberties was to be Griffis' first task and the prerequisite to a change of policy.

The President left the January NSC meeting (at which the Spain policy paper was presented) still in substantial disagreement with its recommendations, which had been accepted by Secretaries Acheson and Marshall.

Enter Admiral Sherman

Admiral Forrest P. Sherman had been appointed Chief of Naval Operations in the fall of 1949—a fitting climax to a brilliant career. Sherman practically symbolized the drive for unification of the military services. As Deputy Chief of Naval Operations from 1945 to 1947 he, with General Lauris Norstad, had negotiated and bargained the basis of the original unification act. Sherman, unlike many Navy men, did not believe that full unification signalled the doom of the Navy's peacetime mission and imperilled its wartime fitness. His independent position was rewarded first by appointment for two years as Commander of the Sixth Fleet in the Mediterranean and, after that tour of duty, assignment as Chief of Naval Operations. In this new assignment, as ranking officer in the Navy, he succeeded in overcoming the hostilities of an embittered, bickering service.

Admiral Sherman was a well-known advocate of closer relations with Spain. While in command of the Sixth Fleet, sailing at the very edge of the Western sphere of influence, he had been convinced that his force's presence had had a deterrent effect on Russian moves in the Mediterranean.

In 1949 Sherman had unsuccessfully requested permission from the President on several occasions to visit Madrid, where his son-in-law was assistant naval attaché. In 1950, while on an official visit to Portugal as Chief of Naval Operations, Sherman renewed his request. This time the State Department replied that it would approve a visit in civilian clothes, but that any official mission was out of the question.

Of Sherman's colleagues on the Joint Chiefs of Staff, General Omar Bradley particularly remained cool to the Spanish idea. According to former Secretary of Defense Johnson, Bradley's position changed in response to Sherman's forceful argument. An important consideration on Bradley's part was that Sherman would probably replace him as Chairman of JCS on his retirement.

From this time forth, the Spanish policy was a "piece of unification which worked," with Sherman as its spokesman. President Truman met frequently and religiously with his Joint Chiefs, often calling them to the White House in between their regular weekly meetings. Once Acheson removed his own name from the roster of opposition, Sherman increased his entreaties to the President. How vigorously and often Admiral Sherman broached the subject of Spain with the President will never be fully known. But there is no doubt that Sherman, working with Secretary of Defense Marshall, provided the critical force to change the President's mind. Reluctantly, the President did change it.

On several occasions over lunch at the Army-Navy Club, Sherman discussed Spain with his friend Louis Johnson (now returned to his private law practice), who had urged Sherman's appointment as Chief of Naval Operations. Sherman, by late spring of 1951, had been encouraged in his talks with Truman to believe that on his forthcoming tour of Europe he would finally be authorized to call formally on the Spanish government. In early July Johnson saw Sherman for the last time. Within two weeks the admiral was to depart for the long-planned European tour. Sherman told Johnson that he still hoped for word from "the President on Spain."

On the morning of July 16, 1951, Sherman departed for Europe. To Johnson he wrote, "I have delayed answering your letter to let my plans clarify. They have now done so and I am taking off this morning for Spain, France, England, and Italy."

The New Policy Is Announced

Later on the same day, July 16, Admiral Sherman descended on Madrid, substantially to the surprise of everyone, including Ambassador Griffis. Defense Department press releases for the July 15 to 19 newspapers explained that Sherman was on a week's tour to familiarize himself with European military conditions in preparation for the September meeting of the NATO defense ministers. Spain was mentioned in these reports, but this aspect of the journey was not stressed.

On July 18 Acheson confirmed all hopes and fears. His statement is quoted at length here because it is strongly indicative of what had gone on in secret for so many months:

> Admiral Sherman's interview with General Franco on Monday has caused widespread speculation in the press both here and abroad. The facts are as follows:
>
> Military authorities are in general agreement that Spain is of strategic importance to the general defense of Western Europe. As a natural corollary to this generally accepted conclusion, tentative and exploratory conversations have been undertaken with the Spanish Government with the sole purpose of ascertaining what Spain might be willing and able to do which would contribute to the strengthening of the common defense against possible aggression.
>
> We have been talking with the British and French Governments for many months about the possible role of Spain in relation to the general defense of Western Europe. We have not been able to find a common position on this subject with these Governments for reasons of which we are

> aware and understand. However, for strategic reasons outlined above, the United States has initiated these exploratory conversations.
>
> Any understanding which may ultimately be reached will supplement our basic policy of building the defensive strength of the West. It has been and is our firm intention to see to it that if Western Europe is attacked it will be defended—and not liberated. The presence of American armed forces in Western Europe bears witness to this intent as does the appointment, at the request of our NATO allies, of General Eisenhower as Supreme Commander.
>
> We are sending vast amounts of military and other aid to these Allies for whom a clear priority has been established. There will be no change in this procedure. In other words, the North Atlantic Treaty is fundamental to our policy in Europe and the closest possible cooperation with our NATO Allies will remain the keystone of this policy.

Truman delayed comment until his press conference on the day following Acheson's statement. With characteristic frankness, the President acknowledged that the administration had officially changed its policy toward Spain. The President further affirmed that the policy had been shifted as a "result of advice by the Department of Defense."

Concluding Steps

Strategic considerations had prevailed. In the words of Secretary of State Acheson, the military authorities were "in general agreement," an agreement, however, that did not simplify the future of the Spanish bases. Part of that future was reflected in Secretary Acheson's statement. As he saw it, the real problem in

1951 was the same as it had been in 1948, to rearm and unify Europe. The essence of the Acheson statement was its reassurance to the NATO countries that aid to Spain would in no way interfere with the commitment of the United States to NATO. The secretary also attempted to settle the issue of the Pyrenees: the United States would continue to station American troops in Europe, and, as a corollary, would defend Europe at its farthest eastern point in the free world.

Strategic considerations were also victorious over the President. The advice of the Defense Department to which he so openly referred may not have been contrary to his better judgment by July 1951, but it had certainly gone against strong emotions. At a press conference on February 7, 1952, just as negotiations were getting underway, the President stated flatly—to the great embarrassment of the State Department and the United States mission in Spain—that he was still "not fond of" General Franco. Thus a new policy was inaugurated without the full concurrence of the Western allies or the wholehearted approval of President Truman.

In July 1951, as has been said, Admiral Sherman arrived in Madrid. A week later, in Naples, the Admiral died. Within that week, Sherman, in the presence of his son-in-law, Lieutenant Commander John Fitzpatrick, Ambassador Griffis, and an interpreter, managed to clarify the positions of the two countries well enough to get planning underway. When the conversations came to an end, it appeared that Franco was willing to negotiate. However, the Generalissimo asserted that base privileges would be of little use unless military arrangements were accompanied by enough economic aid to make the bases efficient (a statement which could hardly come as an overwhelming surprise to the Americans).

As evidenced by subsequent events, Franco also agreed to allow American economic and military experts to study the situation preparatory to negotiations. For, now that the United States had made the decision to negotiate with the Spanish leader, it had to decide what it wanted and how much it was willing to pay for it.

The $450 Million Question

Consequently, before the climactic month of July 1951 had passed, Assistant Secretary of State George S. Perkins outlined the plan before Senate hearings on the Mutual Security bill.

> [We] will start off by talking with the Spaniards about our ability to use certain facilities in Spain, not to establish bases at the present time, but that we would have the right to use some of their air and naval facilities.
>
> In doing that it is probably going to be necessary to make some improvements in some of those facilities to make them useful for our purposes.

On August 20 a Temporary Military Survey Team was dispatched from Washington. This team, composed of high-ranking personnel from all three armed services, was headed by Air Force Major General James W. Spry. Spry had been transferred from the command of the Atlantic Division of the Military Air Transport Service. Attached to the team were two Army generals and a lieutenant general, a rear admiral and a captain from the Navy, and an Air Force colonel. There were seventy in all, counting aides of lesser rank.

Three days later, the Temporary Economic Study Group—headed by Professor Sydney C. Sufrin, representing the ECA—departed for Spain. Sufrin, on leave from his post as director of the Business and Economic Research Center at Syracuse University, was accompanied by two officials of the Export-Import Bank and a small staff.

The two groups set to work immediately, with the full cooperation of the Spanish authorities. In November and December 1951 respectively, the military and economic reports were completed, and the two groups returned to Washington. The texts of these reports were never made public. The military report was kept so close to the Pentagon that copies of it were not made available to many highly placed State Department officials until late in January. The general substance of the economic report, however, was made fully available to the press.

Professor Sufrin's feelings on the economic situation in Spain were mixed. His general conclusion was that the Spanish economy was "being held together by baling wire and hope." The railroads were in "terrible shape" and the iron and steel industry was in "dreadful shape." But the situation was not hopeless. If there was to be a substantial increase in Spain's role in Western defense, Sufrin argued, it would be necessary to support Spain with large loans, possibly $450 million over a three-year period. Sufrin warned against a large immediate investment. An enormous dose overnight, he said, would be inflationary, and there were simply not enough trained people in Spain to build an efficient operation on a large scale. In return, Sufrin argued, Spain must make some long-run, drastic, political and social reforms if the general standard of living was to be raised. If private investors were to be encouraged, he said, they would have to be given assurances that ownership and income rights would not be violated.

The Spry report apparently was an even more pessimistic document. While it reaffirmed the strategic value of selected air and naval bases, it pointed to one unanswered question: would land bases, once established in Spain, always remain available to the United States? This was a question that

two years of negotiations and five years of construction did not answer.

Negotiations with Spain

The overall effect of the two surveys was to turn two of the military departments back essentially to their former positions. The Air Force and the Army waded back from what appeared to them to be quicksand. Many of their officers were dismayed at the apparent obstacles. The Army held to NATO, where base utilization rights were more certain. Air Force Secretary Finletter continued to propound his view that Spanish air bases were impractical and undependable. According to him, the effectiveness of bases was drastically reduced to the extent that delays in direct use of them were encountered in cases of emergency. As long as these difficulties could be foreseen, Finletter was content to rely on the North African bases, which were being built at a feverish pace, as a supplement to NATO.

But the Navy was undaunted. After a call at Valencia on January 10, 1952, Vice Admiral Gardner, in command of the Sixth Fleet, proclaimed that the use of Spanish bases would "undoubtedly facilitate the tasks of NATO in the Mediterranean."

At the same time Vice Admiral Cassady declared that "Spain stands out as a bastion of defense, a vital link in the lifeline of a free and peaceful Europe." Admiral Cassady said he considered that one of his "primary missions" was to further closer understanding between Spain and the Sixth Fleet. Pursuant to this mission, Admiral Cassady six months later presented to the Spaniards a portrait of Admiral Farragut (of Spanish ancestry) who, in Cassady's words, "brought to America the finest traditions of Spanish dash and gallantry."

The State Department was faced with the embarrassing problem of what to do with $100 million allocated to Spain in the Mutual Security Act of 1951 (it had been followed by another $25 million in the 1952 MSA). If only because other departments had backed up slightly, the State Department appeared to be in the lead.

Spain's friend, Ambassador Griffis, announced his resignation and retirement on January 21, 1952, much to the dismay of the Spanish. Griffis stated to the press on that occasion that his main task, "to develop the beginning phase of Spanish-American relationships and understanding, has been completed." The second phase, he thought, was that of completing the work done by Sherman, Spry, and Sufrin for full collaboration. "The decision," said Griffis, "hinges on the Department of Defense." Appointed in Griffis' place was Lincoln MacVeagh, who had served a good many years in various ambassadorial posts, most recently as Ambassador to Portugal.

On March 12, 1952, amid President Truman's professions of unfriendliness, the Navy's proclamations of cordiality, and a general feeling of impatience and confusion, Secretary Acheson announced the formal opening of negotiations:

> Preparations have now been completed for negotiations with the Spanish Government regarding the use of military facilities in Spain.
>
> . . . After thorough study of the reports of these survey groups, the Department of State, with the Department of Defense and the Mutual Security Agency, have made preparations for negotiations with the Spanish Government. These negotiations will involve the use by the United States of military facilities in Spain and, in that connection, the use of the $100 million already voted by the Congress for aid to Spain.
>
> Negotiations will be opened with the Spanish Government immediately after the arrangements of Ambassador MacVeagh. Military advisers have been appointed to assist the Ambassador. They will be headed by Maj. Gen. August W. Kissner, U.S. Air Force . . .

The Kissner "advisory group," which was to do the everyday negotiating, included a second Air Force officer and one representative each from the Navy and the Army. A three-man economic advisory group also accompanied Ambassador MacVeagh. This group was headed by George F. Train of the Mutual Security Agency, who had been with MacVeagh in Portugal on an ECA mission.

For the time being, the responsibility no longer rested on the Secretary of State. And, in view of the supercharged atmosphere, the Spanish problem was one burden that could be delegated without regrets. The Spanish bases became an Air Force project. In fact the Secretary of State chose Kissner and delegated the responsibility primarily to the Air Force virtually without warning to Secretary of the Air Force Finletter. As in the matter of Sherman's mission and Spry's appointment, the Kissner group was formed without Finletter's advice and counsel.

No sooner had negotiations got underway than they bogged down: another presidential election was at hand. Spring and summer of 1952 brought forth a series of contrasting statements—now agreements had been made, then there was no program. The Spanish press was utterly confused.

A New Administration Takes Over

After he took office in 1953, President Eisenhower made only one change in the Spanish negotiating team, the replacement of Ambassador MacVeagh by James C. Dunn. With thirty years' experience, Dunn had served in many posts in the Foreign Service and had been Assistant Secretary of State. His most recent assignment before taking the post at Madrid was Ambassador to France.

There was no doubt that the Eisenhower administration was more eagerly resolved to consummate a deal with Spain than its predecessor had been. The pace quickened soon after the inauguration:

March 14, 1953. General Vandenberg, Air Force Chief of Staff, arrived in Spain for conferences with the United States military mission.

April 9. Ambassador Dunn held an unusually long conference with Franco and Foreign Minister Artajo. Afterwards, Dunn made the first official statement of the Eisenhower administration on Spain. With a new cordiality, Dunn indicated in no uncertain terms that the current administration laid more importance on the bases than had the Truman administration. "We want the bases," the Ambassador said. Dunn affirmed the intention of the United States "to strengthen the cordial relations existing between our countries" and the belief that these relations were "an important bulwark" in the defense of Western Europe.

May 1. Ambassador Dunn, with Train and Kissner, returned to Washington to confer with top officials, including President Eisenhower. Following these conferences, the State Department announced that the outlook was so good that an agreement could be expected before summer.

August 20. General Kissner returned to Washington for talks before the signing of an agreement. This time there seemed to be no doubt that something definite would be accomplished. In early September Ambassador Dunn flew to Washington for talks with President Eisenhower and returned to Madrid with the President's personal approval of the text of the agreement.

On September 26, 1953—two years after the Sherman visit and nineteen months after the beginning of negotiations—Ambassador Dunn and Foreign Minister Artajo signed three bilateral agreements. The first concerned the construction and use of military facilities by the United States in Spain; the second covered economic assistance; and the third dealt with military assistance. In sum, the United States agreed to provide $141 million for military end-item assistance and $85 million for "defense support" assistance, a total of $226 million. In return Spain agreed to authorize the United States, "subject to terms and conditions to be agreed, to develop . . . jointly with Spain such areas and facilities in Spain as may be agreed upon by competent authorities of both governments." One final stipulation by Spain was that all areas and facilities were to remain under Spanish jurisdiction and that the manner of utilization of such facilities in the event of war "will be mutually agreed upon."

After nineteen months of negotiations, the question of utilization of the bases in case of emergency had not been solved. Either General Franco had simply worn down the American negotiators, or the bases themselves appeared of such importance to the United States that doubtful use was better than no use at all. Or, perhaps, the Eisenhower administration wished to avoid the embarrassment of a failure to reach agreement.

Thus it happened that on August 25, 1953, when consummation was in sight, Senator Pat McCarran was presented with the Grand Cross of the Order of Isabella la Católica by Ambassador José Felix de Lequerica "for his efforts to improve Spanish-American relations."

Epilogue

With the bases agreement signed and sealed, the military services returned to the planning stage for another six months. Unpredictable Spanish weather—which was to delay building operations for two succeeding winters—and lack of skilled workers were later to make the plans that emerged appear ludicrously optimistic. But by 1954 the Korean crisis had passed. The base program got underway in an atmosphere of relative calm, unlike the circumstances surrounding the Moroccan bases. And the Americans carried out their tasks with utmost delicacy, to avoid any suggestion that a second Napoleonic empire was occupying Spain. For the first time since Napoleon, Spain had qualified her territorial neutrality, a concession to which the Americans were instructed to show great deference.

On September 23, 1956 Secretary of the Air Force Donald Quarles landed at Torrejon Airdrome with Ambassador John Davis Lodge to open officially the first United States installation in Spain, an emergency air base fifteen miles north of Madrid. Although this event was unheralded in the press, it was an important milestone.

In the spring of 1957, four years had passed since the signing of the Spanish-American treaty. An ambitious program was in progress, the pivot point of which was the naval base at Rota, near Cadiz on the Atlantic. It was to be the headquarters of the Sixth Fleet, which had recently been relying on Villefranche, France, and Naples. This base, the largest of the installations, was then expected to cost over $120 million of the total of $400 million allotted for base construction. Completion of the base was expected by the fall of 1958, although a nucleus base was to be in operation before that.[5] The air bases ran along a diagonal 500 miles northeast from Rota. Three of the bases were to be built for large bombers of the Strategic Air Command. An oil pipeline would connect all of these installations with a "tank farm" in Rota. Other marginal features included ammunition and supply dumps and a program of improving Spain's own airstrips. Over $280 million in economic aid was made available between 1953 and 1957, and an additional $250 million in surplus commodities was sold to Spain for Spanish currency.

United States Rights in Spain

The United States flag did not fly over any of the bases, and every American base was under nominal command of a Spanish officer. That United States rights to these bases were tenuous was discovered by Air Force Secretary Harold Talbott on November 2, 1953, greatly to his surprise. On a visit to Spain he remarked to the press that the

---

[5] By March 1958 work on the United States air bases was 80 percent completed, according to an estimate in the *New York Times*. The next year a $10 million Navy installation was opened at Cartagena. In January 1960 work was completed on the naval base at Rota—Ed.

United States would stock its bases in Spain with atomic bombs. A furious Spanish reaction had all of Washington awhirl. On November 3 President Eisenhower summoned the Secretaries of State and Defense to the White House to demand that they get their departments together on public statements. After the meeting Secretary of State John Foster Dulles told the press that the United States had no plan to store atomic bombs in Spain. Later, Secretary of Defense Charles E. Wilson stated that he was "completely in line with the Secretary of State on this matter." Talbott later insisted that he meant only that "we will eventually . . . have atomic bombs in Spain. This will be subject to the approval of the Spanish government."

Early in 1954 Secretary Talbott again discovered the strict limits of the Spanish agreement. At a press conference attended by himself, Secretary Wilson, and others, when asked by a reporter whether the Spanish bases provided for wartime or only peacetime use, Talbott replied, "Well, who's going to stop us? There are certain agreements on the use of the bases, but when the balloon goes up, we are going to use them." Later the secretary had to explain gingerly, "I wish to clarify the statement attributed to me at Mr. Wilson's press conference this afternoon. The United States has every intention of living up to its agreements made between the United States and those foreign countries that have granted air bases to our country."

These political rhubarbs illustrated beyond any doubt that the Spaniards had not signed a treaty giving the United States inalienable rights. In an emergency Spain alone could decide whether the emergency affected her. The basic program was to be completed by June 1958, five years after the signing of the ten-year pact. In 1963 either party could withdraw if a year's notice was given.

Nevertheless, the Eisenhower administration considered the Spanish agreement well worth the trouble. The Eisenhower policy toward Spain contrasted sharply with that of 1950 and 1951, when Truman instructed Ambassador Griffis to insist on the liberalization of the Spanish regime toward the exercise of elementary individual rights. On November 1, 1955 Secretary of State Dulles, after a special trip to Madrid to visit Franco, described the feeling of the United States as one of "frankest cordiality and reciprocal understanding," showing "American friendship for Spain" and "the spirit of collaboration."

Bibliographical Note

The published sources for this study are not voluminous. The *State Department Bulletin* and various press releases of both State and Defense Departments contain essential material, as do the various hearings before a number of congressional committees and the *Congressional Record* itself. There are important details on the early stages in President Truman's *Memoirs,* Vol. II, *Years of Trial and Hope* and in *The Forrestal Diaries,* edited by Walter Millis. Some material on the later stages has been gleaned from Stanton Griffis' *Lying in State* and Herbert L. Matthews' *The Yoke and the Arrows.*

A far more important source than any of these has been the newspapers: the *Washington Post,* the *Christian Science Monitor,* the *New York Herald-Tribune,* and, above all,—the *New York Times.*

For obvious reasons, no archival materials were accessible. In lieu thereof, the writer has had the great good fortune to receive generous aid from participants in these events. An expression of deep gratitude is due the following, without whose gracious assistance this story could not have been written: Louis A. Johnson, Robert A. Lovett, Thomas K. Finletter, John Floberg, James Clement Dunn, Stanton Griffis, Frank Nash, Paul Nitze, James Wilson, William Dunham, Admiral Richard L. Conolly, Charles Patrick Clark, Senator John Sparkman, and Representative Albert Rains. Responsibility for the interpretation and treatment of their remarks, however, is entirely the author's.

The President's Economic Advisers

CORINNE SILVERMAN

In 1946, in accordance with the Employment Act passed that year, three economists were named members of the Council of Economic Advisers and installed in the Executive Office of the President. Their principal duty was to advise President Truman on economic matters and to prepare reports which the President would consider in drawing up his annual economic message to the Congress now required by the new act.

As the CEA began its work, there were many who hoped it would strengthen the quality and rationality of economic decision-making in the government by injecting at the White House level the advice of three professional economists. The three men who were appointed to inaugurate the CEA had similar hopes, but they soon found themselves confronted with procedural problems which raised questions about the extent to which, and the manner by which, professional expertise can be effectively incorporated in the making of major policy decisions in a political democracy.

The three economists differed on some major economic policy matters. This made it harder for them to resolve their difference on one of the important procedural problems they confronted—the question of whether the three CEA members should testify before congressional committees on economic matters after they had rendered advice privately to the President. Was their role solely that of privy adviser to the chief executive or should they also serve as advocates of the policies he finally decided to pursue? If the President ignored his advice, was a CEA member nevertheless obliged to support White House policies at congressional hearings at the expense of his professional conscience? How neutral and confidential could a professional adviser of the President be and still exercise effective influence on policy-making within the executive branch and in the governmental process as a whole?

The three economists who faced these issues were Edwin G. Nourse, Leon H. Keyserling, and John B. Clark.[1] As the first members of the CEA they were conscious that their actions would set precedents for their successors. This case study describes their actions and then goes on to show how their first successor under the Eisenhower administration—Arthur F. Burns—attempted to resolve the same problems in 1953–1954.

---

[1] This case was reviewed by the three members of the first Council of Economic Advisers. Some of their comments appear as footnotes to the text.

The Employment Act of 1946

As the Second World War drew to a close, many economists of all types—government officials, labor union and trade association economists, bank advisers, and academicians—issued predictions of a postwar depression. The general tenor of their analyses, which were accepted in the main by government officials, was that the layoffs from defense plants, disappearance of overtime wages, and the unemployment of returning veterans, would result in a sharp fall in personal incomes. This in turn would restrict consumer purchasing power and result in a business spiral into depression. Predictions of unemployment ranged from 8,000,000 to the Federal Reserve Bulletin's 20,000,000.[2] It was in this atmosphere that the Employment Act was debated and passed, becoming law on February 20, 1946. The congressmen sponsoring the bill saw it as a means of asserting the responsibility of government to promote full employment. They hoped that one of the long-run results of the act would be an unprecedented peacetime total of 60,000,000 jobs.

However, the economists' predictions soon proved wrong. There was an unexpectedly smooth transition from wartime to peacetime production. By May 1946 total employment had risen to 55,000,000 from the war-end level of 52,000,000. Only 2,000,000 were unemployed. As consumers rushed to buy the cars, houses, and washing machines they had been waiting for, it appeared that a major postwar economic problem was not to be unemployment but inflation.

But the Employment Act was by no means obsolete. The act had been cast in a larger frame than guaranteeing full or maximum employment. It had been conceived fundamentally as an expression of a new consensus about government responsibility for the economy—a consensus achieved after the debates and trials-and-errors of the thirties.

The act had received much of its support in Congress because few disagreed with its basic premises: first, that the country could not afford, nor would public opinion accept, another great depression; and second, that positive government action could and should prevent extended periods of economic distress. Debate in Congress had centered on the more difficult questions of when the government should take action, how much government action was possible or desirable, and what kinds of policies would be effective in which situations.

The final declaration of policy of the Employment Act was a cumbersome sentence of over 100 words, riddled with many qualifications resulting from legislative compromises:

> The Congress hereby declares that it is the continuing policy and responsibility of the Federal Government to use all practicable means consistent with its needs and obligations and other essential considerations of national policy, with the assistance and cooperation of industry, agriculture, labor, and state and local governments to coordinate and utilize all its plans, functions, and resources for the purpose of creating and maintaining, in a manner calculated to foster and promote free competitive enterprise and the general welfare, conditions under which there will be afforded useful employment opportunities, including self-employment for those able, willing, and seeking to work, and to promote maximum employment, production, and purchasing power. (*Public Law 304, 79th Congress, Sec. 2*)

---

[2] *Keyserling comments:* "I think you should add that there were some economists who did not expect large unemployment after World War II, and that I was among them."

Apart from the underlying thesis that the federal government was to assume some kind of responsibility for the economic health of the country, this declaration of policy was all things to all people—and indeed the Employment Act passed the Senate unanimously. Those interested in fostering government planning read in loud tones the phrase which enjoined the government to "coordinate and utilize all its plans, functions and resources. . . ." Those who tended more to laissez-faire saw in italics the phrase ". . . in a manner calculated to foster and promote free competitive enterprise. . . ." What the role of the government was to be under the act would emerge only from the way in which the purposes of the new legislation were carried out.

The New Obligations of the Federal Government

Although the act was ambiguous about the scope and nature of the new policy obligations of the government, it was clear about the machinery to be established. It called upon the President to present an annual Economic Report to Congress in addition to the traditional State of the Union and Budget messages. It also established the Council of Economic Advisers in the Executive Office of the President, and a Joint Committee on the Economic Report in the Congress. The Joint Committee was to receive the President's economic message and to report to the House and Senate its own recommendations on each of the major proposals in the President's message.

The council's principal tasks were to assist the President in drawing up his new annual message, to advise him on economic trends, to appraise current economic policies, and to develop and to recommend to the President national economic policies. The council was also to collect from existing governmental agencies statistical information on economic developments and trends.

There had been considerable debate in Congress on whether a separate council was desirable. The Treasury Department already reported directly to the President on the state of the economy and recommended fiscal policies. The Bureau of the Budget also reported to the President on the effect of current and proposed economic policies, including the impact on the economy of the total federal budget. However, neither of the two agencies wished the other to be designated as the top adviser and co-ordinator of economic policies, and so a separate Council of Economic Advisers was established.

In the next year or two the Executive Office of the President was to be expanded further by the creation, for example, of the National Security Council and the re-location in the Executive Office of the Joint Chiefs of Staff. But the Council of Economic Advisers had to break new ground in deciding whether it would act solely as privy adviser to the President with no dealings with Congress on policy issues, or whether it would follow the example of the Bureau of the Budget. The Bureau was also part of the Executive Office,[3] but it had a single head and its director had always worked closely with congressional committees and testified at congressional hearings in support of presidential policies.

[3] The Executive Office of the President may be divided into (1) the President and his personal staff, and (2) the other more formal agencies such as the Bureau of the Budget and the CEA. Traditionally, there is a confidential relationship between the President and his personal staff. Unlike CEA appointments, the President's appointments of his personal staff aides and of the Director of the Bureau of the Budget do not require Senate confirmation.

The Members of the Council

The Employment Act was passed in February 1946. President Truman offered positions on the council to a number of economists, but it was not until July 25, 1946 that he received three acceptances. Edwin G. Nourse accepted the position of chairman, Leon H. Keyserling became vice-chairman, and John D. Clark filled the third place. The act did not specifically invest the chairman with any extra powers or duties. None of the three had met before being nominated to the council.

Edwin G. Nourse was then 63. He had taught at a number of universities until 1923 when he became associated with The Brookings Institution, a non-profit research foundation in Washington. He became director of Brookings' Institute of Economics in 1929, and was vice-president of The Brookings Institution at the time his appointment to CEA was announced. He had served as president of the American Farm Economic Association in 1924 and of the American Economic Association in 1942, and had been chairman of the Social Science Research Council from 1942 to 1945. He was generally regarded as middle-of-the-road to conservative. Politically, Nourse claimed he was "non-political" and "non-partisan." His father had been a member of the Prohibition Party, and Nourse himself had voted only twice in presidential elections, once for a Republican and once for a Democrat. (Since the 1920s, as a resident of the District of Columbia, he had been unable to vote.)

John D. Clark, then 62, was generally considered to be the most conservative of the three. He had had a rather unusual career, starting as a lawyer, at one time serving as counsel for the Midwest Refining Company. Then he became vice-president of Standard Oil of Indiana. Successful in business,

he decided to turn to teaching. He resigned from Standard Oil, returned to college, and received a Ph.D. in economics in 1931. He taught economics for ten years at the University of Denver and at the University of Nebraska, and then he became dean of the College of Business Administration at the University of Nebraska. Sandwiched between these academic posts was a short stint as a Democratic representative in the Wyoming Legislature. During the 1940s he was appointed to a number of political committees or commissions. His political activities in Wyoming had brought him close to Wyoming's Democratic Senator Joseph O'Mahoney, one of the co-sponsors of the Employment Act, and he was regarded by some as the Senator's protegé. Clark did not consider himself a "conservative" economist, and his position on questions pondered by the Council of Economic Advisers seemed to confirm this estimate of himself.

Leon H. Keyserling, only 38 when he was appointed to the council, had a reputation as one of Washington's "boy wonders." His professional training had been in both law and economics. He had received a degree from Harvard Law School, and he had also completed two years of graduate courses in economics at Columbia University. He entered government service as a lawyer for the Agricultural Adjustment Administration in 1933 and almost immediately became legislative assistant to New York's Democratic Senator Robert F. Wagner. He remained associated with Wagner until 1937 when he became general counsel of the United States Housing Authority. He rose to be acting administrator of the Authority and then general counsel of the National Housing Agency. During this period Keyserling had his fingers in almost every pie baking in the New Deal ovens. He became involved in the drafting of the National Industrial Recovery Act, various public works, farm, and banking acts, the Social Security Act, and the National Labor Relations Act. He also did staff work on economic questions for a number of congressional committees. As direct qualifications for nomination to the Council of Economic Advisers, Keyserling had assisted in drafting the bill which ultimately became the Employment Act of 1946; and he had maintained close connections with Senator Wagner, one of the co-sponsors of the original bill. Also, Keyserling had attracted attention when he won the second prize of $10,000 in the Pabst Brewing Company's postwar employment essay contest in 1944.[4]

These background sketches do not shed any light on the personalities of the three men, nor on how they fit together. There were people who had the opportunity to assess the members: the council had a professional staff of twenty or so economists; also there were liaison personnel between the council and the White House, the Bureau of the Budget, the Federal Reserve Board, and the Treasury Department. This case will draw on the recollections of four such persons.

Commentator A described the council members this way:

> Nourse's reputation with us was that he was a wise man with scholarly achievements. His views on policy were limited: he had been in agricultural economics most of his life. He was relatively conservative—not when

viewed on the spectrum of economists, but when viewed as an appointee of a Democratic administration. He was personally liked and respected.

He was also known as relatively inflexible on substantive economic matters. This was the major reason why there were difficulties. He was willing to recognize political realities—for example, the Democratic platform might have said something about price supports which Nourse was not in favor of, but he was willing to go along. However, he chafed under it. He was not used to the kind of policy-making where there is discussion and dissension over policy, then a decision is made, and thereafter the ranks close behind the decision.

Keyserling had no difficulty with this problem, partly because his views were nearer the President's, partly because he was by training a lawyer and government official. Keyserling was regarded as a hard-working man with a somewhat abrupt and sometimes abrasive manner.

Clark was the dark horse. He turned out to be a man who had spent most of his life in business and had just about retired. He had a vigorous mind and unorthodox ideas. He suffered from the narrowness of his background. He was the easiest personality of the three.

On administrative policy issues the Council often split with Keyserling and Clark against Nourse. But it is very important to remember that on economic questions they agreed about eighty percent of the time.

Commentator B observed:

> Nourse was a formalistic thinker. That's one reason why he and Keyserling didn't get along very well. Keyserling didn't have a Ph.D. in economics so Nourse sometimes acted as though he didn't know anything about economics. Of course Keyserling resented this attitude.

[4] One of Keyserling's theses in this essay was that planning and development of economic policies should be a joint executive-legislative function. He suggested the establishment of a continuing American Economic Committee, which, Keyserling wrote, should be composed of representatives from the Senate, House, Cabinet, industry, labor, and agriculture.

This latter observation was repeated in substance by several persons close to the council. It may or may not have been accurate. But the fact that others placed this interpretation on Nourse's opinion of Keyserling made for strain between the two.

Relations with the White House

The council members were formally appointed in August 1946. By October a staff had been recruited, and CEA offices were set up in the Executive Office Building, near the White House. The Bureau of the Budget was also located in this building.

The council's first substantive task was preparing the draft of the President's first economic message to Congress—the draft containing the council's analysis of "foreseeable economic trends" and its suggestions for national economic policy and program.

Here, the newness of the council presented difficulties. The CEA had no regular channels for co-ordinating its proposed recommendations with those in the drafts of the other two messages which were to be presented to Congress in the first week of January—the State of the Union and the Budget messages. The procedure this first year was somewhat disorganized, with co-ordination coming only the last two weeks in December through the joint efforts of the council and members of the staff of John Steelman, the Assistant to the President.

In the following years a rift developed within the White House staff between John Steelman and Clark Clifford, the President's legal counsel. In time, each of the CEA members, along with many other government officials, found he was relying on a different person to serve as a channel of communication with the President. Nourse felt Steelman was more receptive to his

way of thinking; Keyserling had more of a bond with Clifford. Clark found easier access through influential members of Congress. On economic questions to be discussed in presidential messages co-ordination was effected by the establishment of work groups comprised of staff members from the White House office, the Bureau of the Budget, and the CEA. Many of these staff people had been trained in the Bureau of the Budget. The work groups, forming a network of people who knew each other and had worked together, not only bridged the cleavage between Steelman and Clifford, but connected the Bureau of the Budget, the Treasury, the CEA, and the White House, as well as any department concerned with a major economic matter that would be mentioned in a presidential message.

Keyserling and Clark had no difficulty with this system. Nourse, however, had been disturbed by the extent to which responsibility for the draft of the first economic message had been delegated by the President to members of the White House staff. In 1953, quoting from a diary which he kept during his council years, Nourse referred to an interview he had had with the President in November 1946, during the preparation of the first draft of the economic message:

> There was nothing in this half-hour interview which in any way suggested that the President was interested in the content of the work our staff was doing or in the conclusions toward which we were moving. . . .

Writing in his diary in 1947, Nourse again expressed dissatisfaction:

> While he has accepted the material which we have presented to him for use in the Economic Reports and passed it on without material change

and with only minor omissions, there is no clear evidence that at any juncture we have had any tangible influence on the formation of policy or the adoption of any course of action or feature of a program.[5]

And, Nourse wrote:

. . . When it came to using the Council as an intellectual staff arm of the Presidency . . . the President was quite evidently at sea.

These relationships between the council members and the President were seen by Commentator A in this way:

There was really no basis for Nourse's feeling that the Council was rejected by the President. The White House took the Council members very seriously. Their views were sought and listened to on every occasion they should have been. But Nourse may have wished the Council was something it was not and couldn't hope to be. It was set up as a separate, advisory agency with no control or

power.[6] It was not part of a regular flow of procedures and documents. The Council had to make new connections or else wait until people came to consult it—things did not flow across its path in the same way as things routed through the Bureau of the Budget. One of the original ideas had been to give the responsibility to the Bureau of the Budget, making the Council a special section within the Bureau. If that had been done, the Council would have had a more direct way of having its views made effective through influencing the budget.

However, the Council did have the initiative when it came to the draft of the economic message. That was a device for approaching issues on the Council's terms. There the Council didn't have to wait to see whether it was invited in.

The real question in determining whether anyone paid proper attention to the Council is whether it was consulted in time to have its views considered, and whether it had access to the information it needed to formulate its views. On these scores the Council had no complaints.

Commentator C saw the relationship between them in this way:

It was all a matter of temperament. The President was a man who knew his limitations. He knew he was not a scholar. He was a politician. He was somewhat awed by expertise. He just couldn't sit down and jaw with a man

---

[5] *Keyserling comments:* "Dr. Nourse's habitual assertions that he was not accorded the utmost considerate treatment by President Truman is in my opinion one of the most extreme cases of unfair treatment of a President by a disgruntled former official on record. Dr. Nourse could see the President whenever he wanted to. The President gave him a great deal of time. . . . Dr. Nourse was simply unable to adjust himself to the nature and the problems of the Presidency. He could never understand that the President of the United States has too many things to do to engage in long bull sessions on economics of the kind that take place at The Brookings Institution. He could never understand that the President must delegate, must have confidence in his principal officers, and that these officers have no just cause for complaint when the President not only remains accessible to them but also accepts practically everything that they recommend to him."

[6] *Nourse comments:* "I did wish for the Council to be something it was not—that is, a purely advisory agency of the highest professional competence and political detachment. But the implication of this passage— that I wished it to be an agency of 'control or power' is completely erroneous, as is abundantly shown in other parts of this document."

Clark comments: "Mr. Keyserling and I wanted the Council to be a powerful influence in devising and securing the understanding and acceptance of sound economic policies to save prosperity."

with the scholarly reputation and mien of Dr. Nourse. Nourse, on the other hand, wanted to sit down and "ponder" problems with the President.

And Commentator D observed:

That's the way Truman worked. You had to work through his subordinates. Nourse never really accepted this, so the other members of the Council were sometimes able to outflank him by using White House staff channels more effectively.

Relations with Congress

The Employment Act had provided that the Joint Committee on the Economic Report, aided by a professional staff, should review the President's economic message and present a report of its own to Congress. The Joint Committee was composed of seven senators appointed by the President of the Senate, and seven representatives appointed by the Speaker of the House. The party composition reflected roughly the party division in each of the two houses. The first Joint Committee included many of the senators and representatives who had played an active role in the debate and passage of the Employment Act. Democratic Senator Joseph O'Mahoney, who had been one of the co-sponsors of the bill, was expected to be the committee's first chairman. However, the Republicans gained a majority in Congress in the 1946 elections, and Senator Robert A. Taft became chairman.

The President delivered his first economic message in January 1947, but the members of the Joint Committee were occupied primarily with problems attendant on the shift of party control. They did not hold extensive hearings on the 1947 message or prepare more than a mimeographed report of a few pages. Although the Joint Committee began to hold hearings during 1947 on a variety of subjects, the issue of the relationship of the Council of Economic Advisers to congressional committees arose first with the Senate Foreign Relations Committee.

In June 1947, Secretary of State George C. Marshall delivered his famous Commencement Address at Harvard, suggesting a program of economic aid to Europe. That same month President Truman set in motion three studies on the impact of a foreign aid program upon the domestic economy. One of these studies was made by the Council of Economic Advisers, which submitted its report to the President in October of that year.

The next month the Foreign Relations Committee scheduled hearings on the European Recovery Plan and tentatively scheduled appearances before the committee by the chairman of the CEA. When Nourse was advised by the committee secretary of the proposed invitation, he explained that he would be "embarrassed by a formal invitation to testify" and that he had taken the position that council members should not appear, even before the Joint Committee on the Economic Report.

Nourse stated that he had taken this position to protect the relationship between council members and the President. He had explained his views to his colleagues and to the President: the Joint Committee on the Economic Report might try to draw council members into a discussion of policy positions taken by the President in his economic message, and some of these policy positions might not have followed the drafted recommendations of the council. Or, the council members might disagree among themselves about the advisability of some of the President's positions. To date, there had been no major divergence between the council and the President, and only minor disagreements among council members, but, Nourse explained, either situation might arise in the future and cause embarrassment both to the President and to the council members. It would be wise, he felt, to establish precedents to prevent such mutual embarrassment.

The President indicated to Nourse, when the subject was first raised, that he agreed that the council should protect itself against such situations, but he added that at the same time the council should not remain aloof from the work of the Joint Committee.

Neither of Nourse's two colleagues was happy with the chairman's position. Clark, for one, argued that a "policy of aloofness from congressional committees" such as Nourse suggested would impede "the machinery set up by the Employment Act of 1946 to secure congressional approval of economic policies recommended by the President upon the advice of the Council of Economic Advisers." When the issue arose on the question of testifying before the Senate Foreign Relations Committee, Nourse's point of view was accepted by the committee. Keyserling and Clark deferred to this view although they disagreed with it.

From time to time, the members of the CEA were invited by various congressional committees to testify on economic matters, and in each instance Nourse's view prevailed, and invitations were declined. By 1948 the issue of testifying or not had become a source of considerable tension among the council members.

The President Recalls Congress

This was an election year. Harry Truman, regarded by many as a "caretaker" and President only by accident, was almost alone in feeling he had any chance of being re-elected. In July,

President Truman, when accepting the Democratic nomination, made a surprise announcement to the convention: he was going to call back into session the Republican-controlled 80th Congress to consider his eight-point emergency program for inflation control. Inflation was still a serious problem, and Truman seized on this tactic to dramatize his idea that responsibility lay with Congress.

Keyserling and Clark were firmly convinced council members should testify before congressional committees at the special session. Clark felt the council was on probation, since the House Appropriations Committee had just cut the council budget sharply. He still had ringing in his ears the words of the report of the Appropriations subcommittee:

> The testimony of this agency was lamentably weak. There was strong sentiment in the committee for the complete elimination of all funds for the agency. . . . There is little evidence of any important results from its work of interpretation, and it takes the position that its views and recommendations are confidential except to the President, unless released by him.

Nourse did not agree with Keyserling and Clark that their reduced budget was a result of their refusal to testify. He interpreted it as a reflection of the Republican majority's antagonism to President Truman and his advisers, and its dislike of the Employment Act.

The issue of testimony by council members was finally resolved. Nourse described the decision process in this way: "After numerous telephone conversations with Mr. Steelman, Mr. Clifford, Mr. [Paul] Porter [7] and Mr.

---

[7] Paul Porter had been the last head of the wartime Office of Price Administration. He was at that time one of Truman's principal campaign advisers and was co-ordinat-

[Robert] Turner,[8] and with lengthy conferences on the *Williamsburg* [the President's yacht] between the President, the White House aides, and Mr. Porter, and after positions had been taken and reversed, as I recall it, four times within the week, the President's final decision was given me in his letter of August 13." The letter read:

Dear Dr. Nourse,

Mr. Paul Porter has raised with me the question of whether I would regard it as appropriate for members of the Council of Economic Advisers to testify before Congressional committees concerning the anti-inflation program I have recommended to the Congress.

As you know, I have considered from time to time in the past the question. . . . I am aware of the difference between your views on this subject and the views held by your colleagues on the Council. I respect these varying views, which I am sure all of you hold most conscientiously.

Under these circumstances, it seems that the wisest course in the present instance is to permit the members of the Council to be guided by their own convictions. Accordingly, I do not wish to induce any member of the Council to testify if he feels it inappropriate for him to do so; nor do I wish to restrain any member from testifying if he feels that to be an appropriate part of his duties.

I am informing Mr. Porter of this letter, with the expectation that he will make arrangements for testimony by

the members of the Council if any testimony is to be presented by them.
Sincerely,
/s/ Harry S. Truman

Keyserling appeared before the Senate Banking and Currency Committee a few days later. Nourse was invited to appear but was excused by the committee chairman. This became the practice during the rest of 1948 and in 1949. Keyserling and Clark appeared before several committees; Nourse was invited, but he declined and was excused.[9]

Nourse's Letter of Resignation

Immediately after the election of 1948 Nourse submitted his resignation to President Truman. He wrote two drafts of his resignation. The first draft, which he never sent to the President,

---

ing presentations to congressional committees at the special sessions.

[8] Robert Turner had been director of the Foreign Division of the War Production Board during World War II, had been a staff member of the Office of War Mobilization and Reconversion, and was then assistant to John Steelman. He was one of the principal liaison men between the White House staff and the CEA.

[9] *Keyserling comments:* "The important thing is that I refrained from appearing before Congressional committees during the first year of the Council operations, and thus made the concession to Dr. Nourse of being bound by his views, although they were the minority view. I would have been willing to do this throughout the period of our joint service on the Council. But even though I made this concession, Dr. Nourse persisted in making a public issue of it, which was entirely inappropriate on a matter of Council procedure, and which violated his own profession of desire to avoid public controversy. He made a speech on this subject to the National Planning Association before I had ever testified. He carried stories on the disagreement into the public press. He imputed political motivation to his colleagues. I frequently pointed out to him how entirely unreasonable and inconsiderate this was, in view of the concession which the other members of the Council at that time were making to his views. But he persisted in this course of personal attack and disparagement in public forums, and it was this which led me ultimately to the view that nothing was to be gained by refraining further from appearing before Congressional committees, a position which I believed to be correct in substance, and which in fact was held by a majority of the Council."

included the thought that if the council was "in any way to be assigned a political role or to be allowed to stray over into political activities or lay itself open to political influences, you would want an entirely different kind of chairman, and I would want to be relieved of the position at once. . . ." In the second draft—the one the President received in December 1948—Nourse said principally that in view of his age and the hard work and tensions involved in the job, he hoped he could be relieved soon.

The President did not respond to the letter of resignation, and Nourse did not actually resign until a year later. However, during the year the issue of testifying became more and more a source of bitter argument among the council members. Nourse clung to his view that any appearances before Congress meant that the council was taking on a political role. Keyserling and Clark were convinced that it was the duty of the council to be the President's economic ambassadors to and tutors of Congress.

Tensions grew, also, over the kinds of public speeches both Nourse and Keyserling were making. Nourse had taken the position that he did not want to be forced into criticizing the President before congressional committees. Yet, Keyserling pointed out, Nourse did not seem to hesitate to criticize the President's position in public speeches. Nourse's reply was that he could choose his own ground in making speeches, but he could not choose which questions to answer in congressional hearings. In turn, he criticized Keyserling for appearing before such partisan groups as the Americans for Democratic Action. Public appearances, Nourse felt, should be limited to academic, civic, business, labor, or agricultural organizations. (The organizations before which Nourse had appeared included such groups as the

Controllers Institute of America, the United States Chamber of Commerce, the Executives Club of Chicago, and the Illinois Tech Alumni Association.) For his part, Keyserling felt the audience was less important than the content of the speech. Early in 1949 Nourse received considerable press attention for his public criticism of a pending presidential proposal. Keyserling wrote Nourse a memorandum pointing out that his own actions had never drawn attention for such a reason. Nourse replied that on several occasions in the past he had been "deeply concerned" when Keyserling or Clark had made speeches conveying the impression that their personal professional views were in fact the positions of the council.

Economic Differences

The separate economic orientations of the two men also made for difficulties. These professional differences began to be felt late in 1948 and during 1949. A split first developed over the moot question of how much the nation could spend on national defense without increasing inflationary pressures to a dangerous extent. Nourse took the position that a thirteen billion dollar defense program was close to the outer limit of safety—presumably a safety defined in terms of economic stability. Keyserling argued that the economy could stand a substantial increase in the defense effort if this should prove necessary for national security. President Truman asserted his desire for a fifteen billion dollar ceiling on defense spending—much closer to Nourse's position than to Keyserling's—and the defense budget was held under that limit until the outbreak of the Korean War shot defense expenditures to $22 billion in 1951 and $45 billion in 1952.

Another source of disagreement

among the council members began to be felt during 1949 when production, employment, and prices all declined. By mid-June 1949 unemployment was over 3,000,000. The government policy Nourse favored was allowing the recession to find its own bottom. He opposed expansion of the government expenditures as a means of pumping buying power into the economy. Inflationary deficit spending by the government, he believed, was not the way to cope with the recession. Keyserling favored more aggressive anti-slump policies.[10] In his mid-year economic message to Congress, President Truman said, "We cannot have prosperity by getting adjusted to the idea of a depression." The President went on to repeat his January requests, including improved supports for farm income, an increase in the minimum wage, more unemployment and old age assistance. He specifically rejected any increase in taxation. This program of increased benefits with no additional revenue portended a budget deficit for the coming year.

A Single Head?

In January 1949 the first of the Hoover Commission reports appeared —the Report on General Management of the Executive Branch. (Under the chairmanship of former President Her-

bert Hoover, the non-partisan commission prepared a series of reports—recommending specific reorganization plans—aimed at improving the administrative efficiency of government departments.) The Hoover Commission's comments and recommendations concerning the CEA reflected much of the general feeling that the council's problems were at least partly tied to its organizational structure. The report recommended that the CEA be replaced by an Office of the Economic Adviser and that it have a single head:

> . . . at least potentially it is handicapped by being a multiheaded body, with the requirement that its members be confirmed by the Senate.
>
> To put a full-time board at the head of a staff agency is to run the risk of inviting public disagreements among its members and of transplanting within the President's Office the disagreements on policy issues that grow up in the executive departments or in Congress. It also makes cooperation with related staff agencies more difficult.[11]

In 1949 the council broke with another practice. Previously, in its quarterly reports to the President on economic policies, or in its annual and mid-year drafts of presidential economic messages, the council members had attempted to reconcile differences of opinion and present a single viewpoint to the President. However, in

---

[10] *Nourse comments:* "There is a faulty implication of laissez faire in saying: 'Nourse favored allowing the recession to find its own bottom. . . .' The fact was that I was urging on both labor and management that they had a responsibility for working out sound wage and price adjustments for checking recession and quickening recovery rather than looking to the government for the inflationary devices of deficit spending."

Keyserling comments: "An increase in expenditures without an increase in tax rates does not necessarily portend a budget deficit if it produces sufficient economic recovery to enlarge tax receipts through an enlarged national income. This is standard economics."

[11] *Keyserling comments:* "It is significant that the Hoover Commission's recommendation was preceded by discussions between representatives of that Commission and Dr. Nourse, but no effort was made to obtain the views of the other members of the Council. Further, Dr. Nourse never informed the other members of the Council of his discussions on this point, which is to my mind one example of his improper concept of the relationships among the three members of the Council."

the preparation of the draft of the President's mid-year report in 1949, Nourse found he differed with his colleagues to such an extent that he wrote a minority report.

Finally, on September 9, 1949 Nourse wrote Truman that "if the work of the Council is to be kept from serious demoralization," he felt he should tell his colleagues that he wished to retire so that they could get on with the job of preparing the draft of the 1950 economic message. This time Nourse's resignation was accepted, and he left the council on November 1. Leon Keyserling became acting chairman and subsequently was appointed the second chairman.

Commentator C said of Nourse's resignation:

> Nourse . . . wanted to avoid a possible difficult situation which actually never was a real situation. Nourse, so far as I could tell, diverged from the President's position only on very minor points. But Nourse felt the Council members were confidential advisers.
>
> Keyserling felt they were arms of the President. Like other agencies, they were established by Congress to do a certain job and were confirmed in their positions by Congress. They were, he felt, accountable to Congress.
>
> But behind those positions was another factor—the personalities of the two. Nourse didn't like the limelight. Keyserling loved it.

Many public sources attributed Nourse's resignation more to a combination of reasons. The influential British weekly, *The Economist,* reported on October 29:

> The open split in the Council between Dr. Nourse on the one hand, and Mr. Keyserling and Dr. Clark on the other, has for over a year made it likely that Dr. Nourse would resign.

Their disagreement is merely the latest of a series over economic policy and practice which has plagued Washington since the scope and responsibilities of government began to grow under the impact of the great depression nearly twenty years ago.

. . . .

> It was in a speech last week that Dr. Nourse most bluntly outlined the reasons for his determination to press his resignation and made it inevitable that the President should accept it . . . his bitterest criticism was reserved for the apparent willingness to accept deficit financing as a "way of life." . . .
>
> . . . That [the CEA] should split was perhaps inevitable, but is nevertheless regrettable. Dr. Nourse is far from a proponent of laissez faire, but he has a caution as to the extent of government activity which is not shared by the other two members. . . . He likewise holds the conviction that a council appointed to advise the President should do exactly that and no more, while the other two believe its functions should include open advocacy . . . [of] policies felt to be appropriate. The proper character of the new organization has therefore also been an issue.

The *Washington Post* sympathized editorially with Nourse's view that the council should be politically neutral. But, the *Post* went on,

> . . . we think that Dr. Nourse seriously impaired his influence with the President by delivering speeches in which he openly criticized some Administration policies and made it quite plain that he did not agree with the views of his colleagues on various important issues. If he had stuck to his thesis that a presidential adviser should reserve his opinions for the council table, it is our belief that he would have been more effective as a dissenter, and might still be in a position to render useful service as a member of the Advisory Council.

As Keyserling Saw It

In 1952 Leon Keyserling, then chairman of the CEA, was testifying before a subcommittee of the Joint Committee on the Economic Report. He was asked by Senator Paul Douglas to explain exactly what his position was on this issue: was not the council primarily an adviser to the President, Douglas asked, and if this was true could council members be frank with Congress? Keyserling answered with this statement:

> It is . . . clear that the members of the Council are employees of and advisers to the President, and that they are not employees of and advisers to the Congress in the same sense.
>
> But this does not mean, in my opinion, that the members of the Council cannot or should not testify before, cooperate and consult with, and in a sense give advice to, committees of the Congress, just as this is done by heads of other agencies in the executive branch, and even other agencies in the Executive Office of the President. . . .
> . . . In all of these cases . . . none of these officials, except in rare instances, makes available to the public or to the Congress the nature of the advice he gives to the President while he is assisting and advising the President in the preparation of such Presidential messages and the recommendations contained therein; and likewise, it is only in rare instances that such officials make it known to the public or even to the Congress if there is a variance between the advice they give to the President and the extent to which the President follows that advice. . . . Nonetheless after the Presidential message in question and the recommendations contained therein are sent to the Congress . . . it has been practically the universal custom and is entirely appropriate for those officials whose statutory responsibility makes it clear that they have been advisers to the President in the field covered by such Presidential message and recommendations to appear before such congressional committees, to discuss and analyze the matters involved, and in fact to amplify and support the recommendations made by the President and the analysis underlying it. In addition, it has been the almost universal custom and entirely appropriate for such officials to appear before congressional committees and to make analyses and give advice in the fields in which they operate under statute, even when this has not been preceded by a Presidential message. . . .
>
> In appearing before committees of the Congress in this role, I cannot see where the Council of Economic Advisers is doing any different or appearing in any different light from what is done by heads of other agencies working in different fields. . . . Certainly, the distinction cannot be that members of the Council deal with economic problems, because many heads of many other agencies deal with economic problems, or even predominantly with economic problems.
>
> That this construction of the Council's role is correct is supported by the legislative history of the Employment Act, by the expressed views of some of the legislative sponsors of the Act, by the fact that the Joint Committee on the Economic Report and other congressional committees have frequently invited the members of the Council to appear before them for this purpose, and by the fact that doing so is in accord with the Council's responsibilities as defined by the President. More important, it is in accord with the whole tenor of the American system of government, and I believe it a good and healthy thing that public officials should be subjected to the questioning and testing of their views by congressional committees, particularly when these public officials have been appointed and confirmed under acts of Congress to deal with the very subject matters which these committees are considering and to help in the prepara-

tion of the very reports and recommendations which the President sends to these committees.

The next phase of the question is whether the members of the Council are in a position to express themselves frankly and fully to congressional committees, in view of the fact that they are advisers to the President, and in view of the fact that the advice and recommendations that they give to the President may at times not be exactly the same as the advice and recommendations which the President transmits to the Congress. There has been considerable interest in this subject, and I am glad of this opportunity to express my views.

I believe that members of the Council of Economic Advisers are in exactly the same position, with respect to expressing themselves frankly and fully before congressional committees, as any other agency heads of integrity who had advised the President in important fields in which the President makes recommendations to the Congress. Under our system, no responsible official in such a position, while working for the President, parades before the public or before congressional committees the differences of viewpoint that there may be between himself and the President on matters under consideration by the Congress. If these differences are minor in character, the responsible public official does not feel entitled to the luxury of self-satisfaction of having the President agree with him in every detail; government could not function if that were expected. But if the President, in his recommendations to the Congress, were to depart from the analysis and advice given him by the official in question to the extent that it could be regarded as a fundamental repudiation of that official's views, the official of integrity should resign where under all the circumstances he believes it in the national interest to do so. But it seems to me incorrect to say that a public official in this kind of job can place himself in open conflict with the President for whom he works, and at the same time stay on the job. Obviously, also, a man of integrity should resign if the President for whom he works should ask him to go before a congressional committee or anywhere else and stultify himself by making analyses or supporting policies which this official believes to be against the national interest.

The view has been expressed in some quarters, that members of the Council of Economic Advisers, in order never to be faced with a choice based upon the situation described above, should solve the problem by advising the President but by refusing to appear before congressional committees to analyze and support those recommendations by the President to the Congress which are in accord with the advice they have given him. I can see no more reason why the members of the Council should duck their basic responsibilities by so doing than why other officials should thus avoid their responsibilities. Under our system, if it is to function and if congressional committees are intelligently to process reports and recommendations sent to them by the President, there must be and there always has been someone from the executive branch available and ready to come before the congressional committees and to work with them in the customary fashion. With respect to analyses and recommendations sent by the President to the Congress in those areas of economic policy which are the province of the Council as defined by statute, if the members of the Council are not the proper persons to come before the congressional committees for this purpose, then who are the proper persons?

If my analysis is at all correct, it seems to me that for a member of a congressional committee to raise a question about my freedom to be frank, or whether I agree with the recommendations made by the President, or whether after the President has sent up recommendations I am estopped from expressing my own views, is the same as asking that question of the head of some other statutory agency of government appearing before a congressional committee.

My own answer to the question is as follows: I always have and always will try to speak frankly and deal fairly with congressional committees. I ask the subcommittee to assume what is in fact the truth, that the analyses and recommendations which I make to it are consistent with the analyses and recommendations which I make to the President. So long as the recommendations made by the President to the Congress conform in the main to the recommendations which I have given him, I feel privileged and duty-bound in appearing before a congressional committee to give my reasons for supporting those recommendations. If the President were to fundamentally repudiate my views as to what is in the nation's economic interest, and were to send recommendations to the Congress in basic conflict with them, then I would resign. That situation has not arisen. At all times, consequently, I hope this subcommittee will feel that the analyses and recommendations I present to it represent my honest convictions. I would not present them if they did not.

As Nourse Saw It

Nourse explained his point of view in this way: [12]

One of the most important considerations, I felt, was for us to build the precedents properly. The Executive Office was only seven years old, and the Council was a completely new agency. I felt I should think ahead carefully. I was impressed that other people would have to sleep in the bed I was making.

I felt there were, theoretically, three levels on which the Council could op-

erate. The first would be for us to draw up abstract economic analyses. The second would be for us to make our analyses, taking into consideration the impact on the various institutional structures of the country—the labor institutions, the banking setup, and so forth. This I considered to be economically realistic, and this is what I attempted to do. The third level would be to make analyses taking into account the different pressure groups which bear on an issue and try to make analyses which would be accepted by them. This, I felt, was none of our business. This was the role of the politician. Keyserling and Clark disagreed with me.[13]

The sharpest difference between me and my colleagues was that I differentiated clearly between economic analysis and political synthesis. Keyserling and Clark wanted to be policy makers. But I saw the Council as an apex of economic thought, with us processing problems for the President's consideration. Our role was to give the President a notion of how professional economic thought was dividing on a

---

[13] *Keyserling comments:* "No evidence can be brought to bear to support the allegation that either Clark or I took positions in which we did not substantively believe. . . . Dr. Clark and I did, of course, take account of the practicality of policy recommendations from the viewpoint of their institutional acceptability, and this is within the proper scope of economics in the public service. . . . Dr. Nourse's statement . . . that Keyserling and Clark wanted to be policy makers is also categorically false. We recognized that policy had to be determined by the President. We, of course, sought to urge him to adopt the policies in which we believed, but so did Dr. Nourse, and so would anyone else in our position. Further, Dr. Nourse went all around the country making speeches to all kinds of groups, urging upon them the policies in which he believed. Sometimes he did this before the President had made a determination of policy, and sometimes, after the President had made a determination of policy, Dr. Nourse made speeches to the contrary. Clark and I believed this to be inappropriate for reasons fully set forth in your quotation of my views."

---

[12] Based on a transcript of a recorded interview, July 1958.

question, and then give him our best judgment on it. If the President, for political considerations, formulated a policy that led to bad economic policy, the role of the Council was then to show him the least bad way to apply bad policy. I made this point in my speech before the American Philosophical Society. I said:

". . . the economist must be spiritually capable of bringing the choicest pearls of scientific work to cast before the politically motivated and politically conditioned policy makers of the executive branch. He must be prepared to see these carefully fabricated materials rejected or distorted, and still carry on the same process of preparation and submission again tomorrow, unperturbed and unabashed. He must all the while be aware that his professional brethren and the public will hold him accountable for the final compromised product while he, by virtue of his relationship with the Executive Office, is estopped from saying anything in explanation or vindication of his own workmanship." [14]

Now that is where the problem came in testifying before Congress. If we were all in agreement—we three and the President—we could go up and explain to Congress what the economic needs were and how the decisions had been arrived at. But you'd be establishing a precedent. What happens when a policy comes up which you don't think is good economics— and they're bound to come because the President can't be expected always to follow the advice of the Council when he takes into account all factors in the political decision-making process. What would I do then? That was the question I was asking. Do I go ahead as a professional economist and argue for the President's position? That came up and I said, "I can't do that." That, in my judgment, was an entirely differ-

ent role from the one I envisioned as a member of the President's Council.

Take my situation. Suppose the President took a position for, say, selective price or wage controls and that I have to go before Congress and defend it. Then some smart senator on the Joint Committee like O'Mahoney, Douglas, Sparkman —there were plenty of them—says, "That's a very interesting case you make for this policy, Dr. Nourse. Now I notice that on page 486 of your book, *America's Capacity to Produce,* you deplore government controls in these words. Now, do you think the situation has changed?" What am I going to do? Someone else might make a forty-minute speech showing how conditions had changed. I couldn't operate on that basis.

I felt, as I read the Act, that the Congress had provided for dual implementation—we were to advise the President and the Joint Committee was to advise Congress. There was no necessity for us to go before Congress. Congress had its own advisers with their own staff.

Mr. Keyserling, though, felt we were responsible in a sense to Congress, partly because we had had senatorial confirmation, partly because as the President's advisers we should speak for him, and partly because he wanted to wield that influence. On the first score, I had always felt that the situation would be clarified if we did not need senatorial confirmation. We weren't presiding over any action programs. On the second score, although we were the President's advisers he didn't always follow our advice. Our advice was only one factor he took into account. On the third score, I was content being "schulmeister" to the White House. I didn't feel I needed the larger class on the Hill also.

Of course, I wasn't completely happy with the relations we did have with the President. There was never a time when I called Matt Connally, the President's appointment secretary, when there was the slightest difficulty

[14] Edwin G. Nourse, *Proceedings of the American Philosophical Society* (R.A.F. Penrose, Jr., Memorial Lecture), Vol. 94, No. 4, 1950.

in getting an appointment. He would say, "Will fifteen minutes be all right?" And I would say, "No, I need a half hour." Then Connally would say, "Well, we've got a lot of cash customers this morning; we'll have to move some of them around." And they were moved. There was never more than a day's lapse before I was sitting at the President's desk, and that was excellent. But when I got there, the President was always very gracious, friendly and nice—too nice, in fact. He wasn't business-like enough. He'd tell me what happened on his walk that morning, or tell me chit-chat about his family—wasting minutes of this precious appointment. As I think back, I can honestly say that I think I never had a real intellectual exchange with the President, that I was opening my mind to analysis with him, that he was following me. And the situation wasn't much better when I sent him reports. On the occasion when we turned in a majority and minority report the President took them and said, "Thank you for making this report. I'll study it with great care." But the next day he saw Clark Clifford in the morning and he said, "Well, I asked these guys for a report, and they give me two reports. You take them and see if you can make anything out of them." You see, that was the frustrating part of it. I felt there was little opportunity to become more effective.

But the important thing was to establish the Council as a professional body immune from political influence. And, in fact, if the Council could pass from one administration to the next with some continuity of personnel, I felt that would firmly establish the precedent. As I said once or twice before, "It will take time for successive Presidents to learn how to use a nonpolitical advisory staff agency effectively. It will take time for successive Council members to learn how to bring the most competent and realistic analysis of economic problems simply and effectively to the President's aid."

Blough's View

After Keyserling became chairman, council members appeared frequently at congressional hearings. The new council member appointed to fill the vacancy left by Nourse's resignation was Dr. Roy Blough, then professor of economics and political science at the University of Chicago. Blough joined in these appearances but differed from Keyserling about the kinds of testimony a council member should give. This difference emerged publicly at the 1952 subcommittee hearing referred to above, when Senator Douglas asked Blough whether he advised Congress to cut expenditures by five billion dollars or whether he preferred not to answer. In reply Blough stated:

> . . . I consider myself completely at liberty to discuss with Congress economic trends and developments, the effects and implications of governmental policies, and the different ways in which various policy objectives can be achieved. I am very pleased to have an opportunity to do this, and I try to do it in as objective a manner as my basic attitudes permit. However, . . . a definite recommendation on expenditures, it seems to me, is advice that I can more properly give to the Executive than to Congress.

Blough subsequently enlarged on this statement to the effect that the advisory relationship to the President clearly precludes the council member from openly expressing views adverse to the President's recommendations. Accordingly, Blough felt, it is unwise for a council member to serve as an advocate of administration programs. Congressmen will not receive his frank opinion on matters of policy, but they should be able to rely on the objectivity of his statements as an economist.

The CEA Under Eisenhower

In January 1953, when Republican President Dwight Eisenhower took office, he inherited an unusual situation. In 1952 the Congress, uncertain whether the council should be continued, had provided it only enough money to function for nine months. Thus, council funds were due to run out in March 1953. In February 1953 Sherman Adams, the Assistant to the President, advised the chairman of the House Appropriations Committee that President Eisenhower considered it important that the council continue to function, and asked that the committee consider a supplemental appropriation to carry the council through the rest of the fiscal year.

At the same time, President Eisenhower asked Dr. Arthur F. Burns if he would serve as chairman of the Council of Economic Advisers. Burns was at that time professor of economics at Columbia University and director of research of the National Bureau of Economic Research. Burns thought back over some of the difficulties in CEA operations during the Truman administration and looked ahead to the kind of CEA on which he would be serving if he accepted the appointment. He advised the White House that he would accept the nomination provided he had the right to review the other two appointments. His condition was met. Early in March his nomination was presented to the Senate, which confirmed it on March 18. A few days later Congress approved the Supplementary Appropriation Act which provided only for the establishment of one Economic Adviser to the President and appropriated $50,000 for this adviser and a small staff.

The CEA's forty-member economic and clerical staff was almost entirely dispersed. Only two or three economists remained.

Burns considered his first task to be an evaluation of the structure of the council as it had functioned in the Truman administration. In the course of his evaluation he concluded that many of the CEA's difficulties had resulted from defects in the legislation. He agreed with the Hoover Commission that the council had been handicapped "by being a multiheaded body" whose three members had held identical powers and responsibilities. The chairman, as such, had no added powers at all. All administrative problems had to be decided by all three members.

The second defect which Burns detected in the basic legislation was the absence of established channels between the council and other agencies within the government. This deficiency had caused at least two problems: (1) It had been difficult for the council to influence the making of economic policy throughout the government. (2) There had been many accusations of "intrigue" between council members and officials of other agencies. Burns felt that if there had been any "intriguing," one reason was the necessity to by-pass the blocks in the institutional arrangements. He therefore proposed a reorganization of the council, which was approved by the President and which became Reorganization Plan Number 9, approved by Congress on August 1, 1953. This plan placed administrative responsibility for the CEA in the council chairman, who also had the sole responsibility for reporting to the President. The position of vice-chairman was abolished.

In his letter transmitting the reorganization plan to Congress, President Eisenhower indicated that he was also asking the heads of several departments and agencies, or their representatives, to serve as an Advisory Board on Economic Growth and Stability under the chairmanship of the chairman of the CEA. This request was in line with Burns's notion that regular channels of communication between government agencies should be institutionalized. Burns's original idea had been to have an economic cabinet, presided over by the CEA chairman and composed of the Chairman of the Federal Reserve Board, the Secretary of the Treasury, and other Cabinet-level officials with major responsibility in the economic field. However, Burns recommended that rather than leap directly to this high-level economic cabinet, it might be well to try the idea first with an advisory board composed of officials from the policy-making level immediately below that of secretary.

In June 1953 the Advisory Board on Economic Growth and Stability was set up with Burns as chairman. The other seven members were under secretaries, assistant secretaries, and officials of similar rank from the departments of the Treasury, Agriculture, Commerce, and Labor, and the Bureau of the Budget and the Federal Reserve Board. The White House was represented by Gabriel Hauge, an Administrative Assistant to the President with responsibility for briefing the President on details of economic matters.

Burns now had a council reconstituted on his terms: administrative responsibility was centralized in the chairman; there was an inter-agency board for co-ordinating economic policy under CEA direction; the two other members of the council were men specifically approved by Burns. (In September 1953 Burns was joined on the council by Dr. Neil H. Jacoby, Dean of the School of Business Administration at the University of California at Los Angeles, and in December by Dr.

Walter W. Stewart of the Institute for Advanced Study in Princeton.)

Burns also had strong backing from the President. Eisenhower repeatedly told his Cabinet members that he wished them to consult the CEA chairman on all important economic matters and policies. While this did not give Burns veto power, of course, it lent weight to his position and provided him with another channel for putting forward his views. Besides consulting with the heads of departments and agencies individually, Burns attended Cabinet meetings regularly and participated in debates on economic issues.

Under the reorganization plan Burns alone was responsible for reporting to the President on the workings of the CEA and on economic policy recommendations. Burns had a scheduled weekly meeting with Eisenhower, generally attended also by Hauge. Burns made it clear to his two colleagues, however, that although he had sole administrative responsibility for procedural matters, he considered that all three members of the CEA shared equally the responsibility for advising on substantive economic problems.

Burns also discontinued the practice of having the council issue separate annual economic surveys. These were now made part of the President's economic messages.

The problem of the relationship of the CEA to Congress arose immediately. During the hearings before the Senate Banking and Currency Committee on the confirmation of Burns as CEA chairman in March 1953, Senator John Sparkman put a question to Burns: "Is it your feeling that you should testify before a congressional committee, or will you keep yourself aloof from congressional committees?" Burns replied: "Senator Sparkman, it is perfectly plain to me that the Congress has the full right to call upon any citizen within or outside the Government to testify at any time. . . . My own personal . . . inclination would be to stay out of the limelight, make my recommendations to the President, indicate to him what the basis for the recommendation is . . . and then having done that, to remain eternally quiet."

Burns's Position

Burns later gave considerable thought to the position he should take. To a large extent he agreed with Nourse's feeling that it would be difficult for an economic adviser to maintain his usefulness to the President if he had to answer all questions put to him by a political group. However, he felt Nourse had carried this position too far. There were several categories of aid which could be given without interfering with his advisory relationship to the President. First, there might be a request for the CEA to aid the Congress in understanding the Employment Act of 1946. Such a request would call upon council members in their function as administrators of an act passed by Congress, and it would be completely appropriate for council members to testify freely. Secondly, a congressional committee might wish testimony on some technical problem, such as an analysis of the statistical units of all government departments. This too would be a legitimate request which should be honored. Third, council members certainly should appear before the Appropriations Committee to defend budget requests for the council itself.[15]

The difficulty arose when an invitation was proffered by a congressional committee dealing with economic conditions and policy. Here, Burns felt, there were at least two major dangers in testifying.

First, in some cases the President had to adopt policies that he didn't like and that I didn't like. He had to do it for reasons of overall political policy, but his heart was bleeding over it. What should I do before a committee of Congress in such a case? Should I criticize the President when I happen to know that he shares my views? Would that be fair? In any case, how could I critize the President publicly and still remain a useful member of his administration? On the other hand, how could I say to a congressional committee that something is sound when I believed otherwise?

The other major danger in testifying is that once an adviser takes a strong position in public, he is apt to become a prisoner of that position. I wanted to give the President the fullest benefit of my knowledge and thought. Hence I wanted to be free to advise the President one way one day, and yet be able

House committees to defend the Council's budget. When, in May 1947, Senator Taft, as chairman of the Joint Economic Committee, extended us an invitation to meet with that committee to discuss interpretation of the Employment Act and, in a broad way, means for its implementation, I unhesitatingly accepted. The Committee's report had been made several months before. The session was well along on the legislative program, and our discussion was entirely free of debate over policy recommendations of the President or specific issues then involved in Congressional debate. We cooperated fully on the staff level in inquiries initiated by the Joint Economic Committee as to 'statistical gaps' and if, at any time, we had been invited to join with the committee in mutual conferences within this field, I am sure I would have been glad to participate. Not having the statistical competence that Burns had, I was not in a position to exercise the leadership in this important area which he subsequently contributed."

[15] *Nourse comments:* "With these three propositions I am, of course, in complete agreement. I only wish I had been smart enough to differentiate these cases as explicitly as Burns has done from the fourth issue—the one on which I took my stand. Naturally, I appeared before Senate and

if necessary to go in the next day and say, "I've been thinking it over. What I told you yesterday was wrong. I overlooked some important points. What really ought to be done is thus and so."

Burns decided that he ought to testify despite these dangers, because good citizenship required it. He also decided that he would express to the congressional committee, if it dealt with economic policy, a preference as to the method of testifying. Burns preferred that he be permitted to testify in executive session with no transcript made of the remarks. But if the congressional committee would not agree to this method, Burns decided, he would testify anyway. "Maybe I'd have to resign after I got off the stand, but that would be one of the chances I knew I would be taking."

In 1954 the Joint Committee on the Economic Report called upon Burns to testify. At that time the Republicans controlled Congress, and Republican Jesse Wolcott was chairman of the Joint Committee. Wolcott and the committee, with its majority of Republicans, acceded to Burns's request that the testimony be taken in executive session with no transcript.

The election of 1954 resulted in the Democrats gaining control of Congress, and in 1955 Democrat Paul Douglas was chairman of the Joint Committee with its new Democratic majority. Again, Burns was asked to testify, and again he expressed his preference. Douglas replied that although he would agree to an executive session, he would want a transcript made of the testimony. However, Douglas went on, this transcript would not be part of the public record. Burns replied that if a transcript were to be made at all, he would want the transcript made public. Accordingly, in 1955 the testimony was given in executive session, and the

transcript was made a part of the printed record.

The next year Douglas was still chairman, and Burns again expressed his original preference. This time some Democrats on the Joint Committee voted with the Republicans, and Burns's testimony was taken in executive session with no transcript made.

So Burns established his policy. He would clearly express his preference to the congressional committees dealing with economic issues. If the committee in question accepted his preference, that was all to the good. However, if the committee insisted on different terms, Burns would accept those terms.

There was another major change in the workings of the Employment Act in the first years of the Eisenhower administration. The Joint Congressional Committee, which up to this time usually issued partisan majority and minority reports, issued a unanimous report in 1954 and again in 1955. By 1956 there were those who felt that the Joint Committee was no longer "a fifth wheel" and that its hearings and reports were as significant as those of the CEA.

Burns resigned from the council in December 1956 and returned to his post as professor of economics at Columbia University, becoming at the same time president of the National Bureau of Economic Research. In 1958, looking back over his years as chairman, and evaluating his policy against that of the first council members, Burns said:

> Keyserling took an extreme position and in the process ignored a vital distinction. Cabinet officers are directly responsible to Congress. Their responsibilities are largely defined by Congress. But the Council is not an administrative agency. It is advisory only—advisory to the President by

law, and advisory to the Presidency by practice.

Nourse also took a rigid position. To the extent that the Council had duties defined by law it is responsible to Congress and must answer to it— that is why I placed no conditions on my testifying on proposed changes of the Employment Act or on the statistical gathering functions of the government or on the defense of the Council's budget.

But I want to add this: if there had only been the type of Council that Keyserling envisaged, I never would have accepted the appointment. I would have taken it for granted that the Council Chairman must, as a practical matter, support the President's views at public hearings, and I would not place myself in that position. But because there had been a Nourse I could conceive of there being a practical alternative and could try to find it. So Nourse did more than make my job easier by taking the position he did; because there had been a Nourse my job was possible.

Not everyone agreed that Burns had solved the problems. Harvard economist Alvin H. Hansen, for one, considered that Burns's solution had been to sidestep the dilemma Nourse had feared by restricting his activities "more nearly, though not quite exclusively" to assisting and advising the President. Hansen felt that Burns had not really met the question (raised earlier by Keyserling) that the Democratic members of the Joint Committee posed in this manner in the committee's Supplementary Report of March 1955:

A sound and consistent position for the Council must be agreed upon; either it acts solely as an anonymous professional body advising the President or as the spokesmen before Congress and the public for the President's economic analyses and programs. If the first alternative is adopted, then some other spokesman for the President's overall economic position must be established.

SIX

Government, Science, and the Economy

CASE **9**

The Battery Additive Controversy

SAMUEL A. LAWRENCE

Editor's Introduction

In 1953 the new Republican administration of President Dwight Eisenhower was grappling with a host of high policy decisions, many of which involved complex scientific matters. These ranged from atomic energy and space missiles to medical research and hydrological criteria for multipurpose water projects. Some members of the public, and some officials, expected that referring these questions to scientists would yield one correct "scientific" answer. Yet during this period officials in both the executive and legislative branches of government became enmeshed in a national controversy that started in a seemingly simple scientific question about an ordinary storage battery—or, to be more precise, about the effects of a commercial battery additive powder known as AD-X2 on the performance of storage batteries.

The AD-X2 controversy arose out of the actions of federal agencies charged with one aspect of government regulation of business: the prevention of unfair and deceptive business practices—specifically, misleading advertising. The case originated with the efforts of Jess M. Ritchie to market, through Pioneers Inc., a battery additive that he had discovered and which, he claimed, prolonged battery life. The trade name AD-X2 was derived, he said, from the fact that the preparation was an additive and that it contained an unspecified catalyst (X) in addition to two sulfates (sodium and magnesium) commonly used in other additives.

Ritchie's efforts to market his product resulted in complaints from battery manufacturers and from the National Better Business Bureau. Two federal agencies thereupon moved against Pioneers Inc. One was the Federal Trade Commission, an independent regulatory agency with statutory responsibilities for acting against false and misleading advertising. The second was the Post Office Department. The Postmaster General was authorized by law "upon evidence satisfactory to him, to deny use of the mails to any person or company [who] is conducting any scheme or device for obtaining money . . . through the mails by means of false or fraudulent pretenses, representations, or promises."

The legislation giving these powers to the Postmaster General (in 1890) and to the FTC (in 1914 and 1938) had been the product of public sentiments that citizens and honest businessmen should be protected from unscrupulous operators. However, there remained in the laws and in expressions of public opinion a wide area for disagreement about the extent to which the federal government should police and control business practices. A clash of philosophies regarding the proper scope of such federal powers is a feature of this story.

In 1953, when the Eisenhower administration took office, Republican officials began attempting to "change the climate" of the government's activities affecting business to one more favorable to development and prosperity. Ritchie's complaint that his product had received a "raw deal" from the National Bureau of Standards in the Department of Commerce was one of the early matters to engage the attention of Eisenhower's new Secretary of Commerce, Sinclair Weeks. The Secretary, presiding over a large staff of permanent officials and bureau chiefs who had served the previous (Democratic) administration, wanted to redirect his department's policies toward small, unproven businesses. He re-

quested the resignation of the Director of the National Bureau of Standards.

The National Bureau of Standards had played a critical role in the AD-X2 matter. It was, among other things, the government's testing agency. Not itself a regulatory agency, it provided scientific advice on products to the FTC, the Post Office Department, other government agencies, and the public generally. Its scientists had tested battery additives for decades and held that they were generally worthless. This opinion by the government's preeminent scientific authority in the field had appeared to spell economic disaster and federal prosecution for Ritchie.

But Ritchie had refused to give way. Aggressively he had sought support for his product from battery users, senior officials, newspapers, congressmen, and scientists. He charged the Bureau of Standards with bias and inaccuracy, and he took his charges to the Senate Small Business Committee, which subsequently arranged tests at the Massachusetts Institute of Technology. The committee and Ritchie interpreted the MIT tests as vindication of AD-X2. The controversy had led Weeks to investigate the matter and then to ask for the resignation of the bureau's director.

Weeks' action, interpreted widely as a blow against objective scientific inquiry, caused an uproar that overshadowed Ritchie's case. The Secretary was charged with sacrificing the objectivity of science on the altar of Republican political philosophy. Various groups of scientists vigorously supported the Bureau of Standards. Weeks finally reinstated the director. A committee of eminent scientists was then appointed to assess the quality of the bureau's testing of AD-X2. It reported the bureau's work to have been excellent and supported its evaluation of AD-X2.

It was then left to the Post Office and the FTC to deal with the original question of whether to proceed against Ritchie on the ground that his additive was worthless. Confronting them were (1) scientists who claimed that bureau laboratory investigations proved that the additive could have no significant effect on battery life; (2) a number of large users of batteries who testified that the additive had in fact prolonged the service of their batteries.

The AD-X2 case cannot be described as a "typical" instance of government regulation. It might have been if Ritchie had followed the usual course, had remained on the defensive in the face of prosecution, and had used only the range of rights (such as testimony and evidence at hearings) and appeals (inside the agencies and then to the federal courts) that regulatory procedures afforded to insure due process. But Ritchie's extraordinary aggressiveness and resourcefulness led him to surmount these defensive procedures and to seize the offensive. He took his case to the Congress, to the public, and to higher levels in the executive branch. He turned the tables on his "regulators" and sought to put them on trial.

If, in fact, Ritchie had reason to believe that his material was without merit, his attacks on the government agencies that opposed him could be considered masterfully audacious, cynical, and unscrupulous. If, on the other hand, AD-X2 actually did prolong battery life, the question arises whether the federal agencies were persecuting a venturesome and innovating small businessman. Between these two extremes, the unfolding of the AD-X2 case in the following pages affords a number of additional possibilities that would picture neither side as pure saint or complete devil. The different possibilities existed in the AD-X2 case because, in a period when the public was looking to "science" for advice on major national decisions, a precise picture of just what did happen when a storage battery ages was still not a matter of complete agreement among scientists and experts. Nor was it clear where the course of regulatory justice lay when laboratory tests were contradicted by sworn testimony from many persons who used large quantities of a white crystalline additive powder in actual field situations.

The story of the AD-X2 controversy thus has many facets. It describes an episode of government regulation of business, regulation which, in this case, was encouraged by some elements of the business community itself. It indicates some aspects of the relationship between a new department head and the scientific staff of one of the bureaus in his department. It shows a congressional committee seeking a constructive role in a matter ordinarily handled outside the legislative branch by more formal processes. It depicts the transformation of a commercial regulatory question into a political matter that attracted nationwide interest and caused scientific groups to enter the political policy-making arena in order to protect a scientist and his bureau from a political-administrative decision.

AD-X2 and The National Bureau of Standards

Among the correspondence that came to the desk of Dr. George W. Vinal, chief of the electrochemistry section of the Electricity Division at the National Bureau of Standards late in April 1948, was a letter written by Dr. Merle Randall of Oakland, California. Dr. Randall explained that he was writing in the capacity of technical consultant to Jess M. Ritchie, who had recently purchased the equities in a patent application covering AD-X2.[1] The letter continued, in the manner of a scientist sharing with a colleague his most recent investigations:

> The battery AD-X2 process involves the addition of a powder mixture of anhydrous sodium sulfate and a slightly basic, nearly anhydrous, magnesium sulfate to the water while it is filled with standard sulfuric acid electrolyte. Curiously, the result is quite different from that when equivalent amounts of sodium sulfate and epsom salts are added. . . .

> Actual large scale fleet operational tests . . . as well as my own observations, indicate a remarkable improvement in the service of both new batteries and those discarded as sulfated in use or on the shelf. Reduction of 85, 90, and, in one instance, 95 percent in annual battery expense during the past year has been reported by large firms, some of which have always had an intelligent battery service program. These operational service results are, after all, not wholly to be disregarded.

> I am calling this matter to your attention because of the enormous potential effect which these developments can have in connection with the servicing of the "mothball fleet" and the Army reserve equipment, as well as its effect on the practical conservation of lead, one of our vitally essential materials.

The correspondents were familiar with each other's work in the field of

---

[1] The trade name "AD-X2" is used throughout this study. Actually, the name was not coined until July 1948. The patent application purchased by Ritchie covered a material called Protector-charge.

electrochemistry. Dr. Randall had achieved a solid reputation for scholarship in thermodynamics, being coauthor with G. N. Lewis of *Thermodynamics and the Free Energy of Chemical Substances* (1923). He was an emeritus professor of chemistry of the University of California at Berkeley. Dr. Vinal was considered one of the Bureau of Standards' most eminent scientists. His *Storage Batteries* was an authoritative work on lead-acid storage batteries. He was also chiefly responsible for designing the "life-cycle" test, which had been accepted as the measure for capacity by the Association of American Battery Manufacturers.

The National Bureau of Standards

Vinal's 41 years of service covered all but 16 years of the entire life of the National Bureau of Standards (NBS), which had been established in 1901 as a bureau in the Treasury Department to succeed the tiny Office of Weights and Measures, which then had custody over the nation's limited number of official standards. The bureau's standards—there were in 1958 over seven hundred—provided a common denominator for mass production, mass marketing, and scientific research. The importance of this function to the nation's commerce caused the bureau to be transferred to the newly established Department of Commerce in 1913.

As an arm of the Commerce Department, the bureau was requested to expand its services to consumers and industry. Active programs were undertaken to promote trade agreements to simplify product lines, meet quality standards, and label goods adequately. These activities were looked upon by bureau scientists as trade rather than scientific policy, and were undertaken with considerable reluctance. Since its inception, the bureau regarded itself as a scientific agency. Its directors were scientists who had neither commercial nor political experience. Its first director consciously developed a campus-like atmosphere away from the Commerce Department in downtown Washington so that NBS facilities might be conducive to basic research and attract outstanding scientists.

The bureau was called upon to play a leading role in military research and weapons development in World War II. The Korean conflict renewed emphasis on weaponry, and by 1953 this function had grown to 85 percent of the bureau's activity. Only one percent of NBS's resources was devoted to product testing, and only about $25,000 a year was spent for tests performed for regulatory agencies.

The dominance of military work affected the bureau's relations with the Department of Commerce and with Congress. Since much of its military-type work was paid for by other agencies, it was not completely dependent on direct congressional appropriations. The shift in the nature of its work meant that the bureau's activities were increasingly divorced from the main interests of the Department of Commerce and the congressional committees to which the department reported.

The Bureau's Work
with Battery Additives

When Randall's letter arrived, Vinal was engaged in technical investigations for the Navy. "I have been extremely busy with matters . . . important for national defense," he wrote another person shortly thereafter. "I do not feel I can take too much time . . . on these rather troublesome bat-tery compounds." Vinal added the Randall letter to his unit's large file on battery additives without preparing an immediate answer.

Vinal's experience with additives dated from the 1920s. Hundreds of products of the additive family, claiming to lengthen battery life or pep up battery performance, had been introduced without either commercial success or scientific recognition. NBS had tested about one hundred. Shortly after World War II NBS had conducted a two-year research project to find a material that would reduce damage to military batteries during wet storage. Five more additives had been tested in 1947; two in 1948. In none of these tests had Dr. Vinal been able to discover any beneficial effect.

Much of the bureau's work with battery additives had been undertaken at the request of the FTC and the Post Office Dept. Altogether NBS had made 47 negative reports on some 35 separate materials; the products were subsequently withdrawn from commerce.

The results of its first decade of research with additives appeared in a 1931 circular (L.C. 302) cautioning against their use. Magnesium and sodium sulfates, the two basic ingredients of AD-X2 and many other additives tested by the bureau, were discussed and condemned. The bureau's experience, supported by the research of private individuals and groups, tended to discredit the entire concept of battery additives. As some were clearly harmful, their use generally voided battery guarantees.

The Workings of
The Mysterious Storage Battery

Though practical electrical tests of many battery additives provided a firm basis for the bureau's conclusions about additives, scientists are not able to explain completely the nature of the electrochemical processes of lead-acid batteries or the effects of altering the content of the battery electrolyte.[2] The efficiency of a battery is impeded by local electrochemical action at the plates, imperfect insulation between battery elements, and inability of the electrolyte to penetrate the active material on the plates. These effects cause energy to be dissipated as heat, which in turn accelerates crystallization of the lead sulfates on the plates. It was Randall's claim that AD-X2 would reduce formation of this hard lead sulfate and increase the porosity of the active material on old plates.

Scientists acknowledge that the introduction of salts into the electrolyte may help the decomposition of hardened sulfate, chiefly during the early stages of charging a heavily sulfated, severely discharged battery. But the advantage gained during this portion of the charge had been found to be offset by a negative effect in the latter portion of the charging period. Furthermore, additives had been found to decrease the adhesion of lead sulfate to the plates, causing the material to be shed and to collect in the base of the battery as "mud." This could cause short circuiting of the battery.

Scientists do not agree, however, on the extent or exact nature of the effects alluded to above, the effect of pernicious sulfation on battery operation, or the validity of laboratory methods for reproducing conditions of battery usage found in the field. Dr. Vinal, for

example, believed that sulfation itself was not a major cause of battery failure, but that more often failure was caused by the mechanical consequences of sulfation—broken separators, ruptured plates, and short circuiting—which could not possibly be corrected by introduction of an additive.

Jess Ritchie and His Limejuice Cocktail

The man who developed AD-X2, and on whose behalf Dr. Randall wrote the NBS, was Jess M. Ritchie. Ritchie, a self-educated engineer, was born in 1909 in Sharpe County, Arkansas. He supplemented a sixth-grade education with correspondence courses, then worked as a certified bulldozer operator and as a journeyman diesel engineer. During World War II he worked as a civilian in charge of various defense contracts and in 1946 joined the Drake-Utah-Grove construction combine on an $80,000,000 Army Engineer contract, serving as general superintendent of construction with headquarters in the Philippines. In 1945 he qualified as a Class A general contractor in California. In 1953 he listed himself as a "Psychologist-Specialist in Alcoholism" in the phone directory in Oakland, California. By this time, too, he was able to claim a Doctor of Psychology degree from a Chicago institution called the College of Universal Truth.

In the Philippines, Ritchie relates, he had encountered severe battery troubles. Thousands of war surplus batteries stockpiled in the islands were sulfated to the point where their plates were absolutely inert. By squeezing the juice of wild limes into the electrolyte, Ritchie said, he made these batteries take a charge. After a few days the active material was shed from the plates and the battery ruined, but with

---

[2] In physics, an electrolyte is a type of electrical conductor in which, when traversed by an electric current, there is a liberation of matter at the electrodes. In an ordinary battery the electrolyte is dilute sulfuric acid, a solution that conducts electricity.

plenty of batteries and plenty of limes, Ritchie continued this operation until the end of his overseas tour in 1947.

Returning to California, Ritchie bought a partnership in a firm that manufactured and distributed a battery additive. However, the mixture severely damaged many batteries, and Ritchie found himself with a crowd of dissatisfied customers.

It was this experience, Ritchie reports, that led him to seek the assistance of Dr. Randall, senior partner in a firm of chemical engineering consultants. Together they searched the literature on the electrochemical processes of battery operation and initiated a series of tests to try to find an additive that worked. Their experiments led to the accidental discovery of AD-X2 in October 1947.

Ritchie has written of that moment:

> We grew more tense with each passing hour, and stepped up our testing. All that Dr. Randall could say was "Amazing! Amazing!" Fortunately, we had been keeping accurate notes on everything and we had exact details of that accidentally processed batch of chemicals.

Ritchie did not patent the mixture. He has protected the product by refusing steadfastly to reveal the additive's contents or its manner of preparation. He bought out his previous associates and established the business as Pioneers Inc., with himself as president.

The new mixture was marketed immediately to large industrial users— many of whom employed experienced battery maintenance engineers and had controlled accounts from which they could ascertain battery costs. Advertising was placed only in trade journals, and the claims made for AD-X2, in contrast to those made on behalf of most previous additives, were modest. The material was sold with a one-year, "satisfaction-or-your-money back" guarantee. A three-dollar package was sufficient to treat an ordinary car battery.

At first, sales were slow, less than 1,000 packages per month. However, Ritchie's expectations that his customers would find the additive beneficial were confirmed, and business was brisk by 1948. Ritchie also persuaded a number of military installations to experiment with his material, and early test results appeared satisfactory.

The Better Business Bureau Turns to the NBS

Ritchie looked forward to even larger sales. But he soon learned that the additive business was a hazardous one, largely because of the longstanding and widespread suspicion of earlier additives. During the two decades before 1950 many a fast operator had "discovered" a battery additive, mass-produced it on a shoestring, and sold it at a high markup. So many flamboyantly advertised products had been put on the market that, since the 1920s, the National Better Business Bureau had condemned the whole additive business as a racket.

The National Better Business Bureau (NBBB) is an association of business and commercial firms, manufacturers, and national advertising agencies formed to promote high standards in national advertising. Dedicated to "building and conserving public confidence in advertising and business generally," it was organized in 1911 with headquarters in New York. Local better business bureaus located in most large cities are wholly autonomous. Oakland, Ritchie's home city, had a local bureau. Local bureaus are supported by local commercial interests; the national bureau by organizations with national business.

Although the NBBB had commissioned numerous tests of additives, it relied on test findings of the National Bureau of Standards to condemn additives in general. Additives were covered in a NBBB publication, *Facts About Battery Dopes,* issued around 1940, in which the NBS Director was quoted as saying that various compounds of salts "under a seemingly endless variety of trade names . . . have come and gone without attaining any permanent acceptance by the public or the battery industry." The NBBB fact sheet called the bureau "the highest impartial scientific authority in the U.S. on storage batteries."

Ritchie Tries for NBBB Support

Ritchie's position was that AD-X2 was a vastly different product from the run of quack additives. He had two objectives at this time: (1) to get NBS to make tests to "clear" AD-X2 and (2) to gain the support of the Better Business Bureaus. Randall reviewed all claims made for AD-X2 in its advertising and submitted them to the Oakland Better Business Bureau for its information. In addition he wrote the national office in New York and asked that the *Battery Dopes* sheet make an exception for AD-X2.

Ritchie and Randall often asked NBS to test AD-X2 to back their claim that it was not an ordinary additive. NBS officials believed they failed to provide data adequate to support their claims for AD-X2. Once Randall sent data from an experiment on a single battery. Vinal considered the results unreliable. Then in Dec. 1948 Vinal received a copy of a chemical analysis of AD-X2 made for Pioneers Inc. by a private west coast laboratory. NBS scientists did not think the analysis showed anything to distinguish AD-X2

from other sodium and magnesium sulfate mixtures.

NBBB was also occupied at this time with other additives bearing colorful trade names—Hi-Charge, Pepgo, Sure Start, Duble Power, Ever-Start, and Ever-Charge. Hoping to clarify the status of all additives, Kenneth B. Willson, executive director, suggested to Vinal that NBS issue a new circular on additives, stating the latest scientific findings in the field since its last circular in 1931.

Working relationships between the NBS and the NBBB were close, and consultation between top officials was frequent. NBS officials saw nothing improper in these arangements. NBS' basic legislation authorized the publication of scientific and technical findings when the information was deemed important to scientific or manufacturing interests. The NBBB, these officials said, "represents as broad a consensus of business interests as you can find in this country." And, although NBS was authorized to distribute bulletins of consumer interest, it rarely did so. It relied on private groups to publicize its findings.

Dr. Vinal agreed that a new circular would be desirable. On June 25, 1948 he wrote Willson that he had had this "in mind for some time and in the new circular [I hope] to incorporate some of the data more recently obtained." He did not mention AD-X2.

Vinal began work on the draft statement. During the period of its incubation, he discussed the technical contents—in line with established bureau custom—with several battery manufacturers who were in Washington attending a meeting of the Association of American Battery Manufacturers. NBS officials defended this type of consultation on grounds that the people "best qualified to comment and appraise methods of evaluating battery performance are the technical engineers and scientists in the battery industry."

At this stage, a sharp difference of opinion began to develop between the local and national Better Business Bureau offices. The Oakland office, on the basis of Randall's submissions and its own investigations, which included sample tests and interviews with users, concluded that both the NBS and its own national office were unfairly discriminating against Pioneers Inc. Oakland BBB manager Jack Harris felt that Ritchie's troubles stemmed from the fact that NBS, without having tested AD-X2, had lumped it unfairly into the category of prior, unsatisfactory additives. He wrote Vinal on December 1, 1948 and asked the bureau to test AD-X2. At the same time, he forwarded samples for making the tests.

Oakland also urged other business bureaus in the western states to support a resolution to the national bureau opposing prior condemnation of any new product by generalized circulars. Harris asked them to support AD-X2 regardless of NBS statements.

Vinal spelled out the NBS position on testing a specific commercial product in a letter dated December 22, 1948 to the Oakland Better Business Bureau. He made these points: (1) no tests had been made on AD-X2 because Pioneers' consultant, Dr. Randall, had failed to distinguish it from standard additives; (2) "this Bureau does not make commercial tests of batteries or battery materials, and it is an established policy of the Bureau not to endorse commercial products or to permit the results of its tests to be used for advertising purposes"; (3) tests were already being made at the Signal Corps Laboratory at Ft. Monmouth, New Jersey, and at the New York and Mare Island Navy Yards. "These are competent laboratories dealing with large numbers of batteries. In view of the above fact, it does not seem desirable for a fourth Government Agency, that is, this Bureau, to spend the time urgently needed for Army and Navy work to make further tests of these materials."

Results of the military tests reached the Bureau of Standards early in 1949. They were contradictory and did not satisfy any of the parties to the dispute. The Detroit Arsenal, the New York Navy Shipyard, and the Squire Signal Laboratory at Ft. Monmouth all reported negatively. Benecia Arsenal and the Aberdeen Proving Ground tests were favorable. However, the latter two were conducted in a manner Vinal considered unsuitable. It is not clear whether Vinal had access to the test data or only to summaries of the results.

Military agencies suspended purchase of AD-X2 after the Ft. Monmouth and New York Navy Yard tests. Tests in progress at McClelland Field and Wright-Patterson Air Force Base, which Ritchie claimed were favorable to his product, were also stopped. Because most of the military tests were classified as restricted to government personnel only, Ritchie complained that he was unable to examine or criticize them.

The receipt of the military data accelerated the correspondence between Vinal and the NBBB. Anxious over whether NBBB was absolutely correct in its statements in *Facts About Battery Dopes,* Willson wanted NBS to make a confirming statement.

Late in 1948 Senator William F. Knowland also requested NBS to test AD-X2 "so that this product could stand on its own merits." Knowland's home was in Oakland, California, and Ritchie had forwarded him a file on AD-X2.

NBS Tests AD-X2

Accordingly in January 1949 Vinal, for his own information, undertook a limited test of AD-X2, along with another additive being tested at the request of the Federal Trade Commission. This test included a chemical analysis and observation of the electrical performance of one new and one old sulfated battery treated with AD-X2. The analysis indicated to Vinal: (1) that the material was a simple mixture of magnesium and sodium sulfates; and (2) that the trace elements in AD-X2 included nothing not ordinarily found in the sodium and magnesium sulfates in other additives or in battery electrolytes.

Earlier, in the fall of 1948, Vinal had drafted a revision of L.C. 302 and submitted it to the NBS Editorial Committee for approval. With the spurt of interest in AD-X2 and other additives, NBS officials decided that a more complete and formal publication should be prepared. To answer the NBBB's immediate request, however, NBS in March 1949 issued an interim statement on additives over the signature of Dr. Edward U. Condon, NBS Director.

The Condon statement did not refer to any additive by trade name. It expressed the hope that eventually some material might be found to "relieve the difficulties arising from abnormal operation of storage batteries, but none of the exploited materials which have been tested here have had any such merits." It concluded that "the best electrolyte for a storage battery is that presently used by the battery manufacturers, since years of research and experience have shown no other materials superior to the customary sulphuric acid electrolyte of proper specific gravity."

A reprint of its 1931 circular (L.C. 302) on additives was issued by the bureau on March 31, 1949. The new circular recommended against the use of all additives. It contained general information about the effect of sodium and magnesium sulfates on the performance of lead-acid batteries and discussed techniques and procedures for evaluating battery performance. This circular, in line with NBS practice, did not refer to consumer experience, and it did not refer to additives by trade name.

This re-issue of the circular by NBS took care of the NBBB concern about whether its statements in *Facts About Battery Dopes* were still sound. The reprint of L.C. 302 also provided ammunition to battery manufacturing companies interested in policing false claims for additives. Six of the nation's largest battery manufacturing companies were members of the NBBB.

FTC Begins Investigation

The National Better Business Bureau felt justified at this time in lodging a complaint with the Federal Trade Commission, and on June 17, 1949 it asked the FTC to take action against AD-X2 on the ground that the advertising claims of Pioneers Inc. were false. The FTC ordered a field investigation by its San Francisco office. Willson of NBBB notified Dr. Vinal that his organization was complaining to the FTC.

This action by the national office angered the Oakland Better Business Bureau, and on August 30, 1949 Oakland manager Jack Harris wrote a sharply critical letter to Willson:

> Here, Ken, is the issue as I see it. In my opinion, neither you nor the National Better Business Bureau, nor any other organization in God's green earth, have the right to participate in

preventing a man from carrying on free enterprise by direct or indirect means, unless there is a reasonable basis for such action.

Pioneers Inc. continued to make sales gains. Ritchie expanded his business by collecting junked batteries, which he salvaged and rebuilt. This operation, coupled with the growing acceptance of AD-X2, exacerbated the alarm of the established battery manufacturers. One manufacturer, Keystone Batteries, Inc., wrote the Association of American Battery Manufacturers on February 10, 1950:

> This is a serious situation. We know that we have lost a considerable amount of business for last month alone, and the loss of business to large manufacturers must run into thousands. We feel sure that with the cooperation of the association and all its members we will be able to lick this thing.

The association forwarded this letter to the FTC on March 10, 1950, with a request that the FTC "take some action . . . in the interest of both battery manufacturers and consumers. Before doing so, a careful analysis of this material should be made. . . ."

The FTC field investigation was already underway. Instead of unearthing complaints, its San Francisco office found wide acceptance for AD-X2 in and around the Bay Area. The proponents included technical personnel at military installations, the Oakland Chamber of Commerce, the Oakland BBB, and many individual customers.

In view of the nature of the support and the caliber of the supporters, the San Francisco office of the FTC suggested to Washington in February 1950 that new tests of AD-X2 would be desirable. The FTC made such a request of NBS on March 22, 1950.

Vinal's earlier experiments with two batteries treated with AD-X2, augmented by chemical analyses of AD-X2 made in April 1950, formed the basis for the results NBS reported to the FTC on May 11. Dr. Vinal told the FTC that "a series of tests" had failed to demonstrate any "significant reduction in harmful sulfation. . . ." NBS conducted no field tests—tests performed under conditions for which the product was to be used.

While the NBS was preparing its report on AD-X2 for the FTC, correspondence had been continuing between Dr. Vinal and Kenneth Willson of the NBBB. The NBS was preparing to issue a revision of its battery additive circular and to incorporate in it the research of the past several years. NBBB was collecting material for a new publication of its own on additives.

Both Vinal and Willson were aware that Ritchie, in his promotional literature, claimed that the blanket statements made in the NBS and NBBB literature did not and could not apply to AD-X2, since AD-X2 had not been tested. As a result, the NBBB was flooded with inquiries about whether AD-X2 was or was not a safe and effective additive.

Willson began to press the NBS. He told Vinal that the number and nature of the inquiries obliged the NBBB to issue a statement on the subject. Finally, on March 29 he informed Vinal that Pioneers was collecting evidence to initiate a damage suit against NBBB or the battery manufacturers because of distribution of the NBBB publication. Neither the Bureau of Standards, as a government agency, nor Vinal individually, when acting in an official capacity, might be sued. The NBBB did not enjoy this immunity. Willson knew that the bureau was preparing to issue a revision of its battery additive

circular which incorporated the research of recent years. He continued:

> However, Dr. Vinal, there would be
> no need for us to issue any statement
> to battery manufacturers, or to any-
> one else, on this subject if you would
> permit us to inform Pioneers Inc. that
> you have now concluded a compre-
> hensive test of AD-X2. . . .
>
> If we can now tell Pioneers Inc. that
> you have tested this product and found
> it wanting, they may continue to dis-
> pute your findings and conclusions,
> but they cannot claim that they are
> based on theory and not on intimate
> knowledge of the product.

The policy of the Bureau of Standards was to avoid endorsing or condemning any proprietary product by
name. Since silence on its part might
be interpreted as an endorsement for
AD-X2, Ritchie's tactic (i.e., claiming in his advertising that NBS condemnation of additives could not apply
to AD-X2) placed NBS in a quan-
dary. Its officials felt that Ritchie's allegations were untrue, that NBS' integrity was being impugned, and that
the public was being exposed to exaggerated claims for a worthless additive.

NBS Disagrees Publicly with Ritchie

On April 5, 1950 Vinal gave in and
granted Willson permission to tell Pioneers Inc. that tests had been made
on AD-X2. On July 24 the NBS abandoned its policy altogether when it
authorized NBBB to issue a public
statement that NBS had tested AD-X2
and found it to be without merit. In the
NBBB publication there was also a direct rebuttal by Ritchie of the NBS
statement, which the NBBB had included to avoid a possible legal suit
by Pioneers, Inc.

In August 1950 the NBBB issued a
new publication on additives entitled
Battery Compounds and Solutions, a
leaflet that incorporated the Condon
statement of March 1949, parts of revised L.C. 302, and subsequent bureau
statements that referred specifically and
negatively to AD-X2. Battery manufacturers made wide use of it to answer
inquiries about additives.

Although the NBBB distributed 50,-
000 copies of its own publication,
Willson was eager to stimulate circulation of the new NBS circular on additives then being planned. On October
31, 1950 Willson wrote NBS that his
organization "would be glad to see that
battery manufacturers, automotive publications, all better business bureaus
and similar firms . . . receive a copy
along with our recommendation that it
be brought to the attention of their particular audience. It should reach every
battery manufacturer, dealer, supply
house, and trade paper in the automotive field, and all concerned with the
use of batteries in any field."

Before NBS got out the revision of
its additive circular, Ritchie's sales
soared when *Newsweek* magazine carried an article in December 1950 prais-
ing the beneficial effects reported by
AD-X2 users. The magazine had been
alerted to the controversy by the dispute evident in NBBB's *Battery Compounds and Solutions*—particularly
Ritchie's statement that the NBS was
wrong about his additive. *Newsweek*
quoted from tests favorable to AD-X2
and from satisfied customers. Ritchie
reported that Pioneers received 8,000
letters shortly after publication of the
article.

Meantime the Federal Trade Commission continued its investigation of
Pioneers. Its San Francisco attorney-
examiner did not consider the NBS test
results conclusive. He felt that the NBS
report would have had greater effect
if actual service tests had been made.

He felt that the overwhelmingly satisfactory experience of many Bay Area users, reinforced by tests approving AD-X2 made at the University of San Francisco, outweighed the NBS findings. He therefore recommended on December 8, 1950 that the FTC drop its case "without prejudice to the right of the Commission to reopen if and when warranted by facts."

The FTC examiner was overruled by reviewing officials in both Washington and San Francisco who felt that the laboratory tests at NBS were more competent and conclusive than the experience of users. Attempts were then made to work out a stipulation under which Ritchie would modify some of his advertising claims. Ritchie refused to accept any restrictions on his advertising. The FTC investigation then continued.

NBS Issues Its Definitive Circular

NBS spelled out its position on additives in complete and apparently authoritative detail with publication of a new circular on January 10, 1951. L.C. 504, a formal study with test data, was accompanied by a press release. This was followed in April 1951 by a technical report suitable for publication in scientific magazines. Finally, in May 1951 one of NBS' subscription periodicals carried a reprint of the technical report.

Ritchie described the NBS publications on additives as "a perpetual news release." They were extensively publicized in such journals as *Transport Topics, Powerplant Engineer,* and *Chemical and Engineering News.*

In trying to combat the unfavorable publicity, Ritchie was thwarted on several fronts. He first asked magazines that had published the NBS findings to carry Pioneers' side of the issue. One reply, characteristic of several, came from *Chemical and Engineering News:* "Our June 11 [1951] issue carried a factual report and news release by the Bureau of Standards. If you are in disagreement with the research as reported by the Bureau, I would suggest that you contact them directly."

At the same time the battery industry took steps to cut off AD-X2 advertising. One publisher wrote Pioneers that the advertising agency representing a nationally advertised battery had protested its acceptance of Pioneers' ads in view of the absence of NBS approval. The usual procedure, the *Commercial Car Journal* publisher wrote (October 19, 1951), "and the one which we must follow in this case—is to hold everything in abeyance until the accused manufacturer has an opportunity to make a statement in his own behalf. In this case the statement would have to be that the product has been approved by the U.S. Bureau of Standards, because in its department it is the Supreme Court."

Norman Goodwin, Pioneers' aggressive Boston distributor, reported an alleged incident of planned harassment that occurred when he made a talk on AD-X2 at a meeting of the International Municipal Signalmen's Association in Boston. During the 30-minute period set aside for questions,

> The New England manager for a large national battery manufacturer stood up, and he and his assistant took up the whole question period reading the National Bureau of Standards Circular 504. As one man would stop, the other would start—for the full thirty minutes. Why? What had they to fear if AD-X2 was no good?

Business began to slacken as 1951 advanced. Despite the favorable *Newsweek* article, the effect of L.C. 504 and the resulting publicity was to severely discourage promotion and sales of AD-X2. From a quarterly peak of $75,000 following the *Newsweek* publicity, sales dropped to $40,000 in the last quarter of 1951. They dipped further to $15,000 in the first quarter of 1952. And neither Ritchie nor Randall, nor the good offices of the Oakland BBB, nor the requests of California's Senator Knowland had been sufficient to persuade NBS that there was a need for further testing of AD-X2. Ritchie began to cast about for ways to bring political pressure to bear on NBS.

Ritchie Attacks the Bureau

He began by issuing a nine-page memo on August 21, 1951 to AD-X2 "distributors, prospective distributors and interested parties." It said:

> We are now trying to bring sufficient pressure to cause a Senate investigation of the National Bureau of Standards. We certainly have reason to believe that an investigation and perhaps a shakeup are in order. A few days ago . . . Dr. Edward U. Condon . . . suddenly resigned. We like to believe that we had something to do with the resignation.[3]

Ritchie's appeal stirred the recipients to action. A number of them reported the seemingly intransigent attitude of NBS to their senators and congressmen. They also bombarded NBS with requests that its unfavorable judgment of AD-X2 be reversed.

---

[3] Dr. Condon had encountered another opponent besides Ritchie. The "McCarthy era" was at its height, and the late Representative J. Parnell Thomas, chairman of the House Un-American Activities Committee, had publicly denounced Condon as "the weakest link in our atomic security chain." The bureau's advanced research in weapons made the unsubstantiated charge seem serious.

Ritchie summed up his political campaign this way:

> The way we got action was the distributors wrote to the senators, the senators wrote to the Bureau of Standards, the Bureau of Standards wrote back to the senators, and the senators sent it back to their constituent, who was our distributor, and they sent it to us, and we could see how they were thinking. That is the way 24 senators got tangled up in it.

Many of the senators and congressmen wrote a second and third time. To handle the volume of correspondence, NBS issued a mimeographed leaflet in August 1951. It described the tests reported in L.C. 504 as yielding "unambiguous results."

Three factors contributed to the bureau's adamant stand. First, it believed it was right. However, neither the NBS nor NBBB had had any personal contact with Ritchie, his organization, or customers. Their opposition was founded on the theory of battery operation, analogy to the performance of other salts, tests performed by the Detroit Arsenal and the New York Navy Shipyard, one or two chemical analyses, and electrical tests on two batteries—one new, one used. Although AD-X2 appeared to be gaining satisfied users, NBS did not take the favorable user evidence seriously enough to perform more extensive tests. Also the bureau's chemical analysis indicated not only that the material was largely magnesium and sodium sulfates, but that there was a high degree of variability in their mixture from batch to batch. Vinal's attitude remained essentially the way he had described it in 1949:

> None [of a great many tests] have shown that either $MgSO_4$ or Na_2SO_4 or their combination . . . has been the answer. It is up to Randall

[Ritchie's scientific consultant, who died in 1950] to prove that his sodium and magnesium sulfate can behave differently than any other. As yet we have seen nothing that indicates this.

Second, the bureau's handling of congressional inquiries was not merely a product of its thirty years' experience with battery additives. It had a long tradition of freedom from political pressure. Unlike most executive agencies, NBS, with its large volume of reimbursable contract work, even enjoyed some independence from congressional appropriations. Finally, there was the possibility that the AD-X2 question might lead to demands from others for reconsideration of their products. The bureau had also to consider the priorities among many urgent demands upon its time and facilities. It did not appear likely that further testing of AD-X2 would be productive.

Ritchie Goes To Washington

On March 2, 1952 Ritchie received a registered letter from the Post Office Department in Washington. From its contents he learned that he stood accused of "conducting an unlawful enterprise through the mails." He was ordered to appear in Washington on April 26 to answer the charge before an official complaint was issued. Ritchie packed his bags, determined to camp in Washington until he had won his case.

In Washington Ritchie first hired lawyers. Next he sought the help of the Senate Small Business Committee and its counterpart in the House of Representatives. When he endeavored to engage a technical staff, he ran into some difficulty because, he said later, "all the men recognized as authorities in the battery field were connected with the battery industry." After surveying about 200 names, Ritchie located and obtained the services of Dr. Keith Laidler, a young and promising associate professor of chemistry at Catholic University and author of a recognized study of catalytic action.

Ritchie and his attorney also visited the Massachusetts Institute of Technology to try to enlist the technical support of Dr. Harold C. Weber, professor of chemical engineering. Weber had known of AD-X2 since 1948 and more recently had become acquainted with Pioneers' Boston distributor, Norman Goodwin. He had subsequently run some preliminary tests of AD-X2. When Ritchie talked to Weber in April 1952, he found him "very sympathetic and very understanding of our problem." Ritchie said Weber promised to serve as an unpaid consultant to the Senate Small Business Committee on the AD-X2 case.

The Small Business Committee

Ritchie got help from both the House and Senate Small Business Committees [4] early in 1952. The House Committee was the first to act. On March 11, 1952 it requested NBS to test AD-X2. When the Senate committee began to take a more active interest in the case, the House unit withdrew from the controversy.

---

[4] Both committees at the time were directed by Democratic chairmen, but the Small Business Committees continued to assist Ritchie under the leadership of both parties. The allegiance of many congressional committees to a certain committee point of view on matters within their special cognizance is often stronger than differences in party philosophy.

The Senate Select Committee on Small Business had been organized as a permanent body in 1950 to "study and survey . . . all problems of American small business enterprise." The committee had no legislative jurisdiction and was not empowered to report bills. It maintained a six-man professional staff whose efforts were largely directed to seeking redress of the complaints of individual small businessmen about their relations with the federal government. Senators found the committee a useful body to which to refer the problems of constituents who were small businessmen.

The committee's staff operated virtually free of supervision in these cases. When Ritchie sought the committee's assistance, he was referred to Blake O'Connor, Harvard-educated, former journalist and employee of various government agencies including the Department of Commerce, a staff member of the committee since 1950.

Ritchie had arrived at the right place at the right time. The committee and its staff were looking for an opportunity to do more than they had been doing. The staff started by treating the Ritchie case as another routine request from a small businessman. As time went on, however, O'Connor saw in the AD-X2 matter a dramatic example of what the committee later described as "the problems of small businessmen who find themselves at odds with any government body which . . . holds life-or-death power over them."

To O'Connor, the fact that the large battery manufacturers regarded AD-X2 as a threat was an indication that the additive did work. He came to see in AD-X2 a test for the committee: "Would the committee be content merely to make more or less innocuous studies of small business problems and file reports for the record or would the

committee turn when needed into an aggressive champion of the right of the nation's small businessman?"

Requests for
New Tests at NBS

Ritchie wanted NBS to test his additive again. This request was being echoed in many other quarters, as a result of Ritchie's letter-writing barrage of the year before. Even before this, Senators Richard Nixon of California and Henry Dworshak of Idaho had written the Federal Trade Commission to ask if tests might be conducted by some independent laboratory or if the dispute could be placed before some independent scientific referee. The FTC had deemed this proposal inappropriate and perhaps harmful to its future relationships with the Bureau of Standards.

However, the FTC wanted more conclusive tests, which it felt were needed to sustain a complaint against Pioneers Inc. On February 26, 1952 it requested the NBS to perform the tests, specifying that the design of the tests "duplicate, in so far as possible, the conditions for which the product is represented as being effective."

The Post Office Department, in the course of its investigation of Pioneers begun some six months earlier, had also asked NBS for tests of AD-X2. The Post Office postponed its April hearing on Ritchie's case to await the test results.

To fulfill these requests, Walter J. Hamer, Vinal's successor as chief of the NBS electrochemistry section,[5] de-

---

[5] After retiring from the NBS in 1951, Dr. Vinal was employed as a consultant to a number of firms, including a Philadelphia battery manufacturing company. To Ritchie, such employment proved his otherwise unsubstantiated charge that NBS personnel acted as agents for the battery industry when they refused to find merit in AD-X2.

cided to use the so-called Randall method for the new test beginning Mar. 19, 1952. Eighteen discarded batteries and six new batteries—a total of 72 cells—were used. Since the discarded batteries were old, Hamer felt Randall's method (which involved overcharging prior to the test) could validly be applied. For the new batteries, the severe precharge was omitted and the batteries cycled at a low amperage to equalize their starting capacity. The test ran for two weeks. Hamer found no beneficial effect associated with AD-X2 treatment.

Pioneers Inc. was not told that this test was being conducted. When, some time later, he heard of its results, Ritchie vigorously protested the use of the Randall test procedure. He claimed that the low pretest charge given the new batteries returned the cells to perfect condition before AD-X2 was added and that the subsequent test period was too short to reveal any differences caused by treatment. Of the eighteen old batteries, six were dismantled and inspected before the test. Ritchie claimed those which were not already mechanically unsound were probably ruined by the severe overcharge which was a feature of the Randall test.

A New Director and a Public Test

The bureau now had a new director. Dr. Allen V. Astin had been named acting director when Dr. Condon had resigned late in 1951. He would become permanent director in June 1952. Educated at the University of Utah and at New York University, Dr. Astin had been with NBS since 1930. He was a distinguished scientist, well known for his contributions to the development of the proximity fuse in World War II.

The large file of correspondence, now augmented by a request from the Senate Small Business Committee for further tests, soon forced AD-X2 into the new director's attention. He determined that the additive should be given a public "demonstration" test independent of the confidential tests that Hamer was then performing for the Post Office and the FTC.

Ritchie's agreement on specific phases of the test method was then secured through correspondence and conferences. One matter, discussed orally, concerned the specific gravity of the electrolyte. NBS had stipulated in a letter of May 23 that no adjustments should be made to the electrolyte during charge. Ritchie's suggested procedure called for drawing off acid and adding water if the specific gravity increased during the charge to more than 1.280. A compromise was reached to cut the acid only if the specific gravity exceeded 1.325, and this procedure was used in the test.

It was Astin's hope to end the AD-X2 controversy with this test series, and he attempted to get Ritchie to agree that the new test results would be conclusive. On May 23 he wrote Ritchie:

> If the tests do not establish definitely the usefulness of your product, I will expect you to concur that it has not been possible to demonstrate the value of [it]. If the results show conclusively that your product is of value, then the Bureau's position will have to be modified.

Astin's plan to make the test public with results binding upon both parties had the effect of placing the bureau unofficially in a regulatory role, bypassing both the FTC and the Post Office. Based partly on oral agreements which could evaporate, and without any formal legal standing, the arrangement went beyond what it was within the power of the bureau to enforce.

The test, conducted in June 1952, was the bureau's first public experiment with AD-X2. A representative of Pioneers was permitted to observe a portion of it, and Ritchie, along with two associates, participated with NBS personnel in a visual evaluation of the condition of the battery plates after the test was completed. The conclusion, reported by NBS on July 15, was that "the battery additive tested has no beneficial effect on the properties or performance of batteries."

Astin's hope that this test would be conclusive proved false. Ritchie declared that he "could scarcely believe his eyes" to find electrolyte specific gravity readings from .1297 to .1315, that he had never agreed to this compromise, and that the deviations in test method were ruinous. Ritchie stated that the bureau had made ten unwarranted modifications in the test methods agreed upon. However, Astin believed that full agreement had been reached with Ritchie. Otherwise, he said, the bureau would not have consented to conduct the tests.

During the next few weeks a series of conferences took place between Ritchie's scientific consultant, Dr. Keith Laidler, and Dr. Astin, during which Laidler attempted to demonstrate alleged technical flaws in the NBS test procedures.

The Small Business Committee Acts

The Senate Small Business Committee now began to intervene actively in the person of its staff member, Blake O'Connor, who supported Ritchie's view that the test was unsatisfactory.

At O'Connor's request a meeting

was held on September 29 in Dr. Astin's office at the bureau. Its purpose, according to O'Connor, was to "clear the air." In attendance were Dr. Astin, O'Connor, Ritchie, Laidler, two representatives of the Post Office Department, a representative of the Department of Justice,[6] and several NBS scientists. Also present was Dr. Harold C. Weber, the chemical engineering professor from MIT, who reported favorable results from some preliminary tests of AD-X2 he had run on his own initiative. The bureau men listened but conceded no points. Although it was generally agreed that additional tests of AD-X2 were desirable, there was no definite decision about who would conduct them.

Tests at MIT

Ritchie stated at the September 29 meeting that he had no interest in further tests with NBS scientists in charge. During the meeting it was suggested that Dr. Weber should continue his testing at the Massachusetts Institute of Technology and that NBS scientists should observe the work. There was, furthermore, agreement that the chief of the NBS statistical section should estimate the number of tests necessary to provide a proper basis for statistical analysis.

On the basis of these suggestions, O'Connor wrote on October 8 to Dr. Julius Stratton, Provost of MIT, to re-

---

[6] The department was preparing an antitrust case against the Association of American Battery Manufacturers for conspiracy to prevent resale of used battery lead. Information on this matter had been received from Ritchie, who in the previous year had also suggested to the Department of Justice that the battery manufacturers had attempted to influence NBS judgment of battery additives. The department was not officially interested in AD-X2.

quest that university's cooperation in permitting Weber to continue and even to expand his tests at the MIT laboratories.

It was contrary to MIT's general policies to permit the use of its facilities for the evaluation of commercial products. Moreover, in view of the controversial history of battery additives, MIT authorities were not eager to become involved in the investigation. However, at this time they apparently believed that the tests would be conducted with the cooperation of NBS and "solely for the purpose of shedding additional light on technical aspects of the problem." As Dr. Stratton later explained:

> The request was made by a select committee of the United States Senate, and the Institute was informed that no funds were available through which the services of a commercial testing laboratory might be engaged. In view of these facts, MIT concluded that it was obligated to place its facilities at the disposal of the committee. . . .

With university permission granted, Dr. Weber resumed testing. Although the bureau originally had signified willingness to participate—at least to the extent of agreeing to advise on the number and type of tests that Weber should make—it later decided to abstain. "A major factor influencing this decision," Dr. Astin said, "was Mr. Ritchie's attitude toward the Bureau. . . . We concluded it would be better if MIT carried out its tests completely independently."

Weber formulated his own scheme for testing. His key decision was to report all changes in the batteries which resulted from treatment with AD-X2 irrespective of their practical application. He directed his experimental work toward establishing a test design that would reveal any physical effect associated with introduction of AD-X2 into battery electrolytes.

Later, when it became clear that NBS would not participate in the tests, Weber had already performed about half of his experiments. He recommended to the MIT administration that the tests should continue, and the university wrote to O'Connor that it was agreeable to having Weber perform the tests independently.

The Post Office Proceeding

While Ritchie and his adherents were engrossed with the tests at MIT, the Post Office Department moved to prosecute Pioneers for using the mails to defraud. It had asked NBS for test data, and it had conducted test correspondence to establish that AD-X2 was advertised and marketed through the mails. On March 18, 1952 it had issued the hearing notice that brought Ritchie to Washington. It had asked the bureau for additional test data that month. These tests, reported to the Post Office Department in July, had been run in connection with the eighteen battery tests for the FTC. The original hearing date of April 26 had been postponed on motion of Ritchie's attorneys and was now set for October 13. This hearing and its deliberations coincided with the testing at MIT. The charge was that Pioneers Inc. had violated Section 259 (Chapter 6) of Title 39 of the United States Code, which prohibited any scheme or device "for obtaining money . . . through the mails by means of false or fraudulent pretenses, representations or promises."

The Post Office Department, as well as the FTC, had previously taken action against vendors of other battery additives. Thirty-five additives had been withdrawn from the market either by cease-and-desist order or stipulation.

It has been suggested that the issuance of a complaint by the Post Office against Pioneers while the company was under investigation by the Federal Trade Commission placed Pioneers in double jeopardy. Lawyers point out, however, that the two agencies were interested in different facets of Ritchie's operation for violation of different statutes. The FTC is entrusted with protecting the public from deceptive advertising practices; the Post Office Department has the function of policing fraudulent activities carried on through the mails. The regulatory jurisdictions of the two sometimes overlap, but their purposes, procedures, and statutory authority are dissimilar. The Post Office must prove intent to defraud, but from the standpoint of a layman, its procedures are faster and somewhat less formal. Respondents in such Post Office cases have no power to subpoena witnesses.

Because the Post Office, to prove its case, had to show intent, Ritchie felt

> . . . it wasn't a case for the Post Office. The reason for this is simply that we had credible, responsible, scientific evidence which we were convinced indicated that the material did everything claimed for it. . . . It is certainly not the function of the Postmaster General to act as an arbitrator in a technical dispute.

Nevertheless, said Ritchie, he "found people in the Post Office Department working harder to convict us than would even the most ambitious and vindictive prosecuting attorney." He believed that the Bureau of Standards was the moving force behind the Post Office investigation. The Post Office does not require either consumer complaints—there were none in this case— or advice from another government de-partment to institute a fraud action. Many cases of potential fraud are initiated as the result of postal inspectors' reviews of published advertising claims.

In the course of informal negotiations, an Assistant Post Office Solicitor, William C. O'Brien, offered Ritchie a compromise which entailed his giving up his mail order business. Ritchie refused, as he had also refused to alter his position when the FTC tried to work out a stipulation involving some modification of his advertising claims. He estimated that mail orders constituted one percent of his gross sales.

On October 1, 1952 Ritchie again conferred with O'Brien to get his advice regarding Ritchie's defense. Ritchie had, inexplicably, dismissed his lawyers. He suggested to O'Brien that since he could not subpoena his witnesses, it might be advantageous to default the hearing and later, when the test at MIT was completed, appeal to the courts. O'Brien advised him that if he did not exhaust his administrative remedies, it was unlikely that the courts would entertain the appeal. Ritchie said that this information "settled the matter as far as I was concerned." O'Brien, however, interpreted Ritchie's remarks as indicating that he intended to let the hearing go by default.

Ritchie failed to appear at the hearing. Just ten days before the scheduled date, he left Washington for California. On October 11 he telephoned from California to say he was forwarding testimonials to support Pioneers' claims and to request that O'Brien present them at the hearing.[7]

O'Brien has sworn by affidavit that it was definitely clear to Ritchie that

---

[7] Such statements were not admissible as evidence. The Post Office Rules of Practice stated: "Affidavits concerning opinions or statements of an affiant will not be received in evidence, [unless] the witness whose state-

the hearing would go forward as scheduled. Ritchie, however, claimed that he intended to contest the Post Office action but did not realize the hearings were to be held immediately as scheduled.[8] However, on October 13 Ritchie again telephoned O'Brien and learned that the case was being heard at that moment. He requested that the hearing be kept open until he could fly to Washington. O'Brien told him this could not be done.

At the hearing Dr. Astin and seven top scientists from NBS were present to testify in support of the complaint. Nobody was present to enter Pioneers' defense. For such eventualities the Post Office Rules of Practice specify that "the hearing examiner shall receive such proof as he deems proper in support of the complaint, and shall make and file a decision from which there shall be no appeal." The hearing was concluded the following morning.

When it became clear to Ritchie that the formal record strongly supported the complaint, that his testimonials had no evidentiary status, and that the decision to be rendered on this record would be final, he immediately sought to reopen the case. With a new hearing, Ritchie hoped to utilize the findings at MIT.

Report on Tests at MIT

The tests at MIT were concluded November 7. As anticipated, certain physical effects were found to be associated with the use of AD-X2. However, the results were not necessarily

incompatible with the NBS findings, since the objective of the tests and the conditions under which they were made were radically different from the bureau's procedures. Weber had aimed at identifying and reporting *any* differences (rather than only significant differences) resulting from treatment with AD-X2. He had the help of three MIT colleagues in making the tests, two statisticians and a professor of chemistry.

When the analyses were completed in December 1952, the Weber group discussed the contents of the report with university authorities. Since the summer months of 1952, Weber had served without fee as a consultant to the Small Business Committee in connection with AD-X2 and had kept the administrative officers at MIT fully informed of his services.

The first portion of the report was devoted to the eight physical effects found to be associated with use of AD-X2. They included larger discharge capacity, cooler operation during charging, decreased sediment, less loss of electrolyte, and increased conductivity of the electrolyte. They were listed without reservation; qualifications—which were substantial—were discussed later. The report did not claim that any practical benefits were associated with the observed effects. Unlike the NBS tests, Weber's tests had been performed on batteries that were generally below the charge level for normal automobile operations. This suited Weber's experimental purpose, which was to identify *any* changes caused by introduction of AD-X2. In addition, the report did not claim that the same effects recorded in its earlier pages would not be found when using similarly composed additives. Finally, it stated that more extensive laboratory and field investigations should be made to establish conclusive results:

---

ment is offered shall testify under oath at the hearing that the statement is in all respects true."

[8] He later presented four affidavits (from Laidler, O'Connor, Weber, and an official in the Justice Department) to the effect that it had been understood that the hearing was to be postponed until after the test at MIT.

. . . Usually, an evaluation of how a product will act under field conditions can be obtained only after extensive laboratory experimentation. Even after such experimentation, it is common practice in engineering work to subject products to field tests. How a given innovation will perform under use conditions is the true test of its worth. For this reason, laboratory findings must be supplemented by field use data if a true evaluation is to be obtained.

The report carried the full authority and prestige of MIT. The letter of transmittal to the Senate Small Business Committee was written on December 16, 1952 by Provost Stratton:

. . . while we were reluctant to become involved in a controversial issue, we felt that we should make our facilities available to you in the public interest. All expenses in connection with these tests were covered by MIT. The MIT staff members who worked on the tests received no compensation from any source, and they have no financial or consulting interest in the product tested. . . .

We are making the results . . . available solely to the . . . Committee . . . MIT will make no public statement in connection with this investigation.

As suggested by the committee, the report was turned over to Pioneers' Boston distributer, Norman Goodwin, who personally delivered a sealed copy to the committee on December 17.

Publicity For MIT Tests

The supporters of AD-X2 were primed for the arrival of the report; the Bureau of Standards was not. That same day, even while a photostat of the report was being run off for the bureau, the committee was putting the finishing touches on a press release for Thursday morning's newspapers.

The press release proclaimed that the tests at MIT completely supported the manufacturer's claims. By concentrating on the eight effects Weber had found and by playing down the qualifying details, it managed to give the impression that the tests constituted an endorsement of AD-X2. Finally, it concluded with a 15-page critique and commentary under the name of Dr. Keith Laidler, the committee's unpaid consultant, who had until recently been Ritchie's scientific adviser and would be again, in 1953.

The Laidler commentary extolled AD-X2 and attacked the Bureau of Standards scientists:

The MIT tests . . . constitute by far the most thorough scientific tests of the effectiveness of AD-X2. They demonstrate without reasonable doubt that this material is in fact valuable, and give complete support to the claims of the manufacturer.

. . . .

These findings are in sharp contrast to the results of tests conducted. . . by the National Bureau of Standards.

. . . .

Our present concern is how the Bureau could dare to make such grave errors. Several of the Bureau staff working on the tests are men of considerable scientific distinction. All are experienced with batteries. Vinal and Howard, indeed, the authors of Circular 504, have now left the Bureau and are employed by battery companies. It seems to the writer to be possible that it is this very close association with batteries that has made these workers suspicious of new advances in the field.

Laidler later explained how this report came to be issued:

After the MIT report was issued Mr. O'Connor asked me to make a critical evaluation of it and to draw conclusions from it. The MIT people had deliberately refrained from drawing conclusions with respect to the practical advantages of AD-X2; they presented their facts in such a way that such conclusions could readily be drawn by anyone with the least technical knowledge of batteries and their action. On several occasions Dr. Weber [had] expressed to me the private opinion that of course his experiments showed the additive to be effective. . . .

My report for the committee was written hastily, at Mr. O'Connor's request, and it was my impression that I was preparing background material on the basis of which the Committee would pursue its investigations. . . . Instead the Committee decided to issue a report immediately, and to incorporate my notes in them . . . I still stand behind the opinions expressed in my report, but I should have worded the report differently if I had known it was for publication. . . .

The last paragraph [starting with] "Our present concern . . ." was not written by me. I would never have written non-scientific comments of this kind. The first sentence . . . sounds more like something that Ritchie would have written. . . . My recollection is that at the end of my report someone added a section entitled "Concluding Remarks". . . . This section . . . was certainly not mine.

The Public Quandary

The committee's news release was widely reported by press and radio. The fact that the tests were made at MIT, together with the emphasis in the committee's release, appeared to put the controversy on the level of one highly reputable scientific institution disputing another equally reputable one. MIT ignored the controversy and made no comment, even on Laidler's interpretation of the significance of Weber's work. Weber later noted that no one at MIT saw the Laidler report until "a considerable period of time had elapsed."

An assumption that "the scientific method" establishes facts absolutely and indisputably underlay much of the newspaper reporting on the issue. As a result there appeared a suspicion that the "contradictory" tests results grew out of some bias or interest on the part of either the Bureau of Standards or MIT. It was not widely appreciated that the apparent contradiction between the two sets of results lay in differences of interpretation rather than differences of fact. These questions of judgment included: (1) what characteristics of battery operations were significant? (2) what was the relevance of the effects observed on adding AD-X2? (3) what was the magnitude of effect that would establish commercial value, and (4) could laboratory results be completely reliable without confirmation from field experience?

Action By the Republican Administration

During the fall of 1952, while the Post Office hearings were taking place, the Republicans had been campaigning to elect a presidential administration that would "clean up the mess in Washington." The substance of the charge was that the incumbent Democratic administration was so entrenched it had become irresponsible in the use of its powers. Among other things, it was charged that the federal bureaucracy was running roughshod over the rights of businessmen.

When the Post Office issued its complaint, it seemed to Ritchie that the federal bureaucracy was indeed ganging up on him. Then its handling of the case confirmed, to him, his belief that the administrative agencies were working to put him out of business.

Ritchie's story seemed tailormade to sustain the Republican charges, and after the Eisenhower victory Ritchie was keenly aware of a possible change in fortune if he could find a sympathetic ear in the new administration.

When it was announced in Dec. 1952 that Sinclair Weeks of Boston would be appointed the new Sec. of Commerce, Ritchie and his distributors flooded his mail with material describing AD-X2 and its harsh treatment by the Washington bureaucracy. Weeks was impressed.

> My mail in Boston was heavy with letters from people telling me that an outfit in Oakland, California, making a product called AD-X2 to prolong battery life through reducing sulfation, was having tough sledding in Washington.

By what can only be termed the long arm of coincidence, the United-Carr Fastener Co., of which Weeks was a director, had had strikingly satisfactory results with AD-X2. This company had bought a $1,300 battery that had failed to work. After replacing it, Weeks said, "these battery AD-X2 people came along," and the old battery was revived.

Weeks's background was in business. He was described as a believer in fair and tough competition. Graduating from Harvard in 1914, he entered banking, became a bank director. Devoting himself to manufacturing, he was elevated to the directorship of several companies. In 1938–1939 he was a director of the National Association of Manufacturers. His political career included service as treasurer of the Republican National Committee, mayor of his home town of Newton, Mass., and part of a term as United States Senator from that state.

Weeks's approach as Commerce Secretary was direct and forceful. "We shall clean up the mess," he promised in his first public statement. "The administration has the backbone to do the job. . . . Shrill cries will be heard as the ax is swung on deadwood and poison ivy." This pledge was followed by replacement of five high-level officials: the Asst. Sec. for Administration, the Asst. Sec. for Domestic Affairs, the General Counsel, and two bureau chiefs. (These officials are often replaced when the new President is of a different party than his predecessor.) During Weeks's first six months, total department personnel was reduced by 1,330, mostly by the liquidation of the National Production Authority, which had mobilized industry during the Korean conflict. This energetic attack on the department's staffing and its reorientation to a Republican philosophy caused *Fortune* to describe Weeks as "the economy-minded Eisenhower administration's prize exhibit."

Appointed by Weeks to be Assistant Secretary for Domestic Affairs, which included supervision of NBS, was Craig R. Sheaffer, former president of the Sheaffer Pen Co. Sheaffer was reported harboring something of a grudge against federal regulatory commissions because of an earlier FTC investigation of advertising of the Sheaffer "lifetime" pen. However, the commission had not issued a complaint, and contrary to some press reports NBS had not conducted tests of the Sheaffer pen.[9]

By virtue of Ritchie's mail campaign and his own firm's experience with AD-X2, Secretary Weeks was already aware of the controversy growing out of the NBS tests. One of the first assignments Weeks gave Sheaffer was to investigate the AD-X2 case. During the investigation, Ritchie was in frequent contact with Sheaffer and his staff.

The Post Office Halts Ritchie's Mail

At about the same time Ritchie, with the active assistance of the staff of the Senate Small Business Committee, was also continuing his efforts to get the Post Office Department to reopen the case.

The Post Office hearing examiner assigned to the case, acting through Blake O'Connor, advised Ritchie to file an "Application for Correction of Default." On the basis of this document, further conversation with O'Connor, and at least a cursory inspection of the MIT report, the examiner notified Ritchie:

> Upon mutual consent of the Solicitor and Mr. Blake O'Connor appearing for Pioneers Inc. . . . January 15, 1953, is hereby set as the date for the filing by respondent of a new petition to reopen the hearing in this case for the reception of evidence in behalf of the respondent.

Ritchie's petition argued that the public interest would not suffer by reopening the case. The Post Office So-

licitor's answering petition, however, asserted that Ritchie's default had been intentional—an "arrogant flouting of Departmental procedures"—and that the MIT tests were "unsubstantial from any evidential standpoint."

The decision was handed down on February 18, 1953. The findings were that Ritchie had defaulted deliberately and that "neither the tests made at MIT nor the Laidler commentary thereon . . . go to establish the validity of the respondent's advertising claims." On these grounds the petition to reopen was denied. Regarding the substance of the complaint, the decision continued:

> Proof of fraudulent purposes on the part of the respondents in promulgating claims so wholly unsupportable by scientific knowledge and experience with respect to their product . . . may be inferred from this fact alone. . . . There is attached hereto the appropriate order for execution by the Postmaster General in order to suppress the fraudulent enterprise herein found.

With the approval of these documents on February 24, 1953, the fraud order went into effect. From this day on, mail for Ritchie's business would be returned to the sender marked "Fraudulent." This stigma spelled ruin for Pioneers Inc. With the entry of the final order, the normal administrative procedures for evaluating AD-X2 were closed. Ritchie's battle from this point could be fought only through the courts or through an extraordinary appeal at the political level.

The Post Office Suspends Its Order

Ritchie went immediately to the Senate Small Business Committee and was able to persuade its new chairman, Republican Senator Edward J. Thye of

---

[9] Drew Pearson wrote (April 10, 1953): "When Sheaffer first came to Washington he told friends that one of the first things he planned to do was shake up the National Bureau of Standards. He further said that the Bureau had been high-handed in testing a Sheaffer pen."

Minnesota, to come to his aid. (The committee staff remained the same with the Republican changeover in 1953.) Three days after the fraud order went into effect, Ritchie's attorneys prepared a final petition to the Postmaster General, Arthur Summerfield, to vacate the order. Senator Thye wrote a transmittal letter to accompany the petition, adding his voice to that of Ritchie's attorneys in asking the Post Office to set aside the fraud order. Instead of using the mails to reach the Postmaster General, Blake O'Connor delivered the documents late Friday night, February 27, to Summerfield at his Connecticut Avenue apartment. Secretary Weeks also requested in writing that the order be suspended.

The following Monday, Secretary Weeks and Assistant Secretary Sheaffer conferred the entire morning with the Postmaster General. Top aides in both the Commerce and Post Office Departments were present. A phone call to the Attorney General confirmed the fact that Summerfield had authority to suspend the order. Late that afternoon, March 2, Summerfield acceded and signed the directive suspending the fraud order until further notice. Pioneers Inc. began receiving mail again that evening.

Astin Tries to See Weeks

As soon as the MIT report had reached its hands, NBS had undertaken a further series of tests using the methods employed at MIT. By using heavily sulfated plates and dilute electrolyte it also had been able to identify a slight advantage to treated battery cells early in the charging period. The effect was found to be cancelled by a slight negative effect during the latter portion of the charge.[10]

The bureau reported these findings on February 10, 1953 to the House Committee on Interstate and Foreign Commerce, which had requested information on tests of AD-X2 in connection with carrying out its assigned legislative jurisdiction over the Bureau of Standards. The bureau's report to the committee emphasized that neither the Weber-MIT test nor its own test in the same style had any practical relevance to normal battery operation.

Despite the fact that Assistant Secretary Sheaffer and his aides, on orders from Secretary Weeks, were then investigating the bureau and delving into file after file concerning AD-X2, NBS scientists did not clear the report for the House committee with these new top officials at the Commerce Department. Instead they followed routine bureau clearance procedure. When Sheaffer learned about the report, he ordered that further copies be impounded. He also wrote a letter to a trade journal that had carried a condensation of the NBS report and which reported:

> The new administration officials of the Department of Commerce report that they have not had time to complete their study of the questions of battery additives. Therefore, they have not yet made a final decision as to their attitude on previous opinions of the National Bureau of Standards on the value of such additives.
>
> They say the recent NBS report submitted to the House Interstate and Foreign Commerce Committee . . . was released prior to clearance by the current Department of Commerce officials.

Although the latest test of AD-X2 demonstrated the same results as the

---

[10] Original data for these tests were not identified in the record presented to the FTC

at its later hearings. Ritchie maintains that "No one has been able to find any test . . . data . . . by the NBS . . . that had any bearing on the MIT test—all statements by NBS personnel to the contrary."

first, Astin felt that still further scientific confirmation of the bureau's work would be desirable, particularly in view of Sheaffer's virtual repudiation of the latest findings. On two occasions in March he endeavored to get through to Secretary Weeks for direction. In a memorandum dated March 4 he suggested that Weeks invite advice from the bureau's top scientific policy body, the NBS Visiting Committee, on plans for additional scientific confirmation of the bureau's work. Later, he requested general guidance from Weeks on materials that should be published in bureau circulars. Weeks did not respond to either of these overtures. At no time did Weeks speak personally to Astin on the AD-X2 matter. He dealt with NBS exclusively through Assistant Secretary Sheaffer.

As a result of his investigation and conversation, Sheaffer had become more convinced than ever that the bureau had mishandled the AD-X2 affair. His objections were based not on scientific but procedural matters. In particular, he viewed as improper the bureau's close working relations with individuals and organizations such as the NBBB and the Association of American Battery Manufacturers. He also felt that NBS had encouraged the Post Office and the FTC to investigate AD-X2, as Ritchie had charged. Sheaffer reported these views to Weeks along with recommendations for action.

In their administration of the Department of Commerce, Weeks and Sheaffer wanted to be sure that businessmen got a fair break. Weeks believed that the government's regulatory powers with respect to consumer products should be invoked only if the public's interests were clearly and seriously threatened. In the case of AD-X2, its users apparently thought that the product was good and had saved them money. Many user testimonials had been produced—not only by Ritchie

but from Weeks's own former Boston firm. Moreover, Weeks and Sheaffer were aware of the strong feelings of Republican Senator Thye and other senators on the Small Business Committee. Sheaffer also reported that in his search of the files he had not been able to find one user complaint. Finally, Sheaffer and Weeks were mindful of other commercial cases in which businessmen had charged NBS with high-handedness.

Astin Is Asked to Resign

After getting Sheaffer's views and recommendations, Weeks made his decisions. First, he determined that there were grounds for the department itself to express doubt about the reliability of the NBS tests, a step Sheaffer had already indicated the department might take. Second, he decided to remove Dr. Astin and replace him with someone who held views more compatible with those of himself and Sheaffer.

The secretary continued to act through his assistant secretary. On March 24 Sheaffer asked Dr. Astin to resign. Though the AD-X2 affair was evidently prominent in the minds of Sheaffer and Weeks, there was no immediate evidence that they regarded their action as being more than a part of the general housecleaning which Weeks was pursuing so vigorously throughout the department. Even Astin appears to have regarded his dismissal in this light. Though he was given no hearing with Weeks, and was not told the reason for this action against him, he did not resist Sheaffer's request. (The Director of the Bureau of Standards serves at the pleasure of the President and is appointed by the President subject to Senate confirmation. The post carries the top civil service grade but is not subject to civil service rules and procedures.) By March 31 Astin's letter of resignation had cleared the department and was at the White House awaiting the President's approval.

On that day the quiet effectiveness of Weeks's "housecleaning" was rudely shattered. The morning editions of the *Washington Post* and other newspapers throughout the country carried a column by Drew Pearson in which he "exposed" Astin's forced resignation.

> Last week Dr. Astin suddenly was summoned to the Commerce Department by Assistant Secretary Craig Sheaffer . . . and was fired. He was asked to turn in his resignation within three days. . . . He also was lectured regarding the National Bureau of Standards diagnosis of battery additives . . . Sheaffer didn't like this diagnosis and told Dr. Astin the Bureau of Standards in the future was to be run on a businessman's basis.

Weeks's Public Explanation

That afternoon the Senate Small Business Committee held a hearing on AD-X2 at which Secretary Weeks was the sole witness. His prepared statement was sharply critical of the bureau's handling of AD-X2, but he did not mention Astin. The entire hearing took 35 minutes.

Weeks made these points:

1. That the bureau, while distributing technical information to the public condemning all battery additives, had resisted Ritchie's efforts to have it perform a test that might demonstrate the merits of AD-X2. When tests finally were performed, they deviated in ten ways from procedures hitherto agreed upon.

2. That NBS had activated the FTC and the Post Office, causing both agencies to docket cases against Pioneers even though they had received no consumer complaints.

3. That the bureau's product-testing activities should be re-examined:

> The Bureau, which is supposed neither to approve nor condemn a product, has, by its very setup, the power to make the introduction of a new product on the market very difficult, to prevent a product's being advertised by the Federal Trade Commission action, and to have people labeled "fraud" and denied the use of the mails.

4. That the NBS refusal to consider consumer testimony limited the efficacy of its testing methods.

5. Weeks also questioned the propriety of NBS scientists cooperating closely with the National Better Business Bureau and the battery manufacturers:

> I am not a man of science, and I do not wish to enter into a technical discussion or be accused of overruling the findings of any laboratory. But as a practical man, I think that the National Bureau of Standards has not been sufficiently objective, because they discount entirely the play of the market place and have placed themselves in a vulnerable position by discussing the nature and scope of their prospective reports with the very people who might not want to see the additive [AD-X2] remain on the market, and when their reports and results of tests were questioned, discussed the matter with other scientists, engaged by your committee to make separate, objective findings.
>
> I cannot help but wonder how many similar cases have never been heard about—how many entrepreneurs who were convinced they have a good thing for the people, who, whether they knew it or not, were licked before they started—and by their very own Government to whom they paid high taxes! . . .
>
> In this particular case I think the subject company has not been given

fair treatment and I hope to organize the Department . . . so that little businesses like this can get a fair break. . . .

Weeks promised the Small Business Committee that he would take two steps. First, he would have the Bureau of Standards examined and re-evaluated by the "best brains I can find." Second, he would have more tests made of AD-X2, by impartial scientists, "even to the extent of field tests in actual operations." He added that he was withdrawing the bureau's Circular 504 on battery additives.

There were few questions. Senator Thye, committee chairman, merely rephrased portions of Weeks's testimony to allow him to give additional emphasis at some points. Only two of the senators seemed concerned about the removal of Astin. Senator Saltonstall (R, Massachusetts), who was the first to mention it, wondered whether the secretary had interviewed anyone in the bureau before making these charges. And Senator Hunt (R, Wyoming) pointed to the bureau's peerless reputation and reflected that it seemed "a little tough to ask the man to get out because of one mistake."

Assistant Secretary Sheaffer, who sat next to Weeks, cited unnamed "other reasons" behind the Astin firing. When Senator Hunt asked what they might be, Sheaffer refused to go further. Weeks occasionally called on Sheaffer to clear up questions that arose during the hearing.

Committee aides denied that the hearing had been scheduled to give the secretary a favorable opportunity to criticize the bureau and to blame Astin for its alleged bungling.

Weeks Is Attacked

Unaccustomed to Washington, Weeks was stunned by the force of the searing and critical reaction to news of his dismissal of Astin. Scientists, congressmen, civil service groups, consumer organizations, newspapers, and private citizens attacked the summary action. The Catholic journal *America* charged Weeks with "Lysenkoism." It said: "We should hate to see the National Bureau of Standards run like the Soviet Academy of Science, whose members 'find' what is politically healthy to find—or else."

Weeks was accused of valuing political patronage more than the integrity of the government's foremost scientific laboratory,[11] of failing to follow rudimentary rules of fair play by allowing Astin to know and answer charges, and of implying that NBS was a tool of established manufacturers who wanted to suppress new inventions that threatened their products.

Many congressmen in both houses defended Astin. Three senators called for a thorough investigation, either by the Small Business Committee or by the Interstate and Foreign Commerce Committee. Senator Thye promised to hold hearings soon and indicated that he would ask Dr. Astin for his side of the story. His committee members denied that they had had anything to do with Weeks's action.

Technical personnel at NBS construed the Astin dismissal as a threat. Already demoralized by security investigations and in great demand by industry, about 400 scientists, or over ten percent of the bureau's technical complement, told newspaper reporters they planned to resign in protest.

In an editorial entitled "Packing the Courts of Science?" the *Bulletin of the Atomic Scientists* said:

> The point we want to make is that even if it should turn out that the

---

[11] Dr. Astin actually was a registered Republican in Montgomery County, Maryland.

Bureau's conclusions had been erroneous, this gives no one (including the Secretary of Commerce) the right to assert—without a most thorough investigation and convincing proof—that this error was the result of any considerations other than an attempt to get at the truth. To accuse a scientist of being moved by other considerations is like accusing a judge of acting under undue outside influence. . . . If the case of Dr. Astin is not resolved in full fairness to him and the Bureau, not only will the government have a hard time finding a reputable scientist to serve in Dr. Astin's position in the future, but the perennial reluctance of many good scientists to accept positions in government research agencies will be justifiably enhanced. Those accepting or staying in such employment will begin to ask themselves, when approaching a research problem, not "What is the truth?" but "What is it they want us to find?"

The Federation of American Scientists called the Astin firing a "major issue in the relationships of science and government."

Quips making the rounds in Washington included that of the puzzled radio commentator who wondered how he would be sure that his twelve-inch ruler really measured twelve inches. Another story concerned the supposed new protocol at NBS requiring scientists who received a new assignment to communicate with Secretary Weeks to learn what results he wanted.

The *Denver Post* suggested Weeks himself "should be bounced" if indepedent scientific analysis confirmed bureau findings on AD-X2. The *Washington Post* observed that Weeks should have gotten his independent evaluation of the bureau and of AD-X2 before dismissing Astin.

Weeks's action was not universally condemned, however. There was some feeling that the NBS was "a scientific Snug Harbor." The *Christian Science Monitor* (April 2) interpreted the action as a boost to small business generally. "The shake-up in the Bureau of Standards should open this subject up to public examination, not only in this but in other government agencies who favor big business over small." The *Boston Herald* (April 22, 1953) called NBS a "backwater of bureaucracy constantly adding new jobs without getting rid of old ones. . . . The emphasis has been on routine instead of efficiency."

The Scientific Community Saves Astin

President Eisenhower accepted Astin's resignation on April 2 (it was due to take effect on April 15) with the comment that Weeks "would be the last person to be arbitrary or unjust." But the President's words could not still the growing storm of criticism and protest directed at the secretary. The press was becoming increasingly critical. The Democrats were making capital of Weeks's apparent efforts to cause the triumph of "politics over science." A congressional investigation seemed likely.

In explaining his actions to the Small Business Committee, Weeks had promised that he would secure the best scientific talents available (1) to inquire into the work of the Bureau of Standards and (2) to make an independent examination of the AD-X2 matter. It now appeared that the only way the secretary could extricate himself from the boiling controversy without being permanently labeled as a man who placed commerce and politics over science was to secure the support of scientists with outstanding national reputations in fulfilling his pledge. Since a number of scientific groups were already attacking him, this might not be an easy thing to do. With the criticism mounting, the secretary turned to the Visiting Committee of the National Bureau of Standards.

The Visiting Committee was a group of five non-government scientists who served in an advisory capacity to the secretary on matters concerning NBS. They were appointed by the secretary and served without salary. The body had been created in the act that had created the bureau itself. Its members were expected to "visit the Bureau at least once a year, and report to the Secretary of Commerce upon the efficiency of its scientific work and the condition of its equipment."

Two of the principal members of the Visiting Committee were Dr. Detlev W. Bronk, its chairman, and Dr. Mervin J. Kelly. Bronk was president of Johns Hopkins University. Kelly was president of Bell Telephone Laboratories. Both were members of the National Academy of Sciences; Bronk, in fact, was president of the academy. The National Academy of Sciences was the most celebrated national scientific association in the country. It had received a charter from Congress in 1863 to give scientific advice to the government. Its limited membership was composed of eminent scientists with outstanding reputations.

The scientific community, still smarting from the security investigations of the preceding years, was intensely sensitive to any apparent governmental intrusion on scientific freedoms. To many scientists—even some who did not admire NBS—Weeks's action appeared to represent a sacrifice of scientific objectivity to business interest and a rejection of scientific research in favor of "practical" results obtained and interpreted by laymen.

However, scientific organizations followed different tactics in the Weeks-Astin controversy. Members of the Federation of American Scientists and of the Washington chapter of the Association of Atomic Scientists (largely physicists) mounted a frontal assault. They issued angry press releases, called meetings, badgered the administration, and sought to call public attention to the government's alleged assault on science. The members of the National Academy of Sciences, on the other hand, were generally more senior and more conservative. Academy leaders like Bronk and Kelly were upset by the Astin matter, but they decided against public outcry. They did not wish to add to the embarrassment of the administration, and they believed that they could help the bureau more effectively by working quietly within the administration and through established channels.

Weeks invited Bronk and Kelly to his office and for two hours explored with them the crisis caused by the removal of Dr. Astin. It was agreed that a meeting of the full Visiting Committee would be convened on April 14.

On the morning of April 14 Weeks received a stiff letter from Dr. Bronk in which, for the first time, it was suggested that Weeks countermand the dismissal of Astin, "at least" until the issues could be fully studied. Bronk told the secretary that "the integrity of scientific effort and the national interest" demanded that Astin's departure should be postponed. Dr. Bronk's dual position as Chairman of the Visiting Committee and President of the National Academy of Sciences gave the letter considerable weight. This weight was increased by the proceedings at the meeting of the secretary with the full Visiting Committee. For Weeks wanted the National Academy of Sciences to establish a committee that would render a definitive report on the manner in which the Bureau of Standards had dealt with AD-X2. Dr. Bronk, in the interest of fair play and scientific integrity, refused to accept such a responsibility for the National Academy unless Weeks agreed to retain Dr. Astin on a temporary basis.

On April 17 Weeks announced that Dr. Astin (whose resignation was to become effective that day) would remain temporarily as Director of the Bureau—probably until late in the summer. Thus the Academy's cooperation in making an evaluation of AD-X2 was secured.

A second announcement made by Weeks was that Dr. Kelly had agreed to chair a committee that would undertake an evaluation of the bureau's general situation. Telegrams had been sent to heads of seven scientific and technical societies asking them to appoint a member to this committee. Weeks pointed out that Dr. Kelly had made clear to him the "desirability" of retaining Astin until the study was completed. "No question is involved of Dr. Astin's permanent retention," Weeks emphasized. He added, however, that in dismissing the director he had never intended "to cast reflection on the integrity of the Bureau or on the professional competence or integrity of Dr. Astin." Their differences, he said, resulted "from a conflict with respect to administrative viewpoint and procedure."

Dr. Astin then issued a statement announcing his willingness to stay on "regardless of my personal opinions or wishes." He continued to draw his salary but was unable to act officially as bureau director, since his resignation had been accepted. The decision to retain Astin temporarily provided the administration an avenue for orderly retreat, but it was a disheartening defeat to the secretary and, even more, to Assistant Secretary Sheaffer.

The day before it was announced that Dr. Astin would stay on, MIT first released the full text of its report on tests of AD-X2, along with Dr. Stratton's covering letter. Publication served to clarify some of the misunderstanding that had been created by the Senate committee's press release and the appended commentary by Dr. Laidler on the conclusions MIT supposedly had reached. One newspaper, the *Christian Science Monitor,* commented: "Now MIT says publicly what it told the Senate Committee from the beginning: that its tests made no evaluation about the performance of AD-X2 whatsoever. The report merely set forth the results of the tests with no evaluation of their meaning."

The Many Courts of Inquiry

The case of Ritchie's battery additive had extended itself beyond normal administrative channels of government regulation and had become commingled with larger political questions. The fate of AD-X2 would now be affected by the actions of a variety of governmental and private bodies, not merely the regulatory proceedings of the Post Office Department and the Federal Trade Commission. Dr. Astin's temporary reinstatement quieted the storms of protest, but the questions of what would happen to the Bureau of Standards, the Secretary of Commerce, and AD-X2 were still undecided. The Weeks-Astin controversy had not changed the formal position of AD-X2 with the Post Office. The Postmaster General, on the urging of Secretary Weeks and the Small Business Committee, had agreed to suspend the fraud order temporarily, but he had not dismissed it.

Congressional Investigation

The congressional investigation threatened in the wake of the Astin dismissal did not materialize immediately. Although two other Senate committees—Appropriations and Interstate and Foreign Commerce—evinced interest, both yielded to the Small Business Committee, which announced plans to continue its investigations. The SBC's active role in the AD-X2 matter was well known. Its staff had arranged the MIT tests, procured the major military test data, visited Ritchie's operations in California, and interviewed numerous AD-X2 users.

Ritchie, who had been dismayed by the furor over Astin's dismissal ("the whole thing was getting more confused every minute"), resumed his pressure on the Small Business Committee to air the matter publicly. Senator Thye, at first undecided whether hearings should be held, was moved to act by a report from his farm manager that AD-X2 had resuscitated a failing tractor battery.

After several postponements, the Small Business Committee opened hearings on June 22. Senator Thye explained that public hearings were necessary to review Ritchie's problems as a small businessman and to determine "whether or not the agencies of the Government have been fair and just" in their treatment of him and his product. He said the Post Office fraud order "in fairness to all parties, should not be allowed to be held in abeyance indefinitely. Such an order, even though suspended, does damage to a man's good name and to his company."

The first witness was Jess M. Ritchie, who, equipped with demonstration batteries, sheaves of testimonials, correspondence and tests, testified before the committee for almost five hours. A voluble witness, he reviewed his charges that the NBS test procedures were designed to discredit AD-X2, that the favorable results found by other laboratories proved his charge, that NBS went out of its way to hamper new business, and that the NBS had instigated the Post Office complaint.

Ritchie was followed by Dr. Allen V. Astin, whose testimony was equally extensive. Dr. Astin defended the testing procedures and cited the bureau's long experience with additives, described the difficulty of reaching a conclusive agreement with Ritchie on test methods. He defended the association of bureau personnel with scientists employed by battery manufacturers and the consultation between the bureau and the National Better Business Bureau. Responding to questions, he denied that the bureau exercised regulatory authority, either directly or indirectly, or that it was responsible for the charges filed by the Post Office Department.

Dr. Weber of MIT followed. In more abbreviated testimony, he voiced doubt that the MIT tests had "covered enough ground." He also said of the Laidler interpretation of the MIT report: "It was not my opinion. He expressed an opinion of his own." And, although his own tests failed to show an "unfavorable effect for this material," he was not willing to endorse the free interpretation made by the committee's staff that the tests proved favorable to AD-X2. "They were drawing a conclusion we did not draw," he said.

During the hearings, nine civilian and four military users of AD-X2 testified to satisfactory experience with it. The hearings occupied four days, and the record comprised 785 pages.

The committee did not issue a report on its hearings and took no action regarding the issues highlighted by the AD-X2 affair. However, it gave another boost to Pioneers' fortunes by requesting the Department of Defense and the Navy to resume testing AD-X2 in submarine batteries. At the hearings glowing reports had been given of the successful use of AD-X2 in a submarine battery at the New York Submarine Base, and Thye expressed great interest in this application of the product.

Senator Thye personally believed that the Post Office fraud order should be "expunged" from the record, but in view of the contradictory evidence presented he did not urge the committee to make this recommendation.

The *Washington Post* (July 1, 1953) editorialized:

> A request to the Post Office to abolish the fraud order against AD-X2 would constitute an outright whitewash of Ritchie's product, a flagrant disregard for the facts, and an altogether unwarranted stigmatization of NBS. It would amount, in short, to an outrageous attempt on the part of the Senate Small Business Committee to vindicate itself.

The Senate committee forwarded a copy of the hearings to the Postmaster General with a letter dated July 2 stating:

> The Committee has concluded that further hearings should not be held for the time being. It could not, in the present state of the testimony, make a finding of its own . . . this Committee sends you for whatever consideration you care to give it, the testimony presented at its hearings. The decision as to what action your department should take with relation to the suspended fraud order, the Committee emphasizes, is yours.

There was no immediate response from the Post Office Department, which appeared inclined to await the findings of the committee of the National Academy of Sciences before taking action on its suspended fraud order. The committee staff brought this situation to the attention of Senator Thye and urged the Post Office informally to remove the fraud order. The Post Office appears to have responded to this informal pressure, but it was hesitant to strike the order without some documentation to show cause. This was supplied by the committee staff, and summarized in a memorandum stating its view of the testimony, which concluded:

> . . . it would appear that we can draw the following conclusions:
>
> 1. A scientific controversy does exist over the merits of AD-X2.
> 2. The military and commercial users of AD-X2 feel very strongly that this product does all that the manufacturer claims it should do and that they are satisfied that the product can effect large savings in terms of time and money.
> 3. No one who has used this product feels in any way that he has been defrauded, either by the manufacturer or by the product.
> 4. That Mr. Ritchie's advertising is conservative and that his product does exactly what his advertising claims.

NBS Functions Reshaped

Meanwhile, Dr. Kelly's committee directed its attention to finding ways to support and expand the bureau's basic programs. The committee's deliberations continued throughout the summer, and it recommended two reforms before issuing its final report. First, it concluded that the bureau's large weapons program, which had grown vast during World War II, was not a proper bureau activity. It recommended that this work be transferred to the Department of Defense. Weeks concurred and, with the Secretary of Defense, initiated the changeover in July.

Secondly, the committee members believed that some of the problems that arose in the AD-X2 controversy might be avoided in the future if responsibility for product testing were shared between the bureau and the Department of Commerce. Consequently it recommended that the director of the bureau continue to be responsible for the technical side of product testing but that the Secretary of Commerce bear the responsibility for the "policy and the establishment of the non-technical procedures on commercial product tests." With Astin's concurrence, Weeks moved to carry out this recommendation immediately. As a final step, he transferred the NBS from the jurisdiction of Assistant Secretary (for Domestic Affairs) Sheaffer to the Assistant Secretary of Commerce for Administration.

By this time, Secretary Weeks had learned a great deal about the bureau. And he had come to respect Dr. Astin and to understand some of the problems Astin had faced in the AD-X2 matter. Dr. Astin's careful and scrupulously correct conduct, as the summer advanced, had served to win Weeks's confidence. Throughout his suspension, Astin showed no rancor or disloyalty toward his departmental superiors. He had strongly discouraged protest resignations from the bureau and had cleared all his public statements before release. On one occasion he had even shared the speakers platform before the Weights and Measures Conference with Assistant Secretary Sheaffer.

Two Problems Resolved

On August 20 one phase of the controversy came to an end. The Post Office Department cancelled the fraud order against AD-X2. In its announcement it stated:

> There is a substantial disagreement as to the relative benefits of AD-X2.
>
> That the Department of Commerce has authorized further study and investigation of the merits of battery additives.
>
> That based upon all of the evidence . . . [thus far], there is insufficient proof of an actual intent by Ritchie to deceive which is required to warrant and maintain a fraud order.

The following day, a solution was reached on another point of controversy. Secretary Weeks announced the permanent reinstatement of Dr. Astin as Director of the Bureau of Standards. In deciding to retain Dr. Astin as "a member of my team," Weeks said he believed it to be "in the best interests of the Bureau and the public." The preliminary draft of the Kelly committee's report, delivered to Weeks earlier, convinced him that the bureau was a recognized and respected agency, vested with vital responsibilities, and that its staff was loyal and competent. He noted that the members of the Visiting Committee whom he had asked to recommend possible candidates for the directorship were in "unanimous agreement" to retain Astin.

Two of the most aggrieved groups were placated by these solutions— science and small business. Senator Thye commended the Post Office and said it had acted "justly and wisely in view of all the evidence that had been presented." Ritchie was elated over the voiding of the fraud order and proclaimed that he was "going to pour this material into every battery in the U.S."

In a move widely ascribed to his dissatisfaction with the Weeks-Astin rapprochement, Sheaffer resigned the following month. With all obstacles to a reconciliation removed, Weeks became one of the bureau's strongest supporters.

Academy Scientists Evaluate AD-X2

For a specific evaluation of the worth of AD-X2, Weeks had turned to the National Academy of Sciences and to Dr. Bronk, its president. After the secretary had agreed in April to retain Astin temporarily, Bronk had agreed to set up an academy committee of eminent scientists to handle this task. In selecting the members, it was important not only to find persons with appropriate qualifications but also those free of prior involvement or emotional bias regarding AD-X2. This Bronk found to be a difficult task. Bronk himself had deplored Astin's forced resignation, and his stand was endorsed by the National Academy at its annual meeting on April 28. (Scientists' gossip had it even then that Astin was saved. The May issue of the *Bulletin of the Atomic Scientists* predicted that "there is a good chance that Astin will eventually be returned to his job on a permanent basis.")

The task Weeks laid before the academy committee was outlined in his letter of May 3, 1953, to Bronk:

> Although the matter has been discussed over the phone and otherwise on an informal basis, I find that I have not yet formally requested that you do appoint a committee to objectively appraise the quality of the work performed by the National Bureau of Standards in relation to battery additive AD-X2. The study of this com-

> mittee is to include tests *both in the laboratory and in the field*. [Emphasis added.]

Bronk named Dr. Zay Jeffries, retired vice-president of the chemical division of General Electric, chairman of this second committee. The remaining eight members were prominent chemists, statisticians, and electrical engineers. Bronk did not include any persons specifically trained in battery chemistry and testing. His appointments, it seemed, were aimed at establishing a broad-gauge committee capable of critical evaluation of prior work. Weeks had in mind that the academy committee would actually conduct tests. But Bronk apparently disagreed with this idea in his letter to Jeffries setting out the terms of reference of the committee:

> I would wish you and the members of your Academy committee to consider the work of the Bureau of Standards relating to Battery AD-X2, to proceed as you think best. . . . It was my thought, however, that the committee would . . . appraise the Bureau's work and procedures in this regard, but would not actually test the additive or supervise its testing unless that seemed to the committee to be necessary and desirable.

The committee found it unnecessary to conduct additional tests because of the wealth of laboratory data already available from MIT, from the Bureau of Standards, and from tests that Ritchie himself had commissioned at commercial testing laboratories.

The committee held a two-day meeting with the principals in the case on July 15–16, 1953. It heard from NBS representatives (including Drs. Vinal and Howard); from representatives of MIT, and from Ritchie and his scientific consultant, Dr. Laidler. The committee did not feel that the data received at this meeting were conclusive and requested further information for study, including tests performed for Ritchie by the U.S. Testing Company (a commercial testing organization)—tests which demonstrated larger capacities for batteries treated with AD-X2.

At Jeffries' suggestion two manufacturers' representatives and a representative of the Association of American Battery Manufacturers attended the July meeting and joined in the committee's deliberations.

The Jeffries Committee Reports

The work of the Jeffries committee continued into the fall. The committee's study of all the laboratory reports extended over several months. Its analyses dispelled the impression held by some scientists that the scientific work at NBS was routine and perfunctory. It concluded that the NBS scientists had done a thoroughly high-quality job on testing AD-X2. The group reviewed the evidence of the MIT tests and came to the conclusion that Weber's laboratory data were not incompatible with a judgment that AD-X2 was without value.

The members of the Jeffries group found Ritchie an enormously persuasive man whose work on the care and improvement of batteries over the years had given him a vast amount of practical battery "know-how." They considered that the directions on battery care included in each package of AD-X2 were of considerable practical value and, if followed, might by themselves have led to longer battery life.

The committee concluded that the NBS work had been of high quality and that AD-X2 was worthless. Its report, filed October 30, 1953, analyzed each major test of AD-X2 and ruled on its value. "No tests have come to our attention which have, under proper controlled conditions, shown advantages for AD-X2," the committee stated.

Of the favorable effects found by the U.S. Testing Company, it said that although two statistically significant effects appeared in the data, neither was of any practical effect. The committee found the MIT test "too limited for evaluation purposes" and claimed that it was "not well designed for old batteries differing markedly in the characteristics of the cells" since "in the majority of the cell pairings it happened that the better cells were treated with AD-X2." The committee did not evaluate Ritchie's testimonials.

The report noted, perhaps with conscious irony, that the least harmful substance, other than distilled water, that could be added to a battery was AD-X2, since it was virtually an inert substance.

The unanimous conclusions of the committee were:

> The relevant data now available to the Committee on the effects of AD-X2 are adequate to support the position of the Bureau of Standards that the material is without merit. . . . The quality of the work of the National Bureau of Standards in the field of lead-acid battery testing is excellent [and] the Committee recommends that no additional tests on the merit of AD-X2 be undertaken by it or under its supervision.

Two weeks later, on November 13, the Department of Commerce released the committee's report along with a comment by Secretary Weeks. The conclusions regarding the excellence of the bureau's testing "are a source of satisfaction to me and the Bureau. I shall do all in my power to aid the Bureau in maintaining this high level of scientific service." When the report was published, Ritchie threatened to sue each member of the committee but failed to carry out the threat. He also made much of a criminal conviction for violation of the anti-trust statutes entered against Jeffries as an officer of General Electric in 1949 and charged that he had spent his life promoting monopoly.

The Federal Trade Commission Acts

Scientists and scientific societies hailed the Jeffries report. The Federation of American Scientists, one of the most vociferous bodies when Dr. Astin was first removed, pointed out that the National Academy, "the highest scientific Court of Appeals," found the bureau "not guilty."

With this high-level clearance of NBS test results, government officials were once again confronted with a decision on how to move against Pioneers' advertising. The *Washington Post* reported on November 19, 1953 that the Post Office and the FTC were "momentarily playing Alphonse and Gaston" with respect to Pioneers Inc.

The FTC became the agency to act. As an independent regulatory commission, it was free to proceed without the suspicion that the executive branch was trying to justify the Bureau of Standards. Most important, the commission's case could be limited to establishing that the merits claimed for AD-X2 in its advertising did not exist. It was not necessary for the FTC to prove the material to be harmful or to show intent to defraud.

The FTC had been relatively inactive since 1951 after failing to get Ritchie to accept any restrictions on Pioneers' advertising. At that time it had tried to reach agreement with Ritchie through stipulation. The FTC investigation had been kept open be-

cause of the inconclusiveness of the continuing tests of AD-X2.

The National Academy of Sciences report attesting the validity of NBS tests provided the FTC with evidence to renew its investigation. However, it was not a case the commission embraced with enthusiasm. There were no complaints on record from dissatisfied users. Hence the assessment of Ritchie's claims would have to depend primarily on opinion testimony and on the NBS tests.

The FTC renewed its investigation and issued a complaint on March 11, 1954 charging that by means of "false, misleading and deceptive claims, statements and representations," Pioneers Inc. had induced the public to buy AD-X2 and was continuing to expand its sales by such claims. It charged that such acts constituted "unfair and deceptive acts and practices in commerce within the intent and meaning of the Federal Trade Commission Act."

Hearings began in Washington on July 26 before the FTC hearing examiner. The commission's attorneys opened their case with presentation of scientific evidence supporting the complaint. The first witnesses were scientists from the Bureau of Standards, the National Academy of Sciences, and three persons who had made independent tests of AD-X2 confirming the bureau's results.

FTC attorneys hit a snag at the outset. When they attempted to introduce the report of the National Academy of Sciences (Jeffries) committee, Ritchie's lawyers challenged it as second-degree evidence, hearsay, and immaterial. They were supported by the hearing examiner, who ruled it inadmissible as evidence, since the committee had not conducted any tests of its own but had simply studied the records of tests made by NBS, MIT, and others.

The FTC attorneys were able to regain some ground by calling Dr. Zay Jeffries and Dr. Lewis G. Longsworth, two members of the committee. Through their testimony most of the report was made part of the record. However, the two witnesses were not able to give testimony on the competency of any of the tests standing alone. Ritchie's attorneys also brought out the fact that none of the scientists on the Jeffries committee was a battery expert. Ritchie and his attorneys also brought up an alleged statement by Jeffries that the fate of AD-X2 was of secondary importance compared with the fate of NBS.

In the second phase of the case the FTC attempted to enter evidence by dissatisfied users of AD-X2. The commission's Bureau of Investigation had sought to develop evidence from persons throughout the country who were known to have used AD-X2. FTC attorneys said the investigation reports contained information "extremely important, helpful, and necessary."

The commission's user testimony was entered in the record through a series of itinerant hearings held in thirteen cities: Boston, New Haven, New York, Allentown, Pittsburgh, Cleveland, Detroit, Grand Rapids, Chicago, Indianapolis, Knoxville, Oakland, and Washington. Eleven witnesses supporting the complaint testified to their unsatisfactory use of not more than one hundred packets of AD-X2. However, the value of their testimony was dissipated when, on cross-examination, three acknowledged that they had not followed the manufacturer's instructions; one had apparently not used AD-X2; and another had subsequently ordered more of the material.

By the time the FTC had presented evidence in eleven cities and nine states, Ritchie came into possession of a document he considered highly damaging

to the FTC. He had found it, he said, in his own briefcase after the hearing in Knoxville, Tennessee. He explained that he did not know who put it there but that it was only one of many helpful bits and pieces of information turned over to him by persons in and out of government who felt he had had a raw deal.

The document was the FTC internal memo asking for a field investigation to dig up user complaints against AD-X2. The memorandum revealed that the staff had lined up dissatisfied consumer witnesses in 23 states. "For obvious reasons," the memo noted, "it was felt that the survey should be widespread. . . . Hence, the said list of users covered the territory of all the offices of the Commission with the exception of the San Francisco office, which is the home area of the respondents." (It was at Ritchie's insistence that the FTC scheduled hearings in Oakland, too.)

The document seemed to Ritchie to constitute clear proof that the commission intended to exhaust his resources by conducting hearings all over the country.[12] Ritchie copied the memo, returned it to the FTC, and then telephoned the commission to report that he had uncovered its scheme to exhaust his resources by endless hearings. According to Norman Goodwin, FTC attorneys hotly accused Ritchie of having

---

[12] The cost both of prosecuting and of defending a false advertising charge was a vital element. Only a few "small" businessmen would have the resources to defend a charge for the length of time the AD-X2 case dragged on. The same problem sometimes has faced the government. A former FTC chairman, Edward F. Howrey, has said that the commission cannot afford to prosecute apparently false advertising of the major oil companies in their claims for the effects of their gasoline additives: NBS test costs alone would amount to hundreds of thousands of dollars.

stolen the memo. In any event, the commission then closed its side of the case.

It was now Ritchie's turn to present his defense, which was also based on both scientific and user testimony. Although the National Academy report had failed as evidence, Ritchie was successful in introducing the reports made by MIT and by the U.S. Testing Company. In addition, Ritchie employed two expert witnesses, Drs. Brian E. Conway and S. E. El Wakkad. Conway, a Canadian, was at the time assistant professor of chemistry, and El Wakkad a research assistant, at the University of Pennsylvania. Both testified to the merit of AD-X2 and the inadequacy of the NBS tests.

(Laidler subsequently wrote of the testimony of himself, Conway, and El Wakkad on behalf of Ritchie before the Jeffries committee and the FTC: "No one else was available to Ritchie at this time because the situation had developed in such a way that people were afraid of the consequences. Only some non-American scientists, Conway, El Wakkad, and myself, were prepared to speak for Ritchie; we knew that our subsequent careers were not entirely dependent on U.S. scientific opinion, and all of us left the U.S. shortly afterwards.")

The basic defense, however, was the testimony of Ritchie's customers. Some 45 of them filled over 5,000 pages of the record with testimony of their successful experience with AD-X2. While FTC user testimony had described the use of less than 100 packets, the successful experience that Ritchie's witnesses testified to covered the use of tens of thousands of packets. As witness after witness took the stand to attest to the value of AD-X2 to his battery problems, newspapers predicted that the FTC would not be able to sustain the complaint.

The Examiner
Dismisses the Complaint

To the irritation of the academy scientists, the hearing examiner dismissed the complaint on November 9, 1955. He acknowledged the stature of both the Bureau of Standards and MIT and found that the greater weight of the *scientific* evidence supported the bureau's position that AD-X2 was without merit. But, regarding the user testimony, the examiner's opinion was:

The overwhelming weight of the user testimony is with the respondents. And it is highly important to recognize that in this case the user testimony is not mere "consumer" or "public" testimony as those terms are usually understood in Federal Trade Commission proceedings . . . with few exceptions they are plant superintendents, shop foremen, chief electricians, master mechanics, battery shop operators, etc. They are, from a practical point of view, experts on lead-acid batteries. Their aggregate experience with the respondents' product includes thousands of batteries. No other case has come to the examiner's attention in which so large a volume of substantial and reliable user testimony was adduced.

From a scientific viewpoint there are of course valid objections to this user testimony. . . . But after recognizing the validity of these objections and discounting the testimony accordingly, there still remains a very substantial body of reliable and probative evidence attesting to the merit of the product. And such evidence would appear to be particularly significant and helpful in the present case in view of the conflict in the scientific evidence.

Faced with this conflict between field and laboratory evidence—the same conflict which had characterized the case since 1948—the examiner applied the rule of the weight of evidence. In ordering the complaint dismissed, the examiner found the legal principle of burden of proof, which lay with the commission, to be decisive in the case.

Final Appeal

Commission attorneys appealed the examiner's decision. So did Ritchie, his complaint being that a portion of the examiner's decision upheld the NBS tests. On May 16, 1956, over two years after issuance of the complaint and after 103 hearing sessions, the full Federal Trade Commission returned a 4–0 decision dismissing the complaint.

The commission was thus able to come to a decision that at least had the merit of finality. On the other hand, by admitting a conflict of evidence, the commission's decision failed to come

to grips with the problem of whether, consistently, the introduction of AD-X2 into a battery had any measurable effect on its performance. To the academy scientists, a ruling based on weight of evidence, when that evidence contained user testimony unreconciled with laboratory studies, appeared to indicate that the FTC's processes were unable to yield any decision at all.

In contrast to the Federal Trade Commission, the National Academy committee had attempted to give an absolutely definitive ruling on AD-X2. The committee's report was emphatic and uncluttered, but it literally did not "stand up in court." Technically the report failed to meet the rules of evidence, which lawyers viewed as an indictment of the report and scientists viewed as an indictment of the rules of evidence as legalistically applied by the FTC.

Conclusion?

In its eight years of existence, AD-X2 cut a wide swath through the government. Respected personalities and institutions were challenged; accepted procedures were shaken, re-examined, and sometimes simply defended without re-examination. Almost all varieties of government institutions—and many private ones—had become involved in what began as a routine instance of government regulation. To the participants, the implications of the case on their reputations and work made the controversy a serious matter.

The Bureau of Standards

The impact of AD-X2 fell most heavily upon the Bureau of Standards. After the public challenge for scientific inaccuracy by Ritchie, the bureau felt

the force of Weeks's and Sheaffer's personalities and their efforts to improve the attitudes of Commerce bureaus toward businessmen. NBS was badly shaken by reductions made by Congress in its appropriations and by executive action which tended to cut off its reimbursable contract work for other agencies. But it could be said that perhaps AD-X2 was a catalyst that stimulated reconversion of the bureau's work to a peacetime basis. The controversy caused Weeks to devote much attention to the bureau, and the Kelly committee report caused him to correct the maladjustments in its operations resulting from its wartime activities.

The FTC, The Post Office

Ritchie attacked the Federal Trade Commission in the press and before the Senate Small Business, the Interstate and Foreign Commerce, and the Appropriations Committees. His complaints were that the FTC had relied unduly upon the technical advice of the Bureau of Standards, unfairly singled out small businessmen for prosecution, and then exhausted their resources through protracted administrative proceedings.

An FTC study of litigation procedures, made at the urging of the Small Business Committee, resulted in procedural amendments to limit trial itineraries, accept a larger number of written depositions in lieu of calling witnesses, and assign trial attorneys to its branch offices. In general the AD-X2 case reinforced the impression, reported also by other congressional committees, that FTC procedures were slow and cumbersome.

The editor of *Consumer's Research Bulletin* wrote in September 1956: "There is no doubt that the handling of the AD-X2 case has severely damaged the Federal Trade Commission's prestige and ability to provide the American consumer with effective protection against misleading advertising." Kenneth B. Willson of the National Better Business Bureau concurred: "As a result of the AD-X2 affair, I feel that the Government's protection of the consumer has definitely been impaired." Even Ritchie lamented the commission's failure to prosecute other additives that had come on the market after 1954 and which he claimed were falsely advertised.

The Post Office Department weathered the storm with little or no damage. Senator Thye had said at the conclusion of his Small Business Committee's hearing on AD-X2: "Only . . . if the Postmaster General feels the mail fraud order should not be set aside, would it be necessary to find out why the order was ever issued." By complying with Thye's desire, the Post Office escaped congressional investigation.

Careers

The AD-X2 controversy affected variously the lives and reputations of its principal participants. Many were bruised but not permanently damaged.

The careers of several scientists close to the AD-X2 matter were affected. Ritchie charged that NBS personnel tried to defame and intimidate his scientific witnesses and consultants. He threatened legal action against Dr. Wallace Brode, an Associate Director of NBS, who suggested that Drs. Conway and El Wakkad deliberately distorted and misrepresented NBS work in their expert testimony before the FTC. Both El Wakkad and Conway left the University of Pennsylvana shortly after their testimony supporting AD-X2, Conway to join the staff of the University of Ottawa, and El Wakkad to return to Egypt.

Dr. Keith Laidler, Pioneers' consultant during 1952 and 1953, indicated that the bureau attempted to put pressure on him to withdraw his support of AD-X2. Laidler's colleagues at Catholic University publicly disassociated themselves from his views regarding AD-X2. A year later, Laidler became a professor of chemistry at the University of Ottawa.

The Federation of American Scientists warmly supported the Bureau of Standards and its electrochemistry personnel who conducted the bureau's work on AD-X2 after 1950, Drs. W. J. Hamer and D. H. Craig. A paper on the battery charging process—in effect a scientific justification of their work on AD-X2—presented by these men before the winter meeting of the American Institute of Electrical Engineers, was recognized as the prize-winning paper for 1954.

Jess Ritchie

Ritchie himself emerged from the controversy a national figure. Trading on the wide publicity he had gained as a man who "dared to stand up to the whole U.S. Government," Ritchie in 1954 won the Republican nomination as a candidate for Congress from the Eighth California district. Although defeated, Ritchie's political ambitions were whetted and his views sharpened. In 1956 he joined the right-wing Constitution Party and became assistant state chairman. The following year he was elected the party's national chairman. Ritchie also organized the National Small Business Foundation through which the problems of persons in difficulty with administrative agencies were brought to the attention of sympathetic government officials.

Ritchie charged that damages, losses, and expenses in fighting for AD-X2 amounted to over two million dollars. His claim against the federal government for damages of this amount was referred to the United States Court of Claims by means of a private bill introduced by his congressman and passed by the House in July 1958.[13] On December 15, 1961, the Court of Claims dismissed the suit "with prejudice," which meant that this particular claim could never be revived. The *New York Times* story of the dismissal stated that Ritchie "abandoned the claim shortly after lawyers for the Justice Department served notice that they would contest it to the finish with

---

13 There was no provision in law authorizing Ritchie to go into court and claim damages in an instance of this kind. However, either house of Congress, by a resolution, could direct a claim like Ritchie's to the United States Court of Claims.

evidence collected in three years of investigation." The *Times* story quoted one of Ritchie's attorneys as saying that his client "just didn't have the funds to finance the long and extensive hearings that the case seemed likely to entail." It also quoted Dr. Astin as congratulating the Justice Department and as claiming that Ritchie had sought dismissal of the case "after being advised in pre-trial conferences of the nature of the Government's defense."

AD-X2

As if to demonstrate that entrepreneurial determination and government regulation are eternal and immutable aspects of life, newspapers in Washington and other cities in 1959 carried advertisements for AD-X2 that claimed that the white additive powder was "GOVERNMENT TESTED AND PROVED." In another instance, Pioneers' advertising asserted that AD-X2 was "PROVED before the FEDERAL TRADE COMMISSION." In the spring of 1960 Ritchie reported that the FTC had taken exception to these claims and was again proceeding against Pioneers Inc. Ritchie maintained that a considerable number of the 2,000 governmental units in the United States had purchased and were regularly using AD-X2, and that there was a substantial difference between the words "proved" and "approved." This time, however, he agreed to drop the disputed language. On the basis of a stipulation, the FTC entered an order on July 19, 1960 calling on Pioneers Inc.

forthwith [to] cease and desist from representing, directly or by implication: That said product has been proved before or tested or approved by the Federal Trade Commission, or that said product has been Government tested and approved.

Ritchie also reported that much of his time in the spring of 1960 was taken up in exploring the development of an oil filter that would make it unnecessary ever to change the oil in an automobile.